Knowledge of the *Pragmatici*

Max Planck Studies in Global Legal History of the Iberian Worlds

Editor

Thomas Duve

The volumes published in the *Max Planck Studies in Global Legal History of the Iberian Worlds* are dedicated to the legal histories of areas which have been in contact with the Iberian empires during the early modern and modern periods – in Europe, the Americas, Asia and Africa. Its focus is global in the sense that it is not limited to the imperial spaces as such but goes beyond to look at the globalisation and localisation of normative knowledge within the spaces related to these imperial formations. It is global also in another sense: The volumes in the series pay special attention to the cultural translations of normative knowledge in different places and moments, decentering classical approaches on legal history and opening up new perspectives on the production of normative knowledge.

All of the monographs, edited volumes and text editions in the series are peer reviewed and published in print and online.

Brill's Open Access books are distributed free of charge in Brill's E-Book Collections and can be found via DOAB, OAPEN and JSTOR.

VOLUME 1

The titles published in this series are listed at *brill.com/mpiw*

Knowledge of the *Pragmatici*

Legal and Moral Theological Literature and the Formation of Early Modern Ibero-America

Edited by

Thomas Duve
Otto Danwerth

BRILL
NIJHOFF

LEIDEN | BOSTON

Cover illustration: Lemma "Pragmatici", in Johann Kahl, *Magnum Lexicon Juridicum*, Köln 1759, vol. 2, 301 (Photo: Thomas Duve); "Escrivano de cabildo nombrado de Sv M[agesta]d, quilcay camayoc", in Felipe Guaman Poma de Ayala, *El primer nueva corónica y buen gobierno* (1615/1616), 814 [828] (Det Kongelige Bibliotek, Copenhagen).

Library of Congress Cataloging-in-Publication Data is available online at http://catalog.loc.gov
LC record available at https://lccn.loc.gov/2020005908
LC ebook record available at https://lccn.loc.gov/2020005909

Typeface for the Latin, Greek, and Cyrillic scripts: "Brill". See and download: brill.com/brill-typeface.

ISSN 2590-3292
ISBN 978-90-04-42162-2 (hardback)
ISBN 978-90-04-42573-6 (e-book)

This book is printed on acid-free paper and produced in a sustainable manner.

Printed by Printforce, the Netherlands

Contents

Preface

For a long time, the legal history of early modern colonial Ibero-America has focused on royal legislation, law treatises or other legal sources from the Iberian tradition and, more recently, from *ius commune*. In the last two decades, there has been an impressive growth of research in the 'History of Justice', with important contributions from social and cultural history, usually concentrating on court practice and local law. That historiography, however, did only rarely take into consideration a topic, which is crucial for understanding the formation of Ibero-American normative orders between the 16th and 18th centuries: the use of normative knowledge, specific practical reasoning and normative practices from the religious field. It has also failed to examine systematically a literary genre that we call 'pragmatic normative literature', meaning those books written for the orientation and use of legal practitioners, crown officials, or for persons in charge of the *cura animarum*, the missionaries, priests, and other office-holders in ecclesiastical institutions.

Our book builds on the hypothesis that this 'pragmatic normative literature', in particular the strand that refers back to the tradition of moral theology, can be a key to an important dimension of colonial legal culture: the formation of colonial normative orders through the legal and normative knowledge from the religious field. This literature, which has received scarce attention also in European legal history, has special significance and functionality not only in the remote *frontier* context of the early modern empire. It was used in the colonial centres and it accompanied missionaries, but also laymen, to regions where no crown official could take office. It contained the basic moral precepts of early modern society and dealt with many aspects which are commonly considered 'legal': contracts, usury, property, crime, responsibility, etc. As Thomas Duve shows in his introductory chapter, these texts – such as manuals for confessors, catechisms, and moral theological instructions – and their importance have to be understood as part of a specific historical formation, the 16th and 17th century Ibero-American regime of production of normative knowledge. They allowed localisations and cultural translations and enabled erudite as well as non-erudite actors to teach and enforce the moral and legal obligations, codes of conduct and world visions both to the local indigenous and to the European population. They represent an important source for explaining the complex construction of the colonial normative order, and they are key to understand how a basic 'normative literacy' emerged that made communication about normativity possible, not least between the different groups and peoples living in the vast territories occupied by the European invaders and settlers.

The book brings to light not just the practical significance and functionality of this genre, but also its intellectual weight. Despite its perceived 'popular' nature, pragmatic literature does not merely represent – as is often assumed – a form of vulgarisation; on the contrary, it reflects conscious and considerable works of abstraction. In order to analyse this and to better understand how normative knowledge was condensed, we refer to the phenomenon of 'epitomisation' – an intellectual procedure well known in Roman and canon law from late Antiquity to early modern times, as explained in a chapter written by Christoph Meyer. The *longue durée* perspective is crucial for understanding early modern pragmatic literature, fruit of a scholarly practice deeply rooted in medieval practices and, at the same time, undergoing important transformations due to media change and European expansion.

While the two initial contributions of the volume are dedicated to methodology and overarching legal historical perspectives, a second group of articles deals with the presence of pragmatic literature in Ibero-America. After a chapter on the European exportation and dispersion of pragmatic literature in different parts of Spanish America (Otto Danwerth), two contributions discuss the distribution and use of pragmatic literature in broad regional perspectives both for the Andes and for Brazil. In a chapter on Habsburg Peru, Renzo Honores stresses the relevance of these normative texts for the emergence of colonial legal culture and juridical categories. A subsequent treatment of Jesuit pragmatic books in Portuguese America, up to the 18th century, offers important comparative perspectives for central topics of the European, Iberian and Spanish American chapters (Gustavo Machado Cabral).

The last part of the book presents six case studies – examining particular authors, genres and contexts – that highlight essential aspects of pragmatic literature. Each proposes new insights into the elaboration of pragmatic texts, their function, use and interpretation, on the Iberian peninsula as well as in Mesoamerica and South America. Manuela Bragagnolo analyses Martín de Azpilcueta's *Manual for Confessors*, illustrating the complex phenomenon of epitomisation in the work of this eminent 16th century canon lawyer and moral theologian. Three other chapters deal with normative texts in New Spain. José Luis Egío offers a close reading of early colonial catechisms in the Age of Reformation before the Council of Trent had ended, while Osvaldo Moutin examines the relationship between the constitutions of the Third Mexican Provincial Council and other normative devices it produced. How normative knowledge was implemented by Franciscan missionaries in frontier regions, is the subject of David Rex Galindo's article. The two final contributions shed light on further pragmatic genres in South American regions during the 17th and 18th centuries. An essay about devotional literature for "simple people" and Inquisitorial trials focuses on Cartagena de Indias/New Granada (Pilar Mejía). Taking up the perspective of a Spanish American periphery, Agustín Casagrande's discussion of *forensic practices* in late colonial Río de la Plata closes the volume.

The authors of the chapters take up recurring themes in their contributions in order to offer a consolidated, interconnected treatment of normativity and its media, the phenomenom of epitomisation, the circulation of pragmatic normative texts as well as the variety and functions of these works in different regional contexts. Among the authors are Argentine, Brazilian, Colombian, German, Italian, Peruvian and Spanish contributors, representing different disciplines, such as legal history, cultural history, social history and ethnohistory. The authors have been drawn together through their link to Department II of the Max Planck Institute for European Legal History in Frankfurt, either as researchers housed at the Institute or as affiliated researchers in the field of Ibero-American legal history; while others have come from their home countries to spend longer research stays as guests at the Institute.

The close integration of the book chapters into a common analytical framework was possible because the book presents the results of a research project conducted from 2016 to 2018 as part of the DFG-funded Collaborative Research Centre (SFB 1095) at Goethe University, Frankfurt ("Discourses of Weakness and Resource Regimes"), in a sub-project "Knowledge of the *pragmatici*: Presence and significance of pragmatic normative literature in Ibero-America (16th–17th centuries)". Research results of the group were presented at various conferences, e.g. at the 'XIX Congreso del Instituto Internacional de Historia del Derecho Indiano' (Berlin, Aug. 31–Sept. 4, 2016). The 'pragmatici' team organised various workshops like one on 'Practical and Pragmatic Literature in Legal and Science History', in cooperation with the Max Planck Institute for the History of Science in Berlin on Nov. 30, 2016, and a Research Colloquium at the Max Planck Institute for European Legal History on 'Knowledge and information regimes in early modern times' in the winter term 2016–2017. Some draft chapters of our book were discussed in Frankfurt (June 1–2, 2017) with Oracio Condorelli, Tamar Herzog, John F. Schwaller, Carlos Alberto González Sánchez, and Pedro Rueda Ramírez. We are very grateful to them and many colleagues especially from the Max Planck Institute for European Legal History for these opportunities to discuss our ideas.

Thomas Duve and Otto Danwerth
Frankfurt am Main, March 2020

Illustrations

Figures

Tables

Notes on Contributors

Manuela Bragagnolo
is Researcher at the Max Planck Institute for European Legal History (Frankfurt am Main).

Agustín Casagrande
is Assistant Professor of Legal Sociology at the Universidad Nacional de La Plata/Argentina (Law Faculty) and Affiliate Researcher at the Max Planck Institute for European Legal History (Frankfurt am Main).

Otto Danwerth
is Head of Editorial Department at the Max Planck Institute for European Legal History (Frankfurt am Main).

Thomas Duve
is Director at the Max Planck Institute for European Legal History and Professor of Comparative Legal History, Goethe University (Frankfurt am Main).

José Luis Egío
is Researcher of the project "The School of Salamanca" (Academy of Sciences and Literature Mainz, Max Planck Institute for European Legal History, and Goethe University, Frankfurt am Main).

Renzo Honores
is Researcher at the Instituto Internacional de Derecho y Sociedad (Lima/Peru).

Gustavo César Machado Cabral
is Professor at the Law Faculty of the Universidade Federal do Ceará (Fortaleza/Brazil) and Affiliate Researcher at the Max Planck Institute for European Legal History (Frankfurt am Main).

Pilar Mejía
is Researcher at the Max Planck Institute for European Legal History (Frankfurt am Main).

Christoph H.F. Meyer
is Researcher at the Max Planck Institute for European Legal History (Frankfurt am Main).

Osvaldo R. Moutin
is Researcher at the Max Planck Institute for European Legal History (Frankfurt am Main).

David Rex Galindo
is Assistant Professor of History, Universidad Adolfo Ibáñez (Santiago/Chile).

CHAPTER 1

Pragmatic Normative Literature and the Production of Normative Knowledge in the Early Modern Iberian Empires (16th–17th Centuries)

Thomas Duve

1 Introduction

Normative orders are a social and cultural construction, produced and transformed in a continuous process by a multitude of actors. They are created, modified and stabilised by the production, storage, processing, legitimisation – and thus also by the delegitimisation and forgetting – of normative information. This process of continuous translation of normative information into normative knowledge results in historical normative orders which take their shape through the normative information available, through the contingent configuration of actors and actants, the power relations between them, as well as through the social, cultural and material conditions peculiar to a concrete historical setting.

Legal historical and general historical research have increasingly provided us with information about many of these elements. Due to this, we can aspire to understand why a normative order has historically become what it is, why, for example, certain regimes of governance, diversity, dependency etc., have emerged in a more or less specific space and at a more or less specific time. Reconstructing the elements that make up these historical regimes, how they interact and change and understanding their transformation and intertwinement in time is at the core of legal historical research.

This book, however, does not deal with any of these specific historical regimes.[1] It does not reconstruct the history of forced labour, property or other institutions as historical formations in the 16th or 17th century Iberian worlds. It focuses on a different aspect: understanding how the production

1 The term 'historical regime' is understood here as a more or less stabilised historical formation of specific practices, rules, principles and norms in a certain field of action. This definition takes up the conceptual debate going back to Krasner, "Structural causes and regime consequences", that was further developed in various cultural and social scientific disciplines. See on this the survey of List, "Regimetheorie".

DOI:10.1163/9789004425736_002

of normative knowledge in the early modern Ibero-American colonial world worked as such and what role a literary genre, conceptualised in this book as 'pragmatic normative literature', played in this process. Phrased in knowledge-historical terms, the object of this book is the reconstruction of an historical regime of knowledge production in the field of normativity and the functionality of a specific medium therein.[2]

Due to the need to reduce the scale of observation and considering the importance of normative knowledge from the field of religion in the 16th and 17th century Ibero-American worlds, most of the chapters of this book study pragmatic literature related to moral theology and canon law and its making and use by theologians, missionaries and Church officials. They provide insights into the fundamental role actors from the religious field had in establishing something like a colonial normative literacy, a capacity of managing a basic understanding of the rules of colonial social life.[3] They can thus help to understand how normative knowledge reached a wider audience and was translated in everyday interactions, a fundamental question of colonial legal history that often remains unanswered if we focus only on action or patterns of behaviour without asking for the underlying knowledge. In this sense, they are, just like the whole volume, a contribution to a broader intellectual project aiming to understand Iberian colonial legal history as part of an historical process of 'glocal' knowledge production, driven by different, flexible and overlapping epistemic communities and communities of practice with their

2 The 'historical regime of knowledge production in the field of normativity' can be understood as a more or less stabilised historical formation of specific practices, rules, principles and norms of producing normative knowledge. This definition takes up and specifies the definition of 'knowledge regimes', developed by Wehling, "Wissensregime", 704. See on knowledge regimes also Böschen, *Hybride Wissensregime*. In general terms, we have opted for the concept 'historical regimes of knowledge' and not for 'Wissenskulturen' discussed especially in German academia in the 1990s because of the proximity of the debate about 'knowledge regime' to the field of historical epistemology and praxeology, developed not least in the history of science. For a survey of the use of 'Wissenskulturen', see Zittel, "Wissenskulturen, Wissensgeschichte und historische Epistemologie". On 'legal knowledge' see the inspiring observations of James Boyd White, describing legal knowledge "as an activity of mind, a way of doing something with the rules and cases and other materials of law, an activity that is itself not reducible to a set of directions or any fixed description. It is a species of cultural competence, like learning a language", White, "Legal Knowledge", 1399. On the reasons why we prefer to speak of "normative" knowledge and not "legal knowledge" see from a legal theoretical perspective Möllers, *Die Möglichkeit der Normen*, and from a legal historical perspective Duve, "Was ist ›Multinormativität‹?".

3 See for this aspect recently the contributions in Owensby and Ross (eds.), *Justice in a New World*.

own communicative spheres, with special emphasis on normative knowledge produced by actors from the religious field.[4]

The aim of this chapter is to introduce some basic features of this historical regime of knowledge production, to showcase how legal history could be seen as a process of knowledge production and to suggest a definition of 'pragmatic normative literature' as one important medium in this specific historical regime.[5] It therefore starts with an attempt to present the legal history of the Iberian empires as part of a legal tradition that can be understood as a huge diachronic process of intertextuality (2), a long history of reiterating acts of translation of normative information into normative knowledge (3). It sketches out why normative knowledge produced by religious actors was of overwhelming significance within the knowledge economy of the 16th and 17th century Iberian empires and how practical theology, normative practices and pragmatic literature were intertwined (4, 5). From this reconstruction of certain basic characteristics, it is possible to suggest a definition of 'pragmatic normative literature' (6), to summarise the state of the art on the media comprised in this genre in the historiography of law, canon law and moral theology (7) and to conclude with some remarks on why pragmatic literature might have been of special significance for governing an empire (8).

4 See for this perspective Duve, "Katholisches Kirchenrecht" and Duve, "Salamanca in Amerika". It also underlies the collective volume dedicated to Salamanca as a phenomenon of global knowledge production, to be published in 2020: Duve, Egío García and Birr (eds.), *The School of Salamanca: A case of global knowledge production?* It is part of an attempt to set European legal history into a global perspective, see with further references Duve, "Global Legal History: Setting Europe in Perspective", Duve, "Global Legal History – A Methodological Approach". From the perspective of the history of knowledge, important contributions have been developed by Jürgen Renn, especially in the volume Renn (ed.), *The Globalization of Knowledge in History*. On the relevance and potential for interaction between global legal history and history of knowledge see Renn, "The Globalization of Knowledge in History and its Normative Challenges". On the methodological assumptions underlying the idea of "communicative spheres" close to what is called here "communities of practice" and "epistemic communities" see Hespanha, "Southern Europe".

5 For a general introduction into the field 'history of knowledge' see Burke, *What is the History of Knowledge?* with further references. For a good introduction into the discussion about the relation between a history of science and a history of knowledge, as well as into the concepts of 'knowledge' see Renn, "From the History of Science to the History of Knowledge"; Lorraine Daston reflects about risks and opportunities of the opening of history of science towards a history of knowledge which could, *mutatis mutandis*, also apply to the legal historical field, Daston, "The History of Science and the History of Knowledge". A good introduction is also Müller-Wille, Reinhardt and Sommer, "Wissenschaftsgeschichte und Wissensgeschichte".

2 Legal History as a Process of Diachronic Intertextuality

Legal history in Europe can be interpreted as a huge process of diachronic translation of normative information and thus also as a history of recursive processes of closure and differentiation of bodies of normative knowledge. Although inseparable from the secular sphere, the Church, her institutions and personnel and the media produced by them were perhaps the most important drivers in this process. Centuries of research have been dedicated to the reconstruction of this history, often presented as the formation of a distinct western legal tradition. Whereas this history has traditionally been written with a clear focus on the rediscovery of Roman law in the Middle Ages and seen as a cultural-historical process of scientification, secularisation and professionalisation that led to modern statehood, in the last three decades important contributions have emphasised the fundamental role of canon law, Church actors and Religion in this history.[6]

Without being able to engage deeper into this large and complex history, it might be sufficient for the purpose of this chapter to point out that it was, not least, the continuous updating through selection and addition in an epistemic network that guaranteed the identity and, simultaneously, the dynamics and thus functionality of these normative orders through time.

Already in the early medieval legal cultures, built around a smaller amount of written texts and produced in complex constellations with orality,

6 Due to the vast period covered and the introductory character of this chapter, bibliographical references have to be kept to a minimum, especially on questions of method and specific references to pragmatic literature. For a general outline of Western or European legal history and, despite their shortcomings resulting from a Eurocentric perspective as well as their focus on the learned law tradition and the need to reduce complexity, the masterly accounts of Wieacker, *A History of Private Law in Europe*; Grossi, *A History of European Law*; Berman, *Law and Revolution*, provide the reader with a good introduction into the field. With special attention to the religious dimension and the practice of administering justice, see Prodi, *Una storia della giustizia*; Hespanha, *A cultura jurídica europeia* and Herzog, *A Short History of European Law* have presented fresh views on European legal history, including the colonial dimensions. For a first orientation, see also the different chapters in Pihlajamäki, Dubber and Godfrey (eds.), *The Oxford Handbook of European Legal History*. As for the so-called Derecho indiano, the colonial legal history of Spanish-America, the best introduction into its rationality and practices is Tau Anzoátegui, *Casuismo y Sistema*; for the Portuguese Empire see Hespanha, *Como os juristas viam o mundo*; Hespanha, *Filhos da terra*. For a comparative survey of the Hispanic and the Portuguese historiography, see Hespanha, "O 'direito de Índias' no contexto da historiografia das colonizações ibéricas". The combination of translation with an evolutionary perspective presented here is not least indebted to the writings of H.P. Glenn and his conceptualisation of 'legal tradition', see on this more extensively Duve, "Legal traditions".

intertextuality was so strong that some of these 'living texts' have been called "mutating monsters".[7] However, as time went on, more and more new normative knowledge was produced and stored in writing so that the body of accessible normativity continuously grew. By the 11th century, at the latest, theology and law had thus begun to develop a different attitude towards the legacy of these authoritative texts. People undoubtedly still felt bound by the decisions of the past, but they approached them in ways that are commonly seen as the beginning of legal scholarship: new intellectual strategies for coping with the seemingly contradictory parts of the tradition, for example, by using the technique of distinction, were accompanied by the use of new formats and new literary genres, a new organisation of knowledge through a non-chronological order, new finding devices, paratexts etc., all having important effects on the interpretation of the content.

In addition to the constant growth of the existing normative knowledge due to its accumulation over time and despite some losses and forgetting of normativity, the increasingly complex texts with their multiple historical layers – and now also interpretations – became more easily available. Already in the late Middle Ages, the existing as well as new normative texts (the so-called *ius novum*) were copied in increasing numbers due to novel forms of production (such as the *pecia* system) and the general passage "from memory to written record".[8] Manuscripts were used at the many newly founded universities and by a growing number of professionals, stored in libraries and handed over from generation to generation. In other words, the mass of normative information that could be used for producing new normative knowledge became ever larger, the margins of flexibility grew and many attempts of coping with this avalanche of information produced new media in which this information could be stored – and multiplied.

With the use of the printing press, this process of 'looping and feedback' of normative information gained even more momentum, not least because the so-called media revolution coincided with other major developments in late 15th and 16th century Europe such as European expansions, reformations and the emergence of the premodern state. Both Catholic and Protestant scholars now examined the normative knowledge stemming from tradition, whether in theology or in canon law, and prepared ever-new foundational works as well as summaries of their worldviews, their *confessions,* also in the field of law. In part due to this confessionalisation, new universities were founded in many

7 Firey, "Mutating Monsters".
8 Clanchy, *From Memory to Written Record.*

places in Europe and the number of university students increased in large part to supply the growing need for personnel in the huge administrative apparatuses that emerged. Not least in the Iberian monarchies, institutions of governance grew and new practices emerged as a response to imperial dimensions; the same applies to the Roman Curia and the religious orders that became 'global players'.

The European expansions to other continents and its manifold consequences like increasing trade, the need for imperial governance and massive missionary activities, but also the professionalisation in the administration of justice, demanded reproducible compilations of normative knowledge such as confessional and catechetical literature as well as basic information on (canon) law. The mission also brought new intellectual challenges, including questions on how to deal with indigenous peoples and their laws and beliefs, which were unknown to the Catholic world and different from the established categories of *infideles*. These questions motivated many authors and institutions on both sides of the Atlantic, and thereafter in the Pacific parts of the Empires, to edit new texts, drawing on and transforming existing literary traditions both in Europe and in the Americas, as Bragagnolo (Chapter 6), Egío (Chapter 7) and Honores (Chapter 4) illustrate. Bishops (Rex Galindo, Chapter 9) and Church assemblies, in particular the extraordinarily important Third Provincial Councils of Lima (1582/83) and Mexico (1585), saw it as their special responsibility to draft normative texts that were relevant to their diocese and oriented towards the needs of practice. At the same time, they had to respond to the important dogmatic and legislative production carried out in Trent and its intellectual environment. The Third Mexican Provincial Council, for example, produced not only canons, but also one handbook for confessors, three catechisms and a *rituale*, a book that provided all the information required by a priest for his performance of liturgical rites (Moutin, Chapter 8). These pragmatic texts often referred to the need to integrate the reforms discussed in Trent, many of which continued and were implemented after the closure of the Council in 1563.

These examples draw our attention to the expansion of the normative order of the Catholic Church and, at the same time, the need to adapt, clarify and select the relevant normative knowledge for particular areas or groups within this growing Catholic world. In more abstract terms: we can observe that, with the nearly contemporary European expansion and the media revolution, a growing variety of epistemic communities produced bodies of normative knowledge, drawing on the existing texts, modifying or interpreting them, often with specific communities of practice in mind. The epistemic network now spanned over larger territories and the variety of situations led to increasing differentiation. Thus, the so-called 'legal pluralism' inherent to medieval and early modern European law became even more complex: the attempt to provide diverse communities of practice with adequate tools for their task accelerated the continuous processes of differentiation within the overlapping normative orders present in the Catholic world. For example, members of powerful religious orders like the Dominicans or Jesuits followed different opinions on issues of huge practical importance such as usury or restitution. In the same vein, Church Provinces like those of Peru and Mexico started to develop distinct legal politics, for example, with regard to the inclusion or exclusion of indigenous and mestizo populations in the clergy. The specific circumstances of the Americas or the Asian parts of the monarchies led actors to deviate from solutions established in Europe, sustaining that the different circumstances required new solutions to old problems and that these needed specific knowledge that could only be acquired in practice. This is what, for example, the first bishop of Manila, the Dominican friar Domingo de Salazar who had lived for decades in Mexico before arriving in the Philippines, meant when he wrote to the emperor in 1582 that, even if so many excellent advisors from all disciplines served at the Court, to adequately decide over issues of the Indies there is no doubt that "it is necessary to have been there, and not only a few years".[9]

However, even the differentiation, localisations and specifications resulting from this globalisation of the Church and its institutions and the attempt to adapt their normative knowledge to the requirements of each place did not cause a closure of the different legal regimes that emerged. On the contrary, the need to actualise the body of normative knowledge and to answer concrete problems opened these legal regimes up to normative knowledge coming from different fields, regions or regulatory bodies. Mutual observation of what was done in other parts of the polycentric Spanish monarchy or within the widely spread Portuguese Empire was a frequent practice and, as a consequence, where a clear solution lacked in one place, it was possible to argue that a practice that was legitimate in Panamá might also serve for Lima or for Mexico and vice versa. Moreover, as customs were considered a source of law, a *lex non scripta*, and these customs were continuously (re)created and later recognised, daily practice produced new normative knowledge that could eventually be used in other cases as well, enriching the body of normative knowledge upon

9 The memorial of the first Bishop of Manila, Domingo de Salazar, sent to the emperor, is cited in Moutin, " 'Sepamos, Señores, en que ley vivimos y si emos de tener por nuestra regla al Consejo de Indias' ": "Y atrévome a decir esto porque, aunque Vuestra Magestad tiene tan cerca de si tantos y tan excelentes letrados en todas las facultades, pero para determinar muchas cosas de Indias, sin duda es menester haber estado en ellas, y no pocos años".

which actors could draw. Most importantly, kings and popes, intermediate regulatory bodies as well as local officials constantly produced new *reales cédulas*, *provisiones*, bulls, *breves* etc., often directed to specific recipients, but known and taken into account elsewhere. To offer an idea about the productivity of these regulatory bodies, it might be sufficient to keep in mind that the early Spanish recopilations of royal decisions regarding the affairs of the Indies from the late 16th and early 17th centuries (the so-called *Cedulario* of Diego de Encinas from 1596 and the draft of a *Recopilación* by Antonio de León Pinelo from 1636) had taken their selections from an estimated amount of more than 15000 documents. They were motivated not least by the fact that already in the 70s of the 16th century not even the members of the governing body, the *Consejo de Indias*, had a clear picture of the relevant normative framework.[10]

In synthesis, actors on all levels of society saw themselves confronted simultaneously with a need for regulation of new situations as well as with an information overload that could hardly be mastered. There was, as is so often the case in the history of law, simply "too much to know" and, at the same time, a lack of a precise solution to the case in question.[11] This general condition of uncertainty triggered different coping strategies, some of them already known from the past, others newly developed under the conditions of expansions, the printing press, reformation and early modern statehood. A wave of writings about *methodus*, new theories of coping with insecure normative knowledge like the probabilism and its precedents and variants, technical innovations, such as new finding devices, and new literary genres emerged. Early modern states as well as the Curia and the religious orders engaged in far-ranging reforms of their institutional procedures and structures. For the individual, however, the *multitudo* of normative knowledge upon which one could now draw had to be mastered. Not least specialised books providing overviews of the different solutions possible, such as the genre of *differentiae* promised help, and the many *compendia*, epitomisations and *summae* which are at the core of what we call 'pragmatic normative literature' are part of these multiple responses to the early modern information overload and resulting structural insecurity about the relevant knowledge. Meyer's *longue-durée* survey of epitomisation as a scholarly practice and Bragagnolo's case study of one of the bestsellers of the second half of the 16th century, the confession manual of Martín de Azpilcueta, highlight the variety of these coping strategies (Chapters 2, 6).

---

10 See on the *Cedulario de Encinas* García-Gallo, "El cedulario de Encinas", with a panorama of the insecurity of the knowledge in the 1570s. On the later *Recopilación* of Pinelo see Sánchez Bella, "Estudio preliminar", 32.

11 On the early modern information overload, see Blair, *Too Much to Know*.

To summarise, normative orders – at least, but perhaps not only, in the European tradition – can be understood as the result of diachronic and recursive processes of translation of normative knowledge, a textual practice intimately connected to the history of the media in which this knowledge was stored. New normative knowledge was continuously produced by a variety of actors and entered into this process of looping and feedback, giving way to a differentiation and specialisation, localisation and regionalisation by and for specific epistemic communities and communities of practice. At the same time, the practices of translating the knowledge, themselves also part of the normative knowledge, experienced a similar process of stability and adaptation.

3 Translations

The general overview of the evolution of normative orders in time, understood as a continuous process of translation of normative knowledge, shows that there was a need for pragmatic literature as a response to the information overload. It also brings us closer, but does not suffice, for an understanding of how these translations happened on a concrete level and in the specific historical regime of knowledge production we are considering. At least for analytical purposes, it might be helpful to distinguish two moments. First, when normative information is translated into normative knowledge by certain epistemic communities through the embedding of this information into a different context and, second, when this newly generated normative knowledge is translated by members of a community of practice deciding upon a specific case.

3.1 *From Normative Information to Normative Knowledge*

The first translation occurs when normative information is captured and thus inserted into a specific context. This transformation of information into knowledge is closely linked to the mediality, for the storage in a certain medium combines the normative information with a certain field of action and thus adds a new layer of significance to the information.[12]

12 Within the vast debate about 'information' and 'knowledge' and the definition of these two, we have opted for a distinction that considers information as the basic unit, understood as data with a general relevance and purpose. Information is converted into knowledge as soon as it is contextualised and integrated into a field of action, opening possibilities for action. As such, knowledge can be understood as the entirety of all the propositions which the members of a group consider to be true or which are considered to be true in a sufficient amount of texts in this group, comprising all kind of patterns of thought, orientation and action. It comprises also implicit knowledge, embedded in

This embedding into a more or less specific context can be seen as a first translation in the broad sense of the term because the normative information, disembedded from its original temporal and factual context through the storage in a medium, is likely to acquire new meaning. For example, embedding normative information stemming from the religious sphere in a legal medium makes it likely that the normative information will now be read as a legal one, with not unimportant consequences for the methods and practices of interpretation to be used. In other cases, the embedding in a specific institutional context, for instance, as ordinances formulated by bishops and approved by the king (Rex Galindo, Chapter 9) or as an instruction authorised by the Inquisition (Mejía, Chapter 10), entails that the normative information included in the medium now enjoys the authority attributed to this format or to its editors, compilers or to the authorities that recommended its use. The normative knowledge included in the selection is thus charged with authority, while other normative options become less authoritative. For colonial Hispanic America, the most famous example for this charging with authority of some texts and de-authorising others might be the *Recopilación de Leyes de los Reinos de las Indias* from 1680, a collection that did not derogate the royal legislation not included but had a clear bottle-neck-effect for the survival of normative knowledge.

Often this authorising and de-authorising of normative knowledge does not happen through selection or simply local writing, as Honores shows (Chapter 4) but explicitly, for example, in deliberations about different possible solutions for a problem, a typical mode of reasoning not only in the tradition of scholastic argumentation. Notwithstanding the fact that this playing out of authorities against each other was specific for erudite literature, not least in the scholastic tradition, we can also find these authorisations and de-authorisations in smaller texts, including in those we focus on in this volume. "I do not approve the opinion of those who [...]", writes, for instance, the first bishop of Mexico in his *Doctrina breve y muy provechosa* (1543–1544), as Egío (Chapter 7) shows, making

practices, organisational routines; see on the different definitions, for example, Neumann, "Kulturelles Wissen", 811 and the bibliography cited above, especially Wehling, "Wissensregime" It is a narrower definition than the one used by Renn and Hyman, "The Globalization of Knowledge in History: An Introduction", 21–44 who define knowledge as the capacity of an individual, a group, or a society to solve problems and to mentally anticipate the necessary actions, a problem-solving potential; they give an interesting list of forms of knowledge representations and forms of transmission. For a systematic overview see also Abel, "Knowledge Research". 'Normative' knowledge refers to knowledge as positively labelled possibilities, a definition that Christoph Möllers develops in his book *Die Möglichkeit der Normen*.

clear that a doctrine formulated for the *infideles* in Europe was not to apply to indigenous peoples in his diocese.[13] Other chapters in this volume contain similar examples of authorisations, for example, in the Third Mexican Provincial Council of 1585 (Chapter 8). In short, individuals or groups that can be considered, for many reasons, as part of epistemic communities, like members of a religious order or viceroys selecting relevant norms for their realm, contributed to a translation of normative information into normative knowledge through the action of inserting it into their excerpts, manuscript copies and books. Often these texts were specifically made for practitioners.

3.2 *Normative Knowledge in Practice*

This recontextualised normative knowledge, produced for specific contexts of action and for specific communities of practice, was the starting point for these communities when resolving individual cases. From a modern (and yet justifiably contested) perspective, this process of finding a right solution for a specific case is often understood as a logical operation referred to as subsumption and associated with the notion of syllogism.[14] If one takes a closer look at early modern sources, however, we can identify a completely different mode of reasoning, a special *ars inveniendi*. This mode of reasoning can be understood as a second translation in which the normative framework according to which a decision was made had to be generated from the existing normative knowledge in a moment before the selected authorities were weighed against one another in the light of the specific case, again drawing on normative knowledge often embodied in practices and resulting in the production of a normative statement for the individual case.

The logic of this *ars inveniendi* only becomes understandable if we take into account its underlying epistemological assumption that the texts one could draw upon did not contain ready-made solutions for all cases, but that all these were concretisations, part of and a way to a higher objective truth that could not be accessed directly. As famously put by the Digest at the beginning of its final title (Dig. 50.17.1): *Non ex regula ius sumatur, sed ex iure quod regula fiat* – The law is not derived from the rule, but it is the law from which the rule is derived. It was, in other words, possible to find a just solution for each case by looking through the authoritative texts, and this is why one had to have them, or at least a selection of them, at hand. However,

---

13 See José Luis Egío's contribution in this volume, fn. 59.

14 For a critique of this syllogistic model and a clear introduction into 'concretisation', much closer to what we can observe in early modern practice, see Vesting, *Legal Theory*, 109–114.

the solution could not be plucked directly from the authorities, but had to be found through a rational process that drew on different authorities and critically weighed their applicability and appropriateness for the case in question. Authorities from the past and the current normative production by the sovereigns were obviously weighty arguments. They showed a way, perhaps even the only way, to find the right solution. But they were, in the end, just an aid and not the solution as such. For this process of producing the right solution, scholars developed certain rules, a *methodus* and a theory of legal sources and their authoritative value. We can call this the "theory of practice". According to this theory, it was necessary to search in different places (*loci*, *topoi*) for the normative option whose partial truth seemed most appropriate for the individual case at hand. The philosophical background of this method was – legal, philosophical and theological – early modern *topica* and the resulting procedure, the *dialectica*. The *methodus* provided specific techniques of interpretation.[15]

However, it was not only this theory of practice, the theory of sources and the method that influenced the production of a decision. Of particular importance were the practices of norm production as such, factors far beyond the 'theory of practice', such as established patterns of action, conventions or implicit knowledge about how to proceed rightly. These practices were also part of the normative knowledge.[16] Recent historical research has increasingly paid attention to this normative dimension, i.e., the rules of practice, regulatory rationalities, implicit understandings, aesthetic norms as structures of thought, habitus etc., often summarised under the heading of praxeology.[17] Their significance cannot be overrated in legal historical research, especially in a regime of knowledge production that left large margins of discretion to the actors (as was the case in the early modern Iberian empires), thus sharing a general characteristic that can also be found in the 'theory of practice' with

15 This theory of practice, comprising reflection about the theory of sources of law, the method and the interpretation of law, has been the central object of legal historical research on the history of early modern legal method. On the early modern period, see especially the seminal study of Schröder, *Recht als Wissenschaft*.

16 See very clearly on this James Boyd White who defines legal knowledge "as an activity of mind, a way of doing something with the rules and cases and other materials of law, an activity that is itself not reducible to a set of directions or any fixed description. It is a species of cultural competence, like learning a language; this may in fact be the closest analogy we have, for what a lawyer knows at the center is how to speak and write the language of the law, in actual situations in the world – how to use legal language to create legal meaning", White, "Legal Knowledge", 1399.

17 See on this, with further references, the contributions in Duve, "Was ist ›Multinormativität‹?"

its wide understanding of meaning, wide rules of interpretation and the all-encompassing need to find just solutions.

It is not least these rules inherent in practice, the 'practices of practice', that make up communities of practice: groups that share a certain consensus about how to translate the normative knowledge into a decision for a concrete case. These groups might be identical to the epistemic communities mentioned above that produced pragmatic literature for a special area, group or purpose. However, they might also simply be united by their preferences for certain texts and the way they use them; it is not by chance that, as various chapters in this volume show, Church Councils and religious orders obliged the members of their group to acquire certain texts and to have them close at hand. In any case, whether members of these communities of practice or not, those who had to produce a decision on a specific case, as confessor, judge or consultant, had to use, in their artisanal exercise to find the right answer, certain texts which provided them with the relevant information about the normative knowledge upon which they could draw their task.

If a decision about a specific case was made on the basis of this *ars inveniendi*, which was based on a material, non-formal concept of law and some operational rules (i.e., of a theory of practice) and its corresponding practices (i.e., the rules of practice), then a new normative statement emerged, tailored to the concrete case; a particular casuistic norm. This new normative statement, however, did not only resolve the case. If captured in a medium, like in a collection of decisions or a manuscript that summarised good practice for office holders, precedents etc., it also passed into the general body of normative information, to be then again disembedded and processed into normative knowledge until it becomes, once more, an object of translation by a community of practice. This recursive process is thus continuous, constantly adding to and changing the composition of the normative information processed and converted into normative knowledge: "Legal knowledge is thus constantly created and recreated differently by different minds on different occasions".[18] In some cases, we can observe something like the delocalization of local normative knowledge, for example, when a locally motivated action led to a specific regulation that was later applied to other cases or even included in the collection of royal legislation, such as the *Recopilación*.[19] Even if the change in the composition of the body of normative knowledge caused by these processes of localizing and delocalizing normative knowledge, might have been of homoeopathic dosage

18 White, "Legal Knowledge", 1400.

19 Duve, "El Concilio como instancia de autorización".

and barely noticeable at first, cumulatively and over time it was considerable. It is here where we can also find a clue as to how normative orders change because a multiplicity of actors on micro and meso levels produced normative knowledge in their daily activities, continuously transforming the system through minimal adaptations.

The diversity of regulatory bodies, called here 'epistemic communities', as well as the *ars inveniendi* practiced by them acting as 'communities of practice', are key elements of what some legal historians, looking at the secular sphere, have described as early modern *cultura jurisdiccional*.[20] This jurisdictional culture reflected the 'plural' structure of medieval and early modern societies, mirrored in their multiple *iurisdictiones*, ranging from the jurisdictions of corporate bodies to the royal and imperial jurisdictions. The tension between these jurisdictions was constitutive for early modern societies, because in a normative order without a separation of powers in the modern sense, extending the sphere of jurisdiction basically meant extending power, and correspondingly, for the sovereign, conceding jurisdictional privileges was one of the key tools of governance. He was, however, not free in conceding these privileges, because even the sovereign was bound to respect the law with its many long-established rules about the distribution of jurisdictional competences.

Within the multiplicity of these jurisdictions on different levels, and notwithstanding a certain overstatement of this divide in the legal historiography, it was possible to distinguish jurisdictions belonging to the secular and those belonging to the ecclesiastical sphere. This does not mean that jurisdictional conflicts would only have occurred between these two spheres. On the contrary, under the conditions of the royal patronage, the lines of conflict often did not run along this divide, but followed other logics and historical contingencies. There were, for example, fierce conflicts between religious orders and secular clergy, or between bishops and members of the Inquisition. Most importantly, however, all of these *iurisdictiones*, secular or ecclestiastical, were fundamentally grounded on the idea of an objective divine order from which all other human sub-orders could be derived. Both secular and canon law were subject to this divine order, giving religion an overwhelming importance for the production of normative knowledge in the Iberian empires. For this reason, it was important for the entire knowledge economy underlying

20 See, for example, Garriga Acosta, "Sobre el gobierno" with references to the rich tradition of reflection about the significance of the concept of *iurisdictio* in European legal history developed by Pietro Costa, Paolo Grossi, Bartolomé Clavero, António M. Hespanha, Carlos Petit and Jesús Vallejo during the last decades and further developed by Marta Lorente, Alejandro Agüero and others.

this jurisdictional culture when, in the early 16th century, a new producer of normative knowledge – and an important provider of pragmatic literature – entered the stage: moral theology.

4 Secular and Religious Normative Knowledge

The reasons for the rise of moral theology as an independent scholarly discipline and a producer of normative knowledge are manifold and closely connected with the multiple historical transformations of the first decades of the 16th century mentioned above: reformations, European expansions, the media revolution and the rise of the early modern state, growing not least through the absorption of jurisdictional competences traditionally claimed by the Church.[21]

Without going into details, it is important to highlight that, in this historical situation, the Catholic Church and its law came under considerable pressure. Of course, canon law remained indispensable when people were baptised, were married, fasted, celebrated or were buried; it still marked the passages between the different stages of Christian life. The bishop, whose position was strengthened by the Council of Trent, continued to exercise his jurisdiction in the so-called *forum externum*: in the ecclesiastical court within the framework of his *visitas* or at synods. Delegate judges and a number of ecclesiastical offices, authorities and institutions, such as religious communities, hospitals, poorhouses and many others, continued to live according to canon law on a daily basis.

However, in many respects the Church's jurisdiction was curtailed. In response, the Roman Curia developed a system of indirect governance, including the adoption of administrative and political practices resembling those of early modern secular states, for example, by expanding the system of *nuntii* at kings' and emperors' courts or by intensifying communication with the emerging national Churches. The attempt to standardise normative knowledge, for example, by regulating the production of catechetical works, as discussed in the contribution of Egío (Chapter 7), through devotional literature, as Mejía shows in her chapter the Inquisition in Cartagena de Indias (Chapter 10) or through the requirement of Curial approval of synodal decrees, was part of this.[22]

---

21 For an overview on these processes, see Prodi, *Una storia della giustizia*.

22 Albani and Pizzorusso, "Problematizando el patronato regio".

In this context, the importance of canon law scholarship as a producer of normative knowledge declined, not least because of the strengthening centrality of the Roman Curia and its new institutions, introduced after the Council of Trent, and specific measures like the prohibition of commentary on the council's decrees. The normative knowledge produced by the Church continued to operate beyond the ecclesiastical sphere through the authority of tradition. It remained part of the available normative options upon which one could draw as a source of law, as *ratio scripta* and as a body of juridical learned practices. However, it was was a far cry from the significance it had held in the High Middle Ages.

It was in this historical setting that the normative knowledge developed for the so-called *forum internum* or *forum conscientiae*, often related to the practice of confession but not confined to it, grew in importance and moral theology emerged as a new producer of normative knowledge for this *forum internum*.[23] The normative knowledge produced by this discipline around the *forum internum* was seen to be no less juridical than the canon law practiced in the *forum externum*. The confessor was considered a judge of souls, the *iudex animarum*, and confession was equalised to a judicial procedure: the decrees of the Council of Trent explicitly called the granting of absolution an *actus iudicialis*.[24]

As a consequence, the balance between different normative resources from the religious sphere shifted away from canon law towards a normativity produced for the *forum internum*, which became a key component of the normative economy in the Iberian empires. At the end of the 16th century, whoever was searching for the right answer to a problem had to take note of important moral theological texts. The importance of moral theology as a producer of normative knowledge in Ibero-America emerges particularly clearly in the contributions of Machado Cabral (Chapter 5) on Portuguese America, in the chapters of Egío (Chapter 7), Moutin (Chapter 8) and Rex Galindo (Chapter 9) on Mexico and in Danwerth's research on the presence of these texts in

---

23 On this foundation, see Mahoney, *The Making of Moral Theology*; for the significance of the *forum internum*, see, for example, O'Banion, *The Sacrament of Penance*; Marcocci, "Conscience and Empire".

24 In the text of the session of the Council of Trent dedicated to the sacrament of confession, the penitents are seen as accused facing a trial, "ante hoc tribunal tanquam reos", the confession is equalised to a trial and the confessor to a judge: "ad instar actus iudicialis, quo ab ipso velut a iudice sententia pronunciatur", see Council of Trent, sessio XIV, 25.11.1551, doctrina, cap. II, VI, in the edition of Alberigo, Dossetti et al., *Conciliorum Oecumenicorum Decreta*, edition tertia, 1973, cited according to the text in Wohlmuth (ed.), *Dekrete der ökumenischen Konzilien*, vol. 3, quotations on 704 and 707.

Hispanic America (Chapter 3). They also point to the fact that there was one outstanding institution, also an epistemic community and a community of practice that dominated the production of normative knowledge in this field for more than a century, at least in the Iberian worlds: the so-called "School of Salamanca". A closer look at this school can help us understand the connection between practical (moral) theology, its normative reasoning and thus the function and significance of pragmatic literature therein.

5 Practical Theology and Pragmatic Literature

The significance of the School of Salamanca as a web of normative knowledge production and also of pragmatic literature might, at first glance, seem surprising because we usually associate the school with the big multi-volume treatises, *De iustitia et iure* and *De legibus* by Domingo de Soto, Luis de Molina and Francisco Suárez. However, the theologians at the University of Salamanca and in the Dominican convent of San Esteban, the core of the so-called "School of Salamanca", did not inhabit an ivory tower, producing their theoretical systems in seclusion from the world only for other academics.[25]

Alongside their theoretical work, the theologians in Salamanca and elsewhere were deeply immersed with practice and real life. In the turbulent decades of 16th century expansions, reformations, wars, financial speculation and inflation, people were assailed by moral doubts and they searched for advice. They faced problems of everyday life or high politics, concerning just price, financial transactions and fasting rules. They were insecure as to whether the use of force against insurgent indigenous peoples was justified, whether prisoners taken in the conquests could be enslaved and whether there was a legitimate right to take booty. It was this need for moral advice, the preoccupation with religious questions, eschatological hopes and fears, together with a renewal of theology, as well as the impact of personalities such as Francisco de Vitoria, Domingo de Soto and Melchior Cano, that set the stage for the emergence of Salamanca as one of the centres of a new practical theology.

Of course, many of the problems to be resolved were not new. Usury, war or fraud have been classic topics of normative reflection for centuries. However, the intellectual mobilisation in the Iberian peninsula during the first half of the 16th century, the intense quarrels about the right theological method and the uncertainty caused by the existence of many contradictory authorities that

25 In this section, I am drawing on Duve, "The School of Salamanca".

became more visible with the growing body of normative knowledge stored in ever more books, made a re-thinking of the normative system necessary. Moreover, because finding the right solution meant looking at each case's specific circumstances, taking into account the status of the persons, their knowledge and interests, the object of dispute and the decision's consequences, it needed erudite individuals who could perform this reflection. In cases of doubt, an expert's opinion was indispensable. Francisco de Vitoria stated this clearly at the beginning of his famous *Relectio* on the Indies: "Effectively, for an act to be good, if there is cause for doubt, it is necessary to do it according to a wise man's advice and determination".[26]

The wise men – *sapientes* – were, in the first place, theologians, not least because of their experience in the confessional and their training in practical theology and the *summae confessorum* tradition. The *sapientes* were thus, in fact, also practitioners. Moreover, as theologians, they felt not only entitled, but also obliged to advise the faithful: their chief duty was to ensure the salvation of souls and this empowered them to give their opinion on any issue that involved questions of right or wrong. According to Vitoria, "the task and office of the theologian are so far-reaching that no proof, no consideration, and no topic appears to lie beyond the purview of the theological profession and office".[27] Similar statements can be found in Domingo de Soto[28] or in later texts like Francisco Suárez's *De legibus*, to cite only the most famous authors.[29]

From this general point of view, and especially in cases like that of the native Americans, secular and canon law were mere ancillary sciences for the

26 Francisco de Vitoria, Relectio [...] quam habuit [...] anno a dominica incarnatione millesimo quingentesimo trigesimo nono [...]: "Et in his omnibus ita res se habet, quod si quis antequam deliberauerit, & legitimè illi constiterit tale factum licitum esse, aliquod tale faceret, & fortè secundum se esset licitum: talis peccaret, neque excusaretur per ignorantiam: cùm illa, ut patet, non esset inuincibilis, postquam ille non facit quod in se est, ad examinandum quòd liceat, aut non liceat. Ad hoc enim ut actus sit bonus, oportet si aliâs non est certum, ut fiat secundum diffinitionem & determinationem sapientis. Haec enim est una conditio boni actus [...]". Vitoria, *Relectiones Theologicae XII*, 288.

27 Francisco de Vitoria, Relectio [...] de potestate civili: "OFFICIVM, ac munus Theologi tam latè patet, ut nullum argumentum, nulla disputatio, nullus locus alienus uideatur à theologica professione, & instituto". Vitoria, *Relectiones Theologicae XII*, 174.

28 Soto, *De iustitia et iure*, fol. 5: "Neque vero est quod Theologis vitio detur, hanc sibi assumere provinciam quae Iurisperitis accommodatior videri potest: quandoquidem Canonica iura ex visceribus Theologiae prodiere: Civilia vero ex media morum Philosophia. Theologi ergo est iuris Canonici decreta ad normam Euangelicam exigere; philosphique Ciulia ex principiis philosophiae examinare [...]".

29 Suárez, *De legibus ac Deo legislatore*, Prooemium, 2: "Nulli mirum videri debet, si homini Theologiam profitenti leges incidant disputandae".

theologians. Of course, one needed to know both, if only because of the practical implications, as both jurists and canonists emphasised. Not least the *ius commune* tradition provided important points of view that had to be addressed, as the canonist Martín de Azpilcueta stressed in trying to set a limit to theologians' pretensions.[30] Obviously, the question of who qualified to give opinons on all matters was also a battle between the disciplines dedicated to normativity – secular law, canon law, (moral) theology and philosophy. However, as Vitoria's disciple, Melchior Cano, put it in his fundamental work *De locis theologicis*, in the end, the *auctoritates* of the jurists were irrelevant to theologians in questions of faith and of little or no relevance with respect to norms that could be derived from the *lex evangelica* or *ratio*. The only area where they could be of use was in cases of doubt about *moribus ecclesiae & religionis*.[31] In general, however, the theologians knew it better and this is why it is characteristic of the School that its members gave advice in personal conversations, in written expert opinions or as *iudices animarum* in the confessional, but also through their books with an inherent pragmatic purpose – another exercise of practical theology.

Some of these books were more, others less, useful in practice, depending on what kind of 'practice' was at stake. Even if Domingo de Soto, for example, assured that he wrote his multivolume *De iustitia et iure*, published in 1556, not least because of the pressing need to give orientation on practical matters like usury and for the salvation of the souls,[32] his erudite Latin elaborations might

30 Azpilcueta, *Commentarii in tres de poenitentia distinctiones posteriores, videlicet V, VI et VII*, Dist. 6., cap. I, § caveat, n. 11, 188: "De iustitia enim Theologi generatim discere sciunt, quid illa est, & quotuplex, an sit virtus cardinalis, an omnium moralium potissima, in qua potentia locanda, & alia id genus, quae parum aut nihil confessario conferunt. Quod item iniustitia sit peccatum mortale, facile definire norunt. At definire, quando in iudiciis, in contractibus, in ultimis voluntatibus, et nonnunquam in delictis committatur iniustita in casibus innumeris, qui praeter legem naturae occurrunt, vires Theologi excedit: nisi legum quoque se peritum fecerit".

31 Cano, *De locis theologicis*, lib. VIII, cap. VII, fol. 284: "Prima conclusio: In his, quae ad fidem pertinent, iurisconsultorum auctoritate theologus non eget [...]"; fol. 285: "Secunda conclusio: In his etiam, quae ad mores pertinent, quatenus vel lex evangelica, vel ratio Philosophiae de huiusmodi praescribit, iureconsultorum auctoritas parum aut certe nihil theologo conferrre potest"; fols. 285–286: "Tertia conclusio. In tertio illo genere rerum, ubi scilicet de moribus ecclesiae & religionis institutis per leges [...] iurisperitorum omnium communis consensus concorsque sententia, theologo magnam fidem facere debet".

32 Soto, *De iustitia et iure*, lib. VI, Prooemium, fol. 505: "Eo denique destinati operis perventum nobis est, cuius praecipue gratia de illo coepimus cogitare. Haec inquam usurarum, contractuum, cambiorumque ac simoniarum sylva in animum potisssime nobis induxit, ut tantam operem molem aggrederemur"; see also Soto, *De iustitia et iure*, Prooemium, ante lib. I, fol. 5: "[...] peperit tamen humana libido per temporum iniquitatem, parturitque in

not have served every community of practice. Merchants who wanted to know precisely what kind of contracts were immoral and thus illegitimate might have preferred to look at Tomás de Mercado's *Tratos y contratos de mercaderes*, written by the Mexican Dominican friar on the petition of the merchants of Seville and printed in Salamanca a few years later in 1569.[33] This raises the question of how to define 'pragmatic normative literature'. Why not include, for example, Domingo de Soto's *De iustitia et iure*, and why Thomas de Mercado's *Tratos y contratos* or Martín de Azpilcueta's *Manual de confessores*?

6 Pragmatic Normative Literature: Description and Definition

Taking the function of a text in a concrete context of use as the defining criterion for a type of literature, as literary studies suggest,[34] and following what has been said until now, pragmatic normative literature can be defined as thus: written texts used by practitioners in an immediate way to access the relevant normative knowledge required to produce a normative statement related to the legitimacy of human action.

---

dies novas fraudulentiae formas, quibus contra ius & fas suam quisque expleat insatiabilem avaritiam. Quapropter nihil aliud quam operae pretium arbitrandum est si iniqua pacta & conventa, & cambia, tamquam adeo multa usurae simoniaeque recentia genera in animum nobis induxerunt, nova de re veteri volumina aedere".

33 See the preface in Mercado, *Tratos y contratos de mercaderes y tratantes discididos y determinados*.

34 See Busse, "Text- und Gesprächslinguistik". This criterion has also been used in other fields, for example, in the debate about vernacular literature and its significance in German legal history, see the discussion in Schumann, "Rechts- und Sprachtransfer", 136 or in the research on „pragmatische Schriftlichkeit", see Keller, Grubmüller and Staubach (eds.), *Pragmatische Schriftlichkeit im Mittelalter*. In general terms, surprisingly little attention has been paid in legal historical research to the classification of "types of legal literature" even in the (older) standard works on history of literature, see e.g., Holthöfer, "Die Literatur zum gemeinen und partikularen Recht", 106 ("[the typology] with reference to the traditional forms of the Late Middle Ages [has been formulated] exclusively on the basis of the sources"); in a similar manner Söllner, "Die Literatur zum gemeinen und partikularen Recht", 514 ("The typology follows in general formal criteria"); Troje, "Die Literatur des gemeinen Rechts unter dem Einfluß des Humanismus", 634 places "types of literature" in quotation marks and thereafter uses the word "forms of literature". Attempts to apply quantitative methods and a sociological perspective have not led to a clear picture about the criteria for the definition of types of literature, see, however, Ranieri, "Juristische Literatur aus dem Ancien Régime". Martin Bertram gives an insight into the lack of clear criteria about how to classify what is called here 'pragmatic literature' in the historiography on canon law, Bertram, "Spätmittelalterliches Kirchenrecht", 574.

There are some implications of this definition. First, as 'written text', pragmatic normative literature is distinguished from other media, such as audiovisual media. The latter, for example, in the form of pictorial representations in altarpieces, crucifixes, *lienzos* or performances such as plays and processions, were frequently employed in mission and for catechesis and were thus important for the transportation and implementation of normative ideas. They were an important part of the regime of knowledge production in the early modern Catholic world. No doubt, the pragmatic literature needs to be read in its close connection with these other media, not least in its intertwinement with orality, as in the case of the *sermonarios* discussed by Rex Galindo (Chapter 9). However, these other media generally served educational and catechetical purposes and were generally not directed to those practitioners who were in charge of producing normative statements.

Second, it should be noted that pragmatic normative literature is by no means limited to printed texts. On the contrary, a large part of pragmatic normative literature was probably never printed, but circulated in manuscript form: copies, excerpts, abridgements or compilations of relevant documents made by practitioners or for practitioners. In spite of the low survival rate of these texts and the poor cataloguing of the surviving manuscripts, there are some indications that these manuscript texts were numerous and of huge practical importance.[35] However, because the dissemination of printed works in the period under consideration was already considerably greater than that of individual manuscripts and due to practical constraints, in this volume we concentrate on the printed texts. It would, however, be important to consider manuscripts, especially from practitioners who often assembled a set of documents they found helpful and used them as tools for action.

When we use 'normative', we refer to 'normativity' in a dual sense: first, it refers to the fact that these handbooks are themselves normative, meaning that they give instruction on how to act rightly. This normative character, however, applies to many texts from navigation manuals and books on how to exercise the office of a notary to cooking recipes. Second, and more importantly, they are normative in the sense that they contain specific knowledge for the production of a normative statement. For the latter, we adopt a broad notion of 'normativity' that refers to precepts from law (in a wide, sociological sense) and religion. This broadening seems to be nothing else but the consequence of early modern normative or jurisdictional pluralism and, not least, the importance of religion and the precepts stemming from moral theology for the every

35 See the references by Danwerth (Chapter 3) in this volume.

day administration of justice and decision-making. Thus, pragmatic normative literature includes texts that contain knowledge labelled in a positive way as a possibility of action.[36] It therefore does not only consist of works of secular law, canon law and moral theology, but also might include other texts in which recommendations for right action and conduct were stored, such as catechetical and pastoral literature, collections of sermons and devotional books. The chapters of Machado Cabral (Chapter 5), Mejía (Chapter 10), Moutin (Chapter 8) and Rex Galindo (Chapter 9) provide impressive illustrations of the breadth of the literature that come into play within this widened meaning.[37]

Another assumption underlying the definition is that the addressees of pragmatic literature were principally those who should be well-informed about the relevant normative knowledge because they had to take decisions: the practitioners. It was this group that needed information for the exercise of the *ars inveniendi* described above. Obviously, the range of practitioners can be extremely wide, depending on the community of practice we have in mind. However, in view of the limited literacy and for economic reasons as well as taking into consideration the historical circumstances in the Iberian empires, it might have been, above all, professional users. The studies on book circulation, book ownership (see Danwerth, Chapter 3) and on the use of pragmatic literature in this volume examine different types of practitioners: missionaries, merchants, jurists, but also members of the laity.

In a certain way, the users were *pragmatici,* a term used in 19th century legal historiography by Roderich Stintzing in his path-braking study on popular literature of Roman-canon law until the 16th century.[38] With this, Stintzing, however, resorted to the pejorative use of the word *pragmatici* as *homines quidam forensis professionis* which, at least since the days of humanistic jurisprudence, referred to a person who in some way worked in court practice but lacked erudition.[39] The tools of these practitioners, the so-called 'popular' literature,

---

36 For this broad concept of normativity, see Möllers, *Die Möglichkeit der Normen*. With this, we are employing a broader concept than, for example, Dave De ruysscher in his discussion of merchant guidebooks, De ruysscher, "How Normative were Merchant Guidebooks?".

37 As pragmatic literature is defined according to its function and not from the field, this definition could be applied to a wide range of fields, for example, on pragmatic normative literature for certain professions like notaries, navigators, artisans, or merchants. For the latter, see, for example, the collection Hoock and Jeannin (eds.), *Ars Mercatoria*, vol. 1. If such a handbook for merchants contains knowledge about the legitimacy of certain actions, like contracts, it can be considered as pragmatic normative literature.

38 Stintzing, *Geschichte der populären Literatur des römisch-kanonischen Rechts.*

39 See, for example, Budé, *Annotationes Priores & Posteriores*, Reliquae, fol. 241v, littera H, In capite, Moris: "Pragmatici igitur erant quidam forensis professionis"; this understanding

were characterised accordingly as "tools of the semi-erudite", *Hülfsmittel der Halbgelehrten*, which in a certain sense is close to what the users of pragmatic literature in their respective communities of practice were. However, as the use of the term 'popular' was rooted in a philosophically charged discussion about the reception of learned law in Europe and was constructed as a countermodel to 'learned' law, it was soon criticised as misleading and as carrying a whole lot of implications.[40] For these reasons, the term is not employed here, also to avoid further misunderstandings that might arise due to more recent connotations of 'popular' literature as a specific genre for subaltern actors.

As for the communities of practice that might have been the (intended) users of these texts, we can find a wide variety. Sometimes we know about the community of practice for which these books were written, for example, when they were named explicitly by the authors, as was the case of Tomás de Mercado. However, the chapters in this volume show various examples of a production for specific communities of practice even when these have not been explicitly addressed in the titles. When the first bishop of New Spain, Juan de Zumárraga, for example, produced catechetical literature in a key phase of the history of the Church of Mexico (Egío, Chapter 7) or when half a century later his successors in the Provincial Council of Mexico again had to make a multitude of decisions in order to select, update and adapt the available normative knowledge to the specific regional circumstances, it is clear that they had the members of their clergy in mind. As Moutin shows (Chapter 8), they addressed them and other parts of the population, for example, those who made inquiries with the Council, with different media strategies: by producing council canons, a confessional manual and other texts, which we would today describe as pastoral literature, but which contained normative knowledge framed in different formats. Machado Cabral (Chapter 5) examines the production and use of such texts by the Jesuits in Brazil, and Bragagnolo shows the connection between translations and envisioned audiences: the first version of Azpilcueta's confessional handbook was based on a Portuguese model, whereas the later version integrated the experiences of the first Jesuit missions. From then on, the author himself kept adapting his handbook to meet the needs of different communities of practice (Chapter 6).[41]

---

continued in later reference works, such as Kahl, *Magnum Lexicon Juridicum*, s.v. Pragmatici, vol. 2, 301: "Pragmatici erant homines quidam forensis professionis, qui causarum actores juris ignaros monebant interdum, juris responsa, actionumque formulas subministrantes".

40 See, for example, Below, *Die Ursachen der Rezeption des römischen Rechts in Deutschland*, 110–112; see also Erler, "Populäre Rechtsliteratur", 127–134.

41 Bragagnolo, "Les voyages du droit du Portugal à Rome".

Having these practitioners as the main addressees in mind, it also appears more appropriate to speak of 'pragmatic literature' instead of using the term 'practical literature' employed in more recent studies in the history of science on texts by practitioners for practitioners, for example, when European expansion and advances in astronomy produced innovations in navigation techniques. The production of these texts, a response to the need to provide information for less experienced practitioners, shows some interesting parallels with the attempt to provide missionaries or other officials with pragmatic normative literature. The interest in practical literature by historians of science, however, mainly consists in overcoming the divide between theoretical and practical knowledge. They thus focus, above all, on practice as a form of knowledge production and its contribution to 'science' as the classical object of scholarly interest. In fact, pragmatic normative literature in some cases probably served a similar function –Meyer's chapter on epitomisation points in this direction (Chapter 2) and there might be more examples of how pragmatic literature written for practitioners led to important innovations, for example, through abstraction and condensation of knowledge. However, the pragmatic literature of interest in our context was mostly written by erudite authors (who were also practitioners) with the aim to provide less erudite practitioners with useful tools for the exercise of their search for the right answer. Thus, in a certain way, the legal historical perspective taken here is inverse to the studies on the contribution of non-erudite actors to scientific knowledge.[42]

Finally, the 'pragmatic' character of the books is often expressed in a semantic of pragmatisation, in some cases clearly visible in the titles: *Manual, Práctica, Enchiridion, Memorial, Arte, Norte*,[43] with interesting variations of meaning, as Casagrande shows in his chapter (Chapter 11). Only some of these include the term *epitome*; more use the Latin synonyms such as *compendium*,

42 On early modern practical literature, see the contributions in Valleriani (ed.), *The Structures of Practical Knowledge*; Valleriani, "The Epistemology of Practical Knowledge". The term 'pragmatic' can also build on a somewhat different, but in some aspects related research on *pragmatische Schriftlichkeit*, see on this Keller, Grubmüller and Staubach (eds.), *Pragmatische Schriftlichkeit im Mittelalter*. They define the concept of pragmatic writing (formulated for different contexts) as "all forms of the use of writing and texts which directly serve purposeful action or which are intended to guide human action through the provision of knowledge", Keller, Grubmüller and Staubach (eds.), *Pragmatische Schriftlichkeit im Mittelalter*, 1. On handbooks and manuals, see also Creager, "Learning by the Book". I am grateful to Angela Creager for providing me access to this text.

43 An overview is provided by Barrientos Grandón, "La literatura jurídica indiana y el *ius commune*", especially 260–263.

breviarium and *summarium*. The aim of presenting a selection and summary from the immense treasure of normative information, i.e., of collecting the relevant knowledge, also appears in the subtitles and paratexts: the knowledge shall be presented *breviter, sumariamente, breve y llana, breve y claras*. In Azpilcueta's *Manual* we find expressions like *brevissimamente, summa brevedad, breves y claras, breve memoria*, etc. (Chapter 6) and in the case of the *cartillas* used in the Inquisition in Cartagena de Indias, the diminutive form already indicates their small format (Chapter 10).

These titles might be useful indicators as to whether a book might be considered as pragmatic literature or not, not least because they express clearly to whom the books were addressed. Books entitled *De iustitia et iure*, for example, appealed to a different audience[44] and they did not serve in an immediate way for finding the right solution in a practical exercise. Just like other types of literature, for example, vocabularies and other collections of normative knowledge like commentaries, they might have been used as auxiliary instruments for normative reasoning, but not directly in and for practice. In terms of form, pragmatic literature often contained indices and other *finding devices* that were intended to facilitate use.[45] Even though the works' titles often mentioned their handy format, brevity, and ease of use, this was by no means always true: many of the summaries grew again through continuous expansion and additions and thus were objects of epitomisations. However, as books made for practical use, they were usually of a smaller format.

7 Between Law in Books and Law in Action

It should have become clear by now that pragmatic normative literature fulfilled an important function within the regime of knowledge production in 16th and 17th century Ibero-America. It was an important tool for the *ars inveniendi*, characterised here as a 'second translation' carried out by certain communities of practice in a more or less erudite and learned manner, according to the concrete circumstancees. Through its selectivity, pragmatic literature reduced the scale of normative knowledge to a manageable amount and thus responded to the practitioners' needs. Pragmatic literature authorised some parts of the normative knowledge and de-authorised others, in many cases

44 On these treatises, see Folgado, "Los tratados De legibus y De iustitia et iure"; Barrientos García, "Los Tratados 'De Legibus' y 'De Iustitia et Iure' en la Escuela de Salamanca de los siglos XVI y XVII".

45 Blair, *Too Much to Know*.

viewing the local conditions for which they were made. Thus, it helped to reduce uncertainty about whether one had the relevant normative knowledge at one's disposal. This reduction of uncertainty was also possible because, most probably, pragmatic normative literature was not as expensive as the big books and thus could be acquired from time to time in updated versions; it is not by chance that many of the books belonging to this group saw various editions.

On a systemic level, pragmatic normative literature was a medium produced by epistemic communities for the selection and storage of normative knowledge for concrete fields of action; it was a product of what has been called a 'first translation' that converted normative information into normative knowledge. It thus contributed to the implementation of normative knowledge and its reproduction in different local contexts. It could do so because it specified parts of normative knowledge for certain communities of practice, for example, for the members of religious orders, and therefore triggered processes of regional differentiation.

Looking at these important functions, it is astonishing that legal historians have not paid more attention to pragmatic literature and its role in the historical regimes of knowledge production. Despite of the fact that at least since the days of Stintzing, legal historians studying the *ius commune* and its legal literature have been aware of the existence and historical significance of this literature for practitioners, books we would consider as pragmatic literature have received considerable attention mainly in Germanic legal history, a comparatively small field after World War II.[46] With regard to late medieval canon law, it is only recently that the importance of pragmatic literature has been pointed out and claims have been made to see it as a long-underrated tool for the implementation and regionalisation of normative knowledge.[47] It is briefly mentioned in the reference books as literature on the border between canon law and practical theology[48] and textbooks on the history of canon law list some of the great authors' moral theological works,[49] just as the history of

46 See especially Muther, "Zur Geschichte der mittelalterlichen Rechtsliteratur" and Seckel, *Beiträge zur Geschichte beider Rechte im Mittelalter*, vol. 1. See also more recently Schmidt-Wiegand, "Populärjurisprudenz"; Schumann, "Wissensvermittlung leicht gemacht"; Schumann, "Rechts- und Sprachtransfer"; Wittmann, *"Der da sein Practic auß Teutschen Tractaten will lernen"*; some discussion also in Neuheuser, "Kanonistik, Pragmatik, Archivistik, Historik".

47 Especially Martin Bertram has emphasised the need to study these texts and criticised the state of the art, Bertram, "Spätmittelalterliches Kirchenrecht".

48 Schulte, *Die Geschichte der Quellen und Literatur des Canonischen Rechts von Gratian bis auf die Gegenwart*, vol. 2; Erdö, *Geschichte der Wissenschaft vom kanonischen Recht.*

49 For example, Van Hove, *Prolegomena*, 566.

modern private law occasionally mentions moral-theological pragmatic literature, emphasizing its importance for the reception of Roman-canon law in areas with a lower degree of literacy.[50]

Overall, however, legal historical research, still dominated by the legal-historiographical paradigm of the scientification of law and professionalisation of legal practitioners, has not really looked at these texts in their functionality for the formation of normative orders or even tried to conceptualise them as a genre.[51] They were simply not interesting for a historiography tracing what was seen as the progress of scientific law to modernity, in a certain teleology and with a narrow concept of law.[52]

At the same time, pragmatic normative literature was not cherished by general historiography, because these texts seemed not to reveal anything about what is sometimes called the "law in action", the central object of most historical studies on the colonial Iberian worlds. The manuals for confessors and other moral theological texts have basically been seen as part of the attempt to discipline the population and establish colonial power, a function they definitely also fulfilled. They have, however, only rarely been understood as a carrier of normative knowledge that contributed to a general 'legal' literacy enabling all parts of colonial society, not least also the members of indigenous peoples, to engage in the discourse about their rights, as Honores points out in his chapter in this volume.[53] Pragmatic literature therefore remained largely invisible between an interest in the "law in the books", focusing nearly exclusively on the big authors and texts leading to the modern system, and the search for "law in action" through research on court records and other documents of legal practice. Pragmatic normative literature leads us, however, precisely into the wide field between these two reductionist perspectives and can, if one really wants to employ the established terminology, best be considered as "law books in action".[54]

---

50 Bergfeld, "Katholische Moraltheologie und Naturrechtslehre", 1001; on the importance of pragmatic literature from the School of Salamanca in this context, Bergfeld, "Katholische Moraltheologie und Naturrechtslehre", 1027–1028.

51 More recently, legal commentary literature has received more attention, for example, Jansen, "Kommentare in Recht und Religion"; Kästle-Lamparter, *Welt der Kommentare*. However, these were precisely auxiliary tools for erudite practice, so that again the focus is on the role of this literary genre for the emergence of "scientific" law.

52 See on this the historiographical review of this tradition in Duve, "Von der Europäischen Rechtsgeschichte".

53 On the rights of the indigenous peoples and their participation in the colonial negotiations see Duve, "Indigenous Rights in Latin America".

54 The recent publications on "law books in action", which concentrate mainly on textbooks or treatises from the perspective of common law in the 19th century, focus on

Only scarce attention has been paid to this genre in other fields, such as the research on early modern moral theology. Here, too, scholarship has largely focused on famous authors and their works.[55] Some of the literature from the 19th and early 20th centuries include brief surveys of important moral theological works of the early modern period,[56] mostly selected according to their practical value as *auctores probati* for contemporary juridical use. Some introductory sections of moral-theological textbooks[57] contain some information and sometimes the historical significance of these *opera practica* is highlighted.[58] All these references, however, have remained fairly marginal for the history of the discipline and were not connected to an analysis of the process of production of normative knowledge.

Studies on the history of theology, mission and catechesis in the Americas, examining the production of reception of moral-theological works, have provided some interesting insights but are mostly focused on discipline-specific topics, such as mission theology, sacramental doctrine, etc., and do not look at the genre of pragmatic literature as such.[59] Research on the School of Salamanca has, in the past, also concentrated mostly on the great authors and treatises and only occasionally on the smaller pragmatic handbooks. The connection between practical theology and the production of pragmatic literature has however, as far as I can see, not yet received any scholarly attention.[60]

In the research on the early modern history of law in Latin America, Ismael Sánchez Bella has examined the *literatura jurídica práctica* in an exhaustive study, followed by some others, and more recent works have showcased the importance of pragmatic literature in the field of procedural and criminal law within their studies of jurisdictional culture.[61] Some research has been done

different aspects, periods and areas, see Fernandez and Dubber (eds.), *Law Books in Action*; Fernandez, "Legal History as the History of Legal Texts"; the discussion of textbooks and their authority in Simpson, "The Rise and Fall of the Legal Treatise" retains its seminal importance.

55 See, for example, Vereecke, *Storia della teologia morale moderna*, vol. 2; Vidal, *Historia de la teología moral*, vol. 4.1.

56 Fuchsius, *Institutiones theologiae christianae moralis*, vol. 1, 232–268; Bund, *Catalogus auctorum qui scripserunt de theologia morali et practica*.

57 Bouquillon, *Theologia moralis fundamentalis*, 71–167; Pinckaers, *Les sources de la morale chrétienne*, 264–288.

58 See also Theiner, *Die Entwicklung der Moraltheologie*.

59 Saranyana (ed.), *Teología en América Latina*, vol. 1.

60 See Duve, Egío García and Birr (eds.), *The School of Salamanca: A case of global knowledge production?*

61 Sánchez Bella, "Los comentarios a las leyes de Indias". See, for example, Agüero, *Castigar y perdonar cuando conviene a la República*; Garriga Acosta, "Sobre el gobierno".

on legal reference books and dictionaries[62] as well as on teaching and examination literature.[63] However, none of these studies has looked at these books in their functionality in the early modern regime of production of normative knowledge, linking their form and content to their specific significance as tools of empire.

It was António Manuel Hespanha who showed the intimate connections between form and content in early modern legal literature very clearly, and earlier than others, in an article published in 2008 and who placed the history of the legal method, traditionally reconstructed mostly as a result of theoretical discussions, in a media-historical context. His aim was to draw attention to the fact that what he calls the two dominant techniques of simplification of legal discourse – "reducing dialogue to reason" and "replacing doctrinal law by 'legal law' " – have to be seen as deeply intertwined with changing material conditions.[64] He distinguished between different templates and showed the interdependence between these templates and their content. For him, different strategies to cope with this early modern information overload led to the emergence of different types of literature. Within this, the increasing production of indexes, reference works, and other developments also resulted in what he calls a "trivialisation" of legal books. "Compactness, readability, user-friendliness, order: these now become the qualities of a good legal book, qualities which are stressed in the very titles", like *Liber utilissimus, liber in quo facile explanantur, Manual* etc.[65] It was not least this perspective that many authors of the chapters of this book had in mind when they were examining their pragmatic literature, putting these specific media into a pragmatic context.

8 Big Empires, Small Books?

"Imperial Majesty ought not only to be adorned with arms but also armed with laws, so that it can govern right in both times of peace and of war", Justinian's *Constitutio Imperatoriam* of 533 runs, before claiming to have brought peace and faith to the infidels.[66] In the early modern Spanish empire, these sentences

---

62 Barrero García, "Los Repertorios y Diccionarios jurídicos desde la Edad Media hasta nuestros días".

63 Beck Varela, " 'Memoria de los libros que son necesarios para pasar' ".

64 Hespanha, "Form and content in early modern legal books", 18.

65 Hespanha, "Form and content in early modern legal books", 31.

66 "Imperatoriam maiestatem non solum armis decoratam, sed etiam legibus oportet esse armatam, utrumque tempus et bellorum et pacis recte possit gubernari", see *Constitutio*

from the very beginning of the Institutiones of Justinian resonated not only for jurists. Like so many spolia from Antiquity and Christian tradition, the idea of an emperor who defended the religion, armed with both laws and weapons, had become part of political language and imagery. The symbolum IV in Saavedra Fajardo's collection of emblems[67] illustrates this, just as statements like Castillo de Bovadilla's "The defense of the republic is made by letters, weapons, and religion".[68] It has been rightly said that "Roman law, through its multiple transformations, provided a common language for imperial law-makers; more profoundly, Roman practices of legal rule […] enabled creative, open-ended considerations and refinements of imperial legalism"[69] and a wide range of scholarship has dedicated itself to reconstructing the use of normative knowledge in debates about the legitimisation of the conquest, international law or in more specific contexts.

It was, however, not only Roman law that was translated in an enormous diachronic process. In the 16th and 17th century Ibero American worlds, it was not least normative knowledge from the field of religion that made the empire. It was in everyday life that the colonial normative order was stabilised and actualised again and again, far beyond the frontiers of the "lettered city", by an infinite number of actors on micro and meso levels.[70] This knowledge production took place in many imperial locations such as Madrid, Manila or Mexico as well as in the *reducciones de indios*, in rural regions or in the no-man's lands between the Spanish and Portuguese spheres of influence. This production of normative knowledge did not presuppose any in-depth expertise, but rather elementary normative knowledge. Many studies in this volume show that such elementary knowledge was surprisingly widespread, not just among Euro-Americans, but also among native Americans. A central medium that might have made this basic legal intelligibility – and thus also imperial governance

---

Imperatoriam, prooemium and 1, quoted after the edition by Krüger, available online at https://droitromain.univ-grenoble-alpes.fr/Corpus/just_proem.htm.

67 The Symbolum IV, *Non solum armis*, is contained in *Idea principis christiano-politici, centum symbolis expressa a Didaco Saavedra Faxardo* […], Bruxellae 1649: excudebat Ioannes Mommartius, suis, et Francisci Vivieni sumptibus, 8v, 24, online: http://www.fondiantichi.unimore.it/FA/emblem01/saavg004.html.

68 See Castillo de Bobadilla, *Politica para corregidores y señores de vassallos, en tiempo de paz y de gverra*, vol. 1, lib. I, cap. X, Sumario, 187: "La Defensa de la Republica consiste en letras, armas, y religion".

69 Burbank and Cooper, "Rules of law, politics of empire", 280.

70 On legal literacy, see Owensby and Ross (eds.), *Justice in a New World*; Herzog, *Frontiers of Possession* and more specifically on indigenous literacy, see Rappaport and Cummins (eds.), *Beyond the Lettered City*.

and normative imperialism – possible was the pragmatic normative literature. It was widely distributed and used, as the survey on the circulation and presence of pragmatic books in the chapters written by Otto Danwerth and Renzo Honores and many case studies on their use make very clear.

These findings support the hypothesis that gave rise to the research published in this volume: the pragmatic literature from the religious field is particularly important if we want to understand the emergence of the colonial order as a continuous process of translation of normative knowledge, occurring not only in some imperial centres such as Lima, Mexico, Santo Domingo, but as part of a global knowledge production in the field of normativity, a widely underestimated layer in the glocalisation process that led to the modern world.

Acknowledgements

I am grateful for the comments of the members of the research group "The knowledge of the *pragmatici*", to Nicole Pasakarnis, Christian Pogies and Alexandra Woods for their help in editing this text and their comments, and to Tamar Herzog for her suggestions.

Bibliography

Printed Sources

Azpilcueta, Martín de, *Commentarii in tres de poenitentia distinctiones posteriores, videlicet V, VI et VII*, Lyon 1569: Petri Fradini.

Bouquillon, Thomas, *Theologia moralis fundamentalis*, 3rd ed., Brugis 1903.

Budé, Guillaume, *Annotationes Priores & Posteriores* [...] *in Pandectas* [...], Lutetiae 1556: Michaelis Vascosani (https://archive.org/details/bub_gb_GkZ_VQtvi-QC/page/n509).

Cano, Melchor, *De locis theologicis*, Salamanca 1563: Mathias Gast.

Castillo de Bobadilla, Jerónimo, *Politica para corregidores y señores de vassallos, en tiempo de paz y de gverra*, vol. 1, Madrid 1597: Luis Sanchez.

Kahl, Johann, *Magnum Lexicon Juridicum*, vol. 2, Köln 1759: Cramer.

Mercado, Tomás de, *Tratos y contratos de mercaderes y tratantes discididos y determinados*, eds. Birr, Christiane, Ingo Caesar, David Glück, Anselm Spindler and Andreas Wagner (The School of Salamanca. A Digital Collection of Sources, ed. by Thomas Duve & Matthias Lutz-Bachmann), Mainz [1569] 2019 (https://id.salamanca.school/texts/W0007).

Soto, Domingo de, *De iustitia et iure*, Madrid 1556: Andrés Portonaris.

Suárez, Francisco, *De legibus ac Deo legislatore. Liber primus. De lege in communi eiusque natura, causis et effectibus*, eds. Bach, Oliver, Norbert Brieskorn and Gideon Stiening, Stuttgart-Bad Cannstatt [1613] 2019.

Vitoria, Francisco, *Relectiones Theologicae XII*, eds. Birr, Christiane, Ingo Caesar, David Glück, Anselm Spindler and Andreas Wagner (The School of Salamanca. A Digital Collection of Sources, ed. by Thomas Duve & Matthias Lutz-Bachmann), Mainz [1557] 2018 (https ://id.salamanca.school/texts/W0013).

Literature

Abel, Günter, "Knowledge Research. Rethinking Epistemology", in Sandkühler, Hans Jörg (ed.), *Wissen. Wissenskulturen und die Kontextualität des Wissens*, Frankfurt am Main 2014, 17–37.

Agüero, Alejandro, *Castigar y perdonar cuando conviene a la República. La justicia penal de Córdoba del Tucumán, siglos XVII y XVIII*, Madrid 2008.

Albani, Benedetta and Giovanni Pizzorusso, "Problematizando el patronato regio. Nuevos acercaminentos al gobierno de la Iglesia ibero-americana desde la perspectiva de la Santa Sede", in Duve, Thomas (ed.), *Actas del XIX Congreso del Instituto Internacional de Historia del Derecho Indiano, Berlín 2016*, Madrid 2017, 519–543.

Barrero García, Ana María, "Los Repertorios y Diccionarios jurídicos desde la Edad Media hasta nuestros días", in *Anuario de Historia del Derecho Español* 43 (1973), 311–352 (http://hdl.handle.net/10261/15019).

Barrientos García, José, "Los Tratados 'De Legibus' y 'De Iustitia et Iure' en la Escuela de Salamanca de los siglos XVI y XVII", in *Salamanca* 47 (2001), 371–415.

Barrientos Grandón, Javier, "La literatura jurídica indiana y el *ius commune*", in Alvarado Planas, Javier (ed.), *Historia de la literatura jurídica en la España del antiguo régimen*, vol. 1, Madrid 2000, 199–286.

Beck Varela, Laura, " 'Memoria de los libros que son necesarios para pasar'. Lecturas del jurista en el siglo XVI ibérico", in *CIAN – Revista de Historia de las Universidades* 21:2 (2018), 227–267 (10.20318/cian.2018.4476).

Below, Georg von, *Die Ursachen der Rezeption des römischen Rechts in Deutschland*, München 1905.

Bergfeld, Christoph, "Katholische Moraltheologie und Naturrechtslehre", in Coing, Helmut (ed.), *Handbuch der Quellen und Literatur der neueren europäischen Privatrechtsgeschichte*, vol. 2.1: *Neuere Zeit (1500–1800). Das Zeitalter des gemeinen Rechts*, München 1977, 999–1033.

Berman, Harold J., *Law and Revolution. The Formation of the Western Legal Tradition*, Cambridge, MA 1983.

Bertram, Martin, "Spätmittelalterliches Kirchenrecht: Vier Anmerkungen zur Forschungslage", in *Zeitschrift der Savigny-Stiftung für Rechtsgeschichte. Kanonistische Abteilung* 100:1 (2014), 563–579.

Blair, Ann, *Too Much to Know. Managing Scholarly Information before the Modern Age*, New Haven, CT 2010.

Böschen, Stefan, *Hybride Wissensregime. Skizze einer soziologischen Feldtheorie*, Baden-Baden 2016.

Bragagnolo, Manuela, "Les voyages du droit du Portugal à Rome. Le 'Manual de confessores' de Martín de Azpilcueta (1492–1586) et ses traductions", *Max Planck Institute for European Legal History Research Paper Series* No. 2018–13 (10.2139/ssrn.3287684).

Bund, Jacobo, *Catalogus auctorum qui scripserunt de theologia morali et practica. Compendiosam exhibens notitiam biographicam scriptorum, elenchum operum et judicium criticum de auctoritatis pondere quo singuli auctores in re morali fruuntur*, Rouen 1900.

Burbank, Jane and Frederick Cooper, "Rules of law, politics of empire", in Benton, Lauren and Richard J. Ross (eds.), *Legal Pluralism and Empires, 1500–1850*, New York, NY 2013, 279–293.

Burke, Peter, *What is the History of Knowledge?*, Cambridge 2015.

Busse, Dietrich, "Textsorten des Bereichs Rechtswesen und Justiz", in Brinker, Klaus, Gerd Antos, Wolfgang Heinemann and Sven F. Sager (eds.), *Text- und Gesprächslinguistik. Ein internationales Handbuch zeitgenössischer Forschung*, vol. 1, Berlin 2000, 658–675.

Clanchy, Michael T., *From Memory to Written Record, England 1066–1307*, 2nd ed., Oxford 1993.

Creager, Angela, "Learning by the Book: Manuals and Handbooks in the History of Knowledge. Introduction to the special issue", in *The British Journal for the History of Science – Themes* (forthcoming).

Daston, Lorraine, "The History of Science and the History of Knowledge", in *Know* 1:1 (2017), 131–154 (10.1086/691678).

De ruysscher, Dave, "How Normative were Merchant Guidebooks? Of Customs, Practices, and … Good Advice (Antwerp, Sixteenth Century)", in Pihlajamäki, Heikki, Albrecht Cordes, Serge Dauchy and Dave De ruysscher (eds.), *Understanding the Sources of Early Modern and Modern Commercial Law. Sources, Statutes, Contracts, and Legal Scholarship*, Leiden 2018, 144–165.

Duve, Thomas, "El Concilio como instancia de autorización. La ordenación sacerdotal de mestizos ante el Tercer Concilio Limense (1582/83) y la comunicación sobre el Derecho en la monarquía española", in *Revista de Historia del Derecho* 40 (2010), 1–29 (http://www.scielo.org.ar/pdf/rhd/n40/n40a04.pdf).

Duve, Thomas, "Katholisches Kirchenrecht und Moraltheologie im 16. Jahrhundert: Eine globale normative Ordnung im Schatten schwacher Staatlichkeit", in Kadelbach, Stefan and Klaus Günther (eds.), *Recht ohne Staat? Zur Normativität nichtstaatlicher Rechtsetzung*, Frankfurt am Main 2011, 147–174.

Duve, Thomas, "Von der Europäischen Rechtsgeschichte zu einer Rechtsgeschichte Europas in globalhistorischer Perspektive", in *Rechtsgeschichte – Legal History* 20 (2012), 18–71 (10.12946/rg20/018-071).

Duve, Thomas, "Salamanca in Amerika", in *Zeitschrift der Savigny-Stiftung für Rechtsgeschichte. Germanistische Abteilung* 132 (2015), 116–151 (10.7767/zrgga-2015-0108).

Duve, Thomas, "Global Legal History – A Methodological Approach", *Oxford Handbook Online – Law* 2017 (10.1093/oxfordhb/9780199935352.013.25).

Duve, Thomas, "Was ist ›Multinormativität‹? – Einführende Bemerkungen", in *Rechtsgeschichte – Legal History* 25 (2017), 88–101 (10.12946/rg25/088-101).

Duve, Thomas, "Global Legal History: Setting Europe in Perspective", in Pihlajamäki, Heikki, Markus D. Dubber and Mark Godfrey (eds.), *The Oxford Handbook of European Legal History*, Oxford 2018, 1–29 (10.1093/oxfordhb/9780198785521.013.5).

Duve, Thomas, "Indigenous Rights in Latin America", in Dubber, Markus and Christopher Tomlins (eds.), *The Oxford Handbook of Legal History*, Oxford 2018, 817–837 (10.1093/oxfordhb/9780198794356.013.42).

Duve, Thomas, "Legal traditions. A dialogue between comparative law and comparative legal history", in *Comparative Legal History* 6:1 (2018), 15–33 (10.1080/2049677X.2018.1469271).

Duve, Thomas, "The School of Salamanca: A case of global knowledge production?", in Duve, Thomas, Christiane Birr and José Luis Egío García (eds.), *The School of Salamanca: A case of global knowledge production?*, Leiden (forthcoming).

Duve, Thomas, José Luis Egío García and Christiane Birr (eds.), *The School of Salamanca: A case of global knowledge production?*, Leiden (forthcoming).

Erdö, Péter, *Geschichte der Wissenschaft vom kanonischen Recht. Eine Einführung*, Berlin 2006.

Erler, Adalbert, "Populäre Rechtsliteratur", in Cordes, Albrecht, Bernd Kannowski, Hans-Peter Haferkamp, Heiner Lück, Heinreich de Waal, Dieter Werkmüller and Ruth Schmidt-Wiegand (eds.), *Handwörterbuch zur deutschen Rechtsgeschichte*, vol. 3, Berlin 1984, 1825–1828.

Fernandez, Angela, "Legal History as the History of Legal Texts", in Dubber, Markus and Christopher Tomlins (eds.), *The Oxford Handbook of Legal History*, Oxford 2018, 243–290.

Fernandez, Angela and Markus D. Dubber (eds.), *Law Books in Action. Essays on the Anglo-American Legal Treatise*, Oxford 2012.

Firey, Abigail, "Mutating Monsters: Approaches to "Living Texts" of the Carolingian Era", in *Digital Proceedings of the Lawrence J. Schoenberg Symposium on Manuscript Studies in the Digital Age. Lex scripta: The Manuscript as Witness to the History of Law* 2:1 (2010), 1–14 (https://repository.upenn.edu/ljsproceedings/vol2/iss1/1).

Folgado, Avelino, "Los tratados De legibus y De iustitia et iure en los autores españoles del siglo XVI y primera mitad del XVII", in *La Ciudad de Dios* 72:3 (1959), 275–302.

Fuchsius, Bernhard, *Institutiones theologiae christianae moralis*, vol. 1, Augsburg 1848.

García-Gallo, Alfonso, "El cedulario de Encinas", in García-Gallo, Alfonso (ed.), *Los orígenes españoles de las instituciones americanas. Estudios de derecho indiano*, Madrid 1992, 131–255.

Garriga Acosta, Carlos Antonio, "Sobre el gobierno de la justicia en Indias (Siglos XVI–XVII)", in *Revista de Historia del Derecho* 34 (2006), 67–160 (http://dialnet.unirioja.es/servlet/articulo?codigo=2388772).

Grossi, Paolo, *A History of European Law*, trans. Laurence Hooper, Chichester 2010.

Herzog, Tamar, *Frontiers of Possession. Spain and Portugal in Europe and the Americas*, Cambridge, MA 2015.

Herzog, Tamar, *A Short History of European Law – The Last Two and a Half Millennia*, Cambridge, MA 2018.

Hespanha, António Manuel, "Form and content in early modern legal books. Bridging the gap between material bibliography and the history of legal thought", in *Rechtsgeschichte* 12 (2008), 12–50 (10.12946/rg12/012-050).

Hespanha, António Manuel, *A cultura jurídica europeia. Síntese de un milénio*, Coimbra 2012.

Hespanha, António Manuel, *Como os juristas viam o mundo. 1550–1750. Direitos, estados, coisas, contratos, ações e crimes*, Lisboa 2015.

Hespanha, António Manuel, "O 'direito de Índias' no contexto da historiografia das colonizações ibéricas", in Duve, Thomas (ed.), *Actas del XIX Congreso del Instituto Internacional de Historia del Derecho Indiano, Berlín 2016*, Madrid 2017, 43–83.

Hespanha, António Manuel, "Southern Europe (Italy, Iberian Peninsula, France)", in Pihlajamäki, Heikki, Markus Dubber and Mark Godfrey (eds.), *The Oxford Handbook of European Legal History*, Oxford 2018, 332–356.

Hespanha, António Manuel, *Filhos da terra. Identidades mestiças nos confins da expansão portuguesa*, Lisboa 2019.

Holthöfer, Ernst, "Die Literatur zum gemeinen und partikularen Recht in Italien, Frankreich, Spanien und Portugal", in Coing, Helmut (ed.), *Handbuch der Quellen und Literatur der neueren europäischen Privatrechtsgeschichte*, vol 2.1: *Neuere Zeit (1500–1800). Das Zeitalter des gemeinen Rechts*, München 1977, 103–499.

Hoock, Jochen and Pierre Jeannin (eds.), *Ars Mercatoria. Handbücher und Traktate für den Gebrauch des Kaufmanns / Manuels et traités á l'usage des marchands 1420–1820*, vol. 1: *1470–1600*, Paderborn 1991.

Jansen, Nils, "Kommentare in Recht und Religion", in Kästle, David and Nils Jansen (eds.), *Kommentare in Recht und Religion*, Tübingen 2014, 1–14.

Kästle-Lamparter, David, *Welt der Kommentare. Struktur, Funktion und Stellenwert juristischer Kommentare in Geschichte und Gegenwart*, Tübingen 2016.

Keller, Hagen, Klaus Grubmüller and Nikolaus Staubach (eds.), *Pragmatische Schriftlichkeit im Mittelalter. Erscheinungsformen und Entwicklungsstufen* (Akten des internationalen Kolloquiums, 17.–19. Mai 1989), München 1992.

Krasner, Stephen D., "Structural causes and regime consequences: regimes as intervening variables", in Krasner, Stephen D. (ed.), *International Regimes*, Ithaka, NY 1983, 1–21.

List, Martin, "Regimetheorie", in Benz, Arthur, Susanne Lütz, Uwe Schimank and Georg Simonis (eds.), *Handbuch Governance. Theoretische Grundlagen und empirische Anwendungsfelder*, Wiesbaden 2007, 226–239.

Mahoney, John, *The Making of Moral Theology. A Study of the Roman Catholic Tradition*, Oxford 1987 (repr. Oxford 1989).

Marcocci, Giuseppe, "Conscience and Empire: Politics and Moral Theology in the Early Modern Portuguese World", in *Journal of Early Modern History* 18:5 (2014), 473–494.

Möllers, Christoph, *Die Möglichkeit der Normen. Über eine Praxis jenseits von Moralität und Kausalität*, Berlin 2015.

Moutin, Osvaldo, " 'Sepamos, Señores, en que ley vivimos y si emos de tener por nuestra regla al Consejo de Indias' – Salamanca in the Philppine Islands", in Duve, Thomas, José Luis Egío García and Christiane Birr (eds.), *The School of Salamanca: A case of global knowledge production?*, Leiden (forthcoming).

Müller-Wille, Staffan, Carsten Reinhardt and Marianne Sommer, "Wissenschaftsgeschichte und Wissensgeschichte", in Sommer, Marianne, Staffan Müller-Wilde and Carsten Reinhardt (eds.), *Handbuch Wissensgeschichte*, Stuttgart 2017, 2–18.

Muther, Theodor, "Zur Geschichte der mittelalterlichen Rechtsliteratur für 'pauperes' und 'minores' reprinted version of 1869", in Muther, Theodor (ed.), *Zur Geschichte der Rechtswissenschaft und der Universitäten in Deutschland. Collected essays, Jena 1876*, Amsterdam 1961, 158–200.

Neuheuser, Hanns Peter, "Kanonistik, Pragmatik, Archivistik, Historik. Vom kanonistischen Alltagsdokument zur kirchenrechtsgeschichtlichen Quelle", in Neuheuser, Hanns Peter (ed.), *Pragmatische Quellen der kirchlichen Rechtsgeschichte*, Köln 2011, 1–17.

Neumann, Birigt, "Kulturelles Wissen", in Nünning, Ansgar (ed.), *Metzler Lexikon Literatur- und Kulturtheorie. Ansätze – Personen – Grundbegriffe*, 5th ed., Stuttgart, Weimar 2013, 811.

O'Banion, Patrick J., *The Sacrament of Penance and Religious Life in Golden Age Spain*, University Park, PA 2012.

Owensby, Brian P. and Richard J. Ross (eds.), *Justice in a New World. Negotiating Legal Intelligibility in British, Iberian, and Indigenous America*, New York, NY 2018.

Pihlajamäki, Heikki, Markus Dubber and Mark Godfrey (eds.), *The Oxford Handbook of European Legal History*, Oxford 2018.

Pinckaers, Servais, *Les sources de la morale chrétienne*, Paris 2004.

Prodi, Paolo, *Una storia della giustizia. Dal pluralismo dei fori al moderno dualismo tra coscienza e diritto*, Bologna 2000.

Ranieri, Filippo, "Juristische Literatur aus dem Ancien Régime und historische Literatursoziologie. Einige methodologische Vorüberlegungen", in Bergfeld, Christoph et al. (eds.), *Aspekte europäischer Rechtsgeschichte. Festgabe für Helmut Coing zum 70. Geburtstag*, Frankfurt am Main 1982, 292–322.

Rappaport, Joanne and Tom Cummins (eds.), *Beyond the Lettered City. Indigenous Literacies in the Andes*, Raleigh 2011.

Renn, Jürgen (ed.), *The Globalization of Knowledge in History*, Berlin 2012 (http://edition-open-access.de/studies/1/).

Renn, Jürgen, "The Globalization of Knowledge in History and its Normative Challenges", in *Rechtsgeschichte – Legal History* 22 (2014), 52–60 (https://doi.org/10.12946/rg22/052-060).

Renn, Jürgen, "From the History of Science to the History of Knowledge – and Back", in *Centaurus* 57:1 (2015), 37–53 (10.1111/1600-0498.12075).

Renn, Jürgen and Malcolm H. Hyman, "The Globalization of Knowledge in History: An Introduction", in Renn, Jürgen (ed.), *The Globalization of Knowledge in History*, Berlin 2012, 15–44 (http://www.edition-open-access.de/media/studies/1/5/Studies1ch1.pdf).

Sánchez Bella, Ismael, "Los comentarios a las leyes de Indias", in *Anuario de Historia del Derecho Español* 87 (1954), 381–542 (https://www.boe.es/publicaciones/anuarios_derecho/abrir_pdf.php?id=ANU-H-1954-10038100542).

Sánchez Bella, Ismael, "Estudio preliminar", in Sánchez Bella, Ismael (ed.), *Recopilación de las Indias, por Antonio de Léon Pinelo (1635)*, vol. 1/3, México 1992, 17–64.

Saranyana, Josep Ignasi (ed.), *Teología en América Latina*, vol. 1: *Desde los orígenes a la Guerra de Sucesión (1493–1715)*, Madrid 1999.

Schmidt-Wiegand, Ruth, "Populärjurisprudenz zwischen Artesliteratur und Richterlichem Clagspiegel", in Wich-Reif, Claudia (ed.), *Strukturen und Funktionen in Gegenwart und Geschichte. Festschrift für Franz Simmler zum 65. Geburtstag*, Berlin 2007, 537–554.

Schröder, Jan, *Recht als Wissenschaft. Geschichte der juristischen Methodenlehre in der Neuzeit (1500–1933)*, 2nd ed., München 2012.

Schulte, Johann Friedrich von, *Die Geschichte der Quellen und Literatur des Canonischen Rechts von Gratian bis auf die Gegenwart*, vol. 2: *Von Papst Gregor IX. bis zum Concil von Trient*, Stuttgart 1877.

Schumann, Eva, "Wissensvermittlung leicht gemacht. Die Vermittlung gelehrten Rechts an ungelehrte Rechtspraktiker am Beispiel der volkssprachigen Teufelsprozesse", in

Reich, Björn, Frank Rexroth and Matthias Roick (eds.), *Wissen, maßgeschneidert. Experten und Expertenkulturen im Europa der Vormoderne*, München 2012, 182–213.

Schumann, Eva, "Rechts- und Sprachtransfer am Beispiel der volkssprachigen Praktikerliteratur", in Deutsch, Andreas (ed.), *Historische Rechtssprache des Deutschen*, Heidelberg 2013, 123–174.

Seckel, Emil, *Beiträge zur Geschichte beider Rechte im Mittelalter*, vol. 1: *Zur Geschichte der populären Literatur des römisch-canonischen Rechts*, Tübingen 1898.

Simpson, Alfred William Brian, "The Rise and Fall of the Legal Treatise: Legal Principles and the Forms of Legal Literature", in *The University of Chicago Law Review* 48:3 (1981), 632–679.

Söllner, Alfred, "Die Literatur zum gemeinen und partikularen Recht in Deutschland, Österreich, den Niederlanden und der Schweiz", in Coing, Helmut (ed.), *Handbuch der Quellen und Literatur der neueren europäischen Privatrechtsgeschichte*, vol. 2.1: *Neuere Zeit (1500–1800). Das Zeitalter des gemeinen Rechts*, München 1977, 501–614.

Stintzing, Roderich von, *Geschichte der populären Literatur des römisch-kanonischen Rechts in Deutschland am Ende des fünfzehnten und im Anfang des sechszehnten Jahrhunderts*, Leipzig 1867.

Tau Anzoátegui, Víctor, *Casuismo y Sistema. Indagación histórica sobre el espíritu del Derecho Indiano*, Buenos Aires 1992.

Theiner, Johann, *Die Entwicklung der Moraltheologie zur eigenständigen Disziplin*, Regensburg 1970.

Troje, Hans Erich, "Die Literatur des gemeinen Rechts unter dem Einfluß des Humanismus", in Coing, Helmut (ed.), *Handbuch der Quellen und Literatur der neueren europäischen Privatrechtsgeschichte*, vol. 2.1: *Neuere Zeit (1500–1800). Das Zeitalter des gemeinen Rechts*, München 1977, 615–795.

Valleriani, Matteo, "The Epistemology of Practical Knowledge", in Valleriani, Matteo (ed.), *The Structures of Practical Knowledge*, Dordrecht 2017, 1–19.

Valleriani, Matteo (ed.), *The Structures of Practical Knowledge*, Dordrecht 2017.

Van Hove, Alphonse, *Prolegomena* (*Commentarium Lovaniense in Codicem Iuris Canonici*), Mechelen/Rome 1945.

Vereecke, Louis, *Storia della teologia morale moderna*, vol. 2, Roma 1973.

Vesting, Thomas, *Legal Theory*, München 2018.

Vidal, Marciano, *Historia de la teología moral*, vol. 4.1: *La moral en la edad moderna (ss. XV–XVI). Humanismo y Reforma*, Madrid 2012.

Wehling, Peter, "Wissensregime", in Schützeichel, Rainer (ed.), *Handbuch Wissenssoziologie und Wissensforschung*, Konstanz 2007, 704–712.

White, James Boyd, "Legal Knowledge", in *Harvard Law Review* 115:5 (2002), 1396–1431.

Wieacker, Franz, *A History of Private Law in Europe*, trans. Tony Weir, Oxford 1996.

Wittmann, Piotr, *"Der da sein Practic auß Teutschen Tractaten will lernen". Rechtspraktiker in deutschsprachiger Praktikerliteratur des 16. Jahrhunderts*, Frankfurt am Main 2015.

Wohlmuth, Josef (ed.), *Dekrete der ökumenischen Konzilien. Konzilien der Neuzeit*, vol. 3: *Trient (1545–63) – 1. Vatikanum (1869–70) – 2. Vatikanum (1962–65)*, Paderborn 2001.

Zittel, Claus, "Wissenskulturen, Wissensgeschichte und historische Epistemologie", in Sandkühler, Hans Jörg (ed.), *Wissen. Wissenskulturen und die Kontextualität des Wissens*, Frankfurt am Main 2014, 91–109.

CHAPTER 2

Putting Roman and Canon Law in a Nutshell: Developments in the Epitomisation of Legal Texts between Late Antiquity and the Early Modern Period

Christoph H.F. Meyer

1 Introduction

"The form and manner in which the sources of Roman law were abused in the Frankish Empire [...] such overestimation of juridically inferior material as is expressed in the preference for the epitomes [...] all this characterises in unambiguous fashion the appalling decadence of Roman law [...]".[1] In these remarks of Alfred von Halban (1865–1926), one can detect assumptions that shaped legal historians' ideas about epitomes for a long time. Epitomes were viewed as rather primitive reference works that deprived the sophisticated source texts of their originality and jeopardised their later transmission. In fact, they were frequently held to be symptoms of decline. Some aspects of this perception can be traced back to the humanists.[2] More recent works have judged the epitomes less harshly. However, their improving reputation is only partly due to new insights,[3] since legal historians have examined the phenomenon of epitomisation only sporadically, that is, only with regard to a small number of specific examples.[4]

1 Halban, *Das römische Recht in den germanischen Volksstaaten*, vol. 3, 90. See also Halban, *Das römische Recht in den germanischen Volksstaaten*, vol. 2, 351. For more on the author, see [Anon.,] "Alfred von Halban". Unless otherwise indicated, all translations are the author's.

2 Accordingly, the philologist Isaac Casaubon (1559–1614) condemned the *pestis ... compendiorum et epitomarum confectio*. See [Casaubon,] *Henrico IV. Franciae et Navarrae Regi Christianissimo*, 62. For similar views, see Bacon, *De augmentis scientiarum*, eds. Spedding, Ellis and Denon Heath, lib. II, cap. 6, 506. The negative perception of epitomes occasionally inspired apologetic remarks. See Olearius, *Doctrina theologiae moralis totius*, Preface "Auditoribus suis". On the ancient roots of this view, see Mülke, *Der Autor und sein Text*, 95–108.

3 For a recent, yet traditional view of epitomes, see Meder, *Rechtsgeschichte*, 108.

4 This applies especially to the Roman law of late antiquity and the early Middle Ages (e.g. D. Liebs, H. Siems) as well as the classical canon law of the High and Late Middle Ages. (e.g. J. Rambaud-Buhot, R. Weigand). See: Liebs, *Hermogenians iuris epitomae*; Liebs, " 'Variae

DOI:10.1163/9789004425736_003

2 Epitomes and Epitomisation

Before turning to the question of how to approach the topic of this study, it is important to delineate the research object itself. In line with the present volume's theme, the focus of this contribution will lie on pragmatic normative literature.[5] Like catechisms, glosses and indices, epitomes represent a particular form of generic intertextuality that, as Wolfgang Raible put it, condenses and references a single original work.[6] These characteristics were *mutatis mutandis* already part of the first millennium's understanding of the term. For example, a Greco-Latin glossary (*Scholica Graecarum glossarum*), dating perhaps from the second half of the 9th century, defines epitomes as excerpts or extracts that are compiled from a more extensive *corpus librorum* by means of a selection or florilegium and can be described as a succinct ready-to-use presentation.[7]

In this description, which largely correlates with conventional Latin usage in antiquity,[8] three central characteristics of epitomes become apparent.[9]

---

lectiones' "; Liebs, "Legis Romanae Visigothorum Epitomen Sangallensem"; Liebs, "Römischrechtliche Glut aus dem 8. Jh. für ein Bischofsgericht in Burgund"; Liebs, "Scintilla de libro legum"; Siems, *Handel und Wucher im Spiegel frühmittelalterlicher Rechtsquellen*, 191–200; Rambaud-Buhot, "Les divers types d'abrégés du Décret de Gratien"; Rambaud-Buhot, "L'Abbreviatio Decreti d'Omnebene"; Weigand, "Die frühen kanonistischen Schulen und die Dekretabbreviatio Omnebenes"; Weigand, "Die Dekretabbreviatio 'Quoniam egestas' und ihre Glossen"; Weigand, "Die Dekretabbreviatio 'Exceptiones ecclesiasticarum regularum' und ihre Glossen".

5 See on this generally Thomas Duve's contribution (Chapter 1) in this volume.

6 Raible, "Arten des Kommentierens – Arten der Sinnbildung – Arten des Verstehens", 56–61. See also Doering, "Fort- und Neuschreibung autoritativer Texte und Identitätsbildung im Jubiläenbuch sowie in Texten aus Qumran", 72–73.

7 Laistner, "Notes on Greek from the Lectures of a Ninth Century Monastery Teacher", 436: "Epitome: supercisio quae de maiori corpore librorum carptim ac defloratim excerpitur, quae alio nomine brevis expositio ac succincta potest appellari. Quonomine solent Graecorum auctores succinctas et defloratas ex aliis doctoribus expositiunculas appellare". See also Llauró, "Los glosarios de Ripoll", 358 ll. 199–203. Laistner associated this glossary with the teaching activities of Martin of Laon (819–875), whereas Contreni in particular disputed this attribution (ascribing authorship instead to Heiric of Auxerre). See Contreni, "Three Carolingian Texts from Laon", 805–808; Contreni, "The Biblical Glosses of Haimo of Auxerre and John Scottus Eriugena", 427–428; Contreni, *The Cathedral School of Laon from 850 to 930*, 114, 151 fn. 59.

8 *Thesaurus linguae Latinae*, vol. 5.2, col. 692 ll. 20–75 (s.v. epitome). See also Wölfflin, "Epitome".

9 On epitomes and epitomisation in general, see Galdi, *L'epitome nella letteratura Latina*; Opelt, "Epitome"; Lizzi, "La memoria selettiva"; Horster and Reitz (eds.), *Condensing Texts – Condensed Texts*; Horster and Reitz, "Handbooks, Epitomes and Florilegia"; Dubischar, "Preserved Knowledge"; Dusil, Schwedler and Schwitter (eds.), *Exzerpieren – Kompilieren – Tradieren*.

First, an epitome requires the (pre)existence of a work to serve as its source-text. Second, epitomes provide a shorter version of the original that emerges through a process of selection. Third, the expression *corpus librorum* suggests that the original was a longer single text comprising several books (*libri*). Epitomes could, thus, be usefully distinguished from florilegia, which consisted of excerpts from several different works.[10]

However, the last of these three characteristics is perhaps more ambiguous than it may at first appear. Already the next sentence in the *Scholica Graecarum glossarum*, which states that Greek authors refer to short texts drawn from other scholars' works as 'epitomes', could also be understood as applying the term to works comprising excerpts from a number of different source texts. Such texts could be considered epitomes in a broader sense that includes works epitomising several carefully sifted texts (e.g., by a single author), as well as literary hybrids, to the extent that they also contain other forms of presentation.

Moving from the term to the function of epitomes, the *Thesaurus linguae Latinae* provides the synonyms *compendium*, *breviarium* and *summarium*,[11] which suggest that epitomisation had two formal objectives: brevity and intelligibility. Achieving these goals required the material to be condensed, and the epitomator could do this either by omitting particular passages but otherwise retaining the original wording, or by paraphrasing the source text's content. On a practical level, the first purpose of epitomes was to spare users the trouble of reading the more extensive original texts, saving them time and bother. Moreover, reducing the length of the text also meant lowering the cost of its reproduction. This, however, could result in the excerpt gradually displacing the original. It is also possible that epitomes were consulted alongside the originals to facilitate working with them, or used to make the source texts known more widely.

This review of epitomes' functions also hints at the insights to be gained for historical research. The first point of interest is the relation between the source text and the epitome. The latter, according to Raible, can be considered a commentary on or interpretation of the original, regardless of whether epitomators paraphrased the text in their own words or excerpted passages. This also raises the question of the temporal relation between the original and the epitome, which can reveal diachronic changes. Second, the content of the epitome itself

10 On (Latin) florilegia, see Chadwick, "Florilegium"; Rouse, "Florilegia"; Hamesse, "«Florilège» et «autorité»"; Hess, "Florilegien"; Horster and Reitz, "Handbooks, Epitomes, and Florilegia".

11 See fn. 8.

can provide insights, for example indications of terminological condensation or of the epitome's pragmatic context. A third area of interest lies in exploring the significance of epitomisation for a text's reception and impact as a result of its increased accessibility and dissemination in epitomised form.

This will have to suffice as an introduction to the subject matter. In the following, the phenomenon of epitomisation will be examined more closely in relation to Latin legal texts written between late antiquity and the early modern period. The object of the following brief survey is the technique of epitomisation itself. As can be gathered from the history of legal sources and legal literature, this spanned not only the composition of epitomes of a single original text, that is, epitomes in the narrower sense, but also in the broader sense of epitomes as compilations from multiple texts, as discussed above. Furthermore, it follows from the nature of the subject matter that the questions to be posed here are not limited to the history of sources and literature but also relate to the role that epitomisation played in the development of law, in particular how it affected the adoption, reception and spread of legal knowledge in the so-called premodern era. The answers are likely to come above all from two branches of legal history, which in the following will be considered in more detail: Roman law between late antiquity and the Early Middle Ages and the canon law of the second millennium. These two – historically and substantively rather different – areas of investigation serve to illustrate the complexity of the phenomenon. Of course, the following observations make no claim to comprehensiveness. Rather, they are only a preliminary attempt to describe a phenomenon that remains largely unexplored.

3 Epitomisation of Roman Law Texts in the First Millennium

Turning from the genre and the craft of epitomisation to the role that it played in the Roman law of the first millennium, one must, as far as the transmission of texts is concerned, first distinguish between written laws and collections of laws, on the one hand, and legal literature, on the other. Although both types of sources underwent widespread epitomisation, there is a large temporal gap between these processes.[12] The interval is due to a particularity in the development of Roman law: even though Roman jurisprudence and legal literature reached its apogee in the so-called classical era, which lasted from the second half of the 1st century BC until 235 AD, the great, official collections of imperial

12 Harries, "Roman Law and Legal Culture", 794–795.

constitutions, the *Codex Theodosianus* (438) and the *Codex Justinianus* (529/534), were not compiled until late antiquity.[13]

Of the works of the classical jurists, however, in most cases only excerpts remain, not least due to late antique "catastrophes of forgetting" (Emil Seckel).[14] It seems likely that the literary-historical background of this loss of knowledge lay in the early epitomisation of these sources, which not only gave rise to new works of jurisprudence (e.g., *Pauli Sententiae, Ulpiani Regulae*) based on excerpts of older texts, but also contributed to many early classical works being forgotten.[15]

Was epitomisation, therefore, a symptom of decline? In order to reach a more differentiated assessment of the historical significance of this technique, it seems appropriate to take a closer look at the processes just mentioned. This includes examining specific elements within those broader developments, such as the differences in the continued use of individual late classical works. As post-classical legal writings lacked the extensive casuistry that characterised many classical works, some writings of late classical jurists were still widely consulted and copied even after the 3rd century.[16]

More important than such details, however, is the underlying understanding of the general developments of interest here. People usually consult juridical literature, in order to find out about the current state of the law. When the legal situation changes, older juridical literature becomes obsolete and thus uninteresting for readers – unless, as just discussed, special circumstances provide it with additional relevance.[17] This simple fact takes us back to the "catastrophes of forgetting". Seckel did not intend the term to denote a general cultural decline in late antiquity.[18] Instead, he had in mind a phenomenon that

13 However, this does not mean that laws and legislation played only a tangential role in classical Roman law as Fritz Schulz's famous remark about the Romans might seem to suggest: 'The 'law-inspired nation' is not statute-inspired.' See Schulz, *Principles of Roman Law*, 7. For the historical and ideological background of this viewpoint, see Stagl, "Die Bedeutung von leges publicae im Römischen Recht", 456–458. See also fn. 24–26.

14 Seckel, *Das römische Recht und seine Wissenschaft im Wandel der Jahrhunderte*, 11. See Wieacker, *Textstufen klassischer Juristen*, 151–152.

15 For the development since the 3rd century, see Liebs, "Warum endete gegen Mitte des 3. Jahrhunderts die klassische Rechtsliteratur?"; Liebs, "Jurisprudenz"; Liebs, "Nachklassische römische Rechtsliteratur"; Liebs, "Recht und Rechtsliteratur". On epitomes and epitomisation in classical Roman law see also Schulz, *History of Roman Legal Science*, 184–186; Schiller, *Roman Law*, 388–389.

16 Liebs, "Wenn Fachliteratur Gesetz wird", 401–403.

17 Stolleis, "Vom Umgang mit veralteten Büchern, oder: Mit den Toten sprechen".

18 Wieacker, *Römische Rechtsgeschichte*, 43 fn. 59.

can be observed at different points in legal history.[19] One could also call it the "disappearance of disused law", as Michael Stolleis put it,[20] or perhaps, by analogy to this, the "disappearance of obsolete legal knowledge".

If 'catastrophes of oblivion' are from a legal-historical point of view both necessary and useful, this also affects our assessment of the epitomes that played a part in them. An antiquarian approach that sees epitomisation mostly as a danger, and only rarely as an aid to the survival of sources, cannot do justice to the phenomenon. The role that epitomisation played in shaping legal knowledge also has to be taken into account. This emerges even more clearly if one turns form the juridical literature to the legislative texts, particularly the compilations of the 5th and 6th centuries that provided the second starting point for processes of epitomisation.

Here, too, context is important, particularly a phenomenon that can perhaps be best described through the metaphor of a forest (*silva*).[21] Tertullian, for example, spoke of 'the ancient and rugged forest of laws' (*vetus et squalens silva legum*).[22] This image illustrates a problem that made itself felt already towards the end of the Roman Republic.[23] Owing to the large number of (in part obsolete) laws, someone seeking to understand the current state of the law might easily not be able to see the wood for the trees.

19 According to Seckel, a similar 'catastrophe of forgetting' occurred a thousand years later when the triumph of the Accursian *Glossa ordinaria* caused the works of the high medieval glossators of Roman law to be forgotten. See Seckel, *Das römische Recht und seine Wissenschaft im Wandel der Jahrhunderte*, 18 and Kästle-Lamparter, *Welt der Kommentare*, 178–179. In a lecture given in 1921 ('Das Corpus iuris civilis') Seckel applied the term 'catastrophe of forgetting' also to developments in modern legal history. See "Die Vorträge Emil Seckels in der Berliner Mittwochs-Gesellschaft", ed. Schubert, 371–373 and Spruit, "Visions fugitives", 494–495.

20 Stolleis, "Vom Verschwinden verbrauchten Rechts". See also Guarino, "La rimozione del diritto e l'esperienza romana".

21 On the metaphor of the forest, see Spitz, *Die Metaphorik des geistigen Schriftsinns*, 130–134; Adam, *Poetische und kritische Wälder*, 57–71; Winter, "A Clearing in the Forest"; Kannengiesser, "Tyconius of Carthage, the Earliest Latin Theoretician of Biblical Hermeneutics", 307–308.

22 Tertullianus, *Apologeticum*, IV,7, 93: "Nonne et uos cottidie, experimentis inluminantibus tenebras antiquitatis, totam illam ueterem et squalentem siluam legum nouis principalium rescriptorum et edictorum securibus ruspatis et caeditis?" See Nörr, *Rechtskritik in der römischen Antike*, 58; Nörr, "Zum Traditionalismus der römischen Juristen", 175.

23 Schwind, *Zur Frage der Publikation im Römischen Recht mit Ausblicken in das altgriechische und ptolemäische Rechtsgebiet*, 35; Grosso, "Meditazione su Tacito"; Honsell, "Der Gesetzesstil in der römischen Antike", 1664–1665; Mantovani, "Legum multitudo e dritto privato", 713–717.

Looking at Giovanni Rotondi's (if by now partly outdated) count of Roman laws passed up to the 1st century of the Principate,[24] the respective number – about 800 – appears quite manageable and might seem to suggest that ancient complaints about the 'forest of laws' were just a topos.[25] However, this impression is based on an anachronistic premise and is therefore misleading.[26] For an observer who is familiar with the modern flood of legislation, the number of laws that Romans had to cope with might seem like a negligeable quantity. Nonetheless, the criticism of the multitude of laws referred to a problem that was quite real in the eyes of contemporaries and became increasingly troublesome in the later imperial period.

What, then, was more natural than to thin the forest of laws and legal texts? To Tertullian, the axes of imperial rescripts and edicts had been the right tools for the job. As time went by, however, they came to be part of the problem rather than of its solution. Thus, in late antiquity, a different approach was taken. The first step towards thinning the *silva legum* was to assemble an official collection of laws, such as the *Codex Theodosianus* and the *Codex Justinianus*. These contained the laws still of contemporary relevance, though many were included only in the form of extracts.[27] However, the resulting compilations were expensive to produce and of little use to non-specialists. The second step, then, which took place during the transition from antiquity to the Middle Ages, was the epitomisation of these law books and other legal texts (e.g. the *Novellae*).[28]

---

24 Rotondi, *Leges publicae populi romani*. For the present state of research see Mantovani, "Legum multitudo e dritto privato". In the German translation of the respective article there is an interesting addendum by Mantovani. See Mantovani, *Legum multitudo*.

25 Schulz, *Principles of Roman Law*, 9; Santucci, "Legum inopia e diritto privato", 377, 381.

26 Honsell, "Der Gesetzesstil in der römischen Antike", 1664; Cuena Boy, "Exceso de leyes en Roma"; Mantovani, *Legum multitudo*, 102–107.

27 Leges novellae ad Theodosianum pertinentes, in: *Theodosiani libri XVI*, vol. 2, eds. Mommsen and Meyer, Nov. Theod. 1,1.3, pp. 3–4: "[…] si copia inmensa librorum […] verum egimus negotium temporis nostri et discussis tenebris conpendio brevitatis lumen legibus dedimus […] Quamobrem detersa nube voluminum […] conpendiosam divalium constitutionum scientiam ex divi Constantini temporibus roboramos, […]". See also *Codex Iustinianus*, ed. Krüger, 1,17,2,17 (Const. Tanta §17), p. 73 (a. 533): "Mirabile autem aliquid ex his libris emersit, quod multitudo antiqua praesente brevitate paucior invenitur. […] ut egena quidem antiqua multitudo inveniatur, opulentissima autem brevitas nostra efficiatur". *Codex Iustinianus*, ed. Krüger, 5,4,24, p. 197 (a. 530): "Sic […] immensa librorum volumina ad mediocrem modum tandem pervenient".

28 For the Epitome Juliani, which was the main source for knowledge of Justinian's Novels in the Latin West up to the 12th century, see *Iuliani Epitome latina Novellarum Iustiniani*, ed. Hänel; Kaiser, *Die Epitome Iuliani*; Kaiser, "Wandlungen im Verständnis der Epitome Iuliani von der Spätantike bis zur Gegenwart".

The epitomisation of the *Codex Theodosianus* illustrates this process rather well.[29] After the fall of the Western Roman Empire, an epitome of it was prepared in the Visigothic Kingdom and promulgated and enforced in this form, along with other ancient legal texts (e.g. *Epitome Gai* and *Pauli sententiae*), as a law book for the Roman population living under Visigothic rule in 506 AD.[30] This work, known as the *Lex Romana Visigothorum* or *Breviarium Alarici(anum)*, represented one of the most important sources for the knowledge of Roman law in the Latin early Middle Ages. It also served as a starting point for Gallo-Roman and Frankish editors to compose 'epitomes of epitomes', which were, however, not official legal texts but works for private use.[31]

One of these 'epitomes of epitomes' is the so-called *Epitome Monachi*, prepared by an anonymous monk in the 8th century – probably in Burgundy – on the order of his abbot.[32] Its prologue allows us further insight into the facets of this source type. The author presents his 'little volume' for the reader who does not have the time, or the required knowledge, to study the Roman laws

29 *Theodosiani libri XVI*, 2 vols., eds. Mommsen and Meyer. See Sirks, *The Theodosian Code*; Atzeri, *Gesta sentus Romani de Theodosiano publicando*; Coma Fort, *Codex Theodosianus*.

30 *Lex Romana Visigothorum*, ed. Hänel; *Legis Romanae Wisigothorum fragmenta*. See Nehlsen, "Alarich als Gesetzgeber", 143–203; Lambertini, *La codificazione di Alarico II*; Lambertini, "Sull'«Epitome Gai» nel «Breviarium»"; Liebs, "Zur Überlieferung und Entstehung des Breviarium Alaricianum"; Martini, "Qualche osservazione a proposito della c.d. Epitome Gai"; Nemo-Pekelman, "How did the authors of the Breviarium Alaricianum work?".

31 Conrat (Cohn), *Geschichte der Quellen und Literatur des römischen Rechts im früheren Mittelalter*, vol. 1, 222–240; Schwerin, "Die Epitome Guelferbytana zum Breviarium Alaricianum"; Gaudemet, *Le Bréviaire d'Alaric et les Epitome*; Siems, *Handel und Wucher im Spiegel frühmittelalterlicher Rechtsquellen*, 194–195; Liebs, *Römische Jurisprudenz in Gallien*, 249–254; Ganivet, "L'«epitomé de Lyon»"; Trump, "Römisches Recht in Reims".

32 *Lex Romana Visigothorum*, ed. Hänel, 3 (Epitome Monachi, Prologus): "Quisquis oportuna vacatione minime perfruitur aut capacitate sensus vel prudentia plene imbutus non invenitur, ut iura librorum, id est leges Romanorum plenissime perscrutentur, hoc quod a nobis parvum volumen, quasi de magnis silvis surculum abscissum videtur integre perlegi non aborreat, et videbitur sibi non parvum in huius operis brevitatis inesse compendium, dum sublatis pragmaticis vel longissimis assertionibus et tamen omnes eorum definiciones in hac nostra reperiantur scedula. Volumus etiam omnia capitula legis huius integra admonitione contexere, ut si qua aliqua requirenda sunt, absque mora de hoc Breviario nostro possis in auctorem volum transire. Dignum videtur, ut hoc nostra exemplaria quasi edita subolis suae matris imitetur: [...]". See also Liebs, *Römische Jurisprudenz in Gallien*, 250. On the work and the passages discussed here see Conrat (Cohn), *Geschichte der Quellen und Literatur des römischen Rechts im früheren Mittelalter*, vol. 1, 238–239; Gaudemet, *Le Bréviaire d'Alaric et les Epitome*, 46–47; Siems, *Handel und Wucher im Spiegel frühmittelalterlicher Rechtsquellen*, 194–195; Liebs, *Römische Jurisprudenz in Gallien*, 249–254 (see 250–251); Coma Fort, *Codex Theodosianus*, 331–332.

collected in the *Breviarium Alarici* in detail: like a twig (*surculus*) taken from the large forest of the Breviary, or rather from the Roman laws it contains.[33] He assures the reader that in his *compendium* he has omitted all solemn and long-winded passages, but retained all the *definiciones* contained in them. The work's structure makes clear what exactly he meant by this. Like other epitomisers, the compiler of the *Epitome Monachi* mostly did not provide the actual text of the imperial constitutions contained in the Breviary nor of the *Pauli Sententiae*. Instead, he focused on the so-called *interpretationes*, that is, the excerpts from the older literature on the Theodosian Code preserved in the Breviary.[34] The author claims that one can easily switch between his own work and the source text.[35] This is due above all to the relationship between the two works. In the prologue he compares his text (*exemplaria*) with a newborn offspring (*suboles*) that emulates its mother.

This simile comes from Pope Gregory the Great's letter of dedication to Leandrus at the beginning of his *Moralia in Job*.[36] The pope explains that, as his commentary (*expositio*) derives from the Bible, it is proper that it takes on the appearance of the mother, that is, the language of Scripture. The author of the *Epitome monachi* copied most of this sentence, but substituted *exemplaria* for *expositio*.[37] It is possible that he did not want to suggest that his work was also a commentary.

At first sight, the author's emphasis on the close connection between the Breviary and his epitome appears justified. However, there are also features that seem to support the opposite view, such as the substantial cuts/omissions

33 See also [Hieronymus,] *Epistula Hieronymi adversus Rufinum presbyterum*, ed. Lardet, c. 39, 107 ll. 6–7: "De tanta librorum silua, unum fruticem ac surculum proferre non potes".

34 *Lex Romana Visigothorum*, ed. Hänel, XXIX–XXX; Gaudemet, *Le Bréviaire d'Alaric et les Epitome*, 46; Soliva, "Römisches Recht in Churrätien", 193; Liebs, *Römische Jurisprudenz in Gallien*, 250. On the *interpretationes* see Matthews, "Interpreting the Interpretationes on the Breviarium"; Di Cintio, *L'«Interpretatio Visigothorum» al «Codex Theodosianus»*; Di Cintio, *Nuove ricerche sulla «Interpretatio Visigothorum» al «Codex Theodosianus»*.

35 *Adnotationes codicum domini Justiniani*, ed. Patetta, XLVI–XLVII; Siems, *Handel und Wucher im Spiegel frühmittelalterlicher Rechtsquellen*, 194–195; Siems, "Adsimilare", 153.

36 Gregorius Magnus, *Moralia in Iob*, ed. Adriaen, *Epistola ad Leandrum*, c. 5, 7 ll. 223–225. On this work see Michel, "Wo das Lamm watet und der Elefant schwimmt"; Kessler, "Gregor der Große und seine Theorie der Exegese".

37 Gregorius Magnus, *Moralia in Iob*, ed. Adriaen, *Epistola ad Leandrum*, c. 5, 7 ll. 223–225: "Ex qua nimirum quia *nostra* expositio oritur, *dignum* profecto est, *ut quasi edita soboles* speciem *suae matris imitetur*". See *Lex Romana Visigothorum*, ed. Hänel, 3 (Epitome Monachi, Prolog): "*Dignum* videtur, *ut* hoc *nostra* exemplaria *quasi edita subolis suae matris imitetur*" (emphasis added).

and the above-mentioned remark about the *definiciones*, which suggests that the author thought them the essential part (as Detlef Liebs translated it), that is, the condensed core substance of the text.[38] Furthermore, the metaphor of the twig taken from the forest could be read as criticism of the source text. Perhaps the author of the *Epitome monachi*, which was conceived a priori as a private book of law ("Rechtsbuch", as Liebs put it), deliberately intended to counteract any impression that his *Epitome* strayed too far from its source.[39]

With this in mind, the simile of mother and child could perhaps gain another layer of meaning, as capturing a relationship of similarity that at the same time includes difference. Following this interpretation, one might ask to what extent the *Epitome* detached from its 'parent' not only in its existence as a separate text, but also in terms of content. However, we should not expect too much in this regard. The early medieval epitomisers of the *Breviarium Alarici* generally did not exhibit a deep understanding of their subject matter.[40] This is also true for the author of the *Epitome monachi*, though his work is seen as among the better efforts.[41] Nevertheless, the question of epitomes as potentially independent developments of their source text remains of relevance for the genre overall. We will return to the issue of the extent to which epitomes could – as a result of processes of in-depth reflection and carefully thought-through abstraction – represent distinct, even innovative development of their subject matter at the end of this essay.[42]

Turning back from this individual example to the general progression from the *Codex Theodosianus* to the *Breviarium Alaricianum* and thence to the latter's epitomes, this process is noteworthy in several respects. First among these is its formal aspect; that is, the dynamic development of the text. Instead of being a process completed in a single step, epitomisation could occur more than once. However, successive iterations did not necessarily reduce the quantity of text, as the transmission of the *Codex Justinianus* shows. At first, the Code's length was progressively reduced (*Epitome codicis*), but this condensed Code was subsequently again augmented (*Epitome aucta*).[43]

---

38 Liebs, *Römische Jurisprudenz in Gallien*, 251.

39 Liebs, "Das Verbot von Mischehen im germanisch-römischen Recht", 626.

40 Siems, "Adsimilare", 153.

41 Liebs, *Römische Jurisprudenz in Gallien*, 253.

42 See p. 66.

43 Krüger, *Geschichte der Quellen und Literatur des Römischen Rechts*, 425–428. Radding and Ciaralli have recently argued against Krüger's theory. See Radding and Ciaralli, *The Corpus Iuris Civilis in the Middle Ages*, 133–168. However, Radding and Ciaralli's argument depends on a controversial late dating of many works and texts. See Kaiser, "Verkürzt und wiederaufgefüllt?"; Müller, "Review of: Ch. Radding/A. Ciaralli, The Corpus iuris in the Middle Ages".

Beyond such a purely quantitative observation, the increasing textual reduction witnessed in Alaric's Breviary and its epitomes is also interesting for what it reveals about the improved access to legal knowledge. The tendency evident here actually accorded with traditional Roman ideas about good law. The dictum that laws should be short to make them comprehensible for non-experts appears already in Seneca.[44] The epitomes' brevity also made sense in terms of the post-Roman legal conditions. In the Latin West, jurists became ever rarer through the 6th and especially the 7th centuries, (almost) completely disappearing after this period. Under these circumstances, in which decreasing literacy and knowledge of Latin presented ever-greater obstacles to comprehension in large parts of Europe, a concise text was certainly advantageous, especially when it came to reaching less proficient readers and thus ensuring at least some adherence to the *lex scripta*.[45] In this light the *Breviarium Alaricianum* and its epitomes appear less as signs of decadence or barbarism than as attempts to preserve the utility of at least some of the knowledge contained in a great codification of late antiquity under changing cultural and legal conditions.[46]

This impression grows even stronger when we turn our attention from epitomes' cognitive-medial aspects to their actual legal content, particularly if one looks at the body of norms contained in the epitomes. The Breviary of Alaric reveals clear differences between Roman law in the early 6th-century Visigothic Kingdom and the two Roman (or, rather, Byzantine) Codes. The differences are not exclusively post-Roman; long before the Visigoths, law had been experienced and practiced very differently in the provinces compared to

44 *L. Annaeii Senecae ad Lucilium epistulae morales*, vol. 2, ed. Reynolds, ep. 94,38, 373 ll. 8–9: "Legem enim brevem esse oportet, quo facilius ab inperitis teneatur". On the idea of *brevitas*, which Roman authors held the Law of the Twelve Tables to embody, see Gebhardt, *Sermo Iuris*, 38–40. Other values, such as *simplicitas*, prominently demanded by Justinian, were closely connected to the postulate of *brevitas*, see Schindler, *Justinians Haltung zur Klassik*, 339–341. Schulz observed a general tendency towards simplification in Roman law between the end of the 3rd century AD and the first third of the 6th century; see Schulz, *History of Roman Legal Science*, 289–293. This should not be mistaken for a kind of decadence. See Dusil, Schwedler and Schwitter, "Transformationen des Wissens zwischen Spätantike und Frühmittelalter", 9–10.

45 For a discussion on the effectiveness of legal texts in late antiquity and the early Middle Ages, see Schott, "Pactus, Lex und Recht"; Nehlsen, "Aktualität und Effektivität der ältesten germanischen Rechtsaufzeichnungen"; Siems, "Zu Problemen der Bewertung frühmittelalterlicher Rechtstexte".

46 Paolo Canciani (1725–1810) had perhaps already thought along similar lines. See Canciani, *Praefatio Collectoris*, ed. Canciani, XII–XIII. On Canciani's biography, see Feola, "Canciani, Paolo".

the image of Roman law transmitted in the *Codex Theodosianus* and the *Codex Justinianus*.

Regardless of whether one associates provincial law with the concept of West Roman vulgar law,[47] it should be clear that how the Theodosian Code and the Breviary of Alaric were epitomised cannot be separated from the redactors' ideas regarding what was (still) applicable law. Indeed, such ideas were a prerequisite to any attempt to clear a path through the undergrowth of texts in the forest of laws. This closes the circle to the classical jurists' texts: as different as the epitomes considered here may be, they all represent efforts to update – by means of selection – and adapt the law to changed legal and extra-legal circumstances.[48] In other words, the epitomes were an important instrument to restructure both the literary and the legal landscape and thus helped to ensure the survival of the *lex scripta*. In this sense, epitomisation made it possible to continue working with at least a basic stock of Roman legal texts and to transmit the knowledge they contained during a time of profound institutional change.

This observation brings us back to the question of how to evaluate the process of epitomisation in the first millennium from the perspective of Roman law. As far as the quality of many late antique and early medieval epitomes is concerned, the traditional assessment cannot be entirely dismissed. Passages that represent a useful abridgment of the original text are interspersed with others that clearly betray how little the epitomator understood it. Nonetheless, the traditional wholesale condemnation remains deficient in many ways. It is ahistorical in its application of standards stemming from classical antiquity, its assumed causality is erroneous, and its perception is selective.

4 Epitomes in the Ecclesiastical Legal Culture of the Second Millennium

Moving on from the Roman law of late antiquity and the early Middle Ages, it is clear that epitomised texts played little role in the transmission of contemporary non-Roman secular law.[49] In contrast, they permeated the canon

47 Kaiser, "Vulgarrecht"; Liebs, "Roman Vulgar Law in Late Antiquity"; Sánchez-Moreno Ellart, "Law, 'vulgar' ".

48 Weiß, "Schwund und Konservierung im römischen juristischen Schrifttum"; Schiller, *Roman Law*, 384; Gaudemet, *Le Bréviaire d'Alaric et les Epitome*, 42.

49 On Lombard law, see Moschetti, *Primordi esegetici sulla legislazione longobarda nel sec. IX a Verona*, 151–167; Angelini, "Annotazioni sull'epitome greca dell'Editto di Rotari". For

law of the first millennium.[50] Similar interests and goals explain the existence of epitomes of canon law as in the case of their Roman law counterparts.[51] Epitomisation in the sphere of Church law focused particularly on the acts of Church councils (e.g., the *Breviarium Hipponense*) and, of course, on the collections of canon law (e.g., the *Breviatio canonum* of Fulgentius Ferrandus and the *Epitome Hispana*).[52] Even though the corpus of canon law texts grew and that of Roman law shrunk over the course of the second half of the first millennium, those composing epitomes of canon law faced relatively few problems compared to those assembling corresponding Roman law compendia at that time. From the middle of the 11th century onwards, however, the Gregorian Reform and the Investiture Controversy led to a rapid rise in the number of canon law collections. Before examining the resulting developments in more depth, it is necessary to clarify some fundamental differences between the phenomena discussed so far and the developments during the second millennium that will be considered below.

The codifications of the 5th and 6th centuries were an attempt to create a comprehensive representation of an unwieldy legal architecture, which until then had existed mainly in the minds of jurists, under the supervision of the state. Theodosius' and Justinian's Codes were intended to be the central source of information for those seeking to understand the current state of the law. The general decline in statehood and literacy in the Latin West, however, meant that these texts had little applicability in the barbarian successor states and mostly fell into oblivion. This development is easy to understand if one considers the availability of knowledge of Roman law in the second half of the first millennium. Early medieval scholars only rarely had access to collections of specialist legal literature, and even less to the legal training needed to find one's way through the large Roman law compilations of late antiquity.

---

the isolated epitome *De legibus divinis et humanis* drawn from Isidore's *Etymologiae* see Tardif, "Un abrégé juridique des Étymologies d'Isidore de Séville".

50 For examples of epitomised canon law collections before Gratian's Decree, i.e. before the second third of the 12th century, see Kéry, *Canonical Collections of the Early Middle Ages (ca. 400–1140)*, 11, 21–24, 57–60, 81–82, 147–148, 180–181, 187, 206, 241, 252, 264, 287.

51 In the prologue to the *Collectio Hibernensis*, a systematic collection of canon law from the first half of the 8th century, the compiler states his motivation succinctly as wanting to trim the *ingens silva scriptorum* down to a short, complete and harmonious depiction. See *The Hibernensis*, ed. Flechner, 1.

52 Munier, "La tradition manuscrite de l'Abrégé d'Hippone et le canon des Écritures des églises africaines"; Landau, "Die Breviatio canonum des Ferrandus in der Geschichte des kanonischen Rechts"; Kéry, *Canonical Collections of the Early Middle Ages (ca. 400–1140)*, 23–24, 57–60; Sedano, "Breviarium".

The situation in the early second millennium, with the so-called 12th-century Renaissance and the attendant rebirth of jurisprudence and legal literature, was strikingly different.[53] In Bologna, Irnerius († around 1130) and his followers studied, taught, and commented on the body of Justinianic texts (the Institutes, the Digest, the Code of Justinian and the Novels), later to become known as the *Corpus Juris Civilis*. Not long thereafter, Gratian († probably before 1150) founded a school of canon law, also in Bologna. This rise in the academic study of civil and canon law went hand in hand with a broader trend of flourishing scholarship and a growing library of texts. Consequently, new forms both of intensive and selective reading, textbooks such as Peter Lombard's (†1160) *Sentences*, and numerous aids for readers appeared.[54] Innovations such as these were closely related to the new academic culture of early scholasticism, which was not only *materialiter* marked by the increasing currency of text-based knowledge, but also characterised intellectually by the spirit of literacy and textuality.[55]

These contextual details cast a new light on the phenomena under discussion. Most of the epitomes of Roman law composed at the transition of late antiquity to the early Middle Ages were considerably younger than the source texts. Due to changing cultural and legal conditions, they came to supplant the original text rather than to be used in conjunction with them. They consolidated those aspects of legal knowledge that were still relevant and in this way kept them available. By contrast, many canonistic and theological epitomes of the later Middle Ages were produced not long after their source texts. Their special significance lay in the fact that they provided readers with a point of entry to the more comprehensive originals or served to make their contents better known. Epitomisation in the later Middle Ages was therefore not concerned

53 Otte, "Die Rechtswissenschaft"; Kuttner, "The Revival of Jurisprudence".

54 Petrus Lombardus, *Sententiae in IV libris distinctae*, vol. 1, Prologus n. 5, 4 ll. 23–26: "[…] brevi volumine complicans Patrum sententias, appositis eorum testimoniis, ut non sit necesse quaerenti librorum numerositatem evolvere, cui brevitas collecta quod quaeritur offert sine labore". See Grabmann, *Die Geschichte der scholastischen Methode*, vol. 2, 84–85; Rouse and Rouse, "La naissance des index", 97. On this development in general, see Parkes, "The Influence of the Concepts of Ordinatio and Compilatio on the Development of the Book"; Rouse and Rouse, "Statim invenire"; Hathaway, "Compilatio"; Illich, *In the Vineyard of the Text*; Hamesse, "A propos de quelques techniques d'interprétation et de compilation des textes". On the learned laws see Dolezalek and Weigand, "Das Geheimnis der roten Zeichen"; Montorzi, "Processi di 'standardizzazione' testuale: margaritae, gemmae, tabulae"; Meyer, "Ordnung durch Ordnen", 338–339; L'Engle, "The Pro-Active Reader".

55 Schönberger, *Was ist Scholastik?*, 83–86.

with the preservation of legal knowledge. On the contrary, its condensation served its expansion and diffusion.

This was particularly evident in the field of canon law.[56] Since the mid-12th century it had developed as an academic discipline with its own literature and science based on the interpretation of the *Decretum Gratiani,* completed around 1145 – a private collection of canon law compiled by the abovementioned monk Gratian.[57] Epitomising adaptations of the Decree began to appear afterwards: the so-called 'abbreviationes' (e.g., by Omnibonus (Omnebene)),[58] which largely preserved the original order of the *Decretum's* sources, and the so-called 'transformationes' (e.g., of Laborans),[59] which not only considerably reduced Gratian's text, but also rearranged the sources included.[60]

Three 'abbreviationes' of the *Decretum Gratiani* composed around the turn of the 13th century reveal the quantitative dimension of canonistic epitomisation.[61] It is immediately apparent that all three works excised over 90% of the content of the *Decretum*, though the intensitiy of the epitomisation varied for different parts of Gratian's work. However, these 'abbreviationes' also demonstrate that the epitomators did not simply follow a general scheme, but instead clearly based their decisions on what to include on careful consideration of the text's contents. Finally, the 'abbreviationes' of Gratian's Decree are also interesting in terms of their form and style. Some of them were composed in verse rather than prose.[62] As strange as that may seem today, rendering an

56 For Roman law epitomes in the 12th and 13th centuries, see Weimar, "Die legistische Literatur der Glossatorenzeit", 251–258.

57 Winroth, *The Making of Gratian's Decretum*; Winroth, "Where Gratian Slept"; Landau, "Gratian and the Decretum Gratiani"; Wei, "The Later Development of Gratian's Decretum"; Dusil, "The Decretum of Gratian". On the resemblance of the *Decretum Gratiani* to a florilegium, see Waelkens, "Le Décret de Gratien", 258–259.

58 On Omnibus (Omnebene), see fn. 4 above. See also Vetulani and Uruszczak, "L'œuvre d'Omnebene dans le MS 602 de la Bibliothèque municipale de Cambrai".

59 Martin, *Die 'Compilatio Decretorum' des Kardinals Laborans.*

60 Kuttner, *Repertorium der Kanonistik (1140–1234)*, 257–271; Ullmann, "The Paleae in Cambridge Manuscripts of the Decretum", 175 fn. 26; Zapp, "Abbreviationes"; Beyer, *Lokale Abbreviationen des Decretum Gratiani*; Fransen, "Les abrégés de collections canoniques", 160; Brasington, "The Abbreviatio 'Exceptiones evangelicarum'"; Kimmel, "Abbreviatio des Decretum Gratiani mit Ergänzungen"; Roumy, "Un abrégé inconnu du Décret de Gratien"; Landau, "Gratian and the Decretum Gratiani", 46–47; Pennington and Müller, "The Decretists", 123–125; Larson, "An Abbreviatio of the First Recension of Gratian's Decretum in Munich?"; León, "Abbreviatio".

61 Beyer, *Lokale Abbreviationen des Decretum Gratiani.*

62 Worstbrock, "Libri pauperum", 46–47. See also Schulte, "Zur Geschichte der Literatur über das Dekret Gratians", 26–29; Schmidt-Wiegand, "Rechtsverse"; Black, "Teaching the Mnemonic Bishop in the Medieval Canon Law Classroom".

'abbreviatio' in verse form was clearly intended to aid its memorisation. This raises questions about the use of mnemonic techniques by canon lawyers more generally, which however lies outside the scope of the article.[63]

In contrast to the many 'abbreviationes' that greatly contributed to the spread of Gratian's Decree,[64] the 'transformationes' generated little interest and remained the exception. Both literary genres can be called epitomes of canon law collections in the narrow sense of the term discussed above, because they aim to represent a single original text in its entirety, whether verbatim or in paraphrase. Other canonistic genres emerging at that time (e.g., 'casus' and 'notabilia'), on the other hand, were epitomes of canon law in the broader sense, because they excerpted only from parts of a text, drew on several source texts or contained elements of other canonistic genres, too.[65]

The developments described above essentially took place during the age of the so-called decretists, during which the *Decretum Gratiani* was the focus of interest in canon law (until ca. 1190). However, the landscape changed in the subsequent period of the so-called decretalists. During this period the focus of canonistic scholarship lay on the production of decretal collections and commentaries on them. This is particularly true for the time after the promulgation of the *Liber Extra* (1234). While 'abbreviationes' of the new papal decretal collections were produced, they were relatively few in number.[66] The focus of epitomising activity had started to shift. Most canonistic works of the 12th century were (compared to the *Decretum Gratiani*) not that extensive and therefore did not particularly require the production of abridged versions.[67] In

63 On mnemonic techniques, see Mazzacane, "El jurista y la memoria"; Meyer, "Spuren im Wald der Erinnerung"; Stolleis, "Corpus Iuris Civilis par cœur"; Rivers, "Remembering Canon and Civil Law around 1400"; Rivers, "Learning and Remembering Canon Law in the Fifteenth Century". For the mnemonic function of the scholastic page layout see Frońska, "Memory and the Making of Images"; Frońska, "Turning the Pages of Legal Manuscripts: Reading and Remembering the Law"; Frońska, "The Memory of Roman Law in an Illuminated Manuscript of Justinian's Digest". See also fn. 99–115 below.

64 Landau, "Gratian", col. 533.

65 Kuttner, *Repertorium der Kanonistik (1140–1234)*, 228–239; Figueira, "Ricardus de Mores and his Casus decretalium: the Birth of a Canonistic Genre", 174–175. On the decretalistic genres in question, see Kuttner, *Repertorium der Kanonistik (1140–1234)*, 397–415. On the 'casus', see also Bertram, "Casus legum sive suffragia monachorum".

66 Schulte, *Die Geschichte der Quellen und Literatur des canonischen Rechts*, vol. 2, 66, 492–495; Van Hove, *Prolegomena*, 484–486; Ourliac and Gilles, *La période post-classique (1378–1500)*, vol. 1, 121–123; Pennington, "Decretal Collections", 304. On the 'abbreviationes' of decretal collections before 1234, see Kuttner, *Repertorium der Kanonistik (1140–1234)*, 434–437.

67 However, epitomes of decretist works can also be found, for example, in the context of Simon of Bisignano's *Summa*, written between 1177 and 1179. See *Summa in Decretum*

the course of the 13th century, however, the decretalists produced ever more extensive works. It comes as no surprise, therefore, that epitomes of the most diverse genres of canon law literature gained in significance.[68] Moreover, the increasingly popular genre of canon law repertories also included epitomising elements.[69]

Irrespective of at what time or in which field of high and late medieval canon law or civil law epitomes were composed, one of the main underlying reasons for their production was economic. Many scholars could not afford the extensive and therefore expensive *Libri legales* and the attendant scholarly literature, making them reliant on excerpts of all kinds.[70] That authors of epitomes took note of this concern is apparent even in the titles and opening lines of several works, such as the civil law *Liber pauperum* of Vacarius (c. 1115/20 – c. 1200) and *Quoniam egestas*, an 'abbreviatio' of the *Decretum*.[71]

Sometimes other factors were added to the need for affordability, which led to the development of a particular form of epitomising canonistic literature distinct from those of the works discussed above. A passage drawn from the prologue of the *Casus ad summam Henrici* ('*Labia sacerdotis*') from about 1290 elucidates this particular development.[72] In it, the author, probably a

---

Simonis Bisinianensis, ed. Aimone Braida; Aimone, "Alcune note sulla Abbreviatio Dunelmensis della Summa Simonis Bisinianensis".

68 Schulte, *Die Geschichte der Quellen und Literatur des canonischen Rechts*, vol. 2, 483. Larson, "Géneros literarios canónicos", 191–192. For the role of epitomes in scholastic theology and philosophy, see Michelitsch, *Kommentatoren zur Summa Theologiae des hl. Thomas von Aquin*, 171–176; Grabmann, *Methoden und Hilfsmittel des Aristotelesstudiums im Mittelalter*, 54–104; Grabmann, "Hilfsmittel des Thomasstudiums aus alter Zeit", 425–452.

69 Schulte, *Die Geschichte der Quellen und Literatur des canonischen Rechts*, vol. 2, 485–489; Van Hove, *Prolegomena*, 486–488; Ourliac and Gilles, *La période post-classique (1378–1500)*, vol. 1, 125–126. See also Horn, "Die legistische Literatur der Kommentatoren und der Ausbreitung des gelehrten Rechts", 349–354.

70 Worstbrock, "Libri pauperum", 43–46; Hamesse, "A propos de quelques techniques d'interprétation et de compilation des textes", 23–24.

71 On the *Liber pauperum*, see *The Liber Pauperum of Vacarius*, ed. Zulueta; Taliadoros, *Law and Theology in Twelfth-Century England*. On *Quoniam egestas*, see fn. 4 above as well as León, "La abreviación 'quoniam egestas' del Decreto de Graciano".

72 Kurtscheid, "De studio juris canonici in Ordine Fratrum Minorum saeculo XIII", 168–169: "Cum summam henrici fratribus legerem et quosdam casus lectioni insererem, quos textus eiusdem summule non habebat, fratres multimodis precibus ac importunis instanciis me rogarunt, ut eosdem casus verbis brevibus et simplicibus annotarem, quatenus fratres simplices ad planiciem eorundem casuum expediendis penitencium perplexitatibus recurrerent, qui non possent se ac confitentes sibi in latebrosa silva iuris canonici ad liquidum expedire … Igitur de textu decretalium et decretorum et de summis ac apparatibus magistrorum famosorum ac valde nominatorum in iure canonico

Franciscan working in the German-speaking lands, describes inter alia the origins of his work. Probably in the course of a lecture on Henry of Merseburg's *Summa* of canon law,[73] he also presented those contents (*casus*) of decretals that were not included in Henry's work. Afterwards his fellow friars asked him to "explain the relevant *casus* in short and simple (written) words, so that the simple brothers who can lead neither themselves nor those who confess to them, through the dark forest of canon law and into certainty, can get to the bottom of the respective *casus* and thus be able to alleviate their penitents' difficulties".[74] The author proceeded to compose his *casus* with explanations based on excerpts from the decretals, from Gratian's Decree and the *summae* and gloss apparatuses of renowned scholars of canon law.

This passage from the prologue is interesting for several reasons, first among which is the reference to the 'dark forest of canon law'. As this notion appeared already in the 12th century, it may at first glance not seem particularly worthy of note.[75] For the author of the *Casus*, however, the overgrown *silva* was problematic for a different reason that it had been for earlier canonists or Roman lawyers. He was not concerned by the complexity of the ecclesiastical legal order *per se*,[76] but about one particular aspect of it, as the remark about the 'simple brothers' makes clear. These fellow friars asking him for an accessible work were not simple in that they were uneducated or simpletons;[77] rather, the author was more likely referring to members of the audience of his lectures who

cum magnis laboribus et crebris vigiliis casus quosdam prout potui collegi, et certis titulis prout eorum materie magis videbatur congruere annotavi". See also Kurtscheid, "De studio juris canonici in Ordine Fratrum Minorum saeculo XIII", 169–172 (on the work); Schulte, *Die Geschichte der Quellen und Literatur des canonischen Rechts*, vol. 2, 535–536; Ertl, *Religion und Disziplin*, 410–411 (text); Goering, "The Internal Forum and the Literature of Penance and Confession", 424. On the *casus* as a genre, see fn. 65 above.

73 On Henry of Merseburg and his *Summa*, see Müller, "Heinrich v. Merseburg"; Dannenberg, "Der lange Arm des Gesetzes", 344–347.

74 For a somewhat divergent German translation, see Ertl, *Religion und Disziplin*, 281.

75 As expressed, for example, by the canonist Stephen of Tournai (1128–1203). See Étienne de Tournai, *Lettres*, ed. Desilve, Ep. 274 (a. 1182), 345 (*inextricabilis silva decretalium epistolarum*). The same metaphor appears in the work of Peter of Blois (c. 1135–1211) in reference to the Digest. See Petrus Blesensis, *Epistolae*, Ep. 140, col. 416C (*quam dumosa silva, quam immeabile pelagus sit Pandecta*). On the antique patristic origins, see Alanus de Insulis, *Liber in distinctionibus dictionum theologicalium*, col. 944C. See also Meyer, "Ordnung durch Ordnen", 350–353.

76 On this general problem of canon law before the Code of 1917, see Stickler, *Historia iuris canonici latini*, 371–376.

77 Kuttner, "On the Place of Canon Law in a General History of Roman Law during the Middle Ages", 55. On the normatively charged diction, see Wesjohann, "Simplicitas als franziskanisches Ideal und der Prozeß der Institutionalisierung des Minoritenordens".

were interested in accessible knowledge regarding difficult and extensive legal texts. However, their interest was neither scholarly nor academic. The *fratres* were motivated in their search for instruction by their work as confessors, for which they required practical knowledge of canon law that they petioned the author of the *Casus ad summam Henrici* to provide.

Such a concern was in keeping with the developments at the time. From the second half of the 13th century onwards, we find an increasing number of canonistic epitomes directed at readers who were not specialists and might even have stood outside the world of learning.[78] Such readers would principally include members of the secular clergy and mendicants who required basic practical knowledge of canon law in order to exercise their confessional jurisdiction, i.e. in the so-called *forum internum*.[79] The existence of such a readership, sometimes referred to as *simplices*,[80] indicates the importance of a heterogeneous and underexplored group of writings, which Stintzing has called the 'popular' literature of Roman and canon law and which played a major role in the dissemination of *ius commune*.[81]

Another type of text that belongs to the category of pragmatic writings, are the manuals for confessors, or *Summae confessorum*, that often consisted of excerpts from works of canon law and theology.[82] These were especially popular among theologians looking for a brief summary of canon law.[83] One

78 Schulte, *Die Geschichte der Quellen und Literatur des canonischen Rechts*, vol. 2, 478; Bergfeld, "Katholische Moraltheologie und Naturrechtslehre", 1009. See also Michaud-Quantin, "Les méthodes de la pastorale du XIIIe au XVe siècle"; Furtenbach and Kalb, "Die Rechtsliteratur in volkssprachiger Überlieferung in Österreich".

79 On the *forum internum*, see Kéry, "Forum externum, Forum internum"; Arrieta, "Fuero interno".

80 On the manifold connotations of the term *simplices*, see Bertram, "Casus legum sive suffragia monachorum", 328–329 (51); Brundage, "E pluribus unum", 25. See also fn. 77 above.

81 Stintzing, *Geschichte der populären Literatur des römisch-kanonischen Rechts in Deutschland am Ende des fünfzehnten und im Anfang des sechszehnten Jahrhunderts*; Stintzing, *Geschichte der deutschen Rechtswissenschaft*, vol. 1, 77–85. See also Schmidt-Wiegand, "Populärjurisprudenz zwischen Artesliteratur und Richterlichem Clagspiegel". For a critique of Stintzing and his use of the term 'popular literature', see Trusen, *Anfänge des gelehrten Rechts in Deutschland*, 127–134; Becker, "Das kanonische Recht im vorreformatorischen Zeitalter", 16–18. See also the contrasting view in Wejwoda, *Spätmittelalterliche Jurisprudenz zwischen Rechtspraxis, Universität und kirchlicher Karriere*, 346–347. For a reconsideration of these and related works, see Thomas Duve in this volume (Chapter 1, section 5–6).

82 On this genre, see Boyle, "Summae confessorum"; Schmoeckel, "Beichtstuhljurisprudenz"; Goering, "The Internal Forum and the Literature of Penance and Confession", 418–427.

83 Melchor Cano (1509–1560) provides a 16th-century example. See Canus, *De locis theologicis libri duodecim*, lib. VIII, cap. 6, 283. It applies equally to Martin Luther who first studied the *Summa Angelica* and then, on 10 December 1520, burned it along with

such manual, the *Summa Angelica*, which Angelo Carletti (1410–1495) composed around 1462, accumulated so many *additiones* – above all by Giacomo Ungarelli († 1517) – in (the course of) its 16th-century editions that the result practically constituted a gloss.[84] The connection between excerpting, or rather epitomisation, and glossing, which can be traced back to the 'abbreviationes' of the *Decretum Gratiani* and continued in later centuries, is remarkable for two reasons. First, it testifies to the intellectual potential contained in the process of epitomisation. Epitomators did not merely abridge texts, they also condensed their contents. Second, the resulting greater conceptual depth was often accompanied by the addition of further texts,[85] which reveal epitomes' remarkable potential for expansion.

The above observations about the *Casus ad summam Henrici*, the confessors' manuals and the dynamics of how these texts developed, already provide some clues regarding their *raison d'être*. Their purpose was to furnish clerics involved in pastoral work with the basics of canon law (which, if necessary, could be extended later) as well as key issues of moral theology. Some of them also provided basic insights into secular, more precisely Roman, law. The legal historical significance of such condensed and mobilised knowledge was most visible at some remove from the great centres of canon-law scholarship. In such areas, the literature for the *forum internum* made an important contribution to the spread of learned law, as was the case, for instance, in the late medieval *Regnum Teutonicum*.[86] The detailed workings of this process need not detain us here. Far more interesting is the role played by the literature based on epitomisation in spreading knowledge about canon law and the resulting changes in regional legal cultures. This is true not only of late medieval and

---

the bull declaring his excommunication and parts of the *Corpus Juris Canonici*. See *D. Martin Luthers Werke. Kritische Gesamtausgabe*, vol. 5: *Tischreden aus den Jahren 1544–1544*, 680, n. 6471: *Ego Martinus Lutherus volens cognoscere iura ecclesiastica legi Summam Angelicam*. See also Boehmer, "Luther und der 10. Dezember 1520" and Ohst, *Pflichtbeichte*, 223–224, 295. On the *Summa Angelica* see fn. 84.

84 On the additions and Giacomo Ungarelli, see Schmitt, "Jacques Ungarelli"; Buzzi, "La tradizione teologica milanese tra Cinque e Seicento", 144. The author did not have access to the following monograph: Dell'Olmo and Scuccimarra, *Il beato Angelo Carletti da Chiavasso*. On the *Summa Angelica* in general, see Viora, "La Summa Angelica"; Montanos Ferrín, "A modo de consulta sobre la literatur jurídica del ius commune, III".

85 Ocker, "The Fusion of Papal Ideology and Biblical Exegesis in the Fourteenth Century", 137–139; Ocker, *Johannes Klenkok*, 22 fn. 21.

86 Trusen, "Forum internum und gelehrtes Recht im Spätmittelalter"; Trusen, "Zur Bedeutung des geistlichen Forum internum und externum für die spätmittelalterliche Gesellschaft". On the legistic literature, see Horn, "Die legistische Literatur der Kommentatoren und der Ausbreitung des gelehrten Rechts", 284–285.

early modern Europe, but also of areas outside Europe, as evidenced by the pragmatic normative literature of early modern Ibero-America.[87]

After this brief digression into the pragmatic side of epitomisation the final section focusses on the role of this technique and the related literary genres in the (early) modern period. First of all, we should note that both continued to be present in post-medieval Catholic canon law. However, compared to the age of classical canon law in the 12th to 14th centuries, the emphasis shifted once more. There are few early modern 'abbreviationes' of the great legal collections (*Decretum Gratiani, Liber Extra, Liber Sextus, Constitutiones Clementinae*) that from about 1500 onwards were gathered together in the *Corpus Juris Canonici*.[88] Instead, one encounters *Summae conciliorum* (like that of Bartolomé Carranza y Miranda),[89] excerpts from the great bullaria and occasionally epitomes of monastic rules.[90] Moreover, it is striking that quite a number of works whose titles suggest them to be epitomes of legal sources are little more than indices or repertories.[91]

To the literature of canon law, however, epitomisation continued to be very important. In the field of canon law works of greater scope were subject to epitomisation, if perhaps less frequently than in contemporary Catholic moral theology.[92] Some texts were condensed into such compendia by the authors

87 In the current volume, Manuela Bragagnolo's contribution (Chapter 6, in particular section 5) is of particular interest in reference to epitomisation.

88 See, for example, Mesnartius, *Legum pontificiarum Gregorii noui, seu Decretalium pentateuchus*; Becker, *Compendium juris decretalium*; Becker, *Decretum Gratiani abbreviatum* [...]. As far as the latter two books are concerned, it should be noted that Becker (1724–1790) was more interested in the history of canon law than in its application. See Schulte, *Die Geschichte der Quellen und Literatur des canonischen Rechts*, vol. 3.1, 232–233. See also Holthöfer, "Die Literatur zum gemeinen und partikularen Recht in Italien, Frankreich, Spanien und Portugal", 135, 209–210. The work of Giovanni Battista Scorza (1553–1627) offers much more than a mere epitome. See Scortia, *In selectas summorum pontificum constitutiones epitome*.

89 Duval, "La Summa Conciliorum de Barthélemy Carranza".

90 On the *Summae conciliorum*, see Sieben, *Die katholische Konzilsidee von der Reformation bis zur Aufklärung*, 235–239 (see also 472–476); Sieben, *Kleines Lexikon zur Geschichte der Konzilsidee*, 179–180 (s.v. Summen). On excerpts and repertories of the bullaries, see von Schulte, *Die Geschichte der Quellen und Literatur des canonischen Rechts*, vol. 3.1, 68 fn. 8. Giovannni Domenico Mansi's epitome of the bullary of Benedict XIV is especially noteworthy. See Mansi, *Epitome doctrinae moralis*. On the constitutions of the Jesuits, see Ruiz Jurado, "De las Constituciones S.J. al Epítome".

91 For example, Maranta, *Medulla Decreti*; Rives, *Epitome canonum conciliorum*; Brancatus, *Epitome canonum omnium* [...]; Schram, *Epitome canonum ecclesiasticorum ex conciliis Germaniae*. See Naz, "Tabula alphabetica juris".

92 Already Schulte was able to identify four epitomes of Tomás Sánchez's (1550–1610) *De matrimonio*, which was repeatedly reissued. See Schulte, *Die Geschichte der Quellen und*

themselves.[93] In still other literary genres, like the *paratitla* of canon law, legal sources and the related literature were epitomised together.[94]

Noting that epitomisation was practised in many forms in early modern canon law is not to imply, however, that the technique and the genres it produced were universally approved. Particularly their use in academic instruction at times attracted criticism. For example, the 1598 statutes of the University of Paris prohibited the use of epitomes for teaching purposes in the Faculty of Canon Law, probably to ensure that students read the legal texts themselves (in their entirety) instead of relying on excerpts.[95] The introductory didactic texts of renowned scholars of canon law (e.g. François Florent and Jean Doujat) and theologians (e.g. Martin Gerbert) also warned against the use of epitomes.[96]

It is no coincidence that, over the course of the 18th century, such criticisms were expressed ever more rarely before disappearing completely. Epitomisation presupposes of large (numbers of) texts, and the quantity of canonistic texts being produced shrank drastically over the course of the 18th century. This is also reflected in the most common sizes of books. While folios and quartos dominated at the beginning of the century, its end belonged to octavos and duodecimos. Far-reaching institutional and methodological changes were responsible for the shift. Many provisions of canon law were dead letters long before (and certainly after) the fall of the *ancien régime*, making any in-depth

Literatur des canonischen Rechts, vol. 3.1, 737 fn. 2. On Sánchez, see Carrodeguas, *La sacramentalidad del matrimonio*; Alfieri, *Nella camera degli sposi*. On moral theology, see Grabmann, "Das Weiterwirken des moraltheologischen Schrifttums des hl. Thomas von Aquin im Mittelalter"; Hurtubise, *La casuistique dans tous ses états*, 35–37.

93 For example, Vitus Pichler (1670–1736) first composed his more extensive *Candidatus jurisprudentiae sacrae* from 1716 to 1721 and then his much shorter *Candidatus abbreviatus*, which he first published in 1731. Both works saw several editions. See Pichler, *Candidatus jurisprudentiae sacrae*, 5 vols.; Pichler, *Candidatus abbreviatus jurisprudentiae sacrae*, 2 vols. On Pichler, see Fritsch, *Religiöse Toleranz im Zeitalter der Aufklärung*, 236–247.

94 On this genre, see Scherer, *Handbuch des Kirchenrechtes*, vol. 1, 123; Van Hove, *Prolegomena*, 544–545. For *paratitla* in Antoine de Mouchy's edition of the *Decretum Gratiani* (first printing: 1547), see Landau, "Gratian and the Decretum Gratiani", 50.

95 *Reformation de l'Université de Paris*, Appendix ad reformationem Facultatis iuris Canonici, art. XIV. See Périès, *La Faculté de droit dans l'ancienne Université de Paris (1160–1793)*, 209 fn. 3. This regulation also appears in the 1662 statutes of Reims University (*Statuta facultatis juris academiae Remensis*, art. 17), but directed at the Faculty of Law. See *Archives legislatives de la ville de Reims*, vol. 2.1, ed. Varin, 758.

96 Florens, *Oratio in aperiendis scholis iuris habita*, 63; Doujat, *Praenotionum canonicarum libri quinque*, lib. IV, cap. 21, n. 11, 518; Gerbert, *Apparatus ad eruditionem theologicam*, 118–120.

engagement with the traditional – once intensively discussed – body of norms unnecessary. In addition, further, new methodological approaches introduced rationalistic, deductive modes of representation that replaced the scholastic methods of textual work.[97]

Thus, the traditional canon law epitomes that had condensed lengthy learned discussions to their essentials, therefore lost their *raison d'être*. Furthermore, new ideas valorising authorship and originality made the epitomisation of others' works seem increasingly questionable. However, we find authors writing on canon law condensing their own extensive handbooks into shorter textsbooks also in the 19th and 20th centuries. Moreover, until the end of the 20th century scholarship on canon law and moral theology also produced works that in their titles labelled themselves 'epitomes'.[98] Generally, though, such works would perhaps be better described as summaries of canon law or moral theology based on selected materials. The era of classical epitomes ended once and for all with the Latin Catholic Church's first codification of canon law, the *Codex Iuris Canonici* of 1917, which almost removed the need to refer back to the *Corpus Juris Canonici* or, indeed, to older canonistic literature. The world of the premodern textual culture of canon law in which epitomisation was firmly anchored was no more.

5 Diagrams (*tabulae*) in (Early) Modern Canon Law and Moral Theology

Apart from works composed in running prose another aspect in which the epitomising tradition continued into the modern era remains to be discussed. From 1785 to 1789 Giovanni Devoti (1744–1822) published a textbook on the institutions of canon law in four volumes that, as one of the few works on canon law produced during the late *ancien régime*, went through a number of editions in the 19th century.[99] In 1835, more than a decade after Devoti's death, Camillo Tarquini (1810–1874), who himself went on to become a noteworthy canonist, completed his doctorate in canon law in Rome with an unusual dissertation

97 Meyer, "Kanonistik im Zeitalter von Absolutismus und Aufklärung".

98 For example, Vermeersch and Creusen, *Epitome iuris canonici*, 3 vols.; Serraino, *Epitome juris canonici*. On moral theology, see Telch, *Epitome theologiae moralis*; Ferreres, *Epitome theologiae moralis*. Judging from the titles, only Noldin's adaptation of Telch's textbook can be classified as a real epitome.

99 Devoti, *Institutionum canonicarum libri IV*, 4 vols. See Lauro, "Devoti, Giovanni"; Fantappiè, *Chiesa romana e modernità giuridica*, vol. 1, 121–123.

which he published anonymously in the same year.[100] Forgoing running prose, he had converted Devoti's textbook into tabular diagrams (*tabulae*) instead (see figure 2.1).

Such interest in graphical modes of representation was not exactly new. From the 11th century onwards, we find so-called 'schematic distinctions' in manuscripts of civil as well as canon law. In these, concepts and rules included in legal provisions or *auctoritates* were illustrated, e.g., in the form of marginal glosses.[101] Works on theology included comparable representations from at least the 12th century onwards.[102] The advent of printing made such tabular representations significantly cheaper and easier to produce.[103] As a result, on top of works written in running prose (the most common form), from the 16th century onwards, canonists and moral theologians also made use of *tabulae*, sometimes with additional comments.[104] This practice, which served not least a didactic purpose, continued into the 20th century, particularly in theology.[105]

---

100 [Tarquini,] *Institutionum juris canonici tabulae synopticae*, 1835. For the person, see Fantappiè, *Chiesa romana e modernità giuridica*, vol. 1, 158–163; Nacci, *Origini, sviluppi e caratteri del jus publicum ecclesiasticum*, 60–79.

101 Meyer, *Die Distinktionstechnik in der Kanonistik des 12. Jahrhunderts*; Meyer, "Spuren im Wald der Erinnerung"; Speer, "Verstehenshilfen zum geschriebenen Recht – Medienwandel als Chance", 239–242; Wittekind, "Überlegungen zur Verwendung graphischer Marginalien in Rechtshandschriften ausgehend von Dom-Handschrift 127"; Dusil, "Visuelle Wissensvermittlung in der Gratian-Handschrift Köln, Diözesan- und Dombibliothek, 128". See also Stein, "Alte und neue Übersichtstafeln"; Schadt, *Die Darstellungen der Arbores Consanguinitatis und der Arbores Affinitatis*; Musson, "Seeing Justice: The Visual Culture of the Law and Lawyers"; Blair, *Too Much to Know*, 144–152; Röhl, "(Juristisches) Wissen über Bilder vermitteln".

102 Moore, *The Works of Peter of Poitiers Master in Theology and Chancellor of Paris (1193–1205)*, 81–83; Robert Grosseteste, *Templum dei*, eds. Goering and Mantello.

103 Holthöfer, "Die Literatur zum gemeinen und partikularen Recht in Italien, Frankreich, Spanien und Portugal", 135; Prinz, *Der Bildgebrauch in gedruckten Rechtsbüchern des 15. bis zum Ausgang des 18. Jahrhunderts*. See also Brendecke, "Information in tabellarischer Disposition".

104 See, for example: Girardus, *Tituli totius iuris caesarei et pontificii per tabulas*; Haemstedius, *Tabulae totius sacrosancti iuris canonici*; Tinctus, *Tabulae sive introductiones*; Ugolinus, *De sacramentis novae legis tabulae perutiles*; Pacius a Beriga, *Oeconomia iuris utriusque*; Le Masson, *Theologia practica per tabulas distincta et exposita*, 3 vols.; Kurtz, *Amussis canonica*, 5 vols.; Goritia, *Epitome theologiae canonico-moralis*; Cappelli, *Manuale juris canonici*. For some observations on this practice, see Wex, *Ariadne carolino-canonica*, Tabula IV, membrum IV, pp. 21–22. On Protestant moral theology, see e.g. Olearius, *Doctrina theologiae moralis totius*; Buddeus, *Institutiones theologiae moralis in tabulis synopticis*; Walchius, *Theologiae moralis epitome tabulis analyticis expressa*.

105 See e.g. Manassero, *Tabulae synopticae theologiae moralis*, 4 vols.; Berthier, *Tabulae systematicae et synopticae totius Summae theologicae*. See also [Anon.,] *Rerum canonicarum scriptores*; Santamaria, *Tabulae synopticae Codicis Iuris Canonici*.

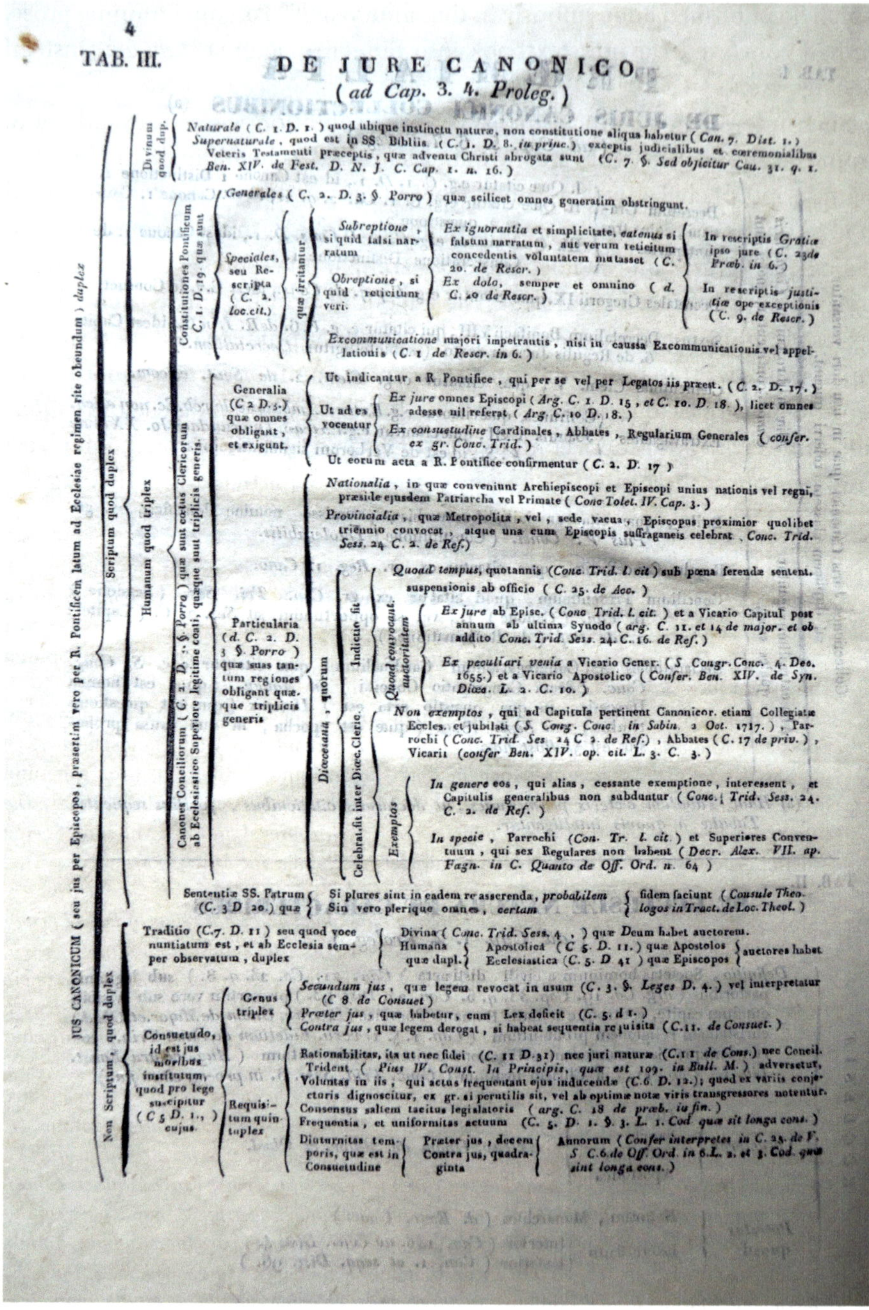

4

TAB. III.

DE JURE CANONICO
(*ad Cap.* 3. 4. *Proleg.*)

JUS CANONICUM (seu jus per Episcopos, præsertim vero per R. Pontificem latum ad Ecclesiae regimen rite obeundum) *duplex*

Scriptum quod duplex

Divinum quod dup.

Naturale (*C.* 1. *D.* 1.) quod ubique instinctu naturæ, non constitutione aliqua habetur (*Can.* 7. *Dist.* 1.)

Supernaturale, quod est in SS. Bibliis (*C.* 1. *D.* 8. *in princ.*) exceptis judicialibus et cœremonialibus Veteris Testamenti præceptis, quæ adventu Christi abrogata sunt (*C.* 7. §. *Sed objicitur Cau.* 31. *q.* 1. *Ben. XIV. de Fest. D. N. J. C. Cap.* 1. *n.* 16.)

Humanum quod triplex

Constitutiones Pontificum C. 1. D. 19. quæ sunt

Generales (*C.* 2. *D.* 3. §. *Porro*) quæ scilicet omnes generatim obstringunt.

Speciales, seu Rescripta (*C.* 2. *loc. cit.*) quæ irritantur

Subreptione, si quid falsi narratum — *Ex ignorantia* et simplicitate, *eatenus* si falsum narratum, aut verum reticitum concedentis voluntatem mutasset (*C.* 20. *de Rescr.*)

Obreptione, si quid reticitum veri. — *Ex dolo*, semper et omnino (*d. C.* 20 *de Rescr.*)

In rescriptis *Gratiæ* ipso jure (*C.* 23 *de Præb. in* 6.)

In rescriptis *justitiæ* ope exceptionis (*C.* 9. *de Rescr.*)

Excommunicatione majori impetrantis, nisi in caussa Excommunicationis vel appellationis (*C.* 1 *de Rescr. in* 6.)

Canones Conciliorum (*C.* 2. *D.* 3. §. *Porro*) quæ sunt cœtus Clericorum ab Ecclesiastico Superiore legitime coati, quæque sunt triplicis generis.

Generalia (*C* 2 *D.* 3.) quæ omnes obligant, et exigunt.

Ut indicantur a R. Pontifice, qui per se vel per Legatos iis præest. (*C.* 2. *D.* 17.)

Ut ad ea vocentur

Ex jure omnes Episcopi (*Arg. C.* 1. *D.* 15, *et C.* 10. *D.* 18.), licet omnes adesse nil referat (*Arg. C.* 10 *D.* 18.)

Ex consuetudine Cardinales, Abbates, Regularium Generales (*confer. ex gr. Conc. Trid.*)

Ut eorum acta a R. Pontifice confirmentur (*C.* 2. *D.* 17)

Particularia (*d. C.* 2. *D.* 3 §. *Porro*) quæ suas tantum regiones obligant quæque triplicis generis

Nationalia, in quæ conveniunt Archiepiscopi et Episcopi unius nationis vel regni, præside ejusdem Patriarcha vel Primate (*Conc Tolet. IV. Cap.* 3.)

Provincialia, quæ Metropolita, vel, sede vacua, Episcopus proximior quolibet triennio convocat, atque una cum Episcopis suffraganeis celebrat. *Conc. Trid. Sess.* 24 *C.* 2. *de Ref.*)

Diœcesana, quorum

Indictio fit

Quoad tempus, quotannis (*Conc. Trid. l. cit*) sub pœna ferendæ sentent. suspensionis ab officio (*C.* 25. *de Acc.*)

Quoad convocant. auctoritatem

Ex jure ab Episc. (*Conc Trid. l. cit.*) et a Vicario Capitul. post annum ab ultima Synodo (*arg. C.* 11. *et* 14 *de major. et ob.* addito *Conc. Trid. Sess.* 24. *C.* 16. *de Ref.*)

Ex peculiari venia a Vicario Gener. (*S. Congr. Conc.* 4. *Dec.* 1655.) et a Vicario Apostolico (*Confer. Ben. XIV. de Syn. Diœc. L.* 2. *C.* 10.)

Celebrat. fit inter Diœc. Cleric.

Non exemptos, qui ad Capitula pertinent Canonicor. etiam Collegiatæ Eccles. et jubilati (*S. Cong. Conc. in Sabin.* 2 *Oct.* 1717.), Parrochi (*Conc. Trid. Ses* 24 *C* 2. *de Ref.*), Abbates (*C.* 17 *de priv.*), Vicarii (*confer Ben. XIV. op. cit. L.* 3. *C.* 3.)

Exemptos

In genere eos, qui alias, cessante exemptione, interessent, et Capitulis generalibus non subduntur (*Conc. Trid. Sess.* 24. *C.* 2. *de Ref.*)

In specie, Parrochi (*Con. Tr. l. cit.*) et Superiores Conventuum, qui sex Regulares non habent (*Decr. Alex. VII. ap. Fagn. in C. Quanto de Off. Ord. n.* 64)

Sententiæ SS. Patrum (*C.* 3 *D* 20.) quæ

Si plures sint in eadem re asserenda, *probabilem* — Sin vero plerique omnes, *certam* — fidem faciunt (*Consule Theologos in Tract. de Loc. Theol.*)

Non Scriptum, quod duplex

Traditio (*C.* 7. *D.* 11) seu quod voce nuntiatum est, et ab Ecclesia semper observatum, duplex

Divina (*Conc. Trid. Sess.* 4,) quæ Deum habet auctorem.

Humana quæ dupl.

Apostolica (*C* 5. *D.* 11.) quæ Apostolos — auctores habet

Ecclesiastica (*C.* 5. *D* 41) quæ Episcopos — auctores habet

Consuetudo, id est jus moribus institutum, quod pro lege suscipitur (*C* 5 *D.* 1.,) cujus

Genus triplex

Secundum jus, quæ legem revocat in usum (*C.* 3. §. *Leges D.* 4.) vel interpretatur (*C* 8. *de Consuet*)

Præter jus, quæ habetur, cum Lex deficit (*C.* 5. *d* 1.)

Contra jus, quæ legem derogat, si habeat sequentia requisita (*C.* 11. *de Consuet.*)

Requisitum quintuplex

Rationabilitas, ita ut nec fidei (*C.* 11 *D.* 31) nec juri naturæ (*C.* 11 *de Cons.*) nec Concil. Trident. (*Pius IV. Const. In Principis, quæ est* 109. *in Bull. M.*) adversetur,

Voluntas in iis, qui actus frequentant ejus inducendæ (*C.* 6. *D.* 12.); quod ex variis conjecturis dignoscitur, ex gr. si perutilis sit, vel ab optimæ notæ viris transgressores notentur.

Consensus saltem tacitus legislatoris (*arg. C.* 18 *de præb. in fin.*)

Frequentia, et uniformitas actuum (*C.* 5. *D.* 1. §. 3. *L.* 1. *Cod. quæ sit longa cons.*)

Diuturnitas temporis, quæ est in Consuetudine — Præter jus, decem / Contra jus, quadraginta — Annorum (*Confer interpretes in C.* 25. *de V. S. C.* 6. *de Off. Ord. in* 6. *L.* 2. *et* 3. *Cod. quæ sint longa cons.*)

FIGURE 2.1 [Camillo Tarquini:] *Institutionum juris canonici tabulae synopticae juxta ordinem habitum a Joanne Devoti*, Rome 1835, 4
PHOTO: OTTO DANWERTH

This brings us back to Tarquini's work, which found readers also in perhaps unexpected quarters. The book was not only reprinted as soon as five years after its publication.[106] It was also published in an annotated and somewhat reworked version by Jean-François-Marie Lequeux (1796–1866).[107] This is particularly remarkable because, unlike Devoti and Tarquini, Lequeux did not belong to the group of Curial authors, but instead was a late representative of Gallicanism.[108] The fact that Lequeux took an interest in Tarquini's tables in the first place, is probably due to his teaching at the Seminary of St. Sulpice in Paris where Devoti's *Institutiones* had been the prescribed textbook for canon law since 1836.[109] In 1845 Lequeux anonymously published a version of Tarquini's tables that met the needs of Gallican readers.[110] The two major changes to the work can already be gathered from the title. First, Lequeux indicated the passages where Gallican Church discipline supposedly differed from common canon law, Lequeux had indicated this by annotations. Second, these footnotes mostly refer to the second edition of his manual of canon law published in 1843–1844.[111] The latter was put on the Index in 1851, immediately after the publication of its third edition (1850–1851).[112]

Lequeux's interest in the *tabulae* only becomes understandable if one takes into account the didactic value he placed on them, not only for beginners but especially for more advanced students of canon law.[113] This leads to the question of the particular characteristics of Tarquini's work. Three aspects are particularly noteworthy in this respect. First, Tarquini started not from the sources of canon law itself; although he provided numerous references to legal sources, these all derived from a single work of canonistic scholarship. Second, he did not work eclectically, but rather focused on producing a graphical and tabular epitome of Devoti's textbook. Third and finally, an epigraph suggests that the work might have been inspired by a treatise of the Protestant philosopher and

106 [Tarquini,] *Institutionum juris canonici tabulae synopticae*, 1840.

107 Aubert, "Lequeux (Jean François Marie)".

108 On Gallicanism in general, see Gaudemet, "Les vicissitudes du Gallicanisme"; Basdevant-Gaudemet, *Histoire du droit canonique et des institutions de l'Église latine*, 486–523.

109 Mosiek, *Die probati auctores in den Ehenichtigkeitsprozessen der S.R. Rota*, 41.

110 [Tarquini,] *Synopsis juris canonici*. For the author, see Hurter, *Nomenclator literarius theologiae catholicae*, vol. 5,1, col. 1353.

111 Lequeux, *Manuale compendium juris canonici ad usum seminariorum*, 4 vols.

112 Gough, *Paris and Rome*, 151–161; De Franceschi, "La papauté intransigeante et ses craintes d'un renouveau de régalisme gallican".

113 [Tarquini,] *Synopsis juris canonici*, I.

jurist Christian Wolff (1679–1754), who had studied the design and use of mnemonic tables a century earlier.[114]

The recourse to mnemonic techniques intended to help readers learn and remember key conceptual matrices of canon law[115] reveals an aspect of epitomisation that raises broader questions about the relationship between text and conceptual content. To the extent that the scholastic method, which predominated in the science of canon law until well into the 18th century, was based on "thinking along the text" (Rolf Schönberger),[116] it would also seem to reflect the particular effect of epitomisation. Accordingly, the key principle was working on the text, which sometimes led to transformations of legal concepts.

Since Tarquini's *tabulae* continued a tradition of schematic, tabular representations that stretched back well into the Middle Ages, epitomisation might have given rise to further benefits. This emerges more clearly if we bear in mind that the *silva legum* was not only a forest of laws, but also a thicket of legal terminology and rules. If an epitomator's schematic representations prove that he had a clear conception of the order of legal concepts and rules, perhaps his work did more than clear a path through the forest of legal texts. This brings us back to the possibilities for abstraction inherent in epitomisation. As already suggested above,[117] it is doubtful that we will find much evidence of this in early medieval epitomes. However, it is not unlikely that in the second millennium, particularly in the early modern and modern periods, we might be able to identify quite a number of such instances. This may be a fruitful subject for further study, particularly considering the important role played by epitomes or texts involving epitomisation in pre-modern legislation.[118]

114 [Tarquini,] *Institutionum juris canonici tabulae synopticae*, 1835, 2: "Ingens sane subsidium memoriae in Tabulis consistit, in quas doctrinae ita referuntur, ut uno quasi conspectu comprehendi earum ambitus possit. Christian. Wolph. Disert. de Tabular. Mnemonic. construct. et usu". See Wolfius, *Tabularum Mnemonicarum constructio et usus*, 470–471. See also Fantappiè, *Chiesa romana e modernità giuridica*, vol. 1, 163 fn. 158.

115 See fn. 63 above. See also Heimann-Seelbach, "Diagrammatik und Gedächtniskunst".

116 Schönberger, *Was ist Scholastik?*, 83 ('Denken am Text').

117 See p. 49.

118 See, for example, the significance of epitomes for late medieval and (early) modern legislation. Thus the *Principia iuris canonici*, a compendium (and popular text book) produced by Georg Ludwig Böhmer (1715–1797), in which he condensed his father Henning Böhmer's (1674–1749) more substantial work, formed the basis of the sections on ecclesiastical law in the General Law Code for the Prussian States (Allgemeines Landrecht für die Preußischen Staaten) of 1794. See Richter, *Beiträge zum Preussischen Kirchenrechte*, 11; Dove, "Aemilius Ludwig Richter", 297 fn. 17; Schulte, *Die Geschichte der Quellen und Literatur des canonischen Rechts*, vol. 3.2–3, 136; Löhr, *Das Preußische Allgemeine Landrecht und die Katholischen Kirchengesellschaften*, 20 fn. 2, 116 fn. 1. For more information on Böhmer

Bibliography

Printed Sources

Adnotationes codicum domini Justiniani (*Summa Perusina*), ed. Patetta, Federico (*Bulletino dell'Istituto di diritto romano* 12 (1900)), Roma 1900.

Alanus de Insulis, *Liber in distinctionibus dictionum theologicalium*, in *Patrologiae cursus completus* [...]. *Series latina, accurante J.-P. Migne*, vol. 210, Paris 1855, col. 685–1012.

[Anon.,] *Rerum canonicarum scriptores. Tabulae synopticae ab anno 1141 ad annum 1564*, in *Jus pontificium* 10 (1930), 83–92.

Archives legislatives de la ville de Reims, vol. 2.1, ed. Varin, Pierre, Paris 1847.

Bacon, Francis, *De augmentis scientiarum*, in *The Works of Francis Bacon*, vol. 1, eds. Spedding, James, Robert Leslie Ellis and Douglas Denon Heath, London 1858, 415–837.

Bartholomaeus Ugolinus, *De sacramentis novae legis tabulae perutiles*, Rimini 1587: Typis Ioannis Simbenei.

Becker, Clemens, *Compendium juris decretalium ex ipsis decretalibus collectum* [...], Munster 1772: Typis et sumptibus Anton. Wilh. Aschendorf.

Becker, Clemens, *Decretum Gratiani abbreviatum* [...], Munster 1781: Typis et sumptibus Anton. Wilh. Aschendorf.

Berthier, Joachim Joseph, *Tabulae systematicae et synopticae totius Summae theologicae juxta ipsammet Doctoris Angelici methodum strictius et clarius exactae*, Paris 1931.

Brancatus, Laurentius, *Epitome canonum omnium* [...], Rome 1659: Typis Mascardi.

Buddeus, Joh. Franciscus, *Institutiones theologiae moralis in tabulis synopticis repraesentatas, in gratiam theologiae studiosorum, ut totum theologiae moralis ambitum, in mappa quasi delineatum, uno conspectu intueri possint, evulgare, ac omnibus doctrinam in compendio amantibus consecrare voluit Joh. Anton Strubberg*, Jena/Leipzig 1721: Apud Johannem Martinum Gollnerum.

Canciani, Paulus, *Praefatio Collectoris*, in *Barbarorum leges antiquae cum notis et glossariis*, vol. 1, ed. Canciani, Paulus, Venice 1781: Apud Sebastianum Coletium et Franciscum Pitterium, IX–XX.

Canus, Melchior, *De locis theologicis libri duodecim*, Salamanca 1563: Excudebat Mathias Gastius.

Cappelli, Aloysius, *Manuale juris canonici quod in usum auditorum quinquaginta tabulis synopticis delineavit et brevibus notis illustravit*, Vilnius 1819.

[Casaubon, Isaac,] *Henrico IV. Franciae et Navarrae Regi Christianissimo, Isaacus Casaubonus S.D.*, in *Isaaci Casauboni epistolae, insertis ad easdem responsionibus*, [...],

père et fils, see De Wall, "Böhmer, Georg Ludwig"; De Wall, "Böhmer, Justus Henning". See also Varga, *Codification as a Socio-Historical Phenomenon*, 298–299.

curante Theodoro Janson. ab Almeloveen, Rotterdam 1709: Typis Casparis Fritsch et Michaelis Böhm, 54–89.

Codex Iustinianus, ed. Krüger, Paul, 15th ed., Dublin 1970.

Devoti, Joannis, *Institutionum canonicarum libri IV*, 4 vols., Rome 1785–1789: Excudebat Giunchi librorum Bibliothecae Vaticanae provisor.

Doujat, Joannes, *Praenotionum canonicarum libri quinque: quibus sacri juris atque universi studi ecclesiastici principia enucleantur*, Venice 1717: Ex typographia Balleonii.

Étienne de Tournai, *Lettres*, ed. Desilve, Jules, Valenciennes 1893.

Ferreres, Juan B., *Epitome theologiae moralis codicis canonici praescriptionibus, ac subsequentibus Sanctae Sedis declarationibus, dispositionibus iuris Hispani ac Lusitani, decretis Concilii Plenarii Americae Latinae necnon I Conc. Prov. Manilani, earundemque regionum legibus peculiaribus etiam civilibus accomodata*, 4th ed., Barcelona 1933.

Florens, Franciscus, *Oratio in aperiendis scholis iuris habita VI. Non. Octob. anno M.DC XXXII. ad IX. tractatum calcem edita anno 1641. De recta iuris canonici discendi ratione*, in *Franciscus Florens: Opera juridica*, vol. 1, Paris 1679: Sumptibus Joannis de la Caille, via Jacobaea, ad insigne Prudentiae, 59–63.

Gerbert, Martinus, *Apparatus ad eruditionem theologicam, institutioni tironum Congregationis S. Blasii O.S.B. in silva nigra destinatus*, Augsburg/Freiburg 1754: Sumptibus Ignatii et Antonii Wagner fratrum, typis Joannis Georgii Felner, Univers. typ.

Girardus, Iacobus, *Tituli totius iuris caesarei et pontificii per tabulas, iuxta literarum ordinem, seiunctim digesti* [...], Lyon 1551: Apud Michaelem Syluium Typographum.

Goritia, Franciscus Antonius a, *Epitome theologiae canonico-moralis omnes seorsim in bis centis triginta tribus tabulis clare distincte ac breviter materias practicas exhibens, confessariorum, examinatorum, necnon examinandorum usibus accommodata*, Rome 1796: In typographio Paleariniano.

Gregorius Magnus, *Moralia in Iob, libri I–X*, ed. Adriaen, Marc (Corpus Christianorum, Series latina, vol. 143), Turnhout 1979.

Grosseteste, Robert, *Templum Dei edited from Ms. 27 of Emmanuel College, Cambridge*, eds. Goering, Joseph and Frank A.C. Mantello, Toronto 1984.

Haemstedius, Hadrianus Cornelius, *Tabulae totius sacrosancti iuris canonici*, Louvain 1552: Prostant apud Martinum Rotarium, Bibliopolam Iuratum.

[Hieronymus,] *Epistula Hieronymi adversus Rufinum presbyterum*, in S. Hieronymi presbyteri opera, *Pars III: Opera polemica*, vol. 1, ed. Lardet, Pierre (Corpus Christianorum, Series latina, vol. 79), Turnhout 1982, 73–116.

Iuliani Epitome latina Novellarum Iustiniani, ed. Hänel, Gustav, Leipzig 1873.

Kurtz, Hermannus, *Amussis canonica titulorum libri* [...] *Gregorii IX. pontificis maximi in tabulis mnemonicis analytice proposita* [...], 5 vols., Prague 1761, 1762, 1764: Typis Archi-Episcopalibus per Jacobum Schweiger Archi-Episcopalem Typographum.

Le Masson, Innocentius, *Theologia practica per tabulas distincta et exposita* [...], 3 vols., Paris 1662–1663: Apud Georgium Josse.

Legis Romanae Wisigothorum fragmenta ex codice palimpsesto sanctae Legionensis ecclesiae prostulit, illustravit ac sumptu publico edidit Regia Historiae Academia Hispana, Madrid 1896.

Lequeux, Jean-François-Marie, *Manuale compendium juris canonici ad usum seminariorum, juxta temporum circumstantias accomodatum*, 4 vols., 2nd ed., Paris 1843–1844.

Lex Romana Visigothorum, ed. Hänel, Gustav, Leipzig 1849 (repr. Aalen 1962).

[Luther, Martin,] *D. Martin Luthers Werke. Kritische Gesamtausgabe*, vol. 5: *Tischreden aus den Jahren 1544–1544*, ed. Komission zur Herausgabe der Werke Martin Luthers, Weimar 1919.

Manassero, Bartholomaeus, *Tabulae synopticae theologiae moralis e probatis auctoribus desumptae*, 4 vols., 2nd ed., Rome 1903–1907.

Mansi, Joannes Dominicus, *Epitome doctrinae moralis, et canonicae ex constitutionibus aliisque operibus felicis recordationis Benedicti XIV. pontificis maximi*, Rome 1763: Sumptibus Remondianis.

Maranta, Carolus, *Medulla Decreti alphabeticis distinctis litteris in qua quicquid in Decreto continetur per propositiones distinctas producitur; atque ex sanctorum patrum et conciliorum verbis fundatur; necnon aliquoties doctorum atque etiam sacrorum theologorum auctoritate fulcitur* [...], Naples 1656: Ex Typographia Camilli Caualli.

Mesnartius, Martinus, *Legum pontificiarum Gregorii noui, seu Decretalium pentateuchus in Epitomen arte et ordine reuocatus, seruata quadantenus antiquae legislationis maiestati et phrasi*, Paris 1555: Apud Carolam Guillard sub sole aureo, et Gulielmum Guillard sub diuae Barbare signo, via Iacobaea.

Olearius, Johannes, *Doctrina theologiae moralis totius, in usum incipientium, certis paediae ac methodi limitibus circumscripta et tabulis LXXII. comprehensa*, Leipzig 1694: Sumptibus Joh. Christ. Wohlfarti, Bibliopol.

Pacius a Beriga, Iulius, *Oeconomia iuris utriusque, tam civilis, quam canonici, perspicuis tabulis ad memoriam iuvandam repraesentata, et annotationibus illustrata*, Lyon 1616: Sumptibus viduae Antonij de Harsy. Ad insigne Scuti Coloniensis.

Petrus Blesensis, *Epistolae*, in *Patrologiae cursus completus* [...]. *Series latina, accurante J.-P. Migne*, vol. 207, Paris 1855, col. 1–560.

Petrus Lombardus, *Sententiae in IV libris distinctae. Liber I et II*, vol. 1, 3rd ed., Grottaferrata 1971.

Pichler, Vitus, *Candidatus jurisprudentiae sacrae, seu juris canonici secundum Gregorii Papae IX. decretalium titulos explanati* [...], 5 vols., Augsburg/Dillingen 1716–1721: Sumptibus Georgij Schlüter et Martini Happach, Bibliop., et typis viduae Joannis Mauritij Körner, Typogr. Episc.

Pichler, Vitus, *Candidatus abbreviatus jurisprudentiae sacrae. Hoc est, juris canonici secundum Gregorii Papae IX. libros V. decretalium explanati summa seu compendium, quod in usum maxime discipulorum suorum ex libris suis collegit auctor ipse* [...], 2 vols., Augsburg 1731: Sumptibus Martini Happach, et Franc. Xav. Schlüter.

Reformation de l'Université de Paris, Paris 1601: Chez I. Mettayer et P. l'Huillier imprimeurs et libraires ordinaires du Roy.

Rives, Gregorius de, *Epitome canonum conciliorum in locos communes per alphabetum digesta* [...], Lyon 1663: Sumpt. Benedicti Coral, in vico Mercatorio sub signo Victoriae.

Santamaria, Alberto, *Tabulae synopticae Codicis Iuris Canonici*, Manila 1949.

Schram, Dominicus, *Epitome canonum ecclesiasticorum ex conciliis Germaniae et aliis fontibus juris ecclesiastici Germanici collecta, ac ordine alphabeti secundum materias distincta*, Augsburg 1774: Sumptibus Matthaei Rieger et filiorum.

Scortia, Joannis Baptista, *In selectas summorum pontificum constitutiones epitome, ac theoremata*, Lyon 1625: Sumpt. Ludovici Prost, haeredis Roville.

[Seneca,] *L. Annaeii Senecae ad Lucilium epistulae morales*, vol. 2, ed. Reynolds, L.D., Oxford 1965.

Serraino, Mario, *Epitome juris canonici. Ad mentem Codicis 1983*, Trapani 1988.

[Simon of Bisignano,] *Summa in Decretum Simonis Bisinianensis*, ed. Aimone Braida, Pier V., Vatican City 2014.

[Tarquini, Camillo,] *Institutionum juris canonici tabulae synopticae juxta ordinem habitum a Joanne Devoti*, Rome 1835.

[Tarquini, Camillo,] *Institutionum juris canonici tabulae synopticae juxta ordinem habitum a Joanne Devoti*, Florence 1840.

[Tarquini, Camillo,] *Synopsis juris canonici communis secundum ordinem institutionum J. Devoti per tabulas disposita. Opusculum e selectissimis doctorum utriusque juris operibus collectum. In hac Parisiensi editione indicantur praecipua disciplinae gallicanae a jure communi discrimina per opportunas remissiones ad Manuale compendium juris canonici D. Lequex majoris seminarii Suessionensis moderatoris*, Paris 1845.

Telch, Carolus, *Epitome theologiae moralis universae per definitiones, divisiones et summaria principia pro recollectione moralis et ad immediatum usum confessarii et parochi excerpta e Summa theol. mor. R.P. Hier. Noldin SJ*, 6th ed., Innsbruck 1924.

Tertullianus, Quintus Septimius Florens, *Apologeticum*, ed. Dekkers, Eligius, in *Quinti Septimi Florentis Tertulliani opera, Pars I* (Corpus Christianorum, Series latina, vol. 1), Turnhout 1950, 77–171.

The Hibernensis. A Study and Edition, ed. Flechner, Roy, Book 1, Washington D.C. 2019.

Theodosiani libri XVI cum constitutionibus Sirmondianis et leges novellae ad Theodosianum pertinentes, 2 vols., eds. Mommsen, Theodor and Paul M. Meyer, 3rd ed., Berlin 1962.

Tinctus, Iulius Caesar, *Tabulae sive introductiones in institution[es] iuris canonici in IIII libros distinctae*, Ferrara 1583: Excudebat Victorius Baldinus.

[Vacarius,] *The Liber Pauperum of Vacarius*, ed. Zulueta, Francis de, London 1927.
Vermeersch, Arthur and Joseph Creusen, *Epitome iuris canonici cum commentariis ad scholas et ad usum privatum*, 3 vols., 7th ed., Mechlin 1949–1956.
Walchius, Ioannis Georgius, *Theologiae moralis epitome tabulis analyticis expressa*, Jena 1758: Apud Io. Rudolph. Croecker. viduam.
Wex, Jacobus, *Ariadne carolino-canonica, seu doctrina theorico-practica ss. canonum*, Augsburg/Dillingen 1708: Apud Joannem Casparum Bencard.
Wolfius, Christianus, *Tabularum Mnemonicarum constructio et usus*, in Wolf, Christian, *Horae subsecivae Marburgenses*, vol. 2, Frankfurt/Leipzig 1732: Prostat in bibliop. Rengeriano, 468–513.

Literature

Adam, Wolfgang, *Poetische und kritische Wälder. Untersuchungen zu Geschichte und Formen des Schreibens „bei Gelegenheit“*, Heidelberg 1988.
Aimone, Pier V., “Alcune note sulla Abbreviatio Dunelmensis della Summa Simonis Bisinianensis”, in Goering, Joseph, Stephan Dusil and Andreas Thier (eds.), *Proceedings of the Fourteenth International Congress of Medieval Canon Law. Toronto, 5–11 August 2012*, Vatican City 2016, 179–197.
Alfieri, Fernanda, *Nella camera degli sposi. Tomás Sánchez, il matrimonio, la sessualità (secoli XVI–XVII)*, Bologna 2010.
Angelini, Paolo, “Annotazioni sull’epitome greca dell’Editto di Rotari”, Historia et ius 3 (2015), 1–13 (http://www.historiaetius.eu/uploads/5/9/4/8/5948821/angelini_7.pdf).
[Anon.,] “Alfred von Halban”, in Österreichischen Akademie der Wissenschaften (ed.), *Österreichisches Biographisches Lexikon 1815–1950*, vol. 2, Graz 1959, 157.
Arrieta, Juan Ignacio, “Fuero interno”, in *Diccionario general de derecho canónico*, vol. 4, Cizur Menor 2012, 139–144.
Atzeri, Lorena, *Gesta sentus Romani de Theodosiano publicando. Il Codice Teodosiano e la sua diffusione ufficiale in Occidente*, Berlin 2008.
Aubert, R., “Lequeux (Jean François Marie)”, in *Dictionnaire d’histoire et de géographie ecclésiastiques*, vol. 31, Paris 2015, col. 856–857.
Basdevant-Gaudemet, Brigitte, *Histoire du droit canonique et des institutions de l’Église latine. XVe–XXe siècle*, Paris 2014.
Becker, Hans-Jürgen, “Das kanonische Recht im vorreformatorischen Zeitalter”, in Boockmann, Hartmut, Ludger Grenzmann, Bernd Moeller and Martin Staehelin (eds.), *Recht und Verfassung im Übergang vom Mittelalter zur Neuzeit*, vol. 1, Göttingen 1998, 9–24.
Bergfeld, Christoph, “Katholische Moraltheologie und Naturrechtslehre”, in Coing, Helmut (ed.), *Handbuch der Quellen und Literatur der neueren europäischen Privatrechtsgeschichte*, vol 2.1: *Neuere Zeit (1500–1800). Das Zeitalter des gemeinen Rechts*, Munich 1977, 999–1033.

Bertram, Martin, "Casus legum sive suffragia monachorum. Legistische Hilfsmittel für Kanonisten im späteren Mittelalter (unter Mitarbeit von Marguerite Duynstee)", in *Tijdschrift voor Rechtsgeschiedenis* 51 (1983), 317–363 (reprint Bertram, Martin, *Kanonisten und ihre Texte (1234 bis Mitte 14. Jh.). 18 Aufsätze und 14 Exkurse*, Leiden 2013, 37–90).

Beyer, Alfred, *Lokale Abbreviationen des Decretum Gratiani. Analyse und Vergleich der Dekretabbreviationen "Omnes leges aut divine" (Bamberg), "Humanum genus duobus regitur" (Pommersfelden) und "De his qui intra clausura monasterii consistunt" (Lichtenthal, Baden-Baden)*, Frankfurt 1998.

Black, Winston, "Teaching the Mnemonic Bishop in the Medieval Canon Law Classroom", in Danielson, Sigrid and Evan A. Gatti (eds.), *Envisioning the Bishop: Images and the Episcopacy in the Middle Ages*, Turnhout 2014, 377–404.

Blair, Ann M., *Too Much to Know. Managing Scholarly Information before the Modern Age*, New Haven, CT 2010.

Boehmer, Heinrich, "Luther und der 10. Dezember 1520", in *Luther-Jahrbuch* 2–3 (1920–1921), 7–53.

Boyle, Leonard E., "Summae confessorum", in Bultot, Robert (ed.), *Les genres littéraires dans les sources théologiques et philosophiques médiévales. Définition, critique et exploitation. Actes du Colloque international de Louvain-la-Neuve 25–27 mai 1981*, Louvain-la-Neuve 1982, 227–237.

Brasington, Bruce C., "The Abbreviatio 'Exceptiones evangelicarum'. A Distinctive Regional Reception of Gratian's Decretum", in *Codices manuscripti* 17 (1994), 95–99.

Brendecke, Arndt, "Information in tabellarischer Disposition", in Grunert, Frank and Anette Syndikus (eds.), *Wissensspeicher der Frühen Neuzeit. Formen und Funktionen*, Berlin 2015, 43–59.

Brundage, James A., "E pluribus unum: Custom, the Professionalization of Medieval Law, and Regional Variations in Marriage Formation", in Korpiola, Mia (ed.), *Regional Variations in Matrimonial Law and Custom in Europe, 1150–1600*, Leiden 2011, 21–41.

Buzzi, Franco, "La tradizione teologica milanese tra Cinque e Seicento", in *Studia Borromaica* 21 (2007), 129–163.

Carrodeguas, Celestino, *La sacramentalidad del matrimonio. Doctrina de Tomás Sánchez, S.J.*, Madrid 2003.

Chadwick, Henry, "Florilegium", in *Reallexikon für Antike und Christentum*, vol. 7, Stuttgart 1969, col. 1131–1160.

Coma Fort, José Maria, *Codex Theodosianus. Historia de un texto*, Madrid 2014.

Conrat (Cohn), Max, *Geschichte der Quellen und Literatur des römischen Rechts im früheren Mittelalter*, vol. 1, Leipzig 1891 (repr. Aalen 1963).

Contreni, John J., "The Biblical Glosses of Haimo of Auxerre and John Scottus Eriugena", in *Speculum* 51 (1976), 411–434.

Contreni, John J., "Three Carolingian Texts from Laon: Reconsiderations", in *Studi medievali* 17 (1976), 797–813.

Contreni, John J., *The Cathedral School of Laon from 850 to 930. Its Manuscripts and Masters*, Munich 1978.

Cuena Boy, Francisco, "Exceso de leyes en Roma: ¿retórica o realidad?", in *Annaeus* 4 (2007), 3–27.

Dannenberg, Lars-Arne, "Der lange Arm des Gesetzes. Zur Stellung der franziskanischen Ordensorganisation im Lichte der Vorgaben des kirchlichen ius commune unter besonderer Berücksichtigung der Titelsumme Heinrichs von Merseburg", in Robson, Michael and Jens Röhrkasten (eds.), *Franciscan Organisation in the Mendicant Context. Formal and informal structures of the friars' lives and ministry in the Middle Ages*, Munster 2010, 331–352.

De Franceschi, Sylvio Hermann, "La papauté intransigeante et ses craintes d'un renouveau de régalisme gallican: La mise à l'Index du Manuale compendium iuris canonici de l'abbé Jean-François-Marie Lequeux", in De Franceschi, Sylvio Hermann and Bernard Hours (eds.), *Droits antiromains. Juridictionalisme catholique et romanité ecclésiale (XVIe–XIXe siècles)*, Lyon 2017, 215–253.

De Wall, Heinrich, "Böhmer, Georg Ludwig", in *Handwörterbuch zur deutschen Rechtsgeschichte*, 2nd ed., Berlin 2008, col. 639.

De Wall, Heinrich, "Böhmer, Justus Henning", in *Handwörterbuch zur deutschen Rechtsgeschichte*, vol. 1, 2nd ed., Berlin 2008, col. 640–641.

Dell'Olmo, Luciano and Rino Scuccimarra, *Il beato Angelo Carletti da Chiavasso e le edizioni della Summa Angelica nei secoli XV e XVI*, Chiavasso 1983.

Di Cintio, Lucia, *L'«Interpretatio Visigothorum» al «Codex Theodosianus». Il libro IX*, Milan 2013.

Di Cintio, Lucia, *Nuove ricerche sulla «Interpretatio Visigothorum» al «Codex Theodosianus». Libri I–II*, Milan 2018.

Doering, Lutz, "Fort- und Neuschreibung autoritativer Texte und Identitätsbildung im Jubiläenbuch sowie in Texten aus Qumran", in Grohmann, Marianne (ed.), *Identität und Schrift. Fortschreibungsprozesse als Mittel religiöser Identitätsbildung*, Göttingen 2017, 69–103.

Dolezalek, Gero and Rudolf Weigand, "Das Geheimnis der roten Zeichen. Ein Beitrag zur Paläographie juristischer Handschriften des zwölften Jahrhunderts", in *Zeitschrift der Savigny-Stiftung für Rechtsgeschichte. Kanonistische Abteilung* 69 (1983), 143–199.

Dove, Richard Wilhelm, "Aemilius Ludwig Richter", in *Zeitschrift für Kirchenrecht* 7 (1867), 273–404.

Dubischar, Markus, "Preserved Knowledge. Summaries and Compilations", in Hose, Martin and David Schenker (eds.), *A Companion to Greek Literature*, Chichester 2016, 427–440.

Dusil, Stephan, "Visuelle Wissensvermittlung in der Gratian-Handschrift Köln, Diözesan- und Dombibliothek, 128", in Horst, Harald (ed.), *Mittelalterliche Handschriften der Kölner Dombibliothek. Siebtes Symposion der Diözesan- und Dombibliothek Köln zu den Dom-Manuskripten (25. und 26. November 2016)*, Cologne 2018, 115–137.

Dusil, Stephan, "The Decretum of Gratian: A Janus-Faced Collection", in Rolker, Christof (ed.), *New Discourses in Medieval Canon Law Research. Challenging the Master Narrative*, Leiden 2019, 127–144.

Dusil, Stephan, Gerald Schwedler and Raphael Schwitter (eds.), *Exzerpieren – Kompilieren – Tradieren. Transformationen des Wissens zwischen Spätantike und Frühmittelalter*, Berlin 2017.

Dusil, Stephan, Gerald Schwedler and Raphael Schwitter, "Transformationen des Wissens zwischen Spätantike und Frühmittelalter. Zur Einführung", in Dusil, Stephan, Gerald Schwedler and Raphael Schwitter (eds.), *Exzerpieren – Kompilieren – Tradieren. Transformationen des Wissens zwischen Spätantike und Frühmittelalter*, Berlin 2017, 1–22.

Duval, André, "La Summa Conciliorum de Barthélemy Carranza", in *Revue des sciences philosophiques et théologiques* 41 (1957), 401–427.

Ertl, Thomas, *Religion und Disziplin. Selbstdeutung und Weltordnung im frühen deutschen Franziskanertum*, Berlin 2006.

Fantappiè, Carlo, *Chiesa romana e modernità giuridica*, vol. 1: *L'edificazione del sistema canonistica (1563–1903)*, Milan 2008.

Feola, Raffaele, "Canciani, Paolo", in *Dizionario biografico degli Italiani*, vol. 17, Rome 1974, 749–751.

Figueira, Robert C., "Ricardus de Mores and his Casus decretalium: the Birth of a Canonistic Genre", in Chodorow, Stanley (ed.), *Proceedings of the Eighth International Congress of Medieval Canon Law. San Diego, University of California at La Jolla, 21–27 August 1988*, Vatican City 1992, 168–187.

Fransen, Gérard, "Les abrégés de collections canoniques. Essai de typologie", in *Revue de droit canonique* 28 (1978), 157–166.

Fritsch, Matthias J., *Religiöse Toleranz im Zeitalter der Aufklärung. Naturrechtliche Begründung – konfessionelle Differenzen*, Hamburg 2004.

Frońska, Joanna, "Memory and the Making of Images: A Case of a Legal Manuscript", in *Manuscripta* 54 (2010), 1–20.

Frońska, Joanna, "Turning the Pages of Legal Manuscripts: Reading and Remembering the Law", in Zchomelidse, Nino and Giovanni Freni (eds.), *Meaning in Motion. Semantics of Movement in Medieval Art*, Princeton, NJ 2011, 191–214.

Frońska, Joanna, "The Memory of Roman Law in an Illuminated Manuscript of Justinian's Digest", in Brenner, Elma, Meredith Cohen and Mary Franklin-Brown (eds.), *Memory and Commemoration in Medieval Culture*, Farnham 2013, 163–179.

Furtenbach, Siegfried and Herbert Kalb, "Die Rechtsliteratur in volkssprachiger Überlieferung in Österreich", in Reiffenstein, Ingo (ed.), *Beiträge zur Überlieferung und Beschreibung deutscher Texte des Mittelalters*, Göppingen 1983, 115–138.

Galdi, Marco, *L'epitome nella letteratura latina*, Naples 1922.

Ganivet, Pierre, "L'«epitomé de Lyon»: un témoin de la réception du Bréviaire dans le Sud-Est de la Gaule au VIe siècle?", in Rouche, Michel and Bruno Dumézil (eds.), *Le Bréviaire d'Alaric. Aux origines du Code civil*, Paris 2008, 279–328.

Gaudemet, Jean, *Le Bréviaire d'Alaric et les Epitome*, Milan 1965.

Gaudemet, Jean, "Les vicissitudes du Gallicanisme", in *Studi in memoria di Pietro Gismondi*, vol. 2, Rome 1991, 43–70 (reprint Gaudemet, Jean, *La doctrine canonique médiévale*, Aldershot 1994, XIII).

Gebhardt, Ulrich C.J., *Sermo Iuris: Rechtssprache und Recht in der augusteischen Dichtung*, Leiden 2009.

Goering, Joseph, "The Internal Forum and the Literature of Penance and Confession", in Hartmann, Wilfried and Kenneth Pennington (eds.), *The History of Medieval Canon Law in the Classical Period, 1140–1234. From Gratian to the Decretals of Pope Gregory IX*, Washington, D.C. 2008, 379–428.

Gough, Austin, *Paris and Rome. The Gallican Church and the Ultramontane Campaign, 1848–1853*, Oxford 1986.

Grabmann, Martin, *Die Geschichte der scholastischen Methode*, vol. 2: *Die scholastische Methode im 12. und beginnenden 13. Jahrhundert*, Freiburg 1911 (repr. Graz 1957).

Grabmann, Martin, "Hilfsmittel des Thomasstudiums aus alter Zeit. (Abbreviationes, Concordantiae, Tabulae). Auf Grund handschriftlicher Forschungen dargestellt", in Grabmann, Martin (ed.), *Mittelalterliches Geistesleben. Abhandlungen zur Geschichte der Scholastik und Mystik*, vol. 2, Munich 1936, 424–489.

Grabmann, Martin, *Methoden und Hilfsmittel des Aristotelesstudiums im Mittelalter*, Munich 1939 (*Sitzungsberichte der Bayerischen Akademie der Wissenschaften. Philosophisch-historische Abteilung*, vol. 5).

Grabmann, Martin, "Das Weiterwirken des moraltheologischen Schrifttums des hl. Thomas von Aquin im Mittelalter", in *Divus Thomas* 24 (1947), 3–28 (reprint Steinbüchel, Theodor and Theodor Müncker (eds.), *Aus Philosophie und Theologie. Festschrift für Fritz Tillmann zu seinem 75. Geburtstag (1. November 1949)*, Dusseldorf 1950, 64–83).

Grosso, Giuseppe, "Meditazione su Tacito, sulla moltiplicazione delle leggi e sugli attuali sviluppi costituzionali", in *Studi in onore di Giuseppe Chiarelli*, vol. 4, Milan 1974, 3509–3519.

Guarino, Antonio, "La rimozione del diritto e l'esperienza romana", in *Labeo* 42 (1996), 7–36.

Halban, Alfred von, *Das römische Recht in den germanischen Volksstaaten*, vol. 2 & vol. 3, Breslau 1901 & 1907.

Hamesse, Jacqueline, "A propos de quelques techniques d'interprétation et de compilation des textes. Paraphrases, florilèges et compendia", in Meirinhos, José Francisco (ed.), *Itinéraires de la raison. Études de philosophie médiévale offertes à Maria Cândida Pacheco*, Louvain-la-Neuve 2005, 11–34.

Hamesse, Jacqueline, "«Florilège» et «autorité»: deux concepts en évolution depuis l'Antiquité jusqu'à la Renaissance", in Ceulemans, Reinhart and Pieter De Leemans (eds.), *On Good Authority. Tradition, Compilation and the Construction of Authority in Literature from Antiquity to the Renaissance*, Turnhout 2015, 199–225.

Harries, Jill, "Roman Law and Legal Culture", in Johnson, Scott Fitzgerald (ed.), *The Oxford Handbook of Late Antiquity*, Oxford 2012, 789–814.

Hathaway, Neil, "Compilatio: From Plagiarism to Compiling", in *Viator* 20 (1989), 19–44.

Heimann-Seelbach, Sabine, "Diagrammatik und Gedächtniskunst. Zur Bedeutung der Schrift für die Ars memorativa im 15. Jahrhundert", in Kintzinger, Martin, Sönke Lorenz and Michael Walter (eds.), *Schule und Schüler im Mittelalter. Beiträge zur europäischen Bildungsgeschichte des 9. bis 15. Jahrhunderts*, Cologne 1996, 385–408.

Hess, Gilbert, "Florilegien. Genese, Wirkungsweisen und Transformationen frühneuzeitlicher Kompilationsliteratur", in Grunert, Frank and Anette Syndikus (eds.), *Wissensspeicher der Frühen Neuzeit. Formen und Funktionen*, Berlin 2015, 97–138.

Holthöfer, Ernst, "Die Literatur zum gemeinen und partikularen Recht in Italien, Frankreich, Spanien und Portugal", in Coing, Helmut (ed.), *Handbuch der Quellen und Literatur der neueren europäischen Privatrechtsgeschichte*, vol 2.1: *Neuere Zeit (1500–1800). Das Zeitalter des gemeinen Rechts*, Munich 1977, 103–499.

Honsell, Heinrich, "Der Gesetzesstil in der römischen Antike", in Giuffrè, Vincenzo (ed.), *Sodalitas. Scritti in onore di Antonio Guarino*, vol. 4, Naples 1984, 1659–1673.

Horn, Norbert, "Die legistische Literatur der Kommentatoren und der Ausbreitung des gelehrten Rechts", in Coing, Helmut (ed.), *Handbuch der Quellen und Literatur der neueren europäischen Privatrechtsgeschichte*, vol. 1: *Mittelalter (1100–1500). Die gelehrten Rechte und die Gesetzgebung*, Munich 1973, 261–364.

Horster, Marietta and Christiane Reitz (eds.), *Condensing Texts – Condensed Texts*, Stuttgart 2010.

Horster, Marietta and Christiane Reitz, "Handbooks, Epitomes, and Florilegia", in McGill, Scott and Edward J. Watts (eds.), *A Companion to Late Antique Literature*, New York 2018, 431–450.

Hurter, Hugo, *Nomenclator literarius theologiae catholicae*, vol. 5,1, 3rd ed., Innsbruck 1911 (repr. New York 1963).

Hurtubise, Pierre, *La casuistique dans tous ses états. De Martin Azpilcueta à Alphonse de Liguori*, Montreal 2005.

Illich, Ivan, *In the Vineyard of the Text. A Commentary to Hugh's Didascalicon*, Chicago, IL 1993.

Kaiser, Wolfgang, "Vulgarrecht", in *Der neue Pauly. Enzyklopädie der Antike*, vol. 12.2, Stuttgart 2002, col. 350–351.

Kaiser, Wolfgang, *Die Epitome Iuliani. Beiträge zum römischen Recht im frühen Mittelalter und zum byzantinischen Rechtsunterricht*, Frankfurt 2004.

Kaiser, Wolfgang, "Verkürzt und wiederaufgefüllt? Review of: Ch. Radding/A. Ciaralli, The Corpus iuris in the Middle Ages. Manuscripts and Transmission from the Sixth Century to the Juristic Revival, Leiden/Boston 2007", in *Rechtsgeschichte* 11 (2007), 182–185.

Kaiser, Wolfgang, "Wandlungen im Verständnis der Epitome Iuliani von der Spätantike bis zur Gegenwart", in Avenarius, Martin (ed.), *Hermeneutik der Quellentexte des Römischen Rechts*, Baden-Baden 2008, 300–353.

Kannengiesser, Charles, "Tyconius of Carthage, the Earliest Latin Theoretician of Biblical Hermeneutics. The current debate", in Maritano, Mario (ed.), *Historiam perscrutari. Miscellanea di studi offerti al prof. Ottorino Pasquato*, Rome 2002, 297–311.

Kästle-Lamparter, David, *Welt der Kommentare. Struktur, Funktion und Stellenwert juristischer Kommentare in Geschichte und Gegenwart*, Tübingen 2016.

Kéry, Lotte, *Canonical Collections of the Early Middle Ages (ca. 400–1140). A Bibliographical Guide to the Manuscripts and Literature*, Washington, D.C. 1999.

Kéry, Lotte, "Forum externum, Forum internum", in *Handwörterbuch zur deutschen Rechtsgeschichte*, vol. 1, 2nd ed., Berlin 2008, col. 1641–1643.

Kessler, Stephan C., "Gregor der Große und seine Theorie der Exegese: die Epistula ad Leandrum", in *L'esegesi dei padri latini. Dalle origini a Gregorio Magno. XXVIII Incontro di studiosi dell'antichità cristiana*, vol. 2, Rome 2000, 691–700.

Kimmel, Christina, "Abbreviatio des Decretum Gratiani mit Ergänzungen", in Berschin, Walter and Kurt Hans Staub (eds.), *Fragmenta Darmstadiensia. Heidelberger Handschriften-Studien des Seminars für Lateinische Philologie des Mittelalters (III)*, Darmstadt 1997, 81–88.

Krüger, Paul, *Geschichte der Quellen und Literatur des Römischen Rechts*, 2nd ed., Munich 1912.

Kurtscheid, Bertrandus, "De studio juris canonici in Ordine Fratrum Minorum saeculo XIII", in *Antonianum* 2 (1927), 157–202.

Kuttner, Stephan, *Repertorium der Kanonistik (1140–1234). Prodromus Corporis Glossarum*, vol. 1, Vatican City 1937.

Kuttner, Stephan, "On the Place of Canon Law in a General History of Roman Law during the Middle Ages", in *Seminar* 13 (1955/1956), 51–55.

Kuttner, Stephan, "The Revival of Jurisprudence", in Benson, Robert L. and Giles Constable (eds.), *Renaissance and Renewal in the Twelfth Century*, Cambridge, MA 1982, 299–323 (reprint Kuttner, Stephan, *Studies in the History of Medieval Canon Law*, Aldershot 1990, (III), 5–7 (Retractationes)).

L'Engle, Susan, "The Pro-Active Reader: Learning to Learn the Law", in *Medieval Manuscripts, Their Makers and Users. A special issue of Viator in honor of Richard and Mary Rouse*, Turnhout 2011, 51–75.

Laistner, Max L.W., "Notes on Greek from the Lectures of a Ninth Century Monastery Teacher", in *Bulletin of the John Rylands Library* 7 (1923), 421–456.

Lambertini, Renzo, *La codificazione di Alarico II*, 2nd ed., Turin 1991.

Lambertini, Renzo, "Sull'«Epitome Gai» nel «Breviarium»", in *Labeo* 41 (1995), 229–238.

Landau, Peter, "Die Breviatio canonum des Ferrandus in der Geschichte des kanonischen Rechts. Zugleich nochmals zur Benutzung der Dionysiana bei Gratian", in Zapp, Hartmut, Andreas Weiß and Stefan Korta (eds.), *Ius canonicum in oriente et occidente. Festschrift für Carl Gerold Fürst zum 70. Geburtstag* Frankfurt 2003, 297–309.

Landau, Peter, "Gratian and the Decretum Gratiani", in Hartmann, Wilfried and Kenneth Pennington (eds.), *The History of Medieval Canon Law in the Classical Period, 1140–1234. From Gratian to the Decretals of Pope Gregory IX*, Washington, D.C. 2008, 22–54.

Landau, Peter, "Gratian", in *Handwörterbuch zur deutschen Rechtsgeschichte*, vol. 2, 2nd ed., Berlin 2012, col. 530–533.

Larson, Atria A., "An Abbreviatio of the First Recension of Gratian's Decretum in Munich?", in *Bulletin of Medieval Canon Law* 29 (2011/2012), 51–118.

Larson, Atria A., "Géneros literarios canónicos", in Otaduy, Javier, Antonio Viana and Joaquín Sedano (eds.), *Diccionario general de derecho* canónico, vol. 4, Cizur Menor 2012, 189–192.

Lauro, Agostino, "Devoti, Giovanni", in *Dizionario biografico degli italiani*, vol. 39, Rome 1991, 598–603.

León, Enrique de, "La abreviación 'quoniam egestas' del Decreto de Graciano", in Erdö, Péter and Szabolcs Anzelm Szuromi (eds.), *Proceedings of the Thirteenth International Congress of Medieval Canon Law. Esztergom, 3–8 August 2008*, Vatican City 2010, 303–310.

León, Enrique de, "Abbreviatio", in *Diccionario general de derecho canónico*, vol. 1, Cizur Menor 2012, 66–68.

Liebs, Detlef, *Hermogenians iuris epitomae. Zum Stand der römischen Jurisprudenz im Zeitalter Diokletians*, Göttingen 1964.

Liebs, Detlef, " 'Variae lectiones' (Zwei Juristenschriften)", in *Studi in onore di Edoardo Volterra*, vol. 5, Milan 1971, 51–88.

Liebs, Detlef, "Recht und Rechtsliteratur", in Herzog, Reinhart (ed.), *Handbuch der lateinischen Literatur der Antike*, vol. 5: *Restauration und Erneuerung. Die lateinische Literatur von 284 bis 374 n.Chr.*, Munich 1989, 55–73.

Liebs, Detlef, "Jurisprudenz", in Sallmann, Klaus (ed.), *Handbuch der lateinischen Literatur der Antike*, vol. 4: *Die Literatur des Umbruchs. Von der römischen zur christlichen Literatur 117 bis 284 n. Chr.*, Munich 1997, 83–217.

Liebs, Detlef, *Römische Jurisprudenz in Gallien (2. bis 8. Jahrhundert)*, Berlin 2002.

Liebs, Detlef, "Zur Überlieferung und Entstehung des Breviarium Alaricianum", in Crifò, Giuliano and Stefano Giglio (eds.), *Atti dell'Accademia romanistica costantiniana. XIV Convegno internazionale in memoria di Guglielmo Nocera*, Naples 2003, 653–671.

Liebs, Detlef, "Nachklassische römische Rechtsliteratur", in Thür, Gerhard (ed.), *Antike Rechtsgeschichte. Einheit und Vielfalt*, Vienna 2005, 27–42.

Liebs, Detlef, "Roman Vulgar Law in Late Antiquity", in Sirks, Boudewijn (ed.), *Aspects of Law in Late Antiquity. Dedicated to A.M. Honoré on the occasion of the sixtieth year of his teaching in Oxford*, Oxford 2008, 35–53.

Liebs, Detlef, "Das Verbot von Mischehen im germanisch-römischen Recht", in Giglio, Stefano (ed.), *Atti dell'Accademia romanistica costantiniana. XVII convegno internazionale in onore di Giuliano Crifò*, vol. 1, Rome 2010, 622–628.

Liebs, Detlef, "Legis Romanae Visigothorum Epitomen Sangallensem traditam in codice 731 bibliothecae dictae Stiftsbibliothek descripto a Vandalgario mense Octobris anni 793 p. Chr. n. (paginis 1–230), cum praefatione ratiocinans transscripsit", in *Zeitschrift der Savigny-Stiftung für Rechtsgeschichte. Romanistische Abteilung* 129 (2012), 1–112.

Liebs, Detlef, "Römischrechtliche Glut aus dem 8. Jh. für ein Bischofsgericht in Burgund", in Liebs, Detlef, *Das Recht der Römer und die Christen. Gesammelte Aufsätze in überarbeiteter Fassung*, Tübingen 2015, 256–274.

Liebs, Detlef, "Scintilla de libro legum. L'Epitome Fuldense del Breviario Alariciano", in Bassanelli Sommariva, Gisella and Simona Tarozzi (eds.), *Ravenna capitale. Codice Teodosiano e tradizioni giuridiche in Occidente. La terra, strumento di arricchimento e sopravivenza*, Santarcangelo di Romagna 2016, 279–304.

Liebs, Detlef, "Warum endete gegen Mitte des 3. Jahrhunderts die klassische Rechtsliteratur?", in Eich, Armin, Stefan Freund, Meike Rühl and Christoph Schubert (eds.), *Das dritte Jahrhundert. Kontinuitäten, Brüche, Übergänge. Ergebnisse der Tagung der Mommsen-Gesellschaft am 21.-22.11.2014 an der Bergischen Universität Wuppertal*, Stuttgart 2017, 57–73.

Liebs, Detlef, "Wenn Fachliteratur Gesetz wird. Inwieweit wurden römische Juristenschriften im Laufe der Jahrhunderte überarbeitet?", in *Zeitschrift der Savigny-Stiftung für Rechtsgeschichte. Romanistische Abteilung* 135 (2018), 395–473.

Lizzi, Rita, "La memoria selettiva", in Cavallo, Guglielmo, Paolo Fedeli and Andrea Giardina (eds.), *Lo spazio letterario di Roma antica*, vol. 3, Rome 1990, 647–676.

Llauró, Juan, "Los glossarios de Ripoll", in *Analecta Sacra Tarraconensia* 3 (1927), 331–389.

Löhr, Joseph, *Das Preußische Allgemeine Landrecht und die Katholischen Kirchengesellschaften*, Paderborn 1917.

Mantovani, Dario, "Legum multitudo e dritto privato. Revisione critica della tesi di Giovanni Rotondi", in Ferrary, Jean-Louis (ed.), *Leges publicae. La legge nell'esperienza giuridica romana*, Pavia 2012, 707–767.

Mantovani, Dario, *Legum multitudo. Die Bedeutung der Gesetze im römischen Privatrecht. Nachwort: Jakob F. Stagl, Juristenrecht und Gesetzesrecht*, Berlin 2018.

Martin, Norbert, *Die 'Compilatio Decretorum' des Kardinals Laborans. Eine Umarbeitung des gratianischen Dekrets aus dem 12. Jahrhundert* (*Ph.D. Thesis*), Heidelberg 1994.

Martini, Remo, "Qualche osservazione a proposito della c.d. Epitome Gai", in Crifò, Giuliano and Stefano Giglio (eds.), *Atti dell'Accademia romanistica costantiniana. XIV Convegno internazionale in memoria di Guglielmo Nocera*, Naples 2003, 615–627.

Matthews, John F., "Interpreting the Interpretationes on the Breviarium", in Mathisen, Ralph W. (ed.), *Law, Society, and Authority in Late Antiquity*, Oxford 2001, 11–32.

Mazzacane, Aldo, "El jurista y la memoria", in Petit, Carlos (ed.), *Pasiones del jurista. Amor, memoria, melancolía, imaginación*, Madrid 1997, 75–102.

Meder, Stephan, *Rechtsgeschichte. Eine Einführung*, 6th ed., Cologne 2017.

Meyer, Christoph H.F., *Die Distinktionstechnik in der Kanonistik des 12. Jahrhunderts. Ein Beitrag zur Wissenschaftsgeschichte des Hochmittelalters*, Louvain 2000.

Meyer, Christoph H.F., "Spuren im Wald der Erinnerung. Zur Mnemotechnik in Theologie und Jurisprudenz des 12. Jahrhunderts", in *Recherches de théologie et philosophie médiévales* 67 (2000), 10–57.

Meyer, Christoph H.F., "Ordnung durch Ordnen. Die Erfassung und Gestaltung des hochmittelalterlichen Kirchenrechts im Spiegel von Texten, Begriffen und Institutionen", in Schneidmüller, Bernd and Stefan Weinfurter (eds.), *Ordnungskonfigurationen im hohen Mittelalter*, Ostfildern 2006, 303–411.

Meyer, Christoph H.F., "Kanonistik im Zeitalter von Absolutismus und Aufklärung: Spielräume und Potentiale einer Disziplin im Spannungsfeld von Kirche, Staat und Publizität", *Max Planck Institute for European Legal History Research Paper Series* No. 2018–6 (https://ssrn.com/abstract=2184754).

Michaud-Quantin, Pierre, "Les méthodes de la pastorale du XIIIe au XVe siècle", in Zimmermann, Albert (ed.), *Methoden in Wissenschaft und Kunst des Mittelalters*, Berlin 1970, 76–91.

Michel, Paul, "Wo das Lamm watet und der Elefant schwimmt. Eine Darstellung von Gregors des Großen Epistola dedicatoria zu den Moralia in Iob", in Herwig, Henriette, Irmgard Wirtz and Stefan Bodo Würffel (eds.), *Lese – Zeichen. Semiotik und Hermeneutik in Raum und Zeit. Festschrift für Peter Rusterholz zum 65. Geburtstag*, Tübingen 1999, 71–86.

Michelitsch, Antonius, *Kommentatoren zur Summa Theologiae des hl. Thomas von Aquin*, Graz 1924 (repr. Hildesheim 1981).

Montanos Ferrín, Emma, "A modo de consulta sobre la literatur jurídica del ius commune, III: summa angelica", in *Anuario da Facultade de Dereito da Universidade da Coruña* 8 (2004), 1114–1146.

Montorzi, Mario, "Processi di 'standardizzazione' testuale: margaritae, gemmae, tabulae. Un primo approccio di studio", in Montorzi, Mario, *Processi istituzionali. Episodi*

di formalizzazione giuridica ed evenienze d'aggregazione istituzionale attorno ed oltro il feudo. Saggi e documenti, Padua 2005, 51–69.
Moore, Philip S., *The Works of Peter of Poitiers Master in Theology and Chancellor of Paris (1193–1205)*, Washington, D.C. 1936.
Moschetti, Guiscardo, *Primordi esegetici sulla legislazione longobarda nel sec. IX a Verona. Secondo il Cod. Vat. Lat. 5359*, Spoleto 1954.
Mosiek, Ulrich, *Die probati auctores in den Ehenichtigkeitsprozessen der S.R. Rota seit Inkrafttreten des Codex Iuris Canonici*, Freiburg 1959.
Mülke, Markus, *Der Autor und sein Text. Die Verfälschung des Originals im Urteil antiker Autoren*, Berlin 2008.
Müller, Jörg, "Heinrich v. Merseburg", in *Lexikon für Kirchen- und Staatskirchenrecht*, vol. 2, Paderborn 2002, col. 232–233.
Müller, Wolfgang P., "Review of: Ch. Radding/A. Ciaralli, The Corpus iuris in the Middle Ages. Manuscripts and Transmission from the Sixth Century to the Juristic Revival, Leiden/Boston 2007", in *Speculum* 83 (2008), 1026–1027.
Munier, Charles, "La tradition manuscrite de l'Abrégé d'Hippone et le canon des Écritures des églises africaines", in *Sacris erudiri* 21 (1972/1973), 43–55 (reprint Munier, Charles, *Vie conciliaire et collections canoniques en Occident, IVe–XIIe siècles*, London 1987, V).
Musson, Anthony, "Seeing Justice: The Visual Culture of the Law and Lawyers", in Speer, Andreas and Guy Guldentops (eds.), *Das Gesetz – The Law – La Loi*, Berlin 2014, 711–721.
Nacci, Matteo, *Origini, sviluppi e caratteri del jus publicum ecclesiasticum*, Vatican City 2010.
Naz, Raoul, "Tabula alphabetica juris", in *Dictionnaire de droit canonique*, vol. 7, Paris 1965, col. 1145–1146.
Nehlsen, Hermann, "Aktualität und Effektivität der ältesten germanischen Rechtsaufzeichnungen", in Classen, Peter (ed.), *Recht und Schrift im Mittelalter*, Sigmaringen 1977, 449–502.
Nehlsen, Hermann, "Alarich als Gesetzgeber. Zur Geschichte der Lex Romana Visigothorum", in Landwehr, Götz (ed.), *Studien zu den germanischen Volksrechten. Gedächtnisschrift für Wilhelm Ebel*, Frankfurt 1982, 143–203.
Nemo-Pekelman, Capucine, "How did the authors of the Breviarium Alaricianum work? The example of the laws on Jews", in *Historical Research* 86 (2013), 408–415.
Nörr, Dieter, *Rechtskritik in der römischen Antike*, Munich 1974.
Nörr, Dieter, "Zum Traditionalismus der römischen Juristen", in Jakobs, Horst Heinrich, Brigitte Knobbe-Keuk, Eduard Picker and Jan Wilhelm (eds.), *Festschrift für Werner Flume zum 70. Geburtstag*, vol. 1, Munich 1978, 153–190.
Ocker, Christopher, "The Fusion of Papal Ideology and Biblical Exegesis in the Fourteenth Century", in Burrows, Mark Stephen (ed.), *Biblical Hermeneutics in Historical*

Perspective. Studies in honor of Karlfried Froehlich, on his sixtieth birthday, Grand Rapids, MI 1991, 131–151.

Ocker, Christopher, *Johannes Klenkok: A Friar's Life, c. 1310–1374*, Philadelphia, PA 1993.

Ohst, Martin, *Pflichtbeichte. Untersuchungen zum Bußwesen im Hohen und Späten Mittelalter*, Tübingen 1995.

Opelt, Ilona, "Epitome", in *Reallexikon für Antike und Christentum*, vol. 5, Stuttgart 1962, col. 944–973.

Otte, Gerhard, "Die Rechtswissenschaft", in Weimar, Peter (ed.), *Die Renaissance der Wissenschaften im 12. Jahrhundert*, Zurich 1981, 123–142.

Ourliac, Paul and Henri Gilles, *La période post-classique (1378–1500)*, vol. 1: *La problématique de l'époche. Les sources* (Histoire du Droit et des Institutions de l'Église en Occident, vol. 13), Paris 1971.

Parkes, Malcolm B., "The Influence of the Concepts of Ordinatio and Compilatio on the Development of the Book", in Alexander, Jonathan J.G. and Margaret T. Gibson (eds.), *Medieval Learning and Literature. Essays presented to Richard Willliam Hunt*, Oxford 1976, 115–141.

Pennington, Kenneth, "Decretal Collections", in Hartmann, Wilfried and Kenneth Pennington (eds.), *The History of Medieval Canon Law in the Classical Period, 1140–1234. From Gratian to the Decretals of Pope Gregory IX*, Washington, D.C. 2008, 293–317.

Pennington, Kenneth and Wolfgang Müller, "The Decretists: The Italian School", in Hartmann, Wilfried and Kenneth Pennington (eds.), *The History of Medieval Canon Law in the Classical Period, 1140–1234. From Gratian to the Decretals of Pope Gregory IX*, Washington, D.C. 2008, 121–173.

Périès, George, *La Faculté de droit dans l'ancienne Université de Paris (1160–1793)*, Paris 1890.

Prinz, Franziska, *Der Bildgebrauch in gedruckten Rechtsbüchern des 15. bis zum Ausgang des 18. Jahrhunderts*, Hamburg 2006.

Radding, Charles A. and Antonio Ciaralli, *The Corpus Iuris Civilis in the Middle Ages. Manuscripts and transmission from the sixth century to the juristic revival*, Leiden 2007.

Raible, Wolfgang, "Arten des Kommentierens – Arten der Sinnbildung – Arten des Verstehens. Spielarten der generischen Intertextualität", in Assmann, Jan and Burkhard Gladigow (eds.), *Text und Kommentar*, Munich 1995, 51–73.

Rambaud-Buhot, Jacqueline, "Les divers types d'abrégés du Décret de Gratien. De la table au commentaire", in *Recueil de travaux offerts à M. Clovis Brunel membre de l'Institut, directeur honnoraire de l'École des chartes*, vol. 2, Paris 1955, 397–411.

Rambaud-Buhot, Jacqueline, "L'Abbreviatio Decreti d'Omnebene", in Kuttner, Stephan and Kenneth Pennington (eds.), *Proceedings of the Sixth International Congress of Medieval Canon Law. Berkeley, California, 28 July-2 August 1980*, Vatican City 1985, 93–107.

Richter, Aemilius Ludwig, *Beiträge zum Preussischen Kirchenrechte*, ed. Hinschius, Paul, Leipzig 1856.

Rivers, Kimberly A., "Remembering Canon and Civil Law around 1400", in *Nottingham Medieval Studies* 56 (2012), 265–280.

Rivers, Kimberly A., "Learning and Remembering Canon Law in the Fifteenth Century: The Ars et doctrina studendi et docendi of Juan Alfonso de Benavente", in Sharp, Tristan (ed.), *From Learning to Love. Schools, Law, and Pastoral Care in the Middle Ages. Essays in Honour of Joseph W. Goering*, Toronto 2017, 266–290.

Röhl, Klaus F., "(Juristisches) Wissen über Bilder vermitteln", in Dausendschön-Gay, Ulrich, Christine Domke and Sören Ohlhus (eds.), *Wissen in (Inter-)Aktion. Verfahren der Wissensgenerierung in unterschiedlichen Praxisfeldern*, Berlin 2010, 281–311.

Rotondi, Giovanni, *Leges publicae populi romani. Elenco cronologico con una introduzione sull' attività legislatoria dei comizi romani. Estratto della Enciclopedia Giuridica Italiana*, Milan 1912 (repr. Hildesheim 1966).

Roumy, Franck, "Un abrégé inconnu du Décret de Gratien", in Bontems, Claude (ed.), *Nonagesimo anno. Mélanges en hommage à Jean Gaudemet*, Paris 1999, 501–519.

Rouse, Mary A., "Florilegia", in *Dictionary of the Middle Ages*, vol. 5, New York 1985, 109–110.

Rouse, Mary A. and Richard H. Rouse, "La naissance des index", in Chartier, Roger and Henri-Jean Martin (eds.), *Histoire de l'édition française*, vol. 1, Paris 1989, 95–108.

Rouse, Richard H. and Mary A. Rouse, "Statim invenire. Schools, Preachers, and New Attitudes to the Page", in Benson, Robert L. and Giles Constable (eds.), *Renaissance and Renewal in the Twelfth Century*, Cambridge, MA 1982, 201–225.

Ruiz Jurado, Manuel, "De las Constituciones S.J. al Epítome", in McCoog, Thomas M. (ed.), *Ite inflammate omnia. Selected historical papers from conferences held at Loyola and Rome in 2006*, Rome 2010, 129–147.

Sánchez-Moreno Ellart, Carlos, "Law, 'vulgar' ", in *The Encyclopedia of Ancient History*, vol. 7, Malden, MA 2013, 3975–3978.

Santucci, Gianni, "Legum inopia e diritto privato. Riflessioni intorno ad un recente contributo", in *Studia et documenta historiae et iuris* 80 (2014), 373–393.

Schadt, Hermann, *Die Darstellungen der Arbores Consanguinitatis und der Arbores Affinitatis. Bildschemata in juristischen Handschriften*, Tübingen 1982.

Scherer, Rudolf von, *Handbuch des Kirchenrechtes*, vol. 1, Graz 1886.

Schiller, Arthur A., *Roman Law. Mechanisms of Development*, The Hague 1978.

Schindler, Karl-Heinz, *Justinians Haltung zur Klassik. Versuch einer Darstellung an Hand seiner Kontroversen entscheidenden Konstitutionen*, Cologne 1966.

Schmidt-Wiegand, Ruth, "Rechtsverse", in *Handwörterbuch zur deutschen Rechtsgeschichte*, vol. 4, Berlin 1990, col. 410–415.

Schmidt-Wiegand, Ruth, "Populärjurisprudenz zwischen Artesliteratur und Richterlichem Clagspiegel", in Wich-Reif, Claudia (ed.), *Strukturen und Funktionen in*

Gegenwart und Geschichte. Festschrift für Franz Simmler zum 65. Geburtstag, Berlin 2007, 537–554.

Schmitt, Cl., "Jacques Ungarelli", in *Catholicisme: hier, auhourd'hui, demain*, vol. 6, Paris 1967, col. 287–288.

Schmoeckel, Mathias, "Beichtstuhljurisprudenz", in *Handwörterbuch zur deutschen Rechtsgeschichte*, vol. 1, 2nd ed., Berlin 2008, col. 505–508.

Schönberger, Rolf, *Was ist Scholastik?*, Hildesheim 1991.

Schott, Clausdieter, "Pactus, Lex und Recht", in Hübener, Wolfgang (ed.), *Die Alemannen in der Frühzeit*, Bühl 1974, 135–168.

Schulte, Johann Friedrich von, "Zur Geschichte der Literatur über das Dekret Gratians. Dritter Beitrag", in *Sitzungsberichte der kaiserlichen Akademie der Wissenschaften Wien. Philosophisch-historische Klasse* 65 (1870), 21–76.

Schulte, Johann Friedrich von, *Die Geschichte der Quellen und Literatur des canonischen Rechts*, vol. 2, Stuttgart 1877 (repr. Graz 1956).

Schulte, Johann Friedrich von, *Die Geschichte der Quellen und Literatur des canonischen Rechts*, vol. 3.1 & vol. 3.2–3, Stuttgart 1880 (repr. Graz 1956).

Schulz, Fritz, *Principles of Roman Law*, Oxford 1936.

Schulz, Fritz, *History of Roman Legal Science*, 2nd ed., Oxford 1953.

Schwerin, Claudius von, "Die Epitome Guelferbytana zum Breviarium Alaricianum", in *Atti del Congresso internazionale di diritto romano* (*Bologna e Roma XVII–XXVII Aprile MCMXXXIII*), vol. 1, Bologna 1934, 167–196.

Schwind, Fritz, *Zur Frage der Publikation im Römischen Recht mit Ausblicken in das altgriechische und ptolemäische Rechtsgebiet*, 2nd ed., Munich 1973.

Seckel, Emil, *Das römische Recht und seine Wissenschaft im Wandel der Jahrhunderte. Rede zum Antritt des Rektorates der Friedrich-Wilhelms-Universität in Berlin gehalten in der Aula am 15. Oktober 1920*, Berlin 1921.

[Seckel, Emil,] "Die Vorträge Emil Seckels in der Berliner Mittwochs-Gesellschaft (Teil 3, X.–XVI.) […], herausgegeben von Werner Schhubert", in *Zeitschrift der Savigny-Stiftung für Rechtsgeschichte. Romanistische Abteilung* 123 (2006), 349–374.

Sedano, Joaquín, "Breviarium", in *Diccionario general de derecho canónico*, vol. 1, Cizur Menor 2012, 753–754.

Sieben, Hermann Josef, *Die katholische Konzilsidee von der Reformation bis zur Aufklärung*, Paderborn 1988.

Sieben, Hermann Josef, *Kleines Lexikon zur Geschichte der Konzilsidee*, Paderborn 2018.

Siems, Harald, "Zu Problemen der Bewertung frühmittelalterlicher Rechtstexte. Zugleich eine Besprechung von R. Kottje, Zum Geltungsbereich der Lex Alamannorum", in *Zeitschrift der Savigny-Stiftung für Rechtsgeschichte. Germanistische Abteilung* 106 (1989), 291–305.

Siems, Harald, *Handel und Wucher im Spiegel frühmittelalterlicher Rechtsquellen*, Hannover 1992.

Siems, Harald, "Adsimilare. Die Analogie als Wegbereiterin zur mittelalterlichen Rechtswissenschaft", in Herbers, Klaus (ed.), *Europa an der Wende vom 11. zum 12. Jahrhundert. Beiträge zu Ehren von Werner Goez*, Stuttgart 2001, 143–170.

Sirks, A.J.B., *The Theodosian Code. A study*, Friedrichsdorf 2007.

Soliva, Claudio, "Römisches Recht in Churrätien", in *Jahrbuch der Historisch-Antiquarischen Gesellschaft von Graubünden* 116 (1986), 189–206.

Speer, Heino, "Verstehenshilfen zum geschriebenen Recht – Medienwandel als Chance. Eine Skizze", in Speer, Heino (ed.), *Wort – Bild – Zeichen. Beiträge zur Semiotik im Recht*, Heidelberg 2012, 225–252.

Spitz, Hans-Jörg, *Die Metaphorik des geistigen Schriftsinns. Ein Beitrag zur allegorischen Bibelauslegung des ersten christlichen Jahrtausends*, Munich 1972.

Spruit, Johannes E., "Visions fugitives", in Feenstra, Robert, Arthur S. Hartkamp, Johannes E. Spruit, Pieter Johannes Sijpesteijn and Laurens C. Winkel (eds.), *Collatio iuris romani. Études dédiées à Hans Ankum à l'occasion de son 65e anniversaire*, vol. 2, Amsterdam 1995, 489–497.

Stagl, Jakob Fortunat, "Die Bedeutung von leges publicae im Römischen Recht: Der Beitrag Mantovanis zur „legum multitudo" und die Frage der Privatautonomie bei den Römern", in *Zeitschrift der Savigny-Stiftung. Romanistische Abteilung* 133 (2016), 445–458.

Stein, Robert, "Alte und neue Übersichtstafeln. Ein Beitrag zur Geschichte der Unterrichtsmittel und eine Anregung zu erneuter Verwendung", in *Deutsche Geschichtsblätter* 17 (1916), 167–192, 226–248.

Stickler, Alphonsus M., *Historia iuris canonici latini. Institutiones academicae*, vol. 1: *Historia fontium*, Turin 1950.

Stintzing, Roderich, *Geschichte der populären Literatur des römisch-kanonischen Rechts in Deutschland am Ende des fünfzehnten und im Anfang des sechszehnten Jahrhunderts*, Leipzig 1867.

Stintzing, Roderich, *Geschichte der deutschen Rechtswissenschaft*, vol. 1, Munich 1880.

Stolleis, Michael, "Vom Verschwinden verbrauchten Rechts", in Kiesow, Rainer Maria, Regina Ogorek and Spiros Simitis (eds.), *Summa. Dieter Simon zum 70. Geburtstag*, Frankfurt 2005, 539–558.

Stolleis, Michael, "Corpus Iuris Civilis par cœur", in Haferkamp, Hans-Peter and Tilman Repgen (eds.), *Usus modernus pandectarum. Römisches Recht, Deutsches Recht und Naturrecht in der Frühen Neuzeit. Klaus Luig zum 70. Geburtstag*, Cologne 2007, 245–269.

Stolleis, Michael, "Vom Umgang mit veralteten Büchern, oder: Mit den Toten sprechen", in Nolte, Jakob, Ralf Poscher and Henner Wolter (eds.), *Die Verfassung als Aufgabe von Wissenschaft, Praxis und Öffentlichkeit. Freundesgabe für Bernhard Schlink zum 70. Geburtstag*, Heidelberg 2014, 15–24.

Taliadoros, John, *Law and Theology in Twelfth-Century England. The Works of Master Vacarius (c. 1115/20–c. 1200)*, Turnhout 2006.

Tardif, Ernest-Joseph, "Un abrégé juridique des Étymologies d'Isidore de Séville", in Tardif, Ernest-Joseph (ed.), *Mélanges Julien Havet. Recueil des travaux d'érudition dédiés à la mémoire de Julien Havet (1853–1893)*, Paris 1895, 659–681.

Thesaurus linguae Latinae, vol. 5.2, Leipzig 1931–1953.

Trump, Dominik, "Römisches Recht in Reims: Ein Exzerpt aus der Epitome Aegidii in der Handschrift Mailand, Biblioteca Ambrosiana, A. 46 inf.", in *Zeitschrift der Savigny-Stiftung für Rechtsgeschichte. Romanistische Abteilung* 133 (2016), 322–371.

Trusen, Winfried, *Anfänge des gelehrten Rechts in Deutschland. Ein Beitrag zur Geschichte der Frührezeption*, Wiesbaden 1962.

Trusen, Winfried, "Forum internum und gelehrtes Recht im Spätmittelalter. Summae confessorum und Traktate als Wegbereiter der Rezeption", in *Zeitschrift der Savigny-Stiftung für Rechtsgeschichte. Kanonistische Abteilung* 57 (1971), 83–126.

Trusen, Winfried, "Zur Bedeutung des geistlichen Forum internum und externum für die spätmittelalterliche Gesellschaft", in *Zeitschrift der Savigny-Stiftung für Rechtsgeschichte. Kanonistische Abteilung* 76 (1990), 254–285.

Ullmann, Walter, "The Paleae in Cambridge Manuscripts of the Decretum", in *Studia Gratiana* 1 (1953), 161–216.

Van Hove, Alphonse, *Prolegomena* (Commentarium Lovaniense in Codicem Iuris Canonici), vol. 1.1, 2nd ed., Mechlin 1945.

Varga, Csaba, *Codification as a Socio-Historical Phenomenon*, Budapest 1991.

Vetulani, Adam and Wacław Uruszczak, "L'œuvre d'Omnebene dans le MS 602 de la Bibliothèque municipale de Cambrai", in Kuttner, Stephan (ed.), *Proceedings of the Fourth International Congress of Medieval Canon Law. Toronto, 21–25 August 1972*, Vatican City 1976, 11–26.

Viora, Mario E., "La Summa Angelica", in *Bollettino storico-bibliografico subalpino* 38 (1936), 443–451.

Waelkens, Laurent, "Le Décret de Gratien, un florilège de textes juridiques des années 1130", in Ceulemans, Reinhart and Pieter de Leemans (eds.), *On Good Authority. Tradition, Compilation and the Construction of Authority in Literature from Antiquity to the Renaissance*, Turnhout 2015, 245–262.

Wei, John C., "The Later Development of Gratian's Decretum", in Goering, Joseph, Stephan Dusil and Andreas Thier (eds.), *Proceedings of the Fourteenth International Congress of Medieval Canon Law. Toronto, 5–11 August 2012*, Vatican City 2016, 149–159.

Weigand, Rudolf, "Die frühen kanonistischen Schulen und die Dekretabbreviatio Omnebenes", in *Archiv für katholisches Kirchenrecht* 155 (1986), 72–91.

Weigand, Rudolf, "Die Dekretabbreviatio 'Quoniam egestas' und ihre Glossen", in Aymans, Winfried, Anna Egler and Joseph Listl (eds.), *Fides et ius. Festschrift für Georg May zum 65. Geburtstag*, Regensburg 1991, 249–265.

Weigand, Rudolf, "Die Dekretabbreviatio 'Exceptiones ecclesiasticarum regularum' und ihre Glossen", in Alzati, Cesare (ed.), *Cristianità ed Europa. Miscellanea di studi in onore di Luigi Prosdocimi, Cesare Alzati*, vol. 1,2, Rome 1994, 511–529.

Weimar, Peter, "Die legistische Literatur der Glossatorenzeit", in Coing, Helmut (ed.), *Handbuch der Quellen und Literatur der neueren europäischen Privatrechtsgeschichte*, vol. 1: *Mittelalter (1100–1500). Die gelehrten Rechte und die Gesetzgebung*, Munich 1973, 129–260.

Weiß, Egon, "Schwund und Konservierung im römischen juristischen Schrifttum", in *Zeitschrift der Savigny-Stiftung für Rechtsgeschichte. Romanistische Abteilung* 67 (1950), 501–511.

Wejwoda, Marek, *Spätmittelalterliche Jurisprudenz zwischen Rechtspraxis, Universität und kirchlicher Karriere. Der Leipziger Jurist und Naumburger Bischof Dietrich von Bocksdorf (ca. 1410–1466)*, Leiden 2012.

Wesjohann, Achim, "Simplicitas als franziskanisches Ideal und der Prozeß der Institutionalisierung des Minoritenordens", in Melville, Gert and Jörg Oberste (eds.), *Die Bettelorden im Aufbau. Beiträge zu Institutionalisierungsprozessen im mittelalterlichen Religiosentum*, Munster 1999, 107–167.

Wieacker, Franz, *Textstufen klassischer Juristen*, Göttingen 1960.

Wieacker, Franz, *Römische Rechtsgeschichte. Zweiter Abschnitt: Die Jurisprudenz vom frühen Prinzipat bis zum Ausgang der Antike im weströmischen Reich und die oströmische Rechtswissenschaft bis zur justinianischen Gesetzgebung. Ein Fragment*, ed. Wolf, Joseph Georg, Munich 2006.

Winroth, Anders, *The Making of Gratian's Decretum*, Cambridge 2000.

Winroth, Anders, "Where Gratian Slept: The Life and Death of the Father of Canon Law", in *Zeitschrift der Savigny-Stiftung für Rechtsgeschichte. Kanonistische Abteilung* 99 (2013), 105–128.

Winter, Steven L., "A Clearing in the Forest", in *Metaphor and Symbolic Activity* 10 (1995), 223–245.

Wittekind, Susanne, "Überlegungen zur Verwendung graphischer Marginalien in Rechtshandschriften ausgehend von Dom-Handschrift 127", in Horst, Harald (ed.), *Mittelalterliche Handschriften der Kölner Dombibliothek. Siebtes Symposion der Diözesan- und Dombibliothek Köln zu den Dom-Manuskripten (25. und 26. November 2016)*, Cologne 2018, 83–114.

Wölfflin, Eduard, "Epitome", in *Archiv für lateinische Lexikographie und Grammatik* 12 (1902), 333–344.

Worstbrock, Franz Josef, "Libri pauperum. Zu Entstehung, Struktur und Gebrauch einiger mittelalterlicher Buchformen der Wissensliteratur seit dem 12. Jahrhundert", in Meier, Christel, Dagmar Hüpper and Hagen Keller (eds.), *Der Codex im Gebrauch*, Munich 1996, 41–60.

Zapp, Hartmut, "Abbreviationes", in *Lexikon des Mittelalters*, vol. 1, Munich 1980, col. 16.

CHAPTER 3

The Circulation of Pragmatic Normative Literature in Spanish America (16th–17th Centuries)

Otto Danwerth

1 Introduction

By the third decade of the 16th century, in the wake of the conquests of Mexico and Peru, the Spanish monarchy was confronted with the task of establishing its dominion over huge populations and across vast distances in Central and South America, albeit with limited human and material resources. In light of the scarcity and the remoteness, great importance was accorded to propagating and implementing codes of conduct – not just among European settlers, but also over the indigenous population.

Which norms and mediatic forms had been put to service by the Spanish sovereign and colonial authorities to regulate codes of conduct in early colonial Spanish America? As set out in Thomas Duve's introductory chapter, the contributors of this volume are exploring the presence and functions of a particular type of normative literature in Ibero-America. To a lesser degree we draw on conventional sources of legal history, i.e., the large stacks of textual collections pertaining to the norm-setting practices of higher authorities or other early modern legal sources from the Castilian tradition and the *ius commune*. Instead, close attention is paid to modalities of normativity addressed to 'practitioners', especially religious ones (such as parish priests or missionaries), and, in particular, we take into consideration sources from the field of moral theology.[1]

As explained in the first chapter, the use of the term 'pragmatic normative literature' was partly inspired by a pioneering work of legal historiography written in the second half of the 19th century. In his *History of Popular Literature of Roman Canon Law in Germany at the End of the 15th and at the Beginning of the 16th Century* (1867),[2] Roderich Stintzing treated diverse types of juridical literature, which had been neglected by the legal historians of his

1 For the multi-normative order constituted by canon law and moral theology in the 16th century, see Duve, "Katholisches Kirchenrecht und Moraltheologie im 16. Jahrhundert".

2 Stintzing, *Geschichte der populären Literatur des römisch-kanonischen Rechts in Deutschland.*

DOI:10.1163/9789004425736_004

time. Sources such as alphabetical collections, instructions on legal procedure, notarial handbooks, compendia of cases, or "ecclesiastical jurisprudence" like *summae confessorum*, and small treatises on confession are good examples of 'pragmatic normative literature', as defined by Duve.

Similar genres have not been considered as particularly relevant sources by legal historians of early colonial Ibero-America, either. We argue, instead, that 'pragmatic normative literature' – especially from the religious field – held a greater significance in the remote *frontier* contexts of an early modern empire. This is in no small part due to the fact that such a body of literature did not represent complex instructions or a sophisticated normative framework, but instead condensed normative knowledge. These texts were perceived as 'weak' given their lack of theoretical complexity compared to erudite scholarly treatises. They were 'strong', however, in a pragmatic sense, as their flexible normative underpinnings enabled them to take up those notions of legitimacy that became a part of the moral economy of the colonial society. Not least in the imperial peripheries, these adaptable pragmatic texts – catechisms, manuals for confession, moral theological instructions, but as well *sermonarios* and *devocionarios* – became particularly important.[3] Even in places where the reach of law was limited, the practice of regulations and notions of 'proper' behaviour were mediated through ecclesiastical institutions and actors, but also through religious symbols and practice.

2 Circulation of Books in Colonial Spanish America: Relevant Features

In order to examine the presence and function of pragmatic normative literature in Spanish America during the 16th and 17th centuries, it is crucial to explore the circulation and distribution of these material resources – mainly books but as well other mediatic forms. The aim of this chapter is to sketch out central aspects of the topic, to offer a historiographic synthesis and to discuss some empirical evidence. Painting in broad strokes, as it were, we will proceed in two steps: First, some basic information about book circulation in colonial Spanish America (sources, historiography, numbers) will be provided. In a second step, a few cases based on the literature and on archival sources will be

3 For a brief typology, see Resines Llorente, *Catecismos americanos del siglo XVI*, vol. 1, 20–21. Saranyana (ed.), *Teología en América Latina*, vol. 1, provides an introduction to some of these sources, which are dealt with in detail in the following chapters of the present volume.

discussed, which might illustrate how the circulation of pragmatic literature in Mexico and Peru can be traced, reconstructed and analysed.

2.1 *The Transatlantic Book Trade as a Knowledge Regime*

The transatlantic book trade from Seville to the New World was a key factor. The Castilian Crown and its institutions established a system of controlled exportation and circulation of books in its territories. This can be construed as a "knowledge regime", i.e., "the structured and (more or less) stabilised interrelation of practices, rules, principles and norms concerning knowledge and different forms of knowledge".[4] One might distinguish two dimensions of knowledge regimes: First, the regulation of the relationship between different forms of knowledge (e.g., between scientific and non-scientific, or erudite and pragmatic knowledge); second, the regulation of knowledge production, distribution, and use by 'external' factors, e.g., political and juridical frameworks, cultural traditions, or technical infrastructures.[5]

In the second sense, at least, our topic is a case in point. The *Casa de la Contratación* (House of Trade) was founded in 1503 in Seville to control navigation, commerce, and migration to the Indies. It aimed to regulate all traffic coming to Spanish America, including ships, goods, and people.[6] Furthermore, the Casa held jurisdiction in commercial matters (with judges and a prison), and it was acknowledged as being a centre of nautical and cartographic knowledge.

Books had to be registered prior to being exported since they were an ambivalent resource:[7] sources of knowledge that at the same time could spread supposedly 'dangerous' Protestant or other heretical ideas to the overseas territories.[8] There are no extant detailed book lists for the first half of the 16th century in the House of Trade's records. In 1550, a royal order issued by Emperor Charles V decreed that each of the books to be exported to the New World was to be mentioned individually in the records – and no longer "en bulto", i.e., in a

4 Wehling, "Wissensregime", 704 (translation, OD).

5 Wehling, "Wissensregime", 704.

6 The classic – and 'pragmatic' – manual about the Trade House is Veitia Linage, *Norte de la Contratación de las Indias occidentales*, first published in Sevilla in 1672. For literature on this topic, see García-Baquero, *La Carrera de Indias: Suma de contratación y océano de negocios*; Acosta Rodríguez, González Rodríguez and Vila Vilar (eds.), *La Casa de la Contratación y la navegación entre España y las Indias*.

7 See Danwerth et al., "Resources in a Social World", 234–236.

8 See González Sánchez, *New World Literacy*, 54–57. The Spanish version of this book was published in 1999 under the title *Los mundos del libro. Medios de difusión de la cultura occidental en las Indias de los siglos XVI y XVII*, Sevilla.

lot.[9] However, only with the publication of Gaspar de Quiroga's *Index of Prohibited Books* in 1583,[10] was this norm complied with more regularly for approximately the next 40 years, so that more homogeneous book lists were issued. From 1620, fiscal reasons made it unnecessary to specify the correct content of boxes to be exported, and from around 1660 detailed registers of books become less frequent in the documentation (figure 3.1).[11] These conditions might explain why especially the last two decades of the 16th century have still a great deal of source material to be examined. To this end our archival work about the export of books concentrates on ship registers from the late 16th and early 17th centuries, which are conserved in the *Archivo General de Indias* (AGI).

In order to prevent the transit of incriminated texts included in the Index of Prohibited Books, the *Casa de la Contratación* cooperated with the Inquisition. Its officials, residing in the castle of Triana, had to approve the cargo lists.[12] For that purpose, evaluators were appointed: friars of different orders, in general Franciscans and Dominicans.[13] The cooperation between the House of Trade and the Holy Office was not without tension, though; furthermore, the inquisitorial censors did not always perform rigid examinations of the book lists. As research has shown, the controls were quite lax during certain periods, when lists were only checked but not compared against the actual books in the boxes. Thus the knowledge regime became permeable, both in Seville and in fact also in the American harbours, given that the inspections of the recently arrived ships was not always conducted in a rigorous manner either.

2.2 *A Historiographic Sketch of Book Circulation in Early Modern Spanish America*

The historiography about the circulation of books in Spanish America during early modern times has its roots in the 19th century. A brief survey of this rich but disperse tradition might be at hand since our work draws strongly on some historiographic contributions. After the Independence period, Latin American scholars in the second half of that century were collecting and

9 *Recopilación de leyes de los reynos de las Indias*, lib. I, tít. XXIV, ley V: "De los libros que se imprimen y pasen a las Indias"; see ley VII as well. Cf. González Sánchez, *New World Literacy*, 50–51.

10 Bujanda, *Index de l'Inquisition espagnole 1583, 1584*.

11 See González Sánchez, *New World Literacy*, 47–53.

12 With regard to this institutional cooperation, see Rueda Ramírez, *Negocio e intercambio cultural*, 61–80. The rest of this paragraph follows his analysis.

13 For example: Petition and license by the Inquisition for books to be sent to Mexico City, Sevilla, 26/27–II–1705, AGI, Contratación 674, no. 2, fols. 241r, 242r; and more licenses in the same *legajo*.

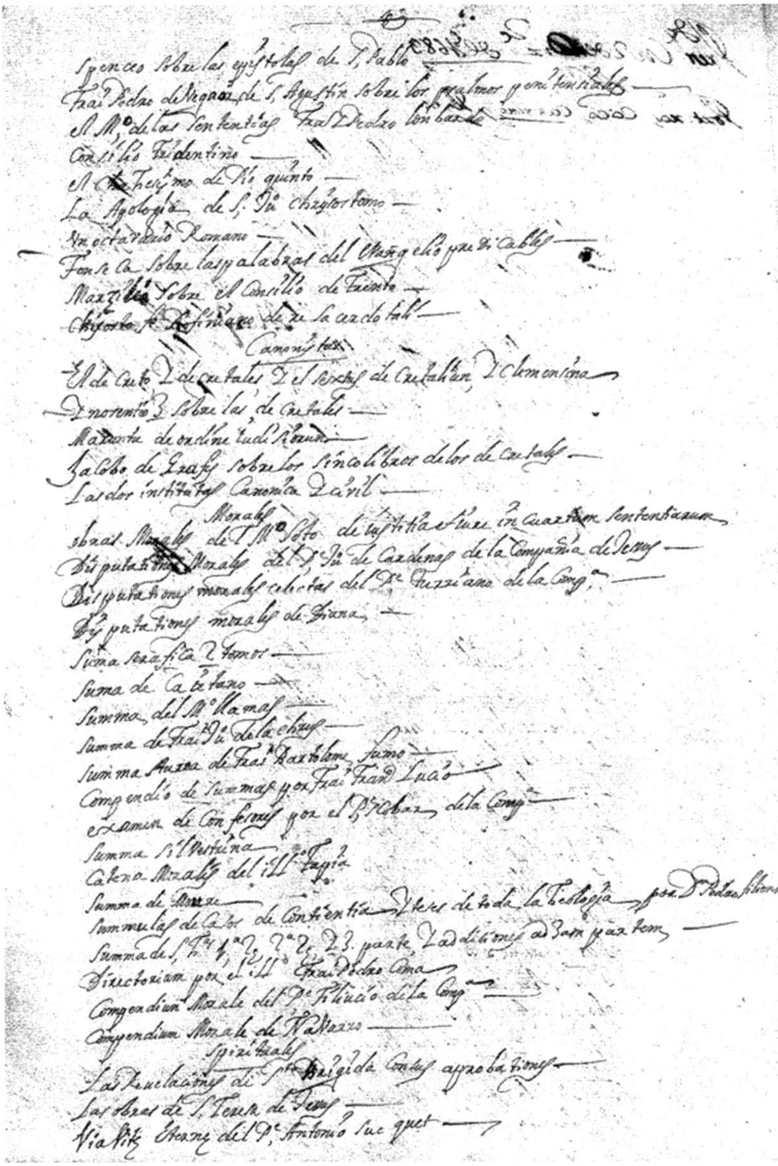

FIGURE 3.1 Ship register with book list "para su venta en los reinos de las Indias", issued by Don Francisco Joseph de la Estrella, priest from Sevilla, indicating book categories ("Canonistas", "Morales"), Sevilla, 2–XII–1689, AGI, Contratación 674, no. 1, fols. 104r–105v, here fol. 104v

composing bibliographic works about the intellectual outputs of their new countries in early modern times. This documentation should be set in the context of nation-building processes, which were accompanied by quite negative depictions of Spanish "repressive" rule in the colonial past.[14] The most eminent representative of that formative period was the Chilean scholar José Toribio Medina (1852–1930), who, among other topics, cultivated the research on Spanish American – and not only regional or national – bibliography. One should mention his books on the American printing presses and the *Biblioteca Hispano-Americana (1493–1810)*, still reference works.[15]

A new generation of researchers, working between the 1930s and 1950s, added fresh evidence and offered new interpretations on the circulation of books in America.[16] They took into consideration the institutional context of transatlantic book trade and found important empirical data in their respective regional as well as in Spanish archives, basing their results on new types of sources: ship registers, contracts, inquisitorial records, etc. Thus, they contested traditional assumptions (e.g., on the effectivity of the inquisitorial control) and highlighted instead the volume of the transatlantic book trade.

In that period, historians from different fields like Edmundo O'Gorman, Guillermo Lohmann Villena, Rubén Vargas Ugarte, Guillermo Furlong Cardiff, Carlos Luque Colombres, Vicente Osvaldo Cutolo, and Javier Malagón Barceló contributed to the field.[17] However, two scholars published landmark books on the topic: the Argentinian José Torre Revello (*El libro, la imprenta y el periodismo en América durante la dominación española*)[18] and the U.S. American Irving Leonard, whose opus magnum *Books of the Brave* appeared in 1949.[19] Among

14 Calvo, "The politics of print", 280.

15 Medina, *Biblioteca hispano-americana (1493–1810)*; plus many works focusing on each of the diverse printing centres. Another landmark work was published posthumously: Medina, *Historia de la imprenta en los antiguos dominios españoles de América y Oceanía*. Cf. Calvo, "The politics of print", 281.

16 See Calvo, "The politics of print", 282–283, who cites two important contributions of the early 20th century: Rodríguez Marín, *El "Quijote" y don Quijote en América*; Fernández del Castillo (ed.), *Libros y libreros en el siglo XVI*.

17 O'Gorman, "Bibliotecas y librerías coloniales, 1585–1694"; Lohmann Villena, "Los libros españoles en Indias"; Vargas Ugarte, *Impresos peruanos*; Furlong Cardiff, *Bibliotecas argentinas durante la dominación hispánica*; Luque Colombres, "Libros de Derecho en bibliotecas particulares cordobesas (1573–1810)"; Osvaldo Cutolo, "Bibliotecas jurídicas en el Buenos Aires del siglo XVII"; Malagón Barceló, *La literatura jurídica española del siglo de oro en la Nueva España*.

18 Torre Revello, *El libro, la imprenta y el periodismo en América durante la dominación española*; see as well his posterior work, e.g., Torre Revello, "Lecturas indianas (siglos XVI–XVIII)".

19 Leonard, *Books of the Brave*.

the articles collected in this classic work, some traced the presence of books that, according to the older historiography, were not supposed to be found in colonial Spanish America, such as picaresque novels or *Don Quixote*.[20] Other contributions, more relevant to our subject, dealt with the book trade in Lima and Mexico, and with their 'bestsellers' in the late 16th century.

The most recent wave of research on our topic started in the late 1980s.[21] In addition to the publication of several comprehensive works, a renaissance of historical book studies can be observed over the past three decades or so in many Latin American countries and in Spain. We can now consult quite a number of book histories for specific countries and overviews of regional research. Moreover, good editions of book inventories are available, mainly issued by individuals from the colonial elites (including Spanish officials, noblemen, clerics, *encomenderos*, and *caciques*), and several by institutions. The majority of these studies are dedicated to the former centres of the viceroyalties New Spain and Peru. Especially in Mexico, investigators open the field of book history to wider issues like literacy, education, and reading.[22]

Not meant as an exhaustive list, the following authors might be mentioned as exemplary figures for the regional historiographies (on the 16th–17th centuries) of the recent decades:

- the Caribbean area: Juan José Sánchez Baena, Ambrosio Fornet;[23]
- New Spain: Javier Barrientos Grandón, Alejandro Mayagoitía, W. Michael Mathes, Magdalena Chocano, Carmen Castañeda, Idalia García, Norah Jiménez, Kenneth Ward;[24]

---

20 See Calvo, "The politics of print", 283.

21 A precursor of that wave was Millares Carlo, "Bibliotecas y difusión del libro en Hispanoamérica colonial". See as well Solano, "Fuentes para la historia cultural: Libros y bibliotecas de la América colonial"; and the exhibition catalogue edited by Greer Johnson, *The Book in the Americas*.

22 See Calvo, "The politics of print", 286–287; González Sánchez, *New World Literacy*, 30–32.

23 Sánchez Baena, "Noticias sobre el mundo del libro en Cuba antes del desarrollo de la imprenta (1525–1763)"; Fornet, *El libro en Cuba, siglos XVIII y XIX*. See as well Hampe Martínez, "Lecturas de un jurista del siglo XVI".

24 Barrientos Grandón, *La cultura jurídica en la Nueva España*; Mayagoitía, "Notas sobre los alegatos impresos novohispanos"; Mathes, "Humanism in Sixteenth and Seventeenth Century Libraries of New Spain"; Chocano Mena, "Colonial Printing and Metropolitan Books"; Castaneda, *Del autor al lector. Historia del libro en México*; García Aguilar, "El conocimiento histórico del libro y la biblioteca novohispanos"; García Aguilar and Rueda Ramírez (eds.), *Leer en tiempos de la colonia*; Jiménez, "Cuentas fallidas, deudas omnipresentes"; Ward, *"Mexico, where they coin money and print books"*. See as well Garone Gravier, "Fuentes para el estudio de la tipografía, la imprenta y el libro antiguo mexicano (1539–1821)"; Luque Talaván, "De los libros surgen las leyes"; Cervantes Bello (ed.), *Libros y Lectores en las sociedades hispanas: España y Nueva España (Siglos XVI–XVIII)*.

- Central America: Pedro Rueda Ramírez;[25]
- New Granada: Ildefonso Leal, José del Rey Fajardo, Mónica Fortich Navarro;[26]
- Peru: Teodoro Hampe Martínez, Carlos Alberto González Sánchez, Pedro Guibovich, Herman Nébias Barreto;[27]
- Charcas: Daisy Rípodas Ardanaz, Josep Barnadas, Marcela Inch;[28]
- the Río de la Plata and interior regions: Daisy Rípodas Ardanaz, Marcela Aspell, Ernesto Maeder, Alejandro Parada, Esteban Llamosas, Silvano Benito Moya, Celina Lértora Mendoza;[29] and
- Chile: Bernardo Bravo Lira, Javier Barrientos Grandón, Carlos Salinas Araneda.[30]

We should not forget important studies coming from Spain. Of special interest are the authors of what might be labelled 'Seville school of book history'. Following the lead of León Carlos Alvarez Santaló and the late Hispanist Klaus Wagner, early modern historians like Carlos Alberto González Sánchez, Pedro Rueda Ramírez, and Natalia Maillard have contributed widely to our

---

25 Rueda Ramírez, "Libros europeos en Centroamérica en los siglos XVI–XVII". For the 18th and 19th centuries, with respect to Costa Rica, see Molina Jiménez, *El que quiera divertirse*.

26 Leal, *Libros y bibliotecas en Venezuela colonial (1633–1767)*; Rey Fajardo, *Las bibliotecas jesuíticas en la Venezuela colonial*; Rey Fajardo and Marín Cortés (eds.), *La biblioteca colonial de la Universidad Javeriana comentada*; Fortich Navarro, *Togados y letrados*; Córdoba-Restrepo (ed.), *Biblioteca antigua. Circulación y conocimiento*. See as well, in this volume, Pilar Mejía's chapter 10 with reference to Cartagena de Indias.

27 Hampe Martínez, *Bibliotecas privadas en el mundo colonial*; Hampe Martínez, "Las bibliotecas virreinales en el Perú y la difusión del saber italiano"; González Sánchez, "La cultura del libro en el Virreinato del Perú en tiempos de Felipe II"; Guibovich Pérez, "The Printing Press in Colonial Peru"; Nébias Barreto, "Legal Culture and Argumentation in the Vice-Reign of Peru from the 16th to the 18th centuries". See as well Dolezalek, "Libros jurídicos anteriores a 1800 en la Biblioteca de la Universidad Nacional Mayor de San Marcos en Lima".

28 Rípodas Ardanaz, "Bibliotecas privadas de funcionarios de la Real Audiencia de Charcas"; Barnadas, *Bibliotheca Boliviana Antiqva*; Inch C., "La Biblioteca Potosina de la Compañía de Jesús".

29 Rípodas Ardanaz, "Libros, bibliotecas y lecturas [cap. 22]"; Aspell de Yanzi Ferreira and Page (eds.), *La Biblioteca Jesuítica de la Universidad Nacional de Córdoba*; Maeder, "Libros, bibliotecas, control de lecturas e imprentas rioplatenses en los siglos XVI al XVIII"; Parada, "Tipología de las bibliotecas Argentinas desde el periodo hispánico hasta 1830"; Llamosas, "Probabilismo, probabiliorismo y rigorismo"; Benito Moya, "Bibliotecas y libros en la cultura universitaria de Córdoba durante los siglos XVII y XVIII"; Lértora Mendoza, "Bibliotecas académicas coloniales".

30 Bravo Lira, "La literatura jurídica indiana en el Barroco"; Barrientos Grandón, *La cultura jurídica en el Reino de Chile*; Salinas Araneda, "Los textos utilizados en la enseñanza del Derecho Canónico en Chile indiano". See as well Argouse, "De libros y otras cosas".

understanding of book circulation in Spain and in the Atlantic world.[31] Their work sheds new light on the commercial networks and the intermediaries (booksellers, merchants) involved. Moreover, there are very good book histories and related issues about the Iberian Peninsula, which further our understanding of the Ibero-American perspective.[32]

Apart from the studies cited above treating major spaces within early modern Ibero-America – other regions have not received as much attention, like former frontier areas or Portuguese America[33] – we have at our disposal a good deal of legal historical scholarship on printing and the commerce of books in Castilian law and *Derecho Indiano*.[34]

After sketching this historiographic background, let us now turn to some of the already mentioned types of sources most relevant for the study of book circulation. They will be discussed following the movement of books from Europe to America.

---

31 For a few of the most recent contributions, see González Sánchez, *Atlantes de papel*; González Sánchez, "La cultura escrita en el Mundo Atlántico colonial"; González Sánchez, "El comercio de libros entre Europa y América en la Sevilla del siglo XVI"; Rueda Ramírez, *Negocio e intercambio cultural*; Rueda Ramírez, "El comercio de libros en Latinoamérica colonial"; Rueda Ramírez (ed.), *El libro en circulación en el mundo moderno en España y Latinoamérica*; García Aguilar and Rueda Ramírez (eds.), *El libro en circulación en la América colonial*; Maillard Alvarez, "Aproximación a la creación de las redes de distribución de libros en América"; Maillard Alvarez (ed.), *Books in the Catholic World during the Early Modern Period.*

32 See, for example, Cátedra and López-Vidriero (eds.), *La memoria de los libros*; Wilkinson (ed.), *Iberian Books*; Wilkinson and Lorenzo (eds.), *Iberian Books*; Wilkinson and Lorenzo (eds.), *A Maturing Market*; Peñalver Gómez (ed.), *América escrita*. On the history of a printer dynasty important for the establishment of the printing press in Mexico, see Griffin, *The Crombergers of Seville*. With respect to Portugal, see the monographic issue *O livro antigo em Portugal e Espanha, séculos XVI–XVIII*; Ramada Curto (ed.), *Bibliografia da História do Livro em Portugal, séculos XV–XIX*; Camarinhas, "Bibliotecas particulares de magistrados no século XVIII"; Palomo, "Anaqueles de sacra erudición"; Guedes de Campos, *Para se achar facilmente o que se busca*; Giurgevich and Leitão, *Clavis bibliothecarum.*

33 See only Moraes, *Livros e bibliotecas no Brasil colonial*; Grover, "The Book and the Conquest"; González Sánchez, "La cultura escrita en el Mundo Atlántico colonial", Agnolin, *L'invenzione del Tupì*; as well as Gustavo Machado Cabral (Chapter 5) in this volume.

34 See Mohler, "Publishing in colonial Spanish America"; Ávila Martel, "La impresión y circulación de libros en el derecho indiano"; Tau Anzoátegui, *Nuevos Horizontes en el estudio histórico del Derecho Indiano*, ch. 5 ("El libro jurídico"), 70–84; Tau Anzoátegui, *El Jurista en el Nuevo Mundo*, 14–16; Reyes Gómez, *El libro en España y América.*

2.3 *The Exportation of Pragmatic Books to the New World*

Despite the restrictions mentioned above and the control mechanisms exercised by civil and ecclesiastical authorities, the transatlantic book trade was a flourishing enterprise. It is estimated that up to 85% of the books circulating in America were imported and of European origin.[35] Of these imported works, the great majority had been printed in Spain, with very few having been printed in other European centres of book-production (France, Flanders, Italy, Portugal, Holy Roman Empire) before arriving in Seville.

The itinerary of the books on the ocean followed the 'Carrera de Indias'. In order to better protect the ships against pirates, a convoy system was established from 1564 onward, with two fleets per year heading for New Spain (Veracruz) and Tierra Firme (Nombre de Dios and Cartagena). Due to the fast growing immigration to Spanish America, the market for books was expanding. In comparison to other goods and merchandise exported from Seville, however, books constituted only a very small portion of the cargo; some researchers calculate that their percentage amounted to 2%, on average.[36]

The ship registers kept in the *Archivo General de Indias* (AGI, Seville) are a central type of source for tracing European books to the New World. Although they were usually studied by economic historians (think, for example, of Pierre Chaunu's work), some 'modern classical' researchers of book history, like Leonard and Torre Revello, already consulted these sources in the middle of the 20th century. In 1973, Helga Kropfinger von Kügelgen dedicated a concise and dense monograph to the complete export lists of books sent to New Spain in one year: 1586.[37]

The analysis of the ship registers provides us with high percentages of religious literature and respective categories; some scribes even organised the lists according to the book sizes (from *folio* to *quarto* and *octavo*).[38]

Carlos Alberto González Sánchez has analyzed the entire book lists for the years 1583–1584 (824 books) and the year 1605 (2098 books). Summing up his findings very briefly, we can state that the percentage of religious books in the

35 See Hampe Martínez, "Historiografía del libro en América hispana", 61.

36 See González Sánchez, *New World Literacy*, 96.

37 Kropfinger von Kügelgen, *Exportación de libros europeos de Sevilla a la Nueva España en el año de 1586*.

38 Ship register with list of books to be sent to New Spain, issued by Fernando Romero y Torres, vecino of Seville, indicating category and size of books ("Libros de q[uar]to theologuicos", "Juridicos de fol[io]"), Seville, 23–VI–1689, AGI, Contratación 674, no. 1, fols. 64r–72r, here fol. 65v; Ship register with list of books "para su venta en los reinos de las Indias", issued by Don Francisco Joseph de la Estrella, presbítero en Sevilla, indicating category of books ("Canonistas", "Morales"), Sevilla, 2–XII–1689, AGI, Contratación 674, no. 1, fols. 104r–105v, here fol. 104v (see figure 3.1).

samples rose from 34% in the 1580s to 77% in 1605. He divides the religious books into the following genres:[39]

Types	Per cent of religious books	
	1583–84	1605
Spiritual	24.6	47.8
Theology	22.8	9.6
Prayer and liturgy	20.3	32
Moral theology	20	1.8
Canon law	5	0.1
Oratory	4.6	2
Hagiography	3.5	6.8

While we cannot refer here to the author's discussions of the works mentioned, we would nevertheless like to stress two points. First, the best-selling author among the spiritual literature was the Dominican Fray Luis de Granada (e.g., *Libro de la oración y de la meditación*). Secondly, regarding manuals of moral theology, González Sánchez' analysis is quite insightful:

> The most numerous are the *Suma de casos morales* by Bartolomé de Medina, with nineteen copies, and the very successful *Suma de casos de conciencia* by the Franciscan Manuel Rodríguez, with fifteen copies. But the most widely distributed was undoubtedly the *Summario* by Martín de Azpilcueta, a disciple of Domingo de Soto, of which I have counted only seven. Others, also widely accepted, were those by Antonio de Córdoba, Juan de Pedraza, and Tomás de Mercado. A special case, with eighteen copies, is the *Director[i]um curatorum* of the Dominican Bishop of Elna, Pedro Martír Coma, a book that is everywhere in ecclesiastical libraries, and that is not a manual of morality in the strict sense, but rather a text aimed at forming priests, though with continual allusions to confession and ethical problems.[40]

This quote shows that detailed reconstructions of book lists might provide clues for contextualising Azpilcueta's work in the second half of the 16th

39 González Sánchez, *New World Literacy*, 100.
40 González Sánchez, *New World Literacy*, 112.

century.[41] Pedro Rueda, in his profound analysis of book trade during the first half of the 17th century, has demonstrated that 'el Navarro', as Azpilcueta was also known, can be found in many exportation documents (figure 3.2). However, other authors of *Sumas morales* were registered more frequently in that period, such as Manuel Rodríguez or Pedro de Ledesma.[42]

2.4 *Books Stemming from American Printing Presses*

Although the great majority of the books circulating in America were imported via Seville, about 15% were printed in the overseas territories. These books were supplied by the few printing presses that had received a royal license in Spanish America: they operated in Mexico City (1539), Lima (1581/1584), Puebla (1640), and Guatemala (1660). In the remaining areas of the vast region called *las Indias*, only from the 18th century onward, printing centres were established, for example, in Havana (1707), Santafé de Bogotá (1736), Quito (1759) and Buenos Aires (1780), followed by Caracas in 1808.[43]

As the printing presses of Mexico and Lima had been explicitly installed to help missionaries in their activities, it should not come as a surprise to find among their production a great many of catechetic books (*catecismos, doctrinas*), confessionaries and sermonaries, including translations into indigenous languages and vocabularies.[44] Think, for example, of the pre-Tridentine *Confessionario mayor en lengua Mexicana y Castellana* by the Franciscan friar Alonso de Molina (Mexico 1565),[45] or of the voluminous 'pastoral texts' published in

41 The *Manual de confessores y penitentes* written by this canon lawyer and moral theologian is examined by Manuela Bragagnolo (Chapter 6) in this volume.

42 Rueda Ramírez, *Negocio e intercambio cultural*, 309–312.

43 A classic is Medina, *Historia de la imprenta en los antiguos dominios españoles de América y Oceanía*. See as well Thompson and Woodbridge, *Printing in Colonial Spanish America*; Maris Fernández, *La imprenta en Hispanoamérica*; Deylen, "Buchdruck, kolonialer, in Lateinamerika". There is abundant literature on the history of imprints in the various American publishing centers. For Mexican literature, just see García Icazbalceta, *Bibliografía mexicana del siglo XVI* (1ª ed. 1886); Zulaica Gárate, *Los franciscanos y la imprenta en México en el siglo XVI*. For Peru, see Vargas Ugarte, *Impresos peruanos*.

44 See, for example, Resines Llorente, *Catecismos americanos del siglo XVI*; Durán, *Monumenta catechética hispanoamericana (siglos XVI–XVIII)*; Gil, *Primeras "doctrinas" del Nuevo Mundo*; Jiménez, "Los libros en lenguas indígenas como un género de las imprentas novohispanas entre los siglos XVI y XVII"; Guibovich Pérez, "The Printing Press in Colonial Peru".

45 Molina, *Confessionario mayor en lengua Mexicana y Castellana*. See Saranyana (ed.), *Teología en América Latina*, vol. 1, 55–59; Durán, *Monumenta catechética hispanoamericana*, vol. 1, 353–541. For pre-Tridentine catechisms edited by bishop Juan de Zumárraga in Mexico, see José Luis Egío (Chapter 7) in this volume.

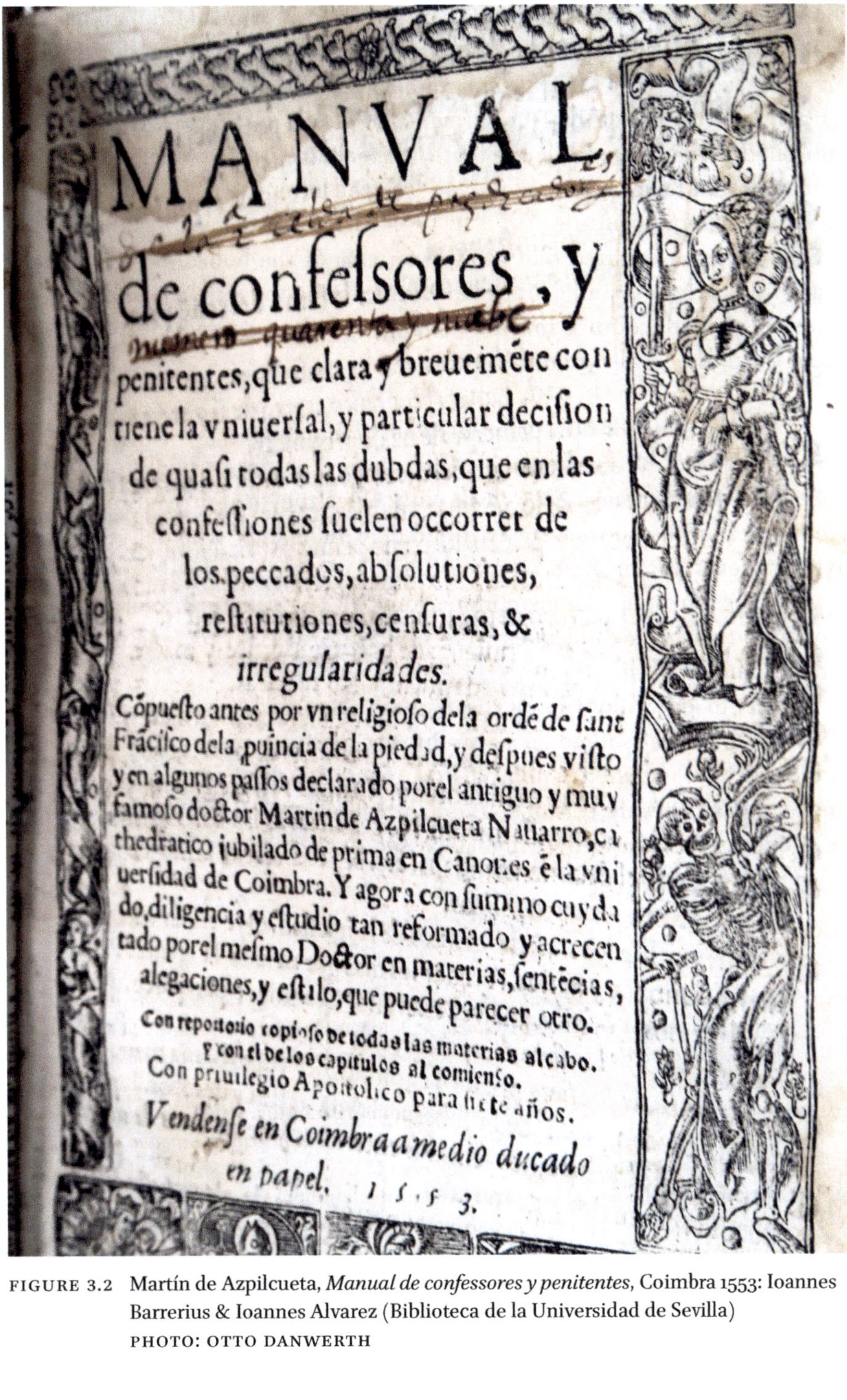

MANVAL,
de confessores, y
penitentes, que clara y breuemēte con
tiene la vniuersal, y particular decision
de quasi todas las dubdas, que en las
confessiones suelen occorrer de
los peccados, absolutiones,
restitutiones, censuras, &
irregularidades.
Cōpuesto antes por vn religioso dela ordē de sant
Frācisco dela ꝓuincia de la piedad, y despues visto
y en algunos passos declarado por el antiguo y muy
famoso doctor Martin de Azpilcueta Nauarro, ca
thedratico jubilado de prima en Canones ē la vni
uersidad de Coimbra. Y agora con summo cuyda
do, diligencia y estudio tan reformado y acrecen
tado por el mesmo Doctor en materias, sentēcias,
alegaciones, y estilo, que puede parecer otro.
Con repertorio copioso de todas las materias al cabo.
Y con el de los capitulos al comienço.
Con priuilegio Apostolico para siete años.
Vendense en Coimbra a medio ducado en papel. 1553.

FIGURE 3.2 Martín de Azpilcueta, *Manual de confessores y penitentes*, Coimbra 1553: Ioannes Barrerius & Ioannes Alvarez (Biblioteca de la Universidad de Sevilla)
PHOTO: OTTO DANWERTH

three languages after the celebration of the Third Provincial Council of Lima (1582–1583) – which was the first book to have left a South American printing press.[46] In contrast, the *catecismos* and the *Directorio de Confesores y Penitentes* written in the course of the Third Provincial Council of Mexico (1585) were not published at that time; while the first were included in the catechetical works of the Fourth Mexican Council only in 1771, the latter even awaited its edition for more than four centuries.[47]

Scholars have counted that more than 31% of the books printed in New Spain were written in indigenous languages during the 16th century. Over the course of the 17th century, this ratio changed profoundly and comprised only about 3% of the locally produced books.[48]

2.5 *Possessing Books in Colonial Spanish America*

Up to this point the – European or American – origins of books circulating in Spanish America have been dealt with. Once they had arrived in the New World, most of the books were distributed by merchants, who delivered them to their clients (for example, religious orders), sold them in bookshops, or sent them to local regions via "economic agents".[49] The American market was so profitable that book catalogues were printed for certain regions in order to promote the book sales there.[50]

In order to know more about the dissemination of the printed works there, one relies on other sources, e.g., inventories of goods owned by individuals. These lists were included in notarial documentation for the living as well as for the dead. Two relevant sets of sources are wills and lists of *bienes de difuntos*, i.e., "goods of the deceased" (who had passed away in Spanish America without

46 *Doctrina christiana, y catecismo para instruccion de los indios, y de las demas personas, que han de ser enseñadas en nuestra sancta fé*, Lima 1584: Antonio Ricardo. See Saranyana (ed.), *Teología en América Latina*, vol. 1, 74–78; Durán, *Monumenta catechética hispanoamericana*, vol. 2, 331–741.

47 See Osvaldo Moutin (Chapter 8) in this volume; Saranyana (ed.), *Teología en América Latina*, vol. 1, 192–203; Durán, *Monumenta catechética hispanoamericana*, vol. 3, 135–578; Poole (ed.): *The Directory for Confessors 1585*.

48 Chocano Mena, "Colonial Printing and Metropolitan Books", 73; see Calvo, "The politics of print", 279. – Recent monographs on book censorship and Inquisition in American tribunals include: Guibovich Pérez, *Censura, libros e Inquisición en el Perú colonial*; Nesvig, *Ideology and Inquisition*; Ramos Soriano, *Los delincuentes de papel*; Campillo Pardo, *Censura, expurgo y control en la biblioteca colonial neogranadina*.

49 González Sánchez, *New World Literacy*, 143.

50 See Rueda Ramírez, "El derecho en los catálogos de venta de los libreros sevillanos".

heirs).[51] Books could be sold or given as gifts during one's lifetime, or sold in an auction after death. These second-hand sales were a good opportunity to buy books at lower prices. Little is known so far about these transactions, which are important for understanding the circulation of books in the American regions; the best information is provided in notarial records.

The circulation of (religious) pragmatic texts contributed to the establishment of knowledge regimes in early modern Hispanic America. Manuals of moral theology, catechisms, and other genres applied above all in missionary contexts were central media for the diffusion of normative orders in an emerging empire. In order to evaluate their distribution in different regions during the 16th and 17th centuries, a vast multidisciplinary bibliography on the production, possession, and circulation of books has been established.[52]

Which types of pragmatic literature can be detected in personal and institutional libraries,[53] and what do we know about the circulation of these resources? Whereas the research on the book possession of bishops, friars and priests, of colonial authorities, and of wealthy settlers offers rich material, the investigation on book collections of institutions and corporations – such as cathedral chapters, monasteries of mendicant orders, Jesuit colleges, the Inquisition as well as parishes – is not that advanced but catching up, as some chapters of this volume show. In particular, library catalogues of institutions and personal book inventories are central sources to grasp the importance of circulating 'pragmatic' normative books for the creation of knowledge structures – especially missionary ones – in imperial contexts of early colonial America.

3 Presence of Pragmatic Books in Spanish America: Some Case Studies

In the final part of this chapter, instead of treating institutional book collections, I would like to present some examples of individuals or pertinent professional groups, who kept pragmatic books in Spanish America.

51 On the topic of this paragraph, see González Sánchez, *New World Literacy*, 37–39; and ch. 5, 185–207.

52 Danwerth, A bibliography on the circulation of books in early modern Ibero-America.

53 From the 17th century onwards, an institutional book collection used to be called 'biblioteca' while the lot of books owned by an individual was often called 'librería'; see Rípodas Ardanaz, "Libros, bibliotecas y lecturas", 256; Carlyon and Guibovich Pérez, "Library [Spain/Spanish America]".

Some book owners distinguished between "theoretical and practical" authors in their libraries, as did a certain Pedro Zamorano. This "vecino de la ciudad de México, corregidor, alcalde mayor and procurador de la Real Audiencia" stated in 1622: "Item declaro que tengo los libros de derecho canonico y ciuil y de los leyes de partida // y nueua recopilacion y de differentes authores assi theoricos como practicos que valdran treçientos pesos pocos mas o menos [...]".[54]

Other inventories and book titles explicitly used the term 'práctica' for certain types of literature; at the same time, it is an analytic category. In diverse fields of knowledge, for instance, in geography, navigation, architecture, metallurgy, or medicine, we find books directed at a non-specialised readership, which transmitted knowledge regarding practical application.[55] Thomas Duve, in his introductory chapter (especially section 6), has discussed the relationship between such practical genres and pragmatic literature.

Besides this technical kind of literature, other practical works of a normative nature were published. Manuals and instructions written for the juridical work of lawyers, notaries, and scribes,[56] using the term 'prácticas' in their titles, were quite common in Spain and in Spanish America.[57] Let us only mention three well-known examples (in their first editions, followed by many more): Juan Bernardo Díaz de Luco's *Practica criminalis canonica*, Lyon, Guillermo de Millis, 1543; Gabriel de Monterroso y Alvarado's *Práctica civil y criminal & instrucción de escribanos*, Valladolid, Francisco Fernández de Córdoua, 1563; and Blasius Flórez Díez de Mena's *Recentiorum practicarum quaestionum iuris canonici, et civilis, ad praxim utrisque fori spectantium libri tres*, Medina del Campo, Juan Godínez de Millis, 1603.[58]

---

54 AGI, México 262, no. 283, fols. 776r–779v, here fol. 778r.

55 To cite but two examples from the late 16th and early 17th centuries: Flores, *Arte de navegar*; García Cavallero, *Theorica y practica de la arte de ensaya*. – See González Sánchez, "Misión náutica".

56 A classic manual was Yrolo Calar, *La política de escrituras* (1st ed. México 1605). – On the literature for scribes and notaries, see Fernández del Castillo, *Historia de la escribanía en la Nueva España*; Luján Múñoz, "La literatura jurídica notarial en Hispanoamérica durante la colonia"; Herzog, *Mediación, archivos y ejercicio*; Duve, "Geschichte des Notariats und Notariatsrechts im frühneuzeitlichen Hispanoamerika und im späteren Argentinien"; Burns, *Into the Archive*; Villalba Pérez and Torné (eds.), *El nervio de la República: el oficio de escribano en el Siglo de Oro*; Presta, "Redes de tinta y poder"; Rubio Hernández, "Los tratados de práctica notarial en las bibliotecas de escribanos neogranadinos del siglo XVIII".

57 See Luque Talaván, *Un universo de opiniones*, 140, 252; Rueda Ramírez, "El derecho en los catálogos de venta de los libreros sevillanos", 467–469. González Sánchez, *New World Literacy*, 121, defines "prácticas" as "collections of empirical knowledge".

58 On the literary genre 'practica criminalis', see Maihold, *Strafe für fremde Schuld?*, 73–81. A stimulating analysis of 18th century "forensic practical literature" is Agustín

In certain cases, authors of "prácticas" explain their motivation for writing their work and thus provide insights into their "methodological" reflections. So did Pedro Pérez Landero Otañez y Castro, who wrote a *Practica de visitas y residencias*, dealing with how to conduct inspections and judgments of residence at the end of an office-holder's term in Peru. In his preliminary remarks to the reader ("al lector"), he distinguishes the sophisticated knowledge learnt by jurists at "school" from the "experimental knowledge" ("conocimiento experimental") acquired by lawyers during the years when practicing at the bar. It is this very "genre of experimental study" he wants to make accessible to his readers from the juridical and administrative field.[59]

However, we do not focus primarily on such juridical texts but on religious pragmatic literature, which sometimes was labeled 'práctica'[60] yet often used other genre titles, such as *manual, compendio, suma, sumario, instrucción, índice, guía, regla breve* etc. In the following section, we will examine the presence of those pragmatic books in the New World drawing on some case studies.

3.1 *A Sample from Peru in the* longue durée *(1550–1700)*

A sample from Peru in the *longue durée* (1550–1700), based on "goods of the deceased" (*bienes de difuntos*) inventories, allows us to reconstruct the book

Casagrande's contribution (Chapter 11) in this volume; see as well Casagrande, "Literatura Práctica en el siglo XVIII. The use of *prácticas* in Peru is discussed by Renzo Honores (Chapter 4) in this volume as well as in Honores, "Litigación en la Audiencia Arzobispal de Lima".

59 Pérez Landero Otañez y Castro, Pedro, *Practica de visitas y residencias apropriada a los reynos del Perù*: "Al letor. No suele ser el mejor Abogado en los estrados el Iurista, que en las Escuelas gano los applausos de mas ingenioso, y sutil; sino el que con muchos años de Abogazia adquirio un conocimiento experimental del modo mas acertado de conducir a feliz expediente los pleytos, y una facilidad, o prontitud erudita, y eloquente para expressar, confirmar, y persuadir el derecho, que patrocina. [...] Para facilitar este genero de estudio experimental, en todas artes se han escrito diuersos libros de practicas, en que los que con mucha fatiga, aplicacion, y desuelo se auentajaron en ellas, deseosos de que su trauajo aliuiase a los que les sucediesen, y que a menos costa, y en menos tiempo aprouechasen mas, dexaron notadas sus obseruaciones, establecido el methodo, que hallaron mas acertado, y con esso superadas grauissimas difficultades, y preuenidos grandes hierros, que sin esta luz se podian facilmente cometer con graue, y a vezes irremediable perjuicio de muchos". I sincerely thank Pedro Rueda for this information and for sharing the quote; he consulted the book in the Biblioteca Universitaria de Salamanca (BG/2791).

60 For example, Vega, *Svmma llamada Sylva y Practica del Foro Interior utilissima para Confessores y Penitentes* [...]. A pertinent 'bestseller' of the 18th century was Murillo Velarde's *Práctica de testamentos* (first published in Manila 1745, later in Mexico 1755, 1765 and 1790, as well as in Madrid 1765 and in Buenos Aires 1792; several editions followed in the 19th century).

possession of diverse social groups (priests, merchants, artisans, functionaries, miners, et al.). What follows is the statistical evidence for the religious books mentioned in the inventories (715 books, which amount to 30% of the total number) studied by González Sánchez:[61]

Types	Per cent of religious books
Spiritual	28
Prayer and liturgy	23.7
Canon law	16.4
Moral theology	12.2
Theology	11.7
Hagiography	6.8
Rhetoric	0.9

Among these religious books, which were possessed by individuals living in the Indies, the percentage of different literary genres resembles those of the book registers known from Seville. The author observes that

> […] the 87 treatises on moral theology are mainly among the possession of the clergy and, exceptionally, among those of four unidentified cases, one doctor, a scribe, and a miner. The fact that these are book manuals used by confessors, work tools of the priestly profession, does not mean they cannot be owned by lay people, no doubt to guide themselves, by reference to the solutions adopted by skilled doctors of theology, during the doubts of conscience arising in their everyday practice (business, vices, behaviour, attitudes, sin, etc.). In any case, it is not my intention to separate rigorously the 'popular' religious books from the professionals […].[62]

Among the books and work materials for the priesthood, especially the repertories of moral casuistry, one can – again – identify 'bestsellers', such as Azpilcueta's *Compendium and Summary of Confessors and Penitents* as well as

61 González Sánchez, *New World Literacy*, 212.
62 González Sánchez, *New World Literacy*, 220.

Summae of Spanish scholastic authors (such as Bartolomé de Medina, Manuel Rodríguez, or Pedro Ciruelo) and certain directories for priests.[63]

Turning to the non-religious books of the sample, it seems that repertories of civil law were more frequently owned by priests than by state functionaries in Peru. These, in sum, possessed only about 18% of the professional books compared to 82% of works classified as leisure literature. One could relate this surprising finding to the following Mexican sample, which we have recently studied in the AGI.

3.2 *Inventories of Royal Officials in a Single Year (Mexico, 1622)*

When the newly appointed Mexican viceroy, Diego Carrillo de Mendoza (Marquis of Gelves), took office in 1621, he was to implement a number of reforms. Executing a royal order issued by Philip IV, he asked the Crown officials serving in New Spain to send inventories of their belongings. (In no other American *Audiencia* was this royal order followed, it seems.) Many royal officials obeyed, as the existence of 1004 inventories in the AGI shows. The documents, all issued in Mexico in a single year (1622), offer insight into the book possession among one specific group: official royal servants, among them high-ranking court officials (*oidores*), *corregidores*, *alcaldes* and public scribes. Less than 4% of the officials owned registered books, the size of the collection ranging between one item and 920 books.[64]

Here is a transcript of an inventory from a public scribe called García Fernández Cabrera, who was "casado con descendiente de conquistador, vecino y

63 González Sánchez, *New World Literacy*, 220. – For confession and pertinent manuals in early modern Spain, see Morgada García, "Pecado y confesión en la España Moderna"; Río Parra, *Cartografías de la conciencia española en la Edad de Oro*; González Polvillo, *El gobierno de los otros*; González Polvillo, *Análisis y repertorio de los tratados y manuales para la confesión en el mundo hispánico*; O'Banion, *The Sacrament of Penance and Religious Life in Golden Age Spain*; Orrego González, *La administración de la conciencia*. On Portuguese literature, see Correia Fernandes, "Do manual de confessores ao guia de penitentes"; Palomo, "Anaqueles de sacra erudición", 138 (on Azpilcueta). For a comparative analysis of German Catholic and Lutheran manuals in the 'confessional age', see Dürr, "Confession as an Instrument of Church Discipline", 215–240. – Some relevant studies on Spanish America are: Azoulai, *Les péchés du nouveau monde*; Martínez Ferrer, *La penitencia en la primera evangelización de México, 1523–1585*; Lira, "Dimensión jurídica de la conciencia"; Roselló Soberón, *Así en la tierra como en el cielo*; Harrison, *Sin and Confession in Colonial Peru*. – Concerning manuals for priests, see Saranyana (ed.), *Teología en América Latina*, vol. 1, cap. XI, 447–479.

64 These *legajos* (AGI, Audiencia de México, 259–263) were studied as well by Manrique Figueroa: "Bibliotecas de funcionarios reales novohispanos de la primera mitad del siglo XVII".

escribano público y de cabildo de la villa de San Ildefonso". In 1622, he declared to own the following books:

- la nueba rrecopilacion primera y segunda y terçera parte que costo treynta y dos pesos
- otro libro yntitulado curia filipica que le costo ocho pesos
- otro libro yntitulado notas de diego de rribera que le costo quatro pesos
- otro libro yntitulado platica de monterrosso que le costo çinco pesos
- otro yntitulado torneo que le costo dos pesos y quatro tomines
- otro yntitulado penas de dilictos que le costo un peso y quatro tomines
- otro yntitulado pulitica de yrolo que le costo tres pesos y quatro tomines
- otros dos libros primera y segunda parte de garibay que le costaron nuebe pesos
- otro llamado biaje de jerusalen que le costo un peso
- otra segunda parte de el picaro que le costo dos pesos y quatro tomines //
- otro cuerpo de libro de la segunda parte de la nueba recopilaçion que le costo dose pesos
- otro libro yntitulado farfaro que le costo tres pesos
- unas [h]oras rromanas que le costaron quatro pesos
- dos flosantorus [Flos Sanctorum] de billegas que costaron dies y nuebe pesos[65]

That scribe possessed a small but decent book collection, which in its majority had a professional value, such as legal classic works and manuals for notaries. However, one may note a misspelling in the fourth item: It reads "Platica" (sermon), while it should read "Prǎctica" de Monterroso.

Moreover, the mentioned inventories include interesting information on book prices in New Spain in comparison to the Old World: Prices for sold books in Mexico were much lower than in Spain, yet prices for new books bought from local Mexican booksellers were three times as high as in Spain. This at least was stated by the high-ranking Dr. Galdós de Valencia ("vecino de la ciudad de México, oidor de la Real Audiencia de México"), who had arrived in New Spain with 30 book boxes and who definitely owned the largest library among his peers there, comprising 920 books. On July 18, 1622 he declared:

> Yten ttengo la libreria que adelante yra declarada que fueron mas de ttreinta caxones de libros y q[ue] en esta ciudad [h]a comprado muy pocos despues q. Vino [...] // Todos estos libros truge qu[and]o pase a estas partes escepto muy pocos que he comprado en esta ciudad de Mejico que

65 AGI, México 259, no. 84, fols. 234r–239v, here fol. 235r–v.

> no se pone[n] los precios porq[ue] si se quisiesen vender no se allaria lo que costaro[n] en españa y si se ubiesen de comprar de libreros costarían tres vezes mas.[66]

3.3 *Libraries in Convents and Monasteries*

Turning to pragmatic books held by religious actors and institutions, book collections of convents and monasteries are of special interest.[67] Dominican friars were present on the Caribbean islands from 1510 and on the American continent from 1526; the first Franciscans arrived in Mexico in 1524, followed by Mercedarians and Augustinians arriving in the 1530s. Later, in 1585, the Carmelites entered the scene. All of these orders established libraries at their American institutions, to a lesser or greater extent (figure 3.3). Books for convents and mission stations were usually ordered by 'comisarios', 'provinciales' or 'procuradores generales' of a particular mendicant order.[68] The Jesuits, who arrived in the New World in 1572, were in great demand of books, in particular for their educative centres. In Seville they had a representative (a so-called *Procurador General de Indias*) who was organising the acquisition and transport of books to the American Jesuit colleges.[69] The books for the church

66 AGI, México 261, no. 84, fols. 213r–226v, here fols. 213v, 220v. – Prices of books in America are discussed by González Sánchez, *New World Literacy*, 203–207.

67 Various catalogues of these libraries are edited. See, for instance, Mathes, *The America's First Academic Library*; Osorio Romero, *Historia de las bibliotecas novohispanas*, 61–118; Rodríguez-Buckingham, "Monastic Libraries and Early Printing in Sixteenth-Century Spanish America"; Llamosas, "Las obras jurídicas en la biblioteca del Colegio Jesuita de Arequipa"; Rey Fajardo, "El papel de las bibliotecas jesuíticas en la fundación de la cultura moderna"; Serrano Prada, *Apuntes al catálogo sistemático de la Biblioteca del Colegio de Misiones de Popayán, siglos XV–XVIII*. Some relevant literature has already been mentioned above in our historiographic sketch (2.2.). Further references are given in Rueda Ramírez, "El comercio de libros en Latinoamérica colonial", 208–210; Palomo, "Cultura religiosa, comunicación y escritura en el mundo ibérico de la Edad Moderna", 63–64.

68 This and the following paragraph draw closely upon Rueda Ramírez, *Negocio e intercambio cultural*, 170–190. See also Rueda Ramírez, "El abastecimiento de libros de la biblioteca conventual de San Agustín de Puebla de los Ángeles a través de la Carrera de Indias (1609–1613)". For book inventories of Franciscan convents in New Spain, see the two catalogues prepared by Morales, *Inventario del Fondo Franciscano*, and Morales, "Cómo se formaron las bibliotecas franciscanas". Some examples from Franciscan mission zones in New Spain are discussed by David Rex Galindo (Chapter 9) in this volume. On the acquisition of books for religious communities in Mexico (not only Francisan ones), see García Aguilar, "'Para que les den libre paso en todas partes sin que los abran ni detengan' ".

69 To mention but one example: For the acquisition of books for the Jesuit *Colegio de San Pablo* (Lima) and their circulation, see Martín, *La conquista intelectual del Perú*, chapter 4, 97–120.

FIGURE 3.3 Library of the Convent La Recoleta, Arequipa
PHOTO: OTTO DANWERTH

buildings or diocesan seminars in Spanish America were usually bought or ordered by the ecclesiastical chapters of the pertinent diocese.[70]

Individual clerics, be they friars or secular priests, evidently needed books: for prayer, for devotion, and for their multiple tasks such as the celebration of mass, preaching, or hearing confessions. Before departing to the Indies, they could stock up in Seville on books and religious artifacts offered by local bookshops and artisans. Textiles, clothes, artefacts and works of art were bought and then brought to the New World, as were their personal books. Some orders, such as the Dominicans from 1508 on, expressly permitted friars to carry their own books – a very common practice among secular clerics.

3.4 *Book Possession of Priests*

As to the question of books in the possession of priests, post-Tridentine canon law had created some pertinent norms: The Third Provincial Councils of Lima (1582–1583) and Mexico (1585), as well as numerous South American synods, stipulated that clerics had to own certain types of pragmatic texts. Apart from canon law decrees, priests were supposed to possess pastoral texts (e.g., on the

70 Books on religious normativity used in post-Tridentine seminars for the education of priests are discussed by Peña Espinosa, "Fuentes, autoridades y normas para la enseñanza del derecho canónico en el seminario de Puebla".

administration of sacraments), catechetic works, and some treatises on moral theology.[71] As Magnus Lundberg puts it succinctly, with regard to New Spain:

> A priest needed a library. In 1646, Bishop Juan de Palafox y Mendoza wrote that every priest should own a number of books to be able to minister properly and compared a curate without books to a soldier without arms. According to Palafox, the essential priestly library included a Vulgate Bible, a missal, a breviary, a sacramental manual, a copy of the Tridentine decrees as well as some handbooks on moral theology. If working in an indigenous parish, he also needed to have access to grammars, vocabularies and sermon books in relevant languages.[72]

Drawn from recent research literature, the following 17th-century examples from different American regions will illustrate that many clerics were law-abiding in this regard.

Based on the investigation of ecclesiastical inspections (*visitas*), the actual presence of books in the parishes and in *doctrina* priests' houses can be verified. Research conducted by Pedro Guibovich on the Archbishopric of Lima in the 17th century has identified in this latter category a diversity of works that even in frontier regions were present: compendia of moral theology, penitential *summae* and manuals, written by authors like Azpilcueta.[73] The smaller the book formats were – *octavo*, *duodecimo* and less – the more convenient they were for everyday use. However, many "manualitos" (a term present in the title of some of these smaller books)[74] were prone to getting lost over the course of time because of their fragility.[75]

---

71 Cf. Río Parra, *Cartografías de la conciencia española en la Edad de Oro*, 191–192.

72 Lundberg: *Church Life between the Metropolitan and the Local*, 117–118.

73 Guibovich Pérez, "Los libros de los doctrineros en el virreinato del Perú, siglos XVI–XVII". Ibero-American historical research could well profit from integrating scholarship on the Iberian peninsula. For relevant works on Portuguese and Spanish "interior missions" – Franciscan and Jesuit ones – see Palomo, "Misioneros, libros y cultura escrita en Portugal y España durante el siglo XVII"; Palomo, "Cultura religiosa, comunicación y escritura en el mundo ibérico de la Edad Moderna".

74 An 18th century example in 24° (consulted at the John Carter Brown Library) is the anonymous *Manualito de las mas usuales bendiciones, que se acostumbran* [...], printed in Mexico.

75 A case in point involves the so-called "cartillas", i.e., small-format leaflets used as teaching aids to learn how to read and/or as catechetic tools explaining articles of faith. Although they were printed in the thousands and circulated extensively, only few exist today. See Infantes, "De la cartilla al libro".

One *doctrinero* studied by Guibovich was *licenciado* Agustín Ortiz Cerrano, *doctrina* priest of Pachacamac, who declared in 1631 to the inspector that he owned the following books:

> El concilio de Trento y los concilios limenses de sesenta y siete y ochenta y tres, y las sinodales del año trece, y el cathecismo romano y la suma de Córdova, de Navarro y el Directorium Curatorum, y el Cathecismo y cartilla y sermonario en la lengua quichua y aymara, y un arte y bocabulario en la lengua y exhibió cantidad de sermones assí en la lengua como en romance.[76]

Even more evidence on the book holdings of a particularly infamous priest from the Southern Peruvian region of Andahuaylas has survived in the *bienes de difuntos* inventories of the AGI, mentioned above (3.1.). In her study of Father Juan Bautista de Albadán, priest of Pampachiri in the first decade of the 17th century, Sabine Hyland dedicates one chapter to his library.[77] It consisted of 62 volumes – a rather large book collection in comparison to the few books owned in general by other rural priests, mostly had at least a missal and a breviary. Among Albadán's books mentioned by Hyland, we might highlight some pragmatic works. At first, two manuals on penal law are striking: Juan Bernardo Díaz de Luco's *Practica criminalis canonica* and Juan de Robles' *Práctica criminal*. With regard to canon law, the priest owned the necessary decrees: those of the Council of Trent as well as those of the Third Provincial Council of Lima; they were accompanied by the "pastoral instruments" produced by the Lima Council, published in 1584 (mentioned above, 2.4).[78] Somewhat surprising is the lack of diocesan synods.

Hyland's summary on the "after-life" of this priest's library vividly describes the dispersion of his works:

76 Guibovich Pérez, "Los libros de los doctrineros en el virreinato del Perú, siglos XVI–XVII", 108, who quotes the following document: Archivo Arzobispal de Lima, Visitas, leg. 7, exp. 15.

77 Hyland, *The Chankas and the Priest*, chapter 4, 54–75, here 60: "Even the humblest Catholic priest in colonial Apurimac owned at least a missal and a breviary".

78 Hyland, *The Chankas and the Priest*, 71–72. Actually they were tri-lingual – in Spanish, Quechua and Aymara. – An interesting and somewhat rare work to be found in Peruvian clerical libraries was written by a French Franciscan who had lived in Mexico: Juan Focher, *Itinerarium Catholicum*, Sevilla 1574. "This work, edited by Focher's native disciple Diego Valadés, describes how to administer the sacraments to indigenous Mexicans; it contains sermons in the native languages [...]". (70).

> After Albadán's death, his goods were auctioned off in Andahuaylas [...]. Forty of his books were sold to the local clergy; the vicar of Andahuaylas, Father Diego Arias de Sotelo, purchased the largest number, including the four volumes by Aquinas, Robles's *Práctica criminal* and Luco's *Practica criminalis canonica* [...]. A local priest, Father Gregorio Fernández de Salcedo, purchased the Roman breviary, the *Vocabulario eclesiástico*, and the three books in Quechua and Spanish: the catechism, the confessional, and the *Tercer catecismo*. Albadán's successor in Pampachiri, Father Alonso de Sigura, bought a book on the Lima councils and another one on // the Council of Trent [...]. After the sale, twelve volumes, including Horace and Juvenal, remained, and they were packed up and carried to Lima, where they were sold by weight.[79]

In sum, down to the local level, books provided resources of pragmatic normativity, and were amply used by those *pragmatici*.[80] Beyond this modern but quite expensive medium, other sources, which were more difficult to grasp yet present in Ibero-America, existed and had a great importance: manuscripts. Manuscript copies or originals of books, called "notebooks by hand" were quite common in the Indies,[81] as they were in Spain or Portugal.[82] Frequently, they included transcriptions of didactic works and texts for professional use (small treatises, reports, synods, sermons, etc.); moreover, prohibited works or texts which had not yet been approved of, could circulate in manuscript form. Looking at erudite culture of Mexico in the 17th century, Magdalena Chocano has suggested that it was more the oral transmission and the presence of

79 Hyland, *The Chankas and the Priest*, 74–75. According to 176, note 30, the inventory of his books and other things is found in AGI, Contratación 305B, no. 1, ramo 6, Bienes del difuncto del Padre Juan Bautista Albadán, 1612.

80 Pragmatic religious texts such as sacramental manuals, rituals and confessionaries are central sources for recent studies on the administration of sacraments to the indigenous population. With regard to marriage, see Latasa, "Tridentine Marriage Ritual in Sixteenth- to Eighteenth-century Peru"; Zaballa Beascoechea, "Indian Marriage Before and After the Council of Trent".

81 See González Rodríguez, "La difusión manuscrita de ideas en Nueva España (Siglo XVI)"; Tau Anzoátegui, *Nuevos Horizontes*, 73–75.

82 For the Middle Ages and the Renaissance, see Johnston and van Dussen (eds.), *The Medieval Manuscript Book*; Richardson, *Manuscript Culture in Renaissance Italy*; Neddermeyer, *Von der Handschrift zum gedruckten Buch*. For early modern manuscript culture and circulation in the Iberian world, see Bouza Alvarez, *Corre manuscrito*; Bouza, *Hétérographies*; Castillo Gómez, *Entre la pluma y la pared*; Palomo, "Misioneros, libros y cultura escrita", 142–143; Palomo, "Written empires".

manuscripts than the written culture that proved decisive for the circulation of ideas.[83]

Magnus Lundberg's research on sacramental manuals for priests – a genre he labels "clerical vademecum" – in mid-colonial New Spain is a case in point. He has shown that a great diversity of those "manuales sacramentales" existed in Mexican dioceses such as Puebla. Particularly in the 1630s and 1640s, secular clerics prepared and wrote such pragmatic texts themselves, as they needed them for the ministry of their Nahuatl and Mazahua-speaking parishioners.[84] These works, which described the priest's work, mainly remained unpublished and circulated in manuscript form:

> In the parish ministry, the priests used the small books they had access to and the linguistic diversity of many parishes meant that curates often had to make recourse to their memory, their own manuscripts or manuscripts that had been compiled by colleagues and circulated.[85]

3.5 *The Use of Books – an Open Question*

Coming to a close, I would like to briefly mention the last aspect of book circulation, which is still – and to a large degree – an open question: the use of pragmatic books and the "focus on the reader as the main performer of every process of reception or creative appropriation of a text in a different context".[86]

The problem of reading (as well as the oral participation of the illiterate as listeners) is one of the most difficult tasks to tackle. Nevertheless, it is on our agenda, especially as regards the use of pragmatic books owned by clergy

83 Chocano Mena, "Colonial Printing and Metropolitan Books", 90; see Calvo, "The politics of print", 279.

84 Lundberg: *Church Life between the Metropolitan and the Local,* 117–144. Examples are the Spanish-Nahuatl *Manual Mexicano de la administración de los santos sacramentos, conforme al Manual Toledano,* by Francisco Lorra Baquio (printed in Mexico 1634), or the *Doctrina y Enseñanza* of Náguera Yanguas.

85 Lundberg: *Church Life between the Metropolitan and the Local,* 143–144; see as well 237. – For 18th century Mexico, see Taylor, *Magistrates of the Sacred,* especially 152–162.

86 Beck, "The Diffusion of Law Books in Early Modern Europe", 201. On the topic of reading, see the rich literature about the Iberian peninsula, for instance, Dadson, *Libros, lectores y lecturas*; Castillo Gómez (ed.), *Libro y lectura en la península ibérica y América (siglos XIII a XVIII)*; Prieto Bernabé, *Lecturas y lectores*; Nalle, "Printing and reading popular religious texts in sixteenth-century Spain"; Palomo, "Cultura religiosa, comunicación y escritura en el mundo ibérico de la Edad Moderna", 85–87; as well as the reflections of Rueda Ramírez, "El comercio de libros en Latinoamérica colonial", 203–205.

FIGURE 3.4 Martín de León, *Manual Breve, y Forma de administrar los Santos Sacramentos à los Indios*, México 1669: Rodriguez Lupercio, with manuscript notes (Linga Library, Hamburg)
PHOTO: OTTO DANWERTH

and friars. One way of answering this question might be provided by studying the personal aspect of reading:[87] examining traces that users left in concrete books, like manuscript notes or glosses. Some of these were detected in select works from the Linga Library, Hamburg, from the John Carter Brown Library, Providence, or from Mexican colonial libraries in Mexico City, Puebla, Oaxaca and Guadalajara – all of them recently consulted (figure 3.4).[88]

Let us end, however, with one example of how some Spanish clerics were suspicious of those indigenous people who knew how to read and write Spanish, so-called *ladinos*. Bartolomé Alvarez, a parish priest from the *Audiencia* of Charcas (Alto Perú), complained in his in memorial to the King (1588) about their lack of Catholic religion:

---

87 The personal aspect of reading is stressed by Tau Anzoátegui, *Nuevos Horizontes*, 78–79; Rípodas Ardanaz, "Libros, bibliotecas y lecturas"; Navarro Bonilla, "Las huellas de la lectura"; and Hespanha, "Form and content in early modern legal books".

88 To mention but one interesting example with manuscript notes (from the Linga Library, Hamburg): León, *Manual Breve, y Forma de administrar los Santos Sacramentos à los Indios*, printed in México in 1669. A select number of those books is available at the Digital Library *De Indiarum Iure*, provided by the Max Planck Institute for European Legal History (https://dlc.mpdl.mpg.de/dlc/collection/escidoc:71437).

> Among the virtues that the *ladinos* pursue is that of bringing a suit and making a petition to lodge an accusation: with this aim, a *ladino* Indian of Andamarca [...] bought a Monterroso, and in another town called Corquemarca another *ladino* bought the *Partidas* of King Alfonso; and this without knowing a word of the Christian doctrine.[89]

This example shows that classic Castilian legal compilations, such as the *Siete Partidas* as well as a typical pragmatic manual like Gabriel de Monterroso y Alvarado's *Práctica civil y criminal & instrucción de escribanos*, were circulating and being consulted by indigenous individuals in the Andean highlands to prepare legal litigation against Spanish officials.[90]

Indians, and not only Spaniards, drew on this resource of normativity, which due to the circulation of books was quite accessible in the New World. How this ambivalent resource was used, however, depended on the colonial actors.

4 Concluding Remarks

Some preliminary results can be drawn from this brief overview on central characteristics of book circulation in Spanish America, and from some case studies of pragmatic books in colonial contexts.

In the first place, the knowledge regime which aimed to strictly control the circulation of books across the Atlantic and in Spanish America, was based on the work carried out by the House of Trade and the Inquisition. Despite the rigid politics of vigilance, the regime became 'permeable' in some aspects. Books were considered an ambivalent resource, offering useful or dangerous knowledge.

The rich historiography on book circulation in Spanish America provides case studies from a variety of disciplines. These studies are based in part on

89 Alvarez, *De las costumbres y conversión de los indios del Perú*, 269; cited from the translation in González Sánchez, *New World Literacy*, 45.

90 See Renzo Honores' contribution in this volume (Chapter 4); as well as Puente Luna and Honores, "Guardianes de la real justicia: alcaldes de indios, costumbre y justicia local en Huarochirí colonial". This innovative case study analyzes the circulation and appropriation of legal knowledge by indigenous *alcaldes* using Castilian judicial practices – and pragmatic literature – in the colonial Andes. Another telling study, drawing on 18th century cases from Northern New Spain, is Cutter, "El imperio 'no letrado'". – For further insightful studies from New Spain and Peru, see Ramos and Yannakakis (eds.), *Indigenous Intellectuals*. The last chapter deals with indigenous notaries and discusses Guaman Poma's illustration depicted on the cover of the present volume; see Burns, "Making Indigenous Archives".

early modern library catalogues, on lists of bought books, on sources stemming from import controls and censorship, as well as on research from book studies and cultural history, providing insight into both the estates of book owners and the book production of the early printing presses in Mexico and Lima.

After an initial analysis of this vast historiography and some archival stays, we find that among the normative resources circulating in Spanish America there was a considerable amount of secular and ecclesiastical pragmatic literature, namely small compendia, summaries of greater moral theological works, and, in part, also of juridical treatises. The books not only reached cities and convents but also rural areas and mission zones.

The circulation of this (religious) pragmatic literature in remote Spanish American regions offered functional resources for establishing a new regime of normativity. How these resources were used in order to implement European normative concepts and codes of conduct in places where 'official' legal sources issued by state authorities were not present, remains to be studied more closely.

Books with a normative content, be they pragmatic or not, cannot be considered as material resources alone. Books and other mediatic forms (manuscripts) refer to immaterial resources – secular and spiritual normativity, morality, knowledge – which are reflected or even embodied in them. This ambivalent potential becomes clear when their use by colonial actors is studied.

Future research on the book circulation in Ibero-America will certainly profit from an intellectual exchange with scholars focusing on similar topics in the Iberian Peninsula, or in other European regions. At the same time, within this field of investigation, legal history and cultural history are encouraged to work together in order to improve our understanding of normative literature genres.

Acknowledgements

This chapter draws on an earlier article published in Spanish: Danwerth, "La circulación de literatura normativa pragmática en Hispanoamérica (siglos XVI–XVII)".

Bibliography

Manuscripts

Archivo General de Indias, Sevilla (AGI), Contratación 674.

AGI, México 259–263.

Printed Sources

Alvarez, Bartolomé, *De las costumbres y conversión de los indios del Perú. Memorial a Felipe II (1588)*, ed. Martín Rubio, María del Carmen, Madrid 1998.

Díaz de Luco, Juan Bernardo, *Practica criminalis canonica*, Lyon 1543: Guillermo de Millis.

Díez de Mena, Blasius Flórez, *Recentiorum practicarum quaestionum iuris canonici, et civilis, ad praxim utrisque fori spectantium libri tres*, Medina del Campo 1603: Juan Godínez de Millis.

Doctrina christiana, y catecismo para instruccion de los indios, y de las demas personas, que han de ser enseñadas en nuestra sancta fé, Lima 1584: Antonio Ricardo.

Flores, Lázaro de, *Arte de navegar. Navegacion astronomica, theorica, y practica. En la qual se contienen tablas nuevas de las declinaciones de el sol* […], [Madrid] 1673: Iulian de Paredes.

García Cavallero, Joseph, *Theorica y practica de la arte de ensaya. Oro, plata, y vellon rico* […], Madrid 1713: Agustín Fernández.

Manualito de las mas usuales bendiciones, que se acostumbran, con experimentado provecho de sanos, y enfermos […], Reimpresso en México 1772: Felipe de Zuñiga y Ontiveros.

Molina, Alonso de, *Confessionario mayor en lengua Mexicana y Castellana*, México, Antonio de Espinosa, 1565.

Monterroso y Alvarado, Gabriel de, *Práctica civil y criminal & instrucción de escribanos*, Valladolid 1563: Francisco Fernández de Córdoua.

Murillo Velarde, Pedro, *Práctica de testamentos*, Manila 1745: Imprenta de la Compañia de Jesus por D. Nicolas de la Cruz Bagay (later editions: Mexico 1755, 1765 and 1790, as well as Madrid 1765 and Buenos Aires 1792; several editions followed in the 19th century).

Pérez Landero Otañez y Castro, Pedro, *Practica de visitas y residencias apropriada a los reynos del Perù y deducida de lo que en ellos se estila*, Napoles 1696: por Nicolas Layno.

Recopilación de leyes de los reynos de las Indias, Madrid 1681: Iulian de Paredes.

Vega, Alonso de la, *Svmma llamada Sylva y Practica del Foro Interior utilissima para Confessores y Penitentes* […], Alcalá de Henares 1594: Íñiguez de Lequerica.

Veitia Linage, Joseph de, *Norte de la Contratación de las Indias occidentales*, Buenos Aires 1945 (1st ed. Sevilla 1672: Juan Francisco de Blas).

Yrolo Calar, Nicolás De, *La política de escrituras*, ed. de Martínez López-Cano, María del Pilar, México 1996 (1st ed. México 1605: Diego Lopez Daualos).

Literature

Acosta Rodríguez, Antonio, Adolfo González Rodríguez, Enriqueta Vila Vilar (eds.), *La Casa de la Contratación y la navegación entre España y las Indias*, Sevilla 2003.

Agnolin, Adone, *L'invenzione del Tupì. Imprese coloniali e catechismi indigeni*, Bologna 2014.

Argouse, Aude, "De libros y otras cosas: el legado del obispo De la Puebla González. Santiago de Chile, 1705", in *Relaciones. Estudios de historia y sociedad* (Zamora/ Michoacán) 36, no. 144 (2015), 13–53.

Aspell de Yanzi Ferreira, Marcela, Carlos Alberto Page (eds.), *La Biblioteca Jesuítica de la Universidad Nacional de Córdoba*, Córdoba 2000.

Ávila Martel, Alamiro de, "La impresión y circulación de libros en el derecho indiano", in *Revista Chilena de Historia del Derecho* (Santiago de Chile) 11 (1985), 189–209.

Azoulai, Martine, *Les péchés du nouveau monde: les manuels pour la confession des Indiens. XVIe–XVIIe siècle*, Paris 1993.

Barnadas, Josep M., *Bibliotheca Boliviana Antiqva. Impresos coloniales (1534–1825)*, 2 vols., Sucre 2008.

Barrientos Grandón, Javier, *La cultura jurídica en el Reino de Chile. Bibliotecas de ministros de la Real Audiencia de Santiago (s. XVII y XVIII)*, Santiago de Chile 1992.

Barrientos Grandón, Javier, *La cultura jurídica en la Nueva España (Sobre la recepción de la tradición jurídica europea en el virreinato)*, México 1993.

Beck, Laura, "The Diffusion of Law Books in Early Modern Europe. A Methodological Approach", in Meccarelli, Massimo and María Julia Solla Sastre (eds.), *Spatial and Temporal Dimensions for Legal History. Research Experiences and Itineraries*, Frankfurt am Main 2016, 195–239.

Benito Moya, Silvano G.A., "Bibliotecas y libros en la cultura universitaria de Córdoba durante los siglos XVII y XVIII", in *Información, cultura y sociedad* (INIBI, Buenos Aires) 26 (2012), 13–39.

Bouza Alvarez, Fernando J., *Corre manuscrito. Una historia cultural del Siglo de Oro*, Madrid 2002.

Bouza, Fernando, *Hétérographies. Formes de l'écrit au siècle d'or espagnol*, Madrid 2010.

Bravo Lira, Bernardino, "La literatura jurídica indiana en el Barroco", in *Revista de Estudios Histórico-Jurídicos* (Valparaíso) 10 (1985), 227–268.

Bujanda, J[esús] M[artínez] de, *Index de l'Inquisition espagnole 1583, 1584*, Sherbrooke/ Geneva 1993.

Burns, Kathryn, *Into the Archive: Writing and Power in Colonial Peru*, Durham, NC 2010.

Burns, Kathryn "Making Indigenous Archives: The Quilcaycamayoq in Colonial Cuzco", in Ramos, Gabriela and Yanna Yannakakis (eds.), *Indigenous Intellectuals.*

Knowledge, Power, and Colonial Culture in Mexico and the Andes, Durham, NC 2014, 237–260.

Calvo, Hortensia, "The politics of print: the historiography of the book in early Spanish America", in *Book History* 6 (2003), 277–305.

Camarinhas, Nuno, "Bibliotecas particulares de magistrados no século XVIII", in *Oficina do Inconfidência* 6, no. 5 (2009), 13–32.

Campillo Pardo, Alberto José, *Censura, expurgo y control en la biblioteca colonial neogranadina*. Bogotá 2017.

Carlyon, Jonathan E. and Pedro Guibovich Pérez, "Library [Spain/Spanish America]", in Levy, Evonne and Kenneth Mills (eds.), *Lexicon of the Hispanic Baroque. Transatlantic Exchange and Transformation*, Austin, TX 2013, 193–199.

Casagrande, Agustín E., "Literatura Práctica en el siglo XVIII. El orden procesal en la historia de la justicia rioplatense", in *Revista de Historia del Derecho* (Buenos Aires) 49 (2015) (http://www.scielo.org.ar/scielo.php?script=sci_arttext&pid=S1853-17842015000100001).

Castañeda, Carmen, *Del autor al lector. Historia del libro en México*, con la colaboración de Myrna Cortés, México 2002.

Castillo Gómez, Antonio, *Entre la pluma y la pared. Una historia social de la escritura en los siglos de oro*, Madrid 2006.

Castillo Gómez, Antonio (ed.), *Libro y lectura en la península ibérica y América (siglos XIII a XVIII)*, Salamanca 2003.

Cátedra, Pedro M., María Luisa López-Vidriero (eds.), *La memoria de los libros: estudios sobre la historia del escrito y de la lectura en Europa y América*, 2 vols., Salamanca 2004.

Cervantes Bello, Francisco Javier (ed.), *Libros y Lectores en las sociedades hispanas: España y Nueva España (Siglos XVI–XVIII)*, Puebla 2016.

Chocano Mena, Magdalena, "Colonial Printing and Metropolitan Books: Printed Texts and the Shaping of Scholarly Culture in New Spain, 1539–1700", in *Colonial Latin American Historical Review* 6 (1997), 69–90.

Córdoba-Restrepo, Juan Felipe (ed.), *Biblioteca antigua. Circulación y conocimiento*, Bogotá 2015.

Cutter, Charles R., "El imperio 'no letrado': En torno al derecho vulgar de la época colonial", in Palacio, Juan Manuel and Manuela Candioti (eds.), *Justicia, política y derechos en América latina*, Buenos Aires 2007, 169–180.

Dadson, Trevor J., *Libros, lectores y lecturas. Estudios sobre bibliotecas particulares españolas del Siglo de Oro*, Madrid 1998.

Danwerth, Otto, "La circulación de literatura normativa pragmática en Hispanoamérica (siglos XVI–XVII)", in Thomas Duve (ed.), *Actas del XIX Congreso del Instituto Internacional de Historia del Derecho Indiano: Berlin 2016*, Madrid 2017, vol. 1, 359–400.

Danwerth, Otto, Teresa Dittmer, Seto Hardjana, Daniel Hausmann, Nicolas Perreaux, Linda Richter, Christian Schleidler, Frederic Steinfeld, David Weidgenannt: "Resources in a Social World", in Amelung, Iwo, Hartmut Leppin and Christian A. Müller (eds.), *Discourses of Weakness and Resource Regimes. Trajectories of a New Research Program*. Frankfurt am Main 2018, 223–253.

Danwerth, Otto, "A bibliography on the circulation of books in early modern Ibero-America", *Max Planck Institute for European Legal History Research Paper Series: subsidia et instrumenta* 2020 (http://dx.doi.org/10.2139/ssrn.3520508).

Deylen, Wiebke von, "Buchdruck, kolonialer, in Lateinamerika", in Hiery, Hermann (ed.), *Lexikon zur Überseegeschichte*, Stuttgart 2015, 135–136.

Dolezalek, Gero, "Libros jurídicos anteriores a 1800 en la Biblioteca de la Universidad Nacional Mayor de San Marcos en Lima. Bases para la formación jurídica de los abogados latinoamericanos del siglo XIX", in *Studi Sassaresi*, serie III, vol. 5: *Diritto romano, codificazioni e unità del sistema giuridico latino-americano*, Milano 1981, 491–518.

Durán, Juan Guillermo, *Monumenta catechética hispanoamericana (siglos XVI–XVIII)*, 3 vols., Buenos Aires 1984–2017.

Dürr, Renate, "Confession as an Instrument of Church Discipline: A Study of Catholic and Lutheran Confessional Manuals from the 16th and 17th Centuries", in Müller, Sigrid and Cornelia Schweiger (eds.), *Between Creativity and Norm-making: Tensions in the Early Modern Era*, Leiden 2013, 215–240.

Duve, Thomas, "Geschichte des Notariats und Notariatsrechts im frühneuzeitlichen Hispanoamerika und im späteren Argentinien", in Schmoeckel, Mathias and Werner Schubert (eds.), *Handbuch zur Geschichte des Notariats der europäischen Tradition*, Baden-Baden 2009, 595–619.

Duve, Thomas, "Katholisches Kirchenrecht und Moraltheologie im 16. Jahrhundert: eine globale normative Ordnung im Schatten schwacher Staatlichkeit", in Günther, Klaus and Stefan Kadelbach (eds.), *Recht ohne Staat?*, Frankfurt am Main 2011, 147–174.

Fernandes, Maria de Lurdes Correia, "Do manual de confessores ao guia de penitentes. Orientações e caminhos da confissão no Portugal pós-Trento", in *Via Spiritus* (Porto) 2 (1995), 47–65.

Fernández del Castillo, Bernardo, *Historia de la escribanía en la Nueva España y el notariado en México*, México 1983.

Fernández del Castillo, Francisco (ed.), *Libros y libreros en el siglo XVI*, 2nd ed., México 1982 (1ª ed. México 1911).

Fornet, Ambrosio, *El libro en Cuba, siglos XVIII y XIX*, Havana 1994.

Fortich Navarro, Mónica Patricia, *Togados y letrados: libros, lecturas y bibliotecas en la formación de los abogados neogranadinos, 1739–1777*, Bogotá 2011.

Furlong Cardiff, Guillermo, *Bibliotecas argentinas durante la dominación hispánica*, Buenos Aires 1944.

García Aguilar, Idalia, "El conocimiento histórico del libro y la biblioteca novohispanos. Representación de las fuentes originales", in *Información, cultura y sociedad* (Buenos Aires, INIBI) 17 (2007), 69–96.

García Aguilar, Idalia, " 'Para que les den libre paso en todas partes sin que los abran ni detengan': Libros para las comunidades religiosas de la Nueva España", in *Cuadernos de Historia Moderna* 42:1 (2017), 151–73.

García Aguilar, Idalia and Pedro Rueda Ramírez (eds.), *Leer en tiempos de la colonia: imprenta, bibliotecas y lectores en la Nueva España*, México 2010.

García Aguilar, Idalia and Pedro Rueda Ramírez (eds.), *El libro en circulación en la América colonial: producción, circuitos de distribución y conformación de bibliotecas en los siglos XVI al XVIII*, México 2014.

García Icazbalceta, Javier, *Bibliografía mexicana del siglo XVI. Catálogo razonado de libros impresos en México de 1539 a 1600*, México 1981 (1st ed. 1886).

García-Baquero, Antonio, *La Carrera de Indias: Suma de contratación y océano de negocios*, Sevilla 1992.

Garone Gravier, "Fuentes para el estudio de la tipografía, la imprenta y el libro antiguo mexicano (1539–1821)", in *Pecia Complutense* 9, núm. 17 (2012), 59–84.

Gil, Fernando, *Primeras "doctrinas" del Nuevo Mundo: estudio histórico-teológico de las obras de fray Juan de Zumárraga (1548)*, Buenos Aires 1993.

Giurgevich, Luana and Henrique Leitão, *Clavis bibliothecarum: Catálogos e inventários de livrarias de instituições religiosas em Portugal até 1834*, Lisbon 2016.

González Polvillo, Antonio, *Análisis y repertorio de los tratados y manuales para la confesión en el mundo hispánico (ss. XV–XVIII)*, Huelva 2010.

González Polvillo, Antonio, *El gobierno de los otros: confesión y control de la conciencia en la España Moderna*, Sevilla 2010.

González Rodríguez, Jaime, "La difusión manuscrita de ideas en Nueva España (Siglo XVI)", in *Revista Complutense de Historia de América* 18 (1992), 89–116.

González Sánchez, Carlos Alberto, "La cultura del libro en el Virreinato del Perú en tiempos de Felipe II", in *Colonial Latin American Review* 9:1 (2000), 63–80.

González Sánchez, Carlos Alberto, *Atlantes de papel. Adoctrinamiento, creación y tipografía en la Monarquía Hispánica de los siglos XVI y XVII*, Barcelona 2008.

González Sánchez, Carlos Alberto, *New World Literacy. Writing and Culture across the Atlantic*, Lewisburg 2011 (Spanish version: *Los mundos del libro. Medios de difusión de la cultura occidental en las Indias de los siglos XVI y XVII*, Sevilla 1999).

González Sánchez, Carlos Alberto, "La cultura escrita en el Mundo Atlántico colonial: Brasil y América del norte. Claves historiográficas, retos y perspectivas", in *Revista de Indias* LXXIII, no. 259 (2013), 633–662.

González Sánchez, Carlos Alberto, "El comercio de libros entre Europa y América en la Sevilla del siglo XVI: Impresores, libreros y mercaderes", in *Colonial Latin American Review* 23:3 (2014), 439–465.

González Sánchez, Carlos Alberto, "Misión náutica. De libros, discursos y prácticas culturales en la Carrera de Indias de los siglos XVI y XVII", in Federico Palomo (ed.), *La memoria del mundo: clero, erudición y cultura escrita en el mundo ibérico (siglos XVI–XVIII)*, Madrid 2014, 71–86.

Greer Johnson, Julie (ed.), *The Book in the Americas. The role of books and printing in the development of culture and society in colonial Latin America*, Providence, RI 1988.

Griffin, Clive, *The Crombergers of Seville. The History of a Printing and Merchant Dynasty*, Oxford 1988.

Grover, "The Book and the Conquest: Jesuit Libraries in Colonial Brazil", in *Libraries and Culture* 28:3, 266–283.

Guedes de Campos, Fernanda Maria, *Para se achar facilmente o que se busca: Bibliotecas, catálogos e leitores no ambiente religioso (séc. XVIII)*, Casal de Cambra 2015.

Guibovich Pérez, Pedro, "The Printing Press in Colonial Peru: Production Process and Literary Categories in Lima, 1584–1699", in *Colonial Latin American Review* 10:2 (2001), 167–188.

Guibovich Pérez, Pedro, *Censura, libros e Inquisición en el Perú colonial, 1570–1754*, Sevilla 2003.

Guibovich Pérez, Pedro M., "Los libros de los doctrineros en el virreinato del Perú, siglos XVI–XVII", in Oesterreicher, Wulf and Roland Schmidt-Riese (eds.), *Esplendores y miserias de la evangelización de América. Antecedentes europeos y alteridad indígena*, Berlin 2010, 97–132.

Hampe Martínez, Teodoro, "Lecturas de un jurista del siglo XVI. La biblioteca del doctor Gregorio González de Cuenca, presidente de la Audiencia de Santo Domingo (1581)", in *Anuario de Estudios Americanos* 41 (1984), 143–193.

Hampe Martínez, Teodoro, *Bibliotecas privadas en el mundo colonial: la difusión de libros e ideas en el virreinato del Perú (siglos XVI–XVII)*, Frankfurt am Main/Madrid 1996.

Hampe Martínez, Teodoro, "Las bibliotecas virreinales en el Perú y la difusión del saber italiano: el caso del virrey Toledo (1582)", in Cantù, Francesca (ed.), *Las Cortes virreinales de la Monarquía española: América e Italia*, Roma 2008, 539–555.

Hampe Martínez, Teodoro, "Historiografía del libro en América hispana: un estado de la cuestión", in García Aguilar, Idalia and Pedro Rueda Ramírez (eds.), *Leer en tiempos de la colonia: imprenta, bibliotecas y lectores en la Nueva España*, México 2010, 55–72.

Harrison, Regina, *Sin and Confession in Colonial Peru. Spanish-Quechua Penitential Texts, 1560–1650*, Austin, TX 2014.

Herzog, Tamar, *Mediación, archivos y ejercicio. Los escribanos de Quito (siglo XVII)*, Frankfurt am Main 1996.

Hespanha, António Manuel, "Form and content in early modern legal books. Bridging the gap between material bibliography and the history of legal thought", in *Rechtsgeschichte – Legal History* 12 (2008), 12–50.

Honores, Renzo, "Litigación en la Audiencia Arzobispal de Lima: Abogados y procuradores de causas en la litigación canónica, 1600–1650", in Otto Danwerth, Benedetta Albani and Thomas Duve (eds.), *Normatividades e instituciones eclesiásticas en el virreinato del Perú, siglos XVI–XIX*, Frankfurt am Main 2019, 69–108 (http://dx.doi.org/10.12946/gplh12).

Hyland, Sabine, *The Chankas and the Priest. A Tale of Murder and Exile in Highland Peru*, University Park, Pennsylvania, PA 2016.

Inch C., Marcela, "La Biblioteca Potosina de la Compañía de Jesús", in *Bibliographica Americana*, Revista Interdisciplinaria de Estudios Coloniales (Buenos Aires) 4 (2007), 1–11 (http ://www.bn.gov.ar/media/page/marcela-inch.pdf).

Infantes, Víctor, "De la cartilla al libro", in *Bulletin Hispanique* 97:1 (1995), 33–66.

Jiménez, Norah Edith, "Los libros en lenguas indígenas como un género de las imprentas novohispanas entre los siglos XVI y XVII", in Jiménez, Norah Edith and Martina Mantilla Trolle (eds.), *Colección de Lenguas Indígenas* (Fondos del Tesoro: Biblioteca Pública del Estado de Jalisco "Juan José Arreola"), Guadalajara 2007, 65–117.

Jiménez, Nora E., "Cuentas fallidas, deudas omnipresentes. Los difíciles comienzos del mercado del libro novohispano", in *Anuario de Estudios Americanos* 71:2 (2014), 423–446.

Johnston, Michael and Michael Van Dussen (eds.), *The Medieval Manuscript Book: Cultural Approaches*, Cambridge 2016.

Kropfinger von Kügelgen, Helga, *Exportación de libros europeos de Sevilla a la Nueva España en el año de 1586*, Wiesbaden 1973.

Latasa, Pilar, "Tridentine Marriage Ritual in Sixteenth- to Eighteenth-century Peru: From Global Procedures to American Idiosyncrasies", in *Rechtsgeschichte – Legal History* 27 (2019), 105–121.

Leal, Ildefonso, *Libros y bibliotecas en Venezuela colonial (1633–1767)*, 2 vols., Caracas 1978.

Leonard, Irving A., *Books of the Brave. Being an account of books and of men in the Spanish Conquest and settlement of the sixteenth-century New World.* With a new introduction by Rolena Adorno, Berkeley and Los Angeles 1992 (1st ed. Cambridge, MA 1949).

Lértora Mendoza, Celina A., "Bibliotecas académicas coloniales. Reconstrucción y puesta en valor", in *Anuario de Historia de la Iglesia* 22 (2013), 259–273.

Lira, Andrés, "Dimensión jurídica de la conciencia. Pecadores y pecados en tres confesionarios de la Nueva España, 1545–1732", in *Historia Mexicana* 55:4 (2006), 1139–1178.

Llamosas, Esteban F., "Las obras jurídicas en la biblioteca del Colegio Jesuita de Arequipa", in *Rudimentos legales* (Jaén) 3 (2002), 95–159.

Llamosas, Esteban F., "Probabilismo, probabiliorismo y rigorismo: La teología moral en la enseñanza universitaria y en la praxis judicial de la Córdoba tardocolonial", in *Cuadernos del Instituto Antonio de Nebrija de Estudios sobre la Universidad* (Madrid) 14:2 (2011), 281–294.

Lohmann Villena, Guillermo, "Los libros españoles en Indias", in *Arbor* (Madrid) 2, no. 6 (1944), 221–249.

Luján Múñoz, Jorge, "La literatura jurídica notarial en Hispanoamérica durante la colonia", in *Revista Interamericana de Bibliografía* 3 (1987), 335–368.

Lundberg, Magnus: *Church Life between the Metropolitan and the Local: Parishes, Parishioners, and Parish Priests in Seventeenth-Century Mexico*. Madrid/Frankfurt am Main 2011.

Luque Colombres, Carlos A., "Libros de Derecho en bibliotecas particulares cordobesas (1573–1810)", in *Para la Historia de Córdoba*, Córdoba 1971, 267–318 (1st ed. 1945 in *Cuadernos de Historia*, Córdoba, no. IX).

Luque Talaván, Miguel, *Un universo de opiniones. La literatura jurídica indiana*, Madrid 2003.

Luque Talaván, Miguel, "De los libros surgen las leyes. Aproximación a los fondos jurídicos de las bibliotecas particulares y públicas novohispanas", in García Aguilar, Idalia (ed.), *Complejidad y materialidad: reflexiones del seminario del libro antiguo*, México 2009, 65–191.

Maeder, Ernesto J.A., "Libros, bibliotecas, control de lecturas e imprentas rioplatenses en los siglos XVI al XVIII", in *Revista Teología* (Buenos Aires) 40, no. 77 (2001), 5–24.

Maihold, Harald, *Strafe für fremde Schuld? Die Systematisierung des Strafbegriffs in der Spanischen Spätscholastik und Naturrechtslehre*, Köln 2005.

Maillard Alvarez, Natalia, "Aproximación a la creación de las redes de distribución de libros en América a través de las fuentes españolas (segunda mitad del siglo XVI)", in *Anuario de Estudios Americanos* 71:2 (2014), 479–503.

Maillard Alvarez, Natalia (ed.), *Books in the Catholic World during the Early Modern Period*, Leiden 2014.

Malagón Barceló, Javier, *La literatura jurídica española del siglo de oro en la Nueva España. Notas para su estudio*, México 1959.

Manrique Figueroa, César, "Bibliotecas de funcionarios reales novohispanos de la primera mitad del siglo XVII", in *Boletín del Instituto de Investigaciones Bibliográficas* (México) 19 (2014), 57–93.

Maris Fernández, Stella, *La imprenta en Hispanoamérica*, Madrid 1977.

Martín, Luis, *La conquista intelectual del Perú. El Colegio Jesuita de San Pablo, 1568–1767*, Barcelona 2001 (1st ed. Fordham 1967).

Martínez Ferrer, Luis, *La penitencia en la primera evangelización de México, 1523–1585*, México 1998.

Mathes, W. Michael, *The America's First Academic Library: Santa Cruz de Tlatelolco*, Sacramento 1985.

Mathes, W. Michael, "Humanism in Sixteenth and Seventeenth Century Libraries of New Spain", in *The Catholic Historical Review* 82 (1996), 412–35.

Mayagoitía, Alejandro, "Notas sobre los alegatos impresos novohispanos", in *Memoria del X Congreso del Instituto Internacional de Historia del Derecho Indiano*, vol. 2, México 1995, 1001–1030.

Medina, José Toribio, *Historia de la imprenta en los antiguos dominios españoles de América y Oceanía*, 2 vols., Santiago de Chile 1958.

Medina, José Toribio, *Biblioteca hispano-americana (1493–1810)*, 7 vols., 2nd reprint, Amsterdam 1968 (1st ed. Santiago de Chile 1898–1907).

Millares Carlo, Agustín, "Bibliotecas y difusión del libro en Hispanoamérica colonial: intento bibliográfico", in *Boletín Histórico* (Caracas) 22 (1970), 25–72.

Mohler, Stephen C., "Publishing in colonial Spanish America", in *Inter-American Review of Bibliography* 28:3 (1978), 259–273.

Molina Jiménez, Iván, *El que quiera divertirse: Libros y sociedad en Costa Rica, 1750–1914*, San José 1995.

Moraes, Rubens Borba de: *Livros e bibliotecas no Brasil colonial*. 2nd ed., Brasília 2006 (1st ed. 1979).

Morales, Francisco, *Inventario del Fondo Franciscano del Museo de Antropología e Historia de México*, vol. 1, con la colaboración de Dorothy Tanck de Estrada, México 1978.

Morales, Francisco, *Inventario del Fondo Franciscano del Archivo Histórico de la Biblioteca Nacional de Antropología e Historia*, vol. 2, México 2008.

Morales, Francisco, "Cómo se formaron las bibliotecas franciscanas: Una mirada a través de la Biblioteca Franciscana de Cholula", in: *Ciencia y Cultura entre dos mundos. Nueva España y Canarias como ejemplos de* knowledge in transit (Actas de congreso, San Sebastián de La Gomera, 2 y 4 de abril de 2009), 14 p. (http://www.fundacionorotava.org/media/web/files/page163__01_Francisco_Morales.pdf).

Morgado García, Arturo, "Pecado y confesión en la España Moderna: Los manuales de confesores", in *Trocadero* (Cádiz) 8–9 (1996–1997), 119–148.

Nalle, Sarah T., "Printing and reading popular religious texts in sixteenth-century Spain", in Lewis, Tom and Francisco J. Sánchez (eds.), *Culture and State in Spain, 1550–1850*, New York/London 1999, 123–156.

Navarro Bonilla, Diego, "Las huellas de la lectura: marcas y anotaciones manuscritas en impresos de los siglos XVI a XVIII", in Castillo Gómez, Antonio (ed.), *Libro y lectura en la península ibérica y América (siglos XIII a XVIII)*, Salamanca 2003, 243–287.

Nébias Barreto, Herman, "Legal Culture and Argumentation in the Vice-Reign of Peru from the 16th to the 18th centuries", in *Clio@Themis*, Révue électronique d'histoire du droit 2 (2009) (http://www.cliothemis.com/Legal-Culture-and-Argumentation-in).

Neddermeyer, Uwe, *Von der Handschrift zum gedruckten Buch. Schriftlichkeit und Leseinteresse im Mittelalter und in der frühen Neuzeit. Quantitative und qualitative Aspekte*, 2 vols., Wiesbaden 1998.

Nesvig, Martin A., *Ideology and Inquisition: The world of the censors in early Mexico*, New Haven, CT 2009.

O livro antigo em Portugal e Espanha, séculos XVI–XVIII, in *Leituras* (Lisboa) 9–10, 2001–2002.

O'Banion, Patrick J., *The Sacrament of Penance and Religious Life in Golden Age Spain*, College Park, MD 2013.

O'Gorman, Edmundo, "Bibliotecas y librerías coloniales, 1585–1694", in *Boletín del Archivo General de la Nación* (México) 10:4 (1939), 661–1006.

Orrego González, Francisco, *La administración de la conciencia. Manuales para confesar y tolerancia cultural en tiempos de la Ilustración ibérica. Siglo XVIII*. Aranjuez (Madrid) 2017.

Osorio Romero, Ignacio, *Historia de las bibliotecas novohispanas*, México 1986.

Osvaldo Cutolo, Vicente, "Bibliotecas jurídicas en el Buenos Aires del siglo XVII", in *Universidad* (Santa Fe) 30 (1955), 105–183.

Palomo, Federico, "Anaqueles de sacra erudición: Libros y lecturas de un predicador jesuita en el Portugal del siglo XVII", in *Lusitania Sacra*, 2ª série, 18 (2006), 117–146.

Palomo, Federico, "Misioneros, libros y cultura escrita en Portugal y España durante el siglo XVII", in Castelnau-L'Estoile, Charlotte de, Marie-Lucie Copete, Aliocha Maldavsky and Ines G. Županov (eds.), *Missions d'évangélisation et circulation des savoirs, XVIe–XVIIIe siècle*, Madrid 2011, 131–150.

Palomo, Federico, "Cultura religiosa, comunicación y escritura en el mundo ibérico de la Edad Moderna", in Serrano Martín, Eliseo (ed.), *De la tierra al cielo. Líneas recientes de la investigación en Historia Moderna*, Zaragoza 2013, 53–88.

Palomo, Federico, "Written Empires: Franciscans, Texts and the Making of Early Modern Iberian Empires [Editorial]", in *Culture & History Digital Journal* 5:2 (2016) (https://doi.org/10.3989/chdj.2016.v5.i2).

Parada, Alejandro E., "Tipología de las bibliotecas Argentinas desde el periodo hispánico hasta 1830: una primera clasificación provisional", in *Información, cultura y sociedad*, (Buenos Aires, INIBI) 9 (2003), 75–94.

Peña Espinosa, Jesús Joel, "Fuentes, autoridades y normas para la enseñanza del derecho canónico en el seminario de Puebla durante la época novohispana", in Albani, Benedetta, Otto Danwerth and Thomas Duve (eds.), *Normatividades e instituciones eclesiásticas en la Nueva España, siglos XVI–XIX*, Frankfurt am Main 2018, 51–67 (http://dx.doi.org/10.12946/gplh5).

Peñalver Gómez, Eduardo (ed.), *América escrita. Fondos americanistas en bibliotecas universitarias españolas. Exposición bibliográfica conmemorativa de los bicentenarios de las independencias de las repúblicas iberoamericanas*, Sevilla 2010.

Poole, Stafford (ed.): *The Directory for Confessors 1585. Implementing the Catholic Reformation in New Spain.* With contributions by John F. Schwaller. Norman, OK 2018.

Presta, Ana María, "Redes de tinta y poder. Escribanos, clero e indígenas en la ciudad de La Plata, siglos XVI–XVII", in *Anuario de estudios bolivianos, archivísticos y bibliográficos* (Sucre) 19 (2013), 351–372.

Prieto Bernabé, José Manuel, *Lecturas y lectores. La cultura del impreso en el Madrid del Siglo de Oro (1550–1650)*, Mérida 2004.

Puente Luna, José Carlos de la and Renzo Honores, "Guardianes de la real justicia: alcaldes de indios, costumbre y justicia local en Huarochirí colonial", in *Histórica* (Lima) 40:2 (2016), 11–47.

Ramada Curto, Diogo (ed.), *Bibliografia da História do Livro em Portugal, séculos XV*–XIX, Lisboa 2003.

Ramos, Gabriela and Yanna Yannakakis (eds.), *Indigenous Intellectuals. Knowledge, Power, and Colonial Culture in Mexico and the Andes*, Durham, NC 2014.

Ramos Núñez, Carlos, *Ius Commune. Libros y juristas en la Biblioteca de la Recoleta. Siglos XVI y XVII*, vol. 1: *Catálogo y estudio preliminar*, Arequipa 2016.

Ramos Soriano, José Abel, *Los delincuentes de papel: Inquisición y libros en la Nueva Espana (1571–1820)*, México 2011.

Resines Llorente, Luis, *Catecismos americanos del siglo XVI*, 2 vols., Valladolid 1992.

Rey Fajardo, José del, *Las bibliotecas jesuíticas en la Venezuela colonial*, 2 vols., Caracas 1999.

Rey Fajardo, José del and Myriam Marín Cortés (eds.), *La biblioteca colonial de la Universidad Javeriana comentada*, Bogotá 2008.

Rey Fajardo, José del, "El papel de las bibliotecas jesuíticas en la fundación de la cultura moderna", in Bianchini, Paolo, Perla Chinchilla Pawling and Antonella Romano (eds.), *De los colegios a las universidades. Los Jesuitas en el ámbito de la educación superior*, México 2013, 125–152.

Reyes Gómez, Fermín de los, *El libro en España y América. Legislación y censura (siglos XV–XVIII)*, 2 vols., Madrid 2000.

Richardson, Brian, *Manuscript Culture in Renaissance Italy*, Cambridge 2014.

Río Parra, Elena del, *Cartografías de la conciencia española en la Edad de Oro*, México 2008.

Rípodas Ardanaz, Daisy, "Bibliotecas privadas de funcionarios de la Real Audiencia de Charcas", in *Memoria del II Congreso Venezolano de Historia*, vol. 2, Caracas 1975, 499–555.

Rípodas Ardanaz, Daisy, "Libros, bibliotecas y lecturas [cap. 22]", in Academia Nacional de la Historia (ed.), *Nueva Historia de la Nación Argentina*, vol. 3, Buenos Aires 1999, 247–279.

Rodrigues, Luiz Fernando Medeiros, "As 'livrarias' dos Jesuítas no Brasil Colonial, segundo os documentos do Archivum Romano [*sic*] Societatis Iesu", in Hofmeister Pich, Roberto, Manuel Lázaro Pulido and Alfredo Santiago Culleton (eds.), *Ideas sin fronteras en los límites de las ideas / Ideias sem fronteiras nos limites das ideias. Scholastica Colonialis: Status Quaestionis*, Cáceres 2012, 285–312.

Rodríguez Marín, Francisco, *El "Quijote" y don Quijote en América*, Madrid 1911.

Rodríguez-Buckingham, Antonio, "Monastic Libraries and Early Printing in Sixteenth-Century Spanish America", in *Libraries and Culture* (Austin) 24:1 (1989), 33–56.

Roselló Soberón, Estela, *Así en la tierra como en el cielo: manifestaciones cotidianas de la culpa y el perdón en la Nueva España de los siglos XVI y XVII*, México 2006.

Rubio Hernández, Alfonso, "Los tratados de práctica notarial en las bibliotecas de escribanos neogranadinos del siglo XVIII", in *Revista Historia Y MEMORIA* (Tunja) 13 (2016), 19–46.

Rueda Ramírez, Pedro José, *Negocio e intercambio cultural: el comercio de libros con América en la Carrera de Indias (siglo XVII)*, Sevilla 2005.

Rueda Ramírez, Pedro José, "El comercio de libros en Latinoamérica colonial: aproximación al estado de la cuestión (siglos XVI–XVIII)", in García Aguilar, Idalia (ed.), *Complejidad y materialidad: Reflexiones del seminario del libro antiguo*, México 2009, 193–279.

Rueda Ramírez, Pedro José, "Libros europeos en Centroamérica en los siglos XVI–XVII", in *Yaxkin* (Tegucigalpa) 25:2 (2009), 151–192.

Rueda Ramírez, Pedro José, "El abastecimiento de libros de la biblioteca conventual de San Agustín de Puebla de los Ángeles a través de la Carrera de Indias (1609–1613)", in *Estudios de Historia Novohispana* 44 (2011), 17–43.

Rueda Ramírez, Pedro (ed.), *El libro en circulación en el mundo moderno en España y Latinoamérica*, Madrid 2012.

Rueda Ramírez, Pedro (ed.), "Dossier: Circulación y venta de libros en el mundo americano de la edad moderna: de los circuitos atlánticos a los mercados locales", in *Anuario de Estudios Americanos* 71:2 (2014), 413–503.

Rueda Ramírez, Pedro, "El derecho en los catálogos de venta de los libreros sevillanos: la circulación de impresos jurídicos en el mundo atlántico (1680–1689)", in Duve, Thomas (ed.), *Actas del XIX Congreso del Instituto Internacional de Historia del Derecho Indiano: Berlin 2016*, vol. 1, Madrid 2017, 453–474.

Salinas Araneda, Carlos, "Los textos utilizados en la enseñanza del Derecho Canónico en Chile indiano", in *Anuario de Historia de la Iglesia* 9 (2000), 215–234.

Sánchez Baena, Juan José, "Noticias sobre el mundo del libro en Cuba antes del desarrollo de la imprenta (1525–1763)", in *Contrastes. Revista de Historia* (Murcia) 9–10 (1994–1997), 181–205.

Saranyana, Josep Ignasi (ed.), *Teología en América Latina*, vol. 1: *Desde los orígenes a la Guerra de Sucesión (1493–1715)*, Madrid 1999.

Serrano Prada, José María, *Apuntes al catálogo sistemático de la Biblioteca del Colegio de Misiones de Popayán, siglos XV–XVIII: historia y evaluación de la colección*, Popayán 2016.

Solano, Francisco de, "Fuentes para la historia cultural: Libros y bibliotecas de la América colonial", in Pino Díaz, Fermín del (ed.), *Ensayos de metodología histórica en el campo americanista*, Madrid 1985, 69–84.

Stintzing, Roderich, *Geschichte der populären Literatur des römisch-kanonischen Rechts in Deutschland am Ende des fünfzehnten und im Anfang des sechszehnten Jahrhunderts*, Leipzig 1867.

Tau Anzoátegui, Victor, *Nuevos Horizontes en el estudio histórico del Derecho Indiano*, Buenos Aires 1997.

Tau Anzoátegui, Victor, *El Jurista en el Nuevo Mundo. Pensamiento. Doctrina. Mentalidad*, Frankfurt am Main 2016.

Taylor, William B., *Magistrates of the Sacred: Priests and Parishioners in Eighteenth-Century Mexico*, Stanford 1996.

Thompson, Laurence Sydney and Hensley Charles Woodbridge, *Printing in Colonial Spanish America*, Troy/New York 1976.

Torre Revello, José, *El libro, la imprenta y el periodismo en América durante la dominación española*, Buenos Aires 1940.

Torre Revello, José, "Lecturas indianas (siglos XVI–XVIII)", in *Thesaurus* (Bogotá) 17 (1962), 1–29.

Vargas Ugarte, Ruben, *Impresos peruanos*, 6 vols., Lima 1953–1957.

Villalba Pérez, Enrique and Emilio Torné (eds.), *El nervio de la República: el oficio de escribano en el Siglo de Oro*, Madrid 2010.

Ward, Kenneth C., *"Mexico, where they coin money and print books": the Calderón dynasty and the Mexican book trade, 1630–1730*, Ph.D. thesis, University of Texas, Austin, TX 2013.

Wehling, Peter, "Wissensregime", in Schützeichel, Rainer (ed.), *Handbuch Wissenssoziologie und Wissensforschung*, Konstanz 2007, 704–712.

Wilkinson, Alexander S. (ed.), *Iberian Books: Books published in Spanish or Portuguese or on the Iberian Peninsula before 1601*, Leiden 2010.

Wilkinson, Alexander S. and Alejandra Ulla Lorenzo (eds.), *Iberian Books, volumes II & III: Books published in Spain, Portugal or elsewhere in Spanish or Portuguese between 1601 and 1650*, Leiden 2016.

Wilkinson, Alexander and Alejandra Ulla Lorenzo (eds.), *A Maturing Market. The Iberian Book in the First Half of the Seventeenth Century*, Leiden 2017.

Zaballa Beascoechea, Ana de, "Indian Marriage Before and After the Council of Trent: From pre-Hispanic Marriage to Christian Marriage in New Spain", in *Rechtsgeschichte – Legal History* 27 (2019), 90–104.

Zulaica Gárate, Román, *Los franciscanos y la imprenta en México en el siglo XVI. Estudio bio-bibliográfico*, México 1991.

CHAPTER 4

Presence and Use of Pragmatic Legal Literature in Habsburg Peru (16th–17th Centuries)

Renzo Honores

1 Introduction

Around 1642, the priest and chronicler Fernando de Montesinos (d. 1652) wrote regretfully how the *Curia Philipica* had been widely used by mestizos and Andeans in litigation.[1] For the author of *Anales*, the consultation and social usage of this procedural manual had rocketed the lawsuits in the *Limeño* Audiencia. His pessimistic view on how "subaltern" groups had mischievously used *prácticas* was a common perspective among other Habsburg colonial authors. Thus, in 1561, the notable jurist Licentiate Polo Ondegardo (1517/1520–1575) condemned acrimoniously how the Andean subjects had appropriated the Castilian law.[2] This phenomenon, he argued, had perverted the sense of justice especially among the natives. As an example, he cited endless opportunities in which Cuzqueño people offered their testimonies for economic returns. His experience as magistrate in the former Inca capital convinced him to propose judicial reforms. Polo's view was not an isolated one. In 1588, Father Bartolomé Alvarez, also in Cuzco, accused the Andean *ladinos* of using irresponsible litigation manuals like Gabriel de Monterroso's *Practica civil y criminal* (of 1563) for

1 His words were eloquent: "[Hevia Bolaños' *Curia Philipica*] a hecho mucho daño en este Reyno, no por mala, sino por bien entendida: todos son letrados; especialmente los mestizos se inclinan a esto [litigation in courts], ya me dicen que los indios también tratan de esto y andan en sus pueblos amenaçando a los corregidores y curas con la *Curia*", in Montesinos, *Anales del Perú*, vol. 2, 222. I thank Herman Barreto for this and other references.

2 Polo Ondegardo was the first Spanish jurist who proposed the recognition of customary law as a means to reduce indigenous litigation in the Andes. He presented the hyper-litigation as the consequence of professional manipulation (by lawyers), cultural misunderstanding, and perversion of the justice's goals. He stated: "que cierto ésta es cosa de lástima verlos enseñados a nuestras trampas, hecho pleitistas por las audiencias, y lo que peor es, que entendida la fuerza de nuestra justicia consistir la mayor parte en testigos, hallando fácil el remedio por la gran facilidad de los indios, ya no piden lo que cada uno cree ser suyo o pertenecerle, sino lo que había menester o le viene a propósito [...] y hase hallado plaza pública de viejos que venían de sus tierras a ganar de comer por testigos, y se sentaban a hora cierta para ser alquilados", in Ondegardo, *Informe del licenciado Polo Ondegardo*, ed. Lamana, 144.

DOI:10.1163/9789004425736_005

their disputes.[3] In the early 17th century, the authors of manuals highlighted the importance of their production for improving and reforming the practice of law. Jurists, priests, and theologians coincided in the opinion that the legal literature should be used to reform the role of experts as guarantors of justice.[4] That period marks the rise of the idea of professionalisation in legal practice but also the dissemination of legal concepts through printed pragmatic production.[5] Legal literature was crucial in the effort for regulating the practice, providing templates for laymen, and guiding the conduct of facilitators.

This preliminary essay explores the circulation of 'pragmatic books' and their juridical categories in the Habsburg Andes. 'Pragmatic' literature refers to legal and moral literature written in vernacular language, a corpus that oriented the professional and local practice producing normative effects.[6] This universe of intellectual production was intended for its daily usage in justice administration, local government, and the spiritual legal/moral order. This corpus generated normative effects on the King's subjects because it regulated their own lives, rights, and patrimonies.[7] In late medieval and early modern Castile, the manuals were called *prácticas* to distinguish them from the legal treatises (*tractatus* in Latin), a more sophisticated body of doctrinal ideas in law.[8] However, pragmatic literature itself incorporated legal categories and helped to disseminate them to a broader audience. While *prácticas* circulated in local spheres, they were also used in seats of Audiencias, the great centres of legal production. This chapter argues that pragmatic legal literature became

3 The *Práctica* had at least eight editions between 1566 and 1609. In 1591, this manual was on sale in Lima's bookstores, see Ondegardo, *Informe del licenciado Polo Ondegardo*, ed. Lamana, 524. Palau y Ducet indicates a first edition dated in 1563 (Palau y Ducet, *Manual del librero hispanoamericano*, vol. 10, 122). On Father Alvarez's words, see his report to Philip II (Alvarez, *De las costumbres y conversión de los indios del Perú*, 268–269), a discussion on this point, in Danwerth, "La circulación de literatura normativa pragmática en Hispanoamérica", 389.

4 Priest Bartolomé Vadillo (1593–1659) postulated a moral model for the advocacy and magistracy in colonial Lima, see his sermon of 1648.

5 By professionalisation, this essay refers to a group of specialists who monopolised (or tried to do so) the legal services in return for economic compensations. In the case of litigation, the experts were the *abogado* (advocate) and the *procurador de causas* (procurator). In colonial Peru, they appeared and proliferated in several cities around the mid-16th century.

6 Danwerth, "La circulación de literatura normativa pragmática en Hispanoamérica".

7 I am indebted to Otto Danwerth for this definition and for providing information on this valuable contribution and its current relevance for studies in legal history. Roderich von Stintzing (1825–1883), lawyer and legal historian, explored the popular legal literature in the late medieval and early modern Holy Roman Empire. The result of his research was his book *Geschichte der populären Literatur des römisch-kanonischen Rechts in Deutschland*, Leipzig 1867.

8 Alonso Romero, "Theoria y Praxis en la enseñanza del Derecho".

part of the legal universe in the Peruvian viceroyalty and was used by legal facilitators and laymen.

By focusing on the first two centuries of Spanish colonialism, this chapter emphasises the significance of that period in the making of a colonial legal culture. The term 'legal culture' refers to the knowledge and social usage of law. The rule of the Habsburg dynasty is considered as an example of pluralism and legal diversity in Europe and the Americas.[9] The Habsburgs were also the leaders of the Counter-Reformation and the crafters of the enduring Spanish "Catholic monarchy". Due to the dimensions of its vast dominions, the production of Italian and Flemish printing presses circulated in the New World. This essay examines the functions of that pragmatic juridical literature in the practice of law. This intellectual production exerted a capital influence on the justice administration, the arguments of professionals and ordinary citizens, and on the construction of a rhetoric of justice and good government. Such a political and legal lexicon was a cornerstone in the design of the Habsburg juridical framework. Legal rhetoric was constructed by various agents, and legal literature epitomised in *prácticas* played a significant role in its making.

This exploratory contribution has been divided into three parts. Part one examines pragmatic legal literature and its consumption in Habsburg Peru. The second part pays attention to the use of these laws and rhetoric in higher and lower courts. Finally, part three analyses the genesis of a legal culture in the colonial Andes, a historic process in which both professionals and litigants participated.

2 The Presence of Pragmatic Literature and the Local Book Market

Since the mid-16th century, a population of consumers of legal publications existed in the Andes. Practitioners settled gradually across several cities. In Lima, for instance, the class of lawyers, procurators, and scribes were already visible in 1538.[10] Other places like Cuzco (in the south) and Trujillo (in the north) held a community of specialists for litigation in the decade of the 1550s. Between the 1560s and 1570s, a growing population of legal experts installed in La Plata

9 Härter, "The Early Modern Holy Roman Empire of the German Nation", 113–122.

10 *Libros de cabildos de Lima. Libro primero*, ed. Lee, 234–235. The two first agents for litigation, procurators, were Alonso de Navarrete and Pedro de Avendaño. The latter developed an impressive career becoming the private secretary of Viceroy Marquis of Cañete (r. 1556–1560) and of the Audiencia of Lima. Pedro de Avendaño was the head of an influential lineage in the city.

(today's Sucre) and later in Potosí. At least in a period of forty years after the conquest, the main centres of Spanish urban presence had a numerous class of professionals. In the early 17th century, the Villa Imperial of Potosí, the largest and most populous Andean metropolis, had such a number of practitioners that it surpassed other cities in this regard.[11]

Notarial records demonstrate the existence of an early book trade for forensic purposes in the mid-16th century. At that time, the production was entirely imported to the new viceroyalty, which benefited from the "boom" of publications in Spain, Spanish Italy and Flanders.[12] Manuals like Gabriel de Monterroso, *Práctica civil and criminal,* ecclesiastical handbooks, treatises and legislation were sold in *Limeño* bookstores.[13] At the end of the century, booksellers were very active in the city and had a fruitful commercial connection with their Sevillian counterparts.[14] Notarial documents show how the market was growing and the literary legal production was manifold, including practical juridical authors. The population of consumers were not exclusively Europeans or settlers. Demographic changes in the viceroyalty caused the rise of a new population of Creoles, who began to be educated in law since 1575.[15] In just a couple of years, they turned into the majority of *Limeño* legal facilitators. The 17th century was the time of the apogee of *Creolism*, and it was clearly visible with regard to political and intellectual actors as well. A significant number of descendants of conquerors became lawyers and played an important role as crafters of legal arguments in courtrooms. They wrote the claims, counterclaims, and pleas in the trials. Some of their libraries illustrate the presence of pragmatic literature. According to the book inventory of Doctor Cipriano de Medina's collection, documented in 1635, he possessed the *Practica Papiensis*

11 [Anon.,] *Descripción de la Villa y minas de Potosí.*

12 In the period of 1500–1520, 40% of the peninsular book production was religious, and the law works reached 11%. The percentages changed little at the end of the century. In the years of 1580–1600: 46% were religious works and 16% books on jurisprudence (or law), see Wilkinson, "Ensayo introductorio. La publicación en la Península Ibérica a principios del Siglo de Oro", XXXVIII and XL.

13 Some of the jurists whose books circulated in mid-16th century Lima were Cino da Pistoia (c. 1270–1336/1337), Baldo degli Ubaldi (1327–1400); legislative publications included *Las Siete Partidas* (1256–1265), *Ordenamiento Real* (or Montalvo, 1484), and *Leyes de Toro* (1505).

14 Leonard, "On the Lima Book Trade, 1591".

15 The first courses of the Faculty of "Leyes y Cánones" was established in 1571 and the curriculum was completed in 1578. The reforms were initiated by viceroy Toledo in a process of secularisation and transformation of the Colegio del Rosario in the decade of the 1570s, see Monsalve, "Del estudio del Rosario a la Real y Pontificia Universidad Mayor de San Marcos", 68–73.

(of Venice in 1549), *Instrucción política y práctica judicial* (of Villadiego in 1612), and *Practica de exsaminar testigos*, among other books.[16]

Likewise, an influential group of native chiefs were literate, bilingual, and educated in colleges (especially in Lima and Cuzco).[17] Some of them, like don Rodrigo de Guzmán Rupaychagua, had been educated in the Jesuit College for caciques in Lima in the 17th century.[18] After his formal education, he became a prominent litigant in civil and canonical tribunals, and a skilful user of legal channels.[19] He was part of a long generation of Andean litigators who date back to the mid-16th century, the time of the legal boom in the Real Audiencia of Lima. The 17th century was the time of a more formal group of trained indigenous scribes and provincial professionals.[20] They were consumers of legal production despite the fact that we only dispose of wills from the 18th century. One important example of a conspicuous leader and legal user was the cacique don Cristóbal Choquecasa, an Andean lord in Huarochirí, located in central Peru, close to Lima. The history of litigating caciques with a skilful command of legal terminology dates back to the early mid-16th century. The first testimonies of these lords show their ability and familiarity in the use of legal institutions.

Whereas the early book trade was dominated by the import of European production, in 1584 a printing press was established in Lima. The printer Antonio Ricardo, an Italian with a long editorial experience in Europe and Mexico, relocated to the viceregal capital. The early local printed production was pastoral. The Third Provincial Council of Lima (1582–1583), the great Church assembly of that century, was the decisive agent for this editorial endeavour.

---

16 Novoa, *The Protectors of Indians in the Royal Audiencia of Lima*, 255.

17 On the education of Andean nobility and the libraries in the cacical colleges, see Alaparrine-Bouyer, "La biblioteca del Colegio de Yngas nobles" and Alaparrine-Bouyer, *La educación de las élites indígenas en el Perú colonial*. Caciques studied Christian doctrine, Spanish, and Latin. Although the "spiritual" education was central in the formation of the young native chiefs, they became familiar in the use and consultation of legal books. Rupaychagua, cacique of Huamatanga, in Canta (in Lima's highlands), is one of the representative examples; see Charles, " 'More Ladino than Necessary' ".

18 Alaparrine-Bouyer, *La educación de las élites indígenas en el Perú colonial*.

19 There were prominent examples of litigating caciques in the 16th century: don Diego de Ataurimache, don Felipe Guagrapaucar (cacique in Jauja and traveler to the court of Madrid in 1563). Don Francisco de Mayontopa (member of the Inca elite and cacique in Ollantaytambo), among other prestigious lords. The best study of Andean litigation and the role of lords is Puente Luna, *Los curacas hechiceros*, 227–273. For transatlantic Andean litigation and the making of an early modern legal culture, see Puente Luna, *Andean Cosmopolitans*, 51–88.

20 Ramos, "Indigenous Intellectuals in Andean Colonial Cities", 26–35.

Confessional manuals, guidelines for evangelisation, and the decisions of the Council were produced in the Ricardian workshop. This pattern of canonical topics was dominant in the rest of the century. Confession manuals were printed for the evangelisation, and contributed to forge a normative order in the Andean parishes. In the High Middle Ages, confession was a central instrument for disciplining the Christian believers. Pope Innocent III (r. 1198–1216) led the assertion of papal authority in Europe promoting the mandatory character of the seven sacraments. The papal revolution aimed at controlling the subjectivity and behaviour of peasants and ordinary citizens.[21] This European experience was replicated in the New World. In the Andes, penitential works and definitions of sins (translated from Spanish to Quechua) were the means for the dissemination of the Christian notions (and values) of sex, family, commerce, and labour.[22] A spiritual legal order that regulated the life and goods of believers emerged from that process.

In the 17th century, a young generation of Peruvian priests (some of them members of the aristocratic elite) penned sermons. They cultivated the art of the sacred oratory as another vehicle for moralising the society.[23] One of the most prolific was Bartolomé Vadillo (1593–1659), an Augustinian friar, considered by his contemporaries as the *pico de oro* (the great rhetorician) of theological thought in mid-17th century Lima. His sermons dealt with everyday life aspects of the city: ethics, legal practice, justice administration, law and order. He supported his reflections by using passages taken from the sacred scripture and Scholastic authors (Thomas Aquinas, for instance). Thus, rather than 'abstract' and vague definitions, Vadillo discussed urgent social problems and employed concrete examples to explain his theological views.[24] He was not the only one of several authors who examined and discussed moral topics. Vadillo was also an author of a manual for testaments, written under the premise of popularising the ways to declare the last will. This production was printed and circulated in Lima. The work on testaments was oriented to the laymen.

21 On canon law and its incidence on private life, see Brundage, *Medieval Canon Law*, 70–97.

22 Harrison, *Sin and Confession in Colonial Peru*, 84–219.

23 Theologians and theology professors were usually asked by the authorities to yield their opinions on indigenous labour in mining. Friar Miguel de Agia, lecturer in theology, wrote his *Tratado que contiene tres pareceres graves en Derecho* to examine the *mita* sytem in Huancavelica, the main producer of mercury. Another important Franciscan, Pedro Muñiz, also lecturer in theology, was the author of a report on indigenous working conditions in mining centres, see Fox, "Pedro Muñiz, Dean of Lima and the Indian Labor Question".

24 Vadillo, *Sermón en el quarto miércoles de quaresma*.

That century was the epoch of a significant local writing in the Peruvian viceroyalty. Guillermo Lohmann Villena and Ella Dunbar Temple have called this momentum the "Golden Age" of intellectual history in colonial Peru.[25] The massive circulation of books, the constitution of impressive conventual and personal libraries, and the intellectual energy of local lawyers, practitioners, and priests contributed to this rise.[26] An Asturian author, Juan de Hevia Bolaños, who worked as legal representative of litigants in the Audiencia, wrote his influential *Curia Philipica,* a manual for litigation in both civil and criminal jurisdictions. Although his handbook was intended as a guide to illustrate the stages of a procedure, in a short time it became a best seller with numerous editions in Lima and the Peninsula. Hevia's work opened up the period of manuals that inundated the *Limeño* presses. In 1640, Domingo Gómez de Silva, judge of minors, published his *Práctica e instrucción para albaceas, tutores y curadores,* with important guidelines for the judicial administration of the minors' patrimony.[27] Litigation on mismanagement of these assets was a common feature in the Audiencia of Lima during the Habsburg era. Manuals for scribes were also part of the repertory of this local production.[28]

Advocates also printed their legal allegations. In the 16th and 17th centuries *Limeño* litigation, legal pleadings were written by hand being inserted into the trial proceedings. In the nascent epoch of Philip III (r. 1598–1621), *Limeño* lawyers (sponsored by their clients) printed out their claims, albeit they were ultimately not included in the proceedings. In these pieces, they pointed out their clientele's rights elaborating long and detailed juridical justifications.[29] In Madrid and Mexico City, the printing of this production was common and prior

25 "El jurista indiano don Gaspar de Escalona y Agüero", 570.

26 On conventual book collections, see the study by Ramos Núñez, *Ius commune,* on La Recoleta in Arequipa. His research explores the 16th and 17th books of that repository. With respect to private libraries, one of the most prominent in 17th century Lima belonged to father Francisco de Avila, a priest associated with the campaign against "indigenous idolatry" in Huarochirí, see Hampe Martínez, *Cultura barroca y extirpación de idolatrías.* Notable *Limeño* jurists also held significant book collections in the 17th century; see Novoa, *The Protectors of Indians in the Royal Audiencia of Lima,* 190–200.

27 On the relevance of Gómez de Silva's *Práctica,* see Premo, *Children of the Father King,* 36–37. Gómez de Silva also included in the second part of his book a selection of the *Partidas* with reference to cases of minors, see Gómez de Silva, *Práctica y Instrucción para albaceas, tutores y curadores que administran bienes de menores.*

28 Such as Diego Pérez Gallego's *Recuerdo para escrivanos de algunas cosas que saben o deven saber en los escritos y contratos,* Lima 1649.

29 An important collection of these printed *informes en Derecho* are stored at the National Library of Peru. They were eloquent examples of the construction of professional legal arguments in the Habsburg Andes. See, for example, Sosa, *Informe en Derecho.*

to the *Limeño* case.[30] These pleadings contained passages in Latin written by prominent European jurists and theologians, but also included numerus sources of law in the argumentation.[31] Influential and wealthy clients, like nobles, traders, mine owners, and religious orders financially supported these prints. Around 1625, Juan Enríquez de Borja, Marquis of Santiago de Oropesa (and on behalf of his wife Ana María Lorenza García Sayri Tupac de Loyola) hired four prominent advocates of the Audiencia of Lima to write and sign in a printed allegation in his case before the *Limeño* court.[32] In 1631, mine owners from Potosí took the services of Licentiate Sebastián de Sandoval y Guzmán, a *Limeño* advocate, to claim the reduction of their tributary duties and the recognition of privileges in the Council of the Indies. Sandoval prolifically cited jurists and passages of their writings to support his arguments.[33] His allegation was virtually a *memorial*, an extended narrative of the main points of their clients.

Publishing works of law was an important factor for the social construction of the colonial legal culture. Moreover, everyday juridical practice transformed

30 Mayagoitia, "Notas sobre los alegatos impresos novohispanos" and Corona González, "Alegaciones e informaciones en Derecho (porcones) en la Castilla del Antiguo Régimen". A list of these *porcones* (allegations of the advocates and legal reports) from the National Library of Spain can be found in García Cubero, *Las alegaciones en Derecho (Porcones) de la Biblioteca Nacional.*

31 Barreto, "Legal Culture and Argumentation in the Vice-Reign of Peru from the 16th to the 18th Centuries" offers a rich discussion on the construction of legal arguments in the early 17th century Peruvian legal literature. On the art of writing in 18th century litigation, see Premo, "Legal Writing, Civil Litigation, and Agents in the 18th-Century Spanish Imperial World". A discussion of the professional roles on the making in trial argumentation, in Tormo Camallonga, "El abogado en el proceso y la argumentación en los informes jurídicos del s. XVIII".

32 Ana María Lorenza, Marchioness of Santiago de Oropesa, was the great-granddaughter of Sayri Tupac (c. 1535–1561), Inca ruler in Vilcabamba and son of Manco Inca (r. 1536–1544). The marquises were involved in numerous lawsuits in the *Limeño* court and the Council of the Indies. Their cases illustrate how litigation was also an important activity of the nobility in the Andean Habsburg, see BNP B 1081, 1614 (barcode: 2000001501). In their allegation, the *letrados* who signed the piece were Dr. Leandro de la Reinaga Salazar, Licentiate Lorenzo Pardo del Castillo, Dr. Francisco Ramos Galván (one of the best lawyers of early 17th century Lima and law professor), and Dr. Diego Messia de Zúñiga. Marquis of Oropesa counted on the services of the best *Limeño* advocates in the early 17th century. On his allegation, see Oropesa, *Por el Maqués de Oropesa.*

33 Sandoval y Guzmán, *Pretensiones de la Villa Imperial de Potosí*, first argument. His text is not paged. Sandoval was an advocate in the Audiencia of Lima, representative of the Potosino mineowners and their petitioner in the Council of the Indies. His *memorial* was published in Madrid in 1634. He travelled to the metropolitan capital city to expose the views of his clients and also claim for a judicial position in the Spanish American Audiencias.

the Andean legal landscape. Courts, notary offices, and the local scenarios of customary justice were the rooms in which those changes took place. In this context, practitioners and clientele rethought the normative order insofar as they provided new meanings of western legal categories.

3 Legal Literature and the Court Scenario

Legal manuals provided guidelines for the daily work of experts. In litigation, *prácticas* covered different topics such as the types of procedures, stages of a trial, evidence, and the templates for the writing of pleas. This legal literature also prescribed the abilities and required duties of scribes and procurators. In some respects, it delineated the features of a good facilitator. In mid-16th century, Gabriel de Monterroso argued that good writing and diligence were main scribal qualities.[34] In the early 17th century, Juan Muñoz, another pragmatic author, enumerated the expected qualities of a good procurator in his *Práctica de procuradores* (1618). Muñoz, who was himself a procurator in Huesca (north-eastern Spain), wrote the foregoing based on his own professional experience.[35] In theory, and in Castilian law, procurators were subordinate to lawyers. In practice, nonetheless, they were the real agents in litigation. They represented their clients before the lower and higher courts and were aware of the state of their cases. Given that personal proximity, procurators gained a plethora of information from litigants driving their cases. It determined that they should follow ethical rules, professional secrecy being one of their most relevant duties.

In Spanish America, two important procedural manuals circulated in the early 17th century: *Curia Philipica* (of 1603) and *Instrucción para litigantes* (of 1612). Juan de Hevia Bolaño, himself a facilitator, dedicated a couple of pages to enumerate the function and duties of advocates and procurators using as its main source the *Siete Partidas*. Afterwards, Hevia detailed the steps and logic of the "ordinary procedure", the model for all procedures in civil and canonical litigation. However, the information on pleas, claims, counterclaims, notifications, times for the submission of pleas, and appeals was common for all procedures.[36] Alonso de Villadiego, for his part, worked as an advocate in Madrid and also as a *corregidor*; he was the author of several books on Castilian law. His *Instrucción*, the first edition of which was printed in 1612, was an important

34 Monterroso y Alvarado, *Práctica civil y criminal e instrucción de escribanos*, fol. 7r.

35 Muñoz, *Práctica de procuradores*, fols. 1r and 14r.

36 Hevia Bolaños, *Curia Philipica, primero y segundo tomo*, vol. 2, 1–176.

manual in which the stages of the trial in the ordinary way (*vía ordinaria*) was described in its first part.[37]

Legal history is also an intersection between intellectual and social history.[38] Law has specific categories that actors and agents use to defend, preserve, or increase their rights. Although specialists were central in the knowledge of law, ordinary litigants had also their own ideas of rights and justice. The three following examples try to illustrate the uses of law by king's subjects and their notions of liberty, good government, and local justice.[39] They appropriated these concepts incorporating them into their legal experience and providing new meanings. This was a process of construction of legal discourses in early colonial Peru. In February 1561, Domyngo "natural de la cibdad de Goa de la Yndia de Portugal", presented himself in the Audiencia of Lima. He claimed to be recognised legally as a free person. Domingo indicated that he had been born in Goa, in southern India. At that time, Goa was an important port city of the Portuguese in the Estado da India. Goa was a central place in the circulation of people, objects, and in the transatlantic trade from Asia to Africa (and then to America). Domingo's advocate, Licentiate Diego de Pineda, also emphasised his condition of "poor" and *miserabilis*, two elements of the legal status of Amerindians.[40] He claimed to be treated under that legal category. It meant in judicial terms to receive specialised legal advice by a lawyer of the Audiencia (private or an officer) and that the case should be under the exclusive jurisdiction of that *Limeño* tribunal. Domingo's petition also indicated that don Francisco Pérez Lezcano, a leading citizen in Trujillo treated him erroneously as "a slave" and tried to sell him.[41]

---

37 Villadiego, *Instrucción politica y practica judicial*, 1–28.

38 For recent debates on methodologies in legal history and the recovery of popular voices, see Musson and Stebbings (eds.), *Making Legal History* and Humfress, *Orthodoxy and the Courts in Late Antiquity*.

39 New Andeanist legal history focuses on the usage of law by subaltern and ordinary litigants, see Dueñas, "Introduction", 4–14. Two important examples in this direction are McKinley, *Fractional Freedoms* and Premo, *The Enlightenment on Trial*.

40 AGN–RA, Causas Civiles, leg. 6, cuad. 34, 1561, fol. 1r, Lima, February 27, 1561. Licentiate Diego de Pineda was at that time also prosecutor in the Audiencia. He had been a private lawyer and consultant of the council of Lima. In the decade of the 1550 he was also Corregidor of the city of Trujillo. Given that circumstance, he met Francisco Pérez Lezcano, *encomendero* in the valley.

41 On Pérez Lezcano he said "se sirve de my como esclavo y a enbiado a mandar al secretario Fran[cis]co de Carvajal como tal esclavo me venda en ella [in Trujillo] siendo como es contra Dro. de vno y yo reclamo libertad por ser como soy libre y no sujeto a cautiberio ninguno", AGN–RA, Causas Civiles, leg. 6, cuad. 34, 1561, fol. 1r.

His petition was contradicted by the legal facilitators[42] of Francisco Pérez Lezcano. His advocate, Licentiate Jerónimo López Guarnido indicated in the counterclaim that Domingo had not been born in the "Yndia de Portugal". Instead, Domingo was "subject of serfdom" having been purchased as a slave.[43] Also, López Guarnido denied the quality of legal party of Domingo in the trial, an example of the use of procedural technicalities in the *Limeño* cases. The legal document of sale, presented by Pérez Lezcano, called Domingo a "negro" being the skin colour an element to emphasise his status as a slave. In that sale contract, Alonso de Escobedo sold Domingo as a slave for 425 pesos in October 1558. In this document, Domingo was defined also as troublemaker and *ladino* having a mark on his face.[44] He was sold due to his improper behaviour.

The ideas of liberty and free personal status were central in Domingo's argumentation. They were also part of a transatlantic rhetoric in a time of debate about the Amerindian rights. Between 1530 and 1550, Amerindian litigants in the Council of the Indies demanded their judicial recognition as free individuals.[45] The struggles for liberty were part of a legal mobilisation (and circulation of ideas and doctrines) on both sides of the Atlantic. Domingo's case also shows how the ideas of ethnicity and legal status mingled. In several pleadings, he emphasised his relationship with the city of Goa and the Portuguese Atlantic world.

Domingo's strategy aimed at pointing out that he had been free since his birth. Most of his six witnesses were members of the nascent Portuguese Atlantic community in Lima.[46] They exemplified the presence of diasporic communities in the Peruvian capital.

---

42 His advocate was Licentiate Jerónimo López Guarnido and his procurator (procedural expert) was Francisco de la Torre (fol. 6r).

43 AGN–RA, Causas Civiles, leg. 6, cuad. 34, 1561, fol. 2r–v, Lima, April 21, 1561. "Y lo otro por q el dicho Domyngo no es de la dicha Yndia de Portugal ni libre, antes es esclavo subjeto a la dha. Servidumbre e como tal le con[pró] mi pte". (fol. 2v).

44 "Un esclavo llamado Domyngo, ladino, de hedad de veynte y siete años poco mas o menos, que tiene un letrero en el rostro que dize Bartolomé Garrido, e lo bendo por ladrón, borracho, huydor e jugador y con las demas tachas", AGN–RA, Causas Civiles, leg. 6, cuad. 34, 1561, fol. 37v. On the question of skin color: "qual dho. Alonso Descobedo my padre ha e tiene contra las personas de quien obo el dho. negro [...] e defender, e hazer cierto e sano e seguro de paz el dho negro" (vid. fol. 38v). The entire document in fols. 37v–39r.

45 Van Deusen, *Global Indios*, 125–146.

46 The declarants were Pedro Diaz (from Algarve), Antón de Cordova (from "Yndia de Portugal"), Jorge Fernandes (from Goa), Manuel Paez (from Trujillo in Peru), Simón de Cáceres (from Goa and "mulatto"), and Manuel de Ribero ("Yndio natural de Goa"), see fols. 2r–4r and fols. 23r–25v. There were two episodes in the declaration of witnesses in March and November of 1561.

Pedro Diaz from Algarve indicated that at least twenty years ago (around the decade of 1540) he was in "la Isla Tercera" and saw how a ship struck a rock and wrecked. He went to help and rescued Don Cristóbal and Domingo, his servant. That ship came from the "Yndia of Portugal" and Domingo was a free servant. Diaz underlined that all inhabitants from "la dicha Yndia" are free people. He also added that Domingo was "poor and miserable".[47] Jorge Fernandes, "of mulatto skin colour", argued that he knew Domingo at least for one year and said that all Indians of the "land of the Prince Juan" had been free. Manuel Paez, another witness, declared that Domingo was from Goa and that people of that community were free. His witnesses asserted that he had been born free, his parents were from Goa, he had embarked to the New World, and that he was a good person. In addition, they backed Domingo's version about his Goan origin, providing the name of his parents and his belonging to the local community. They said that Domingo spoke the local language of Goa. With this information, Domingo's defence insisted on his local origin, his status as a free person, and the idea that he was the result of an error in persona. The central position is that his status was erroneously denied to him and that he was considered being a slave by his owner.

Domingo's case was not the only early case of liberty in the Audiencia. Indeed, historical evidence shows that other cases occurred previously. In 1548, in the time of the Civil War between Pizarrist factions, Francisco, an "Indian of Tenochtitlán" demanded to be recognised legally as a free person.[48] Liberty as a synonym of human dignity was employed as argument in the courts. The central point is that they were born free and erroneously considered slaves despite their status. Francisco used also an argument of natural law, an important ingredient of the legal argumentation in Peruvian colonial courts. Francisco's case exemplifies the relevance and circulation of legal ideas of natural and human dignity. In turn, his owner, Juan de Salamanca, artisan, considered that he was a slave and had a mark on his face.[49] Facial brands signaled the status of certain individuals in the 16th century.

"Good government" was another important political concept in early modern Castile. Of medieval origin, this principle had diverse meanings and political implications. One of them was the "fair" justice administration at local

---

47 His declaration was given on 26 February, 1561. He stated: "Y acudió de los primeros a socorrer el dho navío q se perdió [...] y entre los q[ue] se acuerda q tomó a un caballero q se dezia don Cristóbal e de Domyngo por su criado" (fol. 2r).

48 BNP A–208, 1546 (barcode: 2000000097).

49 "Lo otro dixo q lo de Franco [Francisco] yndio esclavo y te [tiene] en el rostro el hierro del rey", fol. 12r.

level. In colonial times, the *juicio de residencia* (a trial after the ending of an authority's tenure) was the opportunity in which the subjects could denounce abuses and misadministration exercised by the authorities. In the trial of the local authorities of Santa (a small Spanish town in coastal central Peru), subjects, like Juan Díaz Melecio, accused the *alcalde* (the magistrate of the city) Juan de Mata of having denied litigants their access to justice. The *alcalde* had avoided to investigate the criminal accusations of some local residents. Juan Díaz Melecio, "vecino de la dicha villa", gave his testimony, and his words are a privileged vehicle to know his ideas of justice. He told how the *alcalde* cultivated favouritism and rejected to investigate the case of Juan Carrasco's wife. She had requested the intervention of the *alcalde* to order the payment of a debt by Diego de Elena Herrero, who was a close friend of the *alcalde*. Díaz Melercio also enumerated other offenses of the *alcalde*. He narrated his numerous incidents with the aldermen and also his lack of interest to maintain the social morality in the town. Thus, Díaz Melecio pointed out that the *alcalde* had tolerated the *amancebamiento* (cohabitation) of many couples and permitted gambling and card games without punishing all "public sins".[50] During colonial times, the denial and obstruction of justice was considered *corruptela,* an antecedent of what we know today as legal corruption.[51]

Viceroy Francisco de Toledo (r. 1569–1581) reorganised the Andean space relocating the native population in small towns called *reducciones*.[52] The political model utilised was the medieval Castilian municipality made up of *alcaldes* as magistrates (judges and mayors), aldermen, and scribes.[53] In San Damián de Urotambo (in Huarochirí, in Lima's highlands), *alcaldes* solved disputes and scribes recorded them in files. In 1631, in a lawsuit for land, the litigating parties invoked Castilian property law when submitting their suits and pleadings in Spanish.[54] The parties (and probably their legal experts) used all procedural technicalities that were common in litigation in the high courts of justices like the Audiencia of Lima. A written procedure, with specific procedural stages, and recorded in a file, were some of the facets of this dispute. The *alcalde* was don Carlos Marcelo Canchaguaman, a member of the local nobility, and his

---

50 AGN–JR, leg. 1, cuad. 1, fols. 21v–22v.

51 Rosenmüller, "Introduction", 3–7.

52 Mumford, *Vertical Empire*.

53 Moore, *The Cabildo in Peru under the Hapsburgs*, 3–30.

54 BNP B 1483, 1637 (barcode: 2000001898), fol. 2r, April 1637. I thank José Carlos de la Puente Luna for this reference. This file is an important testimony on local justice in the colonial Peruvian countryside, and it is one of the few documents that are still stored in national archives. Unlike in Mesoamerican towns, there are few remaining written dossiers of rural litigation in the Habsburg Andes.

scribe was his father, don Cristóbal Choquecasa,[55] lord and local aristocrat. Don Cristóbal was bilingual, a go-between, fluent in Spanish, and most likely the best informant of Father Francisco de Avila.[56] The latter was the parish priest and a prominent extirpator of idolatry who collected the oral narratives of the local religion in Huarochirí. Don Cristobal Choquecasa's familiarity with Castilian legal institutions illustrates the reutilisation of this legal order in the countryside and its powerful influence over local affairs.

Don Cristóbal Choquesaca's case is especially relevant for observing the transformation and the circulation of legal practices in the Andes. As mentioned, he was especially trained in law. He demonstrated the uses of legal formalism and was familiar with legal practice. He was not only a user of justice – as a litigant – but also a legal expert despite the fact that practicing the legal profession was exclusively in the hands of Europeans. His use of a legal vernacular language shows how the normative experience of Castile, as expressed in the "leyes de estilo", became an important parameter in the resolution of disputes. The comparison of language and the presence of experts sheds light on the participation of a rural community of legal experts in litigation – and in a justice of "sticks and branches", as Yanna Yannakakis and Bianca Premo have called it.[57] A generation of indigenous legal experts emerged from that everyday legal practice in rural and urban areas.[58]

4 The Construction of a Transatlantic Legal Culture in the Andes

The enormous corpus of treatises, manuals, and moral and legal literature that circulated in colonial Peru were important components in the construction of the local legal culture. This concept refers to the general understanding of law (or laws) as well as its social usage. Although some doctrines were dominant in the official scenario (the idea of "two republics", the notions of *miserabilis*/neophyte, and the assumption of a good, benevolent, and fair king), it is also relevant to explore how these and other conceptions were socially assimilated (or "translated") and adapted to local needs. In the classic historiography on books, the main emphasis is on the "collection" (or accumulation) itself

55 On Don Cristóbal Choquecasa's abilities, usage of Castilian law, and his role as legal expert, see the study of Puente Luna, "Choquecasa va a la Audiencia".

56 Or even the author, see Durston, "Cristóbal Choquecasa and the Making of the Huarochirí Manuscript" and Puente Luna, "Choquecasa va a la Audiencia".

57 Premo and Yannakakis, "A Court of Sticks and Branches", 29–31, 33–35.

58 Dueñas, "The Lima Indian Letrados".

rather than on the process of circulation of the ideas that these printed materials contained. Over the last years, historiography interrogates the forms and ways in which ordinary legal users created their own normative imaginaries in a context of aristocratic and traditional social order regimes. A magisterial work by E.P. Thompson, *Customs in Common*, offers a pathway to observe how subaltern people crafted their legal regimes despite the pressures of landlords, monarchies, and local elites.[59] Thus, ordinary subjects developed their juridical thought from the ground up by using their social experience and notions of law.

A normative order conceived in the European experience was exported to the New World. The diversity of peoples in the Andes (indigenous, Europeans, mestizos, Africans, and Asians) was a feature of that society, and it multiplied the perspectives on law. Members of these collective groups selected legal resources and used the courts or other scenarios for their own agendas. Andean people gained the reputation of being litigious since the mid-16th century appropriating the court scenario and technicalities as a space to contest colonialism. Likewise, the peoples of African descent used canon law tribunals with vitality, creativity, and audacity, as Michelle McKinley has demonstrated. The regulations and tribunals of the Catholic Church opened up some avenues for the Afro-Peruvians since the mid-16th century (and mainly in the 17th) to demand their liberty or a just treatment.[60] Both Andeans and Africans brought their demands before civil and canon law tribunals, and made their voices heard in these courts.

The circulation of ideas generated a local legal culture which, although connected with the European origins, was modelled on the American soil. This development should not be conceived as a transplant but as a process of transformation and creation. In the courtrooms, lawyers and litigants were central, but also in other episodes of legal practices. There are several examples of such a circulation of ideas and they not only refer to male actors and litigants but even include women as well. Female litigants were also main actors in the construction of a transatlantic legal culture. It was transatlantic because the elements of the European discourse were appropriated and developed by the subjects in the Andean territories. They added their own voices in an *ancien regime* context. A gigantic universe of printed materials circulated in the Andes since the early period of the Spanish colonisation. The *conquistadores* were accompanied by books and printed material. However, this rich intellectual world was appropriated and translated by several agents in Habsburg Peru. Professionals (advocates, procurators, scribes, solicitors, and paralegals) were

59 Thompson, *Customs in Common*.

60 McKinley, *Fractional Freedoms*.

key in that process. At the same time, however, it was the decision and initiative of the king's subjects because they mobilised that legal order. As recent historiography on law and empire shows, the vast and long-lasting empires relied on the active participation of their subjects.[61] They were the backbone of imperial political edifices. In the Andes, the Castilian tradition in administration, Catholic faith, and legal order transformed king's vassals, but they also transformed the language and the ideas of the empire.

The consequence of that process was the enrichment of Castilian law and its use in the own experience of locals. This process also influenced legal rhetoric. So, gradually, a particular discourse and a characteristic practice of law developed in the American colonies.

5 Conclusions

Since the early period of colonisation, printed books and manuals circulated in the Andes. There were two significant phases in this process: (a) The period of import of European production between 1535 and 1584 and (b) the gradual importance of the locally printed materials since 1584. In 1584, Antonio Ricardo opened his printing workshop in Lima. The first book produced in the Ricardian laboratory was a religious one but law increasingly acquired importance. The 17th century was the time of the Golden Age of *Limeño* local production due to the enthusiastic participation of Creole authors. They wrote memorials, allegations, sermons, manuals, and a diversity of legal materials. Theology played a crucial function since it oriented the moral discourses, which were clearly expressed in preaching and local sermons. This vibrant process of intellectual creativity should also be related to the social practice of law, and the construction of a local legal culture. Evidence shows how the king's subaltern subjects used the lexicon, vocabulary, and legal liturgy of the colonists for their own ends.

The courtroom was a laboratory to test the circulation of legal ideas. Litigation involved several actors in higher and lower courts. These forums allow us to perceive the legal ideas that circulated there, and some were born from below. The colonial subjects created and expanded their own ideas in topics such as liberty rights. A local class of facilitators emerged in the colonial context. In San Damián de Huarochirí, these facilitators made law and used the Castilian legal system.

Pragmatic legal literature and the circulation of ideas were central components in the making of colonial Peru. Procedural activity and the use of courts

61 Duindam, Harries, Humfress and Hurvitz (eds.), *Law and Empire*.

opened an important scenario. In particular, texts written by Hevia and Villadiego circulated in the colonial world. They were manuals and simultaneously texts about the duties of facilitators. Likewise, however, the litigants and legal users employed that channel and developed their own narratives. This type of literature and the atmosphere of the period generated a legal culture that endured for a long time.

Acknowledgements

My thanks to Otto Danwerth, Agnes Gehbald, and Pilar Mejía for their comments, bibliographic suggestions, and critical reading of this essay.

Bibliography

Manuscripts

Archivo General de la Nación, Lima (AGN–JR) (Juicios de residencia), leg. 1, cuad. 1.
Archivo General de la Nación, Lima (AGN–RA) (Real Audiencia), Causas Civiles, leg. 6, cuad. 34, 1561.
Biblioteca Nacional del Perú, Lima (BNP), A–208, 1546 (barcode: 2000000097).
BNP, B 1081, 1614 (barcode: 2000001501).
BNP, B 1483, 1637 (barcode: 2000001898).

Printed Sources

Agia, Miguel de, *Tratado que contiene tres pareceres graves en Derecho, que ha compuesto el Padre Fray Miguel Agia de la Orden del Señor San Francisco* [...], Lima 1604: Antonio Ricardo.
Alvarez, Bartolomé, *De las costumbres y conversión de los indios del Perú. Memorial a Felipe II*, Madrid [1587–1588] 1998.
[Anon.,] *Descripción de la Villa y minas de Potosí*, in *Relaciones geográficas de Indias–Perú*, Madrid [1603] 1965, 372–385.
Libros de cabildos de Lima. Libro primero (años 1534–1539), ed. Lee, Bertram, Lima 1935.
Gómez de Silva, Domingo, *Práctica y Instrucción para albaceas, tutores y curadores que administran bienes de menores*, Lima 1640: Pedro Cabrera.
Hevia Bolaños, Juan de, *Curia Philipica, primero y segundo tomo*, 2 vols., Madrid [1797] 1989.
Monterroso y Alvarado, Gabriel de, *Práctica civil y criminal e instrucción de escribanos*, Valladolid 1563: Francisco Fernández de Córdoba, Impresor de la Majestad Real.
Montesinos, Fernando de, *Anales del Perú*, 2 vols., Lima [1642] 1906.

Muñoz, Juan, *Práctica de procuradores para seguir pleitos civiles, y criminales, hecha y ordenada por Juan Muñoz, procurador de causas en la ciudad de Guesca. Añadida y enmendada en esta impression, y con nuevas adiciones, conforme a la Nueva Recopilación*, Madrid 1618: Diego Flamenco, a costa de Manuel Rodríguez, librero.

Ondegardo, Polo, *Informe del licenciado Polo Ondegardo al licenciado Briviesca de Muñatones* [...], in *Pensamiento colonial crítico. Textos y actos de Polo Ondegardo*, ed. Lamana, Gonzalo, Lima [1561] 2012, 139–204.

Oropesa, Marquis of Santiago de, *Por el Maqués de Oropesa como marido de doña María de Loyola Coya sobre la satisfacción que pretende le haga Su Majestad por los derechos y pretensiones en que viene informado por la Real Audiencia de Lima*, Lima ca. 1625.

Pérez Gallego, Diego, *Recuerdo para escrivanos de algunas cosas que saben o deven saber en las escrituras y contratos*. Lima 1649: Jorge López de Herrera.

Sandoval y Guzmán, Sebastián de, *Pretensiones de la Villa Imperial de Potosí, propuestas en el Real Consejo de las Indias*, Madrid 1634: Por la viuda de Juan Gonzalez.

Sosa, Francisco de, *Informe en Derecho cerca de la validación del testamento del capitán Andrés Cintero, que murió en la Villa de Potosí*, Lima 1648.

Vadillo, Bartolomé, *Sermón en el quarto miércoles de quaresma* [...] *Se intima a los señores juezes y abogados la obligación de su oficio, las causas en las que pueden pecar conforme los sumistas*, Lima 1648: Pedro Cabrera.

Villadiego, Alonso de, *Instrucción politica y practica judicial* [...], Madrid [1612] 1766: Antonio Marin.

Literature

Alaparrine-Bouyer, Monique, “La biblioteca del Colegio de Yngas nobles: San Borja del Cuzco”, in *Histórica* 29:2 (2005), 163–179.

Alaparrine-Bouyer, Monique, *La educación de las élites indígenas en el Perú colonial*, Lima 2007.

Alonso Romero, M. Paz, “Theoria y Praxis en la enseñanza del Derecho: Tratados y prácticas procesales en la Universidad de Salamanca a mediados del siglo XVI”, in *Anuario de Historia del Derecho Español* 60 (1991), 451–547.

Barreto, Herman, “Legal Culture and Argumentation in the Vice-Reign of Peru from the 16th to the 18th Centuries”, in *Clio and Themis* 2 (2009) (http://www.cliothemis.com/Legal-Culture-and-Argumentation-in).

Brundage, James A., *Medieval Canon Law*, London 1995.

Charles, John, “ ‘More Ladino than Necessary’: Indigenous Litigants and the Language Policy debate in Mid-Colonial Peru”, in *Colonial Latin American Review* 16:1 (2007), 23–47.

Corona González, Santos M., “Alegaciones e informaciones en Derecho (porcones) en la Castilla del Antiguo Régimen”, in *Anuario de Historia del Derecho Español* 73 (2003), 165–192.

Danwerth, Otto, "La circulación de literatura normativa pragmática en Hispanoamérica (siglos XVI–XVII)", in Duve, Thomas (ed.), *Actas del XIX Congreso del Instituto Internacional de Historia del Derecho Indiano, Berlín 2016*, vol. 1, Madrid 2017, 359–400.

Dueñas, Alcira, "Introduction: Andeans Articulating Colonial Worlds", in *The Americas* 72:1 (2015), 3–17.

Dueñas, Alcira, "The Lima Indian Letrados: Remaking the República de Indios in the Bourbon Andes", in *The Americas* 72:1 (2015), 55–75.

Duindam, Jeroen, Jill Harries, Caroline Humfress and Nimrod Hurvitz (eds.), *Law and Empire. Ideas, Practices, Actors*, Leiden 2013.

Durston, Alan, "Cristóbal Choquecasa and the Making of the Huarochirí Manuscript", in Ramos, Gabriela and Yanna Yannakakis (eds.), *Indigenous Intellectuals. Knowledge, Power, and Colonial Culture in Mexico and the Andes*, Durham 2014, 151–169.

Fox, K.V., "Pedro Muñiz, Dean of Lima and the Indian Labor Question", in *The Hispanic American Historical Review* 42:1 (1962), 63–88.

García Cubero, Luis, *Las alegaciones en Derecho (Porcones) de la Biblioteca Nacional*, Madrid 2004.

Hampe Martínez, Teodoro, *Cultura barroca y extirpación de idolatrías: La biblioteca de Francisco de Avila (1648)*, Cusco 1996.

Harrison, Regina, *Sin and Confession in Colonial Peru: Spanish-Quechua Penitential Texts, 1560–1650*, Austin, TX 2015.

Härter, Karl, "The Early Modern Holy Roman Empire of the German Nation (1495–1806): A Multi-Layered Legal System", in Duindam, Jeroen, Jill Harries, Caroline Humfress and Nimrod Hurvitz (eds.), *Law and Empire. Ideas, Practices, Actors*, Leiden 2013, 111–131.

Humfress, Caroline, *Orthodoxy and the Courts in Late Antiquity*, Oxford 2007.

Leonard, Irving, "On the Lima Book Trade, 1591", in *The Hispanic American Historical Review* 33:4 (1953), 511–525.

Mayagoitia, Alejandro, "Notas sobre los alegatos impresos novohispanos", in Universidad Nacional Autónoma de México (ed.), *Memoria del IX Congreso del Instituto Internacional de Historia del Derecho Indiano*, México 1995, 1001–1029.

McKinley, Michelle, *Fractional Freedoms: Slavery, Intimacy, and Legal Mobilization in Colonial Lima, 1600–1700*, Cambridge 2016.

Monsalve, Martín, "Del estudio del Rosario a la Real y Pontificia Universidad Mayor de San Marcos", in *Histórica* 22:1 (1998), 53–79.

Moore, John Preston, *The Cabildo in Peru under the Hapsburgs. A Study in the Origins and Powers of the Town Council in the Viceroyalty of Peru 1530–1700*, Durham 1954.

Mumford, Jeremy R., *Vertical Empire. The General Resettlement of Indians in the Colonial Andes*, Durham 2012.

Musson, Anthony and Chantal Stebbings (eds.), *Making Legal History: Approaches and Methodologies*, Cambridge 2012.

Novoa, Mauricio, *The Protectors of Indians in the Royal Audiencia of Lima. History, Careers and Legal Culture, 1575–1775*, Leiden 2016.

Palau y Ducet, Antonio, *Manual del librero hispanoamericano*, vol. 10, Barcelona 1957.

Premo, Bianca, *Children of the Father King: Youth, Authority, and Legal Minority in Colonial Lima*, Chapel Hill, NC 2005.

Premo, Bianca, *The Enlightenment on Trial: Ordinary Litigants and Colonialism in Spanish America*, Oxford 2017.

Premo, Bianca, "Legal Writing, Civil Litigation, and Agents in the 18th-Century Spanish Imperial World", in Beezley, William H. (ed.), *Oxford Research Encyclopedia of Latin American History (online publication)* 2017 (10.1093/acrefore/9780199366439.013.247).

Premo, Bianca and Yanna Yannakakis, "A Court of Sticks and Branches: Indian Jurisdiction in Colonial Mexico and Beyond", in *The American Historical Review* 24:1 (2019), 28–55.

Puente Luna, José Carlos de la, *Los curacas hechiceros. Batallas mágicas y legales en el Perú colonial*, Lima 2007.

Puente Luna, José Carlos de la, "Choquecasa va a la Audiencia: Cronistas, litigantes y el debate sobre la autoría del Manuscrito quechua de Huarochirí", in *Histórica* 39:1 (2015), 139–158.

Puente Luna, José Carlos de la, *Andean Cosmopolitans: Seeking Justice and Reward at the Spanish Royal Court*, Austin, TX 2018.

Ramos, Gabriela, "Indigenous Intellectuals in Andean Colonial Cities", in Ramos, Gabriela and Yanna Yannakakis (eds.), *Indigenous Intellectuals. Knowledge, Power, and Colonial Culture in Mexico and the Andes*, Durham 2014, 21–38.

Ramos Núñez, Carlos, *Ius commune. Libros y juristas en la Biblioteca de La Recoleta. Siglos XVI y XVII*, Arequipa 2016.

Rosenmüller, Christoph, "Introduction: Corruption, Abuse, and Justice in the Iberian Empires", in Rosenmüller, Christoph (ed.), *Corruption in the Iberian Empires. Greed, Custom, and Colonial Networks*, Albuquerque, NM 2017, 1–12.

Temple, Ella D., "El jurista indiano don Gaspar de Escalona y Agüero, graduado en la Universidad de San Marcos", in *Documenta*, vol. II (1949), 545–586.

Thompson, Edward P., *Customs in Common*, New York 1991.

Tormo Camallonga, Carlos, "El abogado en el proceso y la argumentación en los informes jurídicos del s. XVIII", in *Ivs Fvguit* 10–11 (2001–2002), 1079–1131.

Van Deusen, Nancy, *Global Indios. The Indigenous Struggle for Justice in Sixteenth-Century Spain*, Durham 2015.

Wilkinson, Alexander S., "Ensayo introductorio. La publicación en la Península Ibérica a principios del Siglo de Oro, 1472–1600", in Wilkinson, Alexander S. (ed.), *Libros Ibéricos. Libros publicados en español o portugués o en la Península Ibérica antes de 1601*, Leiden 2010, XXXIII–XLVI.

CHAPTER 5

Jesuit Pragmatic Literature and Ecclesiastical Normativity in Portuguese America (16th–18th Centuries)

Gustavo César Machado Cabral

1 Introduction

Studying the legal experience in colonial Brazil is not an easy task.[1] A legal culture strongly influenced by orality, a reduced sphere of institutionalised jurisdiction, the absence of formal juridical education and the prohibition of printing books and journals are some of the most remarkable difficulties a legal historian faces when dealing with this period. Despite the reduced number of written sources, in which the learned legal culture somehow materialised, the few available texts constitute a possible way for analysing this juridical experience.

To provide means for identifying how this erudite knowledge circulated in the colonial space is one of the purposes of this article. Ecclesiastical texts are probably the most useful sources in that respect, particularly the texts produced by the priests of the Society of Jesus, the strongest religious order active in Portuguese America.[2] Facing practical problems during the attempt of building a Christian society in the New World, the Jesuits had a relevant role in the shaping of the juridical framework of colonial Brazil. The writings to be analysed in this article were conceived to resolve practical problems: How can missionaries catechise the native population if they do not speak the same language? Which Christian values are essential for a neophyte to guide oneself in

1 Probably the best text about the elements of colonial law in Brazil is Hespanha, "Porque é que existe e em que é que consiste um direito colonial brasileiro". See also Hespanha, "O 'Direito de Índias' ".

2 Besides the Society of Jesus, other religious orders acted in Portuguese America but were less relevant, such as the Benedictines (1581), the Franciscans (1584), the Capuchins (1642, but there was a French Capuchin mission in Equinoctial France two decades before), the Carmelites (first half of the 17th century), the Oratorians and the Mercedarians (second half of the 17th century).

the social life? Who is obliged to provide spiritual instruction in that society? How can people deal with specific moral problems they were not used to?

Each of these questions constitute a topic of this chapter, which begins with a sketch of the particular background of colonial Brazil. Providing practical solutions for concrete problems is the structural concern these texts share, and that is the reason why catechisms, cases of conscience and sermons can be considered pragmatic sources, in the terms described by Thomas Duve's chapter in this book. In contrast to a form of knowledge structured only in a theoretical perspective, these texts used traditional forms and European learning in order to propose practical answers for questions with juridical relevance and to construct a normative order based on Christianity. These foundations were extremely important for a society where moral and juridical matters could not be neatly distinguished.

2 An Overview on Early Modern Portuguese America

During the first decades of the 16th century, in the wake of the first Portuguese expedition of 1500, the presence of Portuguese and other Europeans was minimal. The establishment of the hereditary captaincy system in 1534, by which the coastal area of Portuguese America was divided into a dozen territories that should be explored and occupied by noblemen who had received the donations, did not lead to an effective occupation of the continent. Previously adopted in smaller territories such as Madeira Island, in the Atlantic Coast of Africa, the hereditary captaincy system was a seigneurial regime in which many rights, especially jurisdictional rights, over a territory were donated by the king, mainly to a nobleman.[3] As the results were not the expected ones, the Crown created royal captaincies in areas not effectively occupied by their donees (*donatários*) and founded the settlement of a General Government in Salvador da Bahia in 1549.[4] The division of Portuguese America into two territories (the State of Brazil and, from 1619 on, the State of Maranhão, which was

3 An explanation of the juridical basis of the hereditary captaincy system can be found in Cabral, "Senhores e ouvidores de capitanias hereditárias".

4 The village of Salvador was located in an area donated in the previous decade to Francisco Pereira Coutinho, who failed in occupying it permanently. In 1548, the Crown bought the territory which became the location of the general administration of the colony. A few years later, in 1565, the same happened to an abandoned area donated in 1534 to Martin Afonso de Sousa: after the expulsion of the French, the Crown created the royal captaincy of Rio de Janeiro in this area.

renamed a couple of times in the following century) did not result in a massive occupation of these areas.

Different from what happened in some territories of Hispanic America, where cities like Mexico and Lima had a population that was compatible with big European cities,[5] in Brazil the numbers were far more modest. According to estimations,[6] only at the turn of the 17th century the first villages (Salvador and Recife) had populations over 10,000 people, not including slaves. Nevertheless, as time went by, the population increased quickly. Except for Vila Rica de Ouro Preto, the most important Brazilian urban area during the so called "gold cycle" in the beginning of the 18th century, all the other relevant villages and cities (Salvador, Recife, Rio de Janeiro, São Paulo, São Luís do Maranhão and Belém do Pará) were located on the seaside or near it.

Moreover, the presence of Portuguese officials was low in America, despite the progressive increase of nominations during the 18th century, as Nuno Camarinhas shows.[7] Only at the end of the 17th century, the Crown introduced the appointment of first and second grade judges (*juízes de fora* and *ouvidores de comarcas*, respectively). Before, the litigation concerning civil matters was decided by the judges appointed by the donee of the hereditary captaincy[8] (*ouvidores de capitania*) or, more often, by the ordinary judges (*juízes ordinários*) elected in municipal councils, who had no formal legal training and even were analphabets in many cases. Analphabetism was also frequent among the *ouvidores de capitanias*.[9] The progressive increase of royal appointments by the Crown of judges with a law degree (*juízes letrados*) was part of a slow and gradual process of enlargement of the Crown jurisdiction, which did not mean the exclusion of the local jurisdiction. In 1609, the *Tribunal da Relação* of Bahia initiated its activities in Salvador da Bahia; due to the Dutch invasion, it was out of function between 1626 and 1652. One hundred years later, in 1751, a second court opened its doors in Rio de Janeiro.[10] The existence of these

5 The case of the city of Mexico (with an estimated population size of around 200,000 people) is particular because of the structure that already existed when the Spaniards conquered Tenochtitlan in 1521.

6 Hallewell, *O livro no Brasil*, 833–835.

7 For an analysis of this process, see Camarinhas, "A administração da justiça em espaços coloniais".

8 Cabral, "Senhores e ouvidores de capitanias hereditárias", 106–112.

9 Saldanha, *As capitanias do Brasil*, 222–223.

10 About the courts (*Tribunais da Relação*) of Bahia and Rio de Janeiro, see Schwartz, *Sovereignty and society in Colonial Brazil*; Wehling and Wehling, *Direito e justiça no Brasil Colonial*.

courts[11] contributed to increase the areas covered by Portuguese law, but the impact seems to have been modest, with most of the conflicts being resolved in local jurisdiction.

Besides this reduced sphere of an erudite jurisdiction in Portuguese America, another important feature of the legal phenomenon in colonial Brazil was the absence of formal legal instruction. Since the first law schools were founded only in 1827 in São Paulo and Olinda, five years after Brazilian Independence, in early modern times no law degree could be earned in Portuguese America. The failed attempt to create a university in Brazil by request of the Municipal Council of Salvador da Bahia in 1663[12] proves that the Portuguese Crown did not intend to expand the number of universities both in the kingdom and overseas.[13]

In this context, it seems important to recognise the role of canon law and moral theology because of the notion of casuistry and the need of resolving social conflicts. As the presence of Crown officials was not high during the first centuries of the Portuguese occupation, the most relevant institution in that time was the Church; not only because of the clergymen, but also, and particularly, because of the missionaries. These matters probably influenced the local authorities, which were responsible for resolving the majority of the juridical conflicts in colonial Brazil, in a social reality quite close to Tamar Herzog's description of the juridical space of Quito during the 17th century.[14] The notion of *arbitrium*[15] explains how the *juízes ordinários* shaped their conviction with regard to the suitable justice for a specific case rather than the pure application of royal law. This rustic world, in a reference to what Hespanha calls "the reverse of the erudite",[16] operated with a logic in which the learned knowledge was not applied directly.

---

11 Actually, there were four courts in colonial Brazil, if one includes the *Tribunais da Relação* of São Luís do Maranhão, founded in 1812, and Pernambuco, founded in 1820. However, their impact was much smaller in comparison with the other two tribunals.

12 The Municipal Council of Salvador tried to attribute the status of university to the Jesuit College of Arts located in that city, but the Crown denied the request. Leite, *História da Companhia de Jesus no Brasil*, vol. 7, 195–199; Silva, *Bahia, a corte da América*, 200–201.

13 Indeed, no university was founded in the Portuguese colonial empire during the Early Modern Age; with respect to mainland Portugal, Coimbra, founded in 1290, was the only university until the University of Évora was erected in 1559 and operated by the Society of Jesus.

14 Herzog, "Sobre la cultura jurídica en la América Colonial".

15 For the notion of *arbitrium* in the Early Modern Age, see Mecarelli, *Arbitrium*.

16 "As fronteiras do poder. O mundo dos rústicos" in Hespanha, *A ordem do mundo e o saber dos juristas*, 199–208.

3 Moral Theology, Conversion and the Linguistic Issue

From the elements described before, understanding the role of canon law and moral theology seems to be indispensable to the comprehension of the juridical phenomenon in Portuguese America. In this context, religious orders, particularly the Society of Jesus, were prominent. Since their arrival, in the same fleet of the first General-Governor Tomé de Sousa, in 1549, until their expulsion, in 1759, the Jesuits were responsible for the creation of spaces for intellectual activities through their colleges, by far the most relevant educational institutions until the first half of the 18th century. The three most important colleges, located in Salvador, Rio de Janeiro and São Luis do Maranhão, provided a liberal arts education deeply influenced by scholastic methodology, including primary instruction and the bachelor degrees of Arts, Philosophy and Theology, as well as professional formation.

The intention of these colleges was both to provide instruction and to catechise indigenous people; in this sense, the linguistic issue was relevant. While the classes at the colleges were held in Latin, the conversion activities predominantly used indigenous languages. Local canon law recognised the relevance of learning indigenous languages for conversion, as the III Provincial Council of Lima (1582–1583) literally enacted.[17] Two influential works written in Spanish America about this issue, José de Acosta's *De procuranda indorum salute* and Alonso de la Peña Montenegro's *Itinerario para párrocos de indios*, also stress the necessity of learning the languages of indigenous people in order to use them as instruments of catechesis. Schlieben-Lange describes the Jesuit linguistic ability and refers to 58 languages learned by them only in South America[18] – in Brazil, the two most important were the Tupi and the Kariri language.

As the first step to a successful conversion was to master the language, instruments such as grammar books were essential. Before the arrival of the

17 "Et quoniam ad Indorum salutem non solum rerum sententiarumq; consensus, sed ipsa etiam sermonis conformatio, plurimum confert, prohibet etiam praeteruersionem ipsius auctiritate factam, atq; editam, tam in precibus, rudimentisq; doctrinae Christianae, quam in cathechismo in linguam Curquensem, vel in Aymaraycam, aliam traductionem, à quo quam fieri, vel aliter facta quem quam vti, atq; vt idem fructus ad caeteros etiam manet, qui diuerso à supradictis idiomate vtuntur, mandat Episcopis omnibus, vt in sua quisq: diocesi, quam primum curet cathechismum eundem per idoneos, & pios interpretes in reliquas linguas suae dioceseos verti: eamque interpretationem ab Episcopo sic approbatam, ab omnibus sine controuersia recipi, non obstante qualibet contraria consuetudine". *Concilium Limense*, 23–24.

18 Schlieben-Lange, "Missionarslinguistik in Lateinamerika", 44–45.

Europeans, there was no homogeneity nor structured rules of the indigenous languages, whose syntactic and semantic standards were only established by missionaries. Standardisation, in this case, also means the creation of a language – systematised, taught and learned with the help of the Jesuits in Brazil.[19] The "lengua general" was a homogeneous language based on common elements of diverse indigenous languages, an artificial creation by the religious orders that was to facilitate the contact with the indigenous people and their conversion. It contributed to a process of homogenisation of the indigenous people – or "tupization" (*Tupisierung*), in the words of Fernando Aymoré.[20] In Spanish America, the conscience of the relevance of the linguistic problem was so intense that the Crown created a specific office, the *lengua general*, to handle it,[21] among other dispositions in the *Recopilación de leyes de los reynos de las Indias*.[22] The linguistic policy and the standardised treatment in early colonial Brazil resulted in what John Monteiro described as the two generic categories of natives during the 16th century. The so-called Tupi group included all the tribes living on the Brazilian coast and those who had direct contact with Portuguese, Spaniards and French settlers; in comparison with the Tupi, the Tapuia, most of them unknown by the Portuguese, were less homogeneous and had different customs.[23]

Since the foundation of the Jesuit Province of Brazil in the 1550s, some missionaries were in charge of mastering the indigenous languages. The pastoral works included the grammar of the Tupi language (e.g., *Arte de gramatica da lingoa mais usada na costa do Brasil*, 1595, by José de Anchieta), catechisms (e.g., *Catecismo na lingoa brasilica*, 1618, by António de Araújo; *Catecismo da doutrina christaa na lingua brasilica da Nacao Kiriri*, 1698, by Luigi Vincenzo Mamiani della Rovere; and *Doutrina crista*, by José de Anchieta), dialogues (*Diálogo sobre a conversão do gentio*, 1556–1557, by Manuel da Nóbrega), and also plays and poems, e.g., those written by José de Anchieta. One can detect their pragmatic essence in realising that their main function was to provide

19 On Tupi as a 'general language' in Portuguese America, see Obermeier, "Die Jesuiten und die brasilianischen Indianersprachen". About the *lenguas generales* in Spanish-America, see Schlieben-Lange, "Missionarslinguistik in Lateinamerika", 47–52.

20 Aymoré, *Die Jesuiten im kolonialen Brasilien*, 321.

21 In the *Recopilación de Leyes de Indias*, the office of *lengua general* is mentioned with respect to the indigenous population of Chile. *Recopilación de Leyes*, lib. 6, tit. 16, ley 8.

22 Two of these dispositions included in this *Recopilación* are particularly interesting: religious men who serve in *doctrinas* are obliged to know the indigenous language (lib. 1, tit. 15, ley 5), and a chair of "lenguas de la tierra" is to be established at the university of Mexico (lib. 1, tit. 22, ley 49).

23 Monteiro, *Negros da terra*, 19–20.

missionaries the adequate instruments for their spiritual and social activities, particularly conversion. Since most of the missionaries were ignorant of the indigenous languages, the manuals intended to supply this knowledge.[24] Within the Tridentine emphasis on confession, including the necessity to confess the sins individually and not in general,[25] it seemed obvious that the missionaries should be able to understand the indigenous languages, at least in an intermediary level.[26]

Mastering the language was an important tool for the catechesis of indigenous people, but it did not guarantee that the missionaries achieved their goals. Many coeval authors commented that indigenous people in Brazil were easy to convert, but that it was extremely hard to keep them in the Christian faith.[27] According to Viveiros de Castro, these difficulties cannot be explained by a lack of curiosity for "the new", but by the incapacity of being indelibly impressed by it:[28] for him, a reconstruction of what he called the memory and the traditions of these societies was necessary to understand some essential elements of their culture.[29] Thus, the 'success' of the conversion depended on many factors and not only on the initial contact with the new faith.

A process of a long and permanent education in Jesuit schools was one of the elements for creating a Christian society in Portuguese America in the context of the Counter-Reformation. Among the courses offered in the Jesuit colleges, the moral theology course was one of the most relevant. Its structure was, according to Serafim Leite, quite similar to the classical manuals

24 Fernandes, "Do manual de confessores ao guia de penitentes", 48–49.

25 "Constat enim sacerdotes iudicium hoc incognita causa exercere non potuisse nec aequitatem quidem illos in poenis iniungendis servare potuisse si in genere dumtaxat et non potius in specie ac sigillatim sua ipsi peccata declarassent". *Concilii Tridentini Canonibus et decretis insertae*, Sessio XIV, Doctrina de sanctissimis Ponitentiae, et extremae Unctionis Sacramentis, cap. V. De confessione.

26 Among the three levels of knowledge, confessors were required to master at least the intermediary one, that is, the capacity of understanding and speaking a little bit the language in which the confession should happen. Castelnau-L'Éstoile, *Operários de uma vinha estéril*, 176.

27 See, for instance, the famous fragment of the *Sermon of the Holy Spirit*, written in 1657 by Father António Vieira: "Há outras nações, pelo contrário – estas são as do Brasil – que recebem tudo o que lhes ensinam com grande docilidade e facilidade, sem argumentar, sem replicar, sem duvidar, sem resistir; mas são estátuas de murta que, em levantando a mão e a tesoura do jardineiro, logo perdem a nova figura, e tornam à bruteza antiga e natural, e a ser mato como dantes eram".

28 "O mármore e a murta: sobre a inconstância da alma selvagem" in Viveiros de Castro, *A inconstância da alma selvagem e outros ensaios de antropologia*, 184.

29 Viveiros de Castro, *A inconstância da alma selvagem e outros ensaios de antropologia*, 181–264.

published in the 16th and 17th centuries. An overview on the tables of contents of Paul Laymann's *Theologia moralis*, one of most-used theological books in colonial Brazil, for example, shows that many juridical themes were discussed in the courses at the colleges, such as the notion of human law (lib. I, tract. IV), justice and law (lib. III, tract. I, cap. I), crimes (lib. III, tract. III, I), contractual obligations (lib. III, tract. III, III), testaments (lib. III, tract. V) and marriage (lib. III, tract. X). The same can be observed in Domingo de Soto's *De Justitia et jure*, whose influence in theological texts of the 16th century was also great: nature, the relation between human and divine law, distributive and commutative justice, murder and usury were treated in the first six books, all of them relevant in the reality of colonial Brazil. The focus of these courses was not only to present the theological discussions in the manuals and monographic books – indeed, a very relevant matter – but also, and probably primarily, to provide answers to concrete problems observed in a specific reality.[30] Therefore, discussions about catechesis, slavery and its theological consequences as well as the sacraments, particularly marriage in relation to indigenous people, were the most common matters.

The first generation of Jesuits in Brazil, who arrived in 1549, was entirely educated at Coimbra and Salamanca. In a few cases, they had close relations to prominent jurists of these universities, and two examples should be mentioned. Priest João de Azpilcueta (c. 1522–1557), Martín de Azpilcueta's (1492–1586) nephew, stayed in Brazil from 1549 until his death and was the first one to translate some catechetical instruments into Tupi language.[31] Priest Manuel da Nóbrega (1517–1570), one of the most remarkable characters of the early Brazilian colonisation, was also Dr. Navarrus' disciple, and to him and to his nephew Azpilcueta dedicated his book *Relectio cap. ita quorundam de iudeis*.[32] Azpilcueta's presence can be presumed not only by his influence as professor of most of the Jesuits and by the close relations with some of them – evident in a letter that Nóbrega wrote him (10/08/1549)[33] – but also because of

30 See Leite, *História da Companhia de Jesus no Brasil*, vol. 7, 175–189.

31 Serafim Leite mentioned the translations of catechetical instruments, such as an explanation on the creation of the world, the commandments, Our Father and a "general confession". Leite, *História da Companhia de Jesus no Brasil*, vol. 2, 546–547. Francisco González-Luis referred to a work entitled *Oraciones y Catequesis en la Lengua General del Brasil* and written by João de Azpilcueta, but there is no evidence of how precise this information is. González-Luis, "La Gramática de la lengua tupí de José de Anchieta", 231.

32 "Quaestiones item illae, quas per doctus Emanuel a Nobrega iam pridem a nobis laurca donatus religione, doctrina, & genere clarus, & Ioannes ab Azpilcueta meus ex fratre nepos carissimus ex Brasiliae [...]". Azpilcueta, *Relectio*, fol. VIr.

33 Leite, "Introdução Geral", 44–57.

the impact of the *Manual de confesores y penitentes* in Portuguese America. Nóbrega received the book, which is discussed in Manuela Bragagnolo's contribution for this volume, just in the beginning of 1550, among other books in a box sent from Portugal by the Portuguese provincial priest Simão Rodrigues (1510–1579),[34] and the text continued to be used in many other works produced in Brazil. The main concern of the book was the confession of a sin, which was part of the judgement of the conscience,[35] and the consequent attribution of a penance. In this perspective, Azpilcueta's work dealt with the following topics: confession as a judgement, the procedure adopted by the confessor, the Ten Commandments, the commandments of the Church,[36] the seven sacraments, the seven capital sins, the five exterior senses and the ecclesiastical censures (interdict and excommunication, as well as the suspension of clerics). All of these topics are present in the catechetical books produced in Brazil.

Canonists and theologians from Coimbra and Salamanca, such as Francisco Suárez and Luis de Molina, were some of the most quoted authors in the examined texts, probably because of their presence in the libraries of the Jesuit colleges. Reviewing documents of the 17th and 18th centuries, Serafim Leite affirms that the libraries of Maranhão and Pará totalled 12,000 volumes in the first half of the 18th century[37] – a very significant number even if we compare it with the presumed 15,000 volumes existing in Salvador by the time of the expulsion, in 1759.[38] In a region with a huge majority of analphabets, low-populated cities, no universities, printings presses or bookshops, these libraries belonged to the few spaces where one could find books related to the matters of interest of the Jesuit missions.[39]

4 Brazilian Pragmatic Literature

Portuguese America was not an ideal place to produce formal legal knowledge. There is no doubt about the circulation of books in colonial Brazil, evidenced

34 Leite, "Introdução Geral", 47.

35 See Prodi, *Una storia della giustizia*, 297–306; Prosperi, *Tribunali della coscienza*, 213–548.

36 To attend mass on Sundays and on holy days, to fast in the prescribed days, to pay the tithes, to confess once a year and to receive the Holy Communion at Easter. See Azpilcueta, *Manual de confesores y penitentes*, 352–385.

37 Leite, *História da Companhia de Jesus no Brasil*, vol. 4, 289.

38 Leite, *História da Companhia de Jesus no Brasil*, vol. 5, 94.

39 For an overview on the Jesuit libraries in Portuguese America, see Rodrigues, "As 'livrarias' dos jesuítas no Brasil Colonial".

by studies on private libraries mentioned in testaments and criminal prosecutions as well as by research on inventories of religious libraries.[40] They highlight the presence of religious books and illustrate the strong censorship, imposed by the Crown, the Church and the Inquisition, and exercised in Brazil by Jesuit *visitadores*.[41] Furthermore, the existence of texts considered inadequate, particularly during the 18th century, was a clear evidence of a clandestine circulation. Since the foundation of the *Real Mesa Censória* (Royal Censorship Board) in 1768, the Portuguese Crown centralised book censorship; every book required a license to be sent to Brazil because, unlike in Hispanic America,[42] there was no institutional control in Portuguese America. Therefore, legally acquiring a book was difficult, expensive and extremely supervised, but it did not exclude the possibility of smuggling.[43]

The reduced market of bookselling, the small number of readers, and especially the prohibition of printing presses contributed considerably to the limited scale of book circulation. Notwithstanding some attempts to operate during the 18th century, the ban of editorial activities in the case of António Isidoro da Fonseca, in 1747, exemplified the attitude of the Portuguese Crown against printing presses during the colonial age.[44] While in Mexico, for example, printers operated since 1539, and published even catechetical books in indigenous languages,[45] publishing in Portugal was the only option for those in Portuguese America who intended to print books.

The few printed sources used in this article appeared in Portugal, but the majority of texts concerned about the particularities of Brazilian cases of conscience were, by that time, manuscripts. This was especially due to the high costs of printing and, as concerned some sources, to the difficulties in reviewing the originals. Even the theses defended in the Jesuit colleges were published in Portugal,[46] but, because of very low print runs, the few extant

---

40 Moraes, *Livros e bibliotecas no Brasil Colonial*; Lessa, "As bibliotecas brasileiras dos tempos coloniais"; Pereira, "O livro e a biblioteca nas mudanças no Brasil Colônia".

41 González Sánchez, "La cultura escrita en el Mundo Atlántico colonial: Brasil y América del norte".

42 Rueda Ramírez, *Negocio e intercambio cultural*.

43 Silva, "O comércio de livros de Portugal para o Brasil e a censura"; Abreu, "Circulação de livros entre Europa e América".

44 Hallewell, *O livro no Brasil*, 85–92.

45 According to the collection of the Count de la Vinaza, 30 works written in indigenous languages were printed in Mexico only between 1539 and 1560. Daher, "Os usos da língua tupi nos séculos XVI e XVII", 361–362.

46 Leite, *História da Companhia de Jesus no Brasil*, vol. 4, 269; Leite, *História da Companhia de Jesus no Brasil*, vol. 7, 209–210.

copies might have been destroyed during the expulsion of the Jesuits in 1759–1760. Among these manuscripts, there are some catechetical books, such as the *Confessionario pella lingoa geral para seconfessar por elle em cazo denesesidade urgente*, which we will examine later. This work, both written in the Tupi language and in Portuguese, circulated in the Jesuit missions of the captaincy of Pará in the middle of the 18th century; it was directly influenced by Alonso de la Peña Montegro's *Itinerario para párrocos de indios*.[47]

Despite so many unfavourable elements, an interesting literature concerning the necessity of resolving conflicts in Portuguese America appeared, but not in the same way as the juridical literature produced in early modern Spanish America. If authors such as Juan de Matienzo, Juan de Solórzano Pereira, Feliciano de Vega y Padilla y Diego de Avendaño were recognised in Spanish America after the publication of their works, the most important juridical texts written in Brazil did not have the same impact. Simão Marques' *Brasilia pontificia* (1749), probably the most complex juridical text written in colonial Brazil, was rarely mentioned in other books although it was published in Lisbon. The circulation of *Cultura e opulência do Brasil por suas Drogas e Minas* (*Culture and wealth of Brazil resulting from its medicinal drugs and mines*), published in 1711 and nowadays a significant source for Brazilian economic history of the late 17th century, was prohibited by the *Desembargo do Paço* just a few days after its publication; researchers did not even pay attention to its juridical relevance.[48]

Some texts related to ecclesiastical normativity are particularly interesting for our purposes. Aiming to provide solutions for cases of conscience, this literature clearly proves the existence of a space where juridical and theological knowledge circulated. At the same time, these texts granted relevant information about the practice of cases of conscience in Portuguese America, offering details on the themes discussed and how they were decided. However, many manuscripts written from the 16th until the 18th centuries are now lost. Serafim Leite found references for the period about collections of cases compiled by the Jesuits Manuel da Fonseca, Manuel Xavier Ribeiro and Jerónimo Moniz, which seem to have disappeared.[49] On the other hand, many available sources can be considered pragmatic literature. Conversion, confession and good Christian manners, as well as the resolution of cases of conscience, clearly express the practical objective of the texts: the creation of an *orbe christiano* in the New World both by teaching Christian principles and by offering solutions for particular cases.

47 Barros and Fonseca, "Passagens do livro 'Itinerário para Párocos de Índios' ".

48 On this aspect, see Cabral, "Antonil jurista?".

49 Leite, *História da Companhia de Jesus no Brasil*, vol. 7, 182.

Pastoral works (conversion dialogues, catechisms, sermons and grammar books) and cases of conscience will be examined in the following paragraphs, as well as a text whose purpose was not addressed to priests or to indigenous people, but to farmers and slave owners. Despite their juridical and theological relevance,[50] the constitutions of the Archbishopric of Bahia, produced by the Synod in Salvador da Bahia in 1707, are not dealt with in this article.[51] The same applies to other important practical juridical works indirectly connected to Portuguese America, such as Antonio Vanguerve Cabral's *Practica judicial* (1730) and Manuel Álvares Pegas' *Allegaçam de direito por parte dos senhores condes do Vimiozo sobre a sucessam da capitania de Pernambuco* (1671). The author mentioned first was a former *ouvidor* in the Captaincy of Itamaracá and reported some cases decided by him. The second text was an *allegatio* written by the most famous Portuguese jurist of the 17th century, it dealt with a lawsuit between the heirs of the hereditary Captaincy of Pernambuco (which was the richer and economically most relevant area of Brazil in the previous century) and the Crown. Both of them were objects of specific papers.[52]

5 Catechisms and Other Pastoral Works

This group of sources highlights the juridical relevance of catechetical books, grammar books of indigenous languages and sermons. The common purpose of all of these texts was primarily to promote the conversion of the "gentiles", as pointed out before. However, some of them aimed at the promotion of Christian virtues (and consequently "educating" their congregation in the principles learned in their studies on moral theology).

That was the case of the sermons. Among them, those written by Father António Vieira (1608–1697) and published under the title of *Sermões*, are without a doubt the most remarkable and relevant – but his geniality seems to be singular in the colonial context. Since this chapter intends to comprehend the mainstream thinking, it would be better to examine the sermons produced by those fathers who preached in Brazilian churches and spread their words by printing or made them circulate in manuscripts. The case of Simão Marques

50 Marciano Vidal, among many others, considers the decrees of the councils and pastoral theology, which includes catechisms, confession manuals and sermons, as literary genres of moral theology. Vidal, *Historia de la Teología Moral*, vol. 4.2, 286.

51 About these Constitutions, see Feitler and Souza, *A Igreja no Brasil*; Cabral, "Ius commune in Portuguese America".

52 Cabral, "Senhores e ouvidores de capitanias hereditárias"; Cabral, "Pegas e Pernambuco".

is singular because he published five of his sermons, all of them in Portugal.[53] The other priests published less, like Lourenço Craveiro's sermon at the College of Bahia (16 February 1665),[54] or the sermons delivered by José de Andrada e Moraes[55] and Manuel Freire Batalha,[56] both in the village of Mariana in 1745, among many other cases.

On the other hand, catechetical works were a relevant genre produced in Portuguese America. The most important texts of this kind, according to the literature,[57] are *Doutrina Christam* (1592), by José de Anchieta, *Catecismo na Lingoa Brasilica* (1618), by Antonio de Araújo, and *Compendio da doutrina christam na lingoa portuguesa & brasílica* (1687), by Johann Philip Bettendorf, to which I would add the *Catecismo da doutrina christãa na lingua Brasilica da Nação Kiriri* (1698), by Luigi Vincenzo Mamiani della Rovere. All of them, with the exception of the first one, were printed during the 17th century, and only Mamiani's work refers to other indigenous language besides the Tupi. Antonio de Araújo's text, the longest and best known,[58] was printed once more in 1686, in a modified version by Bartolomeu de Leão.[59] It was written almost entirely in Tupi, like the *Doutrina Christam*, whose first printed and fully translated version only appeared in 1992.[60] As I have mentioned before, Mamiani della Rovere's *Catecismo* was a bilingual text. Bettendorf, in turn, conceived his *Compendio* to be a short catechism.

Besides their intention of conversion, the other common element of these books was their content. They shared a common structure and dealt with certain topics: the confessionary, the dialogues of conversion, an introduction to the Christian faith (with an explanation about God, Jesus, Mary, the Holy Trinity, etc.), the Ten Commandments, the commandments of the Church, the seven capital sins, and so on. Clearly influenced by the scholastic method, they all used a structure based on questions and answers, trying to facilitate the work of the missionaries.

Antonio de Araújo's *Catecismo na Lingoa Brasilica* was the first printed catechism (1618) among those produced in Portuguese America. Araújo states in the prologue that he had used other catechisms as the base of his work to

---

53 Marques, *Sermão do patriarca S. Ignacio de Loyola*; Marques, *Sermam do grande apóstolo do Oriente S. Francisco Xavier*.

54 Craveiro, *Merenda eucarística e sermão*.

55 Moraes, *Sermão de acçam de graças*.

56 Batalha, *Sermoens, que no dia da presentação de nossa senhora*.

57 Leite, *História da Companhia de Jesus no Brasil*, vol. 4, 312–314; Aymoré, *Die Jesuiten im kolonialen Brasilien*, 272.

58 Navarro, "Tradução do 'Catálogo de todos os dias santos de guarda e de jejum' ".

59 Monserrat, Barros and Mota, "O índio "travesso" em um confessionário jesuítico tupi de 1686".

60 Anchieta, *Doutrina Chistã*, vol. 1.

which he added other contents,[61] which is evidence of the construction and circulation of knowledge concerning catechisms and those related matters. Strategies to achieve a better pronunciation in Tupi, at the beginning of the book, constitute one of the few parts written in Portuguese,[62] while the following pages are all in the *lingua geral*. The contents of the book show his intention to offer a reduced but complete version of the foundations of the Christian doctrine in the standardised indigenous language, introducing those elements and explaining them. When Araújo treats the fasting or the Sunday as a holy day,[63] he offers a theoretical but simple explanation for that, in order to make easier the diffusion among indigenous people. Translated prayers and explanations of the bases of Christianity, such as the Lord's Prayer,[64] as well as the catechism itself, follow; the book opted for a structure in dialogues.

Avoiding complexity and reducing the theological knowledge were the guidelines followed by Araújo in his book. As he intended to make the indigenous people understand the Christian doctrine, nothing should be hard to comprehend or to explain. The rigid formula of a dialogue simplified by the missionary explaining the creation of the world, the passion of Jesus,[65] the Resurrection and even the role of the Catholic Church and of papal jurisdiction.[66] Dialogues were also useful in the catechism to introduce the neophytes into the Ten Commandments and the sacraments. In a recent work, Jaqueline Ferreira da Mota has translated some parts of the confessionary of the *Catecismo na Lingoa Brasilica*, which has not yet entirely been translated into Portuguese. In this Portuguese version, it is possible to understand how the missionaries explained that some practices of this ethnic group were not coherent with the Christian faith. The questions criticised indigenous religious practices in order to convince the audience that these were not correct.

Based on Mota's Portuguese translation of Araújo's confessionary (see table 5.1), I propose a comparative scheme dealing with the questions on the first commandment:

---

61 "[...] que eu o minimo de seus filhos posesse em ordem, pera com a do nosso Reuedenrissimo Padre Geral, se imprimir o Catecismo, que nesta lingoa antigoamente composerao alguns Padres doctos, & bons lingoas, ao qual bem visto, & examinado acrescentei, nao so todas as exortações necessárias nos passos occurentes, & hum copioso confessionário: mas tambem lhe ajuntei tudo o que pertence à ordem de Baptizar, casar, & ungir, & enterrar [...]". Araújo, *Catecismo na lingoa brasílica*.

62 Araújo, *Catecismo na lingoa brasílica*, fols. 1r–2v.

63 Araújo, *Catecismo na lingoa brasílica*, fols. 3r–12v.

64 Araújo, *Catecismo na lingoa brasílica*, fols. 24v–30r.

65 Araújo, *Catecismo na lingoa brasílica*, fols. 51v–64v. Araújo made one dialogue for each station of the Cross.

66 Araújo, *Catecismo na lingoa brasílica*, fols. 49r–51r.

TABLE 5.1 Questions on the first commandment in Araújo's confessionary (1618): comparison of the Tupi, Portuguese and English versions

Q.	Original in Tupi[a]	Portuguese version[b]	English version[c]
1	*Ereimoetepe Tupã opacatu ymoetê piraçocé?*	*Tu honras, tu estimas a Deus sobre todas coisas adoradas?*	Do you honour, do you appreciate God above all the adored things?
2	*Ereimong-etápe Payê marãtecorâmarece Tupã recó cotî nheenga reitíca? Mobipe?*	*Tu pediste ao pajé que fizesse um trabalho, ao mesmo tempo falando mal do mandamento de Deus?*	Did you ask the *pajé*[d] to do work for you while you denigrated God's commandment?
3	*Ererobiápe yetanongaüba? Coipô Caraimonhangâ?*	*Tu acreditas na falsa oferenda ao pajé ou na cerimônia da santidade?*	Do you believe in the false offering to the *pajé* or in the ceremony of the sanctity?
4	*Ererobiápe yagoâra, coi o guîrâ nheẽga morâceya, coipo maraca poraceya? Coipo morãguiguana?*	*Tu acreditas na onça, na fala ou na dança do pássaro, ou na dança do chocalho ou no agouro?*	Do you believe in the jaguar, in the birds' talk or dance or in *chocalho*[e] or in the omen?
5	*Ererobiápe Paye aîba moçanguîjaramo cecô?*	*Tu acreditas no pajé aliado a espírito malfazejo, ele estando na qualidade de feiticeiro?*	Do you believe in the *pajé* allied with bad spirits as a wizard?
6	*Çupixuár ipo Paye ãgaîba erêpe cerobiâ?*	*"Com razão, acredito naquele que costuma ser o pajé mau", disseste?*	Did you say: "Indeed, I believe in the one who usually id the bad *pajé*"?

TABLE 5.1 Questions on the first commandment in Araújo's confessionary (1618): comparison of the Tupi, Portuguese and English versions (*cont.*)

Q.	Original in Tupi[a]	Portuguese version[b]	English version[c]
7	*Erenhemopayêpe enhemoetêbo, epoçubana?*	*Tu te fizeste pajé, tu te honrando, te engrandecendo, tu chupando para curar?*	Did you make yourself *pajé*, honoring yourself, sucking/drinking, in order to cure somebody?
8	*Ereimoripe aba Payê rerobiaragoâma rece?*	*Tu consentiste que alguém?*	Did you agree that anyone did so?
9	*Ereyçubanúçape Payê aiba çûpê?*	*Tu te deixaste chupar pelo pajé mau?*	Did you let the bad *pajé* suck you?
10	*Erexubanucarpe nde raira, coipó nde remirecò, coipò amô abâ?*	*Tu deixaste que chupassem teu filho, ou tua mulher ou algum índio?*	Did you let anyone suck your son or your wife or any indio?
11	*Ereçàirpe nderaîra Iacî cemîpîreme?*	*Tu fizeste incisão no teu filho quando começou a sair a lua?*	Did you make an incision in your son when the moon appeared?
12	*Ereyecuacúpe nde remirecô membîra recè, nde raîra maraârarecè, nderaîjra nhemondîara recê?*	*Praticaste o jejum devido a tua esposa ter dado à luz, por estar filho gravemente doente, ou por causa da primeira menstruação de tua filha?*	Did you fast when your wife gave birth, when your son was seriously ill or because of the first menstruation of your daughter?

[a] Araújo, *Catecismo na lingoa brasílica*, fols. 98v–99r.
[b] Mota, *A confissão tupi*, 237–242.
[c] Translation is mine, based on the mentioned Portuguese translation.
[d] *Pajé* is the spiritual leader of the Tupi people.
[e] *Chocalho* is a musical instrument often used in the religious ceremonies of the Tupi.

A look at questions four and twelve shows that the author of the confessionary was familiar with the indigenous customs and probably knew some of the most frequent practices of the *pajés*, and such a specific knowledge was necessary to establish a successful dialogue. Asking the confessing person about their practices was a form of explaining to them that the *dance of the birds* was a pagan belief that might be avoided, because it violated the Christian faith.

At the end of the 17th century, some years after the publication of a new edition with a linguistic update of Araújo's *Catecismo* by Bartolomeu de Leão, the Jesuit Luigi Vincenzo Mamiani della Rovere published his *Catecismo da doutrina christaa na lingua brasilica da Nação Kiriri*, probably the only printed catechism not in Tupi in Portuguese America. Kariri was a language used in North-eastern Brazil, particularly in the *sertões*. In the prologue, Mamiani explains the reasons why the book has a bilingual structure, with the contents both in Portuguese and in the Kariri language. Those who had the book in their hands could learn the Kariri language, but it was also possible that, if one was not interested in learning the language, one could learn its religious content and use it as an instrument for the conversion and catechesis of people under their responsibility, such as their sons and slaves.[67] This passage clearly demonstrates the author's pragmatic intention in writing a catechism.

As other catechisms, Mamiani's work handles the foundations of the Christian faith in prayers (sign of the Cross, Our Father, Ave Maria, Salve Regina, Credo), the Ten Commandments, the Commandments of the Church, sacraments, capital sins, cardinal and theological virtues and, among some other themes, a general confession. A simple structure in two columns, with the Portuguese text on the right and the Kariri on the left, looks like a glossary or a dictionary, different from the more complex catechism of Araújo. In the second part, the catechism itself, Mamiani applies the scholastic structure of the dialogue between master and disciple to introduce the neophyte in Christian matters, and here, again, he uses texts both in Kariri and in Portuguese. The master (M.) explains some Christian acts, like the sign of the Cross, to the disciple (D.): "M. – Why we do the sign of the Cross? D. – To confess to the Holy Trinity,

67 "Ajuntei neste Catecismo a significação Portugueza correspondente á fraze da língua Kiriri por duas causas. A primeira, para que os novos Missionarios por essa via vendo os exemplos na língua, & a significação no vulgar idioma, possaõ mais facilmente alcançar as frazes, & o modo de falar, & assim aprender mais depressa a língua. A segunda causa he, porque se acaso este livrinho vier ás maõs de quem não sabe a lingua Kiriri, se aproveite também delle, ou para aprender is mysterios, & declaração deles para si; ou para os ensinar com esse metdo aos filhos, escravos, & outros de sua obrigação". Mamiani della Rovere, *Catecismo da doutrina christãa*, fol. 7.

Father, Son, & Holy Spirit, three persons, & only one true God. M. – And what more? D. – To remember the Holy Cross, which redeemed us".[68] Dialogues also served to illustrate themes like the Ten Commandments and the sacraments.[69]

Probably the most interesting part of the text is the fifth chapter entitled "Way to administer the sacrament of marriage" (*Modo para administrar o sacramento do matrimonio*). There, Mamiani's bilingual explanation refers to the most relevant themes on marriage, like the impediments, a glossary on family relationships in the Kariri language[70] and the ceremonial rituals, such as the questions of the father and the answers which bride and bridegroom should repeat during the ceremony.[71]

In the beginning of the fifth chapter (see table 5.2), Mamiani describes the *pregão*, i.e., the public announcement of an upcoming marriage, in order to remind anyone who is aware of impediments to inform the Priest. The author offers a very important document on colonial life, both in Portuguese and in Kariri.[72]

Under the influence of the Constitutions of the Archbishopric of Lisbon, Mamiani informs about a custom in Brazilian dioceses of attributing the penalty of excommunication in the *pregão* for those who did not inform about the impediments or for those who maliciously reported a false one. Nevertheless, the indigenous people did not understand well the nature and the consequences of this excommunication; therefore, the warning against the nature of these acts, which used to happen among those people, was sufficient for Mamiani. The final part of the *pregão*, by its turn, is a clear demonstration of the influence of local customs in the making of institutions: this statement resulted from the usual cohabitation among the indigenous even if they did not get married.[73]

The texts about the impediments follow a particular structure, because they constitute a simplification of the respective canonical dispositions on the theme. At first, Mamiani explains what a "diriment impediment" was,[74] and then in which cases it occurs, always in Portuguese and in Kariri. After analysing the *cognatio* and its cases, he writes a paragraph – only in Portuguese,

---

68 Mamiani della Rovere, *Catecismo da doutrina christãa*, 28–29. In this excerpt, Mamiani used the Portuguese words *Santissima Trinidade* and *Espirito Santo* in the Kariri version of the dialogue; however, when talking about God, he referred to *Tupã*.

69 Mamiani della Rovere, *Catecismo da doutrina christãa*, 110–138.

70 Mamiani della Rovere, *Catecismo da doutrina christãa*, 209–213.

71 Mamiani della Rovere, *Catecismo da doutrina christãa*, 207–208.

72 Mamiani della Rovere, *Catecismo da doutrina christãa*, 193–194.

73 Mamiani della Rovere, *Catecismo da doutrina christãa*, 194.

74 "As pessoas seguintes tem impedimento dirimente para casarem entre si, & se casarem, nao ficao bem casados, & hao-se de apartar". Mamiani della Rovere, *Catecismo da doutrina christãa*, 195.

TABLE 5.2 Questions on the first commandment in Mamiani's Catechism (1698): comparison of the Kariri, Portuguese and English versions

Original in Kariri	Original in Portuguese	English version[a]
Do ighỹde sipiwonhé N.N. inhurae N.N. idehó N.N. inhutidzí N.N. Dunet çorí tokié sii wonheá didehoá, kendébae do Warédi, idzené ibuânghé so Tupã, no imorókié inhádi. No iwakié ibureté idiomon, noríitocriné siiwonheá inaádi idzené ebuângheá so Tupã nodehé. Pihohóde dipiwohnerí diboá codoró siiwhoné kiedeádi bo ibuângheteá	*Quer casar N.N. filho de N.N. com N.N. filha de N.N. quem souber de algum impedimento o descubra ao Padre sobpena de pecado mortal, se o não descobrir. E não havendo algum, ninguém ponha impedimento maliciosamente á execução deste matrimonio debaixo da mesma pena. Os que hao de casar vivirao apartados em quanto não casao, para fugir da ocasião do peccado.*	N.N., son of N.N., wants to marry N.N., daughter of N.N. Anyone who knows of an impediment must inform the Priest about it; on the contrary, he will commit a mortal sin. If there is no impediment, nobody shall maliciously put forward an impediment to the execution of this marriage under the menace of the same penalty. Those who will marry must live apart from each other as long as they are not married yet, in order escape from the situation of sin.

[a] Translation is mine, based on the mentioned Portuguese translation.

probably because it was addressed to the missionaries – to warn that consanguinity is only forbidden in the second grade. To justify it, the author refers to a Papal Bull of Paul III, who decided that impediments of third and fourth grade of consanguinity did not apply for indigenous people. Consequently, dispensations are unnecessary, in those cases: and then he literally quotes Alonso de la Peña Montenegro's *Itinerario para párrocos de indios*.[75] To the other impediments he refers only as those "that only prevent the marriage" (*impedimentos,*

75 "Advirto que aqui não se declara o impedimento de consanguinidade, senão, até o segundo grão inclusive; porque Paulo III por hua Bulla tira aos Indios os impedimentos do terceiro, & quarto grão afim de consanguinidade, como de afinidade; nem há mister dispensação para eles nesses dous grãos, porque como diz o Bispo Montenegro no seu

que sómente impedem o matrimonio), with no definition, but evidently following Thomas Aquinas' view on that matter.[76] After explaining four impediments (*Ecclesiae vetitum, Feriae, Sponsaliae* and *Votum, impediunt fieri, permittunt facta teneri*) in both languages, Mamiani states that the two other impediments of this kind "told by the doctors", the catechism and the crime, were not valid here, because, according to the "common opinion of the authors", the contrary use can abrogate impediments that prevent marriage.[77]

The last text is the anonymous manuscript *Grãmatica da Lingua geral do Brazil, com hum Diccionario dos vocabulos mais uzuaes para a intelligencia da dita Lingua* (1751), which also includes a "doctrine" and a confessionary. In the doctrine, we find Tupi versions of the signal of the cross, Our Father, Hail Mary, Credo, Ten Commandments, commandments of the Church, sacraments and seven capital sins.[78] Just like in other catechisms, some Christian expressions have no translation into Tupi, such as "Sancta Cruz" and "Amen". Jesus and Maria have no correspondence in Tupi; the same happens with the word "peccado" (sin), which appears in the warning before the confession in the *Catecismo na Lingoa Brasilica*[79] probably because the indigenous people did not have any correspondent structure in their culture. On the other hand, the references to "God" have always appeared in the Tupi language with the use of the word "Tupã". As the Jesuits considered Tupã to be the most powerful god according to this tradition,[80] they translated it as "the only god" – a cultural translation of the monotheistic structure to a culture based on polytheism. Since the 16th century catechism written by José de Anchieta, this statement is explicit: when the confessionary treats the first commandment, both the Tupi version (Eimoeté

Itinerario de Parocos de Indios, esta concessão não he meramente privilegio, senão ley municipal Ecclesiastica". Mamiani della Rovere, *Catecismo da doutrina christãa*, 198–199.

76 While the diriment impediments absolutely invalidated the marriage, the impediments that only prevented marriages turned them illicit but valid. Aquinus, *Opera Omnia*, 96–97, Supplementum tertia partis, q. 50. A similar definition is offered by Pedro Murillo Velarde, probably the most systematic canonist of colonial Spanish America: "Sicut in aliis contractibus, sic etiam in matrimonio, aliqua inveniuntur impedimenta inhabilitantia absolute ad matrimonium contrahendum, & dicuntur dirimentia, quia ejus valorem dirimunt. Alia dicuntur impedientia tantum, quia illis stantibus matrimonium validem, tamen illicite contrahitur". Murillo Velarde, *Cursus juris canonici*, vol. 2, 17–18 (lib. 4, tit. 1, n. 27).

77 Mamiani della Rovere, *Catecismo da doutrina christãa*, 206.

78 BUC, *Gramatica da Lingoa Geral do Brazil*, fols. 370–379.

79 "Memẽ tipo nhemogaraîbi pira tecô catû abiára *peccado* Tupã nheengaabí tegoáma yába pupe oanga jucá [...]". Araújo, *Catecismo na lingoa brasílica*, fol. 96v.

80 According to Graciela Chamorro, Tupã was actually a minor god despite its relevance in indigenous thought. Chamorro, "La traducción del lenguaje cristiano al guaraní jesuítico", 254.

ojepé Tupã) and the first question of the confessor to a confident (Ererobiárpe Tupã ojeé, jandé moñangára?) refer to Tupã as "the only God".

In contrast to other catechisms produced in Portuguese America, the confessionary of this manuscript does not have a dialogical structure: written in Tupi, it only contains the questions the confessor might ask the penitent. Some questions are dedicated to each one of the commandments, but, with regard to the fifth and the sixth commandments, the confessionary offers special inquiries about women. Maria Cândida Barros, Ruth Monserrat and Jaqueline Mota, in a paper about the sixth commandment in this confessionary manuscript, propose a translation into Portuguese of all of the pertinent questions (see table 5.3). The specific content of the questions regarding women demonstrates the attention to some particular sexual practices among the native communities. Comparing the questions addressed to men and to women, the authors show that in a few cases the missionaries presuppose a continuity in the actions of the women. However, when they ask similar things to men, the verbal structure denotes an interest only in past actions and not in the continuity of the sin. In other cases, referring to sexual attraction, the questions addressed to women explain many male categories (boy, adult, white man and priest), while the same questions addressed to men only refer to a "more beautiful woman".[81] Some examples of these differences are the following:

TABLE 5.3 Questions on the sixth commandment in the manuscript confessionary (1750): comparison of the Tupi, Portuguese and English versions

Women – Portuguese translation	Women – English version	Men – Portuguese translation	Men – English version
32 – Quando você olhou um rapazinho ou um homem ou um branco ou um Padre você falou para si mesmo tomara que eu copule com ele?	When you look at a young boy or a man or a white man or a priest, did you say to yourself "I hope to copulate with him"?	32 – Ao olhar uma mulher mais bonita você falou para si mesmo tomara que eu a copulasse?	When you look at a more beautiful woman, did you say to yourself: "I hope to copulate with her"?

81 BUC, *Gramatica da Lingoa Geral do Brazil*, fols. 172–176.

Another remarkable aspect of this confessionary is the reference to the devil in the questions on the first commandment (see table 5.4).[82] Jaqueline Mota notices a change in the way the missionaries handle the issue of indigenous diabolic beliefs in this confessionary.[83] In the question *Erarubiãr jurupari recẽ?* (Do you believe in the devil?), they presupposed that the indigenous were able to believe, which was an important assumption in a context when the missionaries were also concerned about fighting the devil. The intention of the anonymous author of the confessionary was to introduce the existence of the devil in order to fight it, and further to connect this abstract character to concrete situations the missionaries believed to be the materialisation of evil, such as the *pajés* and the witches,[84] but using one word (*jurupari*)[85] in the Tupi language. In many questions of this confessionary, this connection becomes evident:

6 Cases of Conscience

Creating a society based on Christian values in the New World, with few European individuals and a more numerous native population, proved very difficult for the first generation of Jesuits. They knew that the situation of Portuguese America in the middle of the 16th century demanded special treatment due to its particularities, but this did not mean abandoning the European traditions. Every difference might not only be thought from but also be compatible with the tradition in which the Jesuits were inserted.

The cases of conscience were precisely those moments when Jesuits reflected about the singularities of the American circumstances. Albert R. Jonsen and Stephen Toulmin, dealing with the medieval origins of the *casus conscientiae* and relating them to the notion of prudence (*prudentia*) especially developed by Thomas Aquinas, drew attention to the possibility of the conscience to be mistaken. If an error arose from ignoring a circumstance which did not result from negligence, the erroneous conscience was excused from sin.[86] This issue is related to the important notion of probabilism, a remarkable issue of moral

82 About the difficulties in achieving a cultural translation of the notion of devil, see Chamorro, "La traducción del lenguaje cristiano al guaraní jesuítico", 256–258.

83 Mota, *A confissão tupi*, 69–73.

84 Mota, *A confissão tupi*, 74–102.

85 In the manuscript of the dictionary found with the same copy of the confessionary, *jurupari* was the Tupi word that corresponded to the Portuguese *diabo* (devil). BUC, *Gramatica da Lingoa Geral do Brazil*, fol. 287r.

86 Jonsen and Toulmin, *The abuse of casuistry*, 129.

TABLE 5.4 Questions on the first commandment in the manuscript confessionary (1750): comparison of the Tupi, Portuguese and English versions

Q.	Original in Tupi[a]	Portuguese version[b]	English version[c]
1	*Ereçauçũb Tupãna nde pỹa çuî catũ?*	*Amas mesmo a Deus, no teu coração?*	Dou you really love God in your heart?
2	*Erarubiãr juruparî recẽ?*	*Crês no diabo?*	Do you believe in the devil?
4	*Erecenõi pecô juruarî, ndepỹa ỹba ramẽ ajubetê teêm nhõte?*	*Invocaste, porventura, o demônio, quando estavas com o coração debilitado, angustiado, ainda que tenha sido apenas à toa, em vão, sem resultados, inutilmente?*	Did you, perhaps, invoke the devil, when your heart was weak, distressed, even if it was only in vain, without results, or, uselessly?
5	*Eremonguetâ pajê amo osecár oaráma, mâ nongára aỹba indébo?*	*Negociaste com algum pajé para que oxalá ele buscasse mal igual para ele?*	Did you negotiate with any *pajé* in order to make him look for the same evil for him?
7	*Nde eropoçanõng ucã, pajẽ amõ çupẽ?*	*Mandaste algum pajé curar?*	Did you ask any *pajé* for a cure?
8	*Erarobiãr, Pajẽ oericõ tecõ juruparî çuî, opaçanõng arãma abã?*	*Acreditas que o pajé tenha hábito com o diabo para curar alguém?*	Do you believe that the *pajé* has a pact with the devil to cure anyone?
9	*Pajẽ pecõ indẽ? = Se for femea = Maracaymbãra?*	*Porventura [és] pajé / Se for fêmea / Porventura [és] feiticeira?*	Are you *pajé*, by chance? [if the confessing person is male] Are you witch? [if the confessing person is female]

[a] BUC, *Gramatica da Lingoa Geral do Brazil*, fols. 384–385.
[b] Mota, *A confissão tupi*, 242–244.
[c] Translation is mine, based on the mentioned Portuguese translation.

theology in the 16th and 17th centuries, present in America[87] as well. With a large scope of action if one analyses the circumstances and follows one's conscience, the prudence and the natural law, the casuistry cannot be separated from the capacity of some people to judge the acts of others, in order to recommend (or not) their actions.[88] As Jonsen and Toulmin resumed, the casuists were offering descriptions of moral behaviour in which the moral precepts and the details of actions were looked at together, prescribing the right act and judging specific situations with their conscience.[89]

In early colonial Brazil, the Jesuits intended to guide morally the population, which included deciding on concrete situations unknown in their particularities to the European tradition. It was not important if they had not yet faced a similar case, because the moral principles and prudence of a Jesuit missionary were considered sufficient to provide an answer for any case of conscience that would appear. From their arrival in the middle of the 16th century until their expulsion, more than two centuries later, the Jesuits were the most relevant casuists in Portuguese America. As already pointed out, the studies of moral theology in the Jesuit colleges were concerned with teaching how to deal with cases of conscience. However, in the first decades of the missions, the necessity of solving these cases was intense and directly proportional to a sentiment of not feeling capable to judge. This is the reason why many priests asked those authorities for the help in whom they trusted, and some of the written answers have survived.

An intriguing source in this respect is the manuscript *Sententiae circa resolutionem aliquorum casum, qui in Brasilia frequenter accurunt*, dated from the 1580s and not yet integrally published.[90] Five years after their arrival in Brazil, some Jesuits asked for the help of their former professors in Coimbra due to the difficulties they were facing with some situations. In this document, the priests Fernão Perez and Gaspar Gil and two of the most relevant theologians of the 16th century, Martín de Azpilcueta and Luis de Molina, answered the consultations in Latin, with the exception of one text written in Spanish by Molina. Five questions are treated in the manuscript: (1) charging more in credit sales than in cash, (2) confession of slaves about their incapacity to speak Portuguese, (3) a general absolution in cases of shipwreck, (4) Portuguese people with "just" titles selling slaves, and (5) priests omitting the bans of marriages. This document illustrates that and how European juridical and theological

87 Ruiz, "Probabilismo e Teologia moral".
88 Jonsen and Toulmin, *The abuse of casuistry*, 135.
89 Jonsen and Toulmin, *The abuse of casuistry*, 136.
90 An excerpt of the text was published by Zeron, *Linha de fé*, 499–505.

traditions directly influenced the formation of a particular juridical space in Brazil; citing an answer given by famous theologians like Azpilcueta and Molina assured a high authority to the solution of the case.

The first question of the *Sententiae* treats usury, a theme in which Luis Molina was a renowned specialist. His response for the consultation offers impressive information about the economic dynamics of the Brazilian sugar production circle in the middle of the 16th century. Molina describes long-term indebtedness to establish *engenhos*, payment not in money but *in natura* (with sugar), the circulation of letters of credit and interest charged by creditors in Portugal; he answers, after an analysis of the contracts, that the system is valid.[91] Azpilcueta answers in the same direction in a likewise complex text with many theoretical aspects about usury and income in mortgage contracts. He does not mention any particularity of Portuguese America, but his opinion refers four times to his *Manual de Confesores* and once to Thomas Aquinas.[92] With regard to the second question, Azpilcueta supports the confession of black slaves made through an interpreter in cases that they do not know the language of the confession[93] – an answer that is perfectly compatible with a quoted opinion he manifested in the *Manual de Confesores*.[94] Here the linguistic problem, a central issue during the first decades of the Portuguese presence in America, appears once more, but the author does not say a word about adopting the strategy of learning the languages of the slaves. Slavery and the issue of the legitimacy of the property title appears in another question; and both Azpilcueta[95] and Molina[96] base their answers on the origins of enslavement, in this case a just war. This argument is compatible with Molina's theory of legitimate slavery, which might result from a just war, a commutation of a death penalty, self-alienation in extreme necessity or birth.[97]

Another example of a written case of conscience deals with the question: "Se um pai pode vender o seu filho ou se alguém pode vender a si mesmo" (If the father could sell his son and if someone could sell himself). It has the structure of a classical *responsa*, a usual genre of juridical literature in the late Middle Ages in which a specialist answered a specific question.[98] In this case,

91 BPE, *Sententiae circa resolutionem*, fols. 120v–123v.

92 BPE, *Sententiae circa resolutionem*, fols. 127r–128v.

93 BPE, *Sententiae circa resolutionem*, fol. 128v.

94 Azpilcueta, *Manual de confesores y penitentes*, 373.

95 BPE, *Sententiae circa resolutionem*, fols. 129r–129v.

96 BPE, *Sententiae circa resolutionem*, fols. 124v–125r.

97 Molina, *De justitia et jure opera omnia*, 87–91 (tit 1, disp. XXXIII).

98 About the genres of European legal literature, see, among other texts, Cabral, *Literatura jurídica na Idade Moderna*, 24–32.

the Jesuit priest Quirício Caxa asks the Provincial priest Manuel da Nóbrega (1517–1570) about the two situations mentioned in the title, which were very common among the natives of Brazil. Nóbrega argues that both are possible and not against natural law, stating that "one can sell himself because everyone is the lord of his own liberty, which can be estimated and, as it is not forbidden by any right, can also be alienated and sold".[99] About the second situation, Nóbrega recognises that there were two conflicting natural laws, and the strongest should prevail: "then, the natural law that orders the conservation of life prevails over the other natural law of conserving the liberty".[100] Only in cases of extreme necessity does natural law allow a father to sell his son.[101] Nóbrega's opinion on indigenous slavery was at the same time critical and somehow tolerant, following the opinions of the theologians, especially Azpilcueta, Soto and the above-mentioned Molina in admitting slavery in exceptional situations.

This text is highly representative of the adoption of a formal structure to provide a solution for a conflict in Portuguese America. Unlike the authors of the *Sententiae circa resolutionem aliquorum casum, qui in Brasilia frequenter accurunt,* Nobrega wrote his *responsa* when he was in Brazil, and that fact is remarkable because of the material content of the answer, which he built by using European legal and moral literature. Nóbrega dealt with particular problems that happened in America but he grounded his opinion on arguments of *ius commune* and theology.

This list of authors used by Nóbrega[102] is quite limited in comparison with other texts produced in Portuguese America,[103] but one point should be stressed. The author of this *responsa* of 1567 was Manuel da Nóbrega, who produced this text less than twenty years after the settlement of the Jesuit Province of Brazil and in a moment when the general conditions of the missions were particularly difficult. Considering that he prepared the text in Brazil – which

99 Nóbrega, *Cartas do Brasil e mais escritos*, 402–403.

100 Nóbrega, *Cartas do Brasil e mais escritos*, 419.

101 Nóbrega, *Cartas do Brasil e mais escritos*, 411–412.

102 The complete list of authors quoted by Manuel da Nóbrega in his text "If the father could sell his son and if someone could sell himself": Abbas Panormitanus, Accursius, Andrea Alciato, Aristotle, Bartolomeo Saliceto, Diego Covarrubias y Leyva, Dino Mugellano, Domingo de Soto, Duns Scotus, Martín de Azpilcueta, Nicholas de Lyra, Richard Middleton, Sylvester Mazzolini, Thomas Aquinas and Tommaso de Vio (Cardinal Cajetan).

103 Despite its limited bibliography, Antonil used many other authors in the more juridical chapter of his *Cultura e opulência no Brasil por suas drogas e minas*, notwithstanding that it was published one-and-a-half centuries later than Nóbrega's text. A table with a complete list of authors quoted by him can be found in Cabral, "Antonil jurista?".

makes it the most ancient Brazilian moral-juridical document, according to Serafim Leite[104] –, it is possible to conclude that Manuel da Nóbrega consulted the quoted books in America, probably in the college library. So these books were available and read in Brazil in the middle of the 16th century, even if this access was limited to the Jesuit colleges. In any case, the example of this *responsa* is sufficient proof that the European juridical and moral literature influenced the way the cases of conscience were decided in early colonial of Brazil.

Cases of conscience had an undoubtedly pragmatic character because they provided a solution for a concrete juridical problem. Despite the inexistence of evidence about the circulation of the answers for these cases of conscience, the hypothesis seems plausible that the content of these proposals, or, more explicitly, the knowledge expressed through these cases of conscience, circulated. Solutions provided for a case could later be adopted in other similar situations, and that would make the Jesuits more confident when facing a case that required moral reflection. So these texts probably contributed to the construction of a legal culture situated between the learned tradition, under the influence of European authors, using the written form and the model of *responsa*, on the one hand, and the oral tradition, applying the solutions to particular cases and transmitting the content of these answers, on the other hand.

7 Advising Masters of Slaves and Promoting Christian Virtues

Jorge Benci, an Italian-born Jesuit, lived in North-eastern Brazil during the last decades of the 17th and the first years of the 18th century. He held many relevant offices in the Jesuit Province of Brazil, and published his book *Economia christaã dos senhores no governo dos escravos* ("Christian economy for the masters in the government of the slaves") in Rome, in 1705. The purpose of the book appears clearly in the preface, in which the author states his intention of imparting the obligations a lord has towards his slaves. That is the reason why he does not use any complex structure or a highly educated tone in his writings, but a simple and clear style, because, as he says, he speaks as a foreign missionary.[105] In other words, his goal was only to make himself understood, facilitating the readers of the book to follow his instructions.

104 Leite, *História da Companhia de Jesus no Brasil*, vol. 7, 184.

105 "Bem creyo que te nao pareceà o estylo tam culto, como quizeras; mas desculpa-me; porque fallo como Missionario, e como Missionario estrangeiro". Benci, *Economia christaã*.

Rafael Marquese rightly observes that only Jesuits, and never a lord of an *engenho*, actually published texts on slavery during the colonial age. As possible reasons for this phenomenon, he mentions the difficulties of printing, the exiguous number of readers and the feeling that the government of slaves was something related to the personal beliefs of every lord.[106] Texts justifying slavery and prescribing good behaviour,[107] of which *Economia christaã* is an example, only appeared at the turn of the 17th century. Social tensions between masters and slaves such as the eruptions of resistance acts like the *quilombo* of Palmares, in the Captaincy of Pernambuco,[108] can explain that scenario, and this is the reason why Jesuits like Benci were so concerned about providing guidelines to the masters of slaves.

After an introduction focusing on the origins of slavery,[109] Benci explains what he considers the correct behaviour a master of slaves should exhibit. A part of the book corresponds to each of the four obligations towards slaves, but three of them (to sustain with food, clothes and health, to punish their faults and to give them work) are not relevant for our chapter, unlike the obligation of introducing them (or providing their introduction) to the Christian faith. As rational creatures, slaves deserved special care for their bodies and souls, so the lords had to sustain both elements.[110] According to the Council of Trent, the spiritual sustainment materialised in accessing the Christian Doctrine, the use of the sacraments and the good example of life, all of them obligations of a lord because the Tridentine decrees, which were primarily addressed to the priests, also reached the lords who somehow were considered *curas* of their servants' souls.[111]

Introducing the Christian doctrine means teaching both the Christian faith in which the servants should believe, and the laws of God, which they should respect. Benci emphasises the master's role as responsible for providing access to Christianity drawing on the opinions of Martín de Azpilcueta, Estevão Fagundez and Saint Augustine.[112] There was no necessity of acting directly and by themselves in this task, because a lord could allow their slaves to attend the Jesuit colleges, where missionaries would teach them in their own language.[113]

---

106 Marquese, *Feitores do corpo, missionários da mente*, 48–49.
107 Vainfas, *Ideologia e escravidão*.
108 Marquese, *Feitores do corpo, missionários da mente*, 49–50.
109 The author's argument to explain slavery was the original sin. Benci, *Economia christaã*, 1–9.
110 Benci, *Economia christaã*, 55.
111 Benci, *Economia christaã*, 56.
112 Benci, *Economia christaã*, 57–62.
113 Benci, *Economia christaã*, 65–66.

In a chapter especially dedicated to the priests, Benci calls on them to participate in the efforts of teaching the slaves the most relevant topics of Christian doctrine, but in a way the slaves could understand, that is to say, with "accommodated words due to their rudeness and their low capacity".[114] In other words, Benci asks the priests to simplify their messages and make their discourse understandable for a particular audience the clergymen were not used to.

Among the objectives of the book, we do not find an explanation about the content and the relevance of the sacraments – these were the matter of catechisms, as previously described. The author justifies the necessity of slaves receiving sacraments, in a first moment baptism, anointment of the sick and confession, finally marriage. Quoting Tomás Sánchez, the author mentions what he calls the revocation of Roman law by canon law in order to admit the possibility of marriage among the slaves, which would be more appropriate to divine and natural law;[115] restrictions of marriages among slaves by their lords meant violating the laws of God. The presence of Sánchez on the topic about marriage is significant: he was the most relevant author on this issue, his book was consulted and used as an authority, and his ideas appeared in the text in a simplified version. Consequently, we can affirm that Sánchez is an example of a theologian whose works circulated and influenced the comprehension of a juridical institution (in this case marriage) in Portuguese America.

Benci also stressed the responsibility of lords to provide good examples and virtues, following the idea that good actions are better than words, and the slaves would imitate their master's actions.[116] In this case, unlike the situations relating to free people, following their master's example was not an incentive but rather an obligation for the slaves.[117] The best way of giving good examples, and consequently helping the slaves to save their souls, was avoiding to sin and not creating situations that might promote sins; hence Benci exemplifies many situations in which lords sin and make their slaves incur in sins, such as the concubinage between a lord and a female slave.[118]

Notwithstanding its character of a simplified text dedicated to an audience of alphabetised people not necessarily familiar with moral discussions, the

114 "Que importa que o Paroco ensine aos escravos as orações, os mysterios da Fé, e os preceitos da Ley de Deos, se os não propõem com palavras accommodadas á rudeza, e pouca capacidade de Negros boçais? Senao uza de semelhanças, e exemplos palpáveis?" Benci, *Economia christaã*, 74.

115 Benci, *Economia christaã*, 86.

116 Benci, *Economia christaã*, 91–94.

117 Benci, *Economia christaã*, 95–96.

118 Benci, *Economia christaã*, 102–121.

book contains some references to important classical authors, theologians and jurists (see table 5.5).[119] Their appearance illustrates the argumentative use of the rhetoric authority of these names, all of them relevant at the end of the 17th century. Besides three mentions of the Council of Trent and a high number of references to the Bible, all the authors quoted in this book are included in the following list.

The strong presence of theologians does not come as a surprise. Nevertheless, next to scholastic theologians and authors associated with the Society of Jesus, there are many references to the Church Fathers, in a clear allusion to early Christianity. It does not seem to be by chance: in the conclusion of the book, Benci recalls that the first Christians freed their slaves as soon as those were baptised. He definitely has no intention to recommend the same action, but he wants to convince the lords to improve the miserable situation of their slaves.[120]

This source clearly shows the author's purpose to instruct the lords about their rights and obligations concerning slavery in colonial Brazil. Lords were also a relevant instrument in the establishment of Christianity in the New World, but they should both expose their slaves to Christian virtues and act according to these values. *Economia christaã* was a book particularly concerned with the practical diffusion of certain matters, all of them discussed with a moral theological background that reflects the mainstream thinking and the predominant interests of the Society of Jesus in Portuguese America.

8 Concluding Remarks

In conclusion, I would like to underscore the relevance of pragmatic literature in the specific period analysed in this chapter. In spaces where the royal power was not always present, the role of ecclesiastical authorities for the regulation of social life was strong. Conflicts always required resolutions, and pragmatic literature was a remarkable instrument for that purpose. Those written sources are important for understanding how Christian mentality developed in Portuguese America, whether by teaching Christian morals or by providing solutions for cases of conscience. The particularities of Portuguese America demanded answers for its specific problems, but the proposed solutions were elaborated in the light of the European legal and theological traditions.

119 In this respect, there are many similarities among the authors quoted by Benci and by other missionaries in Spain. See Palomo, "Misioneros".

120 Benci, *Economia christaã*, 281–282.

TABLE 5.5 Authors cited in Jorge Benci's text *Economia christaã dos senhores no governo dos escravos*, Roma 1705

Author	No. of mentions
John Chrysostom	9
Aristotle	7
Nicholas de Lyra	6
Augustine	6
Thomas Aquinas	5
Cornelius a Lapide	5
Cicero	4
Hugo Etherianis	3
Tomás Sánchez	3
Seneca	3
Ambrose	2
Cyril of Alexandria	2
Bernard of Clairvaux	2
Plutarch	2
Saint Jerome	2
Clement of Alexandria	1
Rabanus Maurus	1
Basil of Seleucia	1
Peter Chrysologus	1
Cyprian	1
Estevão Fagundez	1
Martín de Azpilcueta	1
Fernando de Salazar Chirinos	1
Gratian	1
Domingo de Soto	1
Hugh of Saint-Cher	1
Gaspar Sanchez	1
Luís de Granada	1
Silvestre Mauro	1
Francisco Suárez	1
Tommaso de Vio (Cardinal Cajetan)	1
Philo of Alexandria	1

On the other hand, these texts are also a valuable evidence that learned knowledge circulated in colonial Brazil: both as prints and manuscripts, both written and orally. The analysis of how the authors constructed their arguments, answering cases of conscience or writing pastoral works, indicates that a sphere of formal and somehow erudite juridical life existed in Portuguese America. It was undeniably smaller in comparison with other normative orders, but, even though, one cannot deny its relevance. The structure and contents of sermons, manuals for confessors and cases of conscience, prove the circulation of formal erudite knowledge, albeit in a reduced scale: especially, the authors of cases of conscience used the authority of jurists and theologians in drawing conclusions for particular cases and even asked relevant theologians for help.

Notwithstanding, there are more open questions than answers given. It is hard to evaluate the real influence of moral theology on ordinary colonial life. The influence is presumably high among the people who attended the classes at Jesuit colleges and, probably, those who lived in areas where secular or regular clergymen acted, as well as in the mission areas, but there were vast areas not controlled by the Church. Moreover, the relations between the indigenous people and the religious men were not always friendly, especially regarding native slavery. As to the sources, there are still many challenges: despite the destruction of the Jesuit archives in the wake of the expulsion in 1759, it is possible that documents considered lost by the historiography might be found in certain archives. If, for example, some of the academic theses defended in the colleges, or further *responsa* to cases of conscience were discovered, this process of constructing a new juridical space in colonial Brazil could even be better understood.

Bibliography

Manuscripts

Biblioteca da Universidade de Coimbra, Coimbra (BUC), Gramatica da Lingoa Geral do Brazil. Com hum Diccionario dos vocábulos mais uzuaes para a intelligencia da dita lingua. Pará 1750 (Catálogo de manuscritos, Manuscrito 69).

Biblioteca Pública de Évora, Évora (BPE), Sententiae circa resolutionem aliquorum casum, qui in Brasilia frequenter accurunt, Manuscritos, CXVI/1–33, fols. 109–130.

Printed Sources

Anchieta, José de, *Doutrina Chistã. Catecismo Brasílico*, vol. 1, trans. Armando Cardoso, São Paulo 1992.

Aquinus, Thomas, *Opera Omnia, tomus duodecimus (tertia pars Summae Theologiae)*, Romae 1906.

Araújo, António de, *Catecismo na lingoa brasílica, no qual se contem a summa da doctrina chiristã. Com tudo o que pertence aos Mysterios de nossa Sancta Fè & bons custumes*, Lisboa 1618: Pedro Crasbeeck.

Azpilcueta, Martín de, *Manual de confesores y penitentes*, Valladolid 1570: Francisco Fernandez de Cordoua.

Azpilcueta, Martín de, *Relectio cap. ita quorundam de iudeis, in qua de rebus ad sarracenos deferri prohititis, & censuris ob id ilatis non segniter disputatur composita, & pronunciata in inclyta Conimbricensi academia anno M.D.L.*, Romae 1580: officina Accoltiana.

Batalha, Manuel Freire, *Sermoens, que no dia da presentação de nossa senhora, e nas profissoens da madre Antonio Emereciana Aurelia de Jesus e sua prima a Madre Maria Leodegaria Fabia do Monte Carmo, religiosas do Convento das Carmelitas Calçadas da Esperança e Beja, e naturais de Villa Rica do Ouro Preto das Minas Gerais*, Coimbra 1746: Real Collegio das Artes da Companhia de Jesus.

Benci, Jorge, *Economia christaã dos senhores no governo dos escravos*, Roma 1705: Antonio de Rossi.

Concilium Limense, Celebratum anno 1583, sub Gregoriio XIII. Sum. Pont. autoritate Sixti Quinti Pont. max. approbatum, Madriti 1591: ex officina Petri Madrigalis.

Craveiro, Lourenço, *Merenda eucarística e sermão, que pregou o Lourenço Craveiro da Companhia de Iesus, da Provincia do Brazil, no Collegio da Bahia, no terceiro dia das quarenta horas à tarde em 16. de Fevereiro de 1665*, [without publishing place] 1677.

Laymann, Paulo, *Theologia moralis, in V lib. partita*, Duaci 1635: Gerardum Patte.

Mamiani della Rovere, Luigi Vincenzo, *Catecismo da doutrina christãa na língua Brasilica da Nação Kiriri*, Lisboa 1698: Officina de Miguel Deslandes.

Marques, Simão, *Sermão do patriarca S. Ignacio de Loyola, oferecido ao illustrissimo, e reverendíssimo Senhor D. Fr. Antonio de Guadalupe, Bispo do Rio de Janeyro do Conselho de Sua Magestade*, Lisboa 1735: Miguel Rodrigues.

Marques, Simão, *Sermam do grande apóstolo do Oriente S. Francisco Xavier, padroeyro da Cidade de S. Salvador da Bahia de todos os Santos*, Lisboa 1747: Antonio da Sylva.

Molina, Luis de, *De justitia et jure opera omnia*, Coloniae Allobrogum 1733.

Moraes, José de Andrada e, *Sermão de acçam de graças, que pela continuaçam das melhorias da saúde d'el Rey D. João V, nosso senhor, e pela exaltação da Villa do Carmo das Minas em Cidade Mariana*, Lisboa 1746: Miguel Rodrigues.

Murillo Velarde, Pedro, *Cursus juris canonici, hispani, et incidi in quo, juxta ordinem titularum decretalium non solum canonicae decisiones*, 2 vols., Matriti 1791: Typografhia Vlloae a Romane Ruíz.

Nóbrega, Manuel de, *Cartas do Brasil e mais escritos (opera omnia)*, Coimbra 1955.

Recopilación de Leyes de los reynos de las Indias, 4 vols., Madrid 1681: Iulian de Paredes.

Soto, Domingo de, *De iustitia et iure*, Lugduni 1582: Pesnot.

Literature

Abreu, Márcia, "Circulação de livros entre Europa e América", in *Polifonia* 14 (2007), 161–174.

Aymoré, Fernando Amado, *Die Jesuiten im kolonialen Brasilien: Katechese als Kulturpolitik und Gesellschaftsphänomen (1549–1760)*, Frankfurt am Main 2009.

Barros, Maria Cândida Drumond Mendes and Vitor Manoel Marques da Fonseca, "Passagens do livro 'Itinerário para Párocos de Índios', de Peña Montenegro (1668), em um confessionário jesuítico setecentista da Amazônia", in *Boletim do Museu Paraense Emílio Goeldi. Ciências Humanas* 5:3 (2010), 669–679.

Cabral, Gustavo Cesar Machado, "Senhores e ouvidores de capitanias hereditárias: uma contribuição ao estudo das fontes do Direito Colonial Brasileiro a partir da literatura jurídica (séculos XVI a XVIII)", in Siqueira, Gustavo and Ricardo Fonseca (eds.), *História do direito privado: olhares diacrônicos*, Belo Horizonte 2015, 97–118.

Cabral, Gustavo César Machado, "Ius commune in Portuguese America: criminal issues on local canon law in the 'First Constitutions of the Diocese of Bahia' (1707)", in *Glossae* 13 (2016), 307–327.

Cabral, Gustavo César Machado, "Antonil jurista? Uma contribuição à história da literatura jurídica no Brasil Colonial no século XVIII", in *Fronteiras & Debates* 4:1 (2017), 7–28.

Cabral, Gustavo César Machado, *Literatura jurídica na Idade Moderna: as decisiones no Reino de Portugal (séculos XVI e XVII)*, Rio de Janeiro 2017.

Cabral, Gustavo César Machado, "Pegas e Pernambuco: notas sobre o direito comum e o espaço colonial", in *Revista Direito & Práxis* 9:2 (2018), 697–720.

Camarinhas, Nuno, "A administração da justiça em espaços coloniais. A experiência imperial portuguesa e os seus juízes, na época moderna", in *Jahrbuch für Geschichte Lateinamerikas* 52 (2015), 109–124.

Castelnau-L'Éstoile, Charlotte, *Operários de uma vinha estéril: os jesuítas e a conversão dos índios no Brasil – 1580–1620*, Bauru 2006.

Chamorro, Graciela, "La traducción del lenguaje cristiano al guaraní jesuítico", in Dedenbach-Salazar Sáenz, Sabine (ed.), *La transmisión de conceptos cristianos a las lenguas amerindias: Estudios sobre textos y contextos de la época colonial*, Sankt Augustin 2016, 247–267.

Daher, Andrea, "Os usos da língua tupi nos séculos XVI e XVII", in Algranti, Leila Mezan Algranti and Ana Paula Torres Megiani (eds.), *O Império por escrito: formas de transmissão da cultura letrada no mundo ibérico, séculos XVI–XIX*, São Paulo 2009, 355–374.

Feitler, Bruno and Evergton Sales Souza, *A Igreja no Brasil. Normas e práticas durante a vigência das Constituições Primeiras do Arcebispado do Brasil*, São Paulo 2011.

Fernandes, Maria de Lurdes Correia, "Do manual de confessores ao guia de penitentes. Orientações e caminhos da confissão no Portugal pós-Trento", in *Via spiritus* 2 (1995), 47–65.

González-Luis, Francisco, "La Gramática de la lengua tupí de José de Anchieta y su dependencia de la gramatica latina", in *Fortunae* 4 (1992), 229–244.

González Sánchez, Carlos Alberto, "La cultura escrita en el Mundo Atlántico colonial: Brasil y América del norte. Claves historiográficas, retos y perspectivas", in *Revista de Indias* 73, no. 259 (2013), 633–662.

Hallewell, Laurence, *O livro no Brasil: sua história*, 3rd ed., São Paulo 2012.

Herzog, Tamar, "Sobre la cultura jurídica en la América Colonial (siglos XVI–XVIII)", in *Anuario de historia del derecho español* 65 (1995), 903–912.

Hespanha, António Manuel, "Porque é que existe e em que é que consiste um direito colonial brasileiro", in *Quaderni Fiorentini* 35 (2006), 59–81.

Hespanha, António Manuel, "O 'Direito de Índias' no contexto da historiografia das colonizações ibéricas", in Duve, Thomas (ed.), *Actas del XIX Congreso del Instituto Internacional de Historia del Derecho Indiano*, vol. 1, Madrid 2017, 43–83.

Hespanha, António Manuel, *A ordem do mundo e o saber dos juristas: imaginários do antigo direito europeu*, Lisboa 2017.

Jonsen, Albert R. and Stephen Toulmin, *The abuse of casuistry. A history of moral reasoning*, Berkeley, CA 1989.

Leite, Serafim, *História da Companhia de Jesus no Brasil*, vol. 2: *Século XVI – a obra*, Lisboa 1938.

Leite, Serafim, *História da Companhia de Jesus no Brasil*, vol. 4: *Norte – 2. Obra e assuntos gerais, séculos XVII–XVIII*, Rio de Janeiro 1943.

Leite, Serafim, *História da Companhia de Jesus no Brasil*, vol. 5: *Da Baía ao Nordeste. Estabelecimentos e assuntos locais séculos XVII–XVIII*, Rio de Janeiro 1945.

Leite, Serafim, *História da Companhia de Jesus no Brasil*, vol. 7: *Séculos XVII–XVIII assuntos gerais*, Rio de Janeiro 1949.

Leite, Serafim, "Introdução Geral", in Nóbrega, Manuel de (ed.), *Cartas do Brasil e mais escritos (opera omnia)*, Coimbra 1955, 9–117.

Lessa, Clado Ribeiro de, "As bibliotecas brasileiras dos tempos coloniais", in *Revista do Instituto Histórico e Geographico Brazileiro* 191 (1946), 339–345.

Marquese, Rafael Bivar, *Feitores do corpo, missionários da mente. Senhores, letrados e o controle dos escravos nas Américas, 1660–1860*, São Paulo 2004.

Mecarelli, Massimo, *Arbitrium: un aspetto sistematico degli ordinamenti giuridici in Età di diritto comune*, Milano 1998.

Monteiro, John Manuel, *Negros da terra: índios e bandeirantes nas origens de São Paulo*, São Paulo 1995.

Monserrat, Ruth, Cândida Barros and Jaqueline Mota, "O índio "travesso" em um confessionário jesuítico tupi de 1686", in *Tellus* 11:20 (2011), 261–272.

Moraes, Rubens Borba de, *Livros e bibliotecas no Brasil Colonial*, São Paulo 1979.

Mota, Jaqueline, *A confissão tupi: a problemática dos confessionários jesuítico-tupi nos séculos XVI–XVIII nas missões do Grão-Pará e Maranhão e do Brasil*, São Paulo 2017.

Navarro, Eduardo de Almeida, "Tradução do 'Catálogo de todos os dias santos de guarda e de jejum', texto em Tupi antigo publicado pelo Jesuíta António de Araújo (1618)", in *Língua e literatura* 30 (2010–2012), 351–389.

Obermeier, Franz, "Die Jesuiten und die brasilianischen Indianersprachen. Vom Tupi zur Língua geral", in *Institut Martius-Staden Jahrbuch* 54 (2004), 203–222.

Palomo, Federico, "Misioneros, libros y cultura escrita en Portugal y España durante el Siglo XVII", in Castelnau-L'Estoile, Charlotte de, Marie-Lucie Copete, Aliocha Maldavsky and Ines G. Županov (eds.), *Missions d'évangélisation et circulation des savoirs (XVIe –XVIIIe siècle)*, Madrid 2011, 131–150.

Pereira, Paulo Roberto, "O livro e a biblioteca nas mudanças no Brasil Colônia", in *Revista do Instituto Histórico e Geographico Brazileiro* 160, no. 405 (1999), 813–826.

Prodi, Paolo, *Una storia della giustizia. Dal pluralismo dei fori al moderno dualismo tra coscienza e diritto*, Bologna 2000.

Prosperi, Adriano, *Tribunali della coscienza: inquisitori, confessori, missionari*, Torino 1999.

Rodrigues, Luiz Fernando Medeiros, "As 'livrarias' dos jesuítas no Brasil Colonial, segundo os documentos do Archivum Romano Societatis Iesu", in *Cauriensia* 6 (2011), 285–312.

Rueda Ramírez, Pedro J., *Negocio e intercambio cultural: el comercio de libros con América en la Carrera de Indias (siglo XVII)*, Sevilla 2005.

Ruiz, Rafael, "Probabilismo e Teologia moral, na prática judiciária na América espanhola do século XVII", in *Revista Brasileira de História & Ciências Sociais* 4 (2012), 7–25.

Saldanha, Antonio Vasconcelos de, *As capitanias do Brasil: antecedentes, desenvolvimento e extinção de um fenómeno atlântico*, Lisboa 2011.

Schlieben-Lange, Brigitte, "Missionarslinguistik in Lateinamerika. Zu neueren Veröffentlichungen und einigen offenen Fragen", in *Zeitschrift für Literaturwissenschaft und Linguistik* 116 (1999), 34–61.

Schwartz, Stuart B., *Sovereignty and society in Colonial Brazil: the High Court of Bahia and its judges, 1609–1751*, Berkeley, CA 1973.

Silva, Maria Beatriz Nizza da, "O comércio de livros de Portugal para o Brasil e a censura", in *Revista do Instituto Histórico e Geographico Brazileiro* 164:419 (2003), 195–211.

Silva, Maria Beatriz Nizza da, *Bahia, a corte da América*, São Paulo 2010.

Vainfas, Ronaldo, *Ideologia e escravidão. Os letrados e a sociedade escravista no Brasil Colonial*, Petrópolis 1986.

Vidal, Marciano, *Historia de la Teología Moral*, vol. 4.2: *La moral en la Edad Moderna (ss. XV–XVI). América: "problema moral"*, Madrid 2012.

Viveiros de Castro, Eduardo, *A inconstância da alma selvagem e outros ensaios de antropologia*, São Paulo 2002.

Wehling, Arno and Maria José Wehling, *Direito e justiça no Brasil Colonial: o Tribunal da Relação do Rio de Janeiro (1751–1808)*, Rio de Janeiro 2004.

Zeron, Carlos Alberto, *Linha de fé: a Companhia de Jesus e a escravidão no processo de formação da sociedade colonial (Brasil, séculos XVI e XVII)*, São Paulo 2011.

CHAPTER 6

Managing Legal Knowledge in Early Modern Times: Martín de Azpilcueta's *Manual for Confessors* and the Phenomenon of Epitomisation

Manuela Bragagnolo

1 Introduction: Anatomy of a Pragmatic Book

Pragmatic books related to moral theology, pastoral, and catechetical literature were widespread in the early modern Ibero-American world. But this literary or, we could say, "editorial genre" – to employ a category which scholars have recently been focusing on[1] – did not raise the attention of legal historians for a long time because of its apparent simplicity and lack of learned knowledge.[2] This chapter aims to look inside one of these pragmatic books in order to understand the knowledge base of the *pragmatici*. We will see that pragmatic books, dealing with moral theological topics, could be very learned.

In particular, I propose to analyse one the most famous and most successful pragmatic books, the *Manual for Confessors* (*Manual de Confessores*), written by the celebrated Spanish canon law professor, Martín de Azpilcueta. The text was a real best seller: Emilio Dunoyer counted eighty-one editions printed in Portuguese, Spanish and Latin, between 1549 and 1625, in addition to at least ninety-two editions, if we count the *compendia* and the Italian translations.[3] This incredible number of editions and translations was probably related to both the importance of the author, who was an undeniable authority in his time[4] (named as "iuris monarcha", he was considered as a living legal library),[5]

1 See, for instance, Réach-Gnô, "De la catégorisation bibliothéconomique du livre à la genèse éditoriale de l'oeuvre".

2 For a broad discussion on pragmatic normative literature, see the introduction in the current volume by Thomas Duve (Chapter 1).

3 Dunoyer, *L'Enchiridion Confessariorum' de Navarro*, 77–108.

4 On the relation between "authorship" and "authority" in early modern legal books, see Beck Varela, "The Diffusion of Law Books in Early Modern Europe", 203–213.

5 Ramlotaeus, *Vita excellentissimi iuris monarchae Martini ab Azpilcueta Doctoris Navarri*: "Ipse vero lectione assidua, & meditatione diuturna, pectus suum fecit bibliothecam iuris".

DOI:10.1163/9789004425736_007

and to a series of different factors directly connected to the *Manual*: its peculiar nature of Luso-Spanish and then Roman text, its fundamental value in Counter-Reformation Europe (spreading from the first results of the Council of Trent) and the fact that it was able to meet needs that were considered particularly urgent.

The *Manual*, in fact, soon became a reference work in the courts of conscience both in Europe and in missionary contexts in the frontier regions of the early modern empires. It was a fundamental text for the education of confessors and was also adopted as an official manual by the Jesuits, who used it in their lessons, thus contributing to the development of moral theology as a discipline.[6] Moreover, it was the first manual used in the new Tridentine seminars and the basis for the diocesan discussions established by the Council of Trent on cases of conscience.[7] At the same time, as I said, it was very important in the missionary context of the Spanish and Portuguese Empires.[8] In Goa, as well as in Japan, the *Manual* was a primary resource;[9] moreover, it was a real best seller in the New World, omnipresent in the Mexican and in the Peruvian book trades, in the personal libraries of priests with little formal education, and in seminary libraries.[10] In Mexico and Guatemala, it was highly recommended as a fundamental text for the confession of indigenous people.[11]

It is clear that neither the author nor the *Manual* are a new object of study; many different aspects of Azpilcueta's intellectual production have been deeply analysed on topics ranging from his contribution to economic thinking[12] to his political thought;[13] from the relevance of the *Manual* for the elaboration of

6 Angelozzi, "L'insegnamento dei casi di coscienza nella pratica educativa della Compagnia di Gesù", 143–144; O'Malley, *The First Jesuits*, 146.

7 Prodi, *Settimo non rubare*, 225; O'Banion, " 'A priest who appears good' ", 336.

8 Barros, "Intérpretes e confessionários como expressões de politicas linguísticas da Igreja voltadas à confissão", 293. On the influence of Azpilcueta's *Manual* on the directory for confessors and penitents of the Third Mexican Provincial Council, see the contribution in this volume by Osvaldo R. Moutin (Chapter 8).

9 Barros, "Intérpretes e confessionários como expressões de politicas linguísticas da Igreja voltadas à confissão". See also Wicki (ed.), *Documenta Indica*, vol. 3, 153; Wicki and Gomes (eds.), *Documenta Indica*, vol. 16, 639; López Gay, "La primera biblioteca de los Jesuítas en el Japón (1556)", 364–365.

10 O'Banion, " 'A priest who appears good' ", 336.

11 Barros, "Intérpretes e confessionários como expressões de politicas linguísticas da Igreja voltadas à confissão", 293. Cfr. Baciero, "La obra y sus fuentes", 65.

12 Muñoz de Juana, *Moral y economía en la obra de Martín de Azpilcueta*; Afanaseyev, "La Escuela de Salamanca del siglo XVI".

13 Dios de Dios, "La doctrina sobre el poder del príncipe en Martín de Azpilcueta".

contract law[14] to its contribution to the debate about the validity of positive law in the court of conscience,[15] to mention just a few.

Even though many studies have been conducted, one question still remains: why was this manual so successful? In the following pages, I will try to analyse the reasons for its success, firstly by looking closely into the *Manual*, with an attentive eye to the ways in which knowledge and, in particular, learned normative knowledge (from canon law and civil law) was organised and condensed into a pragmatic manual for confessors. Condensing and epitomising knowledge was a common practice in early modern times, handed down from late antiquity and the Middle Ages. This practice, related to both didactic and professional purposes, was also used in legal and catechetical literature. But this process of condensation from a learned legal text to a pragmatic book did not end, in the case of Azpilcueta, with a static or crystallised work. Studying Azpilcueta's *Manual* as a material object and following its transformations into the different editions and translations, we will see that the *Manual* was a living text, in which canon law was constantly interrogated, interpreted, and updated in order to give answers to the burning questions of a rapidly changing world.

2 Pragmatic Books and Law: Epitomisation of Legal Knowledge in the Early Modern Period

2.1 *Law and Moral Theology: the "Specific" Literature for Confessors*

As I mentioned before, legal historians did not pay much attention to pragmatic literature, whose lack of learned legal knowledge made it appear weak in terms of canon law and theology to a critical eye. This was, even more, the case for a particular kind of pragmatic book, the specific literature for confessors, which was long considered to only relate to the *forum internum*, giving a kind of Catholic deontology, and dealing exclusively with morals. But such was not exactly the case.

Early modern literature dedicated to confession, handed down from the late medieval tradition of *summae confessorum*, was mainly composed of small texts to be used by all priests, especially those who heard confessions. This literature could also count big structured texts with a rich casuistry, but the little manuals were largely more common.[16] These were "practical" books, "designed

14 Decock, *Theologians and Contract Law*.

15 Lavenia, *L'infamia o il perdono*; Condorelli, "Le origini teologico-canonistiche della teoria delle leges mere poenales (secoli XIII–XVI)".

16 Michaud-Quantin, *Sommes de casuistique et manuels de confession au moyen âge*, 9–10.

for use",[17] in which the confessor could find instructions for best administering the sacrament of penance, following, in particular, the order of the seven sins and of the Decalogue. They were compendia of dogmatic-moral principles and, at the same time, practical manuals, with many useful indications – on the process of interrogating a penitent as well as on the penance to be imposed.

During and after the Council of Trent, the attention on the education of priests contributed to a perceived need for tools to implement the decrees on penance. In this respect, numerous practical instructions were printed, to explain the way in which confessors ought to interact with the penitent, such as the *Avvertimenti* by Federico Borromeo (1574).[18] Moreover, many late medieval *summae* were updated in line with the decrees of the Council of Trent, later becoming classics of the post-Tridentine literature.[19] The result was an explosion of manuals for confessors and cases of conscience in the post-Tridentine period, that lead to the need for brevity, selection, and reorganisation of the material in a more efficient way.[20]

A strong intertwining between law and morality characterised this literature for confessors since its origins.[21] Medieval *Summae* and manuals for confessors, in fact, were not only often written by jurists but also contained a juridical discourse with solid theological bases. From the perspective of avoiding sin ("ratio peccati vitandi"), the *Summae confessorum* provided deep analysis of the legal relationships governing medieval Christian societies.[22] The casuistic approach, which characterized many of these works, allowed very profound examination of legal institutions, especially those dealing with *contracts*, which become the most important part of the *summae* concerning the seventh commandment, "do not steal".[23] The solution of moral theological questions was based on civil and canon law.[24]

17 Tentler, *Sin and Confession in the Eve of the Reformation*, 48–53. See also Blanco, *Historia del confesionario*.

18 Boer, *The Conquest of the Soul*.

19 Turrini, *La coscienza e le leggi*, 72.

20 Turrini, *La coscienza e le leggi*, 68.

21 On the legal bases of the literature for confessors, see Michaud-Quantin, *Sommes de casuistique et manuels de confession au moyen âge*; Grossi, "Somme penitenziali, diritto canonico, diritto comune", 1966, then reprinted as Grossi, "Somme penitenziali, diritto canonico, diritto comune", 2013: for this work I consulted this edition; Prodi, *Una storia della giustizia*, 87–92.

22 Grossi, "Somme penitenziali, diritto canonico, diritto comune", 143.

23 Prodi, *Settimo non rubare*, 115–121.

24 It has been stressed that, drawing largely on Roman and Canon law, and, at the same time, being directly related to the concrete practice of confession, this literature became a privileged way in which *ius commune* reached the lower levels of society. See also Goering,

The connection between law and moral theology grew stronger in the Catholic tradition with the Council of Trent, which "affirmed and reinforced the tendency within the late medieval manuals for confessors to use legal argument as an essential tool in solving cases of conscience".[25] But this strong intertwining of canon law, civil law and moral theology, this "symbiosis"[26] between law and morality, was already a trend, particularly in the Spanish legal culture: that can be clearly seen in Azpilcueta's works, namely in his *Manual*.

The portrait depicted by Beyerlinck in his *Magnum theatrum vitae humanae* (1631) is clear in this regard; Azpilcueta was the best theologian among jurists and the best jurist among theologians.[27] What has not been analysed until now, though, is the process through which canon and civil law were transferred and translated from the erudite legal books in universities to practical manuals, which were conceived for use by confessors and penitents. This process, which is the main object of these pages, can be described by the word 'epitomisation'.

2.2 *Epitomising Legal Knowledge*

In the early modern period, epitomising was a common practice. Drawing on traditions from late antiquity and the Middle Ages, this process was greatly developed during the Renaissance.[28] The making of *epitomae* and *compendia* of already existing texts, thus selecting, condensing and briefly summarising them, as well as compiling different works by providing excerpts from them in a convenient and pre-digested way, were among several techniques used for managing scholarly information.[29] The aim of brevity went hand in hand with the will of excerpting only what was considered important and interesting for the reader, while organising the information conveniently in a clear way. This went along with new attitudes toward page layouts (like the creation

"The Internal Forum and the Literature of Penance and Confession", 405–406. See also Decock, *Theologians and Contract Law*, 46.

25 Decock, *Theologians and Contract Law*, 55.

26 Decock, *Theologians and Contract Law*, 44. On the "cross-fertilization between the *ius commune*, the canon law and the moral theological literature" which characterized the "syncretic nature of the Spanish legal culture of the early modern period", see Decock, *Theologians and Contract Law*, 40.

27 Beyerlinck, *Magnum theatrum vitae humanae*, vol. 4, parte II, 468.

28 On the different techniques and aims of epitomisation of Latin legal texts of late antiquity and the early modern period, see Christoph H.F. Meyer's contribution (Chapter 2) in this volume.

29 On "compilers, their motivations and methods", see Blair, *Too Much to Know*, 173–229; Hamesse, "Il modello della lettura nell'età della scolastica", 103–108. See also Minnis, "Late Medieval Discussions on Compilatio and the Role of Compilator", 386–387; Cevolini, *De arte excerpendi*.

of indexes, chapter headings lists, and other finding devices), whose potential was largely developed with the printing press.[30]

Jurists largely practiced the compilation and epitomisation of knowledge. Collecting, selecting and summarising were techniques particularly used in the Middle Ages and in the early modern period, when jurists had to deal with a large number of "universal" corpora of civil and canon law and, for that reason, they elaborated tools and memory devices (like promptuaries, alphabetic dictionaries, *florilegia* and *summae*) for accessing to these corpora, always subscribing to the idea of having an entire library in one book. Therefore, in the 16th century *epitomae* were a specific category for the organisation of knowledge, directly associated with law and the specific literature for confession. That can be illustrated by Conrad Gessner's *Pandectae* (1548–49), the work that organised by subject the huge bibliographic material of his *Bibliotheca Universalis* (1545). In the section dedicated to civil and "Pontifical" law, Gessner mentions the "epitomae in utroque", in which he refers to legal compendia and promptuaries and to the *summae confessorum*.[31]

What Azpilcueta did in writing his manual belonged somehow to this intellectual universe of making *epitomae* and, if we believe Azpilcueta's first biographer, those who possessed the *Manual* could say to have an entire library in their hand.[32] In his *Manual*, in fact, Azpilcueta briefly and clearly explained – "breve", "brevedad", "breves y claras", "brevissimamente", "affectata brevitas", are words quoted more and more often in the paratexts, in the different editions of the book[33] – a large body of knowledge, which was needed to resolve new

30 Rouse and Rouse, "Statim invenire", 201–225.

31 Gessner, *Pandectarum sive partitionum universalium Conradi Gesneri Tigurini*, lib. XIX, tit. II, 336.

32 Ramlotaeus, *Vita excellentissimi iuris monarchae Martini ab Azpilcueta Doctoris Navarri*.

33 The idea of brevity is stressed more and more in the different editions of the Manual. That appears clearly if we look at the prefaces to the readers of the four main editions of the text. In the 1549 edition (El doctor Martín de Azpilcueta Navarro al lector, in: MC1549), Azpilcueta recalls the sweet brevity ("dulce brevedad") with which the anonymous Franciscan friar treated both general and particular matters in this first edition of the Manual. In the 1552 edition (Al pio lector, el doctor Martín de Azpilcueta Navarro. Salud, MC, 1552) the idea of brevity appears much more often, as an effect of the complex process of transformation and revisions he made to the Manual, in which he very briefly ("brevissimamente") gave evidence of the arguments he mentions in the Manual on the hard and huge matters of cases in theology, canon law and civil law. He recalls the briefness needed ("summa brevedad") and describes the pages as brief and clear ("breves y claras"). We can find these two last statements also in the 1556 edition (Al pio Lector, el doctor Martín de Azpilcueta Navarro. Salud. en N.S. Iesu Christo, MC1556), in which Azpilcueta mentions the style of affected brevity ("estilo dela brevedad affectada") which characterised the Manual; he recalls also a special section of the *Reportorio*, added in this

and complicated cases. As we hear in Azpilcueta's own words, confessors were asked to manage a large body of knowledge, especially in larger spaces like a kingdom or in complex and new situations like in the Americas ("En una India"), or in places in which there was no learned person to be consulted for advice.[34] For this reason, having a brief and clear text was particularly important.

However, the *Manual* was addressed not only to confessors (who remained the principal target readers of this kind of books); in fact it was conceived as reaching different kinds of readers and having different levels of reading. As Azpilcueta says in the dedication to the reader, the book was a *Manual* of Christian doctrine for everybody, an inventory and memory tool concerning conscience for learned people, and finally, a treatise with the rules for confessing and being confessed, addressed to both confessors and penitents.[35] And this implied different levels of epitomisation of learned knowledge.

In the specific case of Azpilcueta's *Manual*, the epitomisation of normative knowledge involved different intellectual processes. Not only did it mean collecting, selecting, organising systematically and condensing, but also translating and updating all the normative knowledge concerning conscience in one book (transformed many times), whilst combining the transformations of the text with the self-translation of the *Manual* into different languages. On the one hand, epitomisation went hand in hand with a very special process of cultural translation of legal ideas.[36] While condensing and summarising the content, Azpilcueta translated learned canon law knowledge from the Latin of his university courses to the vernacular language of the *Manual*, thus adapting the technical words of canon and civil law to the practical application in confession. On the other hand, the condensation of normative knowledge was a dynamic and diachronic process, achieved in the many transformations, translations and updates of the *Manual*, which were directly connected with Azpilcueta's travels, as well as with the questions related to newer and more

edition, which could serve as brief memory tool ("breve memoria", "memorial breve") for both penitents (for remembering their sins) and confessors (for examining the penitent). The idea of affected brevity ("affectatae brevitatis") appears twice also in the Latin edition (Candido Pioque lectori, EC1573).

34 MC1552, cap. 4, § 4, 28; MC1556, cap. 4, § 4, 27; EC1573, cap. 4, § 4, 64v.

35 MC1552, Al pio lector, el doctor Martín de Azpilcueta Navarro. Salud: "doctrina Christiana, para todos: memorial y reportorio de lo necessario ala consciencia, para los doctos: Confessionario perfecto, para confessores: espejo de azero, grande y claro para penitentes".

36 On "cultural translation" see Burke, "Cultures of Translation in Early Modern Europe", 9. On the importance of "cultural translation" in legal history, see Duve, "European Legal History".

complicated cases of conscience presented to Doctor Navarrus from both the Old and the New World.

3 Martín de Azpilcueta, "el mayor teólogo de todos los juristas y el mayor jurista de todos los teólogos"

It is probably fair to say that Azpilcueta condensed in the *Manual* the knowledge and the experience of his entire life, a long life in which he was not only a professor of canon law and an advisor, but in which he had the "involuntary chance" to "physically follow" the most relevant passages in the history of the Iberian peninsula and of the Church, moving from one city to another and from a country to another in crucial moments for the religious and political history of the time.[37]

We can identify three moments in Azpilcueta's very long life related to the elaboration, main transformations and translations of the *Manual*, moments in which Azpilcueta was in direct contact – as an adviser – and consultor with the Portuguese and Spanish Crowns and later with the Roman Curia.

The first period can be related to his activity as a professor of canon law, first in Salamanca (1524–1538) and then in Coimbra (1538–1554), where the first edition of the *Manual* appears. Coming from a Spanish noble family of the kingdom of Navarra, Azpilcueta studied theology at Alcalá de Henares and law in Toulouse, where he obtained his doctoral degree in canon law, and started his teaching activity in Toulouse and Cahors. Then he moved to Salamanca, where he obtained a second doctoral degree in canon law and then became a professor, holding first the chair of *Decretum* and then the one of *Prima de Canones*, the most prestigious chair at that University.[38] In Salamanca Azpilcueta already showcased some very special features of his teaching, directly connected to his main scholarly interests. First of all, while his colleagues concentrated their teaching on the canons dedicated to the *forum externum*, namely those matters, which could guarantee an income to canon lawyers, he showed a particular interest for those canons related to spiritual matters and

37 For a comprehensive reconstruction of Azpilcueta's biography and an updated bibliography, see Lavenia, "Martín de Azpilcueta (1592–1586)" (for the quotes, see 71; trans. M.B.); Tejero Tejero, "Azpilcueta, Martín de"; Belda Plans, *Martín de Azpilcueta*. On Azpilcueta, see now Decock, "Martín de Azpilcueta".

38 Some interesting notes on Azpilcueta's teaching activity in Salamanca are to be found in Rodríguez-San Pedro Bezares and Weruaga Prieto (eds.), *Historia de la Universidad de Salamanca*, vol. 5, 391–394. See also García y García, "Juristas Salamantinos", 141–142.

directed to the salvation of the soul. Moreover, he demonstrated his preference for the *ius antiquum* of the *Decretum Gratiani,* the ancient canon law, instead of the *Decretals,* on which, at that time – as he complained many years later, remembering those years – teachers preferred to base their courses, even in the *Decretum* chair.[39] Reading Gratian, Azpilcueta focused particularly on the seven *Distinctiones* on *Penance,* which are the object of his very well-known commentaries on Gratian's *De Poenitentia* (1542).[40] To this period dated also his works on indulgences, his democratic *relectio* on the royal power, as well as his works on exchange and usury: all topics debated within the School of Salamanca, characterised by a deep and constant thinking on the most current topics of the time.[41]

At the moment of Azpilcueta's greatest success in Salamanca, Charles V decided to send his most celebrated professor to Portugal. For this reason, in 1538, Azpilcueta arrived at the new University of Coimbra, reorganised by João III, King of Portugal, to provide an education for the Portuguese future elites. Here Azpilcueta held the chair of *Prima de Canones.* The content of the classes was decided by the University Council (and was particularly dedicated to the second book of the *Decretals*), but he continued to teach extra courses in spiritual matters, which became the bases of his *Manual.* He also gave daily courses on civil law matters related to canon law.[42]

It is also important to stress, once more, that Azpilcueta's canon law courses were directly related to the urgent and contemporaneous religious topics that often originated from the concrete questions, which crossed the Iberian Peninsula and the early modern Empires. Azpilcueta questioned and interpreted canon law at the university in order to offer solutions to the biggest political and legal questions of the time, like, for instance, the topic of trade with Muslims, which was a crucial aspect of the Portuguese imperial life in the middle of the 16th century. In 1550, for instance, Dom João III, urged on by the Jesuit community, asked Azpilcueta to comment, in his university, upon the chapter *Ita quorundam, de judaeis* (X, 5.6.6), established at the III Lateran Council by Alexander III. Behind Azpilcueta's *relectio* there was a concrete question

39 Tejero, "Martín de Azpilcueta en la historia de la doctrina canónica y moral", 455. See Praefatio, in Azpilcueta, *Commentaria in septem distinctiones de Poenitentia,* 3.

40 Azpilcueta, *In tres de poenitentiae distinctiones posteriores commentarii.* The commentaries to all the seven *distinctiones* would be printed in 1581.

41 Tejero Tejero, "Azpilcueta, Martín de", 430.

42 On Azpilcueta's teaching in Coimbra, see Solinas Quijada, "El doctor Martín de Azpilcueta en la Universidad de Coímbra"; Tejero, "Martín de Azpilcueta cinco veces universitario", 859–862.

posed to the King from the frontier regions of the Portuguese Empire (Goa) by the *vicario general*, Fernandes Sardinha.[43] This question raised a huge debate in Portugal and provided Doctor Navarrus the occasion for his lecture, later printed in 1550. In the dedication to Simão Rodrigues (the superior of the Jesuit Province of Portugal), Azpilcueta underlined that several questions related to this topic had also been posed not only by Jesuits in Africa, but also by Manuel da Nóbrega and Azpilcueta's nephew, Juan, in their letters from Brazil.[44] Two years later, Azpilcueta would have constantly referred to this text, as well as to his other books related to his teaching of canon law at the university, in his *Manual for confessors*.

In this period, in fact, Doctor Navarrus was closely connected to the new Jesuit communities. In particular, he was in contact with the Jesuits sent out to set up the first mission in Brazil (1549), namely with Nóbrega, the leader of that mission, and with Azpilcueta's nephew, Juan. Azpilcueta was particularly close to Juan, who had been living together with him, in the same house, for many years.[45] Both Jesuits had been his students in Coimbra and, as we can guess from the mentioned preface to the Reader of the mentioned *Relectio* of 1550, they maintained epistolary communication with their professor and friend as soon as they reached the Brazilian coasts. Azpilcueta, on the other hand, proved to be an important point of reference for the solution of crucial topics in the Portuguese mission in Brazil.

During his stay at Coimbra, Azpilcueta became closely related to the Portuguese Crown, being named the King's advisor in canon law matters as well as the Confessor of Charles V's daughter Doña Juana, the "princess of the Catholic reformation" who was married to Prince João of Portugal in 1552.[46] When the princess of Portugal and Queen of Spain became regent of Castile in 1554, Azpilcueta returned to Spain. These years in Spain (1554–1567), when he became an advisor to the Spanish Crown, mark the second period of Azpilcueta's life.

---

43 Marcocci, *L'invenzione di un impero*, 90–107.

44 Eruditissimo viro magistro Symoni Roderico, in Azpilcueta, *Relectio cap. ita quorundam de Iudaeis*: "Quaestiones item illae, quas perdoctus Emanuel a pridem a nobis laurea donatus, religione, doctrina, & genere clarus, & Ioannes ab Azpilcueta, meus ex fratre nepos chiarissimus ex Brasilia: quo eos ad negotia Iesu Christi agenda misistis, ante annum suis literis interrogarun".

45 Cardoso, "IV Centenario do P. João de Azpilcueta Navarro", 16. On Juan de Azpilcueta see also Palacín, "Azpilcueta (Navarro), Juan de", 317.

46 On Juana de Austria, regent in Spain (1554–1559) during the absence of Philip II, see Bataillon, "Jeanne d'Autriche, Princesse de Portugal", 283.

Finally, in 1567, following the trial of the Archbishop of Toledo, Bartolomé de Carranza, Azpilcueta moved to Rome, where he lived for his remaining 19 years, working as a consultor at the Court of the Apostolic Penitentiary. His stay in Rome (1567–1586) marks the third important phase of our periodisation.

4 The Printing Press as a Tool? Looking at Azpilcueta's *Manual* as a Material Object

I insisted on Azpilcueta's biography because this information is particularly important not only to understand the kind of knowledge Doctor Navarrus condensed in his *Manual*, but also because the most important transformations of the *Manual* are strictly related to his biography and travels. The epitomisation of normative knowledge was a dynamic process, which went hand in hand with, and was made through, these different editions and translations. For this reason, before presenting my hypothesis concerning the strategies that Azpilcueta adopted for epitomising and condensing normative knowledge within the *Manual*, it is important to look at the different editions, and take into account the transformations and the evolution of the book, bearing in mind the author's moves from Portugal to Spain and Rome. I shall consider only a few of those editions which marked major changes, and in which the transformations of the text were accompanied by Azpilcueta's self-translations of the *Manual*. Its author requested, as we will see, the privilege of print for better controlling the editorial process.

4.1 *From a Small Book to a Big One: Self-Translation*

If we turn to the editorial history of the book, from a diachronic perspective we can perceive an evolution of the text, from a small and relatively thin book, printed *in octavo* and written in vernacular language (initially in Portuguese), to a big and much thicker one, *in quarto*, finally written in Latin. What traditionally has been considered "the" *Manual* of Azpilcueta, were, in fact, several different texts. Azpilcueta himself, in the paratexts, took care of informing the reader about the transformations of the text as well as – we will see this later – on the intellectual process, which stood behind them. As we can read in the preface to the reader of the 1556 edition, the *Manual* had grown from a small book, "pequeño", into a big one: "hezimos este grande".[47]

---

47 Martín de Azpilcueta, Al pio Lector, el Doctor Martín de Azpilcueta Navarro, Salud. en N.S. Iesu Christo, in MC1556.

It is particularly important to consider Azpilcueta's *Manual* as a material object, keeping in mind the differences from one edition of the *Manual* to another – not so stressed by the historiography until now – which can help in reconstructing the evolution of the author's thinking. These differences are directly connected to the essential instability of early modern printed books, in which the "fixity" of a text was not an "'inherent' quality", but rather a "'transitive' one".[48] Once printed, early modern books were often rethought and reorganised – also in the light of other books printed at the same time.[49] This instability was a feature, depending not only on the author's intention but also on external reasons more related to the printer's technical and economic needs. The multiplicity of actors involved in the printing process, which somehow complicated the topic of the "authorship" in the early decades of the printing press, contributed to this instability, which also impacted the "readership" of the book and its use. In the case of Azpilcueta's *Manual*, we can add to this instability the author's purpose of transforming and updating the text. Here we can probably adopt Anne Blair's words that the printing press was a "tool", which influenced the author's method as well.[50]

As I said, these main transformations and updates appeared in the translation process, which was – to mention an interesting category to which scholars have recently paid attention – a process of "self-translation" (or, as we will see, a «collaborative» one).[51] Self-translation, "authored by a writer who can compose in different languages and who translates his or her text from one language into another [...] was a common practice in the ambient translingual world of early modern Europe, when bilingualism was the norm and writers increasingly translated between Latin and vernaculars".[52] The self-translator was a kind of cross-cultural interlocutor, a "language broker" between different cultural parties, who

48 Johns, *The Nature of the Book*, 19. Only recently legal historian started to pay attention to legal books as material objects, bringing the gap between material bibliography and the history of legal thought. See in particular Hespanha, "Form and content in early modern legal books"; Beck Varela, "The Diffusion of Law Books in Early Modern Europe".

49 Réach-Ngô, "Du texte au livre, et retour", 33.

50 Blair, "Humanism and Printing Press in the Work of Conrad Gessner", 30.

51 On the several processes of self and collaborative translations of Azpilcueta's Manual, see Bragagnolo, "Les voyages du droit du Portugal à Rome". On "collaborative translation", see Cordingley and Frigau Manning (eds.), *Collaborative Translation*.

52 Hokenson and Munson, *The Bilingual Text*, 1. Bilingualism was the norm between Portuguese and Spanish (both at the Portuguese courts and in the Castilian popular environment) and that not only for the geographical and cultural proximity but also because of the great circulation of people and books. On this point, see Carabias Torres, "Castilla y Portugal". See also Ridruejo, "Castellano y portugués en la época de los descubrimientos"; Buescu, "Aspectos do Bilinguismo Português-Castelhano na época moderna".

accorded to himself much more freedom in the translation process than a normal translator.[53] As we can detect also in Azpilcueta's work, each self-translation produced another version, another "original" of the text, which was connected to the different political and cultural contexts of the author's life (in Portugal, Spain and Rome). The privileges of print granted to Doctor Navarrus for the different editions of the *Manual* that we consider (which however did not prevent several pirate editions and translations that actually appeared in Spain and Italy) show the intertwining and overlapping of the different political powers, whom the author had asked for protection, very probably in order to better control the publication of his works.[54] For instance, in addition to the papal privilege of the 1552 Portuguese edition, printed in Coimbra, Azpilcueta received the privileges of Castile, Aragón and Portugal (as he did for the 1560 Portuguese translation) for the 1556 Spanish edition, printed in Salamanca.[55] While the Spanish updates related to the Council of Trent of the 1570 edition, printed in Valladolid and Zaragoza, went hand in hand with a new privilege of Philip II, the 1573 Latin edition was accompanied by a papal privilege, then renovated for the 1584 edition.

4.2 *Traveling Texts in Space and Time: the* Manual *and its Editorial History*

The *Manual* had a very complex editorial history.[56] The starting point can be identified in the 1549 edition, printed in Coimbra by the printers of that University, Ioão da Barreira and Ioão Alvares: a small *in octavo* book, in Portuguese.[57] Two aspects related to this edition can be considered as particularly interesting. The first interesting aspect of this edition is that its core part was not

---

53 Cordingley, "Introduction", 1.

54 For a description of some elements related to the privileges of print of the editions mentioned in this article, see table 6.2.

55 In Spain, book privileges were mainly granted to authors in order to prevent anyone else but the printer they choose to print the text for a certain time, thus giving to the author the chance to supervise the publication. On the Spanish book privilege system, see Mateu y Llopis, "Licencia"; Simón Díaz, *El libro español antiguo*, 128; Reyes Gómez, "Con privilegio"; Reyes Gómez, "La estructura formal del libro antiguo español", in particular on the privileges granted to Azpilcueta for the 1556 Spanish edition of his *Manual* (that reflected the administrative subdivision of Spain and, as often happened, included also the privilege of Portugal), see 40.

56 For a description of the main editions of Azpilcueta's *Manual de Confessores* quoted in this article, see table 6.1. For a description of the most important sections of the Manual in the different editions, see table 6.3.

57 MC1549. On the contractual relations between the University and Barreira and Alvares, see Fonseca, Antunes, Vaquinhas, Vargues, Torgal and Regateiro, *Imprensa da Universidade de Coimbra*, 13–14.

written by Azpilcueta, but by a Franciscan friar from the Portuguese Provincia da Piedade who, for being extremely humble (humility characterised the members of this Province), remained anonymous.[58] Who was this author? The historiography has identified him as Rodrigo do Porto, but without providing much more information on him and with some incongruence.[59] If his identity at the present state of research remains a mystery, it is possible to reconstruct some information on this Province and its importance for the Portuguese Empire, thus infer some hypothesis on the text and its history.

Founded in 1517 by the Franciscan community who came from Spain to Portugal under the protection of duke D. Jaime de Bragança, the *Provincia da Piedade* (1517) was a Province of strict observance.[60] The province soon provided many of the Franciscan missionaries for the Portuguese Estado da India.[61] According to Ângela Barreto Xavier, the text attributed to Rodrigo could be considered an interesting source of information on the specific models of confession concretely practiced by Franciscans in the missionary context.[62] From this province also came King João III's confessors;[63] moreover, Cardinal Dom Henrique, king João

58 Silva, "A primeira suma portuguesa de teologia moral e sua relação com o «Manual» de Navarro", 368. Azpilcueta himself underlines that the author preferred to remain anonymous due to great humility: "El autor por su humilidad no quiere nõbrarse". Martín de Azpilcueta, Al muy alto, y muy excellente seõor, el Cardenal Infante don Henrique, in MC1552. For some reflections on the relation between the Franciscan friar's work and Azpilcueta's *Manual*, see also Dunoyer, *L'Enchiridion Confessariorum' de Navarro*, 77–84; Fernandes, "Do manual de confessores ao guia de penitentes".

59 See in particular Vilas Boas, *Memorias históricas do ministério do púlpito*, 142; Machado, *Bibliotheca Lusitana*, vol. 3, 654; Machado, *Bibliotheca Lusitana*, vol. 1, 213. On the attribution to Rodrigo do Porto, see also Silva, "A primeira suma portuguesa de teologia moral e sua relação com o «Manual» de Navarro", 368–370. Recently Rodrigo do Porto has been mentioned as a theology teacher (lente) in 1446. Rodrigues (ed.), *Memoria professorum Universitatis Conimbrigensis*, vol. 1, 39. If we believe Azpilcueta's explanation on his collaboration with the author of the 1549 edition for preparing the 1552 edition, this hypothesis seems not to be possible.

60 On the Provincia da Piedade, see Monforte, *Chronica da Provincia da Piedade*. Guedes de Campos, *A ordem das ordens religiosas*, 196–208.

61 Amongst the others, in 1546 João III chose from this province six Franciscan friars, to be sent to the Indian mission; two of these returned to Portugal in 1548. The leader of the group was Antonio do Porto who wrote a detailed report of these events to João III on 7 October 1548. See Rëgo (ed.), *Documentação para a história das missões do padroado português do Oriente*, vol. 3, 258–266, esp. 259–260; Rëgo (ed.), *Documentação para a história das missões do padroado português do Oriente*, vol. 4, 16–22; 59–65.

62 Xavier, "Itinerários Franciscanos na Índia Seiscentista e algumas questões de história e de método", 97.

63 Marques, "Franciscanos e Dominicanos Confessores dos Reis Portugueses das duas Primeiras Dinastias", 58.

III's younger brother, Archbishop of Evora and Inquisitor General of Portugal, was particularly linked to this Province and their members.[64]

It was Dom Henrique who asked Azpilcueta to read and check for the Inquisition the conformity of 'Rodrigo''s text with the Catholic faith, and then to publish it, to connect it with the general reformation of the Portuguese religious life that he aimed at. In fact, not only was Dom Henrique the protagonist of the foundation and spread of the Portuguese Inquisition (1536), which within thirty years had become a powerful machine, but he also promoted the reformation of the religious orders and the secular clergy, paying particular attention to the examination of confessors as well as to the education of the priests, which was perceived as particularly urgent due to the ignorance of the clergy.[65] For that reason, he promoted and often financed the publication of several books, mainly small *promptuaries* for confessors:[66] such as *Arte para bem confessar* (1537) (a Portuguese translation made by Aires da Costa of a treatise composed by an anonymous Spanish friar, belonging to the order of S. Jerome); a new edition of *Sacramental* by Sanchez de Vercial (1539), and the Spanish translation by Paulo de Palacio of the *Summa Caietana* (1557). To these texts, we might add several manuals for confessors, which were more generally printed under the protection of the Portuguese Crown between 1546 and 1552.[67] So Dom Henrique was certainly one of the most active bishops who made a large use of the printing press for the sake of religious reformation in Portugal.[68] Among these editorial initiatives, the *Manual* was, with no doubt, the most successful one.

Returning to the author of the Manual, it can be assumed that the anonymous Franciscan friar knew Azpilcueta's work particularly well. Even if, at the present state of research, it is impossible to distinguish with absolute certainty the different parts of the *Manual* written respectively by 'Rodrigo' and

64 Monforte, *Chronica da Provincia da Piedade*, 340.

65 Polónia, "Espaços de intervenção religiosa do Cardeal Infante D. Henrique"; Polónia, *D. Henrique*.

66 On the manuals promoted by Dom Henrique, see Fernandes, "As artes da Confissão", 76–79. See also Polónia, "Espaços de intervenção religiosa do Cardeal Infante D. Henrique", 19, 23; Marcocci, *I custodi dell'ortodossia*, 155–175.

67 Several manuals were dedicated to João III, King of Portugal: Sancho de Noronha's Tractado da segunda parte do sacramento da penitentia, que he confissam (1547); Enchiridion o Manual de Doctrina Christiana (quae tambien puede servir de confessionario), (1552), written by the Dominican Diego de Ximenez, firstly requested by the Fray Juan de Zumarraga, the first archbishop of Mexico. The king directly commissioned Norte de confessores, by João III's chaplain and preacher, the theologian Francisco de Monzón (1546).

68 Paiva, "Bispos, imprensa, livro e censura no Portugal de Quinhentos", 691.

Azpilcueta (and we have to rely on the printed book), it would not be surprising, for instance, to find him amongst the several Portuguese students who attended his classes at the University of Salamanca or amongst his students in Coimbra.[69] In fact, in the *Manual*, he refers largely to Navarrus' works arising from his teaching activity in Salamanca and in Coimbra, namely his commentary to the three last *distinctiones De Poenitentia* of Gratian's *Decretum* (1542) as well as his commentary on the chapter *Inter verba* (1544), printed only some years before.[70] To 'Rodrigo''s text, Azpilcueta added the explanation of 93 unclear passages of the *Manual*, which he had been asked to clarify once the 27 chapters of the *Manual* were printed but not diffused. In this part, he added further references to his learned works.[71]

Concerning this edition, a second aspect is worth mentioning. This edition, accomplished on 27 July 1549, can be described as particularly instable: it was printed with several variants, at the point that amongst the copies today preserved at the National Library of Portugal, two identical copies do not exist. While differences are mainly formal, sometimes the copies differed also in the content. It is the case, for example, of few copies that showcased a supplementary ending folder, containing specific particular questions asked by some prelates.[72]

This edition was followed by a 1552 Portuguese edition (which was a bit more stable),[73] *in octavo*, which grew bigger, and by a 1553 Spanish close translation of

69 On the important presence of Portuguese students at the University of Salamanca during the 16th century, see Serrão, "Portugueses no Estudo de Salamanca (1250–1550)". The presence of Rodrigo at the University of Salamanca or Coimbra for the moment has to remain a hypothesis. In Serrão's work, in fact, there is no trace of a Rodrigo coming from Porto amongst the Portuguese students in the years in which Azpilcueta was a professor there.

70 The author apparently knew Azpilcueta's other works very well. He frequently quoted "Navarro", namely his work on De Poenitentia (1542) and Inter Verba (1544). See, for example, MC1549, 25 (in which the author refers to "Navarro's" commentary on ch. Consideret of his commentary De Poenitentia); 263 (in which "Navarro's" Inter verba is quoted).

71 Several printing errors characterise this part of the book, namely the numbers of Azpilcueta's explanations: the last one corresponds to number 90, but actually there are three more explanations in the section, not correctly numbered.

72 I examined all the copies of the 1549 edition today preserved at the Biblioteca Nacional de Portugal (BNP): Res. 1060 P.; Res. 1625 P.; Res. 1662 P.; Res. 2929 P.; Res. 2930 P.; Res. 4722 P.; D.S. XVI–19. Among them, only the two last ones showcased the supplementary folder I mentioned, which is also present in a copy preserved in the Biblioteca Publica Municipal do Porto (BPMP): X-1-3-16.

73 The only variant I found concerned a supplementary folder with "Algumas preguntas acerca dos religiosos. E primeiramente dos prelados" showcased, once again, only in

it, *in quarto*. Both of them were published in Coimbra by Barreira and Alvares, who appear in the book as royal printers. This version of 1552/1553 (we know that Azpilcueta and 'Rodrigo' worked contemporarily at the Portuguese and at the Spanish text),[74] which kept the structure in 27 chapters while integrating Azpilcueta's "Declaración", included important revisions of the first text. As we can read in the paratext, Azpilcueta, with the help of 'Rodrigo', worked hard at these modifications, thus producing a completely new version.[75]

After these editions, the text got successively larger and started to be printed mainly *in quarto*, thus revealing probably a shift in the target reader.[76] 1556 saw a new Spanish edition, printed in Salamanca by the well-known Andrea de Portonaris.[77] This revision, made with the help of fray Antonio da Zurara, also coming from the Provincia da Piedade, was requested by the King of Spain and featured some major modifications.[78] Firstly, Azpilcueta added five commentaries on canon law regarding economic matters, printed separately. This edition also contains a sizeable *Repertorium*, which was also printed separately, together with the *Comentarios*. Doctor Navarrus additionally provided more solutions to challenging cases of conscience, and updated the text with further references to the decrees of the ongoing Council of Trent. Thanks to Dom Henrique, the directives of the Council circulated quickly from 1553 in Portugal, when Azpilcueta was there.[79] But Azpilcueta's indirect involvement

---

few copies preserved in the BNP: Res. 1679//1 P.; Res. 1754//1 P.; and in the BPMP: X-1-3-17-1.

74 In the 1552 preface to the reader, Azpilcueta writes about the new 'edition', a revision of the previous one, as being written both in Portuguese and Spanish. MC1552, Al pio Lector, el doctor Martín de Azpilcueta Navarro.

75 For a reconstruction of the co-authorship of the revisions of the Manual (to which Azpilcueta himself refers in the dedication to the reader of the 1552 edition), see Silva, "A primeira suma portuguesa de teologia moral e sua relação com o «Manual» de Navarro", 371–373.

76 On the importance of the 8° format for the definition of the readership in the 16th century, see Infantes, *Del libro áureo*, 137–145. See also McKenzie, *Bibliography and the Sociology of Texts*.

77 MC1556. On Andrea de Portonaris see Ruiz Fidalgo, *La imprenta en Salamanca (1501–1600)*, vol. 1/3, 65–73.

78 Azpilcueta mentions Antonio da Zurara's help in the preface to the reader of the 1556 edition, and also refers to it in the preface of the 1573 Latin edition. In the Latin text, the name of the Franciscan friar changes into Joannes, and Azpilcueta adds that he was asked to make the 1556 revision by Philip II, through the Council of Castile. See Al pio lector, el Doctor Martín de Azpilcueta Navarro, Salud. en. N. s. Iesu Christo, MC1556; Candido, pioque Lectori, EC1573.

79 Polónia, "Recepção do Concilio de Trento em Portugal"; Marcocci, *I custodi dell'ortodossia*, 159.

in the Portuguese participation in the Council began even earlier and dates back at least to 1545, when he was consulted by João III in occasion of the first convocation of the Council.[80] Azpilcueta's profound knowledge of the decrees of the Council (largely and publicly recognized) would appear clearly, once the Council was closed, in the *parascer* Azpilcueta gave to Philip II, on the interpretation of the decree on the episcopal jurisdiction on the cathedral chapters.[81]

In 1560, Azpilcueta also supervised a Portuguese translation of the 1556 text, including the *comentarios* and the *reportorio*, and in 1570, there was an important update to the *Manual*, with a 28th chapter (*capitulo veynte y ocho*), printed in the kingdoms of Castile (Valladolid) and Aragón (Zaragoza) and later in Portugal, which already contained all the references to the Council of Trent to be integrated in each of the 27 chapters of the *Manual*.[82] All the previous modifications would be condensed in the 1573 Latin edition, printed in Rome by Vittorio Eliano in which a more theoretical section, organised in 10 *preludia*, was included.[83] Latin became the final language, preserved also in the last revision, printed in 1584.[84]

These modifications, which transformed the *Manual* into a big, complex and erudite book, led to the need for the numerous *Compendia*, which appeared form 1567 onwards and on which we will come back later.[85] They sometimes also reveal the interest in comparing the different versions of the text. That is particularly clear if we look at a manuscript *compendium*, today preserved at least in two almost identical copies: one at the University Library of Coimbra and the other one in Rome, at the Casanatense Library.[86] As we can see from the title, these two manuscripts contain notes on Azpilcueta's *Manual* (the Coimbra manuscript shows the title "Aliqua adnotata in Manuale Navarri",[87] while the title of the Roman one is "Annotationes quaedam circa D. Nauarri

80 Brandão (ed.), *Actas dos Conselhos da Universidade de 1505 a 1537*, vol. 1, 144.

81 Azpilcueta, "Parescer del Doctor Nauarro".

82 MC1560; CR1560; MC1570; C281570.

83 EC1573. Vittorio Eliano, nephew of Elia Levita, converted in Venice in the 1540s and was a censor of Jewish books and printers; see Casetti Brach, "Eliano, Vittorio".

84 EC1584.

85 On the printed compendia of the manual, see Dunoyer, *L'"Enchiridion Confessariorum' de Navarro*, 100–108. On the importance of the *Compendia* in Ibero-America see Muguruza Roca, "Del confesionario ibérico de la Contrarreforma a los manuales para confesores en la América colonial".

86 UCBG, Ms. 1173, cc. 1r–65r, referenced in Catálogo de Manuscritos, 162; BC, Ms. 740, cc. 3r–203r.

87 UCBG, Ms. 1173, c. 1r.

manuale").[88] Actually, it compares the Spanish and the Latin versions of the *Manual*. Pointing at specific questions discussed in the *Manual*, by precisely referring to passages of the texts via the marginal numbers which marked each paragraph in every chapter, these notes mainly registered the similarities between the two versions: expressions like "tam in manuali latino quam in vulgari [...]";[89] "in utroque manuali [...]"[90] open the major part of them. But they also show the awareness of the differences between these two versions (underlining, for example, when something was added in the last version, "in manuali latino").[91]

4.3 *Finding Devices*

These multiple transformations of the text went hand in hand with the inclusion of some typographical tools, to which it is important to pay attention. These tools, some of which could be described as "finding devices",[92] show us the pragmatic nature of the book, which was meant for practical use by readers.

One of these typographical signs appears already in the 1549 edition. Here the letter "M" stood as an abbreviation for the words "mortal" or "mortally", related to the classification of sins. It was probably an ingenious way the printer adopted for saving space (and money). But it could also have been a way to visualise quickly on the page which behaviour implied a mortal sin.

Beginning with the 1552 edition, many daggers "†" began to appear in the text. It was a typographical sign with different meanings and, since Azpilcueta does not explain it, as he does in other cases, at the present state of research it is difficult to ascertain the meaning he intended to give it in the *Manual*. According to the *Orthographia da lingoa portuguesa*, by Duarte Nunez do Lião (1576), this sign was often used to indicate that the section between daggers was not found in the original text.[93] But it was more likely a device connected to the way in which the books were meant to be read and the information found in the text. These daggers seem to be part of a system of signs, which included marginal numbers and was connected to the table of contents. On the

88 BC, Ms. 740, c. 3r.

89 UCBG, Ms. 1173, c. 1v.

90 UCBG, Ms. 1173, c. 2r.

91 UCBG, Ms. 1173, c. 9r. A similar awareness of the differences between the Spanish and the Latin editions is also present in Francisco de Gouvea's (1540–1628) more critical *Antinavarrus*; see Gouvea, " 'Antinavarrus' ".

92 On early modern finding devices, see Blair, *Too Much to Know*, 132–160.

93 Leão, *Orthographia da lingoa portuguesa, obra util et necessaria assi pera bem escrever a lingoa Hespanhol, como a Latina, & quaesquer outras que da Latina tem origen*, 78.

one hand, the reader could locate in the page the exact place of an argument found in the table of content, which referred to the chapter and to the marginal number: the dagger, placed on the corresponding line, indicated the very place in which this argument started. On the other hand, following the daggers on the page, the reader was able to find the exact point at which the argument started and could maybe jump from one dagger to another in order to follow the main arguments of the reasoning.[94]

But from the point of view of the typographical tools, the 1556 edition is probably the most interesting one. In this edition, the asterisk "*" appears and is used for showing the updated parts of the edition, both in the texts and in the notes, making these changes visible to the reader.[95] That was apparently a common use at that time. The 1536 edition of Nebrija's Castillian-Latin *Dictionarium*, made by his sons, showcased the same device: new entries were marked with an asterisk, thus making the lexical additions immediately visible to the potential buyers.[96] Moreover, from 1556 onward, an extensive *Repertorium* would be added, in which, under the label "Mandamiento", the author listed, in a few pages, all those conducts, which would imply mortal sins against the Decalogue and the Commandments of the Church.[97] As we can read in the "aviso", which closes the dedication to the reader, this part was expressly addressed to both the penitents, who desired a very small tool to quickly remember all their sins, and the confessors, who needed a small practical memory for the examination of the penitent.[98]

94 I would like to thank Alexander Wilkinson and Christiane Birr for their precious help in finding a possible use of daggers.

95 The use of the letter M., as well as of the asterisks is clearly explained in the Aviso, which ends the dedication to the reader of the 1556 edition. Martín de Azpilcueta, Al pio Lector, el Doctor Martín de Azpilcueta, Navarro, Salud. En N.S. Iesu Christo, in MC1556. According to the 16th century Portuguese gramatica, the asterisk was used to show that some words or verses were missing in a text. Leão, *Orthographia da lingoa portuguesa, obra util et necessaria assi pera bem escrever a lingoa Hespanhol, como a Latina, & quaesquer outras que da Latina tem origen*, 78.

96 Ellsworth Hamann, *The Translations of Nebrija*, 25.

97 Reportorio general y muy copioso del Manual de Confessores, y de los cinco Comentarios para su descalacion compuesto, Salamanca, Andrea de Portonariis, 1556 (CR1556), cc3r–cc5v.

98 Martín de Azpilcueta, Al pio Lector, el Doctor Martín de Azpilcueta, Navarro, Salud. En N.S. Iesu Christo, in MC1556: "Al desseo de los penitentes, que desseavan una muy breue memoria para acordarse de todos sus pecados muy presto, se satisfaze en el reportorio con aver puesto muy brevemente en la palabra mandamiento todas las maneras comunes de pecar contra el mãndamiẽto de amar a Dios, y el de amar al proximo, y los otros diez del Decalogo, y los cinco dela yglesia, por su ordẽ, y en cada palabra de cada pecado mortal, y aun de cada otro pecado las maneras comunes de caer en cada uno dellos. Por lo

So, we can assume that particularly this edition of the *Manual* was addressed to different kinds of readers. Also, the use of the marginal notes can contribute towards our understanding in that regard. While in the 1549 edition the not so frequent doctrinal references were embedded in the text (and it will be the same for the Latin edition), the 1552 and the 1556 edition showcased an important apparatus of marginal notes, written in Latin. The learned information and use of Latin for the erudite apparatus of notes (which generally referred to Latin works and was characterised by the complex system of abbreviations with which only erudite people were familiar with) suggests that they were clearly written for learned people, while the rest of the text could be understood by simple penitents and confessors.

4.4 *A Linguistic Travel towards Universality?*

But let us return to the linguistic journey of the text, directly connected to Azpilcueta's own travels from Portugal, to Spain and finally to Rome; what would it mean to move from vernacular to Latin in the second half of the 16th century?

The choice of vernacular was a general trend for the literature for confessors in the 16th century, which tried to satisfy the urgent need for education of confessors, providing all the instruments they needed to fulfil their tasks properly.[99] Azpilcueta's *Manual*, too, at least at the beginning of the story, was probably meant to satisfy this need, in the framework of the religious reformation sought by Dom Henrique in Portugal. That was probably also the reason, which stood behind the Castilian edition, requested by the king of Spain via the Council of Castile, which, on the other hand, as we saw, became more complex and erudite. Here the choice of vernacular language probably accompanied the early awareness of its "Imperial face", following Antonio Nebrija's statement that "language was always the companion of empire".[100]

---

qual mesmo se ha satisfecho tambien alos cõfessores, que desseavan un memorial breve, para pregũtar de todos los pecados con la alegacion del lugar del Manual, donde podran ver si, o quãdo es mortal, o venial: o ni mortal, ni venial. Y asi enel Manual, como enel Reportorio M. significa mortal, o mortalmente".

99 On the large opening to vernacular for the literature for confessors, which marked mainly the second half of the 16th century, see Turrini, *La coscienza e le leggi*, 113. The choice of vernacular for religious education, both of believers and priests was confirmed by the Council of Trent. While Latin still remained the official language of the Church, vernacular was the language chosen for religious education. Concilium Tridentinum, Sessio XXIV (11 Novembris 1563), Decretum De Reformatione, can. VII, in *Conciliorum Oecumenicorum Generaliumque Decreta. The Oecumenical Councils of the Roman Catholic Church. From Trent to Vatican II*, vol. 3, eds. Ganzer, Alberigo and Melloni, 136–137.

100 Burke, *Languages and Communities in Early Modern Europe*, 20.

The final move to Latin, back to the language of the Church, theology and law, suggests perhaps a new and more universal aim of the *Manual*, and also a further shift of the target reader.[101] In his preface to the reader, Azpilcueta, being more than eighty years of age, lists several reasons that pushed him into making the big effort of translating his *Manual* into Latin. First of all, he did not do it for glory but in order to better serve the entire *Respublica Christiana*. Many excellent men from both Spain and Italy had asked him for the Latin translation of his *Manual* and a Latin version so juicy and brief ("tam succiplenae tamque affectatae brevitatis"). Providing the solution of many difficult cases concerning theology, canon and civil law required not only to perfectly know both Latin and Spanish but also a comprehensive knowledge of the three mentioned disciplines which only a few people could reach before old age. Another reason was related to some bad translations into Italian and Latin, which damaged his name, as well as the entire *res christiana*. But the main reason was that Latin was clearer ("clarius verbis") and more suitable for judgment (*aptius sententiis*), and more solid in reasoning ("firmior rationibus") than Spanish. That was even more so for the ten *praeludia* as well as the last updates on penance concerning the Council of Trent which had to be written in Latin in order to preserve the purity of the language ("sermonis castitate"). So, for Azpilcueta, Latin allowed expressing the concepts of law and theology more clearly than Spanish.[102] But it was also more widespread ("communius") than Spanish. The choice of Latin was perhaps also related to the universal aim of the book (conceived to better serve the entire *Respublica Christiana*), and might have corresponded to a further shift of the target reader. We can imagine that while the vernacular *Manual* was mainly addressed to the confessors of the Portuguese and Spanish empires, the Latin *Enchiridion* was written for the erudite people of the entire world.

Such a change in the aims and target readership went hand in hand with Azpilcueta's new role in Rome as a consultor of the Apostolic Penitentiary. This dicastery of the Roman curia, recently reformed by Pius V and Charles Borromeo, administered the sacrament of penance for those particular cases reserved to the Pope as head of the Universal Church. In 1569, Doctor Navarrus

101 On the use of Latin in the early modern period, see Waquet, *Latin or the Empire of a Sign*. On translations from vernacular into Latin in the Renaissance see Burke, "Translations into Latin in early modern Europe"; Fery-Hue (ed.), *Traduire de vernaculaire en latin au Moyen Âge et à la Renaissance*.

102 EC1573, Candido pioque lectori. On the 16th century debates on the use of Latin for theological and spiritual texts, see Fragnito, *La Bibbia al rogo*. For the Spanish context, see Andrés, *La teología española en el siglo XVI*, vol. 2, 570–576.

was appointed jurist of the court[103]; the Latin edition of the *Manual*, which appeared in 1573, right after the reformation of the Penitentiary was completed, became an important tool used by Azpilcueta in his consulting activity. If we look at the posthumously printed *consilia*, which were mainly the fruit of his work in that court, the *Manual* is constantly quoted. But his work as a consultor also contributed to updating the last revision of the *Manual*.[104]

In sum, the small 1549 book, conceived for daily use by confessors and penitents, became – with the Latin edition – the canonist's instrument of work. In this long journey from Portugal to Spain and Papal Rome, Azpilcueta made the book, originally written by an anonymous Franciscan friar, more and more his own work. We can assume that he made this process of appropriation visible by inserting his coat of arms (a parted quarterly shield, with a reversed crescent in the 1° and 4° quarters, and the 2° and 3° chequered quarters) on the front-page of the 1573 edition.[105]

5 Processes of Epitomisation: Condensing and Updating Legal Knowledge[106]

But which kind of knowledge was condensed in the *Manual*? Looking once again at the different editions, we can detect a double process, directly related, on the one hand, to the need for a small and portable text, and, on the other hand, to the importance for confessors to manage an extensive and updated amount of knowledge, which could help in resolving all the concrete and new cases of conscience a confessor might have to deal with.

First of all, we can perceive what we could call a "top-down" process of selection, condensation and reorganisation of learned normative knowledge, in a

103 Borromeo, "Il concilio di Trento e la Riforma postridentina della penitenzeria apostolica (1562–1572)", 131.

104 Azpilcueta, *Consiliorum seu Responsorum*, lib. I, De Iis quae, cons., n. IX, 217–220: 219B. "ut singulariter declaravit Caiet. super 22 S. Tho. q. 189 art 5 quem piget non allegasse in Manual. Confes. hactenus edito ubi tamen citabitur Deo annuente in proxima aeditione". The handwritten Consilium is preserved at the Vatican Archive: ASV, A.A. Arm. I–XVIII, 3129, cc. 1r–7v: 5r.

105 The coat of arm is explicitly attributed to Azpilcueta in the 1584 Roman edition of the *Enchiridion* (EC1584). In the title page verso, in fact, the coat of arm, printed right below Azilcueta's portrait, is provided with the following caption: "Auctoris insegna gentilicia". On Azpilcueta's family coat of arm, see Atienza, *Nobiliario Español*, 394.

106 The analysis of the transformation process of the *Manual* across the editions supervised by Azpilcueta is the object of the project 'Hyperazpilcueta' at the Max Planck Institute for European Legal History: https://www.rg.mpg.de/forschung/hyperazpilcueta.

brief book and in a systematic way, to concretely adapt it for use in confession. But along with brevity, the other requirement of the *Manual* was to provide updated knowledge about conscience. The way in which Azpilcueta reached this goal was by significantly transforming the text from one edition to another. As said before, not only did Doctor Navarrus added progressively more and more references to the Council of Trent – the first sessions of which were coeval to the first editions of the *Manual*. But he also integrated the *Manual*, with more and more solutions to cases of conscience as well as answers to urgent political and religious questions, coming from the global political contexts, in which the different transformations of the *Manual* were conceived. This can be understood as a "bottom-up" process, related to concrete questions Azpilcueta was asked from correspondents from both the Old and the New World.

It is hard to say if these processes of condensing legal knowledge and updating it with answers to those concrete questions marked Azpilcueta's specific contribution to the literature for confessors of the time. But it is probably fairly to say that what distinguished Azpilcueta's *Manual* from other *Manuals for confessors*, at least from those printed under the initiative of the Portuguese Crown in the same years, was the crucial role he attributed to canon law and civil law which he condensed and somehow injected into 'Rodrigo do Porto''s text.

Of course, the need for condensing learned doctrinal knowledge in a brief manual was quite common, expressed particularly in the texts written by learned authors. That was the case, for instance, of the Spanish theologian Francisco de Monzón, belonging to the Dominican order, who was Azpilcueta's colleague at the University of Coimbra and the King's chaplain and preacher. Dedicating to João III his *Norte de confessores* (1546) – which was meant to guide confessors like a compass in the resolutions of complex cases –, he described his books as small in size ("pequeño en el volumen") but very condensed in sentences ("muy compendioso en las sentencias") because it contained the flowers of the doctrine written by the sacred doctors in theology and canon law ("porque contiene las flores de la doctrina que a este proposito escriueron los sagrados doctores teologos y canonistas").[107] But in the case of Azpilcueta's *Manual* we can see something more.

In the preface to the reader of the 1549 edition, in which Azpilcueta largely testified the conformity of the content of 'Rodrigo do Porto''s work with Christian doctrine, we can read what specifically distinguished the text he was publishing from the other manuals that Doctor Navarrus could have seen in his over twenty years of teaching experience on canon law, not only in Portugal

107 Prologo endereçado al mui alto y muy poderoso Rey nuestro segnor don Juan tercero deste nombre, in Monzón, *Norte de confessores*. On Francisco de Monzón and his works see Fernandes, "Francisco de Monzón".

but also in Salamanca and Toulouse. In his opinion, there was no book (with the exception, of course, of the canon law books), neither in Latin nor in vernacular (Portuguese, Castilian or French), which was so "useful and safe" as this book.[108] In fact, some authors of those books spoke unclearly, or in general, without going down to the particular, while others went too much into particular cases, thus becoming obscure for the common knowledge of confessors and penitents.[109] Some of them spoke like "pretores", without referring to reasons, texts or authorities, hoping that their *dicta* had the force of law.[110] While some authors followed false opinions, others did not offer any reference at all – often in order to avoid quoting the "modernos", especially in those texts in which they argued better than the ancients. On the contrary, 'Rodrigo', or, better, the anonymous author of the manual that Azpilcueta was introducing, treated clearly and briefly both the general and the particular cases. Azpilcueta stressed that the author had previously discussed with erudite men and experienced confessors of his Order about all the doubts related to what had been written on penance, both by canonists and theologians, in order to choose the most truthful opinions. And in order to justly give to each one his own, he quoted ("allega") even the most contemporary authors ("aun de los modernissimos") – and amongst them, also Doctor Navarrus himself. According to this preface, 'Rodrigo' did not include offensive references, nor did he silence someone because he belonged to another order or religion, but, with the only desire of serving God, he searched for the truth – and found it – with the simplicity characteristic of the Provincia da Piedade.[111]

108 MC1549, El doctor Martín de Azpilcueta Nauarro al lector: "a mi iuyzo muchos años ha, que ninguna obra de su tamaño se imprimio, ni en latin, ni en romance Portogues, Castellano, ni Frances tan prouechosa, y segura para los confessores y penitentes como esta, sacados los textos de canones".

109 MC1549, El doctor Martín de Azpilcueta Nauarro al lector: "algunos hablan confuso, o en general, sin descender a lo particular, o bien poco. Otros descienden mas: pero por tan luengos y obscuros grados, y escalones de disputationes, que el commun saber de los confessores y penitentes, no los puede andar".

110 MC1549, El doctor Martín de Azpilcueta Nauarro al lector: "Dellos hablan como pretores, sin razon, texto, ni otro autor, queriendo que sus dichos tengan fuerca de editos".

111 MC1549, El doctor Martín de Azpilcueta Nauarro al lector: "El autor empero desta como prudente con gran cordura igual iuyzio & diligencia, todo lo general, y particular ha tocado [...] Y de todos los que en su materia han escripto: assi Canonistas como Theologos, y mixtos, comunicadas las exquisitas dubdas, con muy doctos varones, y muy experimentados confessores, quales los ay cierto en su orden, ha trabaiado de escoger las mas verdaderas opiniones. Y por dar a cada uno lo suyo, como iusto, los lugares aun de los modernissimos, allega sin retener nada delo ageno: como amador de la muy alta pobreza, que professo y guarda. A nadie allega para lo afrentar. A nadie calla por ser de orden, o religion diuersa. Antes con solo amor y desseo de seruir a IESV CHristo, busca y toma la verdad de doquier que se halla: sin ningun sabor de rancor, faction o parcialidad,

As this attitude towards doctrinal allegations was the distinctive character of the first version of the text, by studying the preface to the reader of the 1552 edition we can observe the nature of the intellectual exercise of epitomising learned legal knowledge that both Azpilcueta and 'Rodrigo', in collaboration, performed on the text.

5.1 *An Effort That Almost Killed Him. Azpilcueta's Words on Epitomisation*

In Azpilcueta's preface to the reader of the 1552 edition, we can read in his own words what I called the "top-down" process. He explains the intellectual processes related to the reformation of the 1549 edition of the *Manual* which he carried out in continuous collaboration with the anonymous author of the first version of the text. It comprised, first of all, selecting (he uses the expression *manojo de flores*, bunch of flowers, which directly recalls the legal tradition of *flores legum*) and translating the learned legal knowledge, expressed in Latin, related to his university teaching experience, into a practical manual in vernacular language. We might think about translation here not only in a literal sense; what was at stake was probably a process of adapting learned canon law knowledge to the everyday practice of confessors.

Azpilcueta refers to the great weight and technical complexity of his task, in reforming the 1549 edition, which consisted not only in acknowledging others' opinions in the difficult matters of cases in theology, canon and civil law, but also in articulating these opinions and explaining them very briefly. Moreover, when the available arguments were insufficient, it was necessary to find and offer new ones. He explains that the help of God made him overcome the spiritual anguish and physical suffering, which was related to the great doubts and the fear of erring in his resolutions, as well as to the concern that he could not leave the resolutions of these doubts to the simple confessors.[112] For preserving

---

sin ningun olor de vanidad, inuidia y ambicion, con muchos perfumes de charidad, y prudentissima simplicidad: dignos de las boticas de los padres exemplares dela prouincia dela piedad".

112 MC1552, Al pio Lector, el doctor Martín de Azpilcueta Navarro: "quanto es la [obra] de no solamente referir, los paresceres agenos en infinitas, difficiles, y altas materias de casos quotidianos de las tres soberanas facultades, Theologia, Canones, y Leyes, de tanto peso quanto es dezir si es o no peccado. M. si ay censura o irregularidad, o necessidad de restituir. Pero aun affirmarlos y brevissimamente por la mejor razon, texto, glosa, o authoridad especial, y ciertamente allegada, fundarlos, y hallar y probar nuevos, quando los hallados no bastavan: como con la ayuda de Dios lo hemos hecho o por mejor hemos sido su instrumento a que ha dado esfuerço para suffrir muchas angustias de animo y trassudores del cuerpo, causadas por las grandes dubdas, y ygual temor de errar enla determinacion

and increasing his authority, it would probably have been better (and easier) to have cleaned and revised some material on the *Decretum* and *Decretals*, written in Latin (the most common language), which he had already prepared for his courses and which was largely demanded by his audience. On the contrary, he decided to write the *Manual* in Portuguese and Spanish, therefore doubling his works and writing in two languages "that did not cross the Pyrenees" (but actually crossed the Atlantic!).[113]

So, writing briefly and in vernacular languages what could be more easily expressed in Latin after revising canon law materials already prepared, was an effort that almost killed Azpilcueta ("esto ha sido matarnos"). The *Manual*, in fact, looked simple, because of the extreme brevity required, but it was, indeed, the fruit of very intense efforts. According to Doctor Navarrus, certain half-pages demanded of him the same work and study needed for preparing an entire *repetitio* (which was an academic exercise that usually took days to prepare), and other pages required the same study and work as many good lessons at the most important chair in canon law. Azpilcueta conceded that by looking at those pages written in a vernacular language, and in such a brief and clear manner, one would not surmise that it took so many hours of study. But he insisted that it would not have been possible to accomplish this "pious work" if he had not been so experienced, namely if he had not taught for more than twelve years on matters of theology, civil law, and canon law, from which he took the mentioned decisions. Some of them were offered to the public for the first time in the *Manual*, after the author had been asked "by many excellent confessors of this and other kingdoms".[114]

dellas: y por veer que no convenia a esta edad y opinion de letras remetirla al simple confessor".

113 MC1552, Al pio Lector, el doctor Martín de Azpilcueta Navarro: "y aun porque nos paresciera mas conveniente para la conservacion y augmento de nuestra authoridad (la qual para mas servir a Dios, se deve procurar por las personas publicas) sacar en limpio, con la mitad de trabajo, y estudio, lo que sobre muchas partes del Decreto y Decretales años ha, tenemos en Latin (comun lengua de la mayor parte de Europa) escritos y prometidos a nuestros oyentes, y a otros muchos: y por falta de tiempo para los perfectionar retenidos, que con doblando trabajo y tiempo ocuparnos en hazer esto en romance Portugues y Castellano, que no passa los montes Pyreneos".

114 MC1552, Al pio Lector, el doctor Martín de Azpilcueta Navarro: "Ca en verdad algunas medias paginas ay en esta reformacion, que se ha compuesto con estudio bastante para una repeticion: y muy muchas con bastante para dos, tres, y quatro liciones de prima buenas aun que, por veer las en romance, y tan breve y claras, no os parecera que llevan sendas horas de estudio: y aun os certificamos que no nos bastara esto, diez annos antes, ni aun agora si Dios para tan pio negocio, no proveryera, en que nos hallassemos tan curtidos, con tan vehementes, y continuas liciones, repeticiones, disputaciones, y resoluciones dictadas, y escrita estos diez, o doze años en las materias dela dichas tres facultades, de

Although Azpilcueta's prose was probably following the *topos* of the jurist overwhelmed by his endeavour, this passage reveals the importance of his teaching experience as a fundamental component of the *Manual*, as well as the difficulty of this process of condensing learned legal knowledge into a brief, clear and vernacular text, which also provided new solutions to new problems. Moreover, as I said, Azpilcueta dedicated many learned books to the topics discussed in the *Manual*, and these works, together with many other sources, are constantly quoted in it. The preface, in fact, also makes a reference to Pliny the Elder's opinion about the importance of acknowledging all the sources that were of help to an author.[115] Giving evidence of their statements was, of course, a common practice among jurists. At the same time it can be considered as the other side of epitomisation: providing access to an entire library of selected books on conscience.

5.2 *From the University* Comentarios *to a Practical Manual. Epitomisation in Action*

This process of selection, condensation and translation of learned knowledge in the *Manual* can be demonstrated with regard to one of the most famous of Azpilcueta's learned works, which was related to his teaching experience in Salamanca and Coimbra: his commentary to the section of Gratian's *Decretum* dedicated to penance, the last part of which (the comment on the 5th, 6th, 7th *distinctiones De Poenitentia*) was printed in Latin in 1542, and was the first of Azpilcueta's books to be printed.[116] One of the initial sections of this commentary is dedicated to the fundamental topic of the circumstances of sins, to which confessors paid more and more attention because of their relevance for determining the penance, asking the penitent to clearly describe these circumstances. I am referring to Azpilcueta's commentary to the chapter *consideret*, which opens the 5th *Distinctio*. If we take a brief look at this commentary, comparing it with chapter 6 of the *Manual*, explicitly dedicated to the circumstances of sin, we can gain a first impression into the way in which Azpilcueta transformed and condensed learned legal knowledge.[117]

---

donde se avian de coger las sobredichas determinaciones: alguna delas quales nunca hasta agora osamos dar siendo importunados por palabra y cartas de muchos excellentes confessores destos y otros reinos".

115 MC1556, Al Pio Lector, el Doctor Martín de Azpilcueta Nauarro, Salud. en N.S. Iesu Christo; EC1573, Candido Pioque Lectori. On Pliny's model of organization of knowledge, see Blair, *Too Much to Know*, 18.

116 On the connections between Azpilcueta's Commentary and the Manual, see Lavenia, *L'infamia o il perdono*, 233.

117 For exploring the transformation process of chapter 6 of the *Manual* accross the editions analyzed, I made use of the digital tool LERA: https://lera.uzi.uni-halle.de/?lang=en.

Let us begin with the 1549 edition. The chapter opens saying that the confessor had to expressly ask the penitent for the circumstances that he necessarily had to confess. The text focuses particularly on those aggravating circumstances which transformed a sin into another one, thus modifying the nature of the sin (e.g., committing theft in a sacred place became sacrilege); or those circumstances, which mortally aggravated a sin, meaning a venial sin became a mortal one.[118] Alleviating circumstances are also mentioned later in the chapter but did not necessarily have to be confessed, as well as those aggravating circumstances which recast a small sin as a big (but not a mortal) one.

The same schema is reproduced in the 1552 edition, but here Azpilcueta added something and reorganised the text. Starting from the 1552 edition onwards, Azpilcueta clearly augmented 'Rodrigo do Porto''s text with legal knowledge, then further enriching his legal discourse in the following 1553 and 1556 Spanish editions, as well as in the 1573 Latin edition. In particular Doctor Navarrus translated, condensed and "injected" in the chapter, what he largely developed in the already mentioned commentary to the chapter *consideret*.[119]

First of all, the connection between chapter 6 and Azpilcueta's commentary on chapter *consideret* is clear at first glance if we look at the marginal notes. In fact, in chapter 6 of the *Manual*, Azpilcueta constantly refers to his commentary; one-third of the marginal notes recall explicitly Azpilcueta's commentary to the chapter *Consideret*, using expressions like "as we demonstrated elsewhere" ("segundo que ho declaramos em outra parte"; "como aly ho dissemos").[120]

Epitomisation implied, first of all, a process of selection and translation, from Latin to vernacular. What Azpilcueta added to 'Rodrigo''s chapter was the legal definition of the circumstances of sins, which is totally lacking in the first 1549 version and which is condensed in the two first paragraphs of chapter 6, added in the 1552 edition.

Let us look at these first two paragraphs of chapter 6 of the *Manual*, comparing it with the *Commentary*, starting with the comparison of the summaries (for the summary of the *Manual* we consult the 1556 edition, where the summaries first appear). "Circumstantia quid", which opens the list in the *Commentary*, becomes "Circunstancia que es?" in the 1556 *Manual*. This first point is followed, in the *Manual*, by the statement that there are seven kinds of circumstances "y que ay siete especies della", which recalls the fourth point of

118 MC1549, cap. 6, 23–31. On the aggravating circumstances of sin, see Tentler, *Sin and Confession in the Eve of the Reformation*, 116–120.

119 Azpilcueta, *In tres de poenitentiae distinctiones posteriores commentarii*, 27–73.

120 For instance, MC1552, cap. 6, 32 § 1, § 2.

the Latin summary "circumstantiae septem & quare tot".[121] The Spanish summaries are translated into Latin for the 1573 editions, in which we read "Circunstantia quid nu. 1 & septem eius species".[122]

Chapter 6 of the 1552 edition begins, in fact, with the definition of "circumstance of sin", translating into vernacular (firstly into Portuguese, then into Spanish) the same definition offered in the commentary: "a circumstancia do peccado, segundo a mente de S. Tho[mas] & outros, he hum accidente daquilo, que he peccado",[123] (coming from "circumstantia peccati accidens quoddam ipsius erit peccati").[124] In a marginal note, together with Aquinas, Azpilcueta recalls also the other authors (S. Antoninus of Florence and Jean Gerson) on which he based his commentary to chapter *consideret*, which is expressly quoted in the *Manual*.[125] The same definition is preserved in the Spanish editions (1553, 1556). But by rethinking the text in another language, moving from Portuguese to Spanish, interestingly Azpilcueta makes a little shift: before mentioning the *interpretes*, expressly quoted in the marginal note together with his commentary, he refers to Gratian himself, namely to the chapter *consideret*, stressing that the given definition was, first of all, a legal one: "la circunstancia del pecado, según la mente del derecho y de sus interpretes es un accidente de aquello, que es pecado".[126]

The second paragraph that Azpilcueta adds in the 1552 edition is dedicated to the different types of circumstances of sin, taking them, once again, from his commentary to chapter *consideret*. Both in the *Manual* and in his commentary, Azpilcueta chose the ones proposed by Thomas Aquinas, who enumerated them, as it was usual in the *summae confessorum* recurring to the mnemonic known from Cicero's *Rhetoric*: "Quis, quid, ubi, quibus auxiliis, cur, quomodo, quando" (who, what, where, by what help, why, how, when).[127] In both texts Doctor Navarrus expressed his preference for this classification instead of the

121 MC1556, cap. 6, 30–31. Azpilcueta, *In tres de poenitentiae distinctiones posteriores commentarii*, 28–31.

122 EC1573, cap. 6, 65v.

123 MC1552, cap. 6, 32 § 1.

124 Azpilcueta, *In tres de poenitentiae distinctiones posteriores commentarii*, 32, n. 1.

125 MC1552, cap. 6, 32 § 1 marginal note p). See Azpilcueta, *In tres de poenitentiae distinctiones posteriores commentarii*, 32, princ.

126 MC1556, cap. 6, 31 § 1. Interestingly, this shift in meaning is already present in the 1553 Spanish edition, in which Azpilcueta, for the first time was rethinking the text in another language. MC1553, cap. 6, 19 § 1. The same definition is somehow stabilised in the Latin edition. EC1573, 66r. "Pro fundamento materia praesentis, in primis asserimus circunstantiam peccati iuxta mente iuris [...] esse quoddam accidens rei, quae peccatum est".

127 MC1552, cap. 6, 32 § 2. See S. Thomae de Aquino, *Summa Theologiae, Prima Secundae*, q. 7, a. 3.

one proposed by Pierre de la Palu, in his commentary on Petrus Lombartus' *Sententiae,* who also added the word "quoties", frequently, to his list. In Azpilcueta's mind, this last one was not a circumstance but simply a multiplication of the sin. Interestingly, but not surprisingly, the *Manual* provided not only the Latin version – which, in the Spanish 1553 and 1556 editions, was "enclosed" in a marginal note – but also the vernacular translation of the verse.[128]

But epitomising knowledge also implied a major stylistic modification, directly related, again, to a very attentive selection process: from the scholastic prose of university *relectiones* to a simple, more linear style by choosing only the solution provided for a special doctrinal question. In fact, if the commentary's reasoning is organised in the scholastic way of *pro, contra* and *resolutio*, the *Manual* directly provides a definition and some arguments, which are "declared" or "crumbled" – Azpilcueta uses the expression "de declara",[129] "se desmenuzara"[130] – in corollaries ("ilações", "corolarios"), thus directly proposing the solution instead of showing the dynamics of the reasoning. This is the case, for example, of the explanation of his choice of the expression "de aquello (que es pecado)", instead of using directly the word "pecado", sin, in his definition of circumstances; the reason given by Azpilcueta in the *Manual* was that sometimes a sin could become a sin only because of the circumstances, and was not a sin by itself. This is precisely the translation of the *respondeo* in the first reasoning *pro et contra* of the commentary, located in paragraph 3: Azpilcueta does not recall the entire reasoning, but directly provides the solution of the *respondeo,* to which he refers in marginal note c).[131]

As I said, Azpilcueta also reorganised the text in a new and clearer manner. Right after the mnemonic, a paragraph follows which starts with a clear list of all and the only circumstances ("todas & soos aquellas") that had necessarily to be confessed. Here, once again, he selected, translated and condensed what he said in his *Commentary.*[132] Azpilcueta mentions those circumstances that transformed an action into a mortal sin, and the ones that could change the typological character of a mortal sin. By stressing the mortal nature of the sin, as a fundamental element for necessarily including the circumstances of sin in the practice of confession, Azpilcueta clarified an aspect that was not

128 MC1553, cap. 6, 20 § 2; MC1556 cap. 6, 31 § 2.

129 MC1552, cap. 6, 33 § 3.

130 MC1553, cap. 6, 20 § 3; MC1556, cap. 6, 31 § 3.

131 MC1556, cap. 6, 31 § 1. See Azpilcueta, *In tres de poenitentiae distinctiones posteriores commentarii,* 33 § 3.

132 MC1552, cap. 6, 33 § 3. Azpilcueta, *In tres de poenitentiae distinctiones posteriores commentarii,* 33–34 § 5.

clearly defined in the 1549 edition. It is an interesting point that doctor Navarrus develops in the following transformations of the text, namely enriching the discussion and updating the text with the new canons and chapters of the Council of Trent.

5.3 *Updating and Condensing Knowledge: Azpilcueta and the Council of Trent*

Some early references to the ongoing Council are already present in the 1552 edition, namely to Session VI, of 13 January 1547, which deals with the crucial topic of justification. But the first most important updates of the text with references to the Council of Trent appeared in the 1556 edition, and were made visible by an asterisk "*". In Chapter 6, we can easily identify this kind of addition on the page, inserted right after the paragraph listing the typologies of circumstances that had to be confessed. This is a good example of how Azpilcueta updated the text by translating and interpreting the conciliar norms, and then condensed and injected them into the text. Here Azpilcueta makes references, in particular, to Session XIV, of 24 November 1551, expressly dedicated to the sacrament of penance. He refers namely to Chapter 5 and Canon 7, which deal with the circumstances of sin.

As is stated in the text, doctor Navarrus did not have the possibility to integrate systematically the decisions of Council in the previous editions "* [...] avisamos, que despues que esto se imprimio, declaro por herege el concilio Tridentino, al que dixere, que no somos obligados a confessar la circunstancia, que muda la especie de pecado [...] *". Only after the publication of the *Manual* the Council condemned as heretics those who affirmed that it was not necessary to confess the circumstances that changed the type ("especie") of sin. Here Azpilcueta translated Canon 7,[133] also explaining the way in which this passage should be understood and interpreted. In particular he excluded the need to confess those circumstances that transformed a venal sin into another venal one: "Lo qual *se ha de entender,* de la circunstancia, que muda la especie de pecado venial en mortal, o la del mortal en otra mortal, y no de la que muda en otro venial, que no es necesario confessarlo".[134] Dr. Navarrus, in fact, went beyond the letter of the norm, and elucidated even what the decrees as such did not say. In particular, he added a third type of circumstances to be necessarily

133 "Si quis dixerit, in sacramento poenitentiae ad remissionem peccatorum necessarium non esse iure divino, confiteri omnia et singula peccata mortalia [...] et circumstantias, quae peccati speciem mutat [...]: anathema sit". *Conciliorum Oecumenicorum Decreta*, ed. Istituto per le Scienze Religiose, Sess. XIV, cap. 7, 712.

134 MC1556, cap. 6, 32 (emphasis added, M.B.).

confessed, not mentioned by the Council: those circumstances that made good (or non-bad) behaviour a mortal sin.[135] For grounding his interpretation he referred to a passage taken from the already mentioned chapter five of Session XIV, thus somehow interpreting the Council through the words of the Council itself: the confessor, being a judge, cannot correctly judge the case of the penitent without knowing the circumstances that change the kind of sin.[136]

Azpilcueta refers to the conciliar norms also in the eighth "corollary" of his argumentation and the reference to the Council – this time in the marginal note – is functional to support *a contrario* his idea that it was not necessary to confess all the aggravating circumstances but only the ones responding to the criteria mentioned above.[137] In this way Azpilcueta reinforced his opinion against the theologian Marsilius of Inghen, who affirmed the need to confess also those circumstances that clearly and significantly aggravated the sin.[138]

This point, in which Azpilcueta not surprisingly draws largely on his *Comentario*, was further developed in the section dedicated to chapter six of the *Capitulo veynte y ocho* (1570) and integrated, as well, in the Latin edition.[139] Here doctor Navarrus adds to his eighth "corollary" a discussion with the Dominican Domingo de Soto, a crucial figure of the School of Salamanca, confessor and theologian of Charles V at the Council of Trent. While de Soto in his commentary of Petrus Lombardus' fourth book of *Sentences* (1557) takes side with Marsilius of Inghen,[140] Azpilcueta does not change his position, confirmed by the Council, and his reasoning moves from the doctrinal level to the concrete difficulties of confessors and penitents, in dealing with circumstances in the everyday practice of confession.[141]

---

135 "Y *aunque el concilio no expressa*, sino de la que muda la especie del pecado, pero tambien (y por mas fuerte razon) se ha de entender de la que haze a la obra, que de suyo es buena, o no mala, mortal". MC1556, cap. 6, 32 (emphasis added, M.B.).

136 "Ca la razon que a ello movio al concilio, es que el confessor es juez y no podria bien sencenciar el caso del penitente, sin se le manifestar la circunstancia, que muda la especie del pecado, la qual razon milita en las tres dichas circunstancias *". Cfr. Sess. XIV, cap. 5 "Colligitur praeterea, etiam eas circumstantias in confessione explicandas esse, quae speciem peccati mutant, quod sine illis peccata ipsa nec a poenitentibus integre exponantur, nec iudicibus innotescant, et fieri nequeat, ut de gravitate criminum recte censere possint, et poenam, quam oportet, pro illis poenitentibus imponere". *Conciliorum Oecumenicorum Decreta*, ed. Istituto per le Scienze Religiose, Sess. XIV, cap. 5, 706.

137 MC1556, cap. 6, § 7, 33, note h.

138 Marsilii von Inghen, *Quaestiones super quatuor libros sententiarum*, lib. 4, q. 12, art. 1, corol 4, 572.

139 EC1573, cap. 6, § 7, 67v-68v; See C281570, 9v-10v.

140 Soto, *Commentariorum*, dist. 18, q. 2, art. 4, 763.

141 C281570, 9v-10v; EC1573, cap. 6, § 7, 67v-68v.

5.4 *Updating Knowledge. Questions from the New Worlds and Answers from the Old One*

The condensation of learned legal knowledge was functional, in that it intended to offer confessors the instruments for finding solutions to every concrete case of conscience. Sometimes these cases, analysed by Doctor Navarrus in his *Manual*, arose from concrete questions coming from the Old and the New Worlds. That is what I called the "bottom-up" process.

First of all, as we can read in the 1556 preface to the reader, Azpilcueta was asked by Dom Henrique to answer a lot of questions and doubts ("un montón de questiones y dudas") received mainly from the Archdiocese of Evora, where the text circulated largely. The answer to these questions and doubts were integrated into the new edition, and made visible to the reader, as we have seen, recurring to the typographical sign of the asterisk "*". But this environment, a target of Dom Henrique's reform, seems to feature also earlier: in the "Declaracion de algunos passos dubdosos" that Azpilcueta added to 'Rodrigo do Porto"s text, as well as in the few special copies of the 1549 and 1552 editions of the *Manual*, today preserved at the National Library of Portugal and the Municipal Library of Porto mentioned before. These copies show two folders, at the end of the book, which contain answers to specific new questions concerning priests and friars. These appendices, in which the layout of the page corresponds perfectly to the layout of the editions they are bound to, are clearly related to the *Manual* and they constantly refer to it. Usually the author refers to specific sections with expressions like "polo acima dito", "como acima se disse" and, sometimes, they refer to other Azpilcueta's learned works saying "ou tratou ho doctissimo doutor Navarro".[142]

But also Jesuits, especially those in the New World, asked many questions.[143] I mentioned the relation between Azpilcueta and the first Jesuits sent to Brazil, namely with Manuel da Nóbrega and Juan de Azpilcueta. With both of them Doctor Navarrus entertained an intense epistolary correspondence since the beginning of the mission.[144]

---

142 See, for example, at page 21 § 17 of the supplementary folder of the 1552 edition, referring to Azpilcueta's relectio In Levitico (1550) printed two years before.

143 There is a trace of the questions coming from the Brazilian missions and addressed to the Portuguese jurists and theologians, as well as of their answers in a manuscript preserved in the Public Library of Evora, which contains also the *responsa* on five questions given by Azpilcueta: Sententiae circa resolutionem aliquorum casuum, qui in Brasilia frequenter occurrunt, BPE, cod. CXVI/1–33 (cc. 100–160): cc. 126r–130r. The manuscript is described by Rivara, *Catalogos manuscriptos da biblioteca publica eborense*, vol. 1, 16.

144 See, for example, the letters sent to Dr. Navarro by Nóbrega (10 August 1549) in Leite (ed.), *Monumenta Brasiliae*, vol. 1, 132–143 and the letter addressed by Juan de Azpilcueta to the fathers in Coimbra (19 September 1553), in which he mentions his epistolary contact

Especially Manuel da Nóbrega constantly sent questions to the theologians and jurists in Portugal. We know that he consulted his former professor on several topics, related to the strategies for the conversion of the *indios* or to specific issues connected to the marriage of converted people,[145] as well as about the crucial topic of slavery, namely on the practice of selling the *indios'* children as slaves with their parental assent.[146] If we take a look at these letters, it is possible not only to understand how important Azpilcueta's doctrines were in the New World, but also to understand how the questions raised from the Brazilian missionary context reached Portugal and were integrated into the *Manual.*

An example can be seen in two letters, addressed by Manuel da Nóbrega to the Jesuit Provincial, Simão Rodrigues, in late July and late August 1552, and their possible influences on the evolution of the *Manual* from one edition to another.[147]

The letters to Simão Rodrigues were directly connected to the arrival of the new Bishop in Bahia, who criticised the Jesuits' practice of confessing indigenous people through an interpreter as being a new practice never used in the church before.[148] Nóbrega, replying to these critics, referred to Azpilcueta's commentary *De poenitentia* (1542), namely his commentary on the c. *Fratres* of the fifth *distinctio*, to support – against the Bishop – his argument for the possibility to confess this way, without prejudice to the sacrament of confession. In fact, in the afore-mentioned passage of the commentary on *De Poenitentia* quoted by the Jesuit, Azpilcueta said that even if confession was a secret, it was possible (but not compulsory) for the penitent who did not understand the confessor's language, to confess with the help of an interpreter.[149] Nóbrega recalled the same passage of Azpilcueta's *commentary* also in the second letter in which he asked Rodrigues to send a list of urgent questions to the theologians

---

with his uncle, in Leite (ed.), *Monumenta Brasiliae*, vol. 2, 3–10: 10. On the relations between Azpilcueta and the Jesuits see Lavenia, "Martín de Azpilcueta (1592–1586)", 103–112.

145 Letter sent to Azpilcueta by Nóbrega (10 August 1549) in Leite (ed.), *Monumenta Brasiliae*, vol. 1, 141. On the point, see Castelnau-L'Estoile, "Le mariage des infidèles au XVIe siècle", 112–121.

146 See the letter by Nóbrega to Simão Rodrigues (end of July, 1552) in Leite (ed.), *Monumenta Brasiliae*, vol. 1, 369–375, esp. 370–371.

147 See the letters by Nóbrega to Simao Rodrigues (end of July and end of August, 1552), in Leite (ed.), *Monumenta Brasiliae*, vol. 1, 369–370, 407. On the point, see Cantù, *La conquista spirituale*, 328; Lavenia, "Martín de Azpilcueta (1592–1586)", 109–110.

148 See the letter by the Bishop Pedro Fernandes Sardinha to Simão Rodrigues (late July, 1554) in Leite (ed.), *Monumenta Brasiliae*, vol. 1, 357–366: 361.

149 Azpilcueta, *In tres de poenitentiae distinctiones posteriores commentarii*, cap. Fratres, Distinctio 5, § 85, 130–160: 153.

and jurists of Coimbra. The first one was the problem of confessing with an interpreter.[150]

There is no trace of this topic in the 1549 edition, printed the same year, which saw the arrival of the missionaries in Brazil. But we can imagine that the Jesuits drew very early the canon lawyer's attention to this topic in their letters, or at least that the question was perceived as urgent by Azpilcueta if he felt the need to transpose into Portuguese the mentioned passage of his commentary *De poenitentia*, in the twenty-first chapter of his *Manual* (1552), dedicated to the obligation to confess once a year as a commandment of the Church.[151] The topic was without any doubt amongst the most discussed ones at that time. Two years later, in fact, Doctor Navarrus would have referred to this section of his *Manual*, giving the same answer in one of the five handwritten consultations made to reply to some further questions coming from the Brazilian mission, today preserved at the Biblioteca Publica de Évora, one of which dealt with the topic of confessing black slaves who did not understand Portuguese.[152]

In the 1556 Spanish edition of the *Manual*, the statements on the possibility of confessing with the help of an interpreter was followed by an addition, indicated with an asterisk "*", referring especially to those who claimed that this kind of confession was entirely new and not valid (and we can perhaps find here an allusion to the position taken by the Bishop of Bahia). In fact – Azpilcueta said – not only had the church always confessed in this way, but not confessing with the help of an interpreter could distance persons speaking other languages ("los de la lengua extraña") from confession.[153] This statement of the importance and validity of this kind of confession was finally condensed in the Latin version of 1573.[154]

Even a specific reference to Brazil is already present in the 1552 edition of the *Manual*, in Chapter 23 dedicated to the seven cardinal sins, namely to the fraud (deriving from the sin of avarice) in selling and buying. Here Azpilcueta deals with the topic of the legitimacy of buying and selling *indios* as slaves. Generally speaking, buying someone as a slave, while knowing that he was a free man or that he was not captured in a just war, implied a mortal sin (like in the case of black people or *indios* captured by Christian corsairs and sold

150 Letter by Nóbrega to Simão Rodrigues (end of August, 1552), in Leite (ed.), *Monumenta Brasiliae*, vol. 1, 400–409: 407.

151 MC1552, cap. 21, § 36, 433.

152 BPE, cod. CXVI/1–33 (cc. 100–160): cc. 126r–130r: 128v–129r.

153 MC1556, cap. 21, § 36, 373.

154 EC1573, cap. 21, § 36, 304v.

to Christians as slaves). But this was not the case for those *indios* sold by their enemies as slaves, who kept them with the purpose of eating them – because life was more precious than freedom.[155] Once again, Azpilcueta would have referred to this precise section of his *Manual*, in another of his handwritten consultations preserved in Évora dedicated to the topic of slavery in Brazil.[156]

It is also likely that Juan received guidance regarding new and complicated issues from his uncle, offering Azpilcueta, in return, some important elements for writing the *Manual*. In his short but intense missionary activity, Juan worked tirelessly in the conversion of Brazil's indigenous people. He was not only the first Jesuit who was able to confess in an indigenous language, but he also translated the basics of the Christian doctrine into the Tupi language, recurring also to the music, dancing and typical gestures of the native people.[157]

6 Epilogue

Analizing Azpilcueta's *Manual*, as well as its multiple transformations in the self-translation process, it is possible to identify different processes and levels of epitomisation of learned legal knowledge. Azpilcueta condensed, translated and updated in one material object, a relatively small book, the legal knowledge that confessors and penitents needed for resolving, in the concrete act of confession, new cases of conscience coming from a rapidly changing world.

Epitomising learned legal knowledge in a pragmatic manual for confessors meant, in the case of Azpilcueta, building a bridge between the world of canon law and its concrete everyday practice. This condensation of normative knowledge was always done with the aim of providing immediate solutions to the concrete and contemporary problems which concerned simple priests or Kings, the Old and the New World, the Franciscan and the Jesuit missionary

155 Cfr. MC1552, cap. 23, § 95, 565. Nóbrega had informed Azpilcueta about the anthropophagy of the indios in his first letter from Brazil. Letter sent to Azpilcueta by Nóbrega (10 August 1549) in Leite (ed.), *Monumenta Brasiliae*, vol. 1, 136–137. On the different ways in which native people were captured as slaves (amongst them the "resgates" concerned precisely the case of saving with slavery the indios from the anthropophagic rituals), see Abreu, "O P. Manuel da Nóbrega e a evangelização dos indígenas do Brasil", 165.

156 BPE, cod. CXVI/1–33 (cc. 100–160): cc. 126r–130r: 129r–129v.

157 Leite, *História da Companhia de Jesus no Brasil*, vol. 8, 84. Cfr. Extracto de uma carta do Padre Joao de Azpilcueta Navarro da India do Brasil, (March, 28, 1550) in *Cartas Avulsas*, 76. On the use of Tupi gestures and dancing, see Barros, "Notas sobre os catecismos em línguas vernáculas das colônias portuguesas (séculos XVI–XVII)", 54; Leite, *História da Companhia de Jesus no Brasil*, vol. 2, 299.

experiences, the Portuguese and the Spanish empires. Doctor Navarro then collected and updated these solutions, also considering the new norms of the Council of Trent, which made his *Manual* into a reference work for resolving cases of conscience of the entire *Respublica Christiana*.

Azpilcueta's peculiar narrative on the genesis of each new edition of the text very often stressed the contingent reasons (related to the spread of the printed word that he could not fully control) that generated the need to further work on in. That held particularly true for the last transformation of the text. As we have seen, it was not only the impossibility of finding a good Latin translator for his *Manual*, capable of combining the truth of the doctrine with the clarity and brevity that was needed, that pushed him – an old man – to translate, improve, augment and update the *Enchiridion* himself. Another important factor was the existence of several bad Latin and Italian translations, printed without his consent (which often contradicted what was written in the original text and the true Christian doctrine).[158]

However, this was not the end of the story. If we trust the words used by Azpilcueta to address the King of Spain (and Portugal) in 1586, many people thought that the *Manual*, being published in Spanish, was more useful in the King's very extensive kingdoms ("en sus amplissimos Reynos de España"). For that reason they produced several *compendia* of the Spanish *Manual* without adding, improving and correcting what Azpilcueta added, improved and corrected in his last version and even saying the contrary of what was written there, but still ascribing the text to him.[159] This side effect of the printing revolution – which radically reduced the possibilities for the author to control in advance the correct dissemination of his words – animated, once again, Azpilcueta's pen, compelling doctor Navarrus, aged more than ninety years, to make his own *Compendio*. Doing so, he finally provided the language, (Spanish) and probably also the format (a small *compendium*) more suitable to the needs of simple readers and big empires.

Actually, the *Compendio* immediately appears simpler to the reader's eyes, especially if compared to the last versions of the *Manual*. First of all, the text is much shorter ('only' 562 pages *in quarto*). It retains the structure of the *Enchiridion* (the ten *praeludia* placed at the beginning are summarised and translated into Spanish) but doctrinal references are almost completely eliminated. Some of the very few references in the text (in the form of marginal notes, albeit extremely scarce) refer to the *Manual* and, in this way, the *Compendium*

158 *Candido Pioque lectori*, EC1573; Dedication to the S[acra] C[atólica] R[eal] M[ajestad], in CM1586.

159 SCRM, in CM1586.

appears like a tool for having access to it. The remaining references – generic, with no indication to the pertinent Session, chapters or canons – are mainly to the Council of Trent, but without any allusion to the doctrinal debates related to the canons which had characterised very much the sections added to the 1556 edition as well as the additions of Chapter 28. In fact, they merely focus on those behaviours imposed or condemned by the Council. Also, the organisation of the text within each chapter becomes clearer. The structure of the text in the *Manual* that generally followed the reasoning in numbered corollaries and secondary points is substituted by a linear sequence of numbered arguments.

This becomes evident by a look at chapter 6 of the *Compendio*, dedicated, as said before, to the circumstances of sin. While in the *Manual* and in the *Enchiridion* this chapter is organised into three first points (the legal definition, the seven kinds of circumstances and the circumstances that have to be confessed) and eighteen corollaries (these last ones themselves subdivided into sub-arguments), the *Compendio* simply shows fourteen numbered arguments.[160] Very interestingly, the legal definition of the circumstances of sin that Azpilcueta injected into the text from the 1552 edition onwards, disappears: the most important aspect seems to be the different kinds of circumstances, and the mnemonic (following Thomas Aquinas' version), kept only in the Spanish translation. Doctrinal references are reduced in very simple terms, and more often disappear completely. This is the case, for example, of the entire debate on the circumstances that aggravate notably, but not mortally, the sin. The ideal discussion with Marsilius of Inghen already present in the 1552 edition, as well as the interpretation of Chapter 5 and Canon 7 of Session XVI of the Council of Trent added in the 1556 edition, and the dialogue with Domingo de Soto which we find in the *capitulo veynte y ocho* and which was later integrated into the Latin edition, are radically cut from the text. What remains is only the essential message: the fact that aggravating circumstances are not to be confessed, unless when they transform a venal sin into a mortal one, or when they change the typology of a mortal sin.[161] Likewise the reasons on which Azpilcueta grounded his arguments (the omnipresent "la razon es", "porque" and "ratio est", "quoniam", or "quia" in the Spanish and Latin *Manual*, respectively) are very much reduced. Moreover, the original contexts of the concrete questions answered in the *Manual* are omitted: for example, the fact that a specific question was asked by Antonio de Zurara. With regard to the

160 CM1586, 24r.
161 CM1586, 24v.

TABLE 6.1 Description of the main editions of Azpilcueta's *Manual de Confessores* quoted in the article

	Year	City of print	Printer	Short title	Format	Language	Dedicatee
MC1549	1549, July 27	Coimbra	Ioão da Barreira, Ioão Alvares emprimidores da mesma universidade	Manual de confessores & penitentes	in 8°, 720 pp.[a]	POR	The Reader
MC1552	1552, December 13	Coimbra	Ioannes Barrerius, et Ioannes Alvarez Regii Typographi	Manual de confessores & penitentes	in 8º, 1000 pp.	POR	Dom Henrique The Reader
MC1553	1553, August 30	Coimbra	Ioannes Barrerius, et Ioannes Alvarez Regii Typographi	Manual de confessores y penitentes	in 4º, 588 pp.	SPA	Princess Juana of Austria The Reader
MC1556	1556, July 10	Salamanca	Andrea de Portonariis, Impressor de la S. C. M.	Manual de confessores y penitentes	in 4°, 813 pp.	SPA	Princess Juana of Austria The Reader
CR1556	1556, August 12	Salamanca	Andrea de Portonariis, Impressor de la S. C. M.	Comentario resolutorio de usuras Reportorio general	in 4°, 235 pp.	SPA	Emperor Charles V The Reader
MC1560	1560, January 20	Coimbra	Ioam de Barreyra, Impressor da Universidade, impressor del Rey	Manual de confessores & penitentes	in 4°, 767 pp.	POR	Princess Juana of Austria The Reader

CR1560	–	Coimbra	Ioam de Barreyra, Impressor da universidade	Comentario resolutorio de onzenas	in 4°, 169 pp.	POR	Emperor Charles V The Reader
MC1570	1570	Valladolid	Por Francisco Fernandez de Cordoua impressor de la Magestad Real. Vendese en la Libreria en casa de Antonio Suchet	Manual de confessores y penitentes con cinco Comentarios [...] Nuevamente Revisto, emendado, y añadido el Capitulo veynte y ocho, por el mesmo Autor	in 4°, 1049 pp.	SPA	Princess Juana of Austria The Reader
C281570	1570	Valladolid	Por Adrian Ghemart. Vendese en la Libreria, en casa de Antonio Suchet	Capitulo XXVIII de las Addiciones de los XXVII capitulos del Manual de confessores y penitentes	in 4°, 198 pp.	SPA	–

TABLE 6.1 Description of the main editions of Azpilcueta's *Manual de Confessores* quoted in the article (*cont.*)

	Year	City of print	Printer	Short title	Format	Language	Dedicatee
EC1573	1573	Rome	Victorium Elianum	Enchiridion sive Manuale confessariorum et poenitentium	in 4°, 1136 pp.	LAT	Pope Gregory XIII The Reader
EC1584	1584	Rome	Ex Typographia Georgii Ferrarii, Apud Vincentium Accoltum	Enchiridion, sive Manuale Confessariorum et poenitentium	in 4°, 1107 pp.	LAT	Pope Gregory XIII The Reader
CM1586	1586	Valladolid	En casa de Diego Fernández de Córdoua Impressor de Su Magestad. Por Antonio Suchet	Compendio del Manual de Confessores y Penitentes	in 4°, 562 pp.	SPA	King Philip II

[a] For the sake of consistency, page numbers always comprise the *recto* and the *verso* of the page, even when some original editions only count the folios (*recto*).

TABLE 6.2 Short description of some elements related to the privileges of print of the editions mentioned in the article

	Authority granting the privilege	Year of the privilege	Territory	Years of privilege	Ending-finishing privileges
MC1549	Pope, Paul III: short reference to Paul III's privilege of print granted to Azpilcueta for his lectures, at the end of the *Declaración*	–	–	–	–
MC1552	Pope Paul III: privilege granted for Azpilcueta's lectures	1543, January 8	Entire Christian World (per universum orbem christianum)	7 years	From publication date (1552–1559)
MC1553	Pope Paul III: privilege granted for Azpilcueta's lectures	1543, January 8 (Rome)	Entire Christian World	7 years	From publication date (1553–1560)
MC1556	Princess Juana for the King	I. 1555, May 4 (Valladolid)	Privilege of the king of Castile: territory of Castile	10 years	From the date of the *cédula* (1555–1565)
	Princess Juana	II. 1556, July 3 (Valladolid)	Privilege of Aragon: territory of the crown of Aragon	10 years	From the *cédula* (1556–1566)
	King of Portugal	III. 1554, September 4 (Lisbon)	Privilege of Portugal: territory of Portugal	10 years	From the *alvara* (1554–1564)
CR1556	Pope Paul III: privilege granted for Azpilcueta's lectures	1553, January 8 (Rome)	Papal Privilege: entire Christian World	7 years	From publication date (1556–1563)

TABLE 6.2 Short description of some elements related to the privileges of print of the editions mentioned in the article (*cont.*)

	Authority granting the privilege	Year of the privilege	Territory	Years of privilege	Ending-finishing privileges
MC1560	King of Portugal	I. 1554, August 6; September 4 (Lisbon)	Privilege of Portugal: territory of Portugal	10 years	From the *alvara* (1554–1564)
	Prince of Castile	II. 1554, March 29 (Valladolid)	Privilege of Castile: kingdom of Castile	10 years	From the *cédula* (1554–1564)
	Princess Juana for the King	III. 1555, May 4 (Valladolid)	Privilege of Castile: territory of Castile	10 years	From the *cédula* (1555–1565)
	Princess Juana	IV. 1556 July 3 (Valladolid)	Privilege of Aragon: territory of Aragon	10 years	From the *cédula* (1556–1566)
CR1560	Pope Paul III: privilege granted for Azpilcueta's lectures	1553, January 8 (Rome)	Papal Privilege: entire Christian World	7 years	From publication date (1560–1567)
MC1570	Philip II	I. 1565, December 16	Privilege of Philip II: kingdoms of Philip II	6 years	From end of the previous privilege
	Philip II	II. 1570, March 10	Privilege of Philip II for Manual updated with ch. 28	6 years	From end of the previous privilege
C281570	Philip II	I. 1569, May 10	Licence to every printer to print it once, but in conformity to the Original	Once	

EC1573	Pope Gregory XIII	1572, November 5 (Rome)	Privilege of Pope Gregory XIII + Naples, Venice, Milan, Ferrara and all Italian dominions	7 years	From publication date (1573–1580)
EC1584	Pope Gregory XIII	1581, November 21 (Rome)	Privilege of Pope Gregory XIII + Naples, Venice, and all Italian dominions	10 years	From date of privilege (1581–1591)
CM1586	Philip II	I. 1586, August 2 (Lorenço)	Privilege of Philip II, for territories of Philip II	10 years	From the date of the *cédula*
	Pope Gregory XIII	II. Suma del privilegio del Papa	Recalls the papal privilege of print for EC1584	–	–

TABLE 6.3 Short description of the most important sections of the *Manual* in the different editions mentioned in the article

MC1549	"Declaracion de algunos passos dubdosos, por el mismo doctor Martin de Azpilcueta Navarro"	27 chapters		List of chapter titles: *Seguese a tavoada dos capitulos que em ho presente livro se contem*	
MC1552		27 chapters			Alphabetical table of contents: *Tavoada ou reportorio*
MC1553		27 chapters		List of chapter titles	Alphabetical table of contents: *Tabla o repertorio*
MC1556		27 chapters	5 comentarios (CR1556)	List of chapter titles	Alphabetical table of contents: *Reportorio* (in CR1556)
MC1560		27 Chapters	5 comentarios (CR1560)	List of chapter titles	Alphabetical table of contents: *Reportorio general & muy copioso do Manual de Confessores. E dos cinco comentarios*
MC1570		27 chapters	5 comentarios	List of chapter titles	*Reportorio general & muy copioso do Manual de Confessores. E dos cinco comentarios*

C281570		c. 28		Alphabetical table of contents: *Tabla delo contenido en este capitulo XXVIII*
EC1573	10 *Preludia*	27 chapters	List of chapter titles: *Materia contentorum in hoc libro*	Alphabetical table of contents: *Index copiosissimus*
EC1584	10 *Praeludia*	27 chapters	List of chapter titles: *Elenchus Capitum*	Alphabetical table of contents: *Index copiosissimus*
CM1586	10 *Preludios*	27 chapters		Alphabetical table of contents: *Tabla de lo contenido en este Compendio del Manual de Confessores*

Compendio, more important than the reasons, the debates with other authors, or the motivation that grounded the arguments was the precept in itself, expressed without a margin of doubt.

Extracting the very essence of the updated and revised *Manual* constituted, one might say, the last and ulterior level of epitomisation. What could seem at first glance a simple and small book, with no erudite references, conceived to be understood by simple people, was actually the result of an extremely complex and life-long intellectual process. The famous portrait in the front-page can be understood as its adequate emblem. Traditionally, the picture is said to have been made unbeknown to Azpilcueta in the first years of his Roman stay.[162] (Doctor Navarrus did not want to be portrayed, but his image could not lack in the galleries of *viri illustres* that decorated the libraries of some of the greatest collectors of the time, as well as the illustrated printed biographies of the 16th century.) The engraving of the front-page seems to testify not only to the authorship of the book but also to the fact that the entire erudition of the old and celebrated canonist had been condensed in the *Compendio*.

Bibliography

Manuscripts

Archivio Segreto Vaticano, Città del Vaticano (ASV), A.A. Arm. I–XVIII, 3129, cc. 1r–7v.
Biblioteca Casanatense, Roma (BC), Ms. 740, cc. 3r–203r.
Biblioteca Pública de Évora, Évora (BPE), cod. CXVI/1–33, cc. 100–160.
Universidade de Coimbra. Biblioteca Geral, Coimbra (UCBG), Ms. 1173, cc. 1r–65r.

Printed Sources

a) Azpilcueta's Works

[MC1549] Azpilcueta, Martín de and Rodrigo do Porto, *Manual de confessores & penitentes*, Coimbra 1549: João de Barreira and João Alvares.

162 On Azpilcueta's portrait, dated 1572, which seems to have been commissioned by the Spanish theologian and great collector Alfonso Chacón during his stay in Rome, see Herkolz, "Alfonso Chacón e le gallerie dei ritratti nell'età della Controriforma". See also Ramlotaeus, *Vita excellentissimi iuris monarchae Martini ab Azpilcueta Doctoris Navarri*, who mentions the engraver Philippe de Soye as the artist who secretly sketched the portait, requested by the painter, illustrator, cartographer, print publisher, active in Rome, Antonio Lafreri. The portrait that was sold individually, appears also in some of the iconographic collections of *viri illustres* printed by Lafrery, namely attached to the collection of *Illustrium iureconsultorum imagines* (1566). See Rubach, *Ant. Lafreri Formis Romae*, 370.

[MC1552] Azpilcueta, Martín de, *Manual de confessores & penitentes*, Coimbra 1552: João de Barreira and João Alvares.

[MC1553] Azpilcueta, Martín de, *Manual de confessores y penitentes*, Coimbra 1553: João de Barreira and João Alvares.

[MC1556] Azpilcueta, Martín de, *Manual de confessores y penitentes*, Salamanca 1556: Andrea de Portonariis.

[CR1556] Azpilcueta, Martín de, *Comentario resolutorio de usuras*, Salamanca 1556: Andrea de Portonariis.

[MC1560] Azpilcueta, Martín de, *Manual de confessores & penitentes*, Coimbra 1560: João de Barreira.

[C281570] Azpilcueta, Martín de, *Capitulo XXVIII de las Addiciones de los XXVII capitulos del Manual de confessores y penitentes*, Zaragoza 1570: En casa de la viuda de Bartholome de Nagera.

[MC1570] Azpilcueta, Martín de, *Manual de confessores y penitenets con cinco Comentarios* [...] *Nuevamente Revisto, emendado, y anadido el Capitulo veynte y ocho, por el mesmo Autor*, Valladolid 1570: Francisco Fernandez de Cordoua impressor de la Magestad Real. Vendese en la Libreria en casa de Antonio Suchet.

[EC1573] Azpilcueta, Martín de, *Enchiridion sive Manuale confessariorum et poenitentium*, Romae 1573: Victorium Elianum.

[EC1584] Azpilcueta, Martín de, *Enchiridion, sive Manuale Confessariorum et poenitentium*, Romae 1584: Ex Typographia Georgii Ferrarii.

[CM1586] Azpilcueta, Martín de, *Compendio del Manual de Confessores y Penitentes*, Valladolid 1586: En casa de Diego Fernández de Córdoua Impressor de Su Magestad. Por Antonio Suchet.

Azpilcueta, Martín de, *In tres de poenitentiae distinctiones posteriores commentarii*, Coimbra 1542: João de Barreira and João Alvares.

Azpilcueta, Martín de, *Relectio cap. ita quorundam de Iudaeis*, Conimbricae 1550: Ioannes Barrerius & Ioannes Alvarus.

Azpilcueta, Martín de, *Commentaria in septem distinctiones de Poenitentia*, Romae 1581: Ex typographia Georgii Ferrarii.

Azpilcueta, Martín de, *Consiliorum seu Responsorum*, 2 vols., Venetiis 1601: Apud Ioannem Guerilium.

Azpilcueta, Martín de, "Parescer del Doctor Nauarro sobre el decreto del Tridentino quanto a los cabildos", in Arigita y Lasa, Mariano (ed.), *El doctor Navarro Don Martin de Azpilcueta y sus obras. Estudio histórico-crítico*, Pamplona 1895, 585–600.

b) Other Sources

Beyerlinck, Laurens, *Magnum theatrum vitae humanae*, vol. 4, Lugduni 1665.

Brandão, Mário (ed.), *Actas dos Conselhos da Universidade de 1505 a 1537*, vol. 1, Coimbra 1941.

Cartas Avulsas. Azpilcueta Navarro e outros. Cartas Jesuiticas 2, Coleção reconquista do Brasil. 2ª série, eds. Paim, Antonio, Roque Spencer, Maciel de Barros and Ruy Afonso da Costa Nunes, São Paulo 1988.

Conciliorum Oecumenicorum Decreta, ed. Istituto per le Scienze Religiose, 3rd ed., Bologna 1973.

Conciliorum Oecumenicorum Generaliumque Decreta, vol. 3: *The Oecumenical Councils of the Roman Catholic Church. From Trent to Vatican II (1545–1965)*, eds. Ganzer, Klaus, Giuseppe Alberigo and Alberto Melloni, Turnhout 2010.

Gessner, Conrad, *Pandectarum sive partitionum universalium Conradi Gesneri Tigurini, medici & philosophiae professoris* [...] *libri XXI*, Tiguri 1548: Excudebat Christophorus Froschuerus.

Gouvea, Francisco de, "'Antinavarrus', Introducción y edición de Estanislao Olivares S.I.", in *Archivo teológico granadino* 27 (1964), 271–384.

Leão, Duarte Nunes, *Orthographia da lingoa portuguesa, obra util et necessaria assi pera bem escrever a lingoa Hespanhol, como a Latina, & quaesquer outras que da Latina tem origen*, Lisboa 1576: Ioao de Barreira.

Leite, Serafim (ed.), *Monumenta Brasiliae*, vol. 1: *(1538–1553)*, Roma 1956.

Leite, Serafim (ed.), *Monumenta Brasiliae*, vol 2: *(1553–1558)*, Roma 1957.

Machado, Diogo Barbosa, *Bibliotheca Lusitana*, vol. 1, Lisboa Occidental 1752: Antonio Isidoro da Fonseca.

Machado, Diogo Barbosa, *Bibliotheca Lusitana*, vol. 3, Lisboa 1741: Ignacio Rodriguez.

Marsilii von Inghen, *Quaestiones super quatuor libros sententiarum*, Argentinae 1501: Martinus Flach.

Monforte, Manoel de, *Chronica da Provincia da Piedade primeira Capucha de Toda a ordem, e Regular Observancia de nosso Serafico Padre S. Francisco*, Lisboa 1751: Na Officina de Miguel Manescal da Costa.

Monzón, Francisco de, *Norte de confessores*, Lisboa 1546: En casa de Luis Rodriguez librero del rey.

Ramlotaeus, Simon Magnus, *Vita excellentissimi iuris monarchae Martini ab Azpilcueta Doctoris Navarri*, Romae 1574: Apud Victorium Elianum.

Rëgo, António da Silva (ed.), *Documentação para a história das missões do padroado português do Oriente*, vol. 3: *(1543–1547)*, Lisboa 1950.

Rëgo, António da Silva (ed.), *Documentação para a história das missões do padroado português do Oriente*, vol. 4: *(1548–1550)*, Lisboa 1950.

Soto, Domingo de, *Commentariorum* [...] *in Quartum Sententiarum. Tomus Primus*, Salamanticae 1569: Apud Ioannem Baptistam à Terranova.

Vilas Boas, Manuel do Cenáculo, *Memorias históricas do ministério do púlpito*, Lisboa 1776: Na regia officina typografica.

Wicki, Josef (ed.), *Documenta Indica*, vol. 3: *(1553–1557)*, Romae 1954.

Wicki, Josef and John Gomes (eds.), *Documenta Indica*, vol. 16: *(1592–1594)*, Romae 1984.

Literature

Abreu, Adélio Fernando, "O P. Manuel da Nóbrega e a evangelização dos indígenas do Brasil (1549–1570) (2). Os obstáculos à missão", in *Humanística e Teologia* 34:2 (2013), 149–186.

Afanaseyev, Anton Alexandrovich, "La Escuela de Salamanca del siglo XVI: algunas contribuciones a la ciencia económica", in *Revista Empresa y Humanismo* 19:1 (2016), 7–30.

Andrés, Melquiades, *La teología española en el siglo XVI*, vol. 2, Madrid 1977.

Angelozzi, Giancarlo, "L'insegnamento dei casi di coscienza nella pratica educativa della Compagnia di Gesù", in Brizzi, Gian Paolo (ed.), *La "Ratio Studiorum". Modelli culturali e pratiche educative dei Gesuiti in Italia tra Cinque e Seicento*, Roma 1981, 121–162.

Atienza, Julio de, *Nobiliario Español. Diccionario heráldico de apellidos españoles y de títulos nobiliarios*, Madrid 1948.

Baciero, Carlos, "La obra y sus fuentes", in Baciero, Carlos, Jesús María García Añoveros, Francisco Maseda and Manuel Corrales (eds.), *Alonso de la Peña Montenegro. Itinerario para párrocos de indios. Libros I-II*, Madrid 1995, 57–71.

Barros, Cândida, "Intérpretes e confessionários como expressões de politicas linguísticas da Igreja voltadas à confissão", in DELTA 27:2 (2011), 289–310 (10.1590/S0102-44502011000200005).

Barros, Maria Cândida Drumond Mendes, "Notas sobre os catecismos em línguas vernáculas das colônias portuguesas (séculos XVI–XVII)", in *Iberoromania* 57:1 (2003), 27–63.

Bataillon, Marcel, "Jeanne d'Autriche, Princesse de Portugal", in Bataillon, Marcel (ed.), *Études sur le Portugal au temps de l'humanisme*, Coimbra 1952.

Beck Varela, Laura, "The Diffusion of Law Books in Early Modern Europe: A Methodological Approach", in Meccarelli, Massimo and María Julia Solla Sastre (eds.), *Spatial and Temporal Dimensions for Legal History. Research Experiences and Itineraries*, Frankfurt am Main 2016, 195–239.

Belda Plans, Juan, *Martín de Azpilcueta. El «Doctor Navavarro»*, Madrid 2015 (www.larramendi.es).

Blair, Ann M., *Too Much to Know. Managing Scholarly Information before the Modern Age*, New Haven, CT 2010.

Blair, Ann, "Humanism and Printing Press in the Work of Conrad Gessner", in *Renaissance Quarterly* 70 (2017), 1–37.

Blanco, Arturo, *Historia del confesionario. Razones antropológicas y teológicas de su uso*, Madrid 2000.

Boer, Wietse de, *The Conquest of the Soul: Confession, Discipline, and Public Order in Counter-Reformation Milan*, Leiden 2001.

Borromeo, Agostino, "Il concilio di Trento e la Riforma postridentina della penitenzeria apostolica (1562–1572)", in Sodi, Manlio and Johan Ickx (eds.), *La penitenzeria apostolica e il sacramento della penitenza. Percorsi storici, giuridici, teologici e prospettive pastorali*, Città del Vaticano 2009, 111–134.

Bragagnolo, Manuela, "Les voyages du droit du Portugal à Rome. Le 'Manual de confessores' de Martín de Azpilcueta (1492–1586) et ses traductions (The Travels of Law from Portugal to Rome. Martín de Azpilcueta's 'Manual de confessores' (1492–1586) and its Translations)", *Max Planck Institute for European Legal History Research Paper Series* No. 2018-13 (http://dx.doi.org/10.2139/ssrn.3287684).

Buescu, Ana Isabel, "Aspectos do Bilinguismo Português-Castelhano na época moderna", in *Hispania* 64:1, no. 216 (2004), 13–38.

Burke, Peter, *Languages and Communities in Early Modern Europe*, Cambridge 2004.

Burke, Peter, "Cultures of Translation in Early Modern Europe", in Burke, Peter and Ronnie Po-Chia Hsia (eds.), *Cultural Translation in Early Modern Europe*, Cambridge 2007, 7–38.

Burke, Peter, "Translations into Latin in early modern Europe", in Burke, Peter and Ronnie Po-chia Hsia (eds.), *Cultural Translation in Early Modern Europe*, Cambridge 2007, 65–80.

Cantù, Francesca, *La conquista spirituale. Studi sull'evangelizzazione del Nuovo Mondo*, Roma 2007.

Carabias Torres, Ana María, "Castilla y Portugal: el trajín de la cultura académica", in Espinosa, Rosa María and Julia Montenegro (eds.), *Castilla y Portugal en los albores de la edad moderna*, Valladolid 1997, 31–53.

Cardoso, Armando, "IV Centenario do P. João de Azpilcueta Navarro", in *Verbum* 15 (1958), 15–48.

Casetti Brach, C., "Eliano, Vittorio", in Istituto della Enciclopedia Italiana (ed.), *Dizionario Biografico degli Italiani. Dugoni – Enza*, vol. 42, Roma 1993, 475–477.

Castelnau-L'Estoile, Charlotte de, "Le mariage des infidèles au XVIe siècle: doutes missionnaires et autorité pontificale", in *Mélanges de l'école française de Rome* 121:1 (2009), 95–121.

Cevolini, Alberto, *De arte excerpendi. Imparare a dimenticare nella modernità*, Firenze 2006.

Condorelli, Orazio, "Le origini teologico-canonistiche della teoria delle leges mere poenales (secoli XIII–XVI)", in Schmoeckel, Mathias, Orazio Condorelli and Franck Roumy (eds.), *Der Einfluss der Kanonistik auf die europäische Rechtskultur*, vol. 3: *Straf- und Strafprozessrecht*, Köln 2012, 55–98.

Cordingley, Anthony, "Introduction", in Cordingley, Anthony (ed.), *Self-Translation. Brokering Originality in Hybrid Culture*, London 2013, 1–10.

Cordingley, Anthony and Céline Frigau Manning (eds.), *Collaborative Translation. From the Renaissance to the Digital Age*, London 2017.

Decock, Wim, *Theologians and Contract Law. The Moral Transformation of the Ius Commune (ca. 1500–1650)*, Leiden 2012.

Decock, Wim, "Martín de Azpilcueta", in Domingo, Rafael and Javier Martínez-Torrón (eds.), *Great Christian Jurists in Spanish History*, Cambridge 2018, 116–132.

Dios de Dios, Salustiano de, "La doctrina sobre el poder del príncipe en Martín de Azpilcueta", in Torijano Pérez, Eugenia, Salustiano de Dios de Dios and Javier Infante Miguel-Motta (eds.), *El derecho y los juristas en Salamanca (siglos XVI–XX). En memoria de Francisco Tomás y Valiente*, Salamanca 2004, 461–566.

Dunoyer, Emilio, *L'Enchiridion Confessariorum' de Navarro*, Pamplona 1957.

Duve, Thomas, "European Legal History – Concepts, Methods, Challenges", in Duve, Thomas (ed.), *Entanglements in Legal History: Conceptual Approaches*, Frankfurt am Main 2014, 29–66.

Ellsworth Hamann, Byron, *The Translations of Nebrija. Language, culture, and circulation in the Early Modern World*, Amherst, MA 2015.

Fernandes, Maria de Lurdes Correia, "As artes da Confissão. Em torno dos manuais de confessores do século XVI em Portugal", in *Humanística e Teologia* 11 (1990), 47–80.

Fernandes, Maria de Lurdes Correia, "Do manual de confessores ao guia de penitentes. Orientações e caminhos da confissão non Portugal post-Trento", in *Via Spiritus* 2 (1990), 47–65.

Fernandes, Maria de Lurdes Correia, "Francisco de Monzón, capelão e pregador de D. João III e de D. Sebastião", in *Lusitania Sacra*, 2ª série, 3 (1991), 37–90.

Fery-Hue, Françoise (ed.), *Traduire de vernaculaire en latin au Moyen Âge et à la Renaissance. Méthodes et finalités*, Paris 2013.

Fonseca, Fernando Taveira da, José Antunes, Irene Vaquinhas, Isabel Nobre Vargues, Luís Reis Torgal and Fernando J. Regateiro, *Imprensa da Universidade de Coimbra. Uma história dentro da História*, Coimbra 2001.

Fragnito, Gigliola, *La Bibbia al rogo. La censura ecclesiastica e i volgarizzamenti della sacra scrittura*, Bologna 1997.

García y García, Antonio, "Juristas Salamantinos, siglos XVI–XVII: Manuscritos y impresos", in Rodríguez-San Pedro Bezares, Luis E. and Ángel Weruaga Prieto (eds.), *Historia de la Universidad de Salamanca. Saberes y confluencias*, vol. 3.1, Salamanca 2018, 139–170.

Goering, Joseph, "The Internal Forum and the Literature of Penance and Confession", in Hartmann, Wilfried and Kenneth Pennington (eds.), *The History of Medieval Canon Law in the Classical Period, 1140–1234. From Gratian to the Decretals of Pope Gregory IX*, Washington, D.C. 2008, 379–428.

Grossi, Paolo, "Somme penitenziali, diritto canonico, diritto comune", in *Annali della facoltà giuridica. Università di Macerata* 1 (1966), 94–134.

Grossi, Paolo, "Somme penitenziali, diritto canonico, diritto comune", in Fantappiè, Carlo (ed.), *Scritti canonistici*, vol. 1, Milano 2013, 115–153.

Guedes de Campos, Fernanda Maria, *A ordem das ordens religiosas. Roteiro Identitário de Portugal (Séculos XII–XVIII)*, Casal de Cambra 2017.

Hamesse, Jacqueline, "Il modello della lettura nell'età della scolastica", in Cavallo, Guglielmo and Roger Chartier (eds.), *Storia della lettura nel mondo occidentale*, Laterza 1995, 91–116.

Herkolz, Ingo, "Alfonso Chacón e le gallerie dei ritratti nell'età della Controriforma", in Tosini, Patrizia (ed.), *Arte e committenza nel Lazio nell'età di Cesare Baronio*, Roma 2009, 111–142.

Hespanha, António Manuel, "Form and content in early modern legal books. Bridging the gap between material bibliography and the history of legal thought", in *Rechtsgeschichte* 12 (2008), 12–50.

Hokenson, Jan Walsh and Marcella Munson, *The Bilingual Text. History and Theory of Literary Self-Translation*, Manchester 2007.

Infantes, Víctor, *Del libro áureo*, Madrid 2006.

Johns, Adrian, *The Nature of the Book. Print and Knowledge in the Making*, Chicago, IL 1998.

Lavenia, Vincenzo, "Martín de Azpilcueta (1592–1586). Un profilo", in *Archivio Italiano per la Storia della Pietà* 16 (2003), 15–157.

Lavenia, Vincenzo, *L'infamia o il perdono. Tributi, pene e confessione nella teologia morale della prima età moderna*, Bologna 2004.

Leite, Serafim, *História da Companhia de Jesus no Brasil*, vol. 2: *Século XVI – a obra*, Lisboa 1938.

Leite, Serafim, *História da Companhia de Jesus no Brasil*, vol. 8: *Escritores: de A a M. (Suplemento Biobibliográfico – I)*, Rio de Janeiro 1949.

López Gay, Jesús, "La primera biblioteca de los Jesuítas en el Japón (1556). Su contenido y su influencia", in *Monumenta Nipponica* 15:3–4 (1959–1960), 350–379.

Marcocci, Giuseppe, *I custodi dell'ortodossia. Inquisizione e chiesa nel Portugallo del Cinquecento*, Roma 2004.

Marcocci, Giuseppe, *L'invenzione di un impero. Politica e cultura nel mondo portoghese (1450–1600)*, Roma 2011.

Marques, João Francisco, "Franciscanos e Dominicanos Confessores dos Reis Portugueses das duas Primeiras Dinastias. Espiritualidade e Política", in *Revista da Faculdade de Letras – Línguas e Literatura* Anexo V – Espiritualidade e corte em Portugal (sécs XVI–XVIII) (1993), 53–60.

Mateu y Llopis, Felipe, "Licencia, tasa y privilegio de impresion en la España de los siglos XVI y XVII", in *Gutenberg-Jahrbuch* 40 (1965), 197–200.

McKenzie, D.F., *Bibliography and the Sociology of Texts*, London 1986.

Michaud-Quantin, Pierre, *Sommes de casuistique et manuels de confession au moyen âge (XII–XVI siècles)*, Louvain 1962.

Minnis, A.J., "Late Medieval Discussions on Compilatio and the Role of Compilator", in *Beiträge zur Geschichte der deutschen Sprache und Literatur* 101 (1979), 385–421.

Muguruza Roca, Isabel, "Del confesionario ibérico de la Contrarreforma a los manuales para confesores en la América colonial: el Manual de confesores y penitentes de Martín de Azpilcueta como texto de referencia", in *Indiana* 32:5 (2018), 29–53.

Muñoz de Juana, Rodrigo, *Moral y economía en la obra de Martín de Azpilcueta*, Pamplona 1998.

O'Banion, Patrick J., " 'A priest who appears good'. Manuals of confession and the construction of clerical identity in early modern Spain", in *Dutch Review of Church History* 85:1 (2005), 333–348.

O'Malley, John W., *The First Jesuits*, Cambridge 1993.

Paiva, José Pedro, "Bispos, imprensa, livro e censura no Portugal de Quinhentos", in *Revista de Historia das Ideas* 28 (2007), 687–737.

Palacín, L., "Azpilcueta (Navarro), Juan de", in O'Neill, Charles Edwards and Joaquín María Domínguez (eds.), *Diccionario histórico de la Compañía de Jesús*, vol. 1, Roma 2001, 317.

Polónia, Amélia, "Recepção do Concilio de Trento em Portugal: as normas enviadas pelo Cardeal D. Henrique aos Bispos do reino, em 1553", in *Revista da Faculdade de Letras-Historia*, 2ª série, 7 (1990), 133–143.

Polónia, Amélia, *D. Henrique. O Cardeal-Rei*, Lisboa 2005.

Polónia, Amélia, "Espaços de intervenção religiosa do Cardeal Infante D. Henrique: actuação pastoral, reforma monástica e inquisição", in Amorim, Inês, Helena Osswald and Amélia Polónia (eds.), *Em torno dos espaços religiosos – monásticos e eclesiásticos. Actas do colóquio de homenagem a Frei Geraldo Coelho Dias*, Porto 2005, 17–37.

Prodi, Paolo, *Una storia della giustizia. Dal pluralismo dei fori al moderno dualismo tra coscienza e diritto*, Bologna 2000.

Prodi, Paolo, *Settimo non rubare. Furto e mercato nella storia dell'occidente*, Bologna 2009.

Réach-Gnô, Anne, "De la catégorisation bibliothéconomique du livre à la genèse éditoriale de l'oeuvre: le cas des Trésors imprimés à la Renaissance", in *Seizième Siècle* 10 (2014), 211–224.

Réach-Ngô, Anne, "Du texte au livre, et retour: la production littéraire à la Renaissance, une création collaborative?", in *Genesis* 41 (2005), 29–47.

Reyes Gómez, Fermín de los, "Con privilegio: la exclusiva de edición del libro antiguo español", in *Revista General de Información y Documentación* 11:2 (2001), 163–200.

Reyes Gómez, Fermín de los, "La estructura formal del libro antiguo español", in *Paratesto* 7 (2010).

Ridruejo, Emilio, "Castellano y portugués en la época de los descubrimientos", in Sociedad V Centenario Tratado de Tordesillas (ed.), *La lengua española y su expansión en la época del Tratado de Tordesillas*, Valladolid 1995, 65–78.

Rivara, Joaquim Heliodoro da Cunha, *Catalogos manuscriptos da biblioteca publica eborense*, vol. 1, Lisboa 1850.

Rodrigues, Manuel Augusto (ed.), *Memoria professorum Universitatis Conimbrigensis*, vol. 1: (*1290–1772*), Coimbra 2003.

Rodríguez-San Pedro Bezares, Luis E. and Ángel Weruaga Prieto (eds.), *Historia de la Universidad de Salamanca. Indice y figuras*, vol. 5, Salamanca 2018.

Rouse, Richard H. and Mary A. Rouse, "Statim invenire. Schools, Preachers, and New Attitudes to the Page", in Benson, Robert L. and Giles Constable (eds.), *Renaissance and Renewal in the Twelfth Century*, Cambridge, MA 1982, 201–225.

Rubach, Birte, *Ant. Lafreri Formis Romae. Der Verleger Antonio Lafreri und seine Druckgraphikproduktion*, Berlin 2016.

Ruiz Fidalgo, Lorenzo, *La imprenta en Salamanca (1501–1600)*, vol. 1/3, Madrid 1994.

Serrão, Joaquim Veríssimo, "Portugueses no Estudo de Salamanca (1250–1550)", in *Revista da Faculdade de Letras*, 3ª série, 5 (1962), 1–515.

Silva, António Pereira da, "A primeira suma portuguesa de teologia moral e sua relação com o «Manual» de Navarro", in *Didaskalia* 5:2 (1975), 355–403.

Simón Díaz, José, *El libro español antiguo*, Madrid 2000.

Solinas Quijada, Francisco, "El doctor Martín de Azpilcueta en la Universidad de Coímbra", in *Principe de Viana* 47 (1986), 609–640.

Tejero, Eloy, "Martín de Azpilcueta en la historia de la doctrina canónica y moral", in *Ius Canonicum* 27:54 (1987), 425–492.

Tejero, Eloy, "Martín de Azpilcueta cinco veces universitario", in Linehan, Peter (ed.), *Life, Law and Letter: Historical Studies in Honour of Antonio García y García*, Roma 1998, 839–862.

Tejero Tejero, Eloy, "Azpilcueta, Martín de", in Real Academia de la Historia (ed.), *Diccionario biográfico español*, vol. 6: *De 'Asuero Sáenz de Cenzano' a 'Barco y Gasca'*, Madrid 2009, 430–433.

Tentler, Thomas N., *Sin and Confession in the Eve of the Reformation*, Princeton, NJ 1977.

Turrini, Miriam, *La coscienza e le leggi. Morale e diritto nei testi per la confessione della prima età moderna*, Bologna 1991.

Waquet, Françoise, *Latin or the Empire of a Sign. From the Sixteenth to the Twentieth Century*, trans. John Howe, London 2001.

Xavier, Ângela Barreto, "Itinerários Franciscanos na Índia Seiscentista e algumas questões de história e de método", in *Lusitânia Sacra*, 2ª série, 18 (2016), 87–116.

CHAPTER 7

Pragmatic or Heretic? Editing Catechisms in Mexico in the Age of Discoveries and Reformation (1539–1547)

José Luis Egío

1 Introduction: Paleochristian *passéisme*, Pragmatic Simplicity and Concerns for Orthodoxy in the First American Catechisms

The path toward the definition and implementation of specific points of orthodoxy in the catechetical literature developed for the Early Modern Americas has been studied at length by a number of scholars (Saranyana,[1] Borges,[2] Estenssoro Fuchs,[3] Roulet,[4] Duve,[5] etc.). While the first catechisms and manuals of piety that were used to instruct native Americans in the Christian religion were the result of the individual initiatives of bishops and friars, by the middle of the sixteenth century, responding to the growing concerns about the potential spread of Protestant ideas in the New World and about probable indigenous misunderstandings as to orthodoxy, major steps were taken in order to develop precise and orthodox instruments of indoctrination. The specificities of the missionary context in the Americas, apparently requiring the standardisation of evangelisation tools (catechisms,[6] manuals

1 Saranyana (ed.), *Teología en América Latina*, vol. 1, chapters I–VI, 35–255; Saranyana, "Métodos de catequización".

2 Borges, "Métodos de persuasion" and Borges, "La nueva cristiandad indiana", 573–613.

3 Estenssoro, *Del paganismo a la santidad.*

4 Roulet, *L'évangelisation des Indiens du Mexique*, chapters III & IV, 59–107.

5 Duve, "Catequesis y derecho canónico entre el Viejo y el Nuevo Mundo", 131–145.

6 The historiography on catechetical materials does not always apply homogeneous criteria while classifying the different subgenres of this important field in religious literature. Confusion is prevalent, especially when dealing with *doctrinas* and *catecismos*. While Gil tries to distinguish carefully between *doctrinas* and *catecismos*, Resines considers "ambos términos como equivalentes, pues el uso ha determinado un empleo indistinto". Gil, *Primeras "doctrinas" del Nuevo Mundo*, 275–278; Resines, *Catecismos Americanos del siglo XVI*, vol. 1, 22. In general terms, catechisms have a dialogical structure, that is to say, the exposition is ordered by a series of questions and answers which helps the catechumen to learn the contents by heart. By contrast, with doctrines, the ideas are communicated unilaterally. Nevertheless,

for confessors, prayer books, etc.), converged in the 1550s with a general trend in the Spanish Empire toward the definition of a religious orthodoxy constructed against Protestant and some Erasmian conceptions which had gained great influence in the Spanish universities, Church, cultural circles[7] and even among some of the closest advisers of Charles V (Mercurino Gattinara, Alfonso de Valdés, etc.).[8]

A parallel impulse toward the standardisation of this kind of religious literature came from Rome as well, where, as is well known, shortly after the conclusion of the Council of Trent and following its resolutions, an official catechism was written and approved (1566).[9] For the first time, the popular instruction of Christianity was meticulously and authoritatively established and fixed. This measure had a major impact in the Spanish American dioceses. In fact,

---

this formal denomination does not appear to be clear even for the writers of these different subgenres in the Late-Mediaeval and Early Modern periods, such that no distinction will be made between *catecismos* and *doctrinas* in this present contribution. A conditioning element could be the fact that it is relatively common for a particular book to include contents presented in the form of a *doctrina* as well as in the style of a *catecismo* and, beyond that, even including parts laid out as per other pastoral subgenres (*confesionarios, tratados de oración, artes del buen morir*, etc.). This kind of assembly of heterogeneous materials – which, in fact, made up a kind of manual for priests and missionaries – used to be published under a vague, general title (*Doctrina Cristiana, Regla Cristiana, Libro de la Doctrina Cristiana, Suma de Doctrina Cristiana, Catecismo*, etc.). The very complex *Regla cristiana breve* edited by Juan de Zumárraga – the first Archbishop of Mexico – in 1547 is an illustrative example of this cumulative logic, Zumárraga, *Regla christiana breve*. For the American context, subgenres such as the indigenous vocabularies and *artes de la lengua* are also common components of this kind of catechetical literature. See Zwartjes (ed.), *Las gramáticas misioneras de tradición hispánica (siglos XVI–XVII)*.

7 By the 1520s, not only the humanist University of Alcalá and distinguished teachers at the University of Salamanca such us Nebrija and the Vergara brothers, but also the most prominent Churchmen in Spain, the archbishop of Toledo Alonso de Fonseca and the General Inquisitor, Alonso Manrique, were open sympathisers of Erasmus. After Manrique's fall in disgrace, the Spanish followers of Erasmus began to be prosecuted, accused of being closet supporters of Luther. The increasing repression and confusion of Erasmian and Protestant ideas led to the prohibition of Erasmus' writings in the Spanish *Index* of 1559 (following the criteria adopted by the Roman Inquisition that same year). For a classic perspective on the *Erasmian decades* (1520s–1550s) in Spain, see Kamen, *The Spanish Inquisition*, chapter 3.

8 The experts on the topic are divided between those who consider Erasmus and Valdés as relevant guiding figures in Carlos V's entourage and those who, reducing the importance of religious and ideological principles, give more important to the strategic, military and economic probable motivations for Carlos' enterprises such as the famous *Sacco di Roma* (1527). A contemporary re-appraisal of this debate. Tubau, "Alfonso de Valdés y la política imperial del canciller Gattinara", 17–43.

9 *Catechismus Ex Decreto SS. Concilii Tridentini ad Parochos.*

catechetical materials inspired in the *Roman catechism* of 1566 were approved by most provincial councils and local synods.[10]

The converging dynamic, to which the scholars mentioned above referred in a long diachronic perspective, can also be seen from a synchronic point of view. In fact, if one avoids a teleological perspective regarding the whole process of catechetical uniformisation – taking the Council of Trent, the Spanish and Roman prohibition on Erasmus' writings (1559) and the strengthening of the Spanish Inquisition in the second half of sixteenth century as key explanatory events and predetermined goals – another kind of intriguing convergence can be detected.

On the one hand, the motivations of the different missionary agents, which seem to converge in the significant period between the 1530s and 1540s (the period in which the first serious steps to teach the Gospel to the native Americans were taken),[11] involved the need for brevity and paedagogical simplification, features belonging to catechisms and, in general terms, to all pragmatic religious literature. Even so, the encounter with the *rustic* populations of the Americas led the promoters of their Christianisation to go one step further in the traditional quest for the simplicity that characterises catechetical literature.[12] Given the many uncertainties as to the intellectual capacity of the natives[13] and their own ability to teach the complex mysteries of the Christian

10 A general perspective in Duve, "Catequesis y derecho canónico entre el Viejo y el Nuevo Mundo", 136–140.

11 After the first three decades of Spanish presence in the New World, characterised by an almost purely rhetorical use of Christianity as a set of ideological arguments justifying the war on, plundering and enslavement of the Amerindian populations. According to testimonies of this period such as the chronicles of Gonzalo Fernández de Oviedo, the conversions to Christianism in this period cannot be properly considered as true conversions, given that they were obtained either by force or after a superficial and multitudinous administration of baptism. "É assi parésçeme á mí que para esta creencia desta gente nuevamente allegada á la iglesia, que es más menester de baptiçarlos é dexarlos, pues que sin creer, como lo diçe la mesma verdad evangélica, no se pueden salvar, sino condenar", Fernández de Oviedo, *Historia general y natural*, Section Three, lib. XLII, cap. III, 60.

12 It is important to mention that this kind of catechetical literature was also in vogue in Europe and the Iberian Peninsula just in the period in which the early evangelisation of America took place. See Duve, "Catequesis y derecho canónico entre el Viejo y el Nuevo Mundo", 135.

13 Uncertainties that, until this period, remained even among those who are usually regarded as the most outspoken defenders of the indigenous populations. The case of Vitoria, who, in his *Relectio De Indis prior* (1539), did not manage to give a definite opinion about the supposed mental incapacity of the Indians, is paradigmatic. An English translation in Vitoria, *On the American Indians*, eds. Lawrance and Pagden, Q. 3, Art. 8, § 18, 290–291.

faith in a multitude of unknown, still unwritten, languages,[14] the missionaries were forced to reflect carefully on what the vital essence of the Christian faith at its most basic was. Any possible solution to this catechetical dilemma had to take into account not only the most salvific dogmas and practices but also to envisage, from a pragmatic point of view, which of these eternal truths could be easily communicated.

Looking beyond the American context, just in the decades in which the transcendental choices regarding the Christianisation of the native Americans were to be made, the debate as to what was essential and what were but "human inventions"[15] corrupting Christianity was at its height. In this period, Protestants and Erasmians shared a strong desire to return to a primitive Church, an ideal Church that both of them conceived as essentially simple and pure, standing as such in complete opposition to the corrupt and deformed Church of the era.

As this chapter shows, the ideals of pragmatic simplicity and reformed purification – counterbalanced by the need to maintain a certain distance from the intentionally schismatic approach of the Protestants – came together to establish an uneasy, fragile, short-lived but extremely interesting alliance until the second half of the sixteenth century. Focusing on the Peruvian context, Estenssoro has referred – in other terms – to this problematic alliance as one of the main challenges neglected by previous scholars and which has still to be covered in the historiography regarding catechetical literature.[16] In their books about the missionary strategies and administration of the sacraments in early colonial Mexico, classic scholars such as Robert Ricard[17] and contemporary ones such as Osvaldo Pardo,[18] have also called attention to the way in which these converging but somehow contradictory motivations, polarised the Mendicants when they attempted to define the minimal knowledge that penitents or candidates for baptism had to prove before obtaining absolution or being permitted to receive the first sacrament of the Church. Nevertheless, the

14 See Durston, *Pastoral Quechua. The History of Christian Translation in Colonial Peru, 1550–1650*; Valdeón, *Translation and the Spanish Empire in the Americas*, 111–113.

15 The famous *Institutio Christianae Religionis* of Jean Calvin was published in Latin in 1536 and in French in 1541. Even more than in Luther, the writings of the Genevan reformer show a radical opposition between the true and the false Church, the pure words of God Himself and human idolatrous inventions. Calvin's virulent opinion on this issue can be found in Calvin, *Institution de la religion Chrestienne*, chapter XIII, "Des traditions humaines".

16 Estenssoro, *Del paganismo a la santidad*, 32.

17 Ricard, *La conquista espiritual de México*.

18 Pardo, *The Origins of Mexican Catholicism*, 6–8.

general approach of Ricard and Pardo, trying to synthesize many controversial arguments on baptism, confirmation, penance, confession and the Eucharist having taken place throughout the *long* sixteenth century, led them to review only in passing the concrete collocation of the above-mentioned ideals in the Mexican catechetical literature.

Considering the absence of an intellectual in-depth analysis of the first Mexican doctrines comparable[19] to the works that Estenssoro dedicated to their Peruvian equivalents, this chapter will cover how the ideals of pragmatic simplicity, restoration of the early Church and defence of orthodoxy against the schismatic converge in the short doctrines edited by bishop Juan de Zumárraga in the period of 1539–1547.

2 The Triumphant and Pure Primitive Church. Translation of an Ideal into Mexico by Juan de Zumárraga

Among the catechetical materials developed in America in the first half of 16th century, Zumárraga's doctrines figure among the better examples of this convergence of epochal motivations. First bishop of the diocesis of Mexico and former Franciscan friar, Juan de Zumárraga, is a well-known and well-studied figure.[20] He arrived in Mexico in December of 1528,[21] was consecrated bishop in 1533 (even if he was acting *de facto* as a bishop before his official consecration) and, shortly before his death (1548), was appointed archbishop after the elevation of the Mexican diocese to the category of archdiocese. Zumárraga was responsible for a missionary policy in which the destructive dimension (the bishop took an active role in the demolition and transformation of

19 With regard to the early Mexican doctrines, reliance has, in this contribution, been placed on the important, but, nevertheless, very descriptive studies of scholars such as Gil, *Primeras "doctrinas" del Nuevo Mundo*; Resines, *Catecismos Americanos del siglo XVI*, vol. 1; Saranyana (ed.), *Teología en América Latina*, vol. 1; Alejos-Grau, *Juan de Zumárraga y su "Regla Cristiana breve"*; Medina, *Doctrina cristiana para instrucción de los Indios*; Guillermo Durán, *Monumenta catechetica hispanoamericana (siglos XVI–XVIII)*, 3 vols.; Mira Mira, *Estudio histórico-genético de la "Doctrina breve" (1543–44) de Juan de Zumárraga*; Adeva Martín, "Fray Juan de Zumárraga: Regla Cristiana Breve".

20 See García Icazbalceta, *Don Fray Juan de Zumárraga. Primer obispo y arzobispo de México*, 4 vols.; Greenleaf, *Zumárraga and the Mexican Inquisition, 1536–1543*; Greenleaf and Kaveny, *Zumárraga and his family: letters to Vizcaya 1536–1548*.

21 García Icazbalceta, *Don Fray Juan de Zumárraga. Primer obispo y arzobispo de México*, vol. 1, 34; AGI, México, 1088, L.1, fols. 31v–33v.

temples, burning of codices and annihilation of items related to pre-Hispanic religions)[22] was as important as the creative one.

A very widespread attitude toward Zumárraga's religious commitment is to consider it as a "celo exagerado por mantener la pureza de una religión que apenas se estaba introduciendo en estas partes del mundo". From this perspective, such zeal is regarded as deeply Spanish and closely linked to a caricatured fanaticism "de la España de aquella época" fuelled by the victory over the Muslims of Granada.[23] It is arguable that this historiographical perspective ignores the great complexity of the Spanish and European religious landscape in the first half of the sixteenth century and does not take into account that Zumárraga's *zeal* had little to do with an Andalusian context far away from his experience and motivations. It should, rather, be related to the general trend toward a purer and more authentic Christianity to which many men of this time adhered.

Being a tireless denouncer of the thefts and abuses that unscrupulous friars, churchmen and laymen carried out in his diocese, Zumárraga, longing, after a very idealised fashion, for the discipline prevalent in the early Church, came into contact with Francisco de Vitoria, the famous theology professor at the University of Salamanca, asking him – through Charles V – to make a personal selection from among his more virtuous pupils of twelve *apostles* for the New World[24] and praised the strong discipline that only the Carthusians – faithful custodians of the "santas antigüedades de la Iglesia" – among his contemporaries seemed to respect.[25] It is interesting that, in his disciplinary denunciations,

---

22 Ricard, *La conquista espiritual de México*, 96–108; Greenleaf, *Zumárraga and the Mexican Inquisition, 1536–1543*.

23 Romero Galván, "Review of Sonia Corcuera de Mancera, *De pícaros y malqueridos*", 15–17.

24 "Real Cédula al maestro Fray Francisco de Vitoria, catedrático de Prima en la Universidad de Salamanca, dándole cuenta de que el obispo de México ha escrito que en aquella tierra hay necesidad de clérigos para instruir y convertir a los indios, y que ha sabido que él tiene buenos discípulos, entre los que debe escoger doce, a los que se les proveerá en Sevilla de pasaje y matalotaje para ir a aquellas tierras", 18 April 1539, AGI, Indiferente, 423, L.19, fols. 234v–235r. Edited by Beltrán de Heredia, *Los manuscritos del Maestro Fray Francisco de Vitoria O.P.*, 163.

25 "¡Oh bendita religión, donde los ojos que desean no ver del todo desterradas las santas antigüedades de la Iglesia y hallar algún rastro de ellas, las pueden hallar y ver conservadas como en su primera institución!". "Edicto del obispo Zumárraga exhortando a los vecinos de México a que asistan a la Iglesia". In: García Icazbalceta, *Don Fray Juan de Zumárraga. Primer obispo y arzobispo de México*, vol. 4, n. 28, 266, 269–270. Zumárraga's admiration for the Cartusian discipline and for members of this order such as Denis van Ryckel led him to order the printing of a *Compendio breve que tracta dela manera de como se han de hazer las processiones: compuesto por Dionisio Rickel cartuxano* in 1544.

Zumárraga often blames the instituted Roman Church for its chicanery and the growing contradictory legislation conceding privileges and dispensations regarding even the most elementary "tradiciones santas" of the Ancient Church.[26]

Zumárraga's *passéisme* had not only a disciplinary dimension but was also at the core of his missionary commitment, which drew on the affinity that, from his perspective, existed between the theological condition of the Amerindians and the pagans of apostolic times. To a similar challenge, a similar response: according to Zumárraga, the better catechetical materials were to be found in the historical heritage of the Church, conveniently cleansed of any kind of innovations and excrescences. Zumárraga edited this religious patrimony in several *doctrinas* printed in Mexico between 1539 and 1547, only some of which have survived.[27] The doctrines in which Zumárraga

---

The contemporary Spanish American historiography tends to underscore the influence exerted by late mediaeval mystics such as Denis the Carthusian on Zumárraga's thinking in the context of the reforms launched by Cisneros to impose a strict observance among the Franciscan friars. Josep Ignasi Saranyana, "El impulso editorial de Juan de Zumárraga y sus denuncias proféticas", in Saranyana (ed.), *Teología en América Latina*, vol. 1, 49–55; "Evaluación del 'erasmismo' de Zumárraga", in Gil, *Primeras "doctrinas" del Nuevo Mundo*, 374–384; Alejos-Grau, *Juan de Zumárraga y su "Regla Cristiana breve"*, 62; Guillermo Durán, *Monumenta catechetica hispanoamericana (siglos XVI–XVIII)*, vol. 2, 97. The writings on this matter of Saranyana, Durán, Gil and Alejos Grau seem to be motivated by an explicit will to counter the most widespread French and Anglo-Saxon perspective of an Erasmian Zumárraga, which, in the Spanish American context, was strongly supported in several publications of Almoina, "El erasmismo de Zumárraga"; Almoina, "Introducción". This polemic, a kind of post-mortem trial of Zumárraga's orthodoxy, seems quite sterile. Both influences – late mediaeval mysticism and Erasmian new / old motifs seem to have exercised equal influence on Zumárraga.

26 For example, in the exhortation he addressed to the *vecinos* of Mexico asking them to attend the Church more often, he complains pointedly of the legislation related to private chapels: "[…] en esta nuestra infelicísima edad, en que la soberbia humana y regalo corporal ha ensanchado mucho sus leyes y costumbres con gran derogación de las tradiciones santas que los santísimos padres antiguos hicieron en las cortes que el Espíritu Santo celebró en los concilios de la Iglesia Católica", García Icazbalceta, *Don Fray Juan de Zumárraga. Primer obispo y arzobispo de México*, vol. 4, n. 28, 270.

27 No copies of a *Doctrina cristiana breve para enseñanza de los niños* and a *Doctrina cristiana por preguntas y respuestas* have been preserved, see Wilkinson (ed.), *Iberian Books*, 770. The same would have happened with two other doctrines: First, a *Breve y más compendiosa doctrina christiana en lengua mexicana y castellana* (1539), mentioned by Fernando Gil in his rewriting of the bibliographical repertoires of Icazbalceta and Medina; see Gil, *Primeras "doctrinas" del Nuevo Mundo*, 284–313. Second, a *Doctrina christiana: en que en suma se contiene todo lo principal y necessario que el Cristiano debe saber y obrar* (1545–1546), considered by Resines as the first edition of the later *Doctrina*

played a greater role are the following: *Doctrina cristiana para instrucion y información de los indios: por manera de historia* (1544),[28] *Doctrina breve muy provechosa* (1543–44),[29] *Doctrina christiana mas cierta y verdadera para gente sin erudicion y letras* (1546)[30] and *Regla christiana breve* (1547).[31] Other important catechetical books, such as the influential *Doctrina christiana breve traduzida en lengua Mexicana* (1546)[32] by Alonso de Molina, re-edited on several occasions, were not the work of Zumárraga himself but came to be printed thanks to the explicit support of the bishop. We find echoes of Zumárraga's commitment with his pastoral and formative duties even after his death (1548) and in regions far away from Mexico. For example, as late as 1552, the Dominican Diego Ximénez published in Lisbon an *Enchiridion o Manual de Doctrina Christiana* initially conceived as a doctrine for the Mexican "sheep". According to the foreword of its author, he had begun to write this doctrine in 1541 on request from Zumárraga, assisted by "other friends and bishops from New Spain".[33]

---

cristiana más cierta y verdadera para gente sin erudicion y letras; seeResines, *Catecismos Americanos del siglo XVI*, vol. 2, 409–420. From a *Manual de adultos* printed in 1540 – the very first book published in the New World – only three pages have survived, BNE, R/29333. The website of the Project *Primeros libros de las Américas* (www.primeroslibros.org) also includes some pages of a very synthetic *Cartilla para la enseñanza de la doctrina cristiana en lengua zotzil, latina y castellana*, [México?], [Juan Pablos?], [1547?], which may have been published during Zumárraga's episcopacy. The developers of this ambitious digital library have helped to discard some erroneous data and interpretations found in Gil. For example, it is now clear that the *Doctrina Cristiana in lengua Mexicana* written by Pedro de Gante (1553) was not published during the lifetime of Zumárraga, but rather slightly thereafter.

28 Córdoba, Zumárraga and Betanzos, *Doctrina cristiana para instrucion y información de los indios: por manera de historia.*

29 Zumárraga, *Doctrina breve muy provechosa.*

30 Zumárraga, *Doctrina cristiana: mas cierta y verdadera para gente sin erudicion y letra.*

31 Zumárraga, *Regla christiana breve.*

32 The first pages of these books use to mention that they were printed "por mandado" of Zumárraga. It is the case for Alonso de Molina's doctrine and for the second edition of Pedro de Córdoba's doctrine (1548), a bilingual Castilian-Náhuatl edition of the text that Zumárraga had amended and edited in 1544. Córdoba, Zumárraga and Betanzos, *Declaracion y exposicion de la doctrina christiana en lengua española y Mexicana.* Molina, *Doctrina christiana breve traduzida en lengua Mexicana.*

33 It would be a Herculean task to undertake a thorough and exhaustive search of every one of the doctrines resulting from the firm commitment of Zumárraga. I am very grateful to Manuela Bragagnolo for this curious and telling reference. Ximénez, *Enchiridion o Manual de doctrina christiana*, "Prologo del autor", fol. ✠iiir.

3 The Rewriting of Pedro de Córdoba's Caribbean doctrine, "breve y llana" (1544)

Even if the *Doctrina cristiana para instrucion y informacion de los indios: por manera de historia* (1544) is not usually studied as a substantial part of Zumárraga's catechetical effort,[34] but rather as the printed version of Pedro de Córdoba's and other early Dominican missionaries' perspective,[35] it is clear that, in the twenty-three years following Córdoba's death (1521), many interventions on the part of later Dominican friars – especially, from the province of Santiago de México, Domingo de Betanzos – and of the zealous bishop Juan de Zumárraga contributed to modifications to Cordoba's catechetical legacy. This hypothesis is corroborated by the source itself. In fact, a deeper look into this early *doctrina* – beyond the front pages from which the authors of bibliographical repertoires used to source the information for their accounts – permits the discovery of explicit mentions of the important role played by Betanzos and Zumárraga. In the colophon, it is stated that both of them added "algunas cosas" to the materials used by the Dominican friars to indoctrinate the natives in the Caribbean.[36] Zumárraga's shadow glides over this colophon: he requests "por caridad" of the members of the Orders that they should work on the instruction and conversion of the natives and on the translation into the "lenguas de indios" of this same doctrine. Zumárraga also clarifies the role that the book should play among the different catechetical initiatives that he had launched. While this brief doctrine was very appropriate for preaching to "incipient" catechumens, "the other one", together with the *Tripartito* of John Gerson, would satisfy the special needs of "proficient" neophytes. What *doctrina* this "other one" could, be is still a matter of discussion among scholars. It is arguable that Zumárraga could only be referring to the *Doctrina breve muy provechosa.* Despite its misleading title, it was much longer than the *Doctrina cristiana para instrucion y informacion de los indios,*

34 For instance, Gil dedicates to this book only three descriptive pages of his monograph on Zumárraga's writings, Gil, *Primeras "doctrinas" del Nuevo Mundo*, 294–296.

35 See Guillermo Durán, *Monumenta catechetica hispanoamericana (siglos XVI–XVIII)*, vol. 1, 198–201 and the introductory study to another contemporary edition by Medina, *Doctrina cristiana para instrucción de los Indios.*

36 The colophon of the *Doctrina cristiana para instrucion y informacion de los indios* states: "[…] aquí se acaba la presente doctrina que los padres de la orden de sancto Domingo en principio nombrados ordenaron para el catecismo e instrucion de los indios […]. Y va mas declarada y en algunas cosas añadida por los muy reverendos padres el Obispo de mexico y fray Domingo de betanços".

which was printed this same year,[37] as was the *Tripartito del cristianísimo y consolatorio doctor Juan Gerson de doctrina cristiana*,[38] to which Zumárraga also refers to in the colophon.

Zumárraga does not appeal to the conclusions of a certain *Junta*[39] while justifying the imposition of this sole doctrine. With the warning and rebuking tone to which he would resort in later *doctrinas* – evoking Erasmus to justify his position – he insists on some of the objective pragmatic criteria that were behind his choice:

> El qual [Zumárraga, who had covered the publication expenses] pide y ruega mucho a los padres religiosos que entienden en la instrucion y conversión delos indios: ante todas cosas procuren de les predicar y hazer entender esta doctrina breve y llana: pues conocen su

37 For the purposes of this contribution, Durán's hypothesis is followed. He considers the *Doctrina breve* of 1543–1544 as the doctrine for proficient catechumens, arguing that "es una exposición igualmente sencilla, escrita en estilo llano para común inteligencia, pero su contenido es más denso y sistemático", Guillermo Durán, *Monumenta catechetica hispanoamericana (siglos XVI–XVIII)*, vol. 1, 208. The scholars who put aside the reworking of Córdoba's doctrine from the ensemble of Zumárraga's catechetical initiatives are usually led to confusion by the title of the books. "La *Doctrina breve* (1544), serviría para el primer nivel o principiantes; la *Doctrina Cristiana y su suplemento* (1546), para el segundo nivel, que sería el de los que ya se habían bautizado o se preparaban para ello; y la *Regla cristiana* (1548), para los adelantados o proficientes", Soto Guerrero, *La "Iglesia" en los catecismos mexicanos del siglo XVI editados en México*, 16.

38 Gerson and Zumárraga, *Tripartito del cristianísimo y consolatorio doctor Juan Gerson de doctrina cristiana.*

39 From 1524 to 1546, at least twelve ecclesiastical *Juntas* (meetings of bishops, provincials of mendicant orders and other prominent Churchmen) were held in Mexico. See Saranyana (ed.), *Teología en América Latina*, vol. 1, 93–113. It is common to interpret the doctrines as results of the agreements reached by these *Juntas* as to the way to indoctrinate the natives. Nevertheless, the relationship between the agreements reached by these early meetings of bishops and the catechisms printed in Mexico in the 1540s and the 1550s is not as clear as the one existing between the later Councils in Mexico and Lima and the *official* doctrines that were printed afterwards. Only the colophon of the *Manual de adultos* printed in 1540 states explicitly that the book was financed by the bishops of New Spain and printed by their order, probably following the agreements of the *junta* of 1539 regarding the way and tools to be used in the catechesis of the natives. "Imprimiose este Manual de Adultos en la gran ciudad de Mexico por mandado de los Reverendissimos Señores Obispos de la Nueva España y a sus expensas: en casa de Juan Cromberger. Agno de nacimiento de nuestro señor JesuChristo de mill y quinientos y quarenta. A. xiii. Dias del mes de Deziembre", *Manual de adultos*, [n.p.]. See Gil, *Primeras "doctrinas" del Nuevo Mundo*, 227–229. The other pieces of catechetical literature that are mentioned in this chapter were promoted and financed by the exclusive contribution of Zumárraga, who consequently left his personal and spiritual mark on almost every one of these books.

> capacidad: y que tienen mas necesidad della que de otros sermones que seles predican.[40]

As can be seen, in this first catechetical initiative of 1544, with the printing of a revised edition of the Caribbean doctrine of the Dominicans, Zumárraga is appealing to the need to avoid fancy and motley sermons in favour of focusing on the main articles of the Christian faith related to God and to the humanity of Christ, the Ten Commandments, the seven sacraments, corporal and spiritual works of mercy, main prayers and the rituals of the sign of the Cross – these being the "simple" but "salvific" contents of this *Doctrina cristiana para instrucion y informacion de los indios*. The articles of the faith are introduced by a kind of history of the world since its creation. The chronological and logical order of the narrative is intended to facilitate the assimilation of the doctrines by the natives in a rational and coherent manner (not relying only on a dogmatic learning by heart).[41] It is noteworthy that, even if the natives of New Spain were supposed to be more civilised and intelligent than the *taínos* and other Antillean peoples,[42] Zumárraga made no distinction between them, taking it for granted that they all had in common a low intellectual capacity, insofar, at least, as catechetical methods and indoctrination strategies were concerned. From his perspective, the "brief and plain" doctrine that Pedro de Córboba "de Buena memoria" and his fellow Dominicans had first taught during the foundation period "de la orden de los Predicadores en las yslas del mar Oceano" was still valid and equally useful and proper for the missionaries in continental America. In this case, there is a perfect convergence between Zumárraga's

40 Córdoba, Zumárraga and Betanzos, *Doctrina cristiana para instrucion y información de los indios: por manera de historia*, colophon [n.p.].

41 Following closely some ideas of Borges, Miguel Ángel Medina also considers this method as according to the oral customs and idiosyncrasy of the natives, whose religious pre-Hispanic life was structured in mythical stories related to the origin of their gods (theogonies) and the world (cosmogonies), Medina, *Doctrina cristiana para instrucción de los Indios*, 94.

42 Opting for a methodological uniformity that later missionary agents will criticise. In his *De procuranda Indorum salute*, the Jesuit Acosta distinguishes among three "classes Barbarorum" according to the degree in which they exercise the "recta ratione" and follow the customs of humankind (law of nations). In Acosta sociocultural hierarchy, Mexicans and Peruvians are at a higher level than peoples considered to be composed of "homines sylvestres, feris similes" such as "Carybes", "Chunchos, Chiriguanas, Moxos, Iscaycingas", "Brasilienses" and natives from Florida. On the other hand, Mexicans and Peruvians are surpassed by the Chinese and Japanese. Acosta suggests a specific missionary approach for each of these levels of civilisation. Acosta, *De procuranda indorum salute*, "Prooemium", [n.p.].

aforementioned *passéisme*, his admiration for everything that could be considered a founding act and deed, and the increasingly pragmatic attitude that he would develop as a result of the specific missionary challenges he had faced as first bishop in the diocese of Mexico.

4 Erasmus' *Paraclesis* as Pragmatic Manifesto for the Americas: the *Doctrina Breve muy Provechosa* (1543–1544)

As previously noted, the *Doctrina breve muy provechosa* is much longer than the reworking of Pedro de Córdoba's catechetical materials: lengthy explanations of the fourteen articles of the faith, the seven sacraments, the Ten Commandments, another four commandments of the Church and "del derecho comun", the seven mortal sins, the fourteen works of mercy, the five senses and the three faculties of the soul along with their corresponding virtues are included.[43] Not only the seven sacraments, but also the articles of the faith that, in this period, were discussed by the early reformers or by heterodox Spanish theologians such as Miguel Servet (Mary's virginity and Jesus' conception "sin manzilla por nueva manera de concepción maravillosa y sobre natural",[44] the Trinity,[45] purgatory,[46] etc.) are explained in detail in this 84-folio doctrine.[47]

Despite the detailed character of this early *Doctrina breve muy provechosa*, Zumárraga urges the missionary agents operating in Mexico in a final "Conclusion exortatoria de la obra" to preach the Christian doctrine in the purest and simplest manner, taking the straightforward but salutary and infallible teaching of Jesus as the sole basis of their preaching, and to avoid the subtleties distilled by contemporary theologians and ancient philosophers.[48] Following the idealised perspective – very widespread at this time – on the self-evident and

43 Zumárraga, *Doctrina breve muy provechosa*, [n.p.].

44 Zumárraga, *Doctrina breve muy provechosa*, fol. aIVr.

45 Zumárraga, *Doctrina breve muy provechosa*, fol. aIIIv.

46 Zumárraga, *Doctrina breve muy provechosa*, fol. aVIv.

47 A full bibliographic record and a very detailed analysis of its structure in Gil, *Primeras "doctrinas" del Nuevo Mundo*, 313–329 and 388–410.

48 Zumárraga regards with suspicion not only theological and philosophical knowledge, but also that of lawyers and, in general terms, all non-biblical sources. In the *Doctrina breve muy provechosa* he interrogates his readers in a very rhetorical way: "Porque dan algunos mayor parte de su vida a Avicena: y a Bartolo y Baldo que a los evangelios: Porque casi toda la vida entera de los hombres se gasta en leer scripturas y aprender sciencias y opiniones tan varias de hombres que entre si no concuerdan: y tan poca utilidad: y antes prejudiciales y dañosas para el anima", Zumárraga, *Doctrina breve muy provechosa*, "Conclusion exortatoria de la obra", [n.p.].

non-contradictory character of the doctrine of the Gospel, Zumárraga defines this knowledge as a "manjar simplicissimo", which is simultaneously the highest and the easiest one to be learnt from a few books and pure sources:

> [...] de unos poquitos libros como de fuentes muy claras la podamos sacar, y esto con muy menos trabajo, que sacariamos la doctrina de Aristotiles: de tantos y tan escabrosos libros: y de tanta multitud de comentarios: de interpretes: los quales jamas en uno concuerdan.[49]

As paragraphs such as this make clear, the pragmatic reasoning of Zumárraga is, in fact, a revision and adaptation to the Mexican missionary context of the famous *Paraclesis* of Erasmus, the exhortation written by the Dutch humanist in his 1516 bilingual edition (Greek / Latin) of the New Testament. Zumárraga simplifies Erasmus' *Paraclesis*, removing names and cultural references to Antiquity as well as the history of the Church found in the original text and in the translation into Castilian (1529) attributed to Alonso Fernández de Madrid,[50] but left intact its spirit.

Transposed into the American context, the original appeal of Erasmus' *Paraclesis* became even more intense as a kind of pragmatic manifesto wherein "simplicity" and "earthiness" are considered enhancers of a pure truth to be told in plain language comprehensible to the common people:

> Lo que principalmente deven dessear los que escriven es que la escriptura sea a Gloria de Jesuchristo: y convierta las animas de todos: y para este efecto ninguna necesidad ay de gentilezas ny retoricas: antes la via mas cierta por donde se alcança esto que yo al presente desseo hazer es por la misma verdad: la qual entonces es de mayor fuerça y vigor quando se dize con mas llaneza y simplicidad.[51]

While Erasmus had insisted on the premise that what could be called pragmatic teaching – a simple and solely Bible-based teaching of the Gospel – was what had permitted – in the time of the Apostles – the triumph of the Church over the Jews and pagans, Zumárraga aimed to transpose this victorious strategy into the new missionary field that was the Americas. Simplification, repetition and the exclusive use of the "plain language" of the Bible, avoiding the

49 Zumárraga, *Doctrina breve muy provechosa*, "Conclusion exortatoria de la obra", [n.p.].

50 "Paraclesis", in Erasmus, *Enquiridio o manual del cavallero cristiano*, 1529. See Martín Abad, *La imprenta en Alcalá de Henares*, vol. 3, 1364.

51 Zumárraga, *Doctrina breve muy provechosa*, "Conclusion exortatoria de la obra", [n.p.].

subtleties and nuances later introduced by theologians and doctors of other sciences, were, for Zumárraga, not only the tools that Christian Europe needed in its own process of re-evangelisation, but also those which the emerging Mexican Church would have to use in order to succeed in a context of "childlike" neophytes – "pequeñuelos", in the language of Zumárraga and many other churchmen of the time:

> [...] esta doctrina de JesuChristo a todos ygualmente se comunica, para los pequeños se abaxa y se haze pequeña conformandose con la capacidad dellos. Cria los como con leche: sufre los: recrea los, sostiene los [...]: porque esta doctrina alos pequeños es muy pequeña: y alos grandes mas que grande: ninguna hedad desecha: ni ningún genero: agora sea de hombre: agora de mujeres: ningún estado: y ninguna manera de gente.[52]

Even if the ideals of Erasmian simplicity and austere piety then in vogue appear as one of the main influences on Zumárraga's missionary strategy, it is important to consider that, within the cultural and religious framework to which Zumárraga belonged – the Franciscan order – Erasmism was probably not perceived as a disruptive innovation. More likely, Erasmus' disciplinary denunciations and apostolic nostalgia were seen by observant Franciscans such as Zumárraga as a reinvigoration of the spiritual current toward a return to the primitive Church that Francis of Assisi himself had supported as a preacher, missionary and reformer.[53] Within this long-term timeframe, the reputation earned by Erasmus of Rotterdam for wisdom could serve mostly as a learned confirmation of the simple nature of every salvific truth and piece of knowledge that Francis had preached during his lifetime. Assimilated into this long-term perspective, Erasmus' ideas were spread in Zumárraga's catechetical materials, which include not only the cultural translation of the *Paraclesis*, but also extended quotations and references to the *Enchiridion Militis Christiani* (1503) and others of Erasmus' writings.[54]

---

52 Zumárraga, *Doctrina breve muy provechosa*, "Conclusion exortatoria de la obra", [n.p.].

53 A classic perspective on the impact of the Franciscan spiritual currents in New Spain in: Rubial García, *Notas para el estudio del franciscanismo en Nueva España, 1523–1550*; For an extensive bibliographic account of Franciscan spirituality on the Iberian Peninsula until the late 15th century: Sáenz de Haro, "Franciscanismo y espiritualidad. Bibliografía".

54 On the Erasmian references in the *Doctrina breve* see Josep Ignasi Saranyana, "El impulso editorial de Juan de Zumárraga y sus denuncias proféticas", in Saranyana (ed.), *Teología en América Latina*, vol. 1, 51; Mira Mira, *Estudio histórico-genético de la "Doctrina breve" (1543–44) de Juan de Zumárraga*. For the *Regla cristiana breve*, see Alejos-Grau, *Juan de*

In his cultural translation[55] of the *Paraclesis*, Zumárraga did not limit himself to copying the Castilian translation attributed to Alonso Fernández de Madrid. While rephrasing the ambitious evangelical programme of Erasmus, directed at social groups to this point excluded from the reading and study of the Gospel – especially men from the lowest social classes (farmers, weavers, etc.) and women from every condition – Zumárraga omitted the original references to Turks and Saracens.[56]

Zumárraga, who, as bishop of Mexico, was not especially interested in the Mediterranean infidels, focused instead on the Native Americans as the essential objective of the missionary Church of his time:

> No apruevo la opinion de los que dizen que los ydiotas no leyessen en las divinas letras traduzidas enla lengua que el vulgo usa: porque JesuChristo lo que quiere es que sus secretos muy largamente se divulguen, y assi dessearia yo por cierto que qualquier mugercilla leyesse el Evangelio y las Epistolas de San Pablo. Y aun mas digo: que pluguiesse a Dios que estuviesen traduzidas en todas las lenguas de todos los del mundo: para que no solamente las leyesen los Indios: pero aun otras naciones barbaras: leer y conocer: porque no ay dubda sino que el primer escalon para la christiandad es conocella en alguna manera.[57]

Once again, it seems that the paedagogical religious appeals of Erasmus – idealistic to the point of the ridiculous while dealing with the kind of infidels to

---

Zumárraga y su "Regla Cristiana breve", 62; Adeva Martín, "Fray Juan de Zumárraga: Regla Cristiana Breve". See also Adeva Martín, "Estudio preliminar".

55 On the concept of cultural translation see Burke, "Cultures of Translation in Early Modern Europe". Duve and Foljanty have recently recommended the application of the conceptual framework developed by Burke in cultural studies within a juridical-normative perspective Duve, "European Legal History", 29–66; Foljanty, "Legal Transfers as Processes of Cultural Translation: On the Consequences of a Metaphor".

56 According to Erasmus' very idealistic perspective, Muslims could be more easily won over to the Christian cause having access to vernacular versions of the Gospel: "Dessearia yo por cierto que qualquier mugercilla leyesse el Evangelio, y las Epistolas de S. Pablo, y aun mas digo, que pluguiesse a Dios que estuviesen traduzidas en todas las lenguas de todos los del mundo, para que no solamente las leyesen los de Escocia, y los de Hibernia, pero para que aun los Turcos y los Moros las pudiessen leer y conocer, porque no ay duda, sino que el primer escalon para la Christiandad, es conocella en alguna manera", "Paraclesis", in Erasmus, *Enchiridion o Manual del Cauallero Christiano de D. Erasmo Roterodamo en romance*, 1555, fols. 193r–193v.

57 Erasmus, *Enchiridion o Manual del Cauallero Christiano de D. Erasmo Roterodamo en romance*, 1555, "Paraclesis".

be found in the European context of his time – is better suited to the Mexican context than to their original setting. While Jewish and Muslim rejection of the Christian religion could not be primarily considered as resulting from a lack of knowledge, but rather as a conscious opposition to a rival creed – an element that undermines the applicability of Erasmus' proposals in the European context – most of the Amerindian nations did not demonstrate any kind of open hostility to Christianity. As the theologians of this period stressed,[58] urging warlords to distinguish among types of infidels, native Americans were not open enemies of the Christian religion, but suffered instead from an invincible ignorance of the evangelical truth. Their infidelity was not, therefore, to be punished or fought, but rather cured with appropriate remedies. The translation of previous European catechetical materials and the publication of new doctrines in the languages of the Mexican natives – an initiative also launched by Zumárraga during his lifetime – figure among these remedies and are clearly related to the flourishing printing of this kind of pragmatic literature in the vernacular languages of the Americas.

5 So Simple? Radical Pragmatism and Protestant Silences in Zumárraga's Redrafting of De la Fuente's *Suma de doctrina christiana* (1545-1546)

Zumárraga's utopian republic of readers can be considered one of the attempted missionary strategies that the Roman, Spanish and American Church would discard not only within the context of the New World, but also with regard to the Iberian worshipers.[59] From the second half of the sixteenth century, other approaches would prevail, while the scriptural fixation of Zumárraga and other Erasmian churchmen too close to the Protestant *sola Scriptura* motto would be increasingly regarded as suspicious and untenable.

Among the first Spanish writers of catechetical literature to be arrested, put on trial and condemned by the Inquisition because of such a scriptural approach (in the years 1558–1560), the figure of Constantino de la Fuente, canon-magistral of the cathedral of Seville and court preacher, appears to be closely linked with the missionary perspective of Zumárraga. His life and writings have

58 Since the pioneer treatise *De dominio Regum Hispaniae super Indos* (1512), written by the Dominican friar Matías de Paz. Paz, *Del dominio de los Reyes de España sobre los indios*, 221.

59 See Rodríguez, *El Catecismo romano ante Felipe II y la Inquisición española*, 148–180.

been well studied in abundant and sometimes contradictory – with regard to the religious adherence of De la Fuente – literature.[60] For present purposes, it suffices to note that, before his fall from grace, he was the most prolific author of catechetical books in the Spain of his time.[61]

As is well known, among the *doctrinas* printed by Zumárraga in Mexico, there is also a kind of redrafting in a non-dialogical way of the *Suma de doctrina christiana* (1543) that Constantino de la Fuente had published three years before in Seville.[62] Zumárraga re-edited this *Suma* twice. In 1545–1546, he edited De la Fuente's *Suma* with almost the same title[63] and without major modifications (apart from the minor changes stemming from the adaptation of De la Fuente's dialogical catechism into a monologue, which is characteristic of the doctrines). In 1546, this first re-edition of De la Fuente's catechism was, in turn, re-edited by Zumárraga. A *Suplemento* of 38 pages was added to the 1545–46 edition. It is highly probable that, because of the notorious dogmatic and disciplinary omissions in De la Fuente's catechism to be analysed hereinafter, Zumárraga decided to address them directly, reducing some of the most important gaps and anticipating any kind of future criticism or censorship. The exact differences between these two Mexican re-editions of De la Fuente's catechism are not completely clear. The uncertainties regarding them will probably never be resolved owing to the loss in transit from Toledo to Madrid of the only copy of the 1545–46 edition. Nevertheless, according to the Mexican scholar and bibliographer García Icazbalceta, who acquired a transcription of some paragraphs of the preface, the colophon and the title sections of the book printed in 1545–46, there is some evidence that it was almost identical to

60 A recent overview of his writings and the literature on his person in Giesen, "Audacia y precaución".

61 Wilkinson lists the following titles: *Suma de doctrina christiana en que se contiene todo lo principal y necesario* (Seville, 1543, 1544, 1545, 1551; Antwerp, [1549]); *Catecismo cristiano* (Seville, 1547; Antwerp, 1556); *Doctrina christiana. Parte primera. De los artículos de la fe* (Seville, 1548); *Doctrina christiana en que esta comprehendida toda la informacion que pertenece al hombre que quiere server a Dios* (Antwerp, 1554–1555). Apart from these *doctrinas*, the rest of De la Fuente's literary production is also to be assigned to close subgenres of religious indoctrination, sermons and commentaries on Biblical psalms: *Sermon de nuestro redentor en el monte* (Seville, 1543, 1545 – edited together with the *Suma de doctrina christiana*); *Exposicion del primer psalmo de David* (Seville, 1546, 1548); *Exposición del salmo "Beatus Vir"* (Seville, 1547); *Exposicion del primer psalmus de Daniel* (Antwerp, 1556), Wilkinson (ed.), *Iberian Books*, 587–588.

62 De la Fuente, *Suma de doctrina christiana*.

63 Zumárraga, *Doctrina cristiana: en que en suma se contiene todo lo principal y necessario que el cristiano debe saber y obrar.*

the 1546 edition.[64] It seems that the only substantial change was the *Suplemento* and that Zumárraga opted for this kind of *ad hoc* tool instead of modifying or correcting De la Fuente's text line by line.

The sources, key ideas and, especially, De la Fuente's / Zumárraga's doctrinal omissions make these books much more problematic than the previous doctrines. The apologetic simplicity found in previous catechetical editions of Zumárraga are taken with these re-editions to an extreme in which it is difficult to distinguish the aforementioned pragmatic ideals from a conscious attempt to erase part of the dogmatic and disciplinary patrimony constructed by the Roman Church over centuries.

Omissions, silences and what a zealous reader could consider a contradiction or false expectations while contrasting the promissory title of the books – which explicitly indicates that it "contiene todo lo principal y necesario que el hombre cristiano debe saber y obrar" – and their *de facto* contents are at the core of the criticism aroused by De la Fuente's catechism.[65] It is probable that Zumárraga's doctrine also met with similar reproaches. It would be otherwise difficult to explain why, at the end of 1546, little after its first printing, Zumárraga felt himself compelled to prepare and order the printing of a second, revised edition of this same book. In any case, those precautions were not enough to put an end to any probable suspicion. It is, in fact, known that Zumárraga's unabashed enthusiasm for Erasmus and his call to translate the Bible into every language in the world attracted the attention of his follower in the archbishopric of Mexico, Alonso de Montúfar, who in November of 1559 – this same key

64 Contrasting the information he had received from one of his informants in Spain, Icazbalceta considered that, apart from the *Suplemento,* there was only a minor change – a slight rewording – in one of the paragraphs of the Preface. The contents of the two doctrines were laid out in the same order and even the foliation coincided, García Icazbalceta and Millares Carlo, *Bibliografía mexicana del siglo XVI*, 74–75.

65 The scholars who have dealt with the catechetical writings of De la Fuente himself, have been traditionally divided between those who consider this famous theologian and orator of 16th century Spain as a closet Lutheran (following the influential interpretation of Menéndez Pelayo and his *Historia de los heterodoxo sespañoles*), and the historiographical current which, taking into account the famous findings of Marcel Bataillon in his *Érasme et l'Espagne*, considers De la Fuente, Egidio and other Spanish heterodox religious thinkers of this time closer to Erasmus' ideas and followers of previous Spanish spiritual trends, the movement of the *alumbrados* being the most closely related. Among the most recent accounts on these conflicting interpretations: Pastore, *Una herejía española.* As it is the case for the debates concerning Zumárraga, such labelling and judgments reviewing are quite sterile. A fluid circulation of religious ideas culturally translated into different regions seems to be the dominant note until the end of the Council of Trent and the consolidation of the Christian schism.

turning point in the lives of De la Fuente and Carranza – was able to have those books condemned via a meeting of theologians held in Mexico.[66]

What De la Fuente considered the "breve sciencia" by which both learned and unlettered men had to abide in order to obtain salvation[67] was limited to the symbol and the articles of the faith, the Ten Commandments, the proper way to pray and some of the sacraments (baptism, penance and communion). De la Fuente's *Suma* does not mention the sacraments of confirmation, extreme unction, holy orders and marriage. The catechetical approach of the Sevillian canon-magistral implied a clear break with the systematic expositions of the seven sacraments that had become well established after Radulphus Ardens' *Speculum universale* (11th century), Peter Lombard's *Liber Sententiarum* (12th century), Aquinas' *Summa Theologiae* (13th century) and the conciliar validation of their positions in the Second Council of Lyons (1274)[68] and the later Council of Florence (1439).[69]

The exposition of the ninth article of the faith in the *Suma*, regarding belief in the Holy and Catholic Church could also lead to confusion and give rise to misunderstandings. The hierarchical structure of the Church is something that does not seem to be of interest to De la Fuente. The Church is defined as the "congregation" of the worshipers or as the "mystical body" that they form together with their head, Jesus Christ. With regard to the internal order of this Church, De la Fuente recognised only Christ as "cabeça" and established a minimal difference between "those who serve God" and other Christians.[70] The Pope is therefore another of the great absentees from the *Suma* and later from

66 AGN, Inquisición, vol. 43, exp. 4; *Libros y libreros en el siglo XVI*, ed. Fernández del Castillo, "Censura y prohibición de la *Doctrina cristiana* del Ilustrísimo Don Fray Juan de Zumárraga Obispo de México (1559)", doc. II, 1–2. Nesvig analysed this process in his book, but made a mistake when identifying the book(s) that were condemned by this Mexican *junta*, see Nesvig, *Ideology and Inquisition. The World of the Censors in Early Mexico*, 120–123. A later document from the Spanish Inquisition ("Libros mandados recoger en cumplimiento del Breve de Gregorio XIII de 1573", 1574, doc. X, 246) clarifies the matter and helps to discard other information provided by Nesvig, who erroneously states that the prohibition of Zumárraga's doctrine remained in force until 1579. As can be seen, the *Doctrina christiana* was in circulation again in the territory of New Spain from at least 1574.

67 "A esta breve sciencia se han de atener y con ella se han de salvar los profundos y muy fundados letrados. Y estas letras es menester que sepan sino se quieren perder los rusticos y simples hombres del mundo", De la Fuente, *Suma de doctrina christiana*, fol. ✠vr.

68 Neusner and Dupuis (eds.), *The Christian Faith in the Doctrinal Documents of the Catholic Church*, 19.

69 Bornstain, "Administering the sacraments"; Pardo, *The Origins of Mexican Catholicism*, 11–14.

70 De la Fuente, *Suma de doctrina christiana*, fols. lvv–lviiiv.

De la Fuente's doctrines. Systematic expositions regarding virtues and sins, weaknesses of body and soul and their corresponding works of mercy are also lacking in a catechism where the doctrine of justification by faith alone is stated with a certain rhetorical caution.[71]

As is to be expected, the explanation of the nature and meaning of the Mass is placed by De la Fuente outside the chapters dedicated to the sacraments. It is to be found later in the fifth and final section of the book.[72] With it being confined to a marginal position, the attentive reading of previous paragraphs of the *Suma* indicates that De la Fuente writes about the Mass reluctantly and in order to avoid immediate and certain *scandalum*.[73] Detached from the sacrament of the Eucharist, the Mass appears as a mere "representacion de la passion del redemptor del mundo". The transubstantiation or real presence of the body and blood of Jesus Christ is not mentioned or insinuated at all. With the Mass now deprived of its transcendent significance, the reading of the "doctrina de la epistola y del evangelio"[74] grows in importance. According to this *translatio studii*, the religious orientation provided by De la Fuente is concerned with the care and attention with which the worshipers are to hear the Mass. De la Fuente even recommends a previous individual or group reading "en romance" of the Biblical paragraph and epistle read during the Mass the following day.[75] The scriptural orientation of its teaching – very close, as noted, to Zumárraga's missionary perspective – is evident. From a philosophical and epistemic point of view, a *translatio sensuum* is also something to be considered. Hearing and sight replace the tasting experience associated with the Mass and with the sacrament of communion, an experience that orthodox catechisms regulated explicitly.[76]

71 For example, in the exposition of the first article of the faith: "De aquí es que quien yerra enlo principal dela fe, que es el verdadero conoscimiento de Dios, y en sentir verdadera y acertadamente del y de sus obras, va perdido, porque ha errado la puerta, y ningún camino ay, por donde no se pierda ni obras por donde se salve", De la Fuente, *Suma de doctrina christiana*, fol. xviiir.

72 De la Fuente, *Suma de doctrina christiana*, fols. ✠ivv–✠vr.

73 "Ambrosio: [...] Esta es la doctrina que mi maestro me dio acerca de este sacramento. Dyonisio. Bien se pudiera alargar enella y no se perdiera nada: mas su tiempo se verna. Y mucho mas aveys dicho de lo que pensays: porque vuestro maestro quiso daros essa materia, en que andando el tiempo vereys que teneys bien que pensar", De la Fuente, *Suma de doctrina christiana*, fol. clxr.

74 De la Fuente, *Suma de doctrina christiana*, fol. clxv.

75 De la Fuente, *Suma de doctrina christiana*, fols. clxv–clxir.

76 This is the case in Ripalda's famous catechism. Here, the "manjar espiritual" is no more the salvific knowledge of the Bible – as was it in the case of Erasmus, De la Fuente and Zumárraga – but the body and blood of Jesus Christ that the worshiper received in

Interestingly, while presenting his catechism in the prefatory letter addressed to the archbishop of Seville, García de Loaysa, De la Fuente appealed, precisely, to the need to be pragmatic – that is to speak "plain" and "simple", in the language of his time[77] – in order to transmit to the common man what was strictly necessary for salvation and to reach a wider illiterate public.

De la Fuente seems to rely, in fact, on pragmatism in order to justify a choice of the *ingredients* for redemption very similar, in fact, to the recipes that Luther and Calvin[78] – authors of relatively similar catechisms – had devised, appealing not only to these practical criteria, of lesser interest to both of them, but as an expurgatory and vehement denunciation of what they considered Roman adulterations of the ancient traditions and pure doctrine of the Church. For obvious reasons, this kind of criticism is mentioned only in passing in De la Fuente's introductory letters, almost completely reproduced in Zumárraga's *Doctrina cristiana mas cierta y verdadera*:

> Esta doctrina porque nadie la menosprecie ni tenga en poco: es la que la yglesia catholica en su principio enseñó con grandissimo cuidado a sus hijos. Esta era la predicacion de entonces: y lo que en las publicas y particulares congregaciones se trataba del negocio de JesuChristo redemptor y segnor del mundo. Aquí esta summado y recolegido todo lo que esta sembrado por las escripturas divinas [...].[79]

The last sentences lead the reader to consider De la Fuente's catechism as a kind of epitome of the Holy Scriptures themselves, the truth of which is not only distilled from the "ceguedades" and "variedad de docrinas" introduced

"real substancia" taking Communion, Ripalda, *Doctrina christiana, con una exposición breve*, 27–28.

77 "Doctrina es llana y para gente sin erudicion y letras: mas cierta y verdadera: y el tesoro con que se gana el cielo", De la Fuente, *Suma de doctrina christiana*, fol. ✠iiiv.

78 As does De la Fuente, they deal only with some of the sacraments: baptism and communion. Luther, *Der Kleine Catechismus*; Calvin, *Instruction & confession de foy, dont on use en Leglise de Geneve*.

79 De la Fuente, *Suma de doctrina christiana*, fol. ✠vr. And later on, in paragraphs full of double meanings, which reveal a high degree of self-restraint and self-censorship: "Vengamos al remedio desto: si remedio se puede decir tan blanda medicina como es la que quiere el mundo para tan grandes y tan envegescidas llagas como son las que tiene. Siempre le es cosa aspera y escandalosa dezirle que vuelva ala virtud antigua [...]. Dexemos pues por cosa enojosa y demasiada el verdadero remedio: vengamos a otros mas faciles", fols. ✠viv–✠viir.

later by the "sectas y titulos de theologos" mentioned by De la Fuente shortly after,[80] but also extremely condensed.

Depending on the importance given to the institution of the Papacy, to the missing sacraments or to the aforementioned division between the ceremony of the Mass and the sacrament of the Eucharist, the scholars examining De la Fuente's writings have considered his silences and expository choices as "weak points"[81] in his catechetical writings or, more harshly, as scattered notes of an "underhand and skilful Lutheranism".[82]

The predominant trend in contemporary historiography is to consider the doctrines written by De la Fuente and other related theologians as books perfectly suited to the period in which they were written, that it is to say, for the 1530s and the 1540s, becoming problematic thereafter. From this perspective, De la Fuente and the sympathisers and emulators of his catechetical perspective would have been the victims of the increasing rigour and harshness exerted by the Spanish Inquisition and the Roman Church from the late1550s onwards, especially, after the conclusion of the Council of Trent (1563). The anathemas of Trent would have led to the marginalisation of certain theological approaches, which previously were not only tolerated, but also enjoyed great acceptance.[83]

This historiographical hypothesis seems to contradict the way in which contemporary readers noticed and, sometimes denounced, what they considered as inexcusable omissions. In the case of De la Fuente's doctrines, the Spanish Archivo Histórico Nacional holds two reports that the Inquisition commissioned in 1556 to the Flemish Dominican theologian Jean Hentenius[84] and to another unnamed consultant.[85] Both reports contained similar denunciations of what was considered deliberate ambiguity on the part of De la Fuente regarding almost every one of the doctrinal and disciplinary points disputed with Luther and his followers.[86] Another *parecer* of 1557, perhaps written by Juan de Ovando, *provisor* of the archbishopric of Seville in the 1550s – and later president of the Council of the Indies – or some of the theologians who were close to him and to the *Inquisidor general*, Fernando de Valdés, condemned harshly the *Suma de doctrina christiana* and pointed out that De la Fuente's silences and rhetorical juggling were particularly inappropriate and inexcusable in the catechetical literary genre ("linaje de escriptura"):

80 De la Fuente, *Suma de doctrina christiana*, fol. ✠vv.
81 Guerrero, *Catecismos españoles del siglo XVI*, 307.
82 Resines Llorente, *Catecismos americanos del siglo XVI*, vol. 2, 417.
83 Pastore, *Una herejía española*, 310–313.
84 AHN, Inquisición, Leg. 444, no. 5.
85 AHN, Inquisición, Leg. 444, no. 49.
86 Aspe Ansa, *Constantino Ponce de la Fuente*, 97.

> Item que en estos tiempos en cosa tan importante no basta no dezir la heregía contraria, sino es neccessario dezir la verdad cathólica como contra Erasmo dixo bien Alberto Pío. Item que ya que esa escusa se admitiera en otro linaje de escriptura y de escriptor, no en esta scriptura que él llama Summa de doctrina christiana, en que se contiene todo lo principal y lo neccessario quel hombre christiano deue saber y obrar, y a un escriptor que tan grande cosa promete en el principio. Y en el fin recapitulando dize: «Con la mayor breuedad que nos fue possible comprehendimos en esta summa todo lo principal y lo neccessario que la doctrina christiana contiene» etc. ¿Qué cosa más principal o más neccessaria para el christiano que saber y tener entendido que ha de estar debaxo de la obediencia de la iglesia cathólica, y que la cabeca desta es el papa, successor de san Pedro y bicario de Jesuchristo; y tener entendido que lo que esta iglesia le enseñare es lo verdadero, y que aquellos son los libros de diuina scriptura que esta iglesia señalare por tales, y que aquél es el verdadero sentido de todos ellos y de qualquiera par[te] dellos, que esta iglesia aprobara y diere por verdadero sentido; y todo lo que ella reprobare y diere por falso, es falso y digno de ser reprobado? Éste es el fundamento primero y el A.b.c. de la doctrina christiana, del qual ninguna mención haze este señor.[87]

It can be inferred from the three reports mentioned above that the kind of radical pragmatism and simplicity advocated and recommended by De la Fuente to priests and householders was not unanimously accepted. On the contrary, by 1556–1557, Hentenius and other theologians considered this catechetical perspective as a clear attempt at expurgation of the patrimony of the Church, closely linked to some of the explicit attacks initiated by Luther and other reformers.

6 Approaching Heresy without Falling into It. Zumárraga's Additions and Supplements to the Problematic Doctrines of Córdoba and De la Fuente

What relevance has the American contemporary missionary literature for this intra-European, intra-Spanish and, somehow, intra-Sevillian bitter doctrinal dispute, which, as with many other theoretical quarrels, also covered a struggle for power and influence? The kind of dogmatic and practical

87 "Parecer" transcribed and published by García Pinilla, "Más sobre Constantino Ponce de la Fuente y el Parecer de la Vaticana (Ms. Ottob. Lat.789)", 213–214 quoted. The title of the article is slightly wrong. The "Parecer" is to be found in Ms. Ottob. Lat. 782.

misunderstandings that could arise from the excessive – and sometimes intentional – simplicity of many catechetical materials and exposition models which had circulated for decades in and around Iberia[88] but which became problematic in the new context of a multi-confessional Europe, did not go unnoticed by Zumárraga. Even if his biographers[89] said nothing about his training, or merely supposed that he received only a modest theological education before or after his time as a Franciscan friar, in fact the bishop of Mexico was anything but ignorant or naïve.[90] The troublesome dogmatic perspectives and especially the problematic silences to be found in De la Fuente's *Suma de doctrina christiana*, which would rouse suspicion over the orthodoxy of both book and author ten years later in Spain – leading ultimately to the post-mortem condemnation of De la Fuente as "hereje dogmatizante" in an auto-da-fe held in Madrid in 1560[91] – had already been detected by the attentive Zumárraga. In order to avoid any kind of suspicions and accusations, shortly after the printing of the *Doctrina cristiana* – which, as noted, reproduces De la Fuente's *Suma* without significant changes – Zumárraga published a conscious *Suplemento* of forty pages filling almost every one of the dogmatic and disciplinary gaps that De la Fuente had left open.

The strategy of taking, as a starting point, very simple materials and clarifying them with *ad hoc* additions, confusing paragraphs, missing references to important dogmatic elements or any kind of lacuna that could lead to a disciplinary deviation is not new in Zumárraga's catechetical production. There is ample evidence that Pedro de Córdoba's succinct doctrine was also intensively

88 A useful overview of the extensive Iberian production of catechetical literature in the 15th and 16th centuries is Sánchez Herrero, "Alfabetización y catequesis en España y en América durante el siglo XVI".

89 They do not seem to have discovered much about his obscure childhood and youth since García Icazbalceta's pioneering work. Icazbalceta was astonished by the great mysteries regarding his birthplace, date of birth, the monastery where he took the cloth and his studies, see García Icazbalceta, *Don Fray Juan de Zumárraga. Primer obispo y arzobispo de México*, vol. 1, 13–14.

90 Interpreting Zumárraga's education under the classic glasses of the Manichean division between the Middle Ages / Renaissance, ignorance / wisdom, light / darkness, etc., Greenleaf considered the bishop as "a man of contradiction, a segmented thinker", stating that "although he professed to be a Christian humanist and exhibited an affinity for the ideas of Erasmus, Zumárraga was bound by Thomist orthodoxy. In fact, early sixteenth-century Mexico did not belong to the Renaissance but Dante's World Empire", Greenleaf, *Zumárraga and the Mexican Inquisition, 1536–1543*, 41, 131. Beyond this kind of anachronistic stereotypes, it would be hard to identify which should be the elements of Thomist orthodoxy in Zumárraga's religious thought.

91 Luttikhuizen, *Underground Protestantism in Sixteenth Century Spain*, 12–13, 200–211.

reworked by Betanzos and Zumárraga before its 1544 publication. Even if it is an impossible task to work only with tentative hypotheses – because there is no previous printed edition nor an original manuscript of Córdoba's doctrine – Durán and Medina[92] have identified some clear adaptations to the Mexican missionary context. Scattered throughout the text, those additions are related to the Aztec gods, cults and rites.

The additions that are of interest for the purposes of this contribution are those related to the doctrinal points that were barely mentioned in or altogether absent from the main body of the doctrine. The first has to do with purgatory. The existence and nature of purgatory, which was mentioned in passing in a passage about praying for the deed as a work of mercy, seems to have been clarified by Zumárraga / Betanzos. In fols. dr–dv of their rewriting a detailed topography of the four parts of hell – hell proper, purgatory, hell, a place where the righteous who preceded Jesus were – is provided, while the existence of the souls in purgatory is described and the utility of "alms", "fasts" and "prayers" for friends and relatives – highly criticised by the reformers – is stressed.

A second doctrinal addition (in fols. dv–diir) consists of a reaffirmation of the dogma of Mary's virginity before and after the conception and birth of Jesus. Mary is considered in this paragraph an example, virginity a "great good" in and of itself and a feature which distinguished "clean" women and men from "dirty" lustful individuals. The insistence on Mary's virginity, which had already been mentioned in the exposition of the articles of faith, and this new approach toward some of its moral implications should also be seen as a kind of unsolicited reaction to the Protestant attacks on these dogmatic and moral points.

The third doctrinal addition is an elaborate definition of the Church as "cuerpo mistico" and "ayuntamiento" of the Christian faithful ruled over by the Pope, successor of Saint Peter and Jesus Christ. Such a definition was obviously missing in the catechism written by Luther, Calvin and other reformers.[93] It was also missing, as noted earlier, in De la Fuente / Zumárraga's *Suma* and, as it implies relatively complex political thought and vocabulary, the early American doctrines seem to have avoided getting into details[94] on this matter to

---

92 In their almost identical evaluation of the "Mexican" additions to the *Doctrina christiana para instrucion de los indios* (1544), Guillermo Durán, *Monumenta catechetica hispanoamericana* (*siglos XVI–XVIII*), vol. 1, 209–213; Medina, *Doctrina cristiana para instrucción de los Indios*, 106–111.

93 See, for example, Calvin, *Instruction & confession de foy, dont on use en Leglise de Geneve*, 58–59.

94 Speaking about the *Instrucción de la orden que se ha de tener en la doctrina de los naturales*, written by Bishop Jerónimo de Loayza (1545) in the early Peruvian Church,

the point of having ignored it completely. The high accuracy with which this matter is addressed in the additions to the *Doctrina christiana para instrucion de los Indios* (1544) and the explicit condemnation as heretics of those not recognizing and obeying the authority of the Pope[95] should also be considered against the backdrop of the ongoing debates in Europe throughout this period. It is, incidentally, somehow curious that heretics were gravely threatened in the doctrine, the authors all the while failing to define heresy – another very complex term – anywhere in the entire book.

The *Suplemento* of 1546[96] is also a highly revealing indicator of the anti-Lutheran or anti-Protestant campaign that began to influence the writing of catechetical materials for the New World almost from the very beginning of the first systematic and serious attempts to indoctrinate the natives with the Christian faith.[97] Not by chance, the first paragraph added to the controversial, minimalistic doctrine of 1545–1546 is an explicit expression of commitment to the authority of the Church and to the decisive and binding character of its determination in matters of faith. According to Zumárraga, a full subjection to the authority of the Church was especially important for those "simple persons, who cannot understand every one of the things that the Church believes".[98]

Estenssoro identified similar important doctrinal gaps: "No se trata de la Trinidad bajo ningún aspecto, ni se mencionan jamás los nombres de Cristo, Jesús o María, no se habla de la Iglesia", Estenssoro, *Del paganismo a la santidad*, 56.

95 "Y despues que murio san Pedro: los christianos eligieron otro, y assi en muriendo uno luego elijen otro. Y este que assi es elegido para que govierne la iglesia llamase Papa. Y esta en una ciudad que se llama Roma: y no ay mas de un Papa en el mundo. Y a este emos de obedecer todos los Christianos. El que no tiene al Papa por cabeça y regidor de la iglesia, es herege. Y a este tal hanlo de quemar en el fuego", Córdoba, Zumárraga and Betanzos, *Doctrina cristiana para instrucion y información de los indios: por manera de historia*, fol. diiv.

96 Zumárraga, Juan de, "Suplemento del catecismo o enseñamiento del christiano: con las adiciones que parece que le faltavan. Porque sea doctrina entera y aya conformidad y uniformidad en su enseñamiento". In: Zumárraga, *Doctrina cristiana: mas cierta y verdadera para gente sin erudicion y letra,* fols. livv–nviiir.

97 A detailed analysis of the contents of this *Suplemento* in Guillermo Durán, *Monumenta catechetica hispanoamericana* (*siglos XVI–XVIII*), vol. 2, 206–110. Durán's analysis lacks an interpretation of the materials added by Zumárraga with regard to the European debates between Catholics and Protestants. Following a widespread attitude in Latin-American historiography, the contents of the *Suplemento* are interpreted taking only into account their "utility" or role in the missionary context of the Indies.

98 "Son obligados los que son christianos o lo quieren ser a creer lo que cree y tiene la sancta iglesia catolica romana [...]. E assi es de saber que las personas simples que no pueden alcançar a saber todo lo que cree la iglesia: desseando y procurando de saber lo, en tanto que no lo alcançassen: bastaria para su salvacion creer como es dicho firmemente y sin

Thinking most probably of the indigenous people under his jurisdiction and pastoral care, Zumárraga did not consider a comprehensive knowledge of the Christian faith necessary for salvation. As he states in the *Suplemento*, for these kinds of cases, obedience and acceptance of the Church's criteria were sufficient to obtain salvation.

Zumárraga presents, secondly, a brief overview over some of the most important Christian ritual elements: the meaning of the image of the Cross, instructions on how to cross oneself, the main prayers, attitude and the positions of the worshipers during the Mass. He probably deemed it a useful addition to the original doctrine not only because of the unfamiliarity of the natives to these religious practices newly introduced by the Spaniards, but also because De la Fuente, focusing only on the evangelical-readable part of the Mass, had completely neglected the purely ritualistic facets of the ceremony.

As might be expected, a third addition consists of an explanation of the kind of reverence that Christian worshipers should show for images of the Holy Cross, the Virgin Mary and the saints. Zumárraga addresses explicitly the native worshipers, to whom he wants to explain the difference between an idolatrous adoration *per se* of objects and creatures such as that practised "in this land", and Christian veneration. Zumárraga also explains the proper hierarchy of the images according to what they represent. Even if saints come last in this ranking, the bishop considers it important to have images of a saint – an object of special devotion – in the home "rezar le cada dia alguna oración y el dia de su fiesta hazer algo por su servicio".[99] Although only the natives and the traditional Mexican idolatries are mentioned in this part of the *Suplemento*, it is clear that the long explanation regarding the images intends to fill a notorious void in De la Fuente's doctrine. It can be seen as a counter-reformist defence of Catholic piety taking place, interestingly, long before the conclusion of the Council of Trent. Once again, motivations stemming from the European debates and from the American missionary context meet in a paragraph well worthy of a second glance.

After a half-page dedicated to morning and evening prayers, which the worshiper was to repeat upon rising and before going to bed, Zumárraga attempts to remedy another of the most flagrant omissions in De la Fuente's catechism and introduce a systematic exposition of the seven sacraments in seven pages. In this part of the *Suplemento*, he is guided by the classical order

---

duda alguna lo que tiene la sancta iglesia y rogar a nuestro señor que los alumbre en la fe de los christianos: y esto se debe mucho encomendar a la memoria y dezir cada uno muchas vezes entre si mismo", Zumárraga, *Suplemento*, fol. lvr.

99 Zumárraga, *Suplemento*, fol. lviv.

of exposition found in such writings as the *Speculum universal* of Radulphus Ardens (c. 1200),[100] an established canon whom he had also followed carefully while rewriting Pedro de Córdoba's doctrine. In the long tradition from Ardens to late mediaeval doctrines, sacraments were differentiated according to their necessary or voluntary nature. The common order of exposition – also found in this work of Zumárraga – is as follows: baptism, confirmation, Eucharist, penance, extreme unction (necessary sacraments), holy orders and marriage (voluntary sacraments). Trying to avoid any kind of misunderstanding with regard to the sacraments, Zumárraga also went beyond the previous brief doctrine taken from Pedro de Córdoba and gave further precisions for sacraments such as confirmation, extreme unction and the holy orders, previously epitomized in only one line.[101] Considering the quantity of information on the sacraments, the catechetical approach of the *Suplemento* could be considered as an intermediate position between the very minimalistic explanations of Pedro de Córdoba's and Constantino de la Fuente's rewritten catechisms and doctrines for proficient worshipers such as the *Doctrina breve muy provechosa* (1543–1544) and the later *Regla cristiana breve* (1547).

The moral sections that follow the doctrinal exposition of the sacraments in the *Suplemento* are much shorter and give the impression of being a mere stopgap and formal solution to the suppression of the classical explanations regarding powers and enemies of the soul, sins, theological and cardinal virtues and works of mercy in De la Fuente's catechism. The epitomisation process of erudite theological doctrines reaches an extreme when Zumárraga addresses these issues. Here, the reader of the doctrine does not find any kind of doctrinal or moral explanations, but only a conceptual scheme. For example:

> Potencias del anima, y enemigos del anima, y los tres estados.
>
> Otras cosas ay que debe saber, y son las siguientes. Las potencias del anima son tres, memoria, entendimiento, voluntad. Los enemigos del anima son tres. El demonio, el mundo, la carne. Los estados son tres. Casado bueno, biudo mejor, virgines muy mejor.

---

100 Bornstain, "Administering the sacraments", 133–134.

101 "El segundo sacramento es Confirmación, que se da para que el christiano sea mas fuerte y firme en la fe, y para mayor Gloria [...]. El quinto es Extrema unción. Este sacramento se da alos que se quieren morir, y vale mucho para el perdón de los pecados. El sexto sacramento es Orden. Esta orden se da alos que han de ser ministros dela yglesia, y han de decir missa, y administrar los otros Sacramentos", Córdoba, Zumárraga and Betanzos, *Doctrina cristiana para instrucion y información de los indios: por manera de historia*, fols. ciiiiv–cvr; fol. cviiv. Such an extreme epitomisation could give rise to misunderstandings. The nature and implications of extreme unction seem particularly confusing in this abrupt overview.

> El pecado se comete en tres maneras, por el pensamiento, por la palabra, por la obra. Tres maneras ay de peccados, mortal, venial, original. Pecado mortal es por el qual el que lo comete es obligado al infierno sino haze penitencia del, por el venial al purgatorio, por el original al limbo.[102]

Zumárraga's problem was not the moral dimension of the Christian religion *per se*, but very likely rather the conceptual-rationalistic manner in which it had been taught since the time of Radulphus Ardens. This becomes evident in the last part of the *Suplemento* that shows, moreover, that his final objective was not to provide a highly condensed doctrine. In contrast to the extreme abridgement of the classical schema of virtues, sins, works of mercy, etc., in the following nineteen pages – half of the *Suplemento* – which form the second part of the document are found six moral texts in which Zumárraga addresses at length moral points that, although not indispensable,[103] were of particular interest to him. The first three documents, presented under the subtitle "Documentos para adquirir estado de gracia" are moral reflections addressed by Zumárraga to confessors and sinners who want to do penance, prepare themselves to confess their sins or try hurriedly to "remediar y ordenar su alma"[104] preceding an imminent death. Beyond its being an exhaustive manual for confessors and penitents, it is also a kind of *Ars moriendi* in which Zumárraga stresses the salvific value of two spiritual operations: the rigorous examination of conscience and sincere contrition.

Close to Erasmus' famous *De praeparatione ad mortem* (1534) in his detachment from any kind of theological speculations, his encouragement of an examination of conscience driven "por el amor de dios principalmente y no por el temor de la muerte"[105] and his focus on the spiritual preparation for death – while the sacramental aid of extreme unction is neglected,[106] Zumárraga was also influenced by previous writers of this genre such as Gerson, whose *Opus tripartitum* – in Castilian translation[107] – is explicitly and extensively

102 Zumárraga, *Suplemento*, fol. miiv.

103 Perhaps important for Christian religion, but not necessarily to be found in this kind of *catecismos breves*.

104 Zumárraga, *Suplemento*, fol. mviv.

105 Zumárraga, *Suplemento*, fol. mviv. Both Zumárraga and Erasmus avoided the traditional frightening representations of death and the after-death judgment.

106 See Pabel, "Humanism and Early Modern Catholicism", esp. 32–33.

107 The *Opus tripartitum*, written in the early fifteenth century by Jean Gerson, was first published in Castilian in the translation of Juan de Molina: Gerson, *Confesionario*. Wilkinson lists eight editions of the *Confesionario* or *Tripartito* of Gerson in the Iberian context, among them the one prepared and financed by Zumárraga in Mexico (1544). Wilkinson (ed.), *Iberian Books*, 375.

paraphrased as "confirmación de lo sobredicho"[108] (in the fourth moral text). The same moral and religious values – authenticity of piety, attention to the spiritual ends and detachment from riches, humbleness and modesty [...] – are stressed in the fifth added document, a "brevezica doctrina moral", easily and fluently readable – insofar as it lacks any kind of literary and authoritative references – that, according to Zumárraga, was inspired by Saint Bonaventure's *Espejo de disciplina o doctrina de novicios*.[109] The sixth and last moral text consists of a traditional exposition of parental and filial duties. Two short prayers to be said before and after eating come afterwards. The last of Zumárraga's additions to his second rewriting of De la Fuente's catechism is an abridged version of this same "Conclusion exortatoria" found in the previous *Doctrina breve muy provechosa* (1543–1544). Also, inspired by Erasmus' *Paraclesis*, it is a reaffirmation of the ideals of simplicity, pragmatism and purity (in an evangelical way) to which Zumárraga adhered even if, for obvious reasons, he had to be cautious proposing such personal theological criteria as a general canon for the formation of new Christians in an enormous and promising diocese as Mexico.[110]

Taking into account all concomitant and apparently contradictory elements in Zumárraga's life and writings, it is difficult to evaluate how sincere his anti-Lutheran and anti-Erasmian commitment was. As can be seen, the prefatory letters, colophons and additions that he introduced to the compilations of catechetical writings taken from several sources – as is the case for many other religious texts of this period – should be the object of a careful study. Reading between the lines and interpreting these printed materials in the light of Zumárraga's multifaceted life would be imperative in this case.

With regard to his trajectory as bishop and to his role as apostolic inquisitor in Mexico (1536–1543), even the most critical accounts of his actions recognise that, compared with similar figures of this period, he was very indulgent while dealing with those accused of professing Lutheranism. From the five trials that Greenleaf listed and analysed in his classic *Zumárraga and the Mexican Inquisition*, four concluded with a reprimand, a formal abjuration in the cathedral

108 Zumárraga, *Suplemento*, fol. mviiiv.

109 This text, one of the most popular books attributed to Bonaventure, had been published on the Iberian Peninsula in Latin before the end of the 15th century (*De instructione novitiorum*, Montserrat, Johann Luschner, 1499) and was soon translated into Castilian and printed in Seville, *Espejo de disciplina, o libro de las cosas pequeñas para los novicios*, [Seville], [Estanislao Polono], 1502.

110 Resines, *Catecismos Americanos del siglo XVI*, vol. 1, 39; Resines, *Catecismos Americanos del siglo XVI*, vol. 2, 418.

of Mexico and a relatively low financial penalty: fifty *pesos de oro*. The most severe punishment he imposed was the sentence to perpetual banishment from the Indies and seizure of property dictated against Mateo Alemán. It can be seen as a mild sanction given that Alemán had openly and repeatedly criticised confession, excommunication, the images of the saints, papal bulls, indulgences and pontifical authority, appealing instead to the individual reading and interpretation of the Holy Scriptures and supporting the marriage of priests.[111] The reasons behind the surprising leniency that historians of the Mexican Inquisition such as Greenleaf – almost without ever referring to the catechetical writings of Zumárraga[112] – did not explain could be linked to a mutual adherence to some of the particular beliefs deemed unacceptable at these same trials. In a turbulent and still not clearly defined – in terms of religious orthodoxy – period, inquisitor and accused could have shared some of the ideas and motivations of their age.

As previously noted, the clear additions that Betanzos and Zumárraga made to Pedro de Córdoba's Caribbean doctrine and the *Suplemento* of 1546 constitute an explicit refutation of the Protestant attacks on some key dogmas of the Roman Church (purgatory, utility of the works of mercy, virginity of Mary, pontifical primacy, etc.) and on their usual omission in the writings of Erasmus. Nevertheless, Zumárraga seems somehow reluctant when addressing these controversial topics. The corresponding addenda are very schematic and devoid of the characteristic passionate tone of his writing. Even the title of the *Suplemento* seems in a way tricky, inasmuch as he states that those are "las adiciones que parece que le faltavan", instead of saying clearly and plainly that those were "las adiciones que le faltavan".

On the other hand, the *Suplemento* is the longest piece added to the 1546 re-edition of De la Fuente's catechism, but not the only one – think of the very Erasmian "Conclusion exortatoria" previously mentioned. Another interesting text is found in the index written by the bishop to introduce the book, a little paragraph that Zumárraga repeats again in the following "Prologo al christiano lector", a rewriting of De la Fuente's prefatory epistles to Bishop García de Loaysa and "Al letor christiano". Instead of correcting or moderating De la Fuente's *pastoral minimalism*, Zumárraga reinforces the controversial catechetical choice of the Sevillian canon-magistral and adds a further justification to its restrictive doctrinal choice. The pragmatic considerations of De la

111 Greenleaf, *Zumárraga and the Mexican Inquisition, 1536–1543*, 78–82.

112 Greenleaf did not analyse or use any of the doctrines edited by Zumárraga in the 1540s, dealing only with the inquisitorial trials that he found in the Archivo General de la Nación (Mexico).

Fuente are complemented by an appeal to the authority of Paul and the glory of the Ancient Church:

> Y aun que aya otras doctrinas que tratan delo mismo: mas no tratan las cosas de nuestra fe con la certinidad y firmeza, que cosa tan firme requiere. Y van confusas y prolixas: contra la doctrina de san Pablo que dezia que mas quería predicar en la iglesia solas cinco palabras que tuviesse bien entendidas: para darlas assi a entender a otros: que diez mil que fuesen no bien entendidas, como el poco manjar corporal bien digesto mas aprovecha, y se encorpora mejor al cuerpo, que lo mucho no bien digerido.[113]

7 Concluding Remarks. The First American Doctrines, Exceptional Viewpoints of the Emergent Christian Schism

As Alicia Mayer pointed out in her ground-breaking *Lutero en el Paraíso*,[114] the shadows of Luther, Calvin, Erasmus and other reformers hang over the *American Paradise* influencing the missionary strategies of regular and secular churchmen. On the one hand, there was an evident influence of Erasmus and other coeval reformers – some of them European, but especially Spanish reformers such as Constantino de la Fuente – in some of the catechetical materials devised to indoctrinate the Native Americans in this period. On the other hand, even if often only implicitly – not mentioning Luther and other reformers by name – even the more pragmatic and concise doctrine writers seem to have felt compelled to distance themselves from the attacks against purgatory, Mary's virginity and the pontifical *potestas*.

The case of Zumárraga's doctrines, as the abundant historiography which followed Bataillon's pioneering work attests, figures among the most paradigmatic examples of such an intellectual influence. The re-examination of Zumárraga's brief catechisms in current research on the wide circulation, practical significance and functionality of pragmatic religious literature permits a broadening of knowledge as to the convergence of motivations – practical

113 Zumárraga, *Doctrina cristiana: mas cierta y verdadera para gente sin erudicion y letra*, fol. air. For the purposes of this contribution, the sentences added by Zumárraga to the original phrasing of De la Fuente have been italicised.

114 Mayer does not address Zumárraga's doctrines, but considers a wide range of other textual (theological treatises, sermons, chronicles, etc.) and iconographic elements. Mayer, *Lutero en el Paraíso*.

and theoretical, pragmatic and spiritual – from which the first Mexican doctrines resulted. In the catechetical materials herein reviewed, the ideals of pragmatic simplicity and reformed purification established an uneasy and somewhat fragile alliance. Despite the hesitations and self-censorship that a contemporary reader can easily identify in Zumárraga's texts, the convergence of pragmatism, sobriety and apostolic *passéisme* tended to foster a *catechetical minimalism*. Through the outstanding works of Estenssoro, it is known that Zumárraga found emulators in other regions of the Americas.[115] Even if unable to communicate between themselves, he and his homologue in Lima, Jerónimo de Loayza, operated on similar catechetical choices in the same period and under similar circumstances,[116] plausibly, under the influence of the same authors of reference in catechetical literary subgenres.

A careful examination of Zumárraga's doctrines also has demonstrated that – in contrast to the conclusions of Mayer,[117] Bataillon, Estenssoro and most of the contemporary scholars examining Christian indoctrination and unorthodoxy in early modern America – clear references to the European debates on the tools of indoctrination for use in America can be found in Mexico even before the conclusion of the Council of Trent.[118] Moreover, the emergence of an ideological frontier between orthodoxy and heterodoxy in the American missionary context has become visible. As noted, the consciousness of such a frontier and of the dogmatic and disciplinary aspects which were in dispute

115 In his influential *Del paganismo a la santidad*, Estenssoro called attention to the omissions and silences of the first Peruvian doctrines and suggested that those silences were a kind of singularity of the Peruvian context – Estenssoro, *Del paganismo a la santidad*, 75–76 – and should be understood as a strategy of accommodation to pre-Hispanic beliefs. A detailed comparison between Mexican and Peruvian coeval doctrines shows that such significant omissions have rather to do with the converging pragmatic and spiritual motivations of the missionaries and that silences were very widespread in early American *doctrinas*.

116 In order to ensure that the natives genuinely learnt some important elements of the Christian faith, Loayza and the Council Fathers of the First Council of Lima (1551–1552) focused on baptism, marriage and penance while identifying the doctrinal contents that should be taught to the Indians. The teaching of other sacraments and of the most complex articles of faith was postponed, Estenssoro, *Del paganismo a la santidad*, 58–59, 581.

117 "Es interesante notar que en los catecismos indígenas no encontramos referencia alguna al reformador alemán", Mayer, *Lutero en el Paraíso*, 77. According to her account, one had to wait until the massive importation of Ripalda's catechism (1591) in the 17th century to find a strong and direct opposition to Luther and Lutheranism in New Spain.

118 Like Bataillon, Estenssoro considers it inappropriate to distinguish between orthodox and heterodox catechetical approaches before the 1560s, Estenssoro, *Del paganismo a la santidad*, 74.

with Luther or Erasmus was already intense shortly after the onset of the Reformation movement and from the very beginning of the *spiritual conquest*. The absence of direct references to Luther or to Lutheranism does not imply that, for the missionary agents operating in America, "no tenia caso mostrar a los indios la álgida polémica contra los protestantes que se ventilaba a miles de kilómetros de distancia".[119] On the contrary, even if these intra-European debates could be barely understood by the American catechumens, the close supervision of every printed religious book and, especially, of catechetical materials – the means chosen by most of the reformers in order to introduce and disseminate their ideals – obliged the writers of these literary subgenres to be more and more cautious, explicit and detailed in their rejection of non-orthodox ideas. This is the case of Zumárraga, who, as described, resorted to a conscious self-censorship in the rewriting and editing of the catechetical materials he assembled.

As seen in this chapter, two of the doctrines printed in New Spain by order of Zumárraga, adaptations to the Mexican context of the Caribbean doctrine of Pedro de Córdoba and to De la Fuente's *Suma*, demonstrate that the kind of deficiencies and omissions denounced by the inquisitorial advisors in the late 1550s with regard to De la Fuente's catechism, were clearly already apparent to the bishop and his collaborators by the middle of the 1540s. Despite the evident temptation and need even to be extremely pragmatic, linked with the supposed "weak understanding" of the natives and to the countless difficulties in explaining to them some of the most complicated and illogical mysteries of the Christian faith, Zumárraga did not lose sight of the religious evolution taking place in Spain and Europe and corrected or complemented from the very beginning – more than a decade before the first denunciations of De la Fuente's doctrines – the catechetical materials to be used by the first Mexican *apostles*.

Zumárraga's *minimalistic* doctrines and theological interventions in the doctrines of Córdoba and De la Fuente are, beyond doubt, important milestones in the early modern debate about what could be considered expendable parts of the Church's tradition and what, on the other hand, should be considered as essential elements of the Christian faith and inalienable parts of this same Church's heritage. This is an element of crucial interest which invites a re-examination of the secondary and passive-receptive role that previous historiographical perspectives assigned to America and Mexico in the definition of a clear dogmatic frontier between orthodoxy and heterodoxy that took

119 Mayer, *Lutero en el Paraíso*, 77.

place in this period.[120] A closer look at the global dimension of the formation of confessional cultures may, therefore, also permit a more precise determination of its proper periodisation.

Bibliography

Manuscripts

Archivo General de Indias, Sevilla (AGI), Indiferente, 423, L.19.

AGI, México, 1088, L.1.

Archivo General de la Nación, México D.F. (AGN), Inquisición, vol. 43, exp. 4.

Archivo Histórico Nacional, Madrid (AHN), Inquisición, Leg. 444, n° 5, n° 49.

Biblioteca Nacional de España, Madrid (BNE), R/29333.

Printed Sources

Acosta, José de, *De procuranda indorum salute*, Lyon [1588] 1670: Laurent Anisson.

Beltrán de Heredia, Vicente, *Los manuscritos del Maestro Fray Francisco de Vitoria O.P.: Estudio critico de introducción a sus Lecturas y Relecciones*, Madrid, Valencia 1928.

Calvin, Jean, *Instruction & confession de foy, dont on use en Leglise de Geneve*, [Genève, Köln 1537]: [Wygand].

Calvin, Jean, *Institution de la religion Chrestienne*, Genève 1554: Philbert Hamelin.

Catechismus Ex Decreto SS. Concilii Tridentini ad Parochos, Roma 1566: Paolo Manuzio.

Córdoba, Pedro de, Juan de Zumárraga and Domingo de Betanzos, *Doctrina cristiana para instrucion y información de los indios: por manera de historia*, México 1544: Juan Cromberger [Juan Pablos].

Córdoba, Pedro de, Juan de Zumárraga and Domingo de Betanzos, *Declaracion y exposicion de la doctrina christiana en lengua española y Mexicana, hecha por los religiosos de la orden de sancto Domingo*, México 1548: [Juan Pablos].

De la Fuente, Constantino, *Suma de doctrina christiana en que se contiene todo lo principal y necessario que el hombre christiano deve saber y obrar*, Sevilla 1543: Juan Cromberger.

120 Pastore, Guerrero and other specialists in the study of the European Reformation point to Mexico as one of the distant and exotic places in which the De la Fuente's *Suma* was received and reprinted. None of these scholars took into account the careful and systematic adaptations, corrections and additions made by Zumárraga in order to overcome the most important criticisms that De la Fuente's catechism could spark and that, in fact, arose later in the Spanish context. Pastore, *Una herejía española*, 308–309; Guerrero, *Catecismos españoles del siglo XVI*, 335–339.

Erasmus, *Enquiridio o manual del cavallero cristiano*, trans. Alonso Fernández de Madrid, Alcalá de Henares 1529: [Miguel de Eguía].

Erasmus, *Enchiridion o Manual del Cauallero Christiano de D. Erasmo Roterodamo en romance*, trans. Alonso Fernández de Madrid, Anvers 1555: Martin Nucio.

Fernández de Oviedo, Gonzalo, *Historia general y natural*, Madrid 1851–1855.

Gerson, Jean, *Confesionario*, trans. Juan de Molina, Alcalá de Henares 1519: Arnao Guillén de Brocar.

Gerson, Jean and Juan de Zumárraga, *Tripartito del cristianísimo y consolatorio doctor Juan Gerson de doctrina cristiana: a qualquiera muy prouechosa*, México 1541: [Juan Pablos].

Libros y libreros en el siglo XVI, ed. Fernández del Castillo, Francisco, México 1914.

Luther, Martin, *Der Kleine Catechismus. Fuer die gemeyne Pfarherr vnd Prediger*, Marburg 1529: Rhode.

Medina, Miguel Ángel, *Doctrina cristiana para instrucción de los Indios. Redactada por Fr. Pedro de Córdoba, O.P. y otros religiosos doctos de la misma orden. Impresa en México, 1544 y 1548*, Salamanca 1987.

Molina, Alonso de, *Doctrina christiana breve traduzida en lengua Mexicana*, México 1546.

Paz, Matías de, *Del dominio de los Reyes de España sobre los indios*, México [1512] 1954.

Rickel, Denis van and Juan de Zumárraga, *Compendio breve que tracta dela manera de como se han de hazer las processions: compuesto por Dionisio Rickel cartuxano*, México 1544: Juan Cromberger [Juan Pablos].

Ripalda, Jerónimo, *Doctrina christiana, con una exposición breve*, Madrid [1591] 1909.

Vitoria, Francisco de, *On the American Indians*, in *Vitoria. Political Writings*, eds. Lawrance, Jeremy and Anthony Pagden, Cambridge 1991, 231–292.

Ximénez, Diego, *Enchiridion o Manual de doctrina christiana que tambien puede seruir de confessionario: diuidido en cinco partes* [...] *hecho y copilado de muchos libros de sana doctrina*, Lisboa 1552: German Gallarde.

Zumárraga, Juan de, *Doctrina breve muy provechosa de las cosas que pertenecen a la fe catolica y a nuestra cristiandad en estilo llano para comun inteligencia*, México [1543–1544]: Juan Cromberger [Juan Pablos].

Zumárraga, Juan de [De la Fuente, Constantino], *Doctrina cristiana: en que en suma se contiene todo lo principal y necessario que el cristiano debe saber y obrar*, México 1545–1546: Juan Cromberger.

Zumárraga, Juan de [De la Fuente, Constantino], *Doctrina cristiana: mas cierta y verdadera para gente sin erudicion y letras: en que se contiene el catecismo o informacion para indios con todo lo principal y necessario que el cristiano deve saber y obrar*, México 1546: Juan Cromberger [Juan Pablos].

Zumárraga, Juan de, *Regla christiana breve, para ordenar la vida y tiempo del christiano que se quiere salvar y tener su alma dispuesta, para que Jesuchristo more en ella*, México 1547: [Juan Pablos].

Zumárraga, Juan de?, *Manual de adultos*, México 1540: Juan Cromberger [Juan Pablos].
Zumárraga, Juan de? *Cartilla para la enseñanza de la doctrina cristiana en lengua zotzil, latina y castellana*, [México 1547?]: [Juan Pablos].

Literature

Adeva Martín, Ildefonso, "Estudio preliminar", in Zumárraga, Juan de (ed.), *Regla cristiana breve*, Pamplona 1994, i-cxvi.
Adeva Martín, Ildefonso, "Fray Juan de Zumárraga: Regla Cristiana Breve", in *Hispania Sacra* 47 (1995), 109–117.
Alejos-Grau, Carmen José, *Juan de Zumárraga y su "Regla Cristiana breve" (México 1947): autoría, fuentes y principales tesis teológicas*, Pamplona 1992.
Almoina, José, "El erasmismo de Zumárraga", in *Filosofía y letras* 15 (1948), 93–117.
Almoina, José, "Introducción", in Almoina, José (ed.), *Juan de Zumárraga. Regla cristiana breve*, México 1951.
Aspe Ansa, María Paz, *Constantino Ponce de la Fuente. El hombre y su lenguaje*, Madrid 1975.
Borges, Pedro, "La nueva cristiandad indiana", in Borges, Pedro (ed.), *Historia de la Iglesia en Hispanoamérica y Filipinas (siglos XV–XIX)*, vol. 1: *Aspectos generales*, Madrid 1991, 593–613.
Borges, Pedro, "Métodos de persuasion", in Borges, Pedro (ed.), *Historia de la Iglesia en Hispanoamérica y Filipinas (siglos XV–XIX)*, vol. 1: *Aspectos generales*, Madrid 1991, 573–591.
Bornstain, Daniel, "Administering the sacraments", in Swanson, Robert (ed.), *The Routledge History of Medieval Christianity, 1050–1500*, London 2015, 133–146.
Burke, Peter, "Cultures of Translation in Early Modern Europe", in Burke, Peter and Ronnie Po-Chia Hsia (eds.), *Cultural translation in Early Modern Europe*, Cambridge 2007, 7–38.
Durston, Alan, *Pastoral Quechua. The History of Christian Translation in Colonial Peru, 1550–1650*, Notre Dame, IN 2007.
Duve, Thomas, "Catequesis y derecho canónico entre el Viejo y el Nuevo Mundo", in Schmidt-Riese, Roland (ed.), *Catequesis y Derecho en la América colonial*, Frankfurt am Main, Madrid 2010, 131–145.
Duve, Thomas, "European Legal History – Concepts, Methods, Challenges", in Duve, Thomas (ed.), *Entanglements in Legal History: Conceptual Approaches*, Frankfurt am Main 2014, 29–66.
Estenssoro, Juan Carlos, *Del paganismo a la santidad. La incorporación de los indios del Perú al catolicismo. 1532–1750*, Lima 2003.
Foljanty, Lena, "Legal Transfers as Processes of Cultural Translation: On the Consequences of a Metaphor", *Max Planck Institute for European Legal History Research Paper Series* No. 2015–9 (http://ssrn.com/abstract=2682465).

García Icazbalceta, Joaquín, *Don Fray Juan de Zumárraga. Primer obispo y arzobispo de México*, 4 vols., México 1947.

García Icazbalceta, Joaquín and Agustín Millares Carlo, *Bibliografía mexicana del siglo XVI*, México 1954.

García Pinilla, Ignacio Javier, "Más sobre Constantino Ponce de la Fuente y el Parecer de la Vaticana (Ms. Ottob. Lat.789)", in *Cuadernos de investigación histórica* 17 (1999), 191–226.

Giesen, Christine, "Audacia y precaución: Constantino Ponce de la Fuente, defensor del protestantismo", in *Res Publica* 20:2 (2017), 227–241.

Gil, Fernando, *Primeras "doctrinas" del Nuevo Mundo. Estudio histórico-teológico de las obras de fray Juan de Zumárraga*, Buenos Aires 1993.

Greenleaf, Richard, *Zumárraga and the Mexican Inquisition, 1536–1543*, Washington, D.C. 1962.

Greenleaf, Richard and Neal Kaveny, *Zumárraga and his family: letters to Vizcaya 1536–1548*, Washington, D.C. 1979.

Guerrero, José Ramón, *Catecismos españoles del siglo XVI. La obra catequética del Dr. Constantino Ponce de la Fuente*, Madrid 1969.

Guillermo Durán, Juan, *Monumenta catechetica hispanoamericana (siglos XVI–XVIII)*, 3 vols., Buenos Aires 1984.

Kamen, Henry, *The Spanish Inquisition*, London 1965.

Luttikhuizen, Frances, *Underground Protestantism in Sixteenth Century Spain*, Göttingen, Bristol 2017.

Martín Abad, Julián, *La imprenta en Alcalá de Henares: 1502–1600*, vol. 3: *Catálogo descriptivo (1578–1600)*, Madrid 1991.

Mayer, Alicia, *Lutero en el Paraíso*, México 2008.

Mira Mira, Enrique, *Estudio histórico-genético de la "Doctrina breve" (1543–44) de Juan de Zumárraga*, Pamplona 1989.

Nesvig, Martin, *Ideology and Inquisition. The World of the Censors in Early Mexico*, New Haven (CT), London 2009.

Neusner, Josef and Jacques Dupuis (eds.), *The Christian Faith in the Doctrinal Documents of the Catholic Church*, New York, NY 1982.

Pabel, Hilmar, "Humanism and Early Modern Catholicism: Erasmus of Rotterdam's Ars moriendi", in Comerford, Kathleen and Hilmar Pabel (eds.), *Early Modern Catholicism. Essays in Honour of John O'Malley, S.J.*, Toronto 2001, 26–45.

Pardo, Osvaldo, *The Origins of Mexican Catholicism. Nahua Rituals and Christian Sacraments in Sixteenth-Century*, Ann Arbor, MI 2006.

Pastore, Stefania, *Una herejía española. Conversos, alumbrados e Inquisición (1449–1559)*, Madrid 2010.

Resines, Luis, *Catecismos Americanos del siglo XVI*, 2 vols., Salamanca 1992.

Ricard, Robert, *La conquista espiritual de México. Ensayo sobre el apostolado y los métodos misioneros de las órdenes mendicantes en la Nueva España de 1523–1524 a 1572*, México 2002.

Rodríguez, Pedro, *El Catecismo romano ante Felipe II y la Inquisición española: los problemas de la introducción en España del Catecismo del Concilio de Trento*, Madrid 1998.

Romero Galván, José Rubén, "Review of Sonia Corcuera de Mancera, *De pícaros y malqueridos: huellas de su paso por la Inquisición de Zumárraga (1539–1547)*", in *Históricas. Boletín de información del Instituto de Investigaciones Históricas* 93 (2012), 15–17.

Roulet, Éric, *L'évangelisation des Indiens du Mexique. Impact et réalité de la conquête spirituelle (XVIe siècle)*, Rennes 2008.

Rubial García, Antonio, *Notas para el estudio del franciscanismo en Nueva España, 1523–1550*, México 1975.

Sáenz de Haro, Tomás, "Franciscanismo y espiritualidad. Bibliografía", in Iglesia Duarte, José Ignacio de la, Francisco Javier García Turza and José Ángel García de Cortázar (eds.), *Espiritualidad, órdenes mendicantes y franciscanismo en la Edad Media. VI Semana de Estudios Medievales*, Logroño 1996, 301–336.

Sánchez Herrero, José, "Alfabetización y catequesis en España y en América durante el siglo XVI", in Saranyana, Josep Ignasi, Primitivo Tineo, Antón M. Pazos, Miguel Lluch-Baixaulli and María Pilar Ferrer (eds.), *Evangelización y teología en América (siglo XVI): X Simposio Internacional de Teología de la Universidad de Navarra*, vol. 1, Pamplona 1990, 237–263.

Saranyana, Josep Ignasi, "Métodos de catequización", in Borges, Pedro (ed.), *Historia de la Iglesia en Hispanoamérica y Filipinas (siglos XV–XIX)*, vol. 1: *Aspectos generales*, Madrid 1991, 549–571.

Saranyana, Josep Ignasi (ed.), *Teología en América Latina*, vol. 1: *Desde los orígenes a la Guerra de Sucesión (1493–1715)*, Madrid, Frankfurt am Main 1999.

Soto Guerrero, Antonio, *La "Iglesia" en los catecismos mexicanos del siglo XVI editados en México*, Roma, 1993.

Tubau, Xabier, "Alfonso de Valdés y la política imperial del canciller Gattinara", in *Studia Aurea* 4 (2010), 17–43.

Valdeón, Roberto, *Translation and the Spanish Empire in the Americas*, Amsterdam 2014.

Wilkinson, Alexander S. (ed.), *Iberian Books: Books Published in Spanish or Portuguese or on the Iberian Peninsula before 1601*, Leiden 2010.

Zwartjes, Otto (ed.), *Las gramáticas misioneras de tradición hispánica (siglos XVI–XVII)*, Amsterdam, Atlanta, GA 2000.

CHAPTER 8

Producing Pragmatic Literature in the Third Mexican Provincial Council (1585)

Osvaldo R. Moutin

1 Introduction

On 20 January 1585, the Third Mexican Provincial Council held its opening session.[1] Exactly nine months later, the council promulgated a corpus of decrees[2] and approved the statutes of the cathedral chapter,[3] three catechisms,[4] a directory for confessors and penitents,[5] a list of court fees, and a ritual for administering the sacraments. In addition, the bishops of the Third Mexican Provincial Council sent a long letter to the king and a shorter one to Sixtus V, who had recently been promoted to the Apostolic See, asking for the expeditious approval and recognition of the decrees and the other documents.

Apart from the decrees and statutes of the cathedral chapter, most of the other documents have been considered "pastoral works", and seen as practical, as opposed to legal, productions. In this article, I will examine the authority and value that the bishops claimed for these "pastoral" documents. Considering that, according to canon law, one of the goals of a provincial council was to legislate,[6] I will try to answer the question of why the Third Mexican Provincial Council not only produced decrees, but also other documents. Firstly, I will

1 The main sources of the Third Mexican Council have been edited by Carrillo Cázares, *Manuscritos del Concilio Tercero Provincial Mexicano (1585)*, vols. 1–4.

2 A critical edition of the decrees can be found in Martínez Ferrer, *Decretos del Concilio Tercero Provincial Mexicano 1585*, 2 vols.

3 About the Statutes of Cathedral Chapters in the Third Mexican Provincial Council, see Terráneo, "El llamado 'III Concilio Provincial Mexicano' y los 'Estatutos' de la Santa Iglesia de México' o 'Reglas consuetas de la catedral de México' "; Vidal Gil, *Los Estatutos del Cabildo de la catedral de México elaborados en el Tercer Concilio Provincial Mexicano (1585)*.

4 The catechisms were edited in Durán, "La transmisión de la fe"; Durán, "Los instrumentos americanos de pastoral (siglo XVI)".

5 The directory was published only recently: Carrillo Cázares, *Manuscritos del Concilio Tercero Provincial Mexicano (1585)*, vol. 5; Durán, *Monumenta catechética hispanoamericana*, vol. 3.

6 Although Murphy (1947) focuses on the First Code of Canon Law (1917), his book is instructive, not least because of its sources to Chapter IV: Objects and Methods of Legislation, 53–72. See Murphy, *Legislative Powers of the Provincial Council*.

focus on what a provincial council was, considering its canonical status and its attributions according to the canon law then in force. Here I will use a treatise written by the Franciscan friar Felice Peretti, addressed to the young and recently appointed archbishop of Milan, Charles Borromeo. Fray Peretti would become Pope Sixtus V in 1585, and, in 1589 was to approve the Third Mexican Provincial Council. Secondly, I will examine the "conciliar products" in order to explain their general purpose and why they were considered canonical documents. Finally, I will present some examples of the ways in which different matters were tackled in order to try to understand the normative value they had.

2 What Was a Provincial Council in the Early Modern Period?

Why did the Roman Catholic Church meet in the form of general, provincial councils or diocesan synods to legislate? Unlike in a modern state, there was, and still is, no separation of powers, nor were there any mechanisms for government control apart from its hierarchical structure, with the Roman Pontiff at its head. An initial answer can be found not in law but in theology if we turn our attention to the report or treatise written in 1565 by the Franciscan friar Felice Peretti for Charles Borromeo, entitled "De Concilio Provinciale".[7] This report had been requested in order explain how to celebrate a provincial council according to classical canon law and according to the reform implemented by the Council of Trent, which had been promulgated less than two years before. It is a doctrinal work in which old and new legislation is organised with a particular aim: to explain how a provincial council should be celebrated *de iure canonico*.[8] As was pointed out by the last sentences of the treatise, it had been written in such a way so that the required information could be accessed quickly in order to help the new Milanese bishop celebrate the provincial councils that he intended to, and indeed did celebrate.[9]

Fray Peretti summed up everything that was necessary to know to celebrate a provincial council in twenty chapters. For the purposes of this contribution, I will focus on four of them: the second and the third chapters, which

7 Sala, "Del Concilio Provinciale".

8 A study of the treatise can be found in Grohe, "Der Traktat *De concilio provinciali* (1565) des Felice Peretti (Sixtus V.)".

9 "Haec sunt, Illustrissime et Reverendissime Domine mihi Colen.[mo] quae pro tuo jussu cursim, et in mei longi itineris properatione, scribere potui de Concilio Provinciali, quod tua Illustrissima Dnatio, Domino concedente, celebrare anhelat"., in Sala, "Del Concilio Provinciale", 41.

determined what a provincial council was,[10] and the fifteenth and sixteenth chapters, which singled out the topics for which a provincial council had competence.[11]

So, what was the canonical significance of the provincial council? Fray Peretti wrote that both theologians and canon lawyers knew that there were three types of council: general, provincial, and episcopal. Regarding provincial councils, he explained that these were convoked by the metropolitan bishop who celebrated them with his suffragan bishops for the interests of the ecclesiastical province. He presented three reasons to explain the origins of councils: firstly, in the natural order, when human beings met with their progeny in order to settle any debated doctrine; secondly, drawing on the history of pagan Rome, when meetings were held to reach a decision through deliberation; and finally, because the Church had the promise of Christ that the assistance of the Holy Spirit would be given when two or more gathered in his name (Matthew 18), and so too did the Apostles. He based his arguments for general councils on Acts 15, for provincial councils on Acts 20, and for episcopal gatherings on Acts 21.[12] To sum up, Peretti argued for the necessity of church councils for three reasons: the natural order, the experience of human history, and, finally and decisively, the positive divine law. This interpretation of the Holy Bible, especially in the last case, is not supported by present biblical exegesis. According to modern studies, what has been called the Council of Jerusalem – celebrated between the years 49 and 50 and recorded by Luke in Acts 15 – had never taken place as such but had been the sum of several meetings.[13] However, from the perspective of "Wirkungsgeschichte", the original sense intended by the author or even the events narrated with historical accuracy, were no longer relevant for the interpretation of a text. On the contrary, according to the "Wirkungsgeschichte", what mattered was the impact the text alone had in history. It is through the subject of the read text and the context in which it was read, that it gained its significance.[14] Therefore, Peretti saw the praxis of the

10 Sala, "Del Concilio Provinciale", 33–34.
11 Sala, "Del Concilio Provinciale", 38–39.
12 Sala, "Del Concilio Provinciale", 34.
13 Rivas, "Algunas cuestiones historiográficas en torno al libro de los Hechos de los Apóstoles".
14 Gadamer, *Truth and Method*, 302: "In the sphere of historical understanding, too, we speak of horizons, especially when referring to the claim of historical consciousness to see the past in its own terms, not in terms of our contemporary criteria and prejudices but within its own historical horizon. The task of historical understanding also involves acquiring an appropriate historical horizon from which the traditionary text speaks, we will misunderstand the significance of what it has to say to us. To that extent this seems a legitimate hermeneutical requirement: we must place ourselves in the other situation

primitive church as a rule which had been followed in the practice of medieval and early modern theology and canon law, and as a model of the usage of and need for councils, leaving to ecclesiastical law those norms through which the Church could change and adapt its practice.

Once it had been established that the celebration of councils – general, provincial, or episcopal – were a necessity as well as a resource of divine law, natural law and positive law, Peretti used chapters fifteen and sixteen to determine the competence of a provincial council. When considering for which topics a provincial council had no competence, he stated that everything that related to the definition of the faith was beyond a provincial council's authority.[15] Without getting immersed too deeply in this conclusion, let me list the topics that according to Peretti's chapter 16 were to be treated by a provincial council: Provision for the vacancies of churches, absolution of irregularities, promoting the preaching of the Word of God; that beneficial Churches, as well as exempted ones, monasteries, hospitals, and colleges were to be visited; that churches were strengthened and that the unity of the churches was promoted; that examiners were appointed; that monastic cloisters were regulated; that nuns' monasteries were visited; that religious orders were guarded; that irregular cohabitations were abandoned; that bishops could present cases for trial; that the practice of duels was suppressed; that episcopal seminars were fostered; that laymen gave accounts regarding the administration of pious goods; that residency was observed; what should be established for those who entered sacred ministries; that clandestine marriages were nullified; what was to be observed in marriages, as well as in the mass and the other sacraments, according to the decrees of the Council of Trent; that complaints were heard by those who had been offended; that wicked incidents were investigated; that the lives and sermons of clerics were examined; that notorious crimes were corrected; that approved persons could denounce abuses in the dioceses; that the morality of the laity, especially of those members who induced others to sin, was overseen, as well as those who lurked around churches, including topics such as the adornment of women and similar matters; finally, that the Provincial

in order to understand it. We may wonder, however, whether this phrase is adequate to describe the understanding that is required of us. The same is true of a conservation that we have with someone simply in other to get to know him – i.e., to discover where he is coming from and his horizon. This not a true conversation, that is, we are not seeking agreement on some subject – because the specific contents of the conversation are only a means to get to know the horizon of the other person [...] Historical consciousness is clearly doing something similar when it transposes itself into the situation of the past and thereby claims to have acquired the right horizon".

15 Sala, "Del Concilio Provinciale", 38.

Council should deal with everything that seemed convenient for the ecclesiastical province.[16]

Most of these cases were reinforced by a quotation from the reform canons of sessions 22 to 25 of the Council of Trent, and it is easy to see that these subjects were very broad and provided provincial councils with a wide scope of potential action. Regarding what we could call literary types or juridical forms, Peretti just used the expression "to issue decrees" with no further indication of what other types of "conciliar products" could be issued, but, returning to the list, one can easily see that not everything could be solved by issuing decrees – as the following example will demonstrate.

3 Decrees and Other Products of the Third Mexican Provincial Council

Let us now travel through time and space to Mexico in 1585. Almost fifteen clerics, including seven bishops and a group of theologians and canon lawyers, worked to produce several documents that touched practically every topic on Peretti's list. No source indicates that they knew Peretti's treatise, or any other similar one, but this should not come as a surprise. Most of these clerics had graduated from the best universities of their time – Salamanca, Alcalá de Henares or Granada – and the quality of their education had promoted them to the most important offices in the New World and the Old.

I shall not address the history of this provincial council,[17] but rather briefly introduce those "conciliar products", that is, those documents that were promulgated, before discussing what we know about their genesis. For this purpose, I will examine the manuscripts of the Third Mexican Council, in which a great deal of information is included about the work achieved in the conciliar room.

The conciliar decrees were the most important documents of the council, even simply in terms of their widespread influence and application. First published in 1622,[18] they amounted to almost six hundred paragraphs divided into five books, touching on a wide variety of topics.[19] The importance and

---

16 Sala, "Del Concilio Provinciale", 39.

17 Although a comprehensive history of the Third Mexican Provincial Council of 1585 still has not been published, several topics have been investigated. See Poole, *Pedro Moya de Contreras*, esp. chapters VIII–XI, 201–312.

18 *Sanctum prouinciale concilium Mexici.*

19 On the drafting of the decrees, see Galindo Bustos, *Estudio del Aparato de Fuentes del Concilio Tercero Provincial de México (1585)*; Terráneo, *La recepción de la tradición*

influence of this text is evident because it was quoted and referenced in the registers of episcopal visitations, in treatises and in the legislation and conciliar products of other ecclesiastical provinces of the New World.[20] The statutes of the Cathedral of Mexico were also published in the same volume as the decrees, and these served as a model for all the cathedral churches in the ecclesiastical province.[21]

Along with the conciliar decrees, the council also issued a directory for confessors and penitents. As the title suggests, this work was to provide guidance to ministers and the general public regarding the practice of the sacrament of penance, but it remained unpublished until the first decade of the twenty-first century.[22] This text has been studied extensively by Luis Martínez Ferrer, who identified the Jesuit Juan de la Plaza as its author.[23] It is divided into two major parts: what priests should know in order to pass the examination for a license to hear confession, and a list of moral difficulties arranged according to different types of people, distinguished by their status, job, or duties.

Turning to what the historiography has tended to refer to as "pastoral works", we find three catechisms: a major one, a minor one for rustic and old people, and a third one about how to prepare the soul when death was imminent.[24] A table of fees for ecclesiastical courts was also promulgated but never published.[25] Completing the list of "pastoral works", a ritual was also drafted, but no single copy, manuscript or published, has survived, and we dispose of only a few recommendations and decisions from which to surmise its content.

Apart from the decrees and the "pastoral works", the provincial council wrote two letters. The first one was addressed to King Philip II and included three long *memoriales*, or reports, asking the king to resolve some important

---

conciliar limense en los decretos del III Concilio Provincial Mexicano; Moutin, *Legislar en la América hispánica en la temprana edad moderna*.

20 Cobo Betancourt and Cobo, *La legislación de la arquidiócesis de Santafé en el periodo colonial*.

21 Terráneo, "El llamado 'III Concilio Provincial Mexicano' y los 'Estatutos' de la Santa Iglesia de México' o 'Reglas consuetas de la catedral de México' "; Vidal Gil, *Los Estatutos del Cabildo de la catedral de México elaborados en el Tercer Concilio Provincial Mexicano (1585)*.

22 Carrillo Cázares, *Manuscritos del Concilio Tercero Provincial Mexicano (1585)*, vol. 5; Durán, *Monumenta catechética hispanoamericana*, vol. 3.

23 Martínez Ferrer, *Directorio para confesores y penitentes*.

24 The text of these catechisms: Durán, "Los instrumentos americanos de pastoral (siglo XVI)"; Durán, "La transmisión de la fe"; Carrillo Cázares, *Manuscritos del Concilio Tercero Provincial Mexicano (1585)*, vol. 1, 475–548.

25 Carrillo Cázares, *Manuscritos del Concilio Tercero Provincial Mexicano (1585)*, vol. 3, 237–256.

issues.[26] After concluding the council, on 28 October 1585 the bishops sent a second letter to the recently appointed Pope Sixtus V, previously known as Felice Peretti, the Franciscan Friar who had written the treatise about the holding of provincial councils.[27] In 1589, Sixtus V issued three documents granting recognition or papal approval of the Third Mexican Provincial Council.[28]

4 Pragmatic Literature as a Legal Instrument for Evangelisation

That being said, if canon law ordered the issuing of decrees, why did the bishops of the Third Mexican Provincial Council need other documents?

Five days after the opening of the council, the bishops asked the theological consultants to draft a catechism for *indios*, Africans, and Spaniards, so that they could be instructed in a standardized way. In that logic, this would end the diversity, which experience had taught them was a cause of many obstacles to obedience.[29] From this it can be inferred that there was no lack of catechisms, but that the bishops aimed at a consistent uniformity with regard to the content of faith for old and new Christians alike. In the decrees, the bishops determined that these catechisms, which contained a summary of what Christians were obliged to believe and how this was to be explained, were to be the only ones used for religious instruction, and that every bishop should be in charge of approving the translations to different indigenous languages.

Pedro de Feria, one of the bishops who could not take part in the council, sent a report in which he asked that learned friars and clerics who were experienced in the pastoral care of indigenous people, should write short treatises about the most important contents of faith. He suggested several topics and

26 Carrillo Cázares, *Manuscritos del Concilio Tercero Provincial Mexicano (1585)*, vol. 2, 69–108; 112–156.

27 Carrillo Cázares, *Manuscritos del Concilio Tercero Provincial Mexicano (1585)*, vol. 2, 109–112.

28 Breve Romanum Pontificem given in 28 October 1589, in: Metzler, *America Pontificia. Primi saeculi evangelizationis 1493–1592*, vol. 2, 1398–1400. Sixtus V also ruled that all provincial councils had to receive their *recognitio* from the Sacred Congregation of the Council, see Gómez-Iglesias, "La bula «Immensa Aeterni Dei» de Sixto V (22-1-1588)". On the case of the Third Mexican Provincial Council, see Fornés Azcoyti, *El proceso de la aprobación romana del III Concilio de México, 1585–1589*. On the royal approval, see Martínez Ferrer, "Un "pequeño" conflicto entre Madrid y Roma". For the general political and ecclesiastical context of the reformation of the Church, see García Hernán, "La curia romana, Felipe II y Sixto V".

29 Carrillo Cázares, *Manuscritos del Concilio Tercero Provincial Mexicano (1585)*, vol. 1, 116–118.

recommended that each one should be treated by a different author. However, it is his last recommendation that is the most noteworthy: He proposed that all these treatises were compiled in one single volume written in Spanish. This work should guide priests in Indian parishes and prevent them from using the Latin language and authorities when preaching to Indians – a common practice he had heard from some preachers.[30]

Dionisio de Rivera Flores, prosecutor of the council, also asked for a ritual book to be approved by the provincial council. He explained that both regular and secular priests used several manuscripts to teach the doctrine and to perform liturgical ceremonies, which went against the canons of the Council of Trent.[31] He was not the only one to comment on this situation. Ortiz de Hinojosa, a theological consultant, also wanted prayers to be collected into a single volume, including the ones for priests, along with the psalms, and instructions for administering the sacraments.[32]

So far, I have spoken about the need for the catechism and the ritual, but I will now focus on the other major "pastoral work of the council". The directory for confessors and penitents was even longer than the decrees, and it aimed at providing confessors with sufficient doctrinal knowledge and professional instruction for the exercise of their office, especially for those particular and difficult cases that occurred in the archbishopric and province. All parish priests had to own a copy and follow it, guiding themselves by using its doctrine and erudition.[33]

The directory covered fewer topics than the decrees, referring only to moral and penal questions, and it was drafted by the Jesuit Juan de la Plaza, who had also written the catechisms. However, it was not an entirely new work and the influence of Martin de Azpilcueta's manual, among others, can be perceived easily. According to the decrees, anyone who had an office with *cura animarum*, regardless of whether he was a secular or a regular confessor, had to possess copies of it, one in Spanish and another one in "Mexican". It was to be used not only for the immediate practice of the sacrament of penance but also for the preparation and examination of candidates for the priesthood. As

---

30 Carrillo Cázares, *Manuscritos del Concilio Tercero Provincial Mexicano* (1585), vol. 1, 295–297.

31 Carrillo Cázares, *Manuscritos del Concilio Tercero Provincial Mexicano* (1585), vol. 1, 149–152.

32 Carrillo Cázares, *Manuscritos del Concilio Tercero Provincial Mexicano* (1585), vol. 1, 391.

33 Lib. III, tit. II De Officio rectoris, et plebani, De vigilantia, et cura circa subditos, praesertim in sacramentorum receptione, § 15, in *Sanctum prouinciale concilium Mexici*, 48–49; lib. V, tit. XII De Poenitentiis et remisionibus, § 8, in *Sanctum prouinciale concilium Mexici*, 97–98.

we said above, it consisted of two major parts: one to prepare candidates for the priesthood, and the other one included a catalogue of several offices and the moral risks that they potentially entailed. The directory has been called the first professional ethics book in America.[34]

However, following the spirit of the conciliar decree, the directory was not meant to be an obstacle to erudition by virtue of being a summary. On the contrary, by gathering material from various famous and respected sources, it offered the necessary instruction because it was a guide for learning and for taking the exam to obtain the license for hearing confession. A few examples will help to shed light on this statement.

When the bishops were reviewing the provincial council of Seville of 1512,[35] they ruled that a decree should be drafted to establish what could and what could not be done during a *cessatio a divinis*, a measure closely related to an interdict, which prohibited a priest or a community from celebrating certain sacraments and ceremonies.[36] They wanted to copy exactly what Bartolomé de Medina had written in his instruction for confessors, so a decree was drafted and the disposition was included in the directory.[37] Unlike Medina's work, however, in the directory it was arranged in a question and answer format, which firstly explained the difference between an interdict and a *cessatio a divinis*, then established who could impose it, and, finally, set the penalty for clerics who broke this decree.[38]

This brief example serves to illustrate the practical character of the directory. Those with a superior education in theology or canon law might not have needed this information, but, if necessary, they would have known where to look for it. The directory did not replace erudite knowledge but rather organised it in a systematic way so that it could be easier acquired and applied. Although the Pontifical and Royal University of Mexico had existed for almost thirty years, many of the candidates were thousands of kilometres away or unable to attend university, and so the directory was considered as a vehicle of instruction for these candidates.

---

34 See also Poole, "El Directorio para confesores del III Concilio Mexicano (1585)"; Luque Alcaide, "Ética y teología ante el Nuevo Mundo".

35 Carrillo Cázares, *Manuscritos del Concilio Tercero Provincial Mexicano (1585)*, vol. 1, 770–771.

36 Lib. v, tit. xi De sententia excomunicationis, § 7, in *Sanctum prouinciale concilium Mexici*, 96.

37 Medina, *Breve instruction de como se ha de administrar el Sacrame[n]to de la penitencia*, § 14.

38 Carrillo Cázares, *Manuscritos del Concilio Tercero Provincial Mexicano (1585)*, vol. 5, 144–146.

Something similar happened with regard to the decree on usury. The physician Pedro López had warned the council that several contracts were being used in the commerce of silver and other goods between merchants in Mexico and Spain.[39] The council asked him for a more detailed account of these contracts.[40] Twenty-four cases were submitted to the theological and juridical consultants of the council who responded by outlining the morality of every single one of them.[41] A long decree on usury was drafted, which described and provided solutions to two of these cases.[42] Regarding the remaining cases, the decree stated that the confessor should first consult the directory, where many other cases were explained, and follow those rules in order to condemn or acquit a suspect. If further doubts appeared, they were to consult theologians and jurists in such difficult cases.[43]

5 Concluding Remarks

We have explained that a provincial council was an exercise of the spiritual and jurisdictional *potestas* of the episcopacy, which derived its authority from natural law, positive law, and, above all, from divine positive law promulgated by Christ and being in accordance with the continuous practice of the Church. The main goal of a provincial council was to legislate, and therefore the decrees were its major outcome. Nevertheless, through them, other instruments could become legitimate texts that acquired normative value, as was the case of the catechism or the directory for confessors. If we return to the list made by Pope Sixtus V when he was still Fray Felice Peretti, it becomes clear that most of these topics were addressed by the decrees and by the other documents.

---

39 Carrillo Cázares, *Manuscritos del Concilio Tercero Provincial Mexicano (1585)*, vol. 1, 418–420.

40 Carrillo Cázares, *Manuscritos del Concilio Tercero Provincial Mexicano (1585)*, vol. 1, 431–432.

41 Carrillo Cázares, *Manuscritos del Concilio Tercero Provincial Mexicano (1585)*, vol. 1, 497–535.

42 Lib. V, tit. XI De usuriis, in *Sanctum prouinciale concilium Mexici*, 88–89. About the draft of this decree, see Cummins, "Imperial Policy and Church Income"; Martínez López-Cano, "La usura a la luz de los concilios provinciales mexicanos e instrumentos de pastoral"; Martínez López-Cano, "La Iglesia novohispana ante la usura y las prácticas mercantiles en el siglo XVI"; Martínez López-Cano, "Socialización y religiosidad del médico Pedro López (1527–1597)"; Staples, "Tentaciones de oro y plata"; Moutin, *Legislar en la América hispánica en la temprana edad moderna*, 128–130.

43 Lib. V, tit. XI De usuriis, § 6, in *Sanctum prouinciale concilium Mexici*, 89.

As has been shown, these documents could be the work of individuals, and herein lies the particularity of provincial councils, especially in the New World: apart from the canons produced, they included other normative documents. Nowadays, these historical sources are often classified as "pastoral works", but this – to our mind – is an anachronistic term, which reflects a more recent view that detaches these texts from their juridical origin. As a matter of fact, in the 16th century they were canonical documents arranged for a practical use.

In conclusion, the normative value of these "pastoral works" can only be understood in relation to their conciliar origin. They have been labelled in such an anachronistic manner only because other similar works already existed. In fact, many texts of that type circulated in manuscript and printed copies, but not all of them were considered good, orthodox or appropriate. They created an undesirable diversity, as pragmatic literature of this kind could prove to be dangerous, harmful or simply ineffective. Furthermore, they could result in a waste of resources and effort in places where a lack of personnel and economic provision played a major role. If these "conciliar pastoral works" were useful, it was because they were written by experts at the request of the proper authorities and because they were promulgated by a provincial council. After all, they had "the authority and approval of this council".[44]

Acknowledgements

The author would like to thank Chistiane Birr for the comments and Natalie Cobo for the revision of the text.

Bibliography

Printed Sources

Carrillo Cázares, Alberto, *Manuscritos del Concilio Tercero Provincial Mexicano (1585). Edición, estudio introductorio, notas, versión paleográfica y traducción de textos latinos*, 5 vols., Zamora, México 2006–2011.

Cobo Betancourt, Juan Fernando and Natalie Cobo, *La legislación de la arquidiócesis de Santafé en el periodo colonial*, Bogotá 2018.

44 Lib. V, tit. XI De usuriis, § 6 in fine, in *Sanctum prouinciale concilium Mexici*, 89.

Durán, Juan Guillermo, *Monumenta catechética hispanoamericana*, vol. 3: (*Siglos XVI–XVIII*), Buenos Aires 2017.

Martínez Ferrer, Luis, *Decretos del Concilio Tercero Provincial Mexicano 1585. Edición histórico crítica y estudio preliminar por Luis Martínez Ferrer*, 2 vols., Zamora 2009.

Medina, Bartolomé de, *Breve instruction de como se ha de administrar el Sacrame[n]to de la penitencia: dividida en dos libros compuesta por el padre maestro fray Bartholome de Medina [...]; En la qual se contiene todo lo que ha de saber, y hazer el sabio confessor para curar almas, y todo lo que deue hazer el penite[n]te para conseguir el fructo de tan admirable medicina*, Huesca 1581: Impressa con licẽcia, en casa de Ioan Perez de Valdiuielso.

Metzler, Josef, *America Pontificia*, vol. 2: *Primi saeculi evangelizationis 1493–1592. Documenta Pontificia ex registris et minutis praesertim in Archivo Secreto Vaticano existentibus*, Città del Vaticano 1991.

Sala, Aristide, "Del Concilio Provinciale. Trattatello di Frà Felice da Monte Alto, poi Sisto V", in Sala, Aristide (ed.), *Documenti circa la vita e le gesta di san Carlo Borromeo*, vol. 1, Milano 1857, 33–41.

Sanctum prouinciale concilium Mexici celebratum anno dni millessmo quingentessmo octuagessimo quinto, Mexici 1622: apud Ioannem Ruiz, Excudebatq[ue].

Literature

Cummins, Victoria Hennessey, "Imperial Policy and Church Income: The Sixteenth Century Mexican Church", in *The Americas* 43:1 (1986), 87–103.

Durán, Juan Guillermo, "Los instrumentos americanos de pastoral (siglo XVI)", in Saranyana, Josep Ignasi, Primitivo Tineo, Antón M. Pazos, Miguel Lluch-Baixauli and María Pilar Ferrer (eds.), *Evangelización y teología en América (siglo XVI): X Simposio Internacional de Teología de la Universidad de Navarra*, vol. 2, Pamplona 1990, 747–792.

Durán, Juan Guillermo, "La transmisión de la fe. Misión apostólica, catequesis y catecismos en el Nuevo Mundo (siglo XVI)", in Imbert, Escudero (ed.), *Historia de la Evangelización de América. Trayectoria, identidad y esperanza de un continente. Actas del simposio internacional*, Ciudad del Vaticano 1992, 285–352.

Fornés Azcoyti, Ignacio, *El proceso de la aprobación romana del III Concilio de México, 1585–1589*, Roma 2005.

Gadamer, Hans-Georg, *Truth and Method*, London 2004.

Galindo Bustos, Jesús, *Estudio del Aparato de Fuentes del Concilio Tercero Provincial de México (1585)*, México 2010.

García Hernán, Enrique, "La curia romana, Felipe II y Sixto V", in *Hispania Sacra* 46, no. 94 (1994), 631–649.

Gómez-Iglesias, Valentín, "La bula «Immensa Aeterni Dei» de Sixto V (22-1-1588): la revisión de los decretos de los concilios provinciales", in *L'Année canonique. Hors série* (1992), 409–415.

Grohe, Johannes, "Der Traktat *De concilio provinciali* (1565) des Felice Peretti (Sixtus V.)", in *Annuarium Historiae Conciliorum* 42 (2010), 403–412.

Luque Alcaide, Elisa, "Vida urbana en México (siglo XVI)", in Facultad de Teología San Vicente Ferrer (ed.), *Ética y teología ante el Nuevo Mundo: Valencia y América. Actas del VII Simposio de Teología Histórica (28–30 abril 1992)*, Valencia 1993, 193–212.

Martínez Ferrer, Luis, *Directorio para confesores y penitentes. La Pastoral de la Penitencia en el Tercer Concilio Mexicano (1585)*, Pamplona 1996.

Martínez Ferrer, Luis, "Un 'pequeño' conflicto entre Madrid y Roma. La polémica sobre la inclusión de la jurisdicción civil en el proemio de los Decretos de los terceros concilios de Lima (1582/83) y México (1585)", in Dalla-Corte Caballero, Gabriela, Ricardo Piqueras Céspedes and Meritxell Tous Mata (eds.), *América: Poder, conflicto y política*, Murcia 2013, 1–15.

Martínez López-Cano, María del Pilar, "La usura a la luz de los concilios provinciales mexicanos e instrumentos de pastoral", in Cervantes Bello, Francisco Javier and María del Pilar Martínez López-Cano (eds.), *Los concilios provinciales en Nueva España. Reflexiones e influencias*, México 2005, 285–314.

Martínez López-Cano, María del Pilar, "La Iglesia novohispana ante la usura y las prácticas mercantiles en el siglo XVI: entre el discurso y la práctica", in Cervantes Bello, Francisco Javier, Alicia Tecuanhuey Sandoval and María del Pilar Martínez López-Cano (eds.), *Poder civil y catolicismo en México, siglos XVI al XIX*, Puebla, México D.F. 2008, 75–102.

Martínez López-Cano, María del Pilar, "Pedro López de Medina y la moral mercantil de su tiempo", in Rodríguez-Sala, María Luisa and Luis Martínez Ferrer (eds.), *Socialización y religiosidad del médico Pedro López (1527–1597): de Dueñas (Castilla) a la ciudad de México*, México 2013, 217–247.

Moutin, Osvando Rodolfo, *Legislar en la América hispánica en la temprana edad moderna. Procesos y características de la producción de los Decretos del Tercer Concilio Provincial Mexicano (1585)*, Frankfurt am Main 2016.

Murphy, Francis Joseph, *Legislative Powers of the Provincial Council. A Historical Synopsis and a Commentary*, Washington, D.C. 1947.

Poole, Stafford, "El Directorio para confesores del III Concilio Mexicano (1585): Luz en vida religiosa y social novohispana del siglo XVI", in Mayer, Alicia and Ernesto de la Torre Villar (eds.), *Religión, poder y autoridad en la Nueva España*, México 2004, 111–124.

Poole, Stafford, *Pedro Moya de Contreras. Reforma católica y poder real en la Nueva España, 1571–1591*, trans. Alberto Carrillo Cázares, 2nd ed., México 2012.

Rivas, Luis Heriberto, "Algunas cuestiones historiográficas en torno al libro de los Hechos de los Apóstoles", in *Teología* 68 (1996), 221–236.

Staples, Anne, "Tentaciones de oro y plata", in Lira Gonzalez, Andres, Alberto Carrillo Cazares and Claudia Ferreira Ascencio (eds.), *Derecho, política y sociedad en Nueva España a la luz del Tercer Concilio Provincial Mexicano (1585)*, México 2013, 371–384.

Terráneo, Sebastián, *La recepción de la tradición conciliar limense en los decretos del III Concilio Provincial Mexicano*, Buenos Aires 2010.

Terráneo, Sebastián, "El llamado 'III Concilio Provincial Mexicano' y los 'Estatutos' de la Santa Iglesia de México' o 'Reglas consuetas de la catedral de México' ", in *Revista de Estudios Histórico-Jurídicos* 33 (2011), 613–637.

Vidal Gil, Jesús, *Los Estatutos del Cabildo de la catedral de México elaborados en el Tercer Concilio Provincial Mexicano (1585)*, Roma 2014.

CHAPTER 9

Shaping Colonial Behaviours: Franciscan Missionary Literature and the Implementation of Religious Normative Knowledge in Colonial Mexico (1530s–1640s)

David Rex Galindo

1 Introduction

In 1643, bishop of Michoacán Fray Marcos Ramírez de Prado, a Franciscan friar, conducted a long inspection of his diocese three years after his arrival to its seat in Valladolid (now Morelia). As a result, Ramírez de Prado wrote a series of ordinances or mandates to be observed throughout the diocese. The document, which was approved and signed by King Philip IV, reveals some abuses and negligence of his diocesan clergy, his views on indigenous Catholicism in Michoacán as well as his reformation plans to address shortcomings. Overall, he gave an adverse portrayal of the state of Catholicism in his bishopric. Fray Marcos lamented that neither parishioners nor *doctrina* Indians – those indigenous people still under the stewardship of missionaries – fulfilled the sacramental precepts; there was no decorum in the religious services; and a uniform legal regulation of discipline for the whole diocese was lacking. While he accepted that the flock was large and the ministers were few, Fray Marcos was particularly concerned with the administration of sacraments and the pastoral care of the indigenous communities. He reminded clerics to administer the sacraments – Eucharist, extreme unction, penance, and matrimony – in a timely and proper manner. This meant that his subjects should acquire a verifiable knowledge of the Catholic doctrine before partaking in the sacramental life as Christians. Priests had to hear confessions at least once a year during Lent to fulfil the annual confession requirement. He also urged clerics to check the bride and groom's single state and consanguine requirements to prevent incestuous relations. Michoacán's bishop concluded that priests ought to teach and regularly remind their flock of the path towards salvation through the Christian Gospels and by loving virtues and loathing vices. In other words, as exemplary mirrors and as religious guides, priests should mould the daily lives of their parishioners. Overall, the document is filled with mandatory

 | DOI:10.1163/9789004425736_010

precepts that would regulate the daily lives of his parishioners as much as the cadre of clerics under his authority.[1]

Ramírez de Prado's mandates underpinned a specific normative space to be followed in the diocese over which he ruled. From a juridical viewpoint, his instructions formulated but one layer of various normative levels that regulated the lives of the Spanish monarch's subjects in the early modern Hispanic world. Instructions by ecclesiastical authorities like Ramírez de Prado belonged to the Spanish system of administration of justice that rested on the interpretation and application of customary law, casuistry, legal codes, ecclesiastical normativities, and *ius commune*. Such an early modern multi-normative system or "plurality of rules", to use Paolo Prodi's words, relied on various juridical sources and practices in both the *forum internum* and the *forum externum* that represent the sacred and secular realms. At the backbone of the legal systems of the early modern monarchies were therefore competing juridical practices and normativities that championed the legal text as much as the customary praxis. Concomitantly, canon law, its treatises, and ecclesiastical practices were an essential part of such multinormativities that governed early modern people in Europe.[2]

In Spanish America, this legal culture adapted to and coalesced with local indigenous legal practices and the effervescence of regulations contingent with the colonial process, all of which resulted in a distinct normative regime that has traditionally been identified as "Derecho indiano".[3] Studying the formation of the Spanish colonial legal system in America, scholars have put much attention to investigate the resulting legal institutions, colonial juridical agents and, more recently, how indigenous actors and other colonial subjects not only relied on but also shaped the emerging new American normative orders. They have looked at juridical procedures as a lens into the colonial realities

---

1 "Ordenanzas del Obispo de Michoacán Fray Marcos Ramírez de Prado", AHCM, Fondo Diocesano, Sección Gobierno, Serie Mandatos, Subserie Notificaciones, Caja 6, exp. 18, 1643–1645. These ordinances and Ramírez de Prado's tenure in Michoacán have been studied by Traslosheros, *La reforma de la Iglesia del antiguo Michoacán*, 60–80.

2 Prodi, *Una historia de la justicia*, 99–122; Duve, "Was ist ›Multinormativität‹?", 88–101. Heinz Mohnhaupt writes that "Competing species of norms – such as case law, legal science, customary law and privileges – should also be considered in order to be able to throw light on the status and function of legislation. In doing so we should not focus only on competition between these types of norms, but rather also of complementary points and convergences between them", in Mohnhaupt, "The Object of Interpretation", 63.

3 Good starting points to the study of Derecho Indiano are Tau Anzoátegui, *Casuismo y sistema*; essays in Tau Anzoátegui, *El Jurista en el Nuevo Mundo*; and the collection of legal historical studies in Duve and Pihlajamäki (eds.), *New Horizons in Spanish Colonial Law*.

as well as to the translation of a juridical system into Spanish America.[4] It has been argued that the establishment of the Spanish legal system paved the way for colonial domination. The acts of negotiation, resistance, and conformity manifested themselves explicitly in litigation processes wherein indigenous peoples voiced their complaints to the Spanish authorities, thus appeasing tumultuous intentions and preventing rebellions.[5] While indigenous people litigated early on, the question of how they accessed Spanish juridical knowledge in the early post-conquest period still remains enigmatic. Certainly, close contact between native people and Spaniards catalysed the transmission of normative knowledge between both groups. Because religious men became major interlocutors between the conquered and the conqueror, it seems plausible that such an epistemological exchange occurred in the places of close contact between natives and clerics. In this essay, I show how clerics, with the help of local indigenous peoples, created, stored, and disseminated Catholic normative knowledge to the indigenous communities where they served as missionaries. While catechetical literature was a particular typology that condensed pragmatic religious normative knowledge, orality paved the way to its massive expansion.

---

4 For the English literature, see, for example, Borah, *Justice by Insurance*; Cutter, *The Protector de Indios in Colonial New Mexico*; Cutter, *The Legal Culture of Northern New Spain*; Herzog, *Upholding Justice*; Kellogg, *Law and the Transformation of Aztec Culture, 1500–1700*; Masters, "A Thousand Invisible Architects"; Owensby, *Empire of Law and Indian Justice in Colonial Mexico*; Premo, *The Enlightenment on Trial*; Premo and Yannakakis, "A Court of Sticks and Branches"; the essays in Ruiz Medrano and Kellogg (eds.), *Negotiation within Domination*; Yannakakis, *The Art of Being In-Between*; and Yannakakis and Schrader-Kniffki, "Between the 'Old Law' and the New".

5 In her study of the transformation of Mexican culture among Nahua communities in the aftermath of conquest, Susan Kellogg shows that Spanish colonialism succeeded not just because of direct violence, germs, or technology but because of the subtleties of long-term domination behind cultural hegemonic practices like the colonial legal system that opened space for accommodation, negotiation and dialogue as part of conflict solution. See Kellogg, *Law and the Transformation of Aztec Culture, 1500–1700*, particularly her "Introduction"; and more recently Susan Kellogg, "Introduction – Back to the Future: Law, Politics, and Culture in Colonial Mexican Ethnohistorical Studies", in Ruiz Medrano and Kellogg (eds.), *Negotiation within Domination*, 1–17. Scholars such as Ranajit Guha and Vivek Chibber have pointed out that, in studying agency and resistance to the colonial order, for instance, communal violent resistance should not be taken for granted as most individuals would rather explore all possibilities – particularly through formal, legal appeals and informal complaints to authorities – before risking their lives. Rather than looking at communal thriving forces, these authors showed that to subvert colonial regimes leaders of revolts have to convince individuals to take the risks when other means have failed. See Chibber, *Postcolonial Theory and the Spectre of Capital*, 162–163.

Hence, it is surprising how little attention has been devoted to the normative practices that emanated from religious authorities, especially with regard to canon law and moral theology, which were two pillars of the Spanish legal system implemented among the indigenous communities. Fray Marcos Ramírez de Prado's ordinances are but one example of regulations with exhortative power and of mandatory observance to all subjects in his bishopric that stem from clerical authorities.[6] Thus, the cultural processes of Christian evangelisation seem a worthwhile aspect to pursue in search of how different normative cultures enmeshed during conquest and colonisation. While a variety of Catholic clerical groups worked in the Americas, the mendicant orders, mostly Franciscans, dominated the evangelical landscapes in the first century of Spanish colonialism, especially in Mesoamerica.

The early expansion of the religious orders in New Spain is well-known. The Franciscan friars Pedro Melgarejo, Diego de Altamirano, Johann Van den Auwera, Johann Dekkers, and Pierre de Gand (Pedro de Gante) were the first five missionaries in Mexico, soon followed by the so-called First Twelve or Twelve Apostles, directly sent by the Pope in 1524 to convert the recently conquered Aztecs. With the same aim, Dominicans arrived in 1526 and Augustinians in 1533; Jesuits came in 1572. At the same time, Catholic authorities prompted the establishment of a secular clergy in the Viceroyalty of New Spain (founded in 1535). In any case, since their arrival to Mexico in the wake of Hernán Cortés' conquest of Mexico-Tenochtitlan, Franciscan convents mushroomed throughout the 16th and 17th centuries to become the largest religious order in terms of manpower and extension in New Spain. The Franciscan evangelical programme quickly spread among native communities through the erection of convents and churches, and their administration of Indian parishes (*doctrinas*). Franciscans were quick to occupy an ever-expanding missionary frontier through an iterative process of turning frontier missions into Indian parishes and custodies into independent provinces – for instance, a 1626 census of the Franciscan province of Saint Peter and Saint Paul of Michoacán, established in 1565, lists 135 friars and 33 convents and houses. Hence, in this essay I will focus on Franciscans and their ministry in central New Spain and its northern Michoacán frontiers in the 16th and first half of the 17th centuries to argue that Catholic religious orders were essential to the establishment of colonial normative systems in the Americas due to their close interaction with indigenous communities and their commitment to religious conversion. Frontier

6 One exception is Pardo, *Honor and Personhood in Early Modern Mexico*, who approaches pastoral and catechetical literature as normative knowledge.

realities and the distance from centres of information and knowledge meant that religious men had to be creative in their responses to the new American realities with vast numbers of local peoples to be converted and less evangelical resources available than in Europe (figure 9.1).[7]

True, the processes of acculturation were multidirectional and owe much to the evangelisation ventures wherein both missionaries and indigenous people acted as cultural brokers in defining and re-defining normative orders that stemmed not just from traditional legal systems but also from norms with deep moral significance. Studies of the evangelisation of the Americas highlight the moral dimension of the cultural transfer between the two worlds. Hence, missionaries and indigenous people engaged in "moral dialogues" in which the other's moral concepts were casted within one's own cultural framework and, subsequently, cultural barriers dragged the translation of moral norms from Catholicism into indigenous cultures. As part of these practices, new rituals had to be introduced and behaviours had to be guided.[8] It is also well-known that the Spanish conquest of America wrought havoc to indigenous societies: war, violence, disease. Because Catholic missionaries brought a sense of entitlement and absolute truth, they destroyed elements of local cultures perceived as evil. While it is true that the creation and application of religious normativities among native peoples happened in the midst of a demographic crisis of immense proportions that ravaged the lives of those who endured it, at the same time, however, through the transmission of knowledge, Catholic missionaries gave indigenous peoples the means to engage with the new colonial legal structure.[9]

This chapter gives particular importance to the application of codes of conduct and modes of behavioural control at the community level that stemmed from Franciscan religious men and their knowledge of canon law and moral theology. In the context of Catholic evangelism in early contact situations, I contend that Franciscans (although this might further apply to the other mendicant orders who evangelised in Mexico: Dominicans, Augustinians, and Jesuits), in conjunction with local indigenous peoples, actively participated in creating and applying a religious normative order that, by relying on moral theology, catechetical and pastoral literature (what we call pragmatic normative

---

7 The 1626 Census of the province of Michoacán is in AHFM, Fondo Provincia, Sección Gobierno, Caja 1, Libro de Becerro 1. The process of Franciscan expansion throughout New Spain in the 16th century is well explained in Ricard, *The Spiritual Conquest of Mexico*; and López-Velarde López, *Expansión geográfica franciscana*.

8 Burkhart, *The Slippery Earth*; Lockhart, "Double Mistaken Identity"; Schwaller, "Conversion, Engagement, and Extirpation"; Yannakakis, "Beyond Jurisdictions".

9 One scholar has argued that indigenous people were born to die, see Cook, *Born to Die*.

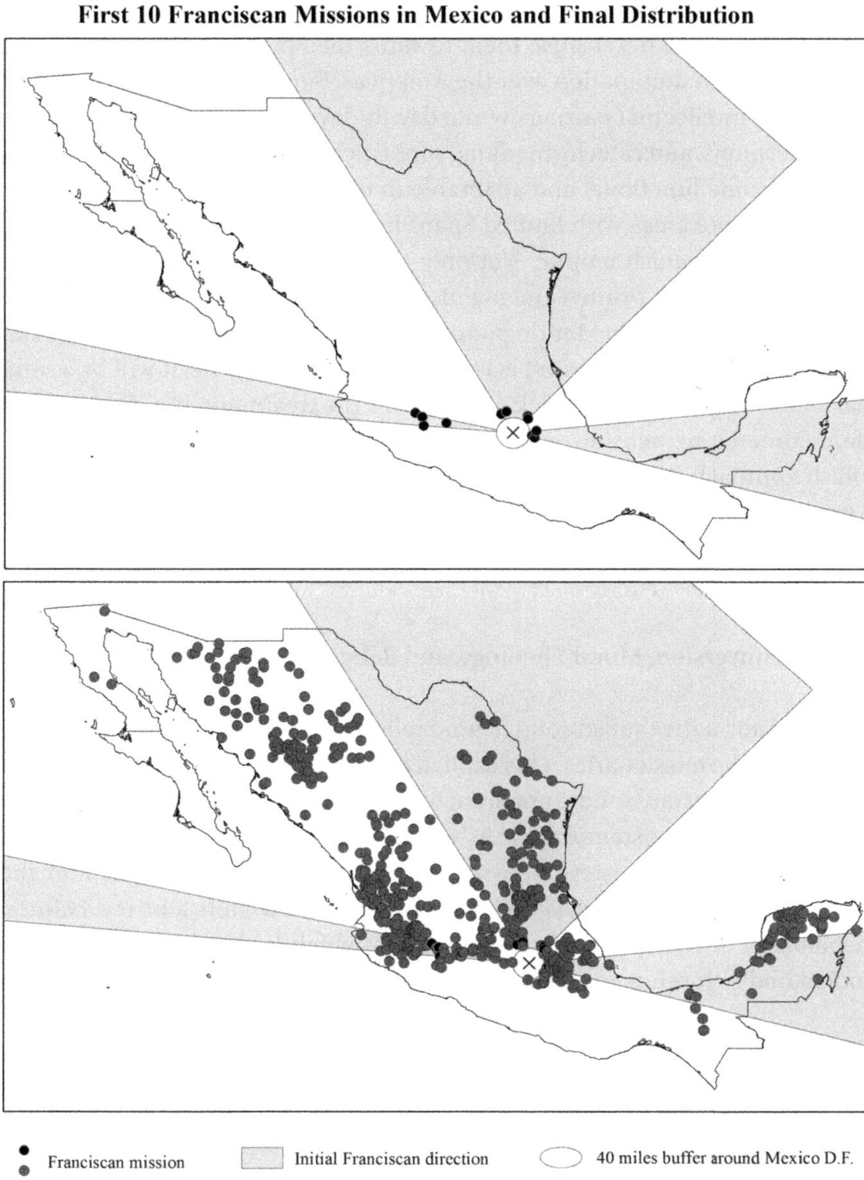

FIGURE 9.1 Map of Franciscan initial conventual and missionary expansion from the first 10 missions outside of Mexico City (see the western direction in Michoacán) and final distribution of doctrinas and missions in Mexico, 1520s–1810s
SOURCE: MARIA WALDINGER, "THE LONG-RUN EFFECTS OF MISSIONARY ORDERS IN MEXICO", *JOURNAL OF DEVELOPMENT ECONOMICS* 127 (2017), 370

literature), indigenous practices, and orality, sought to convert native people to Christianity and desensitise them towards the Spanish culture, ultimately shaping Spanish domination over the Americas. Franciscan scholars and their indigenous intellectual partners wrote day-to-day confessional writings, pamphlets, sermons, and catechisms along sophisticated treatises that, as this book shows, became functional and adaptable to the new colonial settings, particularly in remote areas with limited Spanish government in the context of the early modern Spanish empire. Not only these texts with a theological background circulated in printed and manuscript format throughout the Americas, but, as canonist Osvaldo Moutin points out, "moral theology should be considered a legal source. In many aspects of political and daily life, it will be a seminal factor. Thus, there is no lack of norms for the treatment of Indians, family life, commerce, to mention only some aspects".[10] One aim is henceforth to take a fresh approach to some known catechisms, sermons, and pastoral texts from a normative, juridical perspective while exploring how religious normative knowledge was created, stored, and disseminated in New Spain.

2 Conversion, Moral Theology, and Religious Normativities

There is a normative substratum behind religious conversion, the central focus of the Catholic missionaries. This explicit connection between conversion and normativities becomes more apparent when approaching religious conversion as a process with epistemological as well as behavioural foundations – rather than the fulfilment of rites of passage and devotions such as baptism or the *Via Crucis*. Religious conversion implies a worldview shift and the cultural metabolism of "basic presuppositions upon which both self and others are understood".[11] It refers to the acquisition of certain knowledge as much as to

10 For an overview that approaches the genre of pragmatic normative literature from the perspectives of canon law and moral theology and its relevance to the construction of normative orders in early Ibero-America, see Thomas Duve (Chapter 1) in this volume. On the entanglement between moral theology and Western legal culture, see Prodi, *Una historia de la justicia*; Decock, *Theologians and Contract Law*; Duve, "Catequesis y Derecho Canónico"; and Moutin, *Legislar en la América hispánica en la temprana edad moderna*, quote is on p. 4 (my own translation). A pioneer work in pointing out that the legal culture in the Western tradition had deep roots in ecclesiastical law and moral theology, is Berman, *Law and Revolution*. For a recent reappraisal of Berman's work, see the Forum essays in *Rechtsgeschichte – Legal History* 21 (2013).

11 Buckser (ed.), *The Anthropology of Religious Conversion*, xi. For the following, see Rex Galindo, *To Sin No More*; and Rex Galindo, "Primero hombres, luego cristianos".

a change in a person's conduct. Franciscan missionaries understood religious conversion as a metamorphosis within and without one's faith explicitly related to human behaviour. In other words, religious conversion implies a moral transformation, a change in a person's way of life that, moreover, is not linear because human nature is prone to sin and, hence, relapse prevents conversion from being complete. Religious conversion thereby implicitly comprises a cultural mutation (and adaptation) which could be voluntary but also coerced under the guidance of those who claim to possess the knowledge.

There is always a punitive factor in the conversion process, since those who convert receive the postmortem reward of eternal salvation and those who fail are condemned and punished to eternal suffering.[12] As early modern people knew, the Christian God's punishment was not a rhetorical tool but a taunting reality. Moreover, in the earthly interregnum awaiting the celestial or infernal outcome, the blurred line that separated ecclesiastical from civil jurisdiction in the early modern period manifested vigorously when sinful conducts received spiritual as well as physical chastisement. This theology of fulfilment and chastisement translated to the Americas. For instance, the ordinances for Nahua confraternities Fray Alonso de Molina wrote in Nahuatl (1552) are but one example of the exhortative nature of religious normative texts. Owing to the expansion of the Franciscan missionary scaffold throughout New Spain, Molina's statutes were written as a model for other confraternities in Franciscan hospitals for indigenous peoples in central Mexico. Extending divine punishment of "sinners, idolaters and the haughty and arrogant", to the earthly world, the ordinances admonished those who failed to follow them and prescribed whippings for recidivists. In extreme cases, civil and clerical juridical branches granted justice to what were considered abominable sins that deserve the capital punishment.[13]

It should not be surprising that in an early modern Hispanic world of embroiled civil and ecclesiastical normativities, for those under Franciscan guardianship, moral theology provided the normative arena, setting the norms for the direction of customs; thus, it is considered a fundamental instrument to guide Catholics' behaviour. It focuses on the discussion and establishment of the individual's moral obligations within the framework of the Christian

---

12 See, for instance, Aquinas, *Summa Theologiæ*, 3rd Part, Question 86, Article 1: "Therefore we must say simply that, in this life, every sin can be blotted out by true Penance".

13 *Nahua Confraternities*, ed. Sell, 2, 99. See also Schwaller, "Constitution of the Cofradía". For cases of sodomy punished with death in colonial Peru and the application of entangled civil and ecclesiastical legal cultures in such cases, see Molina, *Cuando amar era pecado*.

God's revelation.[14] Within this context, in his 1643 Chronicle of the Franciscan Province of Michoacán, Fray Alonso de la Rea praised the work of his fellow Franciscan brothers among the native communities of Michoacán, a region to the west of the capital Mexico-Tenochitlán. For de la Rea, the conversion process had a clear beginning and an end. It promised the freedom of Christianity substituting the yoke of servitude of gentiles. Religion brought the law of Christ – "our law" wrote the friar – introducing native peoples into what he viewed as the true religion while condemning the false sects – namely, native American religions. Following this reasoning, friars were "legislators" who introduced the P'urépechas, indigenous people in Michoacán, to "the political and social life" through "establishing towns and the laws of *policia*", that is, a good quotidian order that regulated daily lives.[15] This was more than a rhetorical statement. Since religious conversion had conduct connotations, de la Rea's assertion showcases Franciscan involvement in the setting of normative orders during their evangelical ministry among native peoples. Hence, their pastoral texts, aiming at conversion, maintained a normative stature in Franciscan-indigenous relations.[16]

3 Producing and Storing Religious Normative Knowledge

Clerics produced a good amount of religious texts in America in the colonial period. Scholars have already pointed out that books, both in printed and manuscript versions, circulated widely in the 16th and 17th century Hispanic world.[17] In Mexico, the majority of the printed material consisted of religious texts which aimed at conversion. Besides imported books, early on, local presses also produced books in the Americas. In 1538, Emperor Charles V granted

14 The legal mandate of moral theology was not lost in the early 20th century Catholic Encyclopaedia, which included an entry pointing towards "the rule, or norm, of the moral order, human actions as such, their harmony or disharmony with the laws of the moral order, their consequences, the Divine aids for their right performance". In other words, "as jurisprudence must enable the future judge and lawyer to administer justice in individual cases, so must moral theology enable the spiritual director or confessor to decide matters of conscience in varied cases of everyday life". See Lehmkuhl, "Moral Theology".

15 Rea, *Crónica de la Orden de N. Seráfico P.S. Francisco*, 90–91, 105.

16 Normative orders, whether consensual or imposed, are sets of common norms that define human conduct. Normative orders result from processes of creation, storage, adaptation, legitimisation, and standardisation of norms, that have compelling as well as orderliness natures. See Thomas Duve (Chapter 1) in this volume and MacCormick, *Institutions of Law*, 11–20.

17 See Otto Danwerth (Chapter 3) in this volume.

printer Juan Cromberger permission to publish a catechism in P'urépecha in Sevilla after Bishop Vasco de Quiroga's request. Juan Cromberger soon moved the press to Mexico City, where the first American book, not surprisingly a catechism in Nahuatl, was printed in 1539.[18] Throughout the colonial period, friars and native people wrote extensively in local indigenous languages, predominantly Nahuatl, the *lingua franca* in central Mexico, but also in P'urépecha and Matlazinga, languages of Michoacán, Chontal Maya, and Otomí to name a few. In his study of religious texts written in Maya and Nahuatl languages, Mark Christensen points out that we should not take for granted that all pastoral literature in indigenous languages was the result of intensive cooperation of clerics and Indians. To be sure, printed texts adhered to this interethnic collaboration under the guidance of the religious men. However, some of the unpublished works that circulated in indigenous languages were the sole production of native people, with perhaps slight clerical guidance. Of course, other religious texts were written in Spanish and to a lesser degree in Latin. In terms of their functionality, I would like to distinguish between texts written to train other specialists or to be read by learned readers, particularly confession manuals and theological treatises, and those written to entice a non-erudite audience, particularly catechisms or doctrinal pamphlets, sermons, and speeches (*pláticas*). There is a good amount of scholarly work that shows how these latter pragmatic texts – those with a pastoral and catechetical character – were produced, circulated, and kept in 16th century Mexico.[19]

My own research on inventories of Franciscan conventual libraries in Mexico shows that Franciscan monasteries had copies of pragmatic religious literature in their stacks, such as Martín de Azpilcueta's books – including his bestseller *Manual for confessors and penitents* – as well as bilingual catechisms and dictionaries in indigenous languages. Friars relied on epitomised works such as Azpilcueta's to develop their own pragmatic scholarship.[20] These

18 AGI, Indiferente, 1962, L.6, fols. 127r–v and AGI, Indiferente, 1962, L.6, fol. 128. See also Burkhart, *The Slippery Earth*, 20.

19 Christensen, *Nahua and Maya Catholicisms*, chapter 2. For Nahuatl as the *lingua franca* of central Mexico, see the articles in Schwaller (ed.), *A Language of Empire, a Quotidian Tongue*. For a bibliographical study of catechisms published in America in the 16th century, see Resines Llorente, *Catecismos americanos del siglo XVI*, 2 vols. In his contribution of the present book, José Luis Egío (Chapter 7) shows how under bishop Juan de Zumárraga's ecclesiastical authority, pragmatic catechetical literature was produced in the 1530s and 1540s in New Spain in the context of anti-Protestant and anti-Erasmian politics in Europe before the Council of Trent (1545–1563).

20 For the phenomenon of epitomisation, see Christoph Meyer (Chapter 2) in this volume. For Martín de Azpilcueta, see Manuela Bragagnolo (Chapter 6) in this volume.

inventories are not exhaustive in their bibliographical information, as they commonly list author's last names and title keywords but make no reference to year of publication nor edition. For instance, inventories from the Franciscan convent of Tula – 120 kilometres north of Mexico City – cover the period between 1602 and the late 1620s. According to these inventories, this library was well provided with material necessary for the conversion of native peoples, mostly Otomí and Nahua speakers. The library held some *summae* and *compendia* of Martín de Azpilcueta's works as well as his confession manual, including a Latin edition. Preaching and praying stood out in the stacks, where one could find books of sermons by Dominican Fray Vicente Ferrer (1350–1419) and Franciscan Fray Antonio de Padua (c. 1195–1231), or some of Dominican Fray Luis de Granada's (1504–1588) works on prayers and meditation. The inventory lists bilingual dictionaries in Nahuatl and Spanish as well as Franciscan Fray Juan Bautista de Viseo's book of sermons (which must have been added in 1608) and Fray Alonso de Molina's bestselling confessionary (added in 1611). The library also kept some unidentified manuscripts: two *cartapacios* or binders of unknown topics and seven binders in Otomí language, described as treatises and miscellanea.[21]

General inspections of Franciscan convents conducted in the 1660s in central Mexico also show the bibliographic content of other Franciscan libraries. For instance, the conventual library of Santa María de Atzompan in the current-day town of Ozumba, east of Mexico City, kept two bestsellers in moral theology and confession manuals: Father Antonino Diana's (1585–1663) *Summa and Compendium* (1646) and Franciscan Fray Manuel Rodríguez's (1546–1613) *Explanation of the Bula de la Santa Cruzada* (1589). In his study of confession manuals in the early-modern Hispanic world, historian Antonio González Polvillo cites these books, along with Martín de Azpilcueta's works among the most circulated books across the Atlantic in the 16th and first half of the 17th centuries.[22] The convent of Tepeji del Río, 100 kilometres north of Mexico City, listed a trilingual manuscript manual in Otomí, Nahuatl, and Spanish, a manuscript dictionary of Nahuatl and Spanish, a binder with some cases of conscience, as well as manuscript sermons.[23] Overall, conventual libraries kept

21 BNAH, Fondo Franciscano, vol. 45, Inventarios y memorias del Convento de Tula, passim.

22 BNAH, Fondo Franciscano, vol. 36, Convent of Santa María of Atzompan, 25 January 1661, fols. 22r–v, 51v. Fray Alonso Bravo conducted the inspection. "están cabales los sesenta y tres libros de q.e se compone". For best-selling manuals of confession and moral theology in the Hispanic World, see González Polvillo, *Análisis y repertorio de los tratados y manuales*.

23 BNAH, Fondo Franciscano, vol. 40, fols. 44–48.

Martín de Azpilcueta's various editions of his confession handbook and *compendia*, Fray Alonso de Molina's and Fray Juan Bautista de Viseo's confession handbooks in Nahuatl, Fray Juan Bautista de Viseo's book of sermons in Nahuatl, other printed books of sermons, bilingual dictionaries, as well as manuscript texts: mostly sermons in Nahuatl, Spanish, and even Latin.[24] It should be noted that these inventories of manuscript and printed books do not account for those binders of manuscript texts and printed books kept by individual friars in their cells and those which might have just disappeared.

The bibliographical richness of Franciscan libraries envisages the variety of moral topics discussed and the strategies used during the Franciscan evangelical programme in New Spain. An interesting example emerges from a little-known manuscript in Latin and Spanish titled "Handbook in which many things are noted which are necessary for the priests' quotidian ministry". Composed by Fray Juan de la Concepción in 1597, this handwritten book of 62 sheets compiled an array of sources to help friars deal with practical cases confronted in their ministry such as polygamy, homicides, the intrusion of women into the monasteries, blasphemy, abortions, and the administration of the sacraments. Fray Juan de la Concepción mostly relied on the works of the abovementioned Fray Manuel Rodríguez, a Portuguese Franciscan who wrote extensively on moral cases, and on Martín de Azpilcueta, whom he referred to as Navarro. Texts like de la Concepción's added practical responses by veteran missionaries to real problems the religious confronted in their daily contact with New Spain's diverse communities, including *doctrinas de indios* and missions on the frontiers of the Spanish empire. Serve as an example of the compiler's pragmatism but also the normative nature of these texts, the inclusion of French Franciscan jurist and missionary Fray Juan Focher's brief answers to some practical cases that religious men faced in their daily ministry. It should be noted that Focher, who died in Mexico City in 1572, was a juridical and theological authority in New Spain when Fray Juan de la Concepción compiled his text in the late 16th century. The French missionary extracted his responses from a variety of sources that ranged from the Council of Trent, Paul's letters to the Corinthians, and various papal bulls, to the opinions of the theologians Thomas Aquinas (1225–1274) and John Duns Scotus (1266–1308). The questionnaire consisted of six questions that focus on controversial topics such as the jurisdictional conflicts in the administration of sacraments between regular and secular clergies, redemption of sins among indigenous

24 See other library inventories in the same volume 40 and in BNAH, Fondo Franciscano, vol. 36.

recidivists, Indian marriages, and potential disputes among the missionaries themselves. Friars could conduct marriages of mestizos, blacks and Spaniards within their convents, Focher admitted, but not in other jurisdictions during their visitations, following unnamed papal bulls that had hampered mendicant privileges in Mexico. He further supported that at least in confession, Spaniards and indigenous people should be dispensed alike in cases such as incest if it had been committed with a wife's relative.[25]

The sense of social and moral reform that missionaries wanted to imprint on Catholics and non-Christians alike can be recognised from the confession manuals that proliferated during the 16th century. From a viewpoint of conversion, one function of confession manuals was to distil the religious normativities that missionaries disseminated to Catholics and non-Catholics in the early modern period. The social disciplining ethos of the sacrament of penance has been the focus of various studies in recent decades. A general premise has been that confession and preaching were vehicles to instigate social control and to impose an ecclesiastical normative order aimed at changing people's behaviours.[26] Indeed, this normative pattern behind confession translated to Spanish America. For example, a look at the only confession handbooks published in an indigenous language in the 16th century unveils some of the normative knowledge friars sought to transmit to their Indian parishioners. Fray Alonso de Molina's bilingual confession manual in Nahuatl and Spanish, a bestseller in its own right, went through three editions: 1565, 1569, 1578. The structure of this book is typical and similar to a Christian catechism that he had previously drafted in 1546: the 10 Commandments, the Catholic Church Commandments, Holy Communion, the 7 mortal sins, 14 corporal and spiritual works of mercy, the 5 senses (sight, hearing, taste, smell, and touch), and the virtues. Fray Alonso de Molina's text illustrates the practical concerns priests faced in their daily ministry. For instance, in his lengthy explanation of the 7th commandment "thou shall not steal", he is concerned with the fairness of Indian labour conditions and tribute collection with a clear hierarchical distinction between the *macehuales* (Indian commoners or peasants) and *caciques* (Indian leaders, elites). That *caciques* should be asked by their confessors how they administered the tributes unveils the fluid structures of power in Spanish colonial society. Questions dealt with tax mismanagement, fundamentally unfair increases and diversion of taxes to third parties, the theft of tributes, and irregularities in the distribution of labour to distant mining centres or in

25 BNM, MS.308. For Fray Juan Focher's answers, see fols. 30r–34r.

26 See, for instance, Boer, *The Conquest of the Soul*, 46–47; and Turrini, *La coscienza e le leggi*.

personal services for Spaniards, all of these recurrent problems in the colonial period that contravene royal legislation. Having lived in New Spain since his early teens, Fray Alonso de Molina displayed a familiarity with local practices and languages acquired during his upbringing and his later Franciscan work. Not uncommon with most missionaries, Fray Alonso, however, never acknowledged his tandem work with native Nahuatl-speaking scholars.[27]

We know of Fray Alonso and others' oblivion of Nahua contributions to the writing of pragmatic literature from one of their fellow brethren. Half a century after the publication of Molina's work, Franciscan Fray Juan Bautista de Viseo wrote a more elaborated confession handbook (1660) that addressed topics such as kinship and incest, matrimony, games and cards, fornication, the sale and drinking of *pulque* (a Mexican alcoholic fermented beverage). This Franciscan friar not only credited his collaboration but also acknowledged that other friars had also relied on local knowledge to write their pastoral works. In the prologue to his book of sermons in Nahuatl published in 1606, Bautista de Viseo appreciated the help of his Mexican aides, who had been educated at the Franciscan College of Tlatelolco. It seems as if Mexican Hernando de Ribas – versed in Nahuatl, Latin, and Spanish and an instructor of Nahuatl, who helped various Franciscan missionaries like Fray Alonso de Molina and Fray Joan de Gaona to compose their bilingual works – particularly contributed to Bautista de Viseo's texts. He further praised the support of Joan Berardo, Diego Adriano, Francisco Bautista de Contreras, Esteban Bravo, the famous Antonio Valeriano, and Agustín de la Fuente. Interestingly enough, Bautista de Viseo lists his Mexican collaborators before he owes his intellectual debt to his Franciscan brethren.[28]

Certainly, instead of approaching indoctrination as a unidirectional process, Catholic evangelism became a give and take process with a bi-directional

---

27 Molina, *Confesionario Mayor*, "Acerca del septimo mandamiento de Dios", 35–45. His 1546 *Doctrina Christiana* included basic Christian doctrinal prayers such as explanation of the sign of the cross and its prayer, the Our Father prayer, the Hail Mary, the creed, Salve Regina, the Decalogue, the 5 commandments of the church, the 7 sacraments, 14 articles of the Catholic faith (7 over the blessed divinity of God and 7 over the holy humanity of Jesus), 14 corporal and spiritual works of mercy, general confession, the Eucharist, and the act of contrition; see Molina, *Doctrina Christiana breve traduzida en lengua Mexicana (1546)*, 34–61. Other catechisms added mortal sins and the theological and cardinal virtues to basic Catholic knowledge. Catechetical works published in Europe and America included these basic teachings.

28 Bautista Viseo, *A Iesu Christo S.N. ofrece este Sermonario en lengua Mexicana*, Prólogo. See also Fray Juan Bautista de Viseo, *Advertencias para los confesores de los naturales*, 1600, 2 vols. For a new edition of the first book with an introductory study of the author and his work, see Murillo Gallegos (ed.), *Fray Juan Bautista de Viseo*.

flux. Not only does conversion imply an active role on the part of the converted as much as of the missionary, but also indigenous interpreters and intellectuals played a key role in transforming the message for wide American audiences and thus were crucial in indoctrinating the American populations. The production of Indigenous-language texts was the result of joint-research projects between the friars and local leaders. The best-known example is the co-operation between Franciscan Fray Bernardino de Sahagún and his indigenous collaborators. Sahagún had arrived in Mexico in 1530, where he pursued a long missionary career until his death in 1590. For many years, in the Franciscan College of Tlatelolco (then outside Mexico City), he trained Mexican scholars such as the abovementioned Antonio Valeriano as well as Alonso Begerano, Martín Jacobita, and Andrés Leonardo, who collaborated with the Spanish friars to compose their pastoral literature. Through teamwork, friars and indigenous advisers worked together to produce Christian catechisms and other pastoral texts that contained basic Christian doctrinal prayers. These texts list a series of mandatory religious rituals to be performed regularly. In all, Nahuas had been advising Franciscan missionaries in their writing of pragmatic literature pivotal to the introduction of religious normative knowledge with moral significance.

Other works explicitly aimed at direct catechetical indoctrination. Tactics varied. For instance, friars like Fray Maturino Gilberti in Michoacán used the scholastic dialogue between a master and a student as a method to catechise P'urépecha speakers. In Gilberti's 1559 *Diálogo de Doctrina Christiana* a casual encounter turns into a teaching process. His dialectical pattern echoed other *diálogos de doctrina cristiana,* such as the one by Juan de Valdés (1499–1541) published in 1529, who utilises a conversation among the archbishop of Granada, a priest, and a parishioner. As Fray Maturino Gilberti points out in his prologue to his *Diálogo de Doctrina Christiana*: "It is about what the Christian has to know, believe, do, desire, and hate. The disciple asks the Master".[29] This method reveals a hierarchical flow of knowledge from its possessor (the teacher, the friar) to its receptor (the student) or disciple (the Indian). The disciple is as eager to learn as the master is to teach and correct. Through a Q&A dialectical arrangement, the teacher clarifies Christian concepts whilst applying them to the student's quotidian practices. Ironically, both Valdés and Gilberti were persecuted by the Inquisition. As Moisés Franco Mendoza

29 Title page of Maturino Gilberti's *Diálogo de Doctrina Christiana* (1559): "Trata de lo que ha de saber, creer, hazer, dessear, y aborrecer, el Christiano. Va preguntando el discipulo al Maestro". (my own translation).

points out in his study of Gilberti's P'urépecha corpus, Gilberti proposes a pedagogical model of catechetical implementation based on Christian doctrine through local cultural and linguistic knowledge. He deploys a normative praxis embedded in the teaching of moral precepts that normalize and guide the lives of Christians and potential converts. The teacher is not a mere vehicle of memorised information, he wants to transmit understanding to the Christian normative order. Gilberti like other religious men, might have also worked closely with local people to polish his writing and convey his message in convenient ways.[30]

These indigenous intellectuals, working together with Franciscan missionaries, shared their knowledge in order to bring innovative changes to their communities. As indoctrinators, the thoughts, motives, and intentions of native scholars owed much to the context in which they lived: this included not only their own cultures and institutions, but also those of the new regime that the Spaniards – including the Franciscan missionaries – aimed to implement. In the context of Spanish colonialism wherein actors operate, native people could, and, in many cases, were forced to, innovate the rules that governed their lives. Following other studies that highlight native political preeminence within their own communities under European colonial rule, a similar assertion could be pointed out for the relevance of indigenous legal and theological scholarship in the implementation of a colonial normative order. Certainly, power asymmetries appear, particularly at the macro level of Spanish colonialism in the Americas. But the daily life that involves a deeper knowledge of the internal structures of each community might reveal the way in which a few Catholic missionaries had to deal with communities of dozens, if not hundreds, of Indians. Not only were native scholars "knowledgeable", they were also "enabled" even in the midst of colonial asymmetries.[31] Normative knowledge was transferred through various mechanisms in the early modern period. Besides the dissemination of written texts, communication techniques also included other mass media typologies that had also proved effective in Europe and were transferred to the Americas. I am particularly interested in studying oratory techniques as a means of application of normative knowledge.

30 For Fray Maturino Giberti's work, see Franco Mendoza, *Eráxamakua*, 31–32, 109–114. For Juan de Valdés, see Valdés, *Diálogos de Doctrina Cristiana*.

31 I have discussed these issues in further detail in Rex Galindo, Kalfelis and Nomey, "Agency and Asymmetries", 293–327. For native political pre-eminence in another colonial settings, see, for instance, Hackel, "The Staff of Leadership".

4 Preaching Religious Normative Knowledge

The creation of a juridical system in New Spain mirrored the juxtaposition of oral and written communication traditions with rituals and symbols in the formation of a medieval legal corpus. The works of legal historians such as Gerhard Dilcher illustrate how even in political associations without strong, centralised state structures, conflict regulation rested on undifferentiated oral and written traditions that set the medieval normative orders.[32] Orality, not just in the juridical praxis in court, but as a backbone of jurisprudence and customs translated to Spanish America in the early modern period. In a religious context, oral communication took the form of confession, preaching, and theatrical performances. In fact, confession manuals, theatrical plays, and preaching material attest to the multiple dimensions of the Franciscan evangelical programme in New Spain. This section focuses on the role preaching played in the dissemination of religious normative knowledge.

Through preaching, clerics shaped religious beliefs and set procedures to convey moral, social, and political virtues and loath vices. Even if in early modern America and Europe religious knowledge was distributed through the written word, it was through preaching that knowledge was received. Comparing the power of orality with written texts in his study of English preachers and their listeners in the late 16th and early 17th centuries, historian Arnold Hunt warns us that the written word alone could not transform ordinary peoples' lives, "because it lacked the converting power of the spoken voice".[33] In a period when literacy rates were low, the spoken and visual words were the most important means of mass communication. Religious normative knowledge was produced and applied at two levels: among literate people who wrote and/or read pragmatic texts and among illiterate people who heard, saw, and talked about the subsequent religious normative message. As art historian Samuel Y. Edgerton has shown, to appeal to the senses and convert indigenous peoples, oral skills merged with a visual apparatus produced by local indigenous artisans. Thus, even if ephemeral, preaching was still the most powerful tool to convey messages to wide audiences. It was in a sense the mass media coverage of the early modern period. Thus, in studying preaching, one needs to keep in mind not only the preacher and his message (the text) but the audience, the temporal and spatial context, the language(s), and the reactions. Because of the profound oral traditions on both sides of the Atlantic, preaching became a

32 See, for instance, Dilcher, *Normen zwischen Oralität und Schriftkultur*.

33 Hunt, *The Art of Preaching*, 10.

major means in the transmission of religious norms in 16th- and 17th- century Mexico.[34]

By highlighting the importance of oral traditions in both European and American cultures we may better comprehend the spread and implementation of religious normative knowledge in 16th- and 17th-century Mexico. Orality was a central aspect of the religious life as well as the most important means to convey norms and rules to the general population in Europe. Confession and preaching, major methods to transmit normative ecclesiastical knowledge, owed much to the medieval oral traditions. Franciscan missionaries were above all communicators of the Christian doctrine, who, through an oratory 'science' or *ars praedicandi*, infused their own moral and social codes with the objective of changing their listeners' ways of life. Early on after their arrival in Mexico City in the 1520s, Franciscans ascended the pulpits and temporary stages in plazas, streets, and roads in villages and hamlets in order to introduce their own views over religious conversion and eternal salvation through crafted discourses that reflected intense preparation and meditation.[35] The content of the message and the rhetoric were essential for reaching their audience. Moreover, to entice non-Catholics and Catholics alike to their conversion, friars exhibited a cornucopia of visual effects attached to their verbal message. Missionaries spent long hours in their conventual libraries preparing the content and eloquence of their preaching by reading handwritten and published manuals, sermons, cases of conscience, and other pragmatic texts. These texts

34 I have found the work of the "Italian Voices" Research group at the University of Leeds particularly helpful in understanding the interconnectivities between preaching, oral cultures, orality, and written texts; see, for instance, Dall'Aglio, "Voices under trial"; and the articles in Dall'Aglio, Degl'Innocenti, Richardson, Rospocher and Sbordoni (eds.), *Oral Culture in Early Modern Italy*. I thank Manuela Bragagnolo for these references. Missionaries and local artisans conceptualized architectural designs such as open chapels, paintings, and sculptures to operate in conjunction with the spoken word to appeal to indigenous peoples to their conversion, and hence, to the spread of a colonial normative order with ecclesiastical principles in Spanish America, Edgerton, *Theaters of Conversion*.

35 See, for instance, Carta al emperador por un grupo de franciscanos, entre ellos Motolinia, Cuautitlán, 17 November, 1532, Archivo Histórico Nacional, Madrid, Diversos, no. 14, published in Motolina, *Epistolario (1526–1555)*, ed. Gómez Canedo, 92. This letter was signed by Fray Martín de Valencia, custodio, Fray Ildefonso de Herrera, guardián, Fray Martín de Jesús, guardián, Fray Juan de Padilla, guardián, Fray Antonio Civitatensis, guardián, Fray Francisco Jiménez, Fray Toribio Motolinía, Fray Alonso de Guadalupe, Fray Francisco del Álamo, and Fray Arnaldo de Bazatzio. An almost identical content in Carta al emperador por un grupo de franciscanos, entre ellos Motolinia, Tehuantepec, 18 January 1533, Archivo Histórico Nacional, Madrid, Diversos, no. 16, published in Motolina, *Epistolario (1526–1555)*, ed. Gómez Canedo, 100.

had pedagogic purposes for the listeners as much as for the friars themselves and constituted textbooks for the training of inexperienced preachers and missionaries.[36] Preaching material (*materias predicables*) and the collection of *sermonarios* and *pláticas* held in the libraries reveal that preaching was the main method of bringing the flock to their conversion, and I argue, the means of instilling religious normative knowledge with a strong moral component. Ultimately the goal was to bring men and women to the confessional.

Since the Middle Ages, the art of religious oratory, or *ars praedicandi* (referring to both the craft and the genre) – homiletics as a theological discipline – studied and transmitted the methods and skills of preaching. Printed or manuscript sermons and preaching guides, some written by priests and missionaries to teach future orators, circulated in Europe and crossed the Atlantic to foster evangelical ministry in America. Fray Luis de Granada (1504–1588) and Fray Martín de Velasco (c. 1621 – date of death unknown), who authored the *Retórica augmentativa and arte de escribir sermones*, stand out as representatives of the *ars praedicandi* in the early modern Hispanic world, and their work circulated amply among religious men in colonial Mexico. Friars in Mexico also showed great concern with this genre and topic.[37]

In the viceroyalty of New Spain, the culmination of the *ars preadicandi* definitely came from the hands of a Franciscan mestizo. In 1579, Fray Diego de Valadés, a veteran preacher and missionary in Mexico, published his *Rhetorica Christiana* in Italy, a dense volume in Latin dedicated to the art and practice of preaching. While the book was published as a handbook on preaching techniques, Valadés introduced sections on Mexican culture and the process of evangelisation, with a particular focus on the Franciscan evangelical ministry among the indigenous peoples. Following a motto rooted in the classical works on rhetoric, Fray Diego de Valadés pointed out that preaching had "to teach, to delight, and to motivate". Sermons should be intelligent and delightful, delivered by preachers with obedience. According to this *ars praedicandi*, preaching was an art measured in words as well as in manners. The aim of the sermon, theorists like Valadés emphasised, was to instruct listeners in the rudiments of the Catholic faith and to reform their customs. Valadés pointed out that "the preacher has to do everything in his hand to preach well". Wisdom and knowledge were prerequisites for good preachers. The message had to be poignant in order to affect parishioners' feelings. Of course, it had to be

36 Following theologian Octavio Luna, and historians Federico Palomo and Hilary Dansey Smith, among other scholars, I have discussed this issue in Rex Galindo, *To Sin No More*, 239–240.

37 Rex Galindo, *To Sin No More*, 241.

spoken in the vernacular of the listeners. Besides carefully crafting the content of their sermons, preachers also polished the aesthetics. Valadés' engraving of the preacher on the pulpit and his audience captures the dynamism of preaching (figure 9.2). To translate the basic elements of Catholic doctrine and to help with memorisation, friars instructed Indians with words but also with images. Friars also controlled the preaching spaces. In Valadés' picture, the audience sits in hierarchical and gendered order. In the first row, the indigenous judges show their *varas* as governors of the 'república de indios'.[38]

The Tlaxcalan friar gives hints at the pedagogical tools used during catechetical instruction. One of his most iconic and reproduced engravings on Franciscan activities in the New World is a representation of a conventual patio that offers readers a snapshot into the daily activities of missionaries and their catechumens. In the image, which depicts an idealised open chapel, different aspects of the evangelical agenda are orderly represented. In a composition layout centred on a group of Franciscan missionaries led by Saint Francis transporting the Catholic Church onto Mexico, the friar shows his readers the life of Mexican indigenous peoples from childhood until death under Franciscan missionary care. One can see missionaries instructing native peoples in general knowledge, teaching the Christian doctrine and the sacraments, attending to the sick, and parading the dead. At the base of the engraving, religious men administer the sacraments to the recently converted, and, at the bottom-centre, grant justice. This idealised image seems to be self-complete of a new world in which the friars fulfil their evangelical mission through the spiritual and worldly care of their flock (figure 9.3).

According to Valadés' utopian description of the activities in each Indian town, *indios doctrineros* prayed publicly; children learned how to speak, sing, play instruments, and write; and all attended the sermons. Notwithstanding the idealism of these reflections, oral culture pervaded the Franciscan evangelisation programme, wherein religious men exhorted and preached to

38 Valadés, *Rhetorica Christiana*, 24: "El predicador deber hacer todo lo posible para conseguir hablar bien". "Pues como dice San Gregorio, acepta el oficio de pregonero todo el que sube al sacerdocio para caminar gritando ante la llegada del juez que terriblemente llega". X. Del oficio del predicador: "Mas el que aspira a persuadir por medio de la palabra lo que es bueno, sin desechar ninguna de estas tres cosas, a saber, enseñar, deleitar, conmover, perore y actúe para que sea oído inteligente, gustosa y obedientemente". See pages 211–214 for the engraving of the preacher and an explanation. Preaching theorists agreed that teaching, delighting and motivating were the preachers' three essential tasks to reform their audiences' lives. See, for instance, Smith, *Preaching in the Spanish Golden Age*, 60–61. For the entanglement of visual art and preaching as tools of conversion, see Edgerton, *Theaters of Conversion*.

FIGURE 9.2 Valadés, Fray Diego de, *Rhetorica Christiana*, Perugia 1579, 211

SOURCE: "TYP 525.79.865, HOUGHTON LIBRARY, HARVARD UNIVERSITY"

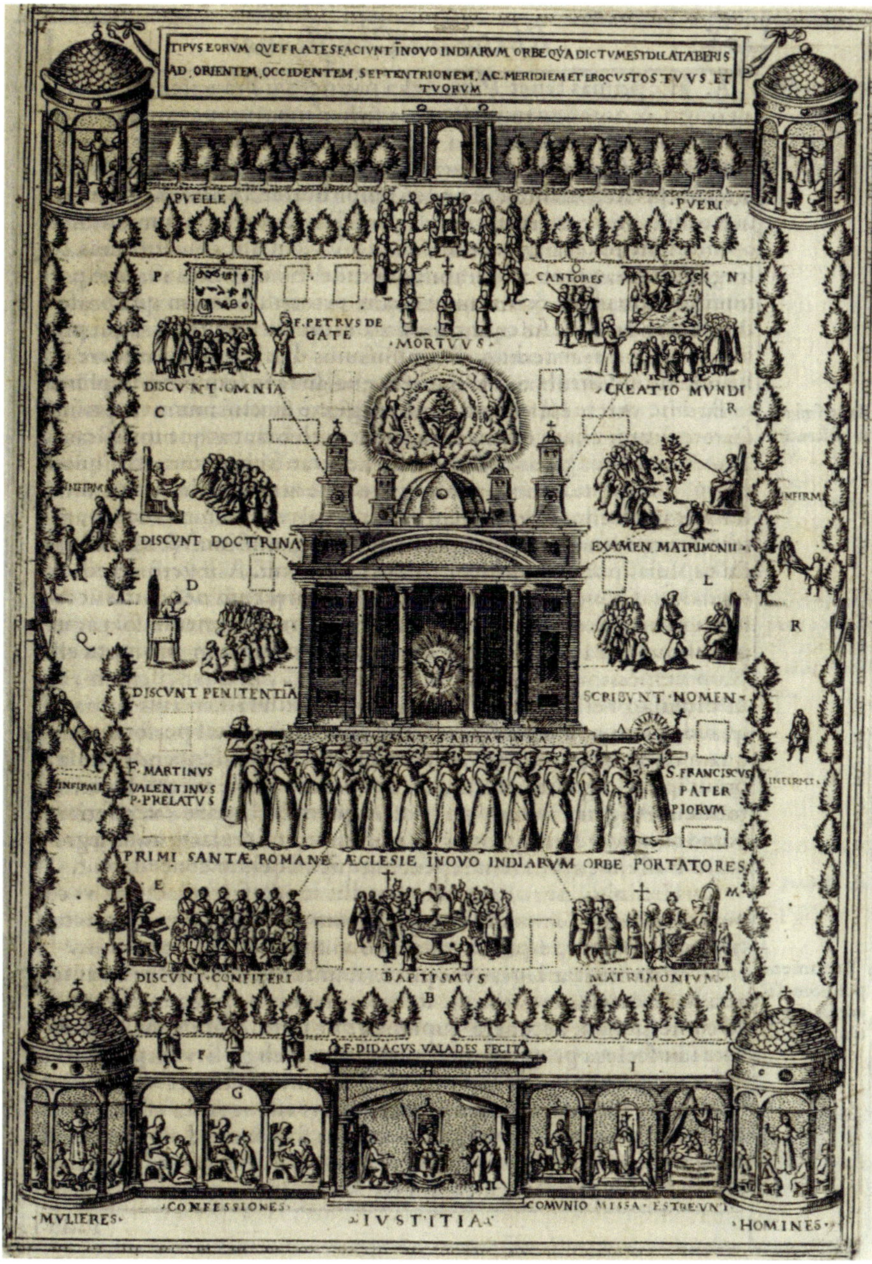

FIGURE 9.3 Valadés, Fray Diego de, *Rhetorica Christiana*, Perugia 1579, 107

emphasise the dichotomy between virtues and eternal reward with sins and punishments. Missionaries became the righteous mediators of divine justice over the American peoples, where the city of God would triumph under the authority of the clerics. It was hence paramount to the missionaries to show that the new justice, which emanated for the Christian God through the Pope, the Catholic monarchy and ultimately the Franciscan missionaries, should supplant the indigenous normative system. The author pointed out that the evangelical pedagogy culminated in a Decalogue-structured questionnaire when listeners counted with "corn seeds or little stones their sins and their number" and friars showed pictures of sinners and sins to deter listeners from the path towards condemnation.[39] Even if an idealised representation, Fray Diego de Valadés' imagery did reflect upon one of various levels of multinormativy that regulated the lives of the Spanish monarch's subjects in the early modern Hispanic world, particularly those catechised by the Franciscan missionaries.

The importance of orality and preaching are ubiquitous in the writings and praxis of the missionaries as well as in native-language texts. The earliest surviving chronicle of Michoacán, written by Fray Diego Muñoz in 1585, emphasised the importance of preaching to the early missionaries of Michoacán. Muñoz's prosopographical study of missionaries highlights his brethren's ability to disseminate the spoken word. True, his words are part of the hagiographic fanfare of his time, but his chronicle (and others) underscores the centrality of orality in the transmission of (normative) knowledge. The first Franciscan missionary in Michoacán, Fray Martín de Jesús, early on "began to preach the evangelical law, and to convert and baptise large numbers of unfaithful, destroying idolatries, erecting crosses and images and teaching the Christian doctrine". Muñoz puts Martín de Jesús at the top of a preaching that ensued: "His successors left, with their entire works, flat and clear the way of preaching to us who followed them".[40] And the list goes on and on to include great orators such as Fray Jacobo Daciano, Fray Maturino Gilberti, Fray Juan de Padilla, or Fray

39 Valadés, *Rhetorica Christiana*, 209–215.

40 Fray Diego Muñoz's manuscript "Descripción de la Provincia de los Apóstoles San Pedro y San Pablo en las Indias de la Nueva España" is in ASOFM, M.33. I have also used Atanasio López's edition of Muñoz's "Descripción de la Provincia de los Apóstoles San Pedro y San Pablo en las Indias de la Nueva España" in López, "Misiones o doctrinas de Michoacán y Jalisco", 393–394: "y comenzó a predicar la ley evangélica y convertir y baptizar grandísimo número de infieles, destruyendo la idolatría, poniendo cruces e imágenes y enseñando la doctrina cristiana".; "sus sucesores dejaron, con sus enteros trabajos, llano y desembarazado el camino de la predicación a los que les sucedimos". (my own translation).

Francisco Lorenzo.[41] The Nahuatl Ordinances of the confraternity of the Immaculate Conception in Mexico City, written in 1552 by Fray Alonso de Molina, were to be read out aloud to all male and female members of the confraternity on the vigil of the feast day so that its members got acquainted with such rules or were reminded of them. Various versions were handwritten probably for such occasions. They requested that the whole confraternity prayed and sang together what had previously been memorised: the *Veni creator spiritus*.[42]

Preaching guides and sermons offered the friars enough material to draft their own orations from an extensive pool of topics that included cornerstone themes of Catholic doctrine such as the Ten Commandments and spiritual devotions to the Virgin Mary in her various avocations and to the saints. Moreover, religious men also distilled preparatory information from sermons, *pláticas*, and references, centred on social and moral issues. In all cases, sermon authors wrote extensively about sexuality, profane spectacles, and gender relations, and to a lesser extent about socio-economic themes. *Sermonarios* from Mexico included a good repertoire of sermons and *pláticas* with a moral and social emphasis, including themes such as lewdness, bad habits, gallantry, drunkenness, dresses, dances, comedies, gender relations, and gambling.[43] Missionaries carried their evangelisation material with themselves – in boxes with pragmatic literature such as compilations of sermons and catechetical works.

---

41 "Descripción de la Provincia de los Apóstoles San Pedro y San Pablo en las Indias de la Nueva España" in López, "Misiones o doctrinas de Michoacán y Jalisco", 396–397 (Fray Jacobo Daciano): "Veniánle los Indios de pueblos muy remotos a ver y comunicar sus trabajos, y él los consolaba y animaba con eficacísimas palabras, en lo cual tenía especial gracia". For Fray Maturini Gilberti, see "Descripción de la Provincia de los Apóstoles San Pedro y San Pablo en las Indias de la Nueva España", in López, "Misiones o doctrinas de Michoacán y Jalisco", 401. For Fray Juan de Padilla, see "Descripción de la Provincia de los Apóstoles San Pedro y San Pablo en las Indias de la Nueva España", López, "Misiones o doctrinas de Michoacán y Jalisco", 403. For Fray Francisco Lorenzo, see "Descripción de la Provincia de los Apóstoles San Pedro y San Pablo en las Indias de la Nueva España", López, "Misiones o doctrinas de Michoacán y Jalisco", 409. Over half a century later, Fray Alonso de la Rea would also describe Muñoz's rhetorical abilities: "Su hablar era poco, pero tan sentencioso y elocuente, que hoy se guardan sus escritos como si fueran de un Justo Lipsio, así por su narración como por su letra, por ser excelente escribano". De la Rea further attests Muñoz's abilities as a moralist: "fue gran sumista, y resolvía con gran destreza los casos más difíciles que ventila la teología moral". Rea, *Crónica de la Orden de N. Seráfico P.S. Francisco*, Capítulo 13, 248–249.

42 *Nahua Confraternities*, ed. Sell, 101.

43 See, for instance, George Baudot's study of Fray Bernardino de Sahagún's sermons and Fray Andrés de Olmos' writings on mortal sins in Baudot, *La pugna Franciscana por México*.

The *ars praedicandi* also had deep roots in American cultures. In central Mexico, civil and spiritual leaders relied on their speeches and rhetorical skills to establish loyalty and spread political and spiritual instructions. Nahuas distinguished the authority of a speech from the word *huehuetlatolli* or "ancient wisdom, speech of the elders", and a distinct glyph. The *huehuetlatolli* was hence a speech of wisdom that emanated from higher authorities and thus had an intrinsic value. In Michoacán, P'urépecha leaders of all levels, from the *cazonzi* or king and *petámuti* or supreme spiritual leader to lesser governors and priests, also used the spoken word as a political tool of control. It was through speeches that leaders could have their messages, mandates and requirements be heard. *Petámuti* in P'urépecha means the "great speaker", and he and his priests, called *curitiecha*, were considered preachers in the *Relación de Michoacán*, and the *hatapatiecha* were town criers who marched and sang in front of war captives.[44] The compiler of the *Relación de Michoacán*, Fray Jerónimo de Ayala, pointed out that his story of P'urépecha leadership owed much to local oratory traditions that stemmed from the *Petámuti*, who orally transmitted the official story of his kingdom to the minor priests or *curitiechas* to spread the narrative to his vassals.[45]

Spaniards were aware of these traditions. Speaking of the P'urépechas in the mid-16th century, the first bishop of Michoacán Vasco de Quiroga exclaimed "Have you heard among illiterate people such eloquent speakers?!" ["¡¿Han oído ustedes, entre gente iletrada, oradores tan elocuentes?!"] Thus, when they arrived in Mexico, European preachers found people already used to giving and listening to normative religious knowledge. Friars relied on local collaborators in the conversion deeds. They elected and trained *fiscales* and *mayordomos* from the local elites to teach the Christian doctrine. In Nueva Galicia, Fray Diego Muñoz wrote that two native Franciscan *donados*, Lucas and Sebastián widely preached to both converted and non-Christian Indians. They even took part in missionary campaigns to New Spain's northern frontiers, where they preached to independent, non-Christian Indians. Nonetheless, the chronicler did not mention the inevitable linguistic problems that these men faced. Lucas was described as a virtuous Christian man although he was never ordained as a friar because he was an Indian.[46] On the other hand, Fray Diego de Valadés,

44 For the Aztecs, see Lockhart, *The Nahuas After the Conquest*, 406. For Michoacán, see Alcalá, *Relación de Michoacán*, Tercera Parte, cap. 2: "En los cués había estos sacerdotes siguientes", 195–196.

45 Martínez Baracs, *Convivencia y utopía*, 87–88.

46 Franco Mendoza, *Eráxamakua*, 147–152. Quiroga's quote on 148. For Diego Muñoz's account on the two native Donados, see López, "Descripción de la Provincia", 403–404.

son of a Tlaxcalan mother and Spanish father, involved himself in catechetical and probably preaching ministry among Nahuatl- and Otomí-speaking peoples, languages that he mastered, prior to his ordination as a friar and priest.[47] Sources and scholars have underlined the reliance on children, particularly the offspring of *caciques*, as cultural-brokers in colonial settings such as 16th century Mexico.[48] The spread of religious norms was hence the result of a multiethnic and multitudinous effort.

Translating posed major challenges, though. Not only did some concepts have no corresponding terms but friars faced difficulties with the message itself. There are some studies on how concepts such as the Holy Trinity, God, Eucharist, and other Catholic concepts, were translated and explained to local communities. Particularly problematic was the explanation of the Holy Trinity in Nahuatl, to which Fray Juan Bautista de Viseo dedicated a whole section in his 1600 *Advertencia para confesores de naturales*. Kinship and differing definitions of incest also concerned the missionaries such as Fray Juan Bautista. In a recent study of an unpublished Nahuatl text on the *Via Crucis* (Stations of the Cross) written around the mid-17th century and attributed to Franciscan fray Agustín de Vetancourt, John Schwaller contrasts the differences between Vetancourt's Nahua text and other Spanish versions of the *Via Crucis*. One striking omission in the second station is the absence of Isaac's sacrifice in his explanation of the Passion of Christ, as it was customary to discuss a troublesome topic in the first decades after the fall of Mexico-Tenochitlan: the eradication of human sacrifice among Mexican nations.[49]

5 Concluding Remarks

By the mid-17th century, theologians and chroniclers who wrote on human sacrifice did so as part of a Mesoamerican past. Only as the frontier unfolded, new instances (even if imaginary) of human sacrifice among peripheral indigenous groups appeared in the sources. Fray Marcos Ramírez de Prado's 1643 ordinances composed for the Christian subjects in his bishopric of Michoacán were mute on this matter. However, some of the themes in his exhortations

47 Esteban J. Palomera, "Introducción", in Valadés, *Rhetorica Christiana*, x.

48 For the use of children as cultural brokers, see "Carta al emperador por un grupo de franciscanos, entre ellos Motolinia", Cuautitlán, 17 November 1532, Archivo Histórico Nacional, Madrid, Diversos, no. 14, published in Motolina, *Epistolario (1526–1555)*, ed. Gómez Canedo, 92.

49 Schwaller, "Fr. Agustín de Vetancurt".

remained an open matter of implementation throughout the colonial period in Mexico. This is directly connected to my understanding of religious conversion (which is ultimately incomplete) as normative implementation.

I think that an explicit connection between religious conversion, moral theology, and normative knowledge offers a venue to address the spread and application of religious norms in colonial Spanish America. I hope to have shown that we can approach Catholic evangelism as a process of creation, propagation, and application of religious normativities that govern peoples' everyday lives in peripheral imperial milieus. As a corollary, we can assume that Catholic religious orders were essential to the establishment of colonial normative systems in the Americas due to their close interaction with indigenous communities and their commitment to religious conversion. But it has further been demonstrated that these processes of normative dissemination were not unidirectional. It was through Christian missionaries and local native aides that European normative ideas were translated to indigenous communities. In many cases, we have seen how these religious normativities were implemented through confession and preaching.

In the midst of weak state control, missionaries and their indigenous partners wrote day-to-day pragmatic confessional writings, pamphlets, sermons, and catechisms along sophisticated treatises that, we believe, became functional and adaptable to the new frontier settings. This "pragmatic normative literature" with a theological, evangelical underpinning gained *ad hoc* significance and functionality in remote areas with limited Spanish government in the context of the early modern Spanish empire. For instance, pragmatic literature encompassed small pastoral works that priests carried in their pockets or under their robes. This literature, with a strong moral component, served as the basis to conversion – not only of the indigenous people, the focus of my chapter – in Spanish America. I suggest that a look at library inventories and a focus on the importance of oral traditions on both sides of the Atlantic may explain the creation, collection, and spread – as uneven as it might have been – of normative religious knowledge in the 16th-century Hispanic world. Both preaching and confession played pivotal roles in the implementation of a normative order. In spite of the corrective nature of confession, ecclesiastical norms were first heard. Both cultures used rhetorical techniques filled with metaphorical symbolism, corporal gestures, and visual symbols to instigate order.

As recent research has pointed out, the process of conversion of Spanish America was incomplete at its best. Some scholars even write about the various *Catholicisms* that Catholic clerics brought and transmitted to native communities. Native people who received the Christian message did it in polyphonic and sometimes distorted ways. Native Americans adapted these multiple voices into their own cosmology to mould their local, individual Catholicism.[50] This means that the implementation of ecclesiastical normative knowledge was irregular and affected indigenous communities in unpredictable ways.

Acknowledgements

I would like to thank Manuela Bragagnolo, Oracio Condorelli, Otto Danwerth, Max Deardorff, Thomas Duve, José Luis Egío, Carlos Alberto González Sánchez, Tamar Herzog, Constanza López, Osvaldo Moutin, Pedro Rueda Ramírez, and John F. Schwaller for the comments and suggestions throughout the elaboration of this essay. My particular gratitude to Thomas Duve for his support while I was a researcher at the Max-Planck-Institut für europäische Rechtsgeschichte and beyond. I am also grateful to Ana María Ruiz Marín, of the Archivo Histórico de la Provincia Franciscana de Michoacán, and the staffs of the Biblioteca Nacional de México, Museo de Antropología e Historia, Archivo Storico dell'Ordine dei Frati Minori, Museo y Archivo Histórico Casa de Morelos, and the Archivo General de Indias for their kind and diligent support in locating documents.

Bibliography

Manuscripts

Archivo General de Indias, Sevilla (AGI), Indiferente, 1962, L.6.

Archivo Histórico Provincial Franciscano de Michoacán, Celaya [México] (AHFM), Fondo Provincia, Sección Gobierno, Caja 1, Libro de Becerro 1.

Archivo Storico dell'Ordine dei Frati Minori, Roma (ASOFM), M.33.

Biblioteca Nacional de Antropología e Historia, México D.F. (BNAH), Fondo Franciscano, vols. 36, 40, 45.

Biblioteca Nacional de México, México D.F. (BNM), MS.308.

Museo y Archivo Histórico Casa de Morelos, Morelia [México] (AHCM), Fondo Diocesano, Sección Gobierno, Serie Mandatos, Subserie Notificaciones, Caja 6, exp. 18, 1643–1645.

50 See, for instance, Christian, *Local Religion in Sixteenth-Century Spain* and the essays in Nesvig, *Local Religion in Colonial Mexico*. For the idea of multiple Catholicisms, see Christensen, *Nahua and Maya Catholicisms*. For the incompleteness of conversion, see Rex Galindo, *To Sin No More*.

Printed Sources

Alcalá, Fray Jerónimo de, *Relación de Michoacán, 1541*, Madrid 2002.

Aquinas, Thomas of, *Summa Theologiæ*, trans. Fathers of the English Dominican Province, 1920 (Online edition 2017: http://www.newadvent.org/summa).

Bautista Viseo, Fray Juan, *A Iesu Christo S.N. ofrece este Sermonario en lengua Mexicana*, Mexico City 1606: En casa de Diego Lopez Daualos, y a su costa.

López, Atanasio, *Misiones y doctrinas de Michoacán y Jalisco*, in *Archivo Ibero-Americano* 18 (1922), 341–425.

Molina, Fray Alonso de, *Confesionario Mayor, en la lengua mexicana y castellana*, México 1569: En Casa de Antonio Espinosa Impressor.

Molina, Fray Alonso de, *Doctrina Christiana breve traduzida en lengua Mexicana (1546)*, in *Códice Franciscano. Siglo XVI*, ed. Icazbalceta, Joaquín García, 2nd ed., México 1941.

Motolina, Fray Toribio, *Epistolario (1526–1555)*, ed. Gómez Canedo, P. Lino, México 1986.

Murillo Gallegos, Verónica (ed.), *Fray Juan Bautista de Viseo y sus Advertencias para los confesores de naturales*, México 2014.

Nahua Confraternities in Early Colonial Mexico: The 1552 Nahuatl Ordinances of Fray Alonso de Molina, OFM, trans. Barry D. Sell, ed. Sell, Barry D. (with contributions by Larissa Taylor and Asunción Lavrin. Introduction by John F. Schwaller), Berkeley, CA 2002.

Rea, Alonso de la, *Crónica de la Orden de N. Seráfico P.S. Francisco, Provincia de San Pedro y San Pablo de Mechoacan en la Nueva España (1639)*, México 1882.

Resines Llorente, Luis, *Catecismos americanos del siglo XVI*, 2 vols., Salamanca 1992.

Valadés, Diego de, *Rhetorica Christiana* (Perugia 1579), México 1989.

Valdés, Juan de, *Diálogos de Doctrina Cristiana*, Alcalá de Henares 1529.

Literature

Baudot, George, *La pugna franciscana por México*, México 1990.

Berman, Harold J., *Law and Revolution: The Formation of the Western Legal Tradition*, Cambridge, MA 1983.

Boer, Wietse de, *The Conquest of the Soul: Confession, Discipline, and Public Order in Counter-Reformation Milan*, Leiden 2001.

Borah, Woodrow, *Justice by Insurance: The General Indian Court of Colonial Mexico and the Legal Aides of the Half-Real*, Berkeley, CA 1983.

Buckser, Andrew, Stephen D. Glazier (ed.), *The Anthropology of Religious Conversion*, Lanham, MD 2003.

Burkhart, Louis M., *The Slippery Earth: Nahua-Christian Moral Dialogue in Sixteenth-Century Mexico*, Tucson, AZ 1989.

Chibber, Vivek, *Postcolonial Theory and the Spectre of Capital*, London 2013.

Christensen, Mark Z., *Nahua and Maya Catholicisms: Texts and Religion in Colonial Central Mexico and Yucatan*, Stanford, CA 2013.

Christian, William A., *Local Religion in Sixteenth-Century Spain*, Princeton, NJ 1981.

Cook, Noble David, *Born to Die: Disease and New World Conquest, 1492–1650*, Cambridge 1998.

Cutter, Charles R., *The Protector de Indios in Colonial New Mexico, 1659–1821*, Albuquerque, NM 1986.

Cutter, Charles R., *The Legal Culture of Northern New Spain*, Albuquerque, NM 1995.

Dall'Aglio, Stefano, "Voices under trial. Inquisition, abjuration, and preachers' orality in sixteenth-century Italy", in *Renaissance Studies* 31:1 (2017), 25–42.

Dall'Aglio, Stefano, Luca Degl'Innocenti, Brian Richardson, Massimo Rospocher and Chiara Sbordoni (eds.), *Oral Culture in Early Modern Italy: Performance, Language, Religion*, in *The Italianist* 34:3 (2014).

Decock, Wim, *Theologians and Contract Law. The Moral Transformation of the Ius Commune (ca. 1500–1650)*, Leiden 2013.

Dilcher, Gerhard, *Normen zwischen Oralität und Schriftkultur: Studien zum mittelalterlichen Rechtsbegriff und zum langobardischen Recht*, Köln, Weimar 2008.

Duve, Thomas, "Catequesis y Derecho Canónico entre el viejo y el nuevo mundo", in Schmidt-Riese, Roland (ed.), *Catequesis y Derecho en la América colonial*, Madrid 2010, 131–145.

Duve, Thomas, "Was ist ›Multinormativität‹? – Einführende Bemerkungen", in *Rechtsgeschichte – Legal History* 25 (2017), 88–101.

Duve, Thomas and Heikki Pihlajamäki (eds.), *New Horizons in Spanish Colonial Law. Contributions to Transnational Early Modern Legal History.* Frankfurt am Main 2015 (10.12946/gplh3).

Edgerton, Samuel Y., *Theaters of Conversion: Religous Architecture and Indian Artisans in Colonial Mexico*, Albuquerque, NM 2001.

Franco Mendoza, Moisés, *Eráxamakua: Utopía de Maturino Gilberti*, Zamora 2016.

González Polvillo, Antonio, *Análisis y repertorio de los tratados y manuales para la confesión en el mundo hispánico (ss. XV–XVIII)*, Huelva 2010.

Hackel, Steven W., "The Staff of Leadership: Indian Authority in the Missions of Alta California", in *The William and Mary Quarterly* 54:2 (1997), 347–376.

Herzog, Tamar, *Upholding Justice: Society, State, and the Penal System in Quito (1650–1750)*, Ann Arbor, MI 2004.

Hunt, Arnold, *The Art of Preaching: English Preachers and their Audiences, 1590–1640*, Cambridge 2010.

Kellogg, Susan, *Law and the Transformation of Aztec Culture, 1500–1700*, Norman, OK 1995.

Lehmkuhl, Augustinus, "Moral Theology", in *The Catholic Encyclopedia* 14 (1912) (http://www.newadvent.org/cathen/14601a.htm).

Lockhart, James, *The Nahuas After the Conquest: A Social and Cultural History of the Indians of Central Mexico, Sixteenth Through Eighteenth Centuries*, Stanford, CA 1992.

Lockhart, James, "Double Mistaken Identity: Some Nahua Concepts in Post Conquest Guide", in Lockhart, James, *Of Things of the Indies: Essays Old and New in Early Latin American History*, Stanford, CA 2000, 98–119.

López-Velarde López, Benito, *Expansión geográfica franciscana en el hoy Norte Central y Oriental de México*, México 1964.

MacCormick, Neil, *Institutions of Law: An Essay in Legal Theory*, Oxford 2007.

Martínez Baracs, Rodrigo, *Convivencia y utopía: El gobierno indio y español de la ciudad de Mechuacan, 1521–1580*, México 2005.

Masters, Adrian, "A Thousand Invisible Architects: Vassals, the Petition and Response System, and the Creation of Spanish Imperial Caste Legislation", in *Hispanic American Historical Review* 98:3 (2018), 377–406.

Mohnhaupt, Heinz, "The Object of Interpretation: Legislation and Competing Normative Sources of Law in Europe During the 16th to 18th Centuries", in Morigiwa, Yasutomo, Michael Stolleis and Jean-Louis Halperin (eds.), *Interpretation of Law in the Age of Enlightenment. From the Rule of the King to the Rule of Law*, Heidelberg 2011, 61–89.

Molina, Fernanda, *Cuando amar era pecado: Sexualidad, poder e identidad entre los sodomitas coloniales (Virreinato del Perú, siglos XVI–XVII)*, Lima 2017.

Moutin, Osvaldo Rodolfo, *Legislar en la América hispánica en la temprana edad moderna. Procesos y características de la producción de los Decretos del Tercer Concilio Provincial Mexicano (1585)*, Frankfurt am Main 2016.

Nesvig, Martin A., *Local Religion in Colonial Mexico*, Albuquerque, NM 2006.

Owensby, Brian P., *Empire of Law and Indian Justice in Colonial Mexico*, Stanford, CA 2008.

Pardo, Osvaldo F., *Honor and Personhood in Early Modern Mexico*, Ann Arbor, MI 2015.

Premo, Bianca, *The Enlightenment on Trial: Ordinary Litigants and Colonialism in the Spanish Empire*, New York, NY 2017.

Premo, Bianca and Yanna Yannakakis, "A Court of Sticks and Branches: Indian Jurisdiction in Colonial Mexico and Beyond", in *The American Historical Review* 124:1 (2019), 28–55.

Prodi, Paolo, *Una historia de la justicia: De la pluralidad de fueros al dualismo moderno entre conciencia y derecho*, trans. Luciano Padilla, Madrid 2008.

Rex Galindo, David, "Primero hombres, luego cristianos: Un análisis sobre la conversión forzosa en la frontera de Texas", in *Colonial Latin American Historical Review* 2:3 (2014), 405–432.

Rex Galindo, David, *To Sin No More: Franciscans and Conversion in the Hispanic World, 1683–1830*, Stanford, CA 2018.

Rex Galindo, David, Melina Kalfelis and José Luis Paz Nomey, "Agency and Asymmetries: Actors and their Access to Resources in Colonial and Developmental Setting", in Amelung, Iwo, Hartmut Leppin and Christian A. Müller (eds.), *Discourses of*

Weakness and Resource Regimes: Trajectories of a New Research Program, Frankfurt am Main 2018.

Ricard, Robert, *The Spiritual Conquest of Mexico: An Essay on the Apostolate and the Evangelizing Methods of the Mendicant Orders in New Spain, 1523–1572*, trans. Lesley Byrd Simpson, Berkeley, CA 1966.

Ruiz Medrano, Ethelia and Susan Kellogg (eds.), *Negotiation within Domination: New Spain's Indian Pueblos Confront the Spanish State,* Boulder, CO 2010.

Schwaller, John F., "Constitution of the Cofradía del Santíssimo Sacramento of Tula, Hidalgo, 1570", in *Estudios de Cultura Nahuatl* 19 (1989), 217–244.

Schwaller, John F., "Conversion, Engagement, and Extirpation: Three Phases of the Evangelization of New Spain, 1524–1650", in Kendall, Calvin B., Oliver Nicholson, Jr. Phillips, William D. and Marguerite Ragnow (eds.), *Conversion to Christianity from Late Antiquity to the Modern Age: Considering the Process in Europe, Asia, and the Americas*, Minneapolis, MN 2009, 259–292.

Schwaller, John F., "Fr. Agustín de Vetancurt: The 'Via crucis en mexicano'", in *The Americas* 74:2 (2017), 119–137.

Schwaller, Robert C. (ed.), *A Language of Empire, a Quotidian Tongue: The Uses of Nahuatl in New Spain* (Special issue of *Ethnohistory* 59:4), Durham, NC 2012.

Smith, Hilary Dansey, *Preaching in the Spanish Golden Age: A Study of Some Preachers of the Reign of Philip III*, Oxford 1978.

Tau Anzoátegui, Víctor, *Casuismo y sistema: Indagación histórica sobre el espíritu del Derecho Indiano*, Buenos Aires 1992.

Tau Anzoátegui, Víctor, *El Jurista en el Nuevo Mundo. Pensamiento. Doctrina. Mentalidad*, Frankfurt am Main 2016 (http://dx.doi.org/10.12946/gplh7).

Traslosheros, Jorge E., *La reforma de la Iglesia del antiguo Michoacán: la gestión de fray Marcos Ramírez de Prado, 1640–1666*, Morelia 1995.

Turrini, Miriam, *La coscienza e le leggi. Morale e diritto nei testi per la confessione della prima età moderna*, Bologna 1991.

Waldinger, Maria, "The long-run effects of missionary orders in Mexico", in *Journal of Development Economics* 127, issue C (2017) 355–378 (https://doi.org/10.1016/j.jdeveco.2016.12.010).

Yannakakis, Yanna, *The Art of Being In-Between: Native Intermediaries, Indian Identity, and Local Rule in Colonial Oaxaca*, Durham, NC 2008.

Yannakakis, Yanna, "Beyond Jurisdictions: Native Agency in the Making of Colonial Legal Cultures. A Review Essay", in *Comparative Studies in Society and History* 57:4 (2015), 1070–1082.

Yannakakis, Yanna and Martina Schrader-Kniffki, "Between the 'Old Law' and the New: Christian Translation, Indian Jurisdiction, and Criminal Justice in Colonial Oaxaca", in *Hispanic American Historical Review* 96:3 (2016), 517–548.

CHAPTER 10

"Just Rules" for a "Religiosity of Simple People": Devotional Literature and Inquisitorial Trials in Cartagena de Indias (17th–18th Centuries)

Pilar Mejía

1 Introduction

The aim of this chapter is to establish a dialogue between the archive of an Inquisition tribunal and the works written, published, translated, abridged, and selected by jurists and theologians in order to explain how to prosecute the different cases, and how to practise the "true" Christian doctrine in daily life. Understanding the activities of the Inquisitorial court is not restricted, then, to what is written in the court's proceedings, nor are the proceedings themselves strictly limited to references to the tribunal. Rather, I shall show that such proceedings must necessarily be associated to other sources useful for the court's everyday work. In particular, I shall take into account some leaflets [*cartillas*] and "small pieces" [*obritas*] which describe the methods used for instructing people and how "remedies were searched" for the "minor heresies" dealt with at the court.

The daily work at this court was not characterised exclusively by prosecutions against the "major heresies" of the Muslim, Jewish or Protestant populations. Rather, it mainly aimed at the practices of people who, in the 17th century of this cosmopolitan Caribbean port, constituted a variegated aggregate of "superstitious" Christians.[1] Based on a detailed analysis of the court's proceedings and reports [*relaciones*], of the available letters exchanged and the books consulted, we see that the court members needed handbooks and "small pieces" [*obritas*] to expound in a short, compiled way and in plain language how "true devotions" should be practised without lapsing into the risks of superficial approaches and religious vices.

1 The Inquisitorial court of Cartagena de Indias had jurisdiction over the New Kingdom of Granada (including the dioceses of Santa Fe de Bogotá, Cartagena, Santa Marta, Panamá, Popayán, Santa Fe de Antioquia, Cáceres, Venezuela, Isla Margarita) as well as over the *Audiencia* de Santo Domingo (Santo Domingo, Trinidad, Jamaica, Puerto Rico, and Santiago de Cuba), see AHN, Inquisición, L.282, 329 fols., fol. 51v.

The purpose of this chapter is, then, to examine the sources used at the Inquisitorial court of the trading port of Cartagena de Indias, with the aim of exploring how their officials tried to encourage and spread pious norms and behaviours among a great number of people charged for their "excesses", "vices", and "offenses". To this end, they used short "leaflets for prosecuting" [*cartillas para procesar*] and also resorted to educational handbooks to instil the practice of licit devotions. In these documents we can observe how the judges and their consultants endeavoured to rectify a series of practices deemed "erroneous" by giving "simple and useful" instructions to "redress" the Christian cult as it was practised in wide portions of the local society. Starting from a brief overview about the kind of "superstitious" practices labelled as "minor" causes or errors, resulting from "ignorance", "trickery" [*embuste*], or "fraud" [*fraude*], we shall try to elucidate the type of moral-theological knowledge adduced by these judges and the remedies they proposed. The changes introduced into prayers and sacred words during the proceedings themselves are very interesting, as well as their direct relation with circulating devotional books, which were one of the instruments chosen to give instruction about oral religious practices. Devotional literature offered practical indications as to how to recite prayers, comply with *novenas*, follow the mass and perform actions involving holy water in domestic premises. It also prescribed how customary usages should be included in the calendar of Christian holidays and the commemoration of the saints. The use of devotional books had the purpose of changing superstitious excesses into pious oral practices. Within a wide range of such books, we will describe the characteristics of those deemed most "effective" and "healthiest" in the context of the Caribbean district.

In what follows, I will analyse the inquisitorial prosecution of minor causes, the forms of regulating sacred prayers and the importance of the devotional books, as a theological and moral response to the practices judged by this tribunal in Cartagena de Indias.

2 The Inquisitional Prosecution of *causas leves* ("minor heresies")

Under the common label of "causas leves", a whole series of cases are listed, including different people prosecuted for "superstitious practices" and "fortune telling" who might have committed "errors in matters of faith" because either they worshipped God in a false way or they performed worship correctly but to false gods. In the theological-legal tradition, such "errors" ("heresies" properly or not) constituted a false way of approaching the Catholic doctrine, and deserved to be condemned because they involved an open or indirect offense to the true God. From the 16th century onwards, we dispose of a corpus of texts[2] (treatises, lectures, disquisitions, epitomes, handbooks, allegations, and "small pieces") dealing with the reprobation of superstitions, which shed light on the subtle and changing borders that delimited different types of "heresies" and "false ways" [*falsas vías*]. From 1510 to 1688 such questions as the "order of causalities", the actions of evil, their effects, the subject's will, the different types of pacts, the parties involved, damages, and possible benefits were intensely discussed, as well as the penalties, correctives, and licit ways of struggling against deviations.[3] Circulating texts emphasised the importance of differentiating "authentic" "sorcerers" and "warlocks" from people who only appeared as such. The presence of the Devil and the source of evil had to be verified; ignorance and errors that might still be amended should also be identified. This debate became more and more complex confronted as it was with American realities, and with the fact that people of different origins – Africans, indigenous people, *mestizos*, and Europeans – were slowly understanding and embracing the expanding Christian practices.

One of the practical difficulties laid in distinguishing "minor" from "major" heresies (*errores leves* from *errores graves*, where this last category qualified the properly called "heresies"), a distinction that entailed complex theological questions discussed in learned texts. Hence, some authors emphasised the need to explanain these subject matters in the form of handbooks for the judges involved, and in a more accessible language, sometimes written in Spanish. When they presented their "small pieces" to their Spanish speaking readers, early theologians justified their work by referring to the confusion derived from the great number of similar works in circulation:

2 Some of the most important sources were the following, arranged in chronological order: Arles y Andosilla, *Tractatus exquisitissimus de Superstitionibus*; Grillandi, *Tractatus de hereticis et sortilegiis*; Castañega, *Tratado de las supersticiones y hechizerias y de la possibilidad y remedio dellas*; Ciruelo, *Reprobación de las supersticiones y hechizerias*; Olmos, *Tratado de Hechicerías y sortilegios*; Vitoria, *De Magica*; Malvetius, *Tractatus de Sortibus*; Pererius, *Adversus fallaces et superstitiosas artes, id est, de magia, de observatione somniorum, et de divinatione astrologica*; Del Río, *Disquisitionum magicarum*; Suárez, *De superstition*; Torreblanca Villalpando, *Epitome Delictorum, Sive De Magia, In Qua Aperta Vel Occulta Invocatio Daemonis intervenit*; Ruiz de Alarcón, *Tratado de las supersticiones y costumbres gentilicias que hoy viven entre los indios naturales de esta Nueva España*; Navarro, *Tribunal de supersticion ladina*; Nieremberg, *Oculta Filosofia*; Blasco Lanuza, *Patronicio de angeles y combate de demonios*; Caldera de Heredia, *Tribunal Medicum Magicum et Politicum*; Noydens, *Práctica de exorcistas, y ministros de la Iglesia*.

3 For an analysis of literature against superstitions, see Campagne, *Homo catholicus, homo superstitiosus*.

> [...] en el presente tratado se ponen mas expresamente y de otra arte. Los puntos que me parece que son necesarias [...] para quitar dudas y escrupulos de muchos coraçones incrédulos destas cosas, por muy vivos y sotiles fundamentos y razones muy artizadas y teologales [f. 5r] [...] y en lengua Castellana, porque a todos se pueda comunicar y cada uno sea mas familiar.
>
> Suplicote amantissimo lector, que no con sola una vez que leas lo dexes leydo, que tornándolo muchas vezes a mirar, siempre hallaras que notas, y quanto mejor entendieres la materia tanto mas lo preciaras e ponderaras muchos puntos que son dignos de ser notados. [f. 6.r] [...] mas agora no esta bien seca la primera tinta del borrador quando ya esta en poder del impresor.[4]
>
> Doctrina muy verdadera a católica sacadas de las entrañas de la más sana filosofía y teología, que por muy ciertas y claras razones arguye reprobando muchas maneras de vanas supersticiones y hechicerías, que en estos tiempos andan muy públicas en nuestra España por la negligencia y descuido de los señores prelados y de los jueces ansi eclesiásticos como seglares; a los cuales va dirigida esta obrecilla.[5]

For the judges entrusted with these matters, doctrine itself was as profuse as casuistry, so that the "sensible reader" of such works sometimes required additional tools in order to dispense justice in the trials. However, in the case of major difficulties or doubts to discern different kinds of heresies in matters of faith, consultation with one or two theologians knowledgeable in such questions was also necessary.[6] These consultants were appointed to qualify the reported offense from the doctrina point of view, and to establish whether the accusation was pertinent, from the very moment in which the defendant was arrested until the final sentence was passed.

However, for the jurisdiction assigned to the court of Cartagena, the presence, advice, and opinion of knowledgeable theologians was not easy to obtain. From the correspondence between the district's bishops and inquisitors, and the Supreme Council of the Inquisition [the *Suprema*] in Madrid, it is

4 Castañega, *Tratado de las supersticiones y hechizerias y de la possibilidad y remedio dellas*, ed. Muro Abad, fols. 5–6.

5 Ciruelo, *Reprobación de las supersticiones y hechizerias*, fol. 6r.

6 They were required to set an example by teaching theology over twelve years, even though this requirement might be dispensed with. See Murillo Velarde, *Curso de derecho canónico hispano e indiano*, vol. 1, eds. Carillo Cázares, Pérez Ramírez and Méndez Hernández, lib. 1, tit. 14, num. 232.

evident that doctors in theology qualified to advise the local Inquisition court were not frequent among the Caribbean clergy.[7] Most inquisitors were born in Spain and held a degree in law from Spanish universities; they often had pursued an ecclesiastical or civil career and had experience in other Inquisition courts. Prosecutors, who were graduate lawyers or held a bachelor's in law, and were in charge of promoting trials by making the necessary inquiries and pronouncing the indictment, learnt their profession by practicing with the inquisitors; the same holds true for most local commissaries of the Inquisition [*comisarios*] and people otherwise connected with the court.[8]

Both the theologians who acted as qualifiers [*calificadores*] and the inquisitors themselves were responsible for distinguishing heresies, offenses, and reprehensible practices in matters of faith. According to the doctrine, the entire People of God was liable to partake in such practices, from the most learned to the most simple and uncultivated person. The criteria used by inquisitors should discern whether the denounced practices involved communication with the Devil or some knowledge of his arts and sciences, or if they were mere "deceptions" [*engaños*], "fraud" [*frauds*], and "trickeries" [*embustes*], derived from various kinds of ignorance,[9] as most cases in Cartagena proved to be.

Specifically, the court had to deal with cases of domestic altars and devotions paid to saints which, added to sacred objects, amulets, indigenous plants, holy water, and unknown words, were used to obtain results "out of proportion", such as finding missing people or objects, knowing what was unknown, distancing some people or bringing them together, and also healing diseases. According to the doctrine, all such practices might be classified as offenses or false paths in the adoration of the true God; however, they were mainly

---

7 Medina, *La imprenta en Bogotá y la Inquisición en Cartagena de Indias*, 406–407, Ceballos Gómez, "Entre el Rey y el Papa. La Inquisición: trayectoria de una institución plurisecular", 16.

8 Secretary of the Secret [*secretario del secreto*], attorneys of the Royal Fiscal Office [*abogados del fisco*] and defence attorneys, prosecuting attorney [*procurador*], notaries of the Secret [*notarios del secreto*], notaries of the sequestered goods [*notarios de secuestros*], general administrator of the tribunal's goods and assets [*receptor general*], accountant [*contador*], messenger [*nuncio*], doorman [*portero*], chief jailer [*alcaide de cárceles*], chief constable [*alguacil mayor*], various constables [*alguaciles*], interpreters, and jailers.

9 Nevertheless, there were several kinds of ignorance: invincible ignorance – liable to accusation – and conquerable ignorance, which included, in its turn, subtle gradations: unforgivable ignorance [*ignorancia crasa*], negligent ignorance [*ignorancia supina*], and ignorance of the law, depending on the defendant's will, knowledge, condition, and the age from which the law considered the subject was liable. See Murillo Velarde, *Curso de derecho canónico hispano e indiano*, vol. 1, eds. Carillo Cázares, Pérez Ramírez and Méndez Hernández, lib. 1, tit. 2, num. 35.

sanctioned as "minor causes" or very slight deviations [*causas leves y levísimas*]. In order to understand why they were judged in this way, we should understand firstly the kind of knowledge and the juridical, theological, and moral rationale expressed in the corresponding dossiers. In this case, we should consider not only that few proceedings were fully recorded and detailed, but also that the vast majority of the causes were very succinctly reported to the *Suprema*, and that in other cases, no sentence was passed or no formal charge was recorded. These "minor causes" for superstition are characterised, even during the preliminary investigation, by the insistence on the "acknowledgement of errors" and "repentance": defendants were told that they could "save their souls" if they replaced their "wrongful" prayers and practices with those admitted by the Church.

In the corresponding records, then, it seems that the emphasis was not on the punishment but rather on repeating these hearings until the defendants repented and showed interest in amending their behaviour, whatever the descriptions of heretical practices might have been. For example, once a group of slaves and women were interrogated, their confession was recorded stressing that they had been "deceived by the devil", "undeceived by the confessor", or that the whole matter was the result of "their own deception".

A distinction between two "false paths" may be found in the documents analysed: the first false path is associated with a bad, deliberate, deception; the second one is associated with a fiction or weakness, away from matters of faith, and most causes were classified as such. The binary thought characteristic of the age tried to distinguish between good, allowed deceptions – like the so-called "ability to ward off trickeries and injustice"[10] – whereas "bad deception" might be mischief itself or a fraud [*dolo*], which involved the intention and will to deceive.[11] Therefore, judges had to investigate the will, the gullibility, or the conviction surrounding the effectiveness of the means used to attain certain ends, both in the case of the defendants and in the case of witnesses.

10 Murillo Velarde, *Curso de derecho canónico hispano e indiano*, vol. 2, eds. Carillo Cázares, Pérez Ramírez and Méndez Hernández, lib. 2, tit. 14, num. 107.

11 Murillo Velarde, *Curso de derecho canónico hispano e indiano*, vol. 2, eds. Carillo Cázares, Pérez Ramírez and Méndez Hernández, lib. 2, tit. 14, num. 107: "Agimus ergo in praesenti de dolo malo, qui est calliditas, fallacia, vel machinatio ad circumveniendum, fallendum, vel dicipiendum alterum adhibita cum alliud simulatur alliud que agitur [...] De dolo malo calliditas committitur tacendo, vel disimulando, fallacia, mentiendo: machinatio fit arte verborum. [...] Dolus ergo provenit ex alterius malitia: in quod differet ab errore & ignorantia; quae quidem naturaliter contingunt; item dolus committitur ex intentione dicipiendi, in quo à culpa differet, quae aperte & sine tale animo commititur".

A series of rather short causes were dealt with by resorting to the legal definition of "trickery" [*embuste*]. Although they neither implied errors in matters of faith nor did they evidence deals with the devil, they were dangerous because the defendants involved were "superstitious tricksters" who harmed the community by suggesting false ways to find lost objects and become rich. They thus propagated false paths which did not lead to the salvation of their souls, although they did not deserve a close investigation (by consultants), to the extent that this step might be omitted. Among the procedural peculiarities of the American courts highlighted in the literature, we should mention the fact that a previous authorisation of the *Suprema* to pass a sentence was no longer needed for certain trials.[12] The votes of theological advisors were all equivalent, and local commissaries of the Inquisition [*comisarios*] took on the task of collecting evidence in their districts, ratifying the witnesses through local honest people. Thus, from the mid-17th century onwards, causes labelled as major sins declined, and the number of disqualified and suspended trials increased as well as venial or slight sins involving trickeries, fraud, insanity, a weakness derived from disease, lack of a purpose or volition, even the improbable involvement of the devil, and ignorance of the doctrine. All this required a complex and open argumentation plus the deployment of the theologians' moral virtues in order to correct the intimate beliefs of the Christian community.

Even though the number of *causas graves* diminished, we cannot assume from this fact that the tribunal was falling into decline: we should take into account its uninterrupted activity on other causes until well into the 18th century. In such causes, the Tribunal of the Holy Office retained its *raison d'être*: the internal redressing of Christians considering, however, that there was not much guilt among the weak, the ignorant, and the sick, so that the court tried to alleviate them by disqualifying, suspending, absolving, and quickly putting an end to their trials. Although the sentence brought an end to the question in need of solving, it was not the only way to address the problem. The process of redressing itself occurred in the course of confession and repentance, which might lead to another kind of remedy that did not require the final closure of the case through a sentence.

It is instructive to highlight these circumstances as they constituted the approach followed in legal proceedings when no further theological reasons were found to label "harmless practices" as heresies. In this respect, the basic tenet of scholasticism should be recalled: every heresy implies an error, but the

12 Maqueda Abreu, *Estado, Iglesia e Inquisición en Indias: un permanente conflicto*, 71; Pérez Villanueva and Escandell Bonet (eds.), *Historia de la Inquisición en España y América*, vol. 2, 652.

converse is false: not every error implies a heresy, unless it is a matter of faith.[13] Thus, at the tribunal of Cartagena there seemed to be decreasingly fewer offenders sentenced for heretical practices, and increasingly more who needed instruction[14] and reconciliation.[15]

The questions, answers, and formulas provided in the "leaflets for prosecuting" [*cartillas para procesar*] issued by the tribunal of Cartagena were strictly followed.[16] The first penalty for all minor suspects was the *abjuratio de levi*, which implied that the defendant explicitly confessed his guilt by swearing on the Gospel that he loathed the offense committed and promised not to relapse. Thus, reconciliation with the true religion was sought.[17] Such a procedure meant that prosecution came to an end because the offender had achieved an agreement as to the fault committed, had repented, and had been pardoned, so that his relationship with God and the community was restored.

However, following the instructions contained in the leaflet could also implied omitting the details of each case, silencing rather than recording, correcting discreetly, and performing smaller *autos particulares* (small celebrations) at the tribunal's chapel, as well as giving instruction on true devotions. Therefore, some women were confined in convents, hospitals, or respectable houses, with the prescription that they should attend mass until its end, recite the entire rosary, pay devotion to the saints and observe their holidays. Having reached this point, it is necessary to complement our reading of court proceedings with the "minor" religious literature barely mentioned in the prosecutions; these texts meant to support procedures and aimed at "restoring" and "redressing" the practices of these subjects by making them learn and repeat prayers, spiritual exercises, novenas, canticles, and signs befitting the "true" Christian.

This type of literature – which also had a practical purpose – was issued in an abridged format, not anymore in Latin but in Spanish, and was written in

13 Soto, *Relección del maestro fray Domingo de Soto, acerca de la herejía*, ed. Sánchez-Lauro Pérez, 52, fol. 204v, quotes St. Augustine's proposition: "Omnis haeresis est error, non tamen viceversa omins error es haeresis, nisi sit circa materiam fidei".

14 In the case of people prosecuted by the Inquisition of Lima, René Millar highlights the efforts made by the tribunal to this end, because the court itself carried out indoctrination activities parallel to those of ecclesiastical institutions. Millar Carvacho, *Inquisición y sociedad en el virreinato peruano*.

15 Álvarez Alonso, *La Inquisición en Cartagena de Indias durante el siglo XVII*, 293 even refers to cases of women who were reconciled a second and a third time.

16 BNC, RM 98.

17 BNC, RM 98, fols. 27v–28v; Murillo Velarde, *Curso de derecho canónico hispano e indiano*, vol. 4, eds. Carillo Cázares, Pérez Ramírez and Méndez Hernández, lib. 5, tit. 34, num. 304.

plain language. The table of contents was brief, and occasional illustrations were included. All these publications had already passed the necessary process of qualification. Inquisitorial consultants told devotees that, besides their internal conviction, they were to avoid excesses, vices, or superficial attitudes in their religious practices. It is rather surprising, therefore, to discover the interest of the Inquisition in regulating oral practices, clearing doubts about the content of prayers, and establishing the legitimate forms of devotion to the saints and various patrons. The authorities tried to spread "effective tools for struggling against superstitions" in the form of "directories on piety" [*directorios de piedad*], compendia, letters, handbooks, exercises for penance, and the repentance processes themselves.

3 Regulating Sacred Formulas

From the first hearing, an oath was required from the defendant and the witnesses: that they will tell the truth, describe their genealogy and life history, and demonstrate their knowledge about doctrine. Therefore, both the Cartagena leaflets and the prosecuting instructions indicated that the judges had to pay attention to the way in which the accused made the sign of the cross, and to find out about the following questions: whether they had good knowledge of prayers; whether they recited them quickly and by heart (in Latin or in Romance); whether they repeated them correctly or committed mistakes; where and how the defendant was baptised; whether they were confirmed, whether they took communion, and if they have studied some science.[18] In the different causes under study, and whatever the cultural differences between the people interrogated, a common trait of the information gained is the use of prayers to mediators in order to solve everyday problems. The manipulation of the supernatural was a common, everyday practice among the prosecuted Christians, derived from the continuous exchange of religious knowledge among them. Far from being an abstract question, in the cases explored, this attitude is reflected in various practices, such as the use of prayers and Christian sacred objects to heal diseases, locate people and objects, induce attraction between people, and alter the weather.

In a corpus of different kinds of documents from 1612 to 1791,[19] 188 cases were found that reveal the use of a series of sacred formulas, the way in

18 Garcia, *Órden que comunmente se guarda en el santo oficio de la inquisicion*, 29; BNC, RG 6981; BNC, RM 98, fol. 5v.

19 Including complete trials, the copies of which were sent to the Council of the *Suprema* at Madrid between 1612 and 1760 (AHN, Inquisición, 1620, 1621, 1623); four books

which redressing was sought, and the inclusion of such formulas as Christian practices. Among the prayers most frequently recorded, which had a greater number of versions in the Cartagena district, we may list prayers to St. Martha [*Santa Marta*],[20] St. Clare [*Santa Clara*], St. Helena [*Santa Elena*], St. Cyprian [*San Cebrián*], St. Erasmus [*San Erasmo*],[21] St. Mark [*San Marcos*],[22] St. Sylvester [*San Silvestre*], the Souls [*las Ánimas*],[23] the Lonely Soul [*el Ánima sola*],[24] the Blessed St. John [*San Juan Bendito*],[25] St. Christopher [*San Cristóbal*], the Holy Lady of Bethlehem [*Santísima Señora de Belén*], and the Lord of the Street [*el Señor de la Calle*],[26] as well as prayers to the Star,[27] the Sun, to the *cigarrón*, to oranges,[28] and many others that do not have a specific name[29] so that in the proceedings they were frequently referred to as spells, incantations, implorations or invocations.[30] All of them are present in the sources; they were either

---

recording *causas de fe* which served as regular summary reports for the Council, dated between 1614 and 1698 (AHN, Inquisición, L.1020; AHN, Inquisición, L.1021; AHN, Inquisición, L.1022; AHN, Inquisición, L.1023). Among the other books and documents belonging to this tribunal, the following should be mentioned: records about the visits of Martin del Real and Pedro Medina Rico between 1643 and 1651 (AHN, Inquisición, 1600, 1601, 1602, 1603); books that contain the letters exchanged between the Council and the Cartagena tribunal between 1610 and 1695 (AHN, Inquisición, L.1008–1019); books bound in calf leather [*libros de becerro*] where the confiscation, inventories, and the public auction of goods were recorded; and books containing the doctrine, decrees, questions, and Instructions; plus a whole series of archive materials about trials on jurisdictional questions, genealogies, and proofs.

20 AHN, Inquisición, L.1022, fol. 498r, also transcribed in Álvarez Alonso, *La Inquisición en Cartagena de Indias durante el siglo XVII*, 202; AHN, Inquisición, L.1022, fol. 54v, fol. 70r. Quezada Ramírez, "Santa Marta en la tradición popular", 228 distinguishes the pleading originated in France from the Mexican one which, from 1622 onwards, makes a distinction between a Good and a Bad St. Martha [*Santa Marta, la Buena y la Mala*]. Ramírez' paper collects a series of variations of these prayers. The versions recorded in Cartagena are, in their turn, variations of the Bad St. Martha.

21 AHN, Inquisición, L.1022, fol. 78r.

22 AHN, Inquisición, L.1020, fol. 27v.

23 AHN, Inquisición, L.1022, fol. 498r, transcribed in Álvarez Alonso, *La Inquisición en Cartagena de Indias durante el siglo XVII*, 202.

24 AHN, Inquisición, 1620, exp. 1, fol. 5v.

25 AHN, Inquisición, L.1023, fol. 66r.

26 AHN, Inquisición, 1620, exp. 1, fol. 28r.

27 AHN, Inquisición, 1620, exp. 1, fols. 2v, 27r, 60r; AHN, Inquisición, L.1022, fol. 79v.

28 AHN, Inquisición, L.1020, fols. 28v, 52r.

29 AHN, Inquisición, L.1022, fols. 69r, 235r; AHN, Inquisición, L.1023, fols. 43r, 243r, 353r; AHN, Inquisición, L.1021, fol. 442r; AHN, Inquisición, 1620, exp. 1, fol. 29v.

30 With regard to the Inquisition Tribunal of México, Campos Moreno (2001) has collected and analysed these magic formulas. He emphasises that neither the judges nor the accused people had a clear idea of the difference between a prayer [*oración*], an incantation [*ensalmo*], and a spell [*conjuro*], although some distinctions may be detected by

mentioned in descriptions of performed practices, or summarised and fragmented as propositions to be qualified by expert theologians. Some of them were identified by "words used in the Consecration of the Mass",[31] others were considered as "incomprehensible prayers".[32] Missing words and the "spells" that the defendant and the witnesses did not remember, or which were not recorded in the proceedings were, in their turn, replaced by or completed with authorised contents, thus generating new prayers and new purposes. Indeed, throughout the entirety of trials under study, we rarely find complete formulas reproduced "exactly as they were pronounced".[33] Instead, we could identify a series of fragments belonging to different versions, where the memory lapses of the accused and of the witnesses replace one another and overlap.

Therefore, the act itself of recording such oral practices caused the prayers to be rewritten and transformed. In order that the theological advisor might qualify the prayers,[34] a new unified version of them was written, sometimes emphasising the heretical character[35] of the formulas,[36] or – in most cases – merely informing that no qualification had been possible or needed because

considering the form and the purpose of the invocation: "En las oraciones y los ensalmos el invocante tiene una actitud más sumisa y rogativa que en los conjuros, actitud que se ve reflejada en el modo de cómo se invoca a las divinidades y como se hace la petición. [...] En los ensalmos, el invocante señala que sólo con la intervención de la divinidad invocada se podrá realizar la curación. [...] En los conjuros, en cambio, invocación y petición adquieren un carácter imperativo" Campos Moreno, *Oraciones, ensalmos y conjuros mágicos del archivo inquisitorial de la Nueva España, 1600–1630*, 34.

31 AHN, Inquisición, L.1022, fol. 34r.

32 AHN, Inquisición, L.1020, fol. 15r.

33 AHN, Inquisición, 1620, exp. 1, fols. 60r–61r.

34 AHN, Inquisición, 1620, exp. 1, fol. 27r. "Los dichos padres aviendo visto la oración conformes dixeron que es sortilegio que sapit heresim manifeste y lo firmaron Hernando Nuñez [rector de la compañía de Jesús], Fray Bartolomé del Toro [de la orden de Santo Domingo], fray Lucas Ramirez [de la de San Francisco], Antonio Agustin [padre de la compañía de Jesús] Fray Sebastian de Chumillas [guardián del convento de San Diego]" AHN, Inquisición, 1620, exp. 1, fols. 27v, 28r, 28v, 29r, 29v.

35 The use of the formula "sapit heresim manifeste" in the quotation above refers to: "Forma sententie inmurationis cum signo hostie rotunde contra persona aliquam, que de et cum corpore Christi sortilegium aut maleficium aloquod perpetravit"; see Hansen, *Quellen und Untersuchungen zur Geschichte des Hexenwahns und der Hexenverfolgung im Mittelalter*, 54.

36 "Al comparar estas dos versiones de la oración, se hace evidente la necesidad inquisitorial de reducir el poder de la oración al distorsionar su contenido pasando de una fuerza de influencia sobre la movilidad y proximidad ajenas a un ejercicio de animalización [que ladre como perro, rebuzne como asno o cante como gallo] que confirmara el pacto con el demonio en términos demonológicos". Díaz Burgos, *Fisuras inquisitoriales, voces femininas y hechicería en Cartagena de Indias*, 217.

the analysed material contained examples of venerated prayers to saints recognised by the Church.

Such prayers and formulas were, nevertheless, problematic when they were associated with additional practices and ingredients that placed them into a new context as regards their religious use. This change was one of the main causes that required not only prosecution, but also qualification and redressing. For example, some of these prayers were combined with the use of holy water, which was taken from the churches to domestic premises with various purposes: to be sprinkled on people and things,[37] to be administered as a medicine, mixed with the holy palm and "eggshells from Asunción",[38] to be transformed into scented water and sprayed on fishnets in order to bring about a rich catch.[39] Similarly, the candles and crosses "taken from a church which had a tabernacle",[40] were thought to have special effects in everyday domestic situations where healing and communication with the supernatural was involved.

Although most prayers and the worship of certain representations of saints and virgins were already known in Europe, as well as their combination with water, candles, and crosses, one of the American peculiarities was their extended use with indigenous herbs. Among the plants most frequently mentioned in the proceedings are the *hayo* or coca, the *bassa*,[41] herbs from the lowlands,[42] those coming from the indigenous village of Tolú, *guaco* plants, other herbs used by Afro-American people of the Mandinga nation,[43] herbs growing in house yards, and many others that Indians had taught Christians to chew in combination with their prayers. The Inquisition especially tried to discover their hallucinatory or therapeutic effects, and to find for them equivalent European or American names,[44] assimilating them to coca, which served ritual and religious purposes and also had healing effects. White and mulatto women and Afro-American people used to pray and chew these herbs, which caused a

---

37 AHN, Inquisición, L.1022, fol. 54v.

38 AHN, Inquisición, L.1021, fol. 409r, see Álvarez Alonso, *La Inquisición en Cartagena de Indias durante el siglo XVII*, 203–204.

39 AHN, Inquisición, L.1022, fol. 510r.

40 AHN, Inquisición, L.1022, fol. 64r.

41 AHN, Inquisición, L.1022, fol. 170r.

42 AHN, Inquisición, L.1022, fol. 150v; "tierra caliente" meaning "tierras bajas".

43 AHN, Inquisición, L.1021, fol. 176.

44 "la vio mascar a indios y blancos y vender en la plaza [... hasta el consejo quizo averiguar] qué manera se tiene por supersticiosa y efectos que obra, y a que hierba corresponde en los Reinos de España", AHN, Inquisición, L.1023, fol. 219v, quoted in Álvarez Alonso, *La Inquisición en Cartagena de Indias durante el siglo XVII*, 204.

heavy slumber; they were also spit on hands,[45] applied to the body,[46] sprinkled on handkerchiefs, and drunk in infusions.[47]

The most widely circulated prayers consisted of simple rhythmic and repetitive structures,[48] which were easy to learn, use, and spread among Christians. Besides these texts so highly appreciated in practice, additional images and pictures in "parchment or coarse paper" [*papelón*] circulated in a "seasoned" [*aderezada*] way among the defendants.[49]

Although in the Iberian peninsula and in other parts of Europe, treatises on astrology, alchemy, and magic, as well as collections of spells, incantations, and magic practices circulated and were condemned by the Inquisition,[50] their usage, presence, and application in American territories is unknown. However, we do know how prayers circulated through novenas, the saints' epitomes, and devotional books[51] – of a portable size and low cost – which explained how and where prayers should be used: they prescribed the correct way of reciting them, at which hours of the day, and that they should observe the calendar of the saints.[52] Inquisitorial proceedings dealt with the use of religious prayers and were also concerned with diffusion of Christian practices, as may be seen in handbooks for priests – so that they might properly perform exorcisms – in

45 "[El Hayo] es el principal y cuasi inseparable medio, misturada con otros ingredientes y aplicada al fuego, escupida en las manos para (por las rayas o caracteres que en ellas deja) decir que vienen en conocimiento de lo que consultan y desean saber por este medio, [...] tan frecuentado en la ciudad de Santa Fe y sus circunvecinas y en la de Popayán y su provincia, que no sólo corre entre personas de ínfima calidad, sino es que toca en algunas de mayores obligaciones". Medina, *La imprenta en Bogotá y la Inquisición en Cartagena de Indias*, 340.

46 AHN, Inquisición, 1620, exp. 1, fol. 6v.

47 AHN, Inquisición, L.1022, fols. 171v–172r.

48 Such as composing anaphoras, epiphoras, parallel constructions, repetitions, and homophone cadences, which are studied in Campos Moreno, *Oraciones, ensalmos y conjuros mágicos del archivo inquisitorial de la Nueva España, 1600–1630*, 38–41.

49 AHN, Inquisición, 1620, exp. 1, fols. 49, 56.

50 Historiography refers permanently to the Key of Solomon [*la Clavícula de Salomón*], the book of Saint Cyprian [*libro de San Cipriano*], the Treasury of prayers and miracles of the Holy Cross at Caravaca [*Tesoro de milagros, oraciones de la cruz de Caravaca*], and the Red Dragon [*el Dragón rojo*].

51 This becomes evident in the listings that include 762 religious and devotional titles; see Álvarez Santaló, "Adoctrinamiento y devoción en las bibliotecas sevillanas del siglo XVIII", 22, 28, 31–32.

52 Pedro Guibovich comments that, being small and of low cost, devotional books were "an attractive source of income for booksellers". Book sales in Hispano-America prove that the belief in the magic power of prayers was widespread in the population. Guibovich Pérez, "Piedad popular y Contrarreforma: los devocionarios en el virreinato del Perú", 225.

the enthusiastic recommendation of *novenas* and relics to heal sick people, or in the transmission of formulas to resolve conflicting relationships.

Among healing practices, a flexible and narrow line dividing accepted pious practices from those censored as superstitious, can be discerned. Such is the case of a whole series of treatments prescribed for various complaints and diseases; these activities should always be preceded by "pious practices: litanies, psalms, recitations of the liturgy",[53] and devout invocations to the Virgin, the Holy Trinity, the Most Blessed Sacrament, the saints, and the sign of the cross in order that healing might be achieved. For the tribunal of Cartagena, some everyday practices aroused special suspicions: medicines for conception,[54] pregnancies, births, and miscarriages,[55] as well as practices carried out by Afro-American slaves[56] to cure people affected by the evil eye,[57] snake bites, ulcers,[58] toothaches, haemorrhages, contutions, fevers, and tertian fevers [*malarias*].[59] In these procedures, the use of Christian symbols played the same role of other remedies in traditional cures – such as herbs, bark, and honey – which were applied until the element symbolising the disease was finally expelled through the wound or through the mouth.[60] In the trials, reference is made to some priests who recommended the use of amulets,[61] to surgeons that cured with holy water, to pious slaves who recovered their health when they commended themselves to a certain image, and also to monks who used indigenous purgatives.

Prayers were also a part of divinatory practices, such as the procedure called the "suerte del huevo" (test of the egg), where the prayer to St. John plus Three

53 Such as headaches, stomach swelling, chronic fatigue, insomnia, sexual impotence, dizziness, anxiety, etc., see Aspell de Yanzi Ferreira, "El Tribunal de la Inquisición en América. Los comisarios del Santo Oficio en Córdoba del Tucumán en el siglo XVIII", 275.

54 Lux Martelo, *Las mujeres de Cartagena de Indias en el Siglo XVII*, 132–133.

55 AHN, Inquisición, L.1022, fols. 509v–510r.

56 Among the main experts in these healings, mention should be made of the following Afro-American people: Francisco and Antonio Mandinga, Pedro Congo, Lorenzo García, Domingo López, Juan de Salcedo.

57 Domingo de la Ascensión cured more than thirty people from the "evil eye" by invocating Jesus, the Virgin and the Eucharist; see Álvarez Alonso, *La Inquisición en Cartagena de Indias durante el siglo XVII*, 204.

58 Lorenzo García used this method to cure an Afro-American woman whose name was Paulita, by applying basil and honey to the sore and making the sign of the cross over it; see Álvarez Alonso, *La Inquisición en Cartagena de Indias durante el siglo XVII*, 204.

59 Ceballos Gómez, *Quyen tal haze que tal pague: Sociedad y prácticas mágicas en el Nuevo Reino de Granada*, 201–202.

60 AHN, Inquisición, L.1021, fols. 176, 304r; AHN, Inquisición, L.1023, fol. 353r.

61 AHN, Inquisición, 1620, exp. 1, fols. 15v–16r.

Creeds recited at certain specific days and hours, contributed to determine the interpretation given to an egg which had been immersed in water. The aspect of the egg determined an affirmative or negative answer to questions about future events, such as the arrival of galleons, the location of missing people, and future weddings.[62]

The Inquisition tried to eliminate the use of sacred prayers for such "vain goals" by imposing spiritual penances, during which the accused people had to repent from the use they had made of prayers and images. Assuming the "attitude of a penitent", they should take part during the next years in pilgrimages to sanctuaries and processions, reciting the Rosary with correctness,[63] regularly and orderly, besides attending the mass regularly, confessing, fasting, and mortifying themselves through humiliation.[64] This procedure sought to transform "slightly superstitious" customs into pious practices toward the saints, devotions, holidays, and other advisable usages – hence, the importance of teaching the correct prayers to the representations accepted by the Church, using the accurate words and the prescribed rhythm, and repeating them the prescribed number of times, as indicated in devotional books. Another aim was to restrict the uses of holy water and the sign of the cross, and also, to spread among the population the custom of saying the grace before meals, and many other "effective instruments to struggle against superstition".[65]

4 Concluding Remarks. Devotional Books as a Juridical, Theological and Moral Response

Within all this literature against superstition, one of the subjects of the greatest concern for theologians was that anyone might use and manipulate the words (prayers) and religious objects meant for God.[66] However, the uninterrupted series of trials for superstition shows differing stances and stages along these two centuries: we find repression among the first 17th-century inquisitors, but also, in proceedings about cures in the 18th century, the acceptance

62 AHN, Inquisición, L.1023, fol. 66r–66v.

63 AHN, Inquisición, L.1021, fol. 396v.

64 Álvarez Alonso, *La Inquisición en Cartagena de Indias durante el siglo XVII*, 192, 216.

65 Campagne, *Homo catholicus, homo superstitiosus*, 428, presents a comparative table of three treatises against superstition and the "rituals that may licitly replace baroque Catholicism".

66 Such as the use of sacred and consecrated objects (holy water, candles, prayers, holy oil, consecrated wine, religious images and relics).

of new uses for prayers, as well as a consequent change of attitude towards religious devotions, contexts, and experiences that were progressively considered harmless for Christianity. Far from being considered the isolated practices of a few Christians, the effectiveness of some patronages, and their presence in domestic, everyday circumstances paved the way to their inclusion into the Christian way of life of the various types of Christians living in the Inquisitorial district of Cartagena de Indias.

Although superstition was defined in the 16th century as an aggregate of practices characterised by excess and an improper way of worshipping the true God, the rectifications and redresses introduced throughout the 17th and 18th centuries meant that those "excesses" were reassessed as another kind of religiosity – one that was considered useful and "healthy" for spreading the Christian way of life among the wider population. It was an activity carried out by religious orders and the secular clergy through the promotion of brotherhoods, the devotion paid to images, religious holidays, and a whole series of pious deeds and daily exercises. Thus, the notion of religiosity began to include doctrine and also the various ways in which religion was lived; it no longer emphasised "errors", "falseness" or the "people's ignorance" but rather the inclusion and the "sedimentation of the official religion"[67] among the various people that were adopting Christianity. Throughout the 17th and 18th centuries, theology as a knowledge specialised in interpreting Christian truths and dogmas had the difficult task of distinguishing between learned devotion and its own progressive differentiation from baroque expressions and manifestations, which gave occasion to the ambiguities and flaws of a different communication with the supernatural. Therefore, in this period of a progressive distancing movement between the "religion of the learned" and the "religiosities of the simple", some very useful books were published about the way of "redressing the devotion of Christian people",[68] as well as directories on piety which accepted different ways of living religion stressing that the limits between these ways and superstitions were rather blurred. Indeed, the role of pious laywomen [*beatas*] as participant witnesses of superstitions proved that those limiting borders were quite narrow; these cases illustrate how much judges and theologians "feared popular piety".[69]

67 "La religiosidad popular no se constituye con los restos de una ignorancia secular del pueblo, sino en el proceso también secular de asentamiento de la religión oficial". García García, "El contexto de la religiosidad popular", 29.

68 Muratori, *La devoción arreglada del christiano*, ed. Perez Pastor.

69 Such is the case of the pious laywomen Francisca Hernández – see Giles (ed.), *Mujeres en la Inquisición*, 99 and Carlota de Esquivel, see Díaz Burgos, *Fisuras inquisitoriales, voces femininas y hechicería en Cartagena de Indias*, 130–131.

Such need to transform "superstitious" practices was also a challenge for theological thought, which had understood how useful it was to express the Christian doctrine in simple devotional works in order to promote pious practices. Devotional books were a form of explaining and impressing the doctrine by means of simple oral practices. It should not come as a surprise, then, that the most widely circulated devotional books in America were written by eminent European theologians and jurists. For example, in the 18th century, copies of the different editions of Muratori's handbook translated into Castilian[70] were catalogued in several private and convent libraries. In the prologue, the translator stresses the usefulness of the book:

> [...] [el pueblo español] carecía hasta ahora de un Libro, que en breve compilase, y diese las mas justas reglas, para conducirse en su devoción. Ninguna Nación (y se puede decir con verdad) tiene Autores mas insignes, y piadosos, y que con mayor pureza hayan guiado a las almas devotas por el seguro camino espiritual.[71]

As Muratori's translator suggested, among such an abundant supply of devotional books and the fast appearance of new publications, "small pieces" were needed to explain how to distinguish between "superficial", "vain devotions" or those having "a substance of superstition", from "true" devotions aimed at instructing.[72] However, the translator warns that the new edition differs from the original in so far as he omitted clauses that only learned theologians might understand, as well as debates "designed for another Nation" and prayers in Latin, so that the book might be more useful for a wider readership, thus accommodated to new contexts, although faithful to the "sound original doctrine".

---

70 "Compuso esta Obrita en el ano 1747, y en el mismo la imprimió en Venecia, donde se reimprimió en los siguientes de 748, y 752: en Florencia, y Trento en 1749, y dos veces en Nápoles, aunque con la data de Trento en 1750. Se traduxo al Aleman en 1753, y al Latin en 1760. La traducción Espanola se ha hecho por la impresion de Venecia de 1748". Nota del traductor Miguel Perez Pastor en: Muratori, *La devoción arreglada del christiano*, ed. Perez Pastor, 2.

71 Muratori, *La devoción arreglada del christiano*, ed. Perez Pastor, 5.

72 "Mi asunto primario en esta Obrita es dar a entender en que consiste justamente la verdadera, y solida devocion, distinguiendola de las devociones superficiales, y apuntando ligeramente otras, que tienen apariencia, o tal vez la substancia de supersticion". Author's Prologue, Muratori, *La devoción arreglada del christiano*, ed. Perez Pastor, 20–21.

> En el capítulo 2 se ha omitido una cláusula, que aunque contiene doctrina sumamente sana, podía al parecer de algunos Teólogos, entenderse mal por el que no estuviese mas que medianamente instruido en la Teología; y por evitar aun este leve tropiezo, pareció medio fácil el omitirla.[73]
>
> No tiene duda que hay grande distancia entre traducir una Misa para sola instrucción de los ignorantes, y el querer que el Sacrificio se celebre en vulgar, o afirmar, que celebrar la Misa en lengua que entendiese el Pueblo, sería más útil que la santa práctica de la Iglesia. [...] En prueba de esta diferencia han sido aprobadas, y tenidas por útiles las traducciones de la Misa.[74]

Devotional books translated and continuously republished were one of the instruments developed by "wise theologians" to instruct "ignorant" people and "train them in the genuine Christian devotion". By the 17th and 18th centuries, however, the task of "regulating devotion" entailed a series of premises about the ideas of "religiosity" and "popular devotion". Learned theologians succeeded in differentiating the way in which they themselves understood the doctrine and the way in which it was most usefully transmitted to and practiced by other Christians who barely had any theological education. Thus, learned devotion would be practised by a small elite of wise men, whereas popular religiosities and devotions – which did not belong exclusively to the "lower" sectors or certain *castas* – would be practised by common people. As evidenced in inquisitorial trials, Spanish, Creole, and *mestizo* elites also took part in such practices, as well as some members of the religious orders and the secular clergy. Beyond their individual condition and trade, all of them had common "moral flaws", and their relation to the supernatural had peculiar external and internal characteristics suitable for their everyday needs, which were impossible to detach from ambiguous notions about disease, healing, affinities, and the future. All these practices implied great challenges, and the devotional literature was in keeping with the moral-theological and juridical updating demanded by the changing local circumstances.

Acknowledgements

I would like to thank Elena Morengo for the careful translation of this article.

73 Muratori, *La devoción arreglada del christiano*, ed. Perez Pastor, 7.

74 Muratori, *La devoción arreglada del christiano*, ed. Perez Pastor, 9.

Bibliography

Manuscripts

Archivo Histórico Nacional, Madrid (AHN), Inquisición, 1620, exp. 1.
AHN, Inquisición, L.282; L.1020; L.1021; L.1022; L.1023.
Biblioteca Nacional de Colombia, Bogotá (BNC), RG 6981; RM 98.

Printed Sources

Arles y Andosilla, Martín de, *Tractatus exquisitissimus de Superstitionibus*, in *Tractatus universi iuris, Tomus XI, Pars II De iudiciis criminalibus S. Inquisitionis*, Venetiis [1510] 1584: Zilettus.

Blasco Lanuza, Francisco de, *Patronicio de angeles y combate de demonios…: Es una ilustración de los beneficios que hazen los Angeles de la Guarda a los hombres. Y tambien de las stucias, y impugnaciones de los demonios*, Real Monasterio de San Juan de la Peña 1652.

Caldera de Heredia, Gaspar, *Tribunal Medicum Magicum et Politicum, pars altera*, Lugduni Batavorum 1657.

Castañega, Martín de, *Tratado de las supersticiones y hechizerias y de la possibilidad y remedio dellas*, ed. Muro Abad, Juan Robert, 3rd ed., Logroño [1529] 1994.

Ciruelo, Pedro, *Reprobación de las supersticiones y hechizerias. Libro muy útil y necesario a todos los buenos christianos*, Medina del Campo 1551: Guillermo de Millis.

Del Río, Martín Antonio, *Disquisitionum magicarum libri sex, quibus continetur accurata curiosarum artium & vanarum superstitionum confutatio, utilis theologis, iurisconsultis, medicis philologis*, Colonia Agrippinae [1599] 1755: Huisch.

Garcia, Pablo, *Órden que comunmente se guarda en el santo oficio de la inquisicion, acerca del processar en las causas que en él se tratan, conforme á lo que está proveido por las instrucciones antiguas y nuevas*, [Madrid] Córdoba [1622] 1843: Imprenta a cargo de Manté (https://books.google.de/books?id=JRYQAAAAIAAJ&printsec=frontcover&dq=Pablo+Garcia+inquis&hl=es-419&sa=X&redir_esc=y#v=onepage&q&f=false).

Grillandi, Paolo, *Tractatus de hereticis et sortilegiis*, in *Tractatus universi iuris Tomus XI, Pars II, De iudiciis criminalibus S. Inquisitionis*, Venetiis [1524] 1584: Zilettus.

Malvetius, Troilus, *Tractatus de Sortibus*, in *Tractatus universi iuris, Tomus XI, Pars II, De iudiciis criminalibus S. Inquisitionis*, Venetiis 1584: Zilettus.

Muratori, Ludovico Antonio, *La devoción arreglada del christiano que escribió Luis Antonio Muratori en el idioma italiano y traducida la publica el Sr. Dr. D. Miguel Perez Pastor*, ed. Perez Pastor, Miguel, 3rd ed., Madrid 1783: Imprenta de la Viuda de Ibarra (http://www.iberoamericadigital.net/BDPI/Search.do;jsessionid=182AA530B34F9C65A32323C5F8A841D5?numfields=1&field1=docId&field1val=bdh0000171543&field1Op=AND&advanced=true&hq=true&important=T%C3%ADtulo%3A+La+devoci%C3%B3n+arreglada+del+christiano).

Murillo Velarde, Pedro, *Curso de derecho canónico hispano e indiano*, 4 vols., trans. Alberto Carillo Cázares, Pascual Guzmán de Alba, Augustín Ayala García, Ignacio Estrella Primo, Eloy Medina Salinas, Augusto Larrauri Jiménez, Jesús Gómez Fregoso, Serafín Alvarez Ruiz and Manuel López Medina, eds. Carillo Cázares, Alberto, Salvador Pérez Ramírez and Silvia Méndez Hernández, Zamora, México [1791] 2004–2005.

Navarro, Gaspar, *Tribunal de superstición ladina, explorador del saber, astucia y poder del demonio: en que se condena lo que suele correr por bueno en hechizos, agueros, ensalmos, vanos saludadores, maleficios, co[n]juros, arte notoria, caualista, y paulina y semejantes acciones vulgares*, Huesca 1631: Pedro Bluson (http://alfama.sim.ucm.es/dioscorides/consulta_libro.asp?ref=B19316914&idioma=0).

Nieremberg, Juan Eusebio, *Oculta Filosofia. De la sympatia y antipatia de las cosas, artificio de la naturaleza, y noticia natural del mundo. Y segunda parte de la curiosa Filosofia. Contiene historias notables. Aueriguanse muchos secretos, y problemas de la naturaleza. Explicanse lugares dificultosos de Escritura*, Madrid 1633: Imprenta del Reyno (https://archive.org/details/bub_gb_1I_bEfkahdAC).

Noydens, Benito Remigio, *Práctica de exorcistas, y ministros de la Iglesia: en qve con mvcha ervdición, y singular claridad, se trata de la instruccion de los exorcismos, para lançar, y ahuyentar los demonios, y curar especialmente todo genero de maleficios, y hechizos*, ed. Santos Vila, Sonia, Valladolid [1693] 2010.

Olmos, Andrés de, *Tratado de Hechicerías y sortilegios*, México [1553] 1990.

Pererius, Benedictus, *Adversus fallaces et superstitiosas artes, id est, de magia, de observatione somniorum, et de divinatione astrologica*, Lugduni [1591] 1592: ex oficina Juntarum.

Ruiz de Alarcón, Hernando, *Tratado de las supersticiones y costumbres gentilicias que hoy viven entre los indios naturales de esta Nueva España*, México [1629] 1953 (http://www.cervantesvirtual.com/obra-visor/tratado-de-las-supersticiones-y-costumbres-gentilicas-que-hoy-viven-entre-los-indios-naturales-de-esta-nueva-espana--0/html/cf187f38-7e62-49f7-bcf3-71d3c710fe4e_2.htm#1).

Soto, Domingo de, *Relección del maestro fray Domingo de Soto, acerca de la herejía*, in *Relecciones y opusculos*, vol. II-2, ed. Sánchez-Lauro Pérez, Sixto, Salamanca [1539] 2011, 23–137.

Suárez, Francisco, *De virtute Religionis*, Tractatus III, Liber II: *De superstitione*, in *Opera Omnia*, Editio Nova, Parisiis 1859: Ludovicum Vivès.

Torreblanca Villalpando, Francisco de, *Epitome Delictorum, Sive De Magia, In Qua Aperta Vel Occulta Invocatio Daemonis intervenit. Editio Novissima Innumeris Mendis Expurgata, necnon indice Rerum & Verborum copiosissimo nunc primùm locupletata*, Lugduni 1678: Joannes Antonij Huguetan.

Vitoria, Francisco de, *De Arte Magica*, in *Relectiones Theologicae XII, Tomus II*, Lugduni 1557: Iacobum Boyerium.

Literature

Álvarez Alonso, Fermina, *La Inquisición en Cartagena de Indias durante el siglo XVII*, Madrid 1999.

Álvarez Santaló, Carlos, "Adoctrinamiento y devoción en las bibliotecas sevillanas del siglo XVIII", in Álvarez Santaló, Carlos, María Jesús Buxó i Rey and Salvador Rodríguez Becerra (eds.), *La religiosidad popular*, vol. 2: *Vida y muerte: La imaginación religiosa*, Barcelona 1989, 21–45.

Aspell de Yanzi Ferreira, Marcela, "El Tribunal de la Inquisición en América. Los comisarios del Santo Oficio en Córdoba del Tucumán en el siglo XVIII", in Martiré, Eduardo (ed.), *La América de Carlos IV. Cuadernos de investigaciones y documentos*, vol. 2, Buenos Aires 2007.

Campagne, Fabián Alejandro, *Homo catholicus, homo superstitiosus: el discurso antisupersticioso en la España de los siglos XV a XVIII*, Madrid 2002.

Campos Moreno, Araceli, *Oraciones, ensalmos y conjuros mágicos del archivo inquisitorial de la Nueva España, 1600–1630*, México 2001.

Ceballos Gómez, Diana Luz, *Quyen tal haze que tal pague: Sociedad y prácticas mágicas en el Nuevo Reino de Granada*, Bogotá 2002.

Ceballos Gómez, Diana Luz, "Entre el Rey y el Papa. La Inquisición: trayectoria de una institución plurisecular", in *Análisis* 83 (2013), 287–304 (http://revistas.usta.edu.co/index.php/analisis/article/view/1049).

Díaz Burgos, Ana María, *Fisuras inquisitoriales, voces femeninas y hechicería en Cartagena de Indias*, Atlanta, GA 2011.

García García, Bernardo José, "El contexto de la religiosidad popular", in Álvarez Santaló, Carlos, María Jesús Buxó i Rey and Salvador Rodríguez Becerra (eds.), *La religiosidad popular*, vol. 1: *Antropología e historia*, Barcelona 1989, 19–29.

Giles, Mary E. (ed.), *Mujeres en la Inquisición. La persecución del Santo Oficio y el Nuevo Mundo*, trans. Alejandra Devoto, Barcelona 2000 (http://dialnet.unirioja.es/servlet/extlib?codigo=1069).

Guibovich Pérez, Pedro M., "Piedad popular y Contrarreforma: los devocionarios en el virreinato del Perú", in Oesterreicher, Wulf and Roland Schmidt-Riese (eds.), *Conquista y conversión. Universos semióticos, textualidad y legitimación de saberes en la América colonial*, Berlin 2014, 215–228.

Hansen, Joseph, *Quellen und Untersuchungen zur Geschichte des Hexenwahns und der Hexenverfolgung im Mittelalter. Mit einer Untersuchung der Geschichte des Wortes Hexe von Johannes Franck*, Hildesheim [1901] 1963.

Lux Martelo, Martha Elisa, *Las mujeres de Cartagena de Indias en el Siglo XVII. Lo que hacían, les hacían y no hacían, y las curas que les prescribían*, Bogotá 2006.

Maqueda Abreu, Consuelo, *Estado, Iglesia e Inquisición en Indias: un permanente conflicto*, Madrid 2000.

Medina, José Toribio, *La imprenta en Bogotá y la Inquisición en Cartagena de Indias:* publicación de la Biblioteca National de Colombia, con motivo del primer centenario del nacimiento del señor José Toribio Medina, Bogotá 1952.
Millar Carvacho, René, *Inquisición y sociedad en el virreinato peruano. Estudios sobre el Tribunal de la Inquisición de Lima*, Santiago de Chile 1998.
Pérez Villanueva, Joaquín and Bartolomé Escandell Bonet (eds.), *Historia de la Inquisición en España y América*, vol. 2: *Las estructuras del Santo Oficio*, Madrid 1993.
Quezada Ramírez, Noemí, "Santa Marta en la tradición popular", in *Anales de Antropología* 10 (1973), 221–240.

CHAPTER 11

Forensic Practices and the "History of Justice" in the 17th and 18th Centuries: a View from a Spanish American Periphery

Agustín Casagrande

1 Introduction

In recent years a tension has emerged between legal historians and social historians in the field of the history of justice. While the former have resorted to legal literature and judicial archives to observe how legal knowledge was applied in the practice of justice, the latter have privileged the field of archives without paying as much attention to the discourses that guided judicial praxis. In the latter case, the fundamental role played by a vital source – the *forensic practices* – has been neglected. This literary genre of the 17th and 18th centuries can serve to reconsider the relationship between legal literature and procedural practice which seems to be disconnected by the diverse prejudices created in pertinent disciplines of the academic field. So, by means of historiographic-methodological analysis, the aim of this chapter is to discuss certain elements to be considered in order to understand the oblivion with respect to the functionality of this type of literature (2 and 3). Such an analysis will then leave room for reconstructing the conceptual, intellectual and political conditions that served as a basis for the production of these texts (4). After a concrete analysis of the form that this type of literature took – by studying its writing conditions (5) – we will finally reflect on the uses that it can provide for writing and understanding the history of justice in marginal territories of the Spanish Monarchy (6) and (7).

2 "Practices": a Meta-Category in the Formation of a Disciplinary Field

One of the greatest tensions in the academic field today can be observed in the dialogue between the history of law and social history; above all, in the point made by social historians as to the lack of research on "practices" conducted by ius-historians. This criticism has a theoretical burden, which is sometimes forgotten due to the subjectivity that is constructed in university training. Thus, this tension must be considered to be part of the logic of the scientific field.[1] In Argentina, this criticism has emerged in conjunction with the "new history of justice", which is based on the assumptions of social history.[2] It can be observed, then, that this critique is defined by two elements. On the one hand, a process of professionalisation of historians has reinforced certain methodologies that are expressed in research topics and questions (popular culture, the lower classes, the actors, etc.). At the same time, this professionalisation was accompanied by a broadening of the social historical agenda towards the study of justice institutions. With respect to these new topics, it is worth noting that the field of justice was not a wasteland, since legal history had hegemonised the knowledge about law and political institutions until the latter half of the 20th century. So one way to address this matter was through criticism.

The correlate of this academic dispute can be found in a critical formula used by social historians, which strategically reduced the procedures and investigations of legal history to a mere recounting of laws under a 19th century state paradigm – discourse – which had forgotten the practices, to be found in judicial archives, and ignored the living experience and reality. In addition to the attraction for the archive, which was constitutive of a disciplinary identity, a theoretical assumption claimed that practices were the only way of reconstructing the everyday experience of law. For that purpose, it was necessary to resort to a lens that isolated (inadvertent) practice from the discourse of normativity and centred it as a privileged object by contrasting it with the former.

In order to do this, historians turned to the sociology of practices. Some drew on the theory of Anthony Giddens, where the capacity of agency appeared as a determinant of a freedom to do things differently from the dictation of orders from above, thus rediscovering the "lost actors"; additionally, they relied on a more determining theory of *habitus*.[3] By obliterating the debate on the crossroads of the actor with the social and institutional structure, it allowed an unusual recovery of the daily practices in the category, no less problematic, of extended practices which were crystallised in the form of the *customary/*

---

1 For the use of this category, see Bourdieu, "Le champ scientifique".

2 From the French and Spanish tradition, see the recent work of Barriera, "La historia de la justicia y las otras historias". Some classic texts from the tradition of the New Legal History are: Buffington, "Introduction"; Aguirre and Salvatore, "Writing the History of Law, Crime, and Punishment in Latin America"; Palacio and Candioti (eds.), *Justicia, política y derechos en América Latina.*

3 Giddens, *The Constitution of Society*. See also Bourdieu, *El sentido práctico*.

habits.[4] Thus, the scientific field produced a contraposition between *practices-custom* versus *discourse-law* which would open a hiatus in the appreciation of the judicial phenomenon.

However, it was not sociology that allowed the social historisation of the juridical but the influence of British cultural Marxism, which reached the pampas through the feverish reading of Edward Palmer Thompson.[5] Following this key author, Argentinian historians began to see custom as the practice that acted in a zone of friction between men and the law. However, in order to define custom, no complex legal concept was used;[6] rather, the semantic content of this legal institution was reduced to an operative category, presenting it as the result of the elementary exchanges of material life, with no connection to the influence of high culture.[7] It can be seen, then, how the theory allowed the appearance of a pure practice underlying the normative power of custom. In this way, beneath the veil of custom the know-how of rural – rustic – people could be revealed. Such "real acts" could only be found in the archives, and mainly in view of the judicial sources, which in their daily life and repetition showed how order and justice were "really" experienced in spaces far away from the high technology of literate knowledge.[8]

This theoretical activity presents a few drawbacks. So, in order to describe them, the theoretical basis for the discovery of pure practices must be deconstructed. Recently, in a criticism of romanticism and the *reification* of the concept of Thompsonian custom, Paola Miceli has pointed out that:

---

4 As an example, see the first pages of Raúl Fradkin's excellent and classic work, "Ley, costumbre y relaciones sociales en la campaña de Buenos Aires (siglos XVIII y XIX)", in Fradkin, *La ley es tela de araña*.

5 Thompson, *Costumbres en Común*. It should be noted that the critical aspect of this essay does not rule out E.P. Thompson's fundamental contribution, especially considering his attempt to rethink the role of superstructural elements in the shaping of legal experience, and thus returning a cultural character to law that had been reduced to a mere response of the economic structure by traditional Marxism. On this last point, see V. Tau Anzoátegui's reflections, referring to Le Goff, in Tau Anzoátegui, *La ley en la América Hispana*, 3–7.

6 On the problem of custom and the exhaustive problematisation of the diverse theoretical keys that surround the phenomenon, Paola Miceli's study is fundamental; see Miceli, *Derecho consuetudinario y memoria*, 27–72.

7 Cerutti, "Histoire pragmatique, ou de la rencontre entre histoire sociale et histoire culturelle", 151.

8 The construction of this particular object – village – emerges from a double isolation. On the one hand, from the bourgeoisie, which becomes an anachronism and, on the other, from the scriptural world, where textuality is isolated from a broad register that coexists with the literate; so a voice reappears that is characteristic of the agent detached from culture. The risk seems to be that this tends to become – through the writing of its history – the "copy of the artefact" that produces it; see De Certeau, *La invención de lo Cotidiano*, 146.

> From the title of his introduction: "Customs and Culture", we can clearly see what is the prevailing notion of custom in Thompson. Custom is the reservoir of tradition, which is used by those who cannot access systematic education. Custom includes the traditional habits and customs of the people as opposed to knowledge transmitted by elitist mechanisms. The relationship that is immediately established is between custom, culture and people. The custom is, thus, popular culture, the set of experiences and practices transmitted from generation to generation as systematic teaching through non-systematic channels. A romantic touch surrounds this statement: for Thompson, custom is an environment of uncontaminated behaviour, the moment or place where human nature is expressed.[9]

The consequence of the link between custom-culture-village and its resulting "uncontaminated sphere of behaviour" as opposed to "knowledge transmitted by elitist mechanisms" produced, as Peter Burke points out, a split between popular culture and high culture.[10] This separation that knocks at the doors of academia would serve to define an analytical procedure. But in Thompson's thought there is something else. By deconstructing it, Simona Cerutti reveals the base of this theoretical scheme:

> The tradition of the School of historical law, which strives to revive the popular roots of law – Thompson's first source of inspiration is Marx, a student of Savigny. From this intellectual tradition, Thompson adopts a crucial presupposition, the popular character of "alternative" cultures; which means the existence of a link between the plebs (the ensemble of groups excluded from power) and conceptions of law that are "other" than those legitimized by the texts.[11]

This sliding from Thompson to Marx, and from Marx to Savigny, facilitates an understanding of the original division between two different cultures, which found in the customary voice a romantic conception of a popular act, serving as a base to construct a dichotomy between the field of pure practices and the textual universe of elites.

9 Miceli, *Práctica jurídica y costumbre en Castilla y León*, 43–44.
10 Burke, *Was ist Kulturgeschichte?*, 38–40.
11 Cerutti, "Histoire pragmatique, ou de la rencontre entre histoire sociale et histoire culturelle", 152.

That theory gave rise to several consequences in Argentina, specifically, in the field of the "new history of justice". The first was the separation between a legal culture – based on practices – and a legal culture – as producer of discourses – which, under the theoretical assumption of corresponding to alternative cultural formations, fragmented the legal phenomenon, making invisible, in some cases, a connection between texts, institutional pressures, forms of knowledge circulation, etc. The second, rather methodological consequence was the difficulty to integrate the use of diverse sources in the same study. That is to say, to compose what can be said of a historical phenomenom beyond the "voice" of the actors, by means of juridical books, legislation, confession manuals, etc. Consequently, given that the production of a lay culture was derived from material relations, any other product was a replica or contamination, something that deserved to be reduced as much as possible.

Thus, the seemingly innocuous expression of "discourses and practices" as organising categories of what can be observed in research has a surplus of meaning, which conceals a dense legal debate on the sources of law originated in the 19th century. If the accusation against a state-oriented legalist history of law resulted in new advances in research, this criticism should not replicate another contribution of the 19th century. Thus, the dismantling of another 19th century foundation – that of the historical school of law – can make some points appear occluded by the category of "pure practices", which deserve to be thematised.

3 "Forensic practices": a History of Oblivion

Beyond those theoretical elements which constitute the institutional logic of social history, a distrustful or even derogatory view of practical literature has also been presented within the literary legal history. This point can find some explanation for the taxonomic impulse of contemporaneity. In the task of isolating and cataloguing books, some genres (such as the forensic practices) have been put in a marginal place after comparing them with the great theoretical and dogmatic works of the time.[12] The fate of this juridical literary genre is not paradoxical, given that although it is recognised as having circulated widely,[13] its little dogmatic importance seems to have condemned these works to occupy the last step of a process that, by traditional juridical history

12 On this subject, see the classic and fundamental work of Tomás y Valiente, *El derecho penal de la Monarquía absoluta*, 139–149.

13 Cutter, *The Legal Culture of Northern New Spain*.

was characterised as vulgarisation.[14] To analyse the role of this kind of literature through this process seems to conceal the rich and complex process of distancing between theory and praxis that would be a characteristic note of the 18th century experience.

However, this is not only attributable to legal historiography. Cultural history has also adopted this perspective with similar effects. As an example, we can refer to a detailed study and evaluation of the legal books held by the capitular clergy of the Toledo cathedral, conducted by Ramón Sánchez González, who states:

> It will be precisely the genre of forensic practices – that is, the attempt to know more about the legal praxis expressed through the formulas mentioned above, which establish a doctrinal corpus with which lawyers acquire fluency in the way of acting but they ignore the scientific foundations of these actions which leads to a process of *cultural impoverishment*.[15]

A brief analysis of these models presents the problem of understanding the emergence of this practical literature as a record of "cultural impoverishment", without stressing that, perhaps, the simple discourses conveyed by these works were the consequence of the action of a context of power that prevented long theoretical excurses. Thus, more than an impoverishment – a word that manifests a certain nostalgic teleology – the extended use of these texts could be indicative of changes in the political-legal power that were inscribed in a particular discursive formation – explicative for other than this literary genre – and that deserves to be reconstructed.

For its part, from the perspective of social history, although the significance of these forensic practices has been recognised, their value as a cultural object worthy of analysis has been reduced by methodological means when compared with the wealth provided by judicial archives.[16] In this second case, the fact of

---

14 Bernal, "Las leyes de indias a la luz de dos comentaristas novohispanos del siglo XVIII". For the analysis of "vulgarization", see Christoph Meyer (Chapter 2) in this volume.

15 Sánchez González, "La cultura de las letras en el clero capitular de la catedral toledana", 193 (italics do not appear in the original). Even a brilliant scholar of the subject like Tomás y Valiente, in his commentary, and in spite of recognising the link between the growth of the King's power and the appearance of such a pragmatic literature, warns that: "These men of the non-university forum are with certain frequency expressedly authors or addressees of some *Prácticas* or *Sumas judiciales* that break with the old style and incur at the same time in the already mentioned scientific mediocrity", in Tomás y Valiente, *El derecho penal de la Monarquía absoluta*, 140.

16 See the excellent work of Barriera, "Voces legas, letras de justicia".

presenting them in close relationship with judicial practice – but no longer as a formative element of it but as a subsidiary factor to interpret the sources available to the researcher – impoverishes the network of referrals between sources.

Based on what has been said in the previous sections, some questions can be postulated. In the first place, and given that the notion of pure practices turned out to be a replica of a 19th-century Savignian "invention of tradition" linked to custom, from the Hispanic legal tradition it is worth asking what was understood by 'practice' and 'custom' in the Castilian and Spanish American world of the 18th century. Correlatively, it is necessary to ask if there was a total discontinuity between lay and literate cultures and, from the revision of this presupposition, it is possible to enquire into the role of a practical literature in the political context of the 18th century. This will try to overcome the forms of teleology that the disciplinary gaze casts on this narrative. So, the juridical matter could be considered as a discourse of power, which allows the supposition of a very pronounced dynamic that includes institutions, actors and discourses in each instance of action. Therefore, we should begin by trying to answer the first question: what was understood by 'practice' in the 18th century?

4 Practice as a Concept: Reassembling the Romantic Prejudices

Given the mentioned difficulty concerning the meaning of two basic concepts of the juridical culture of the 18th century – custom and practice – which extend to the present reinterpreted in the light of the romanticism of the historical school, it is worth carrying out a very brief historical-conceptual exercise to clarify any doubts and to reach the central problem of judicial praxis. To this end, although being aware of the diverse layers of meaning stratified in the concept of custom, the operation proposed here is very simple: to resort to dictionaries. It is worth mentioning that this source must be treated very carefully. Although, methodologically, they had become indexes of concepts inserted in another period, their definitions do not manage to capture the total complexity of a language of a time, which is in constant mutation. Besides, dictionaries were not at all politically innocuous. With this clarification, it cannot be denied that in the dictionaries, 'custom' possesses a large dose of 'practice'. But this practice that sediments custom cannot be defined only by its iterative character. Thus, although in the second entry of the lemma "práctica" of the *Diccionario de Autoridades* of 1737, it can be read that this one "means also the continued use, custom or style of a thing",[17] which seems to confirm the

17 Real Academia Española, *Diccionario de la lengua castellana*, vol. 5, 1737, 344.

Thompsonian sense; in the same work, the second entry of "costumbre" – corresponding to the juridical sense – indicates that:

> It is also valid as a *fuero*, an unwritten right or law, which has the same force, and produces the same effect as it, as long as it is introduced with the circumstances or solemnities provided in law. First, that it be about a point or a thing of which something good is derived. Second, that its use or exercise be public; Third, that it be admitted with the will of all persons who make up the *Pueblo* or Province where it is established, or at least of the greater part; Fourth, that it does not oppose or contradict the rights or laws written; Fifth, that it is permitted or tolerated by the Lord of the *Pueblo*.[18]

The comparison between the second definition of "costumbre" and the second definition of "práctica" – charged with a "solemnity provided in law" – makes visible some elements that need to be explored. From a logical point of view, the dictionary sentence exhibits a tension between written law and custom within the sources of pre-modern law. At this level, although both terms are found in the paragraph, there is a growing weight of the power of the former with respect to the latter, which, while not ruling out the significant role of custom, at least moderated it. There, the power of custom seemed to require a process of juridical qualification, which implied that the habitual and repetitive actions to be converted into law, had to be filtered by a knowledge that was composed of laws and reasons of justice.[19] Indeed, the *Diccionario de Autoridades* stated that there was a recognised custom "when there is no law to the contrary, nor that it repulses reason and justice". Thus, it can be perceived that although every custom required 'practices', not every group of 'practices' *per se* could become custom, but only those that, in dialogue with the law and the concepts of reason, were tolerable. This last point, precisely, invites reflection on the concept of practice, given that if it seems that customary law refers to

---

18 Real Academia Española, *Diccionario de la lengua castellana*, vol. 2, 1729, 643: "vale también fuero, derecho ù ley no escrita, que tiene la misma fuerza, y produce el mismo efecto que ella, con tal, que se introduzca con las circunstancias o solemnidades prevenidas por derecho: Primera, que sea sobre punto ò cosa de que se pueda seguir algún bien; segunda, que su uso ò exercicio sea público; tercera, que se admita con voluntad de todas las personas que componen el Pueblo ò Provincia donde se establece, ò á lo menos de la mayor parte: Cuarta, que no se oponga o contravenga a los derechos o leyes escritas, quinta, que la permita o tolere el Señor del Pueblo [...]".

19 See Thomas, "La valeur des choses", 1449–1450; Miceli, *Derecho consuetudinario y memoria*, 20.

an *ordo iuris*, possibly the practices – the last and formative instances of the former – could present a similar content. That is to say, within this cultural enclave it should not be surprising that the practice possessed a determining relationship with a knowledge that qualified it as such. What, then, did the dictionary say about 'practice'?

The main entry of the 1737 edition described "practice" as "the exercise, or actual execution, according to the rules of some Art or Faculty, which teaches to do something, as a consequence of the theoretical. It is from the Latin *Praxis*, which means the same thing".[20] The close relationship between theory and practice was essential for thinking about exercising something, or simply acting. Instead of projecting a limit on the contamination of an external knowledge to the practices themselves, these could not be conceived without the guidance of rules consistent with a theory. It was just towards the middle of the 19th century, precisely between the edition of the Dictionary of the Royal Academy of 1843 and that of 1857, when this relationship disappeared, leaving a simplified term that is closer to our present understanding: "The exercise of any art or faculty according to its rules. Praxis".[21] Clearly, in the course of little more than a century, the dislocation of a tradition and the conceptual mutation implied by semantic displacement caused the theoretical to be lost as an essential datum that refounded practice in knowledge, finding in its definition the notion of an act according to a simple *rule*.

As it appears at first glance, the course of this voice is complex. Hence, in order to perceive that change that would bring the *praxis* closer to *techné*, it is necessary to observe a greater field where dislocation is generated: politics.[22] The displacement, which took place in the 18th century and which follows a winding road of more than 18 centuries, has the Aristotelian *praxis* as its starting point.[23] At this extreme, it cannot be ignored that, for this tradition, practical philosophy could not be separated from politics. Thus, between ethics and politics there was no distance or dialectic, but rather a continuum based on experience. In this context, *praxis* was a moral action, where acting had an end in itself. This nature separated it from *poiesis*, which approached the action of

---

20 Real Academia Española, *Diccionario de la lengua castellana*, vol. 5, 1737, 344: "El exercicio, ù actual execución, conforme à las reglas de algún Arte o Facultad, que enseña à hacer alguna cosa, como consiguiente à la Theórica. Es del Latino *Praxis*, que significa lo mismo".

21 Real Academia Española, *Diccionario de la lengua castellana*, 1852, 556.

22 This aspect has been intensively studied by Sandro Chignola and Giuseppe Duso. See Chignola and Duso, *Historia de los conceptos y filosofía política*.

23 For a reconstruction of this long evolution, see Bien, Kobusch and Kleger, "Praxis, praktisch".

the craftsman, who produces something that comes into existence outside the agent of his acts. In this sense, it should be remembered that for Aristotelian thought, *praxis* was separate from "simple *techné*", since the former depended on the knowledge applied for a good life. This implied seeing politics as a pedagogical formation of character that led to a *phronesis*, that is, to achieve "a wise understanding of the situation; *phronesis*, on which the tradition of classical politics is based from Cicero's prudence to Burke's Prudence".[24]

Now, simplifying to the extreme the course of philosophical thought, one can see a fundamental logical split established by modern political science, anticipated by Hobbes in the 17th century and developed by the discipline of public law during the 18th century.[25] In this sense, the action of this new knowledge would have an impact on some correlative points. This key voice of *prudence*, seen as a virtue, would be gradually relegated by a knowledge of the political technique intended to ensure the organisation of the State. In this way, knowledge would emerge by abjuring the classical political tradition, and influenced by the sciences of nature and mathematics, leaving *praxis* in a field close to *techné*.[26] Thus, the logic of government would be transformed from prudence to technique, where *praxis* instead of referring to the former would be ordered by the latter. In this context of radical change in modes of thought, it can be seen that the links between practice and theory and between practice and technique encompassed a logic of government that at the same time overlapped with the legal sphere. This shift also is implied in our present understanding; therefore, to make it explicit would serve to recognise a distinctive way of understanding "practice" in a cosmovision still anchored in the old tradition. Besides, it serves as a warning about the complexity that describing and analysing the shifting structure of a rich concept of *praxis* in the selected period is exposed to theoretical problems starting from a conceptualisation loaded with topicality.

At this point, and if this historical-philosophical excursus is of vital importance as context, the categorical-conceptual uses of *praxis* and theory within the judicial field requires other sources where the tense relationship between theory and practice is expressed in a more specific way. It is precisely here that the forensic literature appears. This special juridical literature, which strongly circulated since the beginning of the 18th century and continued to do so throughout the 19th century, takes on a fundamental dimension because it enables the connection of political-juridical knowledge with the judicial sphere,

24 Habermas, *Teoría y praxis*, 49–50.

25 Duso, *La lógica del potere*.

26 Habermas, *Teoría y praxis*, chapter 1.

which in turn leads one to look for the historical-philosophical relation between theory, discourses and practices.

5 Politics and the Emergency of Legal Practice

The complex relationship between theory and *praxis* was a common base for practical literature, which defined its literary status at these crossroads. Thus, in order to judge its quality, it was less the erudition of the author that counted than the more modest characteristic that looked at the "usefulness" of the work. This topic, ubiquitous in the references to the works, did not mean to propose interpretations or new doctrines but it privileged the collection of "disseminated knowledge" in order to present them in a simplified and orderly way, and in a discourse tending towards a concrete end: judicial performance. This purpose defined the substantial problematic of the works, concentrated on know-how, and delimited a style that left little expressive space to the author.[27] Thus, restricted by powers that ordered the discourses – the need for print approvals, as well as the hidden judgments after publication – the authors strove to justify the need for their works. However, in the course of the 17th century and until the end of the 18th century the meaning of judicial action was modulated by the progressive dissolution of a long experience of political government and by the emergence of a judicial practice that sought to conform to the power of law. In those interstices a slow process began that resulted in the reduction of the semantic field of judicial *praxis*.

5.1 *From Theory to Observation: Moments of Practical Knowledge*

Given the theoretical problem, expressed by the distance between "discourses and practices", referred to at the beginning of this chapter, the first point to highlight is the link between forensic practices, especially criminal ones, and the concept of *praxis* with Aristotelian roots, which, as was indicated, could not consider the latter outside the theory. Going back to works written during the 17th century, one observes that such a connection of meaning was decisive. Gerónimo Fernández de Herrera Villarroel expressed this in the "Prologue to the Reader" of his *Criminal Practice* approved in 1671, of which the 1724 edition is used here:

27 As Bajtín, *Estética de la creación verbal*, 252, pointed out, "in the great majority of discursive genres (except literary genres) an individual style does not form part of the intention of the enunciation, it is not its sole purpose but rather it turns out to be, so to speak, an epiphenomenon of the enunciation, a complementary product of it".

> All art, and craft, be it speculative, theoretical, as well as practical, contains in itself science, without obscuring the distinction that there is no such thing without a divine object (reputing even the most famous for mere art) because without contradicting questions, which result from here, I take it for the extension of its common meaning in all genre, which is enough for my attempt; with which I will say, that to obtain the perfect thing of any Art, or business, the one who exerts it must have science of it, because this is the point of the elevation, or the center of the success, its opposite reverse the ignorance: To arrive from this to that, one disposes the desire, but alone it is not enough without continuous fatigue.[28]

This literature came to occupy a space in the judicial world that would free the reader from ignorance. However, the excess of theory also complicated the experience of justice. Thus, the opinion of the various authors could also lead to a problem of their own making. The task of the author of these works seemed to be defined by the gathering of multiple forms of knowledge in order to simplify them. It was precisely this last point that became the subject of Villadiego's work approved in 1609; in his note to the Reader, he said:

> I have tried in this Political Instruction and Judicial Practice, taking advantage of other books of much erudition, reducing here to a compendium and brief *suma* the most substantial, which in them is very extended, and I remember Seneca's sentence, which says that it is more useful to know few precepts of doctrine and wisdom, and to be soon in them, than many, not having them at hand.[29]

Defined between these lines is the problem that the abundance of texts, dogmas and doctrine entailed for the desired judicial action. Hence, without conceiving an act outside the knowledge composed by doctrine, the excessive amount of information seemed to cloud the gaze of justice. With this, the perfect procedural rule sought to harmonise the theory in order not to divert the practice, as well as to avoid the ignorance of the basic knowledge of dispensing justice. Both correlative dimensions of political government were made comprehensible from a community of theory and practice that guided legal prudence, from a politically guided government. Hence, its proximity

---

28 Fernández de Herrera Villarroel, *Practica criminal, instrucción (nueva útil) de substanciar las causas*, Prólogo.

29 Villadiego Valcuñana y Montoya, *Instrucción Política y práctica judicial*, Prólogo.

to the works of the political government such as that of Castillo de Bovadilla was manifest. Political government and judicial practice, as the title of Villadiego's work pointed out without gratuitousness, showed a jurisdictional logic.[30]

Towards the end of the 18th century, this tension was still inscribed in the writers' messages. However, a glance at the everyday life of the courts showed a tendency to see practices repeated by mere observation, which had to be corrected by the guidance of a just doctrine (precisely the doctrine that these same authors promoted). Antonio de Elizondo said, in volume IV of the 1784 edition of his *Práctica Universal Forense*, that:

> The good and the utility of the industrious youth have been the objects, that we propose to attend in this work, where, without the need of resorting to immense commentaries, it is easy to discover a national practice adjusted to the frequent sponsorship of the cases, cutting the occasion to consume the time in investigating the styles, and excusing the young people to beg these news from some people, whose elusive instruction cannot give them more support than that of the simple and naked observation, of how much they saw other *Curiales* perform in their days.[31]

On sharing that cultivating gaze of youth, and being aware of the need to avoid the errors produced by mere "execution" without proper guidance, Alvarez de Posadilla wrote, in his mid-18th century *Práctica Criminal*, that:

> In order that the young people take advantage of it, it has seemed convenient to give it in the form of dialogues, as it was written for the principal and first disciple of this teaching, that read by way of entertainment, insensibly instruct them, and know, at the same time as exercising themselves in practice, the abuses that they see observing their Masters, and avoid receiving the error and abuse of doctrine.[32]

30 On this perspective, see Costa, *Iurisdictio*. With a link to the history of Justice in Spanish American territories, see Agüero, *Castigar y perdonar cuando conviene a la República*; Garriga, "Sobre el gobierno de la justicia en Indias".

31 Elizondo, *Práctica*, vol. 4, VII. Here, "style" resembles a practice that can be observed juridically. So, "estilo" was not only a note of particularity or distinction but, as stated in Real Academia Española, *Diccionario de la lengua castellana*, vol. 3, 1732, 635: "en lo legal es la fórmula de proceder jurídicamente, y el orden y méthodo de actuar".

32 Álvarez de Posadilla, *Práctica criminal por principios*, II.

Instruction for practice is proposed as a remedy for errors learned by observing the masters. Here, it would seem that the problem was not so much ignorance, but rather that the damage came from the "error and abuse of doctrine".

From this vantage point, it becomes clear that between the first written practices of the 17th century and these other ones from the middle of the 18th century a gap opened with regard to the legal understanding of practices. While in the former the knowledge-politics-practice correlation was indispensable, in the latter there was talk of an observation of acts in the Tribunals, which would open a furrow between knowledge and practice, defining new conceptual contents, which were nothing trivial. But this can only be understood within a complex political history of the conceptual formation of practice separated from theory.

5.2 *From Politics to Practices: a Writing Order*

Contextualisation and diachrony allow us to postulate certain premises in order to understand the process of isolation of "practice" with respect to theory within the legal field. In a first level of analysis, and by means of a long-term view, it is possible to comprehend that both this literature and these authors were exposed to a growing process of hermeneutic control that, throughout the 17th and 18th centuries opposed statutory law to the jurisdiction, assessing the Monarch's power in terms of his *potestas legislatorial*.[33]

In this context, and knowing that all these books had to be submitted for approval, the literary structure was modified by the authors, showing that, beyond a process of "vulgarization" or scientific "advancement", it was the dynamics of political power what was incorporated into the mutated discursive structure. For example, it is noteworthy that, by concealing the reference to the prudence of the "authors" and highlighting instead that the procedures were useful to make the "Laws of the Kingdom" operative, a faster edition could be achieved and, at the same time, a consecration by way of a reference book. The sources seem to demonstrate that extreme. While the practices of Villadiego and Fernández de Herrera Villarroel can be seen as being close to political government during the 17th century,[34] in the 18th century the books remarked

33 On this development, see the indispensable study by Mohnhaupt, "Potestas legislatoria und Gesetzesbegriff im Ancien Régime".

34 For example, Villadiego, whose work did not coincidentally include in its title "politics and practice", explained that his book consisted of "the real laws by which lawsuits and causes must be judged and abrogated and substantiated first than by those of *derecho común*" (which left room for the consideration of the literature that conveyed the latter). For his part, Fernández de Herrera Villarroel stated that jurisdiction should be protected against those who altered justice, where prudence and calm were the pillars of a good

that it was the law and its enforcement which guided the strict "administration of justice".[35]

On a second level, this process of mutation can be seen within the dynamics of the juridical literary field, which, without disassociating itself from the political, allowed greater pertinence to analyse the development of a concept of practice within the discipline. In order to do this, it is necessary to bear in mind that the composition of this particular literary genre was determined by the recognition and intertextuality between the works.[36] In this way, the 18th century references to previous texts offer clues to understanding, on the one hand, how the literary tradition was constructed; and, on the other, how a differentiation process would, despite sharing a common core, have an impact on the conceptuality of each work. An example can clarify this dimension. In 1754, Berní wrote in the introduction of his practice, which was widely disseminated:

> Nearly all the laws of the Kingdom seek the extinction of abuses and crimes; and all together they establish right administration of justice. Their glossators adapted infinite doctrines; and for greater clarity, in matters of crimes, Farinacio wrote six volumes of Criminal Practice; Antonio Gomez wrote the third one of several; Mr. Mateu a work de re criminali; Leotardo, one work de usuris & contractibus; and in order to put the penalties into practice, Peguera, Gutierrez, Salcedo and Herrera wrote their books.[37]

Fernández de Herrera Villarroel thus became an antecedent for intertextual connection, but for a mid-18th century author the work of the former was not enough. Thus, Berní later said: "I have read these works, and I form a concept, that the present Practice will not be despicable; because in addition to reducing to an easy and clear method the matter of crimes, penalties, legal presumptions, and defences, with the most solid foundations, the practice observed today in the Royal Courts of Spain is added". Berní discredited Fernández de Herrera Villarroel just as soon as he had been instituted, by placing him on the side of doctrine, which would be discredited in the face of the emergence

judge. A clear jurisdictional culture, of which the indications to be recognised require a heuristic exercise of translation by means of models. For the context, see the great synthesis Agüero, "Las categorías básicas de la cultura jurisdiccional".

35 See Álvarez de Posadilla, *Práctica criminal por principios*, 9 y Berní, *Práctica criminal con nota de los delitos*, 2.

36 Hespanha, "Una historia de textos".

37 Berní, *Práctica criminal con nota de los delitos*, 2.

of a more important knowledge power: *the observed practice of the Courts*. But this should not come as a surprise. Elizondo, in the first volume of his *Practica Universal Forense*, wrote that:

> You will find a plan, that I consecrate to the wise, and to the curious, to delineate in it the brush of the Juridical. Without being able to vanish the novelty of my Work, the writings of Paz, and Villadiego; For if you do me justice, you will know the concession of these in the variety of resources, produced by the diversity of the Tribunals of our Monarchy, their juridical exposition, and other singular things, which I try to demonstrate with the Royal dispositions, subsequent to the Work of those, of Monarchs so exalted with which Spain has boasted.[38]

In contrast with jurisprudential knowledge, the recursive and daily knowledge of the tribunals would appear. This task would be mostly known through *observation*. On the other hand, the force of the legislative power appears to mark that the previous works had not contemplated "the real dispositions" dictated after their publication. This attack shows that the quality of the work resided in the "updated" knowledge of practice and the law of the King. This statute broke the logic of centuries where knowledge was ancient because it was good, while here beyond goodness it was topicality that mattered.[39]

It is interesting, then, to see how the same logic of constitution of a disciplinary field – in this case, the practical one – at the very moment of recognising antecedents for settling down and founding tradition, it carries out a torsion that disqualifies that past in order to justify the present of writing. Consequently, the political ingenuity codified, in part, in the weeding of an abundance of opinions that opened the space for the application of the law, allows us to think of its mediation and functionality in a process of autonomisation of judicial practice with respect to a theory of *iuris opinio*. This history that, with the passage of time, would separate dogmatics from the practice of the courts, had to do with the constitution of a field of knowledge that, having departed from a tradition that did not separate theory and *praxis*, discarded the former, returning the daily life of the judicial task to a set of uses and

38 Elizondo, *Práctica*, vol. 1, Prólogo. The premise for reducing the vast literary universe of *ius commune* was a characteristic that marked the long period from the 18th century to the times of codification. On this subject, see the outstanding study Mohnhaupt, " 'Historia literaria iuris' ".

39 See Duso, *La lógica del potere*, 57: "Il buon diritto antico non era buono perché antico, ma antico perché buono".

practices. So, gradually detaching itself from voices that were becoming more dangerous every day, legal actions – subject to description – lost the knowledge that justified them, turning the process into a form without tradition, a pure form, a practice.

Up to this point, the relations between political and literary cultural formations were evaluated, which allowed, in their timed action, the production of a decentralised practical sense of the theory. However, this had an impact on the discursive formation that conveyed this new knowledge, without ignoring the fact that these rules of writing and the production of knowledge about practices also influenced the political and cultural fields.

5.3 *The Writing of Practices*

As noted, the purpose of these texts was their utility, which referred to advice for everyday judicial practice. This implied, in the first place, reaching those users who could benefit from a practical book. The consideration of the reader, who acted as a horizon of expectation for the practical authors, determined the form of writing.[40] Both elements cannot be separated from a material condition. Since the 17th century, there had been technological and economic reasons that explained the accelerated tendency of the passage in the language of books from Latin to *romance*. This did not necessarily mean that the first texts lost their value – in economic and symbolic sense – in the Castillian linguistic space,[41] but they were linked more to places of status than to rapidly expandable technologies of knowledge. Within this particular literature, Villadiego found a close relationship between language and the influence of "forensic practices" by stating:

> And to go in *romance* this book, has in itself particular grace, and usefulness, so that those who do not know Latin, are not deprived of these matters, and things so common, that it is convenient for them to know; without this seeming to be less, nor profane this science, because in all vulgar languages this is the most abundant, virile, and sonorous, and most common to various nations of the world.[42]

---

40 Chartier, *The order of Books*, 27.

41 Chartier, *El presente del pasado*.

42 Villadiego Valcuñana y Montoya, *Instrucción Política y práctica judicial*, Prólogo. A similar piece of news about this writing practice and the main model that marks the production threshold in Spanish is the classic book by Castillo de Bovadilla, *Política para corregidores*. For an excellent commentary on this author and the production of his work, see Francisco Tomás y Valiente, "Castillo de Bobadilla. Semblanza personal y profesional de

With a more pragmatic vocation based on observation, Fernández de Herrera Villarroel said:

> [...] Scribes of these *Reynos* are not *Latinos*. I believe that some practices that are [written] in that language are no longer useful for the majority of scribes, nor others that in Latin, and Romance annoy those who look at the *Glossa*, do not understand the text, or on the contrary, and that although some and others say what should be done, they lack the when, and why, and the forms of *autos*, and in them many difficulties are not touched that the modern experienced have recognized.[43]

Texts written in Spanish reached an audience that needed to know, through this translation, the theory behind everyday life. This translation was not minor, since although in several works some quotations appeared in Latin, their content, their formulations, the re-submissions sought to reduce "the multitude of allegations, decisions, and consultations scattered in so many books". With this, young people were "pleased with a study, about which, being taught without rules to dispute everything from the beginning, they would surrender a few times later with submission to the just and innocent uses of the forum".[44]

The composition of the page in the simplicity of Spanish also operated as a reflection of the size of the works, which sought to be cultural objects of easy circulation. An example can be found in the authorisation of Joseph Berní's practice: "Perfection, which the Author of this succinct work also obtained from our [laws], making sure with its smallness, and manner accommodated to everybody, that it can go in the hands of everyone, even of those that will not reach them in their originals, because of their high price or their voluminosity".[45] Elizondo warned of the same thing when he said: "[...] it does not serve us as an impulse to write the vain ambition of fame, or any other less patriotic spirit, than that of reducing many volumes to a few, distracting them by a precise order, and dictating them without affectation, subtlety, or darkness in relief of the youth".[46]

However, this romance language opening within the legal literary tradition – written in Latin – deserved an apology from the authors. This compromised

un juez del Antiguo Régimen", in Tomás y Valiente, *Gobierno e instituciones en la España del Antiguo Régimen*, 179–251.

43 Fernández de Herrera Villarroel, *Practica criminal, instrucción (nueva útil) de substanciar las causas*, Prólogo al lector.

44 Elizondo, *Práctica*, vol. 4, VIII.

45 Berní, *Práctica criminal con nota de los delitos*, Authorisation of 22 September 1749.

46 Elizondo, *Práctica*, vol. 1, Prólogo.

situation, faced with the possible reprobation of the lawyers, highlighted the interest of reaching laymen, rescuing the "practical" sense of the book. In Villadiego's work, these elements were synthesised in a flowery paragraph:

> And this book is not of lesser esteem, because it is taken out of other Authors, so that more credit is given to what is written here, and I want it to be understood, than to dare to write, and to bring this work to light. [...] For the taste of the Reader, we have tried to meddle with the things of usefulness that are resolved here, some of them of taste, because what Horatio said is fulfilled, that the perfect work must have *usefulness and taste*.[47]

The same thing happened in the book written by Fernández de Herrera Villarroel, who, after recounting the fear of publishing his work, and the insistence of a friend to do so, said:

> What I surrendered to, was to say, that I did not write for savants, to whom these principles do not take advantage, but is, or for those who ignore (or those who are forgotten) for being as it is true, that so much of this genre has not been gathered so far in our Spanish language. There are so many books that give documents which explain how not to sin, and so many for punishment (which corresponds to the crime after having been committed), but there was none of them about the practice, and theoretical together, that were in between, and led to that purpose.[48]

A double mediation appears here: the first between practical and theoretical; the second between wise and lay. It is also interesting to note the vacuum that his work filled, by presenting his work as a medium. All this indicates that the hiatus was both human and literary.

Towards the middle of the 18th century, Elizondo also debated between both audiences, but with a stronger tone and, given the contextual conditions outlined above, he declared:

> We, far from being resentful of any observation, addition, or correction that the Wise subscribe to, sincerely protest to embrace them with humility and gratitude, knowing that their spirit is not to discredit our works,

47 Villadiego Valcuñana y Montoya, *Instrucción Política y práctica judicial*, Prólogo.

48 Fernández de Herrera Villarroel, *Practica criminal, instrucción (nueva útil) de substanciar las causas*, Prólogo.

> but to help them to perfection, in order to make them more interesting to the Republic of Letters; [...] which would disprove the good intention, which encourages us, and we proposed, of course, to aspire to the common good only of young people.[49]

In the same sense, giving an account of his previous ignorance, Álvarez de Posadilla pointed out that his work was addressed to "those who exercise the office of Notary, to the Ordinary Mayors, and even to new Judges, I have thought it convenient to give it to the press, so that its usefulness is not limited to the disciple to whom it has been given",[50] for his part, as for his person he confessed, "besides the ideas and knowledge acquired from many things that he did not know, to have come out of a great number of errors that as legal practices he had learned from his Master".[51]

The combination of language, size of works and readers in the constitution of the literary genre also impacted on the conceptual logic of forensic practices, which was devalued by their lack of correlation with profound knowledge.[52] This devaluation, however, was, as previously presented, the consequence of a political-cultural change that, far from implying a teleological gaze, evidenced a new form of production of practical knowledge. Now, at this point it seems that this history of books has no correlation with bodies and justice. In order to connect the experience with the cultural field that coded it, the observation has to return to the experience of the Río de la Plata at the end of the 18th century, which will be used here to discern the way in which these practical ideas materialised in Spanish American territories.

6 Transferability of Practices: Know-How and Institutions

The political change inscribed in the two different ways of conceiving the practices would take shape in the ways of organising the spaces of jurisdictional power.[53] For the sake of brevity, here are some clues to understand the territory of the Viceroyalty of the Río de la Plata, especially during the 18th century. When facing a century of profound cultural changes, the effects would be felt dissimilarly in an extended space. In this context, the heuristic model of Mario

49 Elizondo, *Práctica*, vol. 4, IX.

50 Álvarez de Posadilla, *Práctica criminal por principios*, II.

51 Álvarez de Posadilla, *Práctica criminal por principios*, Prólogo.

52 Bajtín, *Estética de la creación verbal.*

53 Barriera, *Abrir puertas a la tierra*; Hespanha, *La Gracia del Derecho.*

Sbriccoli allows us to better understand the development of institutions by opposing a negotiated to a hegemonic justice.[54] This framework serves as a window into the operability of criminal practices, taking into account the conceptual distance between those written during the 17th century – widely circulated and used during the 18th century – with respect to those actually written in the 18th that, as a novelty, would have an impact on the Bourbon reformers.

Within the great framework proposed, the judiciary of the 17th and 18th centuries, in peripheral areas, presents typical traits of a negotiated justice. A justice of neighbours that implied techniques of government, which carried with them centuries of political tradition. The negotiating role, arbitrator of the problems of a political body, was central. Thus, it not only composed problems of the community but also solved dualisms of the legal universe – between the power of law and judgement, between ordinary and extraordinary ways, in the mixture of accusation and inquisition, between punishment and forgiveness.[55] This preeminent role of the judge and the consequent harmonisation composed a grammar where justice, equity and reasonability stood out. If we add to this the fundamentally lay character of the magistracy, it seems that what can be said and practiced in this context depended on the judge. However, this did not imply that the magistrates acted without a guide, and above all, at the time of writing, they were formulating the account of what happened and forwarding the documents from one seat of justice to another, mainly for control or review. This was complicated especially by the possibility of being sanctioned. In that context, the practices functioned as a textual regulator, as evidenced by the similarity documented in the archives.

Precisely, Alejandro Agüero has stated that, in the 18th century, there were three key elements of influence in the work of laymen.[56] The first concerned the notaries. The absence of lawyers functioning as judges required the revision by a legal advisor, who instructed and transmitted knowledge. In the absence of notaries, the dominant ecclesiastical presence established mechanisms of control of what could be done, with a jurisdictional knowledge that modulated the writing of the cases.[57] Finally, Agüero points out that there was "a constant

54 Sbriccoli, "Justicia Criminal"; Meccarelli, "La dimensión doctrinal del proceso desde una perspectiva de historia de la justicia criminal".

55 Meccarelli, "Dimensions of Justice and Ordering Factors in Criminal Law from the Middle Ages till Juridical Modernity", 62–63; Agüero, *Castigar y perdonar cuando conviene a la República*.

56 Agüero, "El testimonio procesal y la administración de justicia penal en la periferia de la Monarquía Católica", 6–7.

57 See Barral, *De sotanas por la Pampa*; Barriera, "Voces legas, letras de justicia", 352–353.

and silent factor: the circulation of legal books and manuals of procedural and notarial practices among the principal members of the neighbourhood".[58] These practical books had a great impact, even if their content escaped the full understanding of high literature. It is precisely because they helped to label the actions of the community in a certain culture of order. Principally, this becomes visible in the body of the texts which not only ordered the crimes, the penalties, the methods of proof, the auxiliaries involved in the substance of the process, etc., but which included the syntactic formulas of writing down the steps of the process: the *autos* and so on. Hence, everyday life was filled with concepts by which the writers transmitted fundamental meanings.

As we enter the 18th century this textual production was conveyed by new institutional ends. Hence, in addition to these three modes of expansion of procedural knowledge of a local character, a growing control device had to be added – from the second half of the 18th century on – that was not only given by the presence of Bourbon officials but also by the *Real Audiencia* of Buenos Aires. As I have analysed in another paper,[59] this Court added several elements of control, motivated by a series of prejudices against laymen. As Agüero points out, these prejudices were – more than being anchored in the lack of jurisdictional precision – activated by a logic of distinction, and functioned as a legitimating discourse of European lawyers faced with a justice exercised by American neighbours.[60] Beyond the veracity or not of the reasons exposed by the *Audiencia* and its criticism of the practices of the laymen, the purpose of empowerment of the Audience can show the close relationship between the texts of the practices and the institutional dynamics.

If utility had produced, towards the middle of the 18th century, a separation of the practice from the theoretical armour that made up its base and essence, the desire for uniformity found an effective control device in malleable practices. In this way, practices were performed as a regulatory task. An example of this is given in a frustrated attempt in 1788. Within the Real Audiencia de Buenos Aires, the Regent Mata Linares projected a "Circular Instruction for the best and shortest dispatch of the formation of criminal cases", which, although never sanctioned by the delay of Prosecutor Márquez de la Plata, sought to

58 Agüero, "El testimonio procesal y la administración de justicia penal en la periferia de la Monarquía Católica", 7.

59 Casagrande, "Erradicando sus rústicos juzgamientos".

60 On this aspect, see Agüero's interesting discussion, referring to a classic work by Mariluz Urquijo on the relations between laymen and lawyers. See Mariluz Urquijo, "La Real Audiencia de Buenos Aires y la Administración de Justicia en lo criminal en el interior del virreinato"; Agüero, "Saber jurídico y técnica procesal en la justicia lega de la periferia".

unify the procedural practice of justice. In this document there was an attempt to normalise the daily practices in order to avoid that the hightest tribunal wasted its time rectifying the actions, and at the same time, in order to avoid the apologies of the subaltern justices who, by their ignorance or malice, harmed the *vindicta pública*. Now, when presenting the *memoria* document to his successor, Mata Linares emphasised that the Instruction had been "taken from what the laws provide and from our best practicians, clear, methodical and comprehensive of the formalities to be observed".[61] One example, which goes back to literary practices, were the forms, which were interspersed between the provisions to be followed by judges in the investigation. Articles 19 and 20 of the above-mentioned draft are an example:

> 19° The office of the Judge will serve as prosecutor in the slight cases, and this until issuing an order of guilt and charge to the defendant, and giving him notification so that he can defend himself in this, or an equivalent form:
>
> 20° In that *Villa* or *Partido*, on that day of that month of that year, Don XXX, etc. Having seen the summary information against XXX, because of this, or of the other crime, he said: That from this information and from the confession, it turns out that said defendant committed such and such of the crimes, and that this, in the best possible way in law, made him guilty, and charged him, and of course he gives him notification, so that within nine days he shall purge himself, and at the end of which he would receive, and I receive the cause for evidence with all charges of conclusion, publication and summons, in order to hear sentence, and that the witnesses of the summary trial be confirmed. And so it was ruled, commanded and signed, acting for me, and before witnesses in the absence of a notary.[62]

The procedural matter was ordered without requiring further knowledge. It was intended for "those who had no appreciation for reading" and yet acted as judges. The regulation that, as a new power was appearing in the territory, sought to give ground to the traditions of the judge-arbitrator guided exclusively by his prudence. The verification of facts, the forms of declarations, etc. prepared a culture of procedural practice that fulfilled the purposes of an administration, which in the scheme of powers was taking away space for mediation and opening the place to mere application.

---

61 Mariluz Urquijo, "La instrucción circular para el mejor y más breve despacho de la formación de las causas criminales", 177.

62 Mariluz Urquijo, "La instrucción circular para el mejor y más breve despacho de la formación de las causas criminales", 186.

7 Conclusion: Beyond the Practices, the Languages

Through institutional analysis, it can be seen how the pragmatic texts of *prácticas criminales* could extend into daily life. These late eighteenth century elements of discursive coercion and normalization make it clear that textual levels are not only related to each other when analyzing the history of books, but rather establish a set of relations of institutional preeminence between legal documents (books, judicial archives, laws, *Bandos de Buen Gobierno*, etc.). This, in turn, had an impact on historical reconstruction, reducing the impression of a total agency attributed to the actors and their practices by social history. As Michel Pêcheux stated:

> Faced with a legal or scientific text, this difficulty [the delimitation of what belongs or does not belong to the corpus] does not seem to arise to the extent that there is, in this case, an institution (legal or scientific, etc.) to which the texts can refer. It is therefore necessary to point out the difference between the documentary analysis, carried out within an institutional reference for purposes that respond, in general, to those of the institutions, and the analysis that we will call "non-institutional". [...] Documentary analysis fundamentally requires that the *equivalence* would be defined a priori by the institutional norm itself.[63]

Thus, the relationships between texts – archives, criminal practice, legislation, etc. – show a structure of analysis that requires to reveal the institutional logic underlying the discursive intersection. Between laymen and literate, between savants and rustic people, between levels of languages, the institutional power and the ends to which they responded – from the political government of the republic to the search for the procedural ordering of the *Audiencia* – produced an order of discourse that, without annihilating the actor, reduced his expressive capacity. At the same time, however, this does not imply a static dimension; rather, the changes in power structures and in the devices deployed to sustain it – jurisdiction, legislation, etc. – did have an impact on the logics of the sources of law. Correspondingly, these changes influenced the values attributed to the documents which are subject of current historiographic research.

In sum, one can observe that this literature and the hypotheses that accompany its composition are only an index of much greater problems, that

63 Pêcheux, *Hacia el análisis automático del discurso*, 29.

escape the procedural legal matter, and when it comes to working between dogmatics, practice and the judicial archive, these texts require double epistemological vigilance. On the one hand, they draw attention to a deeper work on the knowledge covered by judicial saying, concealing a romanticisation of the practices in the daily life of the courts. On the other hand, given the difference between the syntactic structures reproduced by the judges in the cases that make up the archives today, it is possible to relate what is written with intermediate models that conveyed different visions of the political order. This is equivalent to saying that the comparison of the textuality of the archive with respect to the formal procedures of certain practices – Villadiego, Fernández de Herrera Villarroel – refers to knowledge that the present can ignore. Thus, criminal judicial practice is a true sounding box of languages and knowledge, whose reading opens the door to a political anthropology that allows us to recognise the symbolic universe which composed the normative culture in different spaces of the Spanish Monarchy – mainly through literature.[64]

Acknowledgements

This text is a revised version of an article published in Spanish: Casagrande, "Literatura Práctica en el siglo XVIII". The English translations of all the Spanish and French quotations included in this chapter were done by the author.

Bibliography

Printed Sources

Álvarez de Posadilla, Juan, *Práctica criminal por principios o modo y forma de instruir los procesos criminales de las causas de oficio de justicia*, Madrid 1798: Imprenta de la viuda de Ibarra.

Berní, Joseph, *Práctica criminal con nota de los delitos, sus penas, presunciones, y circunstancias que los agravan y disminuyen; y ritual para Juzgar, acriminar*, Valencia 1741: Simón Fauré.

Elizondo, Francisco Antonio de, *Práctica universal forense de los tribunales de España, y de las Indias*, 8 vols., 4th impr., Madrid 1783–1788: D. Joachin Ibarra Impresor de Cámara de S.M.

64 See Martínez and Agüero, "Ein Gespräch mit … Bartolomé Clavero".

Fernández de Herrera Villarroel, Gerónimo, *Practica criminal, instrucción (nueva útil) de substanciar las causas, con distinción de lo que particularmente parece se debe observar, assi en los Consejos, y Sala, como en otros Tribunales superiores, y en los inferiores de Juezes pesquisidores, y ordinarios, por los Escrivanos á quienes suelen cometerse, en que se notan muchas de las dificultades que se ofrecen en el todo, y en parte de ellas*, Madrid 1724: Imprenta de Don Gabriel del Barrio.

Real Academia Española, *Diccionario de la lengua castellana, en que se explica el verdadero sentido de las voces, su naturaleza y calidad, con las phrases o modos de hablar, los proverbios o refranes, y otras cosas convenientes al uso de la lengua* [...]. [*Diccionario de Autoridades*], 6 vols., Madrid 1726–1739.

Real Academia Española, *Diccionario de la lengua castellana* [...], 10th ed., Madrid 1852.

Villadiego Valcuñana y Montoya, Alonso de, *Instrucción Políticay práctica judicial, conforme al estilo de los Consejos, Audiencias, y Tribunales de Corte, y otros ordinarios del Reyno. Utilissima para los Governadores, y Corregidores, y otros juezes ordinarios y de comisión, y para los Abogados, Escrivanos, Procuradores y Litigantes*, Madrid 1720: Imprenta de Juan de Ariztia.

Literature

Agüero, Alejandro, "Saber jurídico y técnica procesal en la justicia lega de la periferia. Reflexiones a partir de documentos judiciales de Córdoba del Tucumán, siglos XVII y XVIII", in Aguilar, M. Torres (ed.), *Actas del XV Congreso del Instituto Internacional de Historia del Derecho Indiano*, vol. 1, Córdoba 2005, 311–332.

Agüero, Alejandro, "Las categorías básicas de la cultura jurisdiccional", in Lorente Sariñena, Marta (ed.), *De justicia de jueces a justicia de leyes: hacia España de 1870*, Madrid 2006, 19–58.

Agüero, Alejandro, *Castigar y perdonar cuando conviene a la República. La justicia penal de Córdoba del Tucumán, siglos XVII y XVIII*, Madrid 2008.

Agüero, Alejandro, "El testimonio procesal y la administración de justicia penal en la periferia de la Monarquía Católica, Siglos XVII y XVIII", in *Fontes* 1 (2014), 3–14.

Aguirre, Carlos and Ricardo Salvatore, "Writing the History of Law, Crime, and Punishment in Latin America", in Salvatore, Ricardo, Carlos Aguirre and Gilbert Joseph (eds.), *Crime and Punishment in Latin America*, Durham 2001, 1–32.

Bajtín, Mijaíl, *Estética de la creación verbal*, Buenos Aires 2002.

Barral, María, *De sotanas por la Pampa. Religión y sociedad en el Buenos Aires rural tardocolonial*, Buenos Aires 2007.

Barriera, Darío, "Voces legas, letras de justicia. Las culturas jurídicas de los legos en el Río de la Plata entre los siglos XVI y XIX", in Mantecón Movellán, Tomás A. (ed.), *Bajtin y la historia de la cultura popular*, Santander 2008, 347–368.

Barriera, Darío, *Abrir puertas a la tierra. Microanálisis de la construcción de un espacio político. Santa Fe, 1573–1640*, Santa Fe, NM 2013.

Barriera, Darío, "La historia de la justicia y las otras historias", in Richard-Jorba, Rodolfo and Marta S. Bonaudo (eds.), *Historia Regional. Enfoques y articulaciones para complejizar una historia nacional*, La Plata 2014, 19–40.

Bernal, Beatriz, "Las leyes de Indias a la luz de dos comentaristas novohispanos del siglo XVIII", in *Revista Chilena de Historia del Derecho* 9 (1983), 325–354.

Bien, Günther, Theo Kobusch and Heinz Kleger, "Praxis, praktisch", in Ritter, Joachim and Karlfried Gründer (eds.), *Historisches Wörterbuch der Philosophie*, vol. 7, Basel 1989, 1277–1307.

Bourdieu, Pierre, "Le champ scientifique", in *Actes de la recherche en sciences sociales* 2 (1976), 88–104.

Bourdieu, Pierre, *El sentido práctico*, trans. Ariel Dilon, Buenos Aires 2007.

Buffington, Robert, "Introduction: Conceptualizing Criminality in Latin America", in Aguirre, Carlos and Robert Buffington (eds.), *Reconstructing Criminality in Latin America*, Wilmington, DE 2000, XI–XIX.

Burke, Peter, *Was ist Kulturgeschichte?*, trans. Michael Bischoff, Bonn 2005.

Casagrande, Agustín, "Erradicando sus rústicos juzgamientos. La Real Audiencia y las justicias menores de Buenos Aires, 1785–1787", in *Sudhistoria* 5 (2012), 15–40.

Casagrande, Agustín E., "Literatura Práctica en el siglo XVIII. El orden procesal en la historia de la justicia rioplatense", Revista de Historia del Derecho 49 (2015), (http://ref.scielo.org/zky3tz).

Cerutti, Simona, "Histoire pragmatique, ou de la rencontre entre histoire sociale et histoire culturelle", in *Tracés* 15 (2008), 147–168 (https://journals.openedition.org/traces/733).

Chartier, Roger, *The order of Books. Readers, Authors, and Libraries in Europe between the Fourteenth and Eighteenth Centuries*, Stanford, CA 1992.

Chartier, Roger, *El presente del pasado. Escritura de la Historia, Historia de lo Escrito*, trans. Marcela Cinta, México 2005.

Chignola, Sandro and Giuseppe Duso, *Historia de los conceptos y filosofía política*, Madrid 2009.

Costa, Pietro, *Iurisdictio: semantica del potere politico nella pubblicistica medievale (1100–1433)*, Milano 2002 (1st ed. 1969).

Cutter, Charles R., *The Legal Culture of Northern New Spain, 1770–1810*, Albuquerque, NM 1995.

De Certeau, Michel, *La invención de lo Cotidiano.Las artes de hacer*, México 2000.

Duso, Giuseppe *La lógica del potere. Storia concettuale come filosofía política*, Milano 2007.

Fradkin, Raúl, *La ley es tela de araña. Ley, justicia y sociedad rural en Buenos Aires, 1780–1830*, Buenos Aires 2009.

Garriga, Carlos, "Sobre el gobierno de la justicia en Indias (Siglos XVI–XVII)", in *Revista de Historia del Derecho* 34 (2006), 67–160.

Giddens, Anthony, *The Constitution of Society. Outline of the Theory of Structuration*, Cambridge 1984.

Habermas, Jürgen, *Teoría y praxis. Estudios de filosofía social*, trans. Salvador Mas Torres, Carlos Moya Espí, Madrid 1987.

Hespanha, António Manuel, "Una historia de textos", in Tomás y Valiente, Francisco (ed.), *Sexo Barroco y otras transgresiones premodernas*, Madrid 1990, 187–196.

Hespanha, António Manuel, *La Gracia del Derecho: Economía de la Cultura en la Edad Moderna*, Madrid 1993.

Mariluz Urquijo, José María, "La Real Audiencia de Buenos Aires y la Administración de Justicia en lo criminal en el interior del virreinato", in *Primer Congreso de Historia de los Pueblos de la Provincia de Buenos Aires*, La Plata 1952, 271–291.

Mariluz Urquijo, José María, "La instrucción circular para el mejor y más breve despacho de la formación de las causas criminales. 1788, proyectada por el Regente Benito de la Mata Linares", in *Revista del Instituto de Historia del Derecho* 12 (1961), 173–198.

Martínez, Fernando and Alejandro Agüero, "Ein Gespräch mit … Bartolomé Clavero", Forum Historiae Iuris (2008), (https://forhistiur.de/2008-03-aguero/).

Meccarelli, Massimo, "La dimensión doctrinal del proceso desde una perspectiva de historia de la justicia criminal, a la luz de la lección historiográfica de Mario Sbriccoli", in Madero, Marta and Emanuele Conte (eds.), *Procesos, inquisiciones, pruebas: homenaje a Mario Sbriccoli*, Buenos Aires 2009, 13–37.

Meccarelli, Massimo, "Dimensions of Justice and Ordering Factors in Criminal Law from the Middle Ages till Juridical Modernity", in Martyn, Georges, Anthony Musson and Heikki Pihlajamäki (eds.), *From the Judge's Arbitrium to the Legality Principle. Legislation as a Source of Law in Criminal Trials*, Berlin 2012, 49–67.

Miceli, Paola, *Derecho consuetudinario y memoria. Práctica jurídica y costumbre en Castilla y León (siglos XI–XIV)*, Madrid 2012.

Miceli, Paola, *Práctica jurídica y costumbre en Castilla y León (siglos XI–XIV)*, Madrid 2012.

Mohnhaupt, Heinz, "Potestas legislatoria und Gesetzesbegriff im Ancien Régime", in Mohnhaupt, Heinz, *Historische Vergleichung im Bereich von Staat und Recht. Gesammelte Aufsätze*, Frankfurt am Main 2000, 221–273.

Mohnhaupt, Heinz, "'Historia literaria iuris: Beispiele juristischer Literaturgeschichten im 18. Jahrhundert ('Historia literaria iuris': Examples of Juridical Literary Histories in the 18th Century)", *Max Planck Institute for European Legal History Research Paper Series* No. 2013–03 (https://ssrn.com/abstract=2256530).

Palacio, Juan Manuel and Magdalena Candioti (eds.), *Justicia, política y derechos en América Latina*, Buenos Aires 2007.

Pêcheux, Michel, *Hacia el análisis automático del discurso*, Madrid 1978.

Sánchez González, Ramón, "La cultura de las letras en el clero capitular de la catedral toledana", in Aranda Pérez, Francisco José (ed.), *Sociedad y élites eclesiásticas en la España moderna*, Cuenca 2000, 163–236.

Sbriccoli, Mario, "Justicia Criminal", in Fioravanti, Maurizio (ed.), *El estado moderno en Europa. Instituciones y derecho*, Madrid 2004, 159–196.

Tau Anzoátegui, Víctor, *La ley en América Hispana: Del descubrimiento a la emancipación*, Buenos Aires 1992.

Thomas, Yan, "La valeur des choses. Le droit romain hors la religion", in *Annales* 57:6 (2002), 1431–1462.

Thompson, Edward P., *Costumbres en Común*, Barcelona 2000.

Tomás y Valiente, Francisco, *El derecho penal de la Monarquía absoluta* (*Siglos XVI–XVII–XVIII*), Madrid 1969.

Tomás y Valiente, Francisco, *Gobierno e instituciones en la España del Antiguo Régimen*, Madrid 1982.

Index

FB
5/23